FERRIES OF AMERICA

A Guide to Adventurous Travel

Sarah Bird Wright

To Vicky and Lynn Fischer, with best wishes and many memories of convivial gatherings in Richmond, and hopes that your California sojourn will be but a prelude to your return to Virginia — With much affection,

Sarah

August 6, 1998 — Midlothian, Virginia

Peachtree Publishers, Ltd.

For Lewis and Alexander

Published by
PEACHTREE PUBLISHERS, LTD.
494 Armour Circle, N.E.
Atlanta, Georgia 30324

Design by Paulette Lambert
Maps by Tom Roberts
Cover photo *The Falcon* ("The Millersburg Ferry") Millersburg, PA,
courtesy Capt. Jack Dillman

Manufactured in the United States of America

1st printing

Library of Congress Catalog Card Number 86-63530

ISBN 0-934601-13-5

CONTENTS

CHAPTER 2
FERRIES OF THE MID-ATLANTIC STATES 113

NOTE: All entries are listed under the state where the ferry office is located. If ferries serve two states, they are cross-referenced in brackets under the second state.

All fares are one-way unless otherwise noted.

INTRODUCTION

A ferry is the most poetical of roads.
— James Ramsay MacDonald

Glastonbury, Connecticut . . . Millersburg, Pennsylvania . . . Constance, Kentucky . . . Sistersville, West Virginia . . . Wheatland, Oregon . . . Virgelle, Montana . . . Guion, Arkansas . . . Merry Point, Virginia — these do not, on the face of it, constitute a list of tourist meccas, yet they are among America's most cherished places: starting points for historic ferries. Ferries also serve an abundance of islands and their satellites, not only such celebrated retreats as Nantucket, Massachusetts, Ocracoke, North Carolina, the San Juans in Washington State, and Santa Catalina, California, but literally dozens of others: Washington Island, Wisconsin, America's last Icelandic outpost; Dog Island, Florida, and Bald Head Island, North Carolina, both in part nature preserves; Matinicus, Maine, where you receive an accolade just for making the monthly trip. Many crossings, such as Akers, Missouri, in the Ozarks, are on National Scenic Riverways, and others are on lakes and within harbors that have attracted vacationers for generations. Some ferries are metaphors for rural life and mirrors of the westward expansion of the frontier. Others are ambulances, mail boats, school buses, and, in some places, what Maine writer Agatha Cabaniss calls "an aquatic Pony Express." They carry Christmas wreaths, commuters, Maine potato seed to Long Island, jurors from the North Carolina Outer Banks to the mainland, night-shift workers from St. Louis home to Calhoun County, Illinois, tortillas from Mexico to Texas, optimistic gamblers from Arizona to Nevada, day trippers in myriad places, corn to Oregon canneries, cement mixers, wedding cakes to Monhegan Island in Maine, and folded crop airplanes in Kentucky. In no place is the ferry more entrenched in ordinary lives than in Washington State, where it is theater, forum, emblem, and hearth, mesmerizing schoolchildren, dominating office schedules, and giving rise to an entire corpus of literature (the latest being Joyce Delbridge's *Ferry Tales from Puget Sound*). More recently, ferries have been revived as a form of urban transport: Manhattan has seen four commuter ferries established in 1986 with more on the horizon, and Bostonians (including South Shore residents) can now sail to Logan Airport in comfort instead of fidgeting their way through the Callahan Tunnel.

Writers and artists have long found inspiration in ferries, perhaps sensing, on board, what Hannah Arendt calls the *nunc stans*, the "gap between past and future . . . a timeless region, an eternal presence in complete quiet, lying beyond human clocks and calendars altogether, the quiet of the Now in the time-pressed, time-tossed existence of man." Ferries have long had a mythological existence, of course. The ferryman Charon took souls across the River Styx and gave Psyche a reprieve; the Norse Farbauti is his counterpart. Baudelaire's Don Juan was ferried across the Styx by Charon. When King David is brought back to Jerusalem by the Israelites, after the death of Absalom, his household is ferried across the River Jordan: "And there went over a ferry boat to carry over the king's household, and to do what he thought good." (2 Sam. 19:18). Today, there is even a Bronx ferry carrying the indigent dead of New York to Potter's Field.

To Clive James, whose poem "The Ferry Token" appeared recently in *The London Review of Books*, the ferry token is a visa for the past: "nostalgia impregnates/This weightless disk as sunlight bleaches wood./ Our past is shallow but it scintillates — /Not gold but some base alloy, it stays good."

In *Wanderings and Excursions*, James Ramsay MacDonald focused on ferries as a welcome refuge from his trying days as Prime Minister. They have been a fruitful subject for American writers, past and present. "We were very tired, we were very merry — /We had gone back and forth all night on the ferry," wrote Edna St. Vincent Millay in "Recuerdo" in 1913. Walt Whitman praised the "glories strung like beads" in the passage over the Brooklyn Ferry. He felt that, on board, he could get a "full sweep, absorbing shows, accompaniments, surroundings"; to him they afforded "inimitable, streaming, never-failing, living poems." Hawthorne revelled in the Fort Ti ferry in the 1840s; the succession of travellers in the waiting room allowed him "just enough time to make their acquaintance, penetrate their mysteries, and be rid of them without the risk of tediousness on either side." Such artists as John Sloan ("In the Wake of the Ferry"), G. K. Richardson ("The Ferry at Brooklyn, New York"), Adrien Moreau ("Crossing the Ferry"), and Charles H. Cooke ("Waiting to be Ferried Across a River") have celebrated them as well.

How does such a mystique develop? In many places, the crossing is established to solve a simple logistical problem, getting a few people from Point A to Point B until traffic justifies a bridge. Somehow, the ferry then burrows its humble way into the hearts of the local citizens with the strength of tensile steel, even though they might not have been on the ferry in years and might not contemplate a crossing for some time to come. The faintest suggestion of a bridge or discontinuation casts an aura about the ferry and unleashes such a missionary zeal in the most lethargic citizens that the beleaguered highway officials call off the accountants and turn to other, more benign, economies.

In 1957, John Perry characterized ferries as an important aspect of American life, one which is "continually on the point of vanishing but which never quite disappears." This is still true today. Several ferries, such as the Anderson Ferry in Kentucky, are National Historic Landmarks; others are on the National Register of Historic Places. So addictive are they that "ferry dynasties" have formed in various places in the country, with several generations of a single family growing to love the business and handing it down. Examples are the Steins, Wronowskis, and Clarks of Long Island; the Richters of Washington Island, Wisconsin; the Hornes of Wolf Island, Ontario, whose family ferry to Cape Vincent, NY, dates back to a lease from King George IV; the Sheplers of Mackinaw City, Michigan; the Plaunts of Cheboygan, Michigan; the Russells of LaPointe, Wisconsin; the Brysons of Harsens Island, Michigan; and the Morrises of Atlantic, NC.

Vessels today range from simple wood floats to the huge ferryliners between Seattle and Skagway, Alaska, which undertake round trips of up to a week. In between are such colorful ships as the sail-assisted *Balmy Days* in Maine, the *Golden Eagle* wooden paddlewheel in Illinois, and the rope-pulled Los Ebanos, Texas, ferry. United States ferries are like a litmus paper absorbing our heritage and giving our cultural and ethnic heritage a common denominator: on any given day, across the country, one may find on one or another vessel the Aleut Indians of Alaska, the gullah schoolchildren of Daufuskie Island, SC, the Lummi Indians of Washington State, or Mexican-Americans in Texas. From their varied locations, they are also, in a sense, a fixative of Americana. They call across the years to Indian pirogues; to Jamestown and the early colonists; to Chautauqua and camp meetings; to Ellis Island, the Statue of Liberty and the hardy immigrants; to the San Francisco Great White Arks with their Ladies' Parlors and grand waiting rooms; to the Lewis and Clark expedition; to the miners and settlers of the Klondike; to the whaling days of New London, New Bedford and Nantucket; to J. P. Barnum at Bridgeport/Port Jefferson; to the era of magnates such as Cornelius Vanderbilt and the *Nautilus*; and to the feisty Mosquito Fleet in Washington.

It is not the purpose of this book to give a chronological account of US ferries from their beginning, which was well done by John Perry in *American Ferryboats* (1957). It is intended rather as a practical guide to those still operating. The book is an outgrowth of two obsessions, one with boats and one with travel. It was written in part to dispel the myth that ferries have become extinct and in part to enable people to find and ride those remaining, so the hapless traveller will not have to repeat the experience of a Georgia highway official who drove his family on a hundred-mile detour to the Ozarks to ride a ferry he remembered, only to find it replaced by a gleaming metal bridge. There are over two hundred ferries remaining, however, so this fate should not befall readers today.

Only those ferries which are entirely within the United States or which have one terminus in this country are listed. For each entry, I have included as much information about the history of that particular ferry as I could find, along with information about local sightseeing, schedules, tolls, onboard facilities, restrictions, capacity, directions, and a contact office and number. Schedules and fares do change, so readers are urged to doublecheck such details. The location of each ferry is roughly indicated on regional maps for the purpose of general planning, but riders will need detailed state maps to find some of the more obscure crossings. Indexes and a bibliography for further reading are also provided.

Henry James once wrote of experience that it is "never limited and never complete." During the months of work on this book, I came to feel he might well have been writing of ferries, for even as the bridge-builders and accountants beaver away in one location to consign a ferry route to oblivion, ecologists, boat captains, shipbuilders, and even board-room chairmen are conceiving and implementing new crossings. I compiled the initial list by writing every state tourist office, combing guide books, searching through the Library of Congress computer-generated bibliography, and interviewing ferry operators and owners. But no sooner did I consider my inventory fixed and immutable than a stray clipping or encounter with someone from another state would disclose another one. The phrase, "I don't know whether you know about the one at X, or Y, or want to include it . . . of course it's an institution to us," reverberated through the months of research. I always did include it, of course, while wondering what others might have escaped my seine. The list of ferries known to me at present is, therefore, of necessity subject to revision, and I would welcome information about errors of omission and commission. I hope the book will not only serve travellers but also convey the romance of ferries to those kindred spirits who will always choose the poetry of lapping waves over the harsh prosody of asphalt.

Sarah Bird Wright
Midlothian, Virginia, 1987

FERRIES
OF
NEW ENGLAND

Ferries of New England

CONNECTICUT

1. Bridgeport-Port Jefferson, LI, NY
2. Chester-Hadlyme
* [Groton-Montauk, LI, NY; see NY]
3. New London-Block Island, RI
4. New London-Fishers Island
5. New London-Orient Point, LI, NY
6. Rocky Hill-Glastonbury

MAINE

1. Bar Harbor-Yarmouth, NS
2. Bass Harbor - Frenchboro, Long Island
3. Bass Harbor-Swans Island
4. Boothbay Harbor-Monhegan Island
5. Boothbay Harbor-Squirrel Island
6. Eastport-Deer Island, NB
7. Lincolnville-Islesboro (Dark Harbor)
8. New Harbor-Monhegan Island
9. Northeast Harbor-Cranberry Isles, Islesford & Sutton
10. Port Clyde-Monhegan Island
11. Portland-Peaks Island and Casco Bay Islands
12. Portland-Yarmouth, NS
13. Rockland-Matinicus
14. Rockland-North Haven
15. Rockland-Vinalhaven
16. Stonington-Isle au Haut

MASSACHUSETTS

1. Boston-Charlestown
2. Boston-George's Island
3. Boston-Gloucester
4. Boston-Hingham (Boston Harbor Commuter Service)
5. Boston-Hingham (Mass Bay Lines)
6. Boston-Hull
7. Boston-Logan Airport
8. Boston-Nantasket Beach
9. Boston-Provincetown
10. Boston-Quincy
11. Falmouth-Martha's Vineyard (Oak Bluffs)
12. Hyannis (Ocean St. Dock)-Martha's Vineyard (Oak Bluffs)
13. Hyannis (Ocean St. Dock)-Nantucket
14. Hyannis (South St. Dock)-Nantucket
15. Martha's Vineyard (Edgartown)-Chappaquiddick Island
16. Martha's Vineyard (Oak Bluffs)-Nantucket
17. New Bedford-Cuttyhunk Island
18. New Bedford-Martha's Vineyard (Vineyard Haven)
19. Woods Hole-Martha's Vineyard (Oak Bluffs)
20. Woods Hole-Martha's Vineyard (Vineyard Haven)
21. Woods Hole-Nantucket

NEW HAMPSHIRE

1. Portsmouth-Isles of Shoals

RHODE ISLAND

* [Block Island-Montauk, LI, NY; see NY]
* [Block Island-New London, CT; see CT]
1. Bristol-Prudence Island-Hog Island
2. Galilee (Point Judith)-Block Island
3. Portsmouth (Bend Boat Basin)-Prudence Island
4. Portsmouth (Melville)-Prudence Island
5. Providence-Newport-Block Island

VERMONT

1. Burlington-Port Kent, NY
2. Charlotte-Essex, NY
3. Grand Isle-Plattsburgh, NY
4. Larrabee's Point, Shoreham-Fort Ticonderoga, NY

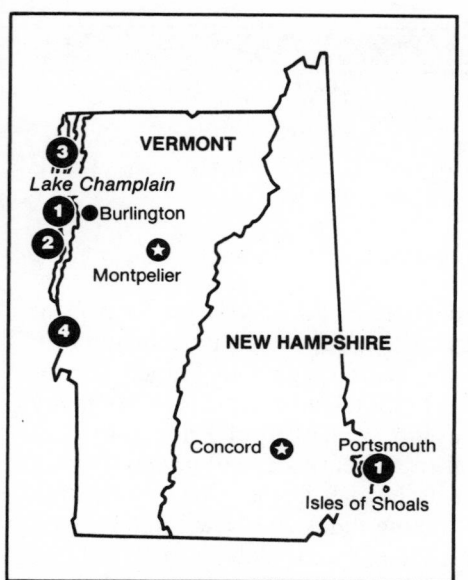

VERMONT

Lake Champlain

③

① ●Burlington

②

★ Montpelier

④

NEW HAMPSHIRE

Concord ★

Portsmouth

①

Isles of Shoals

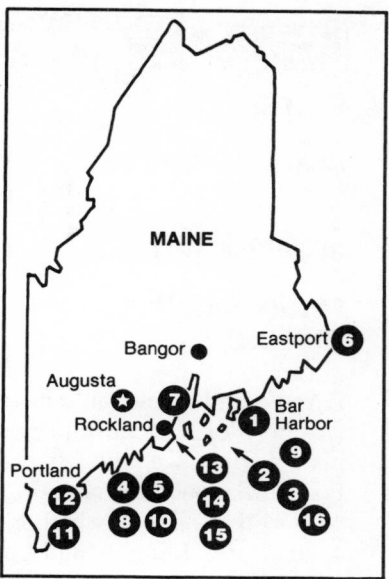

MAINE

Bangor ●

Eastport ⑥

Augusta ★

⑦ Bar Harbor ①

Rockland

Portland

⑬ ⑨

⑫ ④ ⑤ ② ③

⑧ ⑩ ⑭ ⑯

⑪ ⑮

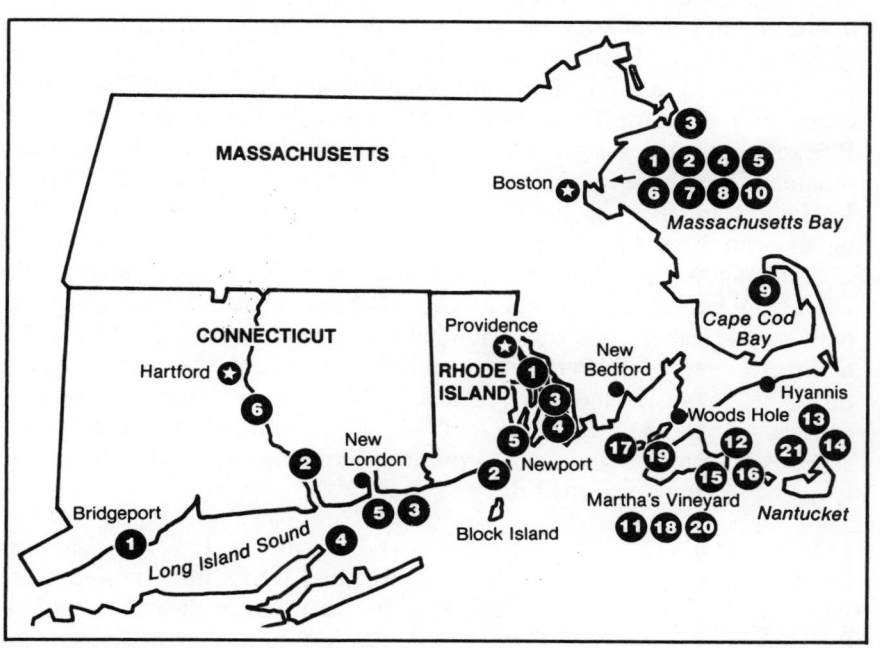

MASSACHUSETTS

③

Boston ★ ① ② ④ ⑤

⑥ ⑦ ⑧ ⑩

Massachusetts Bay

⑨

Cape Cod Bay

CONNECTICUT

Hartford ★

⑥

Providence ★

RHODE ISLAND ①

New Bedford ●

Hyannis ●

⑬

② New London

⑤ ③ ④

Woods Hole

⑫

⑰ ⑲ ㉑ ⑭

Bridgeport

① Long Island Sound

④ ⑤ ③

② Newport

⑮ ⑯

Block Island

Martha's Vineyard Nantucket

⑪ ⑱ ⑳

~7~

STATE:	Connecticut/New York
PLACES SERVED:	Bridgeport, CT—Port Jefferson, Long Island, NY
BODY OF WATER:	Long Island Sound
FERRY SERVICE HISTORY:	The Bridgeport & Port Jefferson Steamboat Company, which celebrated its centennial in 1983, is the lasting legacy of Phineas Taylor

Barnum and a venerable institution on Long Island Sound. The company was born of a friendship between Barnum, a resident of Bridgeport, and his old friend Captain Charles E. Tooker, a deep-water sailor who lived in Port Jefferson. Steamboating was in its heyday at the time, co-existing with sailing packets which had been linking industrial New England with agricultural Long Island since the 1830s. Twenty-seven stockholders founded the company, and Barnum was issued the first stock certificate, for ten shares, in December 1883. The first vessel was the utilitarian steamboat *Nonowantuc,* licensed for 350 passengers; she was considered a fine improvement over the packet ships. Bridgeport merchants would ride over to Long Island to take orders for meat, groceries, and hardware to be delivered in a few days, and Long Island farmers would bring their crops to market in Bridgeport. Long Islanders were also enticed to Bridgeport by the resorts at Savin Rock and Steeplechase Island (later renamed Pleasure Beach). The *Nonowantuc* plied the route until 1902; in 1898 she was joined by the *Park City,* which ran until 1949. Other ships on the run were the *Victor,* the *Long Island,* the *Priscilla Alden,* the *Catskill,* and the *Martha's Vineyard.* The *Grand Republic,* named for the excursion vessel and queen of the McAllister fleet which once ran between the Battery and Bear Mountain, was put in service July 19, 1983. She was greeted with tremendous enthusiasm and, not without reason, is billed as "Long Island's Love Boat." The company took delivery of another vessel, the *Park City,* in 1986, which allowed expansion of the schedule. Motorists are saved a drive of approximately 105 miles, or at least two hours (on a good day).

LOCAL POINTS OF INTEREST:	Bridgeport is known for the Barnum Museum, founded by its most famous resident, P. T. Barnum. Other attractions include

the Beardsley Zoological Gardens and the Museum of Art, Science and Industry.

Port Jefferson has a town marina, and the Benjamin F. Thompson house depicting rural life on Long Island.

CROSSING TIME: 1 hr. 30 mins.

FERRY TYPE: Vehicle

VESSEL CAPACITY: *Grand Republic*: summer 100 cars, 1000 passengers; winter 100 cars, 300 passengers. *Park City*: summer 100 cars, 1000 passengers; winter 100 cars, 500 passengers.

OPERATING SEASON: All year

SCHEDULE: *Subject to change; check with company.* **May-Oct.: Mon.-Thurs. and Sat.: Lv. Port Jefferson** 7 a.m., 10:30, 2:15 p.m., 6; **lv. Bridgeport** 8:45 a.m., 12:15 p.m., 4, 7:45. **Fri. and Sun.: Lv. Port Jefferson** 7 a.m., 10:30, 2:15 p.m., 6, 9:30; **lv. Bridgeport** 8:45 a.m., 12:15 p.m., 4, 7:45, 11. **Nov.-Apr.: Mon.: Lv. Port Jefferson** 7 a.m., 8:45, 10:30, 12:15 p.m., 2:15, 6; **lv. Bridgeport** 8:45 a.m., 10:30, 12:15 p.m., 2:15, 4, 7:45. **Tues., Wed., Thurs.: Lv. Port Jefferson** 7 a.m., 10:30, 2:15 p.m., 6; **lv. Bridgeport** 8:45 a.m., 12:15 p.m., 4, 7:45. **Fri., Sat., Sun.: Lv. Port Jefferson** 7 a.m., 8:45, 10:30, 12:15 p.m., 2:15, 4, 6, *9:30; **lv. Bridgeport** 8:45 a.m., 10:30, 12:15 p.m., 2:15, 4, 6, 7:45, *11. *Except Saturdays. *Holiday schedules vary; check with company.*

RESTRICTIONS: Trailers, pickup-campers, and RVs permitted. Clearance 10 ft. 6 in. Maximum length 26 ft.

FACILITIES: Restrooms, gift shop, snack bar, Steamboat Lounge (cocktails)

FARE: Car and driver $22; adult in vehicle $6; child (under 12) in vehicle $3; adult foot passenger $7; child foot passenger $3.50; trailers $22 minimum plus $2 per foot; special fares for seniors, Ladies' Day (Thurs.) and Gentlemen's Day (Tues.); apply to company for other rates.

RESERVATIONS: Yes, for automobile

DIRECTIONS: In Bridgeport, ferry is at the Union Square Dock; in Port Jefferson, ferry is 102 W. Broadway.

MAP LOCATION: P. 7, CT, 1

CONTACT: Bridgeport & Port Jefferson Steamboat Co., Port Jefferson, NY 11777; CT: (203) 334-5993/(203)334-3043; NY: (516)473-0268

STATE: Connecticut

PLACES SERVED: Chester—Hadlyme

BODY OF WATER: Connecticut River

FERRY SERVICE HISTORY: This ferry is considered the second oldest in the US, after the Glastonbury-Rocky Hill ferry. It uses the same river crossing as the old Warner Ferry, which established service in 1769. From 1884-1924, the *Emily A. Wright* operated on the Chester-Hadlyme run. It was replaced by the *Seldon I* (named in honor of one of the older families in the area). This was followed by the *Seldon II* and, currently, the *Seldon III*, commissioned in March 1950.

LOCAL POINTS OF INTEREST: The ferry crossing is a major attraction for visitors to Gillette Castle State Park in East Haddam (the castle, of medieval Rhenish design, was built by actor William Gillette), the Goodspeed Opera House near East Haddam, and the Nathan Hale Schoolhouse in East Haddam. A circular tour can be planned to take in both this ferry and the one making the Glastonbury-Rocky Hill crossing.

CROSSING TIME: 5 mins.

FERRY TYPE:	Vehicle
VESSEL CAPACITY:	8 cars
OPERATING SEASON:	Apr. 1-Nov. 30, weather permitting
SCHEDULE:	On signal, daily, 7 a.m.-7 p.m.
RESTRICTIONS:	Trailers, pickup-campers, and RVs permitted. Load limit 5 tons. Clearance 7 ft.
FACILITIES:	None
FARE:	Car and driver $0.75; pedestrians $0.25
RESERVATIONS:	No
DIRECTIONS:	Ferry connects SR 148 in Chester with SR 148 in Hadlyme, near East Haddam.
MAP LOCATION:	P. 7, CT, 2
CONTACT:	Write: Director, Bureau of Waterways, State Pier, New London, CT 06320; or call: Dept. of Transportation, Bureau of Waterways, (203)443-3856

STATE:	Connecticut/Rhode Island
PLACES SERVED:	New London, CT—Block Island, RI
BODY OF WATER:	Block Island Sound
FERRY SERVICE HISTORY:	Nelseco Navigation began this service in 1934. The venerable ship *Block Island* has now been replaced by the *Anna C.*, launched

May 3, 1986. It has powerful engines and a new bow design, which have cut the travel time from New London to Block Island in half.

LOCAL POINTS OF INTEREST:	New London, founded in 1646 by a band of Puritans led by John Winthrop, has an excellent deep-water port and has always been a

seagoing town. In 1784, the whaling industry began in New London; it was at its height in the middle of the nineteenth century. The Tale of the

Anna C.

Whale Museum is a former whaling captain's home. Among the many places of historic interest are the Joshua Hempsted House (dating from 1678), the Lyman Allyn Museum, and the Nathan Hale Schoolhouse, where Hale taught. The Connecticut Arboretum is also well worth visiting.

Block Island was named for the Dutch explorer Adriaen Block, who landed here in 1614. Once frequented by pirates and smugglers, and plagued by shipwrecks, today, it attracts artists and summer visitors. Bird migrations cross over in the spring and fall. Mohegan Bluffs, two hundred feet high, affords excellent sea views. Settlers' Rock commemorates the first settlers (1661). There is swimming at Block Island State Beach, and lodging at a few hotels, guesthouses, and rental cottages. Most of these are seasonal, open only from spring through early fall. Ballard's Inn, the Atlantic Inn, and the Harborside Inn all serve breakfast, lunch, and dinner, as does the Samuel Peckham Tavern. For a list of accommodations, write the Tourism Division, RI Department of Economic Development, 7 Jackson Walkway, Providence, RI 02903, as information about the island is not widely distributed.

Galilee is a community on Block Island Sound; the Roger W. Wheeler Memorial Beach is nearby, along with the Galilee Bird Sanctuary. Galilee can be reached from Wakefield, at the northern end of Point Judith Pond. The Point Judith Coast Guard Station is a few miles away.

CROSSING TIME: 1 hr. 30 mins.

FERRY TYPE: Vehicle

VESSEL CAPACITY: 35 cars; 1300 passengers

OPERATING SEASON: June-early Sept.

SCHEDULE: **Daily: Lv. New London** 10 a.m.; **lv. Block Island** 4 p.m.; **extra trip:** From New London on Fridays at 7:15 p.m.; **extra trip:** From Block Island 6 a.m. Saturdays.

RESTRICTIONS: Small trailers permitted. Overhead clearance 9 ft.

FACILITIES: Restrooms, hot-food galley, cocktail bar and soda fountain, dining booths.

FARE: Car $20; adult $10 ($14 same-day round-trip); child under 12 $7 ($8 same-day round-trip); motorcycles $12; bicycles $3.

RESERVATIONS: Advance reservations and full one-way payment essential; cars must be at dock ready to be loaded 30 minutes before scheduled sailing.

DIRECTIONS: From I-95 S: Exit 84 S for "Downtown New London." At 2nd light go left onto Gov. Winthrop Blvd. Go left at end. Take 1st right to ferry entrance. From I-95 N: Exit 83 for "Downtown New London." At 2nd light go left onto Gov. Winthrop Blvd. Go left at end. Take 1st right to ferry entrance. From Rt. 32: After Coast Guard Academy go left at 2nd light onto Gov. Winthrop Blvd. At end go left. Take 1st right to ferry entrance.

MAP LOCATION: P. 7, CT, 3

CONTACT: Nelseco Navigation Co., Box 482, New London, CT 06320, (203)442-7891

STATE: Connecticut/New York

PLACES SERVED: New London, CT—Fishers Island, LI, NY

BODY OF WATER: Fishers Island Sound

FERRY SERVICE HISTORY: Ferries have been serving Fishers Island for approximately one hundred years. Artist Charles Ferguson has painted many of the early ferries, and some of his paintings are displayed aboard the current vessels. The Fishers Island Ferry District has been providing the service since 1949, but the ferries are not publicized. The present vessels are the *Race Point* and the *Munnatawket*.

LOCAL POINTS OF INTEREST:	[For notes on New London, please see entry under New London-Block Island, RI, p. 11.]

Fishers Island, about eight miles long, is eleven miles off the northeastern tip of Long Island, and about seven miles southeast of New London. It is a posh summer resort and residential area, but about three-quarters of the island is privately owned with a gatekeeper preventing unauthorized entry. There are virtually no tourist facilities, though the Pequot Inn in Fishers Island Village (with a population of about six hundred) does have a few rooms, mainly rented to overflow guests of residents. There is no pay telephone, no souvenir shop, no bike rental, and no camping. It has been said that "Strangers generally arrive at Fishers by yacht or by marriage." The Friday ferries are a meeting ground for the weekend. As described in *Town and Country,* everyone "clambering aboard in green espadrilles and worn Shetlands knows each other, each other's children and each other's Labrador retrievers and Jack Russell terriers, by name. Strangers become acutely aware of being strangers. Unless, of course, they are houseguests, in which case they are well-introduced houseguests by the time the ferry docks and the Fishers-folk are whisked off in station wagons down tiny lanes to grandmother's house." If a resilient and determined or unsuspecting and unbefriended person does arrive at Fishers Island, he can walk around the small end of the island, visit a small beach, if he can find it, have lunch at the Pequot Inn (nearly two miles from the village), and take the ferry back before nightfall. (Bikes can be transported, but they cost $5.)

CROSSING TIME:	45 mins.
FERRY TYPE:	Vehicle
VESSEL CAPACITY:	*Munnatawket*: 24 cars *Race Point*: 34 cars
OPERATING SEASON:	All year
SCHEDULE:	Daily, except Christmas. *Check with ferry company for winter schedules; also, special schedules apply on holidays and certain other days.* **May and October: Sun.: Lv.**

New London 7:15 a.m., 11, 1:45 p.m., 3:45, 5:45; **lv. Fishers Island** 8:15 a.m., noon, 3 p.m., 5, 6:45. **Mon., Tues., Thurs., Sat.: Lv. New**

London 7:15 a.m., 11, 3:45 p.m.; **lv. Fishers Island** 8:15 a.m., noon, 4:45 p.m.; **Fri.: Lv. New London** 7:15 a.m., 11, 3:45 p.m., 6:30, 10; **lv. Fishers Island** 8:15 a.m., noon, 4:45 p.m., 7:15, 10:45. **June 1-20: Sun.: Lv. New London** 7:15 a.m., 11, 1:45 p.m., 3:45, 5:45; **lv. Fishers Island** 8:15 a.m., noon, 3 p.m., 5, 7; **Mon., Tues., Wed., Thurs., Sat.: Lv. New London** 7:15 a.m., 11, 3:30 p.m.; **lv. Fishers Island** 8:15 a.m., 12:15 p.m., 4:45. **Fri.: Lv. New London** 7:15 a.m., 11, 3:30 p.m., 6, 8, 10; **lv. Fishers Island** 8:15 a.m., 12:15 p.m., 4:45, 6:45, 8:45, 10:45. **June 21-Sept. 9: Sun.: Lv. New London** 7 a.m., 11, 1:45 p.m., 2:45, 3:45, 4:45; **lv. Fishers Island** 8:15 a.m., 12:15 p.m., 3, 4, 5, 6, 7. **Mon.: Lv. New London** 5:15 a.m., 7, 11, 3:30 p.m.; **lv. Fishers Island** 6:15 a.m., 8:15, 12:15 p.m., 4:45. **Tues, Thurs., Sat.: Lv. New London** 7 a.m., 11, 3:30 p.m., 7; **lv. Fishers Island** 8:15 a.m., 12:15 p.m., 4:45, 7:45. **Wed.: Lv. New London** 7 a.m., 11, 3:30 p.m. **lv. Fishers Island** 8:15 a.m., 12:15 p.m., 4:45. **Fri.: Lv. New London** 7 a.m., 11, 2:15 p.m., 3:30, 5:15, 6:30, 10; **lv. Fishers Island** 8:15 a.m., 12:15 p.m., 3:15, 4:45, 7:15, 8:45, 10:45.

RESTRICTIONS: Trailers, pickup-campers, and RVs permitted. Load limit 35 tons.

FACILITIES: None

FARE: May 1-Oct. 31: Car $8.50; adult $3.50; child under 12 & senior citizen with Ferry District Card $1.75; trailer or pickup-camper $8.50; motorcycle or moped $7.50; bicycle $5. For other rates, please consult published tariffs.

RESERVATIONS: Reservations required for vehicles exceeding 6 ft. 8 in. height. Car must be at dock 15 mins. before scheduled sailing.

DIRECTIONS: Take Exit 83N or 84S from I-95 to New London dock at foot of Captain's Walk.

MAP LOCATION: P. 7, CT, 4

CONTACT: Fishers Island Ferry District, Fishers Island, NY 06390; CT: (203)443-6851; NY: (516)788-7463.

New London

STATE:	Connecticut/New York
PLACES SERVED:	New London, CT—Orient Point, LI, NY
BODY OF WATER:	Long Island Sound

FERRY SERVICE HISTORY: This is a private service which has been under the ownership of the John Wronowski family for over fifty years. An interesting descriptive history of this crossing has been written by Stan Gaby, *The Orient Point Passage*; he gives an account of the ghost legends, islands, and lighthouses near Orient Point. One legend concerns Ernie, an early lighthouse keeper who was said to have leaped from the tower to his death because his wife had run away with a ferryboat captain. The Orient Point ferries run year-round, with many vacationers and tourists during the spring, summer, and fall. The freight is varied, yet closely related to the economy of Long Island. During late February and early March the ferries carry truckers bringing seed from the potato-seed growers of Maine to the famous potato farmers of Long Island. There are four vessels on this run, the *Cape Henlopen*, the *New London,* the *North Star,* and the *Caribbean*. The *Cape Henlopen* was built during World War II as a military landing ship and refurbished; she has belonged to the fleet since 1983 and is the largest vessel, carrying one hundred vehicles and nearly one thousand passengers.

LOCAL POINTS OF INTEREST:	[For notes on New London, please see entry under New London—Block Island, RI, p. 11.]

Orient Point is on the northeastern tip of Long Island, above the Orient Beach State Park and nine miles from Greenport. Greenport is an historic village with a New England ambience, many antique shops, and good restaurants. The drive to Orient Point is especially pretty in the fall, with the foliage changing, and in spring and summer through farmlands filled with vegetables and fruit. This service and those from North Haven to Shelter Island and Shelter Island to Greenport make a pleasant trio of ferries and an appealing way of avoiding a long drive via the congestion of Manhattan (a three-hour drive from Orient Point).

Long Island Sound and Gardiner's Bay are well known as the domain of the British privateer Captain William Kidd, made famous by Robert Louis Stevenson's *Treasure Island*. He was employed by the governor of New York during the seventeenth century to combat piracy but, instead, became an outlaw himself, terrorizing ships, seizing their cargo, and burying it on various islands. Some of his treasure was recovered from Gardiner's Island, off the eastern end of Long Island. He was hanged in England in 1701.

CROSSING TIME:	1 hr. 30 mins.
FERRY TYPE:	Vehicle
VESSEL CAPACITY:	*Cape Henlopen:* 90 cars; *New London:* 47 cars; *North Star:* 33 cars; *Caribbean:* 21 cars
OPERATING SEASON:	All year, except Christmas Day
SCHEDULE:	*Schedule varies each year; check with boat company in advance.* In general, **spring and summer: April-mid-June: Mon.-Thurs.:**

Lv. New London 7:15 a.m., 8:30, 10:45, 12:30 p.m., 2:15, 4:30, 5:45; **lv. Orient Point** 9 a.m., 10:30, 12:30 p.m., 2:30, 4, 6:30, 7:30. **Fri. & Sun.: Lv. New London** 7 a.m., 9, 10, 11, 1 p.m., 2, 3, 5, 6, 7. **Lv. Orient Point** 9 a.m., 11, noon, 1 p.m., 3, 4, 5, 7, 8, 9. **Sat.: Lv. New London** 7 a.m., 8, 9, 11, noon, 1 p.m., 3, 4, 5. **Lv. Orient Point** 9 a.m., 10, 11, 1 p.m., 2, 3, 5, 6, 7. **Mid-June-mid-July (but not July 3-6): Mon.-Thurs.: Lv. New London** 7 a.m., 8:30, 9:30, 11, 12:30 p.m., 1:30, 3, 4:30, 5:30, 7, 9. **Lv. Orient Point** 7 a.m., 9, 10:30, 1 p.m., 2:30, 3:30, 5, 6:30, 7:30, 9. **Fri.-Sun. and also mid-July-Sept. 2:** Hourly service on the hour from New London 7 a.m.-9 p.m.; hourly service on the hour from Orient Point 7 a.m.-10 p.m. *Check company schedule as occasional trips do not operate. Fall and winter schedules reduced. Schedule varies on holidays. No trips Dec. 25.*

RESTRICTIONS: Trailers, pickup-campers, and RVs permitted.

FACILITIES: Restrooms, snack bars, on all vessels

FARE: Car including driver $20.00; adults $7 (same-day round-trip $10); child $3.50; (same-day round-trip $5); car sold one-way only. Tariffs for larger vehicles, such as motorhomes and trucks, on application.

RESERVATIONS: Essential; make by telephoning or applying in person; $10 deposit required. Vehicles with reservations must be at dock 30 mins. before sailing. For refunds a 48-hour notice of cancellation is required. When mailing deposits, include name, return address, phone number, date of departure, time of departure, and point of departure; address written reservations to Cross Sound Ferry Services, Inc., Box 33, New London, CT 06320.

DIRECTIONS: On 95S: Exit 84 for "Downtown New London." At 2nd light go left onto Gov. Winthrop Blvd. Go left at end; take 1st right to ferry entrance. On 95N: Exit 83 for "Downtown New London." At 2nd light go left onto Gov. Winthrop Blvd. Go left at end. Take 1st right to ferry entrance.

MAP LOCATION: P. 7, CT, 5

CONTACT: Cross Sound Ferry Services, Box 33, New London, CT 06320; For reservations from New London telephone (203)443-5281, (203)443-5035, or (203)444-0783; for reservations from Orient Point telephone (516)323-2415, (516)323-2525, or (516)323-2743.

STATE: Connecticut

PLACES SERVED: Rocky Hill—Glastonbury

BODY OF WATER: Connecticut River

FERRY SERVICE HISTORY: This ferry service is the oldest continuously operating one in the United States. The original ferry, in 1655, was a raft poled back and

forth. The ferry was chartered to a Jonathan Smith in 1724 as the South Glastonbury-Rocky Hill ferry. Until 1792 the Smith family and a related Grimes family held the franchise. Elizur Goodrich then succeeded to the ferry privilege. At one time a horse on a treadmill in the center of the craft supplied the motive power. In 1876 the ferry was "modernized" into a steam-driven craft, and it survived in this form until 1920. The service was taken over by the State of Connecticut in 1915. The present vessel is an open flatboat, the *Hollister,* so named because two Hollisters captained the ferry a half-century ago. The diesel towboat which tows the barge is called *Cumberland* in honor of the Duke of Cumberland, who once was granted a two thousand-acre tract in Rocky Hill by his father, George II. Most riders are commuters and tourists.

LOCAL POINTS OF INTEREST: In Hartford, attractions include Nook Farm, which contains the Mark Twain house and the Harriet Beecher Stowe house. Twain's home is a nineteen-room Victorian Gothic mansion in which he resided for many years, and the Stowe house contains a number of artifacts of the author. The Wadsworth Atheneum has paintings, sculpture, bronzes, and other works of art. Families might also enjoy the Museum of Connecticut History and the Children's Museum of Hartford. In Rocky Hill, the Dinosaur Park at West Street draws many visitors.

CROSSING TIME: 4 mins.

FERRY TYPE: Vehicle

VESSEL CAPACITY: 3 cars

OPERATING SEASON:	Apr. 1-Nov. 30, river conditions permitting.
SCHEDULE:	On signal, daily, 7 a.m.-8 p.m.
RESTRICTIONS:	Trailers, pickup-campers, and RVs permitted. Load limit 5 tons.
FACILITIES:	None
FARE:	Car and driver $0.75; pedestrians $0.25 each.
RESERVATIONS:	No
DIRECTIONS:	The ferry is at the intersection of SR 160 and SR 99A; follow signs.
MAP LOCATION:	P. 7, CT, 6
CONTACT:	See CONTACT, p. 11.

STATE:	Maine
PLACES SERVED:	Bar Harbor—Yarmouth, NS
BODY OF WATER:	Bay of Fundy

FERRY SERVICE HISTORY: The steamship *Bluenose* is the former Stena Line *Jutlandica* from Sweden, built in 1973. She entered service in June 1983 after a $2.5 million refit so that the vessel would meet Canadian National Marine specifications. Service was begun on this run twenty-six years ago by another *Bluenose*. The original vessel carried almost 2.5 million passengers across the Bay of Fundy. At least one rider has praised CN Marine for providing "more of a cruise than a crossing," with its cabins, comfortable lounges, and well-appointed dining rooms. Among the amenities are an ample supply of slot machines, as well as a video arcade. Families with small children may wish to bring their own books and games along.

LOCAL POINTS OF INTEREST: Bar Harbor is the largest town on Mt. Desert Island, with a summer population of more than twenty thousand. It is a major resort with many activities, such as horseback riding, hiking, and boating. The juxtaposition of sea, forest, and mountain have made Bar Harbor the summer retreat of choice for generations of affluent Americans.

Bluenose

Yarmouth is situated at the western end of Nova Scotia; it is the province's largest seaport west of Halifax. The town has a long-standing maritime tradition, and many artifacts of its shipping days are exhibited in the Yarmouth County Historical Society Museum on Collins Street. The famous "Runic Stone," which suggests that Norse explorers may have landed nearby, is also on display at the museum. Visitors may continue along Yarmouth County's rugged coast, on the Evangeline Trail (named for Longfellow's poem "Evangeline," written about the expulsion of the Acadians in 1755.)

CROSSING TIME: 6 hours

FERRY TYPE: Vehicle

VESSEL CAPACITY: 250 cars; 1,000 passengers

OPERATING SEASON: All year

SCHEDULE: **Mid-June-mid-Sept.: Daily: lv. Bar Harbor** 8 a.m., **lv. Yarmouth** 4:30 p.m. **Mid-May-mid-June; mid-Sept.-mid-Oct.: Tri-weekly: Lv. Bar Harbor** Mon., Wed., Fri. 8 a.m.; **lv. Yarmouth** Sun., Tues., Thurs. 9 a.m. **Mid-Oct.-mid-May: Tri-weekly: Lv. Bar Harbor** Mon., Wed., Fri. 8:30 a.m.; **lv. Yarmouth** Sun., Tues., Thurs. 3 p.m. **Mid-Oct.-Dec. 1: Triweekly: Lv. Bar Harbor** Mon., Wed., Fri. 11 p.m.; **lv. Yarmouth** Sun., Tues., Thurs. 3 p.m. **Dec. 1-late Apr.: Biweekly: lv Bar Harbor** Mon., Wed. 11 p.m.; **lv. Yarmouth** Sun., Tues. 3 p.m.

RESTRICTIONS: Trailers, pickup-campers, and RVs permitted. Overhead clearance 12 ft.; gas tanks must not be more than 3/4 full when boarding.

FACILITIES: Cabins, restrooms, buffet dining room, cafeteria, casino, quiet lounges, two bars, a newstand and gift shop, two 30-seat private dining rooms, a duty-free boutique, children's play area, non-smoking passenger areas, and facilities for disabled passengers.

FARE: On-season (mid-June-mid-Sept.): Car, pick-up camper $60; adult $26; child (5-12) $13; motorcycle $30; trailer, camper, RV to 22 ft. $99.90; over 22 ft. $133.20. Off-season: Car, pick-up camper $45; adult $19.50; child (5-12) $9.75; motorcycle $22.50; trailer, camper, RV to 22 ft. $82.80; over 22 ft. $110.40.

RESERVATIONS: Required; also car must be at loading dock 1-2 hrs. before scheduled sailing.

DIRECTIONS: In Bar Harbor, the ship leaves from the CN Marine Ferry Terminal, Eden St. In Yarmouth the terminal is near Main St. on the harbor.

MAP LOCATION: P. 7, ME, 1

CONTACT: CN Marine Reservations Bureau, Box 250, North Sydney, NS, B2A 3M3, Canada; Bar Harbor: (207)288-3395, Yarmouth: (902)742-3513, also US except Maine: (800)341-7981, Maine only: (800)432-7344

STATE: Maine

PLACES SERVED: Bass Harbor—Frenchboro, Long Island

BODY OF WATER: Coastal Atlantic Ocean

FERRY SERVICE HISTORY: The Maine State Ferry Service, according to Agatha Cabaniss, publisher of *Linking the D.O.T.s*, is an "arterial system over which goods, services, medical care, and people travel." The ferries linking the six islands to the mainland carry everything from Maine squid and lobster to Christmas wreaths. "No islander," says Ms. Cabaniss, "is dispassionate on the subject of Maine's White Fleet.'' Service to Frenchboro was inaugurated in 1962; Frenchboro and Swans Island share the ferry *Everett Libby,* or, if the *Libby* is in for repairs or substituting elsewhere, the extra vessel, the *William S. Silsby.*

LOCAL POINTS OF INTEREST: Frenchboro is on Long Island, located approximately three miles southeast of Swan's Island. The island was accessible to tourists via steamers from Portland long before the Maine state ferries began running to the island. The area of the island is about one thousand acres. Stone implements, flint arrowheads, and shell heaps suggest that it was settled by the Abnaki Indians long before white men arrived. The coastline is ragged, with sandy beaches; pine groves and shady paths make the island appealing to walkers.

CROSSING TIME: 50 mins.

FERRY TYPE: Vehicle

VESSEL CAPACITY: 12 vehicles; 175 passengers

OPERATING SEASON: All year

SCHEDULE: **Oct.-mid-June: Thurs. and Fri. only: Lv. Bass Harbor** 9 a.m.; **lv. Frenchboro** 10 a.m. **Mid-June-Sept.: Wed. and Thurs. only: Lv. Bass Harbor** 9:15 a.m.; **lv. Frenchboro** 10:15 a.m.

RESTRICTIONS: Trailers, pickup-campers, and RVs permitted. Load limit 38 tons. Overhead clearance 13 ft. 9 in. Maximum length 60 ft.

FACILITIES: Restrooms

FARE: Cars $5.50; passengers $3.75.

RESERVATIONS: Guaranteed space $2.50.

DIRECTIONS: Take US 1 to Ellsworth; SR 3 to Mt. Desert Island; SR 102 to Bass Harbor.

MAP LOCATION: P. 7, ME, 2

CONTACT: Maine State Ferry Service, Box 645, 517-A Main St., Rockland, Maine 04841, (207)594-5543; Bass Harbor office: Bass Harbor, ME 04653, (207)244-3254

Everett Libby

STATE:	Maine
PLACES SERVED:	Bass Harbor—Swans Island
BODY OF WATER:	Blue Hill Bay/Coastal Atlantic Ocean
FERRY SERVICE HISTORY:	The Maine State Ferry Service took over the Swans Island service in 1960. Lloyd Bri-

migion, a Searsport, Maine, historian, who has carried out research for the Penobscot Marine Museum, has investigated the history of the state ferries; he has discovered that the first ferry service taken over by the State Highway Department was the Bath-Woolwich service across the Kennebec River. This ferry was purchased from the Peoples Ferry Company in 1921, and records indicate that it was run by the state until 1927, when the Carlton Bridge was opened. The other ferry services carrying automobiles at that time were Lincolnville to Islesboro, Prospect to Bucksport on the Penobscot River, Sedgwick to Deer Island, and Jonesport to Beals, Maine. All of these were replaced by bridges except the ferry from Lincolnville to Islesboro. In 1957, the State of Maine established the "Maine Port Authority" to provide service to North Haven, Vinalhaven, Islesboro, and Swans Island. The *Everett Libby* serves Swans Island, alternating with the *William S. Silsby* when the *Everett Libby* is being serviced. There are presently six islands, five vessels, and four daily routes, but, if more than one vessel is out of service, the islands must share the ferries. A new thirty-car vessel has been ordered to replace the *Governor Muskie,* which will be sold. Islanders are dependent on the ferry for all of their movements; Maili

Currier, a Swans Island resident, writing in *Linking the D.O.T.s,* says the islanders' way of life and the ferry service are tied in a tightly balanced but "fragile ecosystem." Summer visitors do not always realize the heavy demands made on the ferry service.

LOCAL POINTS OF INTEREST: Swans Island is located five miles southwest of Mt. Desert Island. It was originally called *Brule Côte* (French for "burnt hill.") This and several other islands were bought by Colonel James Swan about 1785, but he failed in his scheme of luring homesteaders with the offer of free eleven hundred-acre tracts. Ferry riders will find that the mountains of Acadia National Park are visible on the trip out. The island has three communities, Atlantic, Minturn, and Swans Island Village, a fishing community of about four hundred people. Minturn has a restaurant and quarry with warm, clear water for swimming. Atlantic, where the ferry arrives, has a library and museum (open Sundays). The Coast Guard lighthouse at Hockamock Head is an interesting site to visit. Camping is not allowed, but Alberta Buswell in Minturn rents rooms and handles reservations for cabins that are available (207/526-4127).

CROSSING TIME: 40 mins.

FERRY TYPE: Vehicle

VESSEL CAPACITY: 12 cars; 175 passengers

OPERATING SEASON: All year

SCHEDULE: **Summer schedule: Mid-June-late Sept., Memorial Day weekend: (Mon.-Sat.): Lv. Swans Island** 7 a.m., 8:30, *10:45, 1:30 p.m., 3, 4:30. **Lv. Bass Harbor** 7:45 a.m., *10, 11:30, 2:15 p.m., 3:45, 5:15. **Late June-Mid-Sept. (Sun.): Lv. Swans Island** 8 a.m., 9:30, 1:30 p.m., 3, 4:30; **lv. Bass Harbor** 8:45 a.m., 10:30, 2:15 p.m., 3:45, 5. **Non-summer schedule: Jan.-mid-June; late Sept.-Dec.: (Mon.-Sat.): Lv. Swans Island** 6:45 a.m., 8:15, 2:15 p.m., 3:45; **lv. Bass Harbor** 7:30 a.m., 11, 3 p.m., 4:30. **Jan.-Mar., Sun.: Lv. Swans Island** 3 p.m.; **lv. Bass Harbor** 3:45 p.m. **April, Sun.: Lv. Swans Island** 2:15 p.m., 3:45; **lv. Bass Harbor** 3 p.m., 4:30. **May-mid-June, late Sept.-Oct., Sun.: Lv. Swans Island** 8:15 a.m., 2:15 p.m., 3:45; **lv. Bass Harbor** 9 a.m., 3 p.m., 4:30. **Nov.-Dec., Sun: Lv. Swans Island** 8:15 a.m., 3 p.m.; **lv. Bass Harbor** 9 a.m., 3:45 p.m. *Does not operate on Wed. & Thurs.

RESTRICTIONS: Trailers, pickup-campers, and RVs permitted. Load limit 38 tons. Overhead clearance 13 ft. 9 in. Maximum length 60 ft.

FACILITIES: Restrooms

FARE: Car and driver $7 ($11.50 round-trip); adult $1.75 ($2.75 round-trip); child (5-11) $1 ($1.75 round-trip), under 5 free. Trailers determined by length. Round-trips good for 30 days. Lower fares Mid-Sept.-mid-June.

RESERVATIONS: You can pay an extra fee of $2.50 for a guaranteed trip.

DIRECTIONS: Take US 1 to Ellsworth; SR 3 to Mt. Desert Island; SR 102 to Bass Harbor.

MAP LOCATION: P. 7, ME, 3

CONTACT: See CONTACT, p. 23.

STATE: Maine

PLACES SERVED: Boothbay Harbor—Monhegan Island

BODY OF WATER: Atlantic Ocean

FERRY SERVICE HISTORY: Talk about ferries! You have hardly been on one until you have ridden the *Balmy Days,* a historical landmark since 1932 in the Boothbay Harbor region. She is a sixty-foot ship powered by two diesel Volvo engines, with a staysail for steadying on a windy day. Capt. Bob Campbell has owned the boat since 1981, when he purchased it from Capt. Bob Fish, who bought it from the original owner, the late Capt. Charles H. Wade, in the early 1970s. Captain Campbell and his son, Capt. Bill Campbell, run the service together. At one time the ship carried mail and freight, but that is now done by the Port Clyde ferry. The boat has been treasured and kept in topnotch shape by its owners, and the original owner, Captain Wade, is considered a legendary figure among the captains of the area. According to Diane Campbell, wife of Capt. Bob Campbell, people still speak of his relationship with the "hermit of Manana Island," who would come to partake of one of his famous meals each day at noon. Captain Wade lived on and worked a farm in Boothbay, and, at Monhegan, while he waited for passengers to hike around the island, he would cook up a fantastic meal of his garden vegetables,

lobsters, and steak. In those days the boat had a full galley and mahogany table. According to Alden P. Stickney, President of the Boothbay Historical Society, the earliest vessel sailing to Monhegan was the *Effort,* a sailing vessel under Capt. William S. Humphrey; she was in operation in 1906 and earlier. In 1907, a three-cornered ferry service, calling at Port Clyde, Monhegan, and Boothbay Harbor, was started by Capt. I. E. Archibald with the steamer *May Archer,* followed in 1916 with the steamer (later converted to diesel) *Gov. Douglas.* Before the days of Captain Wade, there was the *Nereid* under Capt. Earl Starrett and, in the 1920s, the *Novelty* under Capt. Cass Brackett.

Recent passengers, says Diane Campbell, have been a pregnant bunny rabbit from the Fort Cowan Bunny Barracks enroute to take up residence on Monhegan and a variety of dogs.

LOCAL POINTS OF INTEREST: Boothbay Harbor has the flavor of an old New England village, with winding streets and wharves lined with fishing craft. It is also a noted resort area, a mecca for yachtsmen and visitors and a long-established shipbuilding center. The island was sold by the Indians for twenty beaver pelts, surely one of the most disastrous Native American real-estate transactions ever recorded. Boothbay Harbor, with its sheltered deep blue waters, has an ideal yachting harbor and hosts popular summer regattas, including Windjammer Days in mid-July highlighted by the visits of passenger schooners on weekly cruises out of Camden and Rockland. The film *Carousel* was shot on location here in 1955, and it was the home base of Admiral MacMillan's Arctic expeditions on the schooner *Bowdoin.* Places of interest include the Boothbay Region Historical Society Museum, the Grand Banks Schooner Museum, with guided tours of the fishing schooner *Sherman Zwicker,* and the Boothbay Railway

Museum. At McKown Point is Maine's Department of Marine Resources Aquarium. East Boothbay is a picturesque boatbuilding village.

Monhegan Island, a choice island even for Maine, has been a refuge for seafarers for many years; it is still a sailor's haven and fishing center. It is island living at its best, remote but still accessible by boat, homey with window boxes burgeoning with flowers, and free of cars. The island is one and one-half miles long by a half-mile wide, with the highest cliffs on the New England coast. Rockwell Kent formed an artists' colony here in the 1900s, and it is still a mecca for talented painters, potters, and illustrators. If, when you arrive, you have a sense of *deja vu,* it is because it has been depicted by Jamie Wyeth, Paul Henri, and Charles E. Martin (of the *New Yorker*). Many artists today have viewing hours in their studios, and some artists' works are on display at the Plantation Gallery across from the Periwinkle Coffee Shop. Thomas Edison also once vacationed here. Notable sights are its Cathedral Woods, trails, ice pond, and central meadow, which in spring has colorful iris and frost flowers and in fall purple cranberry vines and brown cattails. Advance reservations for lodgings are mandatory; inns include the Trailing Yew, the Offshore Inn (no meals), the Island Inn (Rita White's daily snowy laundry line is a tourist attraction), Monhegan House (no meals), and Hitchcock House (no meals). For quick meals, the Barnacle Upper Deck and Periwinkle are recommended. Note that summer is a better time to visit than in winter, as restaurants are closed off-season and town water is turned off. Those who like beaches best in winter, however, may stay at bed-and-breakfast establishments, such as Tribler Cottages, which has some units where you may prepare simple meals.

CROSSING TIME:	35 mins.
FERRY TYPE:	Passenger
VESSEL CAPACITY:	69 passengers (85 if within a mile of shore)
OPERATING SEASON:	June-September
SCHEDULE:	**Lv. Boothbay Harbor** 9:15 a.m.; **lv. Monhegan Island** 2:55 p.m. [At 2:15, passengers may board the ship for a half-hour cruise to view the cliffs from the water; fee $1.00.]
RESTRICTIONS:	None
FACILITIES:	Restrooms; soda is available
FARE:	$14 (round-trip $18); children under 9 $14 (round-trip $16); small fee for luggage and animals.

RESERVATIONS:	Recommended, with deposit
DIRECTIONS:	Ferry leaves from Boothbay Harbor, Pier 8 (the Chimney Pier on Commercial St.)
MAP LOCATION:	P. 7, ME, 4
CONTACT:	Capt. Bob Campbell, Box 102, Boothbay Harbor, ME 04538, (207)633-2284

STATE:	Maine
PLACES SERVED:	Boothbay Harbor—Squirrel Island
BODY OF WATER:	Atlantic Ocean

FERRY SERVICE HISTORY: Ferry service is provided by the *Maranbo II,* owned by Capt. Bob Campbell, who, with his son Bill, runs the service. She is a lobster-boat hull built in Friendship, ME, in 1947, and originally owned by the Fish Family (MArty, RAmond, ANna, and BOb, whence her name). The ferry service is a blend of domesticity and ingenuity fully appreciated by Squirrel Island residents. Libby Lovatt, writing in the *Boothbay Register* in 1986, commended the *Maranbo* crew, who, on the May 1986 rainy Memorial Day weekend, "gallantly loaded more and more boxes and bags and covered them with tarpaulins. Islanders brought more and more bags and boxes—and dogs, and more dogs, leading to the first of the season's quotable quotes, 'There is an increasing smell of wet dog.' " Throughout the summer season, especially on the Friday afternoon 3 p.m. trip, perks for ferry riders include seeing a travelling zoo with gold fish, dogs, cats, parrots, and other animals. Diane Campbell, wife of Capt. Bob Campbell, says there are sometimes as many as six dogs and two cats; the mate builds a maze of boxes to minimize the pandemonium. Libby Lovatt's dog, Spike, waits for the boat on Squirrel Island with an ice-cream cone and stands on his hind legs waving his paws in a salute when he hears the word "Maranbo." All island festivities are geared to the *Maranbo,* which, luckily, sails "rain, shine, or fog." Diane Campbell, says, "Whenever there is a wedding on the island, at least once a summer, all the champagne glasses, band equipment, flowers, even lilac bushes once, and all the caterer's goodies, are carried on the *Maranbo*." One notable wedding was that of Robert Duvall and Gail Young (in some anonymity, as this was before his Academy Award). The *Maranbo* also provides ferry service to the All Saints by the Sea Episcopal Church on Southport Island as well as the chapel on Squirrel Island during July and August on Sunday mornings for church services. (The cottage of Rachel Carson is on Southport Island, and Cape Island, part of Southport, was the long-time home of the witch in the film *The Wizard of Oz*. Another nearby island, Mouse Island, was the home of Harry Emerson Fosdick.) Summer people in the cottages by the shores of Ocean Point and Spruce Point on the mainland set their clocks by the *Balmy Days* (also owned by the Campbells) as she cruises past bound for Monhegan Island. There is a popular nightlights cruise Tuesday, Thursday, and Saturday past six light-houses with reflections from harbor lights and shore cottages.

LOCAL POINTS OF INTEREST: [For notes on Boothbay Harbor, please see entry under Boothbay Harbor—Monhegan Island, p. 27.]

Squirrel Island is one of the oldest resorts in the Boothbay Harbor area; it has long been the home of college professors and other literary figures. Summers here speak of ideal childhood, of Arthur Ransom and Enid Blyton, of home-grown pageantry in the annual Masquerade, on a plane decidedly superior to most television fare. In 1986, according to Libby Lovatt, the Masquerade theme was "Squirrel Island Characters, Past, Present, and Future," with photographs of "Squirrels from days gone by" available for viewing in the library. The *Maranbo* takes people for all-day picnics, but there are no restaurants or accommodations on the island. Squirrel Island has many day visitors, such as Gail and John Densler of Auburndale, Massachusetts, who return year after year to wander along the tiny paths leading between the Victorian cottages and watch the residents bring small wagons down to the pier to cart home groceries and other cargo from the *Maranbo*.

CROSSING TIME: 30 mins.

FERRY TYPE: Pedestrian

VESSEL CAPACITY: 67 passengers

OPERATING SEASON: All year

SCHEDULE: **Daily: Lv. Boothbay Harbor** at 7 a.m., *9, *11, 12:40 p.m., 1:45, 3, 5:10; **lv. Squirrel Island** 7:30 a.m., 9:30, 11:30, 1:10 p.m., 2:15, 3:30, 5:40. *Sundays 8:45, 9:45, stopping at Squirrel Island and All Saints Southport for 10:30 church services.

RESTRICTIONS:	Limit on building materials carried at one time: 40 bags of cement; 40 bundles of shingles
FACILITIES:	Restrooms; soda is available.
FARE:	Adult $3 (round-trip $4.50); child (11 and under) $2.50 (round-trip $3).
RESERVATIONS:	No
DIRECTIONS:	Ferry leaves from Pier 8, Chimney Pier, in Boothbay Harbor.
MAP LOCATION:	P. 7, ME, 5
CONTACT:	Capt. Bob Campbell, *Maranbo II,* Box 102, Boothbay Harbor, ME 04538, (207)633-2284

STATE:	Maine
PLACES SERVED:	Eastport—Deer Island, NB
BODY OF WATER:	Passamaquoddy Bay

Naskeag Point ? [handwritten annotation]

FERRY SERVICE HISTORY: This route has been called "the Road of the Isles." Ferries have been a feature of the Passamaquoddy Bay area at least since the turn of the century, and probably before. Writing in the "Radar" section of the *Quoddy Tides* of Eastport, Allison G. (Ted) Haskins of Yarmouth, Massachusetts, a former assistant engineer on the *Eastport,* recounted some of the early twentieth-century history of the steam ferries on the Bay. According to Haskins, the *Eastport, Lubec,* and *Campobello* all ran during the summer months, operated by the Passamaquoddy Steam Ferry Company. They served Lubec, North Lubec, Eastport and Welshpool, Campobello Island. The *Lubec* (converted to semi-diesel propulsion) and the *Eastport* held a race on the *Eastport*'s last trip; by what Haskins called "efficient manipulation of the high pressure steam into the low pressure cylinders" the *Eastport* won. In winter the crews toiled to deliver the mail to Eastport, feeling fortunate to make one trip per day. The *Lubec* had a steel prow for icebreaking.

Rover and Deer Island

The current service is the only one linking New Brunswick with the US, though there is ferry service between Deer Island and Campobello and between Deer Island and Letete on the mainland. The vessels are the barge *Rover* (built on Deer Island in 1952) and the tug *Deer Island* (built in Nova Scotia in 1944). The company, East Coast Ferries, Ltd., has been owned by Dale Barteau since 1967. "We're small, and we're old," says Barteau, going on to observe that his wife, Glenna, takes an active part in the service; she "untangles many ferries during telephone calls during the summer, not just ours."

LOCAL POINTS OF INTEREST: Eastport is on Moose Island, named from an old Indian legend. It was settled in 1772 and incorporated as a town in 1798; it was captured and held by the British for four years during the War of 1812. The waterfront is graced by a broad walkway atop a pink granite seawall, defending the shoreline against erosion and storms; the walkway has three small parks, ideal for watching the passing parade of boats. The *Quoddy Tides* is the most easterly newspaper published in the US; it is published for residents on both sides of the border. Eastport also has a marine museum, aquarium, and library. The Cannery Wharf Restaurants at the ferry landing (including the Cannery, the Clam Kibben, and the Pickling Shed) provide, in addition to good seafood, a first-rate view of the harbor and of the fireworks during Eastport's Old Home Week Fourth of July celebration, which draws many former residents home. Weston House (1810), on the National Register of Historic Places, offers bed-and-breakfast accommodations.

Deer Island is one of the Fundy Isles, long popular with artists because of their rugged seascapes and stalwart lighthouses. It has what is claimed to be the world's largest lobster pound and a giant whirlpool known as "The Old Sow." From Deer Island you can take another ferry to Campobello Island, where there is a US Memorial on Canadian soil. Campobello International Park has two Roosevelt summer cottages, including the maroon gambrel-roofed one that Franklin Delano Roosevelt and his wife were given as newlyweds. Here FDR's den even has a megaphone for hailing offshore boats and calling family members in for meals.

CROSSING TIME: 15 min.

FERRY TYPE: Vehicle

VESSEL CAPACITY: 8 cars

OPERATING SEASON: Mid-June-mid-Sept.

SCHEDULE: **Daily: Lv. Eastport** every hour on the half-hour from 9:30 a.m.-6:30 p.m.; **lv. Deer Island** every hour on the hour from 9 a.m.-6 p.m. Additional trip in July & Aug. leaving Deer Island at 7 p.m. and leaving Eastport at 7:30 p.m.

RESTRICTIONS: Trailers, pickup-campers, and RVs permitted. Load limit: Drivers of heavy vehicles, such as trucks or trailers, should contact purser before loading; carried only if weather permits. Overhead clearance 11 ft.

FACILITIES: None

FARE: Car and driver $7; passengers: adults $2; maximum fare $10 per car. Trailer and pickup-campers as per size and load.

RESERVATIONS: No

DIRECTIONS: From Maine: leave Rt. 1 at Whiting, Maine, and take Route 189 to Lubec and Campobello, or leave Rt. 1 at Perry, Maine, and take Route 190 to Eastport. From New Brunswick: Leave Rt. 1 at St. George, NB, and take Route 772 to L'Etete, NB, where free Government ferry leaves for Deer Island. This ferry operates continuously from 7 a.m. to 9 p.m. or later during the summer months.

MAP LOCATION: P. 7, ME, 6

CONTACT: East Coast Ferries, Ltd., Chocolate Cove, Deer Island, NB, Canada, EOG 2GO, (206)747-2168

STATE: Maine

PLACES SERVED: Lincolnville—Islesboro (Dark Harbor)

BODY OF WATER: Penobscot Bay

FERRY SERVICE   The vessel on this run is the *Governor Muskie,*
HISTORY: the oldest and largest of the Maine State Ferries, the only double ender, or Push-Me-Pull-
You. It has wide decks and a center cabin with the pilot house above and can
be used only on the sheltered waters of the Islesboro run. This is the shortest
trip from the mainland. Agatha Cabaniss, publisher of *Linking the D.O.T. s,*
recalls two legendary "worst" trips on the *Muskie*. One was on a stormy
Christmas Eve some years ago when Capt. Stanwood Hinckley called to the
Islesboro ticket office to see if islanders really wanted to come ashore for
Christmas Eve. They said "yes," so he came for them. Water sloshed
through the doors, into the cabin, and up to the hubcaps on the parked cars
on the open deck. An even more memorable trip involved a vehicle not
carried, an occasion long remembered by islanders. The island was infested
with junk cars, and an eighteen-wheel car-crusher came from the mainland,
squashed and loaded many cars, and then started home. The tide was low,
and the ramp was a steep incline. Apparently (there are several versions of
the story), the truck cab made it on to the deck, but not the trailer, which
threatened to capsize the *Muskie*. The captain moved the *Muskie* in the pens
in order to save it, and the rig fell into the water in the pen. "The driver
jumped out onto the deck," says Cabaniss. "The *Muskie* went to Lincolnville and unloaded the cars already on board. It then returned with
passengers, no cars, and anchored in the harbor. People had to be shuttled
back and forth. The truck's dome light was revolving when the mishap
occurred and continued to revolve under the water. Islanders came down to
the ferry that night to stand and stare at the red light circling under the water
in the pen. A barge/platform with a crane and divers came up and the cars
were unloaded one at a time. Then the rig was lifted onto the ferry and taken
to the mainland. No car-crushers have been back since."

Actually, the mishap would never have happened if some Islesboro residents had had their way. Lloyd Bremigion, a historian and researcher for the
Penobscot Marine Museum, Searsport, recalls the controversy that raged
among summer residents about permitting cars on Islesboro in the first
place. The first horseless carriage was brought over in 1912, and from
1913-1933 cars were banned in the interest of preserving the peaceful surroundings on the island (the same prohibition prevailed for a time on the Isle
of Man and in Bermuda). Bremigion states that the self-propelled scow

Red Wing provided service from 1934-1936, then *Governor Brann* and, beginning in 1959, the *Governor Muskie*. The Lincolnville Beach ferry terminal was presided over for many years by the late Malcolm Beckett, known as Mac. He was once described by Agatha Cabaniss as "Islesboro's Gatekeeper, Spokesman, Chamber of Commerce, Source of All Information, Message Service, Car Key Keeper and Exchange, Drop Off and Pick Up and generally Mr. Indispensable operating from his perch on the Ferry Service's Catbird Seat." Mac would straighten out summer people who thought the Maine Turnpike continued on from the island and try to discourage day trippers, but in vain. One famous anecdote about Mac was his reply to a woman who was surprised to find a hearse going to the island to bury someone. She asked, "Do they bury people on the island?" "What do you think they do?" Mac replied. "Recycle them?" Mac will be much missed by islanders.

Cars and ferries are an integral part of life on Islesboro. Kate Waterman, with her husband, purchased and restored the Islesboro Inn in 1983; the Watermans have moved to Islesboro for good. One reason, she says, is that "We like island life very much and have always considered ferry rides one of life's small pleasures." And ferry mishaps, if there are any, are of such a unique nature on Islesboro few residents could protest very much.

LOCAL POINTS OF INTEREST: Lincolnville is six miles north of the yachting center and resort area of Camden, known as "the town where the mountains meet the sea." Here, there are landscaped waterfront parks, a waterfall, a marina, an inner harbor with floats for skiffs, and an outer harbor for pleasure craft of all sizes. Windjammer cruises and other sailing trips leave from here. The charms of Islesboro were recognized in the latter part of the nineteenth-century, according to Kate Waterman, by some wealthy New York, Boston, and Philadelphia banking community members enroute to summer homes in Bar Harbor. They decided Bar Harbor was getting too crowded, and, as they sailed by Islesboro, they thought it very beautiful. They later bought up a large section of the south part of the island, which they sold in lots to other wealthy families (the island had originally been settled by Indians and was a thriving farming and fishing community with some white settlers). Most of the large and elegant mansions, or "cottages" in the Newport sense, still stand and are occupied by private families. They are called the Dark Harbor cottages after Dark Harbor itself (to sailors, a dark harbor is one which cannot be seen easily from the outside). That end of the island is still called Dark Harbor. The charms of the island have become almost too well known, with its coves, evergreens, and views of Penobscot Bay. Bikers, according to Agatha Cabaniss, have become a serious problem. Though the island is flat, the roads are narrow and twisting with sand shoulders. As a result, bikers ride down the middle of the lane, two and three abreast, an increasingly dangerous situation. Bikers are, therefore, discouraged from coming.

Islesboro has no village, but is a long, thin island with many settlements. You may drive up to Pripet, at the north end of the island, or down to Dark Harbor. The Sailors' Memorial Museum in the old Lighthouse and a summer take-out are adjacent to the ferry slip, but pedestrian ferry riders should realize it is a long walk to anything else. The Islesboro Inn is a gracious white structure set above terraced lawns; it was one of the large summer "cottages" and is open May through October. The Dark Harbor House, another former mansion, offers bed and breakfast accommodations.

CROSSING TIME: 25 mins.

FERRY TYPE: Vehicle

VESSEL CAPACITY: 24 cars; 125 passengers

OPERATING SEASON: All year

SCHEDULE: **Daily service. Early Jan.-mid April: Lv. Islesboro** *7:30 a.m., 8:30, 12:30 p.m., 2:30, 4:00; **lv. Lincolnville** *8 a.m., 9, 1 p.m., 3, 4:30. **Late Apr.-late May: Lv. Islesboro** *7:30 a.m., 8:30, 9:30, 12:30 p.m., 1:30, 2:30, 4:30; **lv. Lincolnville** *8 a.m., 9, 10, 1 p.m., 2, 3, 5. **Late May-mid-Sept.: Lv. Islesboro** *7:30 a.m., 8:30, 9:30, 10:30, 12:30 p.m., 1:30, 2:30, 3:30, 4:30; **lv. Lincolnville** *8 a.m., 9, 10, 11, 1 p.m., 2, 3, 4, 5. **Mid-Sept.-mid-Oct.: Lv. Islesboro** *7:30 a.m., 8:30, 9:30, 12:30 p.m., 1:30, 2:30, 4:30; **lv. Lincolnville** *8 a.m., 9, 10, 1 p.m., 2, 3, 5. **Mid-Oct.-late Dec.: Lv. Islesford** *7:30 a.m., 8:30, 12:30 p.m., 2:30, 4; **lv. Lincolnville** *8, 9, 1 p.m., 3, 4:30. **Additional trip operates Thurs.-Sun. during Aug.: Lv. Islesboro** 5:30 p.m.; **lv. Lincolnville** 6 p.m. *Does not operate on Sundays.

RESTRICTIONS: Trailers, pickup-campers, and RVs permitted. Load limit 20 tons. Overhead clearance 13 ft.

FACILITIES: Restrooms

FARE: Fares collected in one direction only; round-trip good for 30 days. Mid-June-mid-Sept.: Car or pickup-camper and driver $5.50; passengers $1.50; children (5-11) $1. Trailers and RVs by length. Mid-Sept.-mid-June: Car or pickup-camper and driver $4.50; passengers $1.25; children (5-11) $0.75

RESERVATIONS: Guaranteed space $2.50

DIRECTIONS: The Lincolnville terminal is located at Lin-
                       colnville Beach on US Route 1.

MAP LOCATION: P. 7, ME, 7

CONTACT: Maine State Ferry Service, Box 645, 517-A
                       Main St., Rockland, Maine, 04841,
                       (207)594-5543; Lincolnville office: Lin-
colnville, ME 04849, (207)789-5611 or (207)734-6935

STATE: Maine

PLACES SERVED: New Harbor—Monhegan Island

BODY OF WATER: Atlantic Ocean

FERRY SERVICE   Service is provided aboard the *Hardy,* owned
HISTORY: by Capt. Vern Lewis. The *Hardy* is a forty-
                       foot wooden lobster style boat, built in the true
Maine tradition; she was designed and built by the Hardys on Little Deer
Isle. Originally intended for the fishing trade, the *Hardy* has devoted most of
her years to ferrying passengers, cargo, and mail to and from the offshore
islands. In addition to the Monhegan ferry service, the *Hardy* also has a
Puffin Cruise during the season, a Lobster Trap Haul, and a sightseeing
cruise to Pemaquid Point lighthouse. Lewis has operated the ferry since the
summer of 1983.

The Maine Audubon Society has an observatory on Eastern Egg Rock,
where the artic puffin nests in summer; there are only three islands in the US
where puffins nest, and this is the closest one to the mainland (five miles).

LOCAL POINTS   New Harbor is a fishing and resort village in
OF INTEREST: the Pemaquid area, on the road leading to
                       Pemaquid Point, on one of the most striking
headlands on the coast. At Pemaquid point is a round fort, a reproduction of
the tower of Fort William Henry; it is now a museum with colonial relics.
The Colonial Pemaquid Restoration is located on a point of land overlooking
the Pemaquid River; foundations thought to be those of seventeenth-century
settlements have been found. The scenic Pemaquid Point Light and Museum
are on a high promontory overlooking the waters of Muscongus Bay.

Thompson Cottages in this area have boats available with rentals; the Gosnold Arms, in New Harbor at the harbor entrance, has cottages. On its return trip from Monhegan, the *Hardy* stops at Duck Rocks so that passengers may view the seventy-five to one hundred seals.

[For notes on Monhegan Island, see description under Boothbay Harbor—Monhegan Island, p. 28.]

CROSSING TIME:	1 hour
FERRY TYPE:	Pedestrian
VESSEL CAPACITY:	49 passengers
OPERATING SEASON:	Mid-June-September
SCHEDULE:	**Daily: Lv. New Harbor** 9 a.m.; **lv. Monhegan** 2:30 p.m.
RESTRICTIONS:	Small animals allowed
FACILITIES:	Restroom
FARE:	Adults $10 (round-trip $15); children $5 (round-trip $8); small animals $2
RESERVATIONS:	No
DIRECTIONS:	Ferry leaves from the Small Bros. Wharf at New Harbor.
MAP LOCATION:	P. 7, ME, 8
CONTACT:	*Hardy* Boat, Small Bros. Wharf, New Harbor, ME 04554, (207)677-2026

STATE:	Maine
PLACES SERVED:	Northeast Harbor—Cranberry Isles, Islesford,* and Sutton (*Islesford is the postal address for Little Cranberry Island.)
BODY OF WATER:	Great Harbor of Mount Desert (Coastal Atlantic)

FERRY SERVICE
HISTORY:
The ferry service has operated since 1950. The present vessels are the *Sea Queen* and the *Double B*. In addition, a mail launch leaves Northeast Harbor daily except Sunday at 11 a.m.

LOCAL POINTS
OF INTEREST:
Northeast Harbor is on Mount Desert Island, termed by the American clergyman and scholar Henry Van Dyke "the most beautiful island in the world." It has been called a geologist's wonder, with the effects of glaciation evident in its jutting peninsulas, islands, bays, and fjord-like inlets. In 1604 the French explorer Samuel de Champlain named the island the *Isle des Monts Deserts* because of the bare mountain tops.

The Cranberry Isles are off Mt. Desert Island; they consist of five islands, Little and Great Cranberry, Sutton, Bear and Baker. At Islesford, the Islesford Historic Museum, operated by the National Park Service, has exhibits on local island history from 1604; it is open daily in July and August. The Blue Duck Ships' Store in Islesford (so named because a blue wooden duck in profile is mounted on the door frame) is of interest. It was built about 1850 by Edwin Hadlock, who, with his sons Gilbert and William operated it as a ship's chandler for about twenty-five years. About 1912 it was purchased by Dr. William Otis Sawtelle, a Haverford College professor, who became interested in maritime New England history and founded the Islesford Historical Society. The Blue Duck and the Islesford Historical Museum became part of Acadia National Park in 1948. The Museum, in a brick and granite building, is open from late June to mid-September. Food service is available at the Islesford Dock Restaurant and the Cranberry Take-Out. Both Great Cranberry and Little Cranberry Islands have small grocery stores and gift shops. The Islesford Ferry Company operates a two-hour Nature Cruise, stopping at Islesford, and a four and one-half-hour Baker Island Cruise from Northeast Harbor's Sea Street Pier, mid-June to Labor Day, visiting osprey and seal habitats. Contact: Islesford Ferry Co., Box 451, RFD 2, Ellsworth, Maine, 04605 (207/244-3366; office hours 9-5:30 p.m.; off-season 207/422-6815).

CROSSING TIME: 30 mins.

FERRY TYPE: Pedestrian

VESSEL CAPACITY: *Sea Queen*: 68 passengers
Double B.: 49 passengers

OPERATING SEASON: All year

SCHEDULE: *Check with company for exact dates each year.*
June 24-Sept. 2: Lv. Islesford for Northeast
Harbor 8:30 a.m., 11, 2 p.m., 4:15, 8; **lv.**
Cranberry for Northeast Harbor 8:45 a.m., 11:15, 1:45 p.m., 4:30, 7:45; **lv.**
Northeast Harbor for Cranberry Isles & Suttons 10 a.m., noon, 3 p.m.,
5:30, 8:30. **June 10-June 23; Sept. 3-Sept. 22: Lv. Islesford** 8:30 a.m.,
1:45 p.m., 3:30; **lv. Cranberry** 8:45, 1:30 p.m., 3:45; **lv. Northeast** 11 a.m.,
2:30 p.m., 4:30. **Late Sept.-early June: Mon.-Sat.: Lv. Islesford** 8:30
a.m., 3:15 p.m.; **lv. Cranberry** 8:45 a.m., 3 p.m.; **lv. Northeast Harbor**
7:30 a.m., 11, 4 p.m. **Sun.: Lv. Islesford** 3:30 p.m.; **lv. Cranberry** 3:15
p.m.; **lv. Northeast Harbor** 4 p.m.

RESTRICTIONS: Light freight & passengers only

FACILITIES: Restrooms

FARE: Adults $1.50; children (under 12) $1.00; children under 3 free.

RESERVATIONS: No

DIRECTIONS: Take US 1 to SR 198.

MAP LOCATION: P. 7, ME, 9

CONTACT: Beal and Bunker, Inc., Cranberry Isles, ME
04625, (207)244-3575: (7:45 a.m.-7:45 p.m.);
after 7:45 p.m.: (207)276-5396

STATE: Maine

PLACES SERVED: Port Clyde—Monhegan Island

BODY OF WATER: Atlantic Ocean

FERRY SERVICE   The boat on this run is a converted Army
HISTORY: T-boat, the *Laura B.*; she carries mail as well
                       as passengers to Monhegan Island. Ferries
have been running from Port Clyde to Monhegan Island for at least one
hundred years; the Barstows have operated the ferry since 1977. The cargoes
carried are frequently out of the ordinary, ranging from goats to sheep,
horses, and cows. Journalist Catherine Foster of the *Christian Science
Monitor* was a passenger in early spring 1986, enroute to Monhegan Island
to do a story on the island's one-room schoolhouse. She says the boat was
"exceptionally cozy, with its wood stove," and that the passengers enjoyed

conversing with the genial captain, Jim Barstow. Barstow recalls one particularly memorable trip, when the late Zero Mostel arrived on Monhegan Island lashed to the mast of the *Laura B*. He shouted to the gathered crowd, "We had a mutiny and we lost!"

LOCAL POINTS OF INTEREST: Port Clyde is a picturesque fishing and resort village on Muscongus Bay, south of Rockland. [For notes on Monhegan Island, please see entry under Boothbay Harbor—Monhegan Island, p. 28.]

CROSSING TIME: 1 hr.

FERRY TYPE: Pedestrian

VESSEL CAPACITY: 93 passengers

OPERATING SEASON: All year

SCHEDULE: **Summer, June 15-Sept.: Daily: Lv. Port Clyde** 10:30 a.m., 2:30 p.m.; **lv. Monhegan** noon, 4 p.m. **Fall, Oct.: Daily: Lv. Port Clyde** 10:30 a.m.; **lv. Monhegan** noon. **Winter, Nov. 1-Apr. 30: Mon., Wed., Fri.: Lv. Port Clyde** 10:30 a.m.; **lv. Monhegan** noon. **Spring, May 1-June 14: Daily except Sun.: Lv. Port Clyde** 10:30 a.m.; **lv. Monhegan** noon. *Special holiday schedules; check with company.*

RESTRICTIONS: Small pets allowed.

FACILITIES: Restrooms

FARE: Adult $8 (round-trip $15); child under 12 $4 (round-trip $8); pets $2.

RESERVATIONS: Required; reservations held until 30 mins. before departure. Deposit of $5.00 per person will hold reservations until 10 mins before departure. Deposits refunded on 24-hr. cancellation notice.

DIRECTIONS: Ferry leaves from Port Clyde, 15 miles down Rt. 131 S from junction at Thomaston.

MAP LOCATION: P. 7, ME, 10

CONTACT: Capt. James Barstow, Monhegan Boat Line, Box 238, Port Clyde, ME 04855, (207)372-8848

STATE: Maine

PLACES SERVED: Portland—Peaks Island and Casco Bay Islands

BODY OF WATER: Casco Bay

FERRY SERVICE HISTORY: As early as 1822, Capt. Seward Porter had placed an engine on a flat-bottomed boat and run a service from Portland to North Yarmouth and the islands of Casco Bay. This vessel, officially named the *Kennebec*, was nicknamed the "Horned Hog," as passengers sometimes had to tread the paddlewheel to get safely home when her engine refused to work. Chartered ferry service to the islands of Casco Bay was created in 1845, over 135 years ago, by the state legislature. This charter document is owned by Casco Bay Lines, making this ferry the oldest firm of its kind in the nation. Ever since 1871, it has provided daily, year-round service to Peaks Island. For many years Peaks and Cushings were the only two islands served by steamers. At the turn of the century, nearly every city of note in Maine had an amusement park, and that for Portland was Greenwood Park, on Peaks Island. Visitors attended the island's theaters to see New York actors and actresses in summer stock productions (many brought to the island by impresario Bart McCullum).

Today, the company is under the management of the Casco Bay Island Transportation District. It operates three passenger ferries and a vehicle ferry to the Casco Bay Islands, including Peaks Island and five other Casco Bay islands (Little Diamond, Great Diamond, Long, Chebeague, and Cliff). The vessels are the *Rebel*, the car ferry, and the *Island Romance*, *Island Holiday*, and *Abenaki*. The same company offers a mail-boat cruise to Cliff, Great Chebeague, Long, Little and Great Diamond, a Bailey Island cruise, a harbor cruise, a sunset cruise, and several others. (Passengers may disembark from the mail boat if they have purchased a one-way or round-trip ticket to a specific island, but if they have just purchased a mail-boat cruise ticket, they must remain on the boat.) The ferries of Casco Bay Lines are recently designed and built specifically for all-season use in Casco Bay.

According to Irene Krechetoff, a summer resident of Peaks Island, a favorite activity of young people from the islands and Portland is to chip in and hire one of the ferries after hours for a "booze cruise" or floating party; wedding receptions, anniversaries and other celebrations are also held aboard one or another of the ferries.

LOCAL POINTS OF INTEREST: Portland, Maine's largest city, is a major oil terminal and shipping port, as well as the home of the University of Southern Maine. It has professional theater groups and its own symphony. Near the waterfront you'll want to explore the Old Port Exchange, an area of attractive shops and taverns housed in restored buildings, many of them former warehouses. The Wadsworth-Longfellow House, the former home of Henry Wadsworth Longfellow, the Portland Museum of Art, and the Portland Headlight, authorized by George Washington and built in 1791, the first lighthouse authorized by the US government, are other places of interest.

Peaks Island is the closest island to Portland, and one of the "Calendar Islands" chain, so-named when an early explorer reported back to his superiors that the bay near Portland "had as many islands as there are days in the year." The island's fifteen hundred year-round population increases to about six thousand in the summer. Island children use the ferry as their school bus. There are three restaurants. On misty (and sunny) mornings, commuters bring coffee from the Cockeyed Gull and Muffin Factory on the ferry, which, later in the day, is often filled with groceries, lumber, shower stalls, and other household provisions. Lodging may be found at the Peaks Island Inn, open year-round. Sightseeing might include a tour of the sandy beach near the ferry landing and the Civil War museum (summer only). Longfellow based the *Wreck of the Hesperus* on the actual destruction of the *Helen Eliza* on the Peaks Island rocks in 1869. Bicycles are available for touring the island's 720 acres.

CROSSING TIME: 20 mins. to Peaks Island

FERRY TYPE: One vehicle; 3 pedestrian vessels

VESSEL CAPACITY: *Rebel*: 9 cars, 70 passengers
Pedestrian ferries: 250 passengers

OPERATING SEASON: All year

SCHEDULE: **Summer (June 21-Sept. 1):** Ferry runs from 5:45 a.m. to 11:50 p.m. every day; hourly service; approximately 6 ferries per day carry vehicles (7 on Fridays). **Fall, Winter, and Spring:** Service is less frequent; consult company schedules for exact off-season crossing times. From 3 to 5 ferries per day carry vehicles off-season, but the time varies.

RESTRICTIONS: Trailers, pickup-campers, and RVs permitted. Passengers may carry aboard only one large personal bag; other items must be shipped as freight. Animals and bicycles are paid for separately. Vehicles are first-come, first-served to Peaks Island except Wednesdays, when reservations are required (at this time, the *Rebel* serves Long Island and larger vehicles).

FACILITIES:	Restrooms; snack bar on some trips
FARE:	Car $8; pick-up camper $9.75 to $34.50; trailers and RVs $17.25-$34.50. Service to other islands $36; prepayment required. Half-

fare for senior citizens, handicapped persons, and children 5-9.

RESERVATIONS:	Needed Wednesdays (see ''Restrictions'' section.)
DIRECTIONS:	The vehicle ferry *Rebel* leaves from Portland Pier; passenger ferries leave from Custom House Wharf, on Commercial St., opposite the

US Custom House, in Portland.

MAP LOCATION:	P. 7, ME, 11
CONTACT:	Casco Bay Lines, Custom House Wharf, Portland, ME 04101, (207)774-7871

STATE:	Maine/Canada
PLACES SERVED:	Portland, ME—Yarmouth, NS
BODY OF WATER:	Atlantic Ocean/Bay of Fundy
FERRY SERVICE HISTORY:	The Prince of Fundy Cruises, Ltd., has operated ships on this route for over a decade. Before the *Scotia Prince*, there was the *Caribe*,

then the *Bolero*, and, before that, the *Prince of Fundy*.

LOCAL POINTS OF INTEREST:	[For notes on Portland, please see Portland— Peaks Island entry, p. 42.]

David Clough has written of the "atmospheric gold" in which Nova Scotia is bathed in autumn; the area is equally appealing in spring and summer, though the temperatures are lower than in most of the US John Cabot arrived at Cape Breton Island in Nova Scotia (or "New Scotland") as early as 1497; the province now has picturesque harbors such as Peggy's Cove, Fortress of Louisbourg National Historic Park, and the spectacular Cabot Trail following the mountainous coastline of the Cape Breton Highlands National Park.

Scotia Prince

CROSSING TIME: 10 hrs. 30 mins.

FERRY TYPE: Vehicle

VESSEL CAPACITY: 250 cars; 1500 passengers

OPERATING SEASON: May-October; no sailings certain days each season, when ship stays overnight; check annual schedule.

SCHEDULE: **Early May-late June and late Sept.-late Oct.: Lv. Portland** 9:30 p.m.; **lv. Yarmouth** 11 a.m.; **late June-late Sept.: Lv. Portland** 9 p.m.; **lv. Yarmouth** 10 a.m.

RESTRICTIONS: None

FACILITIES: Cafeteria, dining room, restrooms, casino, cocktail lounge, English pub, overnight cabins, gift shop; activities include films, bingo, video horseracing.

FARE: Low season: Adults $36; children 5-14 $18; children under 5 free. Cars $65; trailers/campers $6.50/ft.; motorcycles $20; bicycles $6; cabins $15-$95 according to size, facilities, location. High season: Adults $55; children 5-14 $27.50. Cars $80; trailers/campers $8/ft.; motorcycles $26; bicycles $8; cabins $30-$115. 3-6 nt. package plans available.

RESERVATIONS: Required.

DIRECTIONS: Portland: International Terminal; Yarmouth:
                       CN Marine Terminal Bldg., Water St.

MAP LOCATION: P. 7, ME, 12

CONTACT: Prince of Fundy Cruises, Ltd., International
                       Terminal, Portland, ME 04101, USA (except
                       ME): (800)341-7540 ME: (800)482-0955,
                       Portland: 775-5616

STATE: Maine

PLACES SERVED: Rockland—Matinicus Island

BODY OF WATER: Penobscot Bay

FERRY SERVICE   The Matinicus harbor is so shallow only the
HISTORY: *William S. Silsby* or the *North Haven* may enter
                       it and must go on a rising tide. Ferry service is
infrequent, usually only once a month. The vessel on this run is presently
the *William S. Silsby*. The ferry service had been running trips to Matinicus
for quite a number of years, according to Richard Spear of the Maine State
Ferry Service, but in 1981 the state legislature made it mandatory that at least
one trip a month be made to Matinicus.

LOCAL POINTS   Rockland has long been a nucleus of nautical
OF INTEREST: transportation for this section of Maine; years
                       ago the Boston-to-Bangor boat used to dock
here so that passengers could transfer to the smaller vessels which went to
the outer islands. Edna St. Vincent Millay was born in Rockland in 1892; she
gained her first literary recognition in nearby Camden. Among the artists
who have depicted various aspects of the Maine coast, all represented at the
Farnsworth Art Museum, are Andrew Wyeth ("Wood Stove"), Newell
Convers Wyeth ("Cannibal Shore," showing the clashing waves and wind-
swept rocks of the coast), Waldo Peirce ("Children on the Shore"), and
Fairfield Porter ("The Dock.") The public landing is the site of the annual
Maine Lobster Festival the first weekend in August. Rockland has a lighthouse, reached by a granite breakwater, and from the Owl's Head Light, five
miles southeast, good views may be had of Penobscot Bay. Other places of

interest include the Owls Head Transportation Museum, the Shore Village Museum, and the Ureneff Tuberous Begonia Garden. A number of sailing trips leave from Rockland on the coasting schooners *Isaac H. Evans, Lewis R. French and Heritage*, and *Harvey Gamage*.

Matinicus Island, fifteen miles east of Monhegan, is a destination irresistible to ferry lovers. For one thing, the trip is two hours and fifteen minutes, enough to have the sense of a real ocean voyage. For another thing, one has a sense of achievement even catching the ferry, which runs only one day a month and that day subject to availability of the vessel and weather conditions. Most supplies are flown to Matinicus; vehicles and freight wait for the ferry. Norman Hall writes of a trip to Matinicus in *Downeast*: He and his wife waited for the ferry in a Rockland motel; "our proposed trip to Matinicus stamped us with prestige." The trip was foggy; we "listened our way" from one "bobbing bell buoy to the next." On the island, you may climb the rocky path past gardens, over rocks, and around beaches; on a clear day, the rocky headland provides good views of the sea. Matinicus residents depend on lobstering for their livelihood.

CROSSING TIME:	2 hrs. 15 mins.
FERRY TYPE:	Vehicle
VESSEL CAPACITY:	9 cars
OPERATING SEASON:	All year
SCHEDULE:	Once a month, according to availability of vessel and the weather; write for schedule but prepare to wait if the weather is bad.
RESTRICTIONS:	Trailers, pickup-campers, and RVs permitted. Load limit 30 tons. Overhead clearance 13 ft. 9 in.
FACILITIES:	Restrooms
FARE:	Cars $21; passengers $10
RESERVATIONS:	Guaranteed space fee $12
DIRECTIONS:	Take US 1 to the center of Rockland.
MAP LOCATION:	P. 7, ME, 13
CONTACT:	Maine State Ferry Service, Box 645, Rockland, ME 04841, (207)594-5543

STATE: Maine

PLACES SERVED: Rockland—North Haven

BODY OF WATER: Penobscot Bay

FERRY SERVICE   The vessel on this run is the *North Haven*.
HISTORY: Service on this run began in February 1960.

LOCAL POINTS   [For notes on Rockland, please see entry under
OF INTEREST: Rockland—Matinicus, p. 46.]
                         North Haven has a population of fewer than
four hundred during the winter; it triples during the summer season. The
island has a large campground, golf course, and many beautiful summer
estates and cottages. Jon Emerson, writing of North Haven and its ferry in
Linking the D.O.T.s, says, "In the summer months our boat seems to
shrink." The Pulpit Harbor Inn is open all year.

CROSSING TIME: 1 hr., 10 mins.

FERRY TYPE: Vehicle

VESSEL CAPACITY: 9 cars; 125 passengers

OPERATING SEASON: All year

SCHEDULE: **Summer schedule, Mon.-Sat.: Late May-
                         mid-Oct.: Lv. North Haven 8 a.m., 12:15
                         p.m., 3; lv. Rockland 9:20 a.m., 1:30 p.m.,**
4:20. **Sun.: Late May-Aug.: Lv. North Haven** 8 a.m., 4:20 p.m.; **lv.
Rockland** 9:20 a.m., 5:40 p.m. **Non-summer schedule, Mon.-Sat.: Late
Oct.-Mar. 1: Lv. North Haven** 8:15 a.m., *12:15 p.m.; **lv. Rockland** 9:45
a.m., **3 p.m.. *Departs 1:40 p.m. Tuesdays. **Departs 3:30 p.m. Dec.
11:24. **Early Mar.-late May and mid-Oct.-late Oct.: Lv. North Haven**
8:15 a.m., *12:15 p.m.; **lv. Rockland** 9:45 a.m., 4 p.m. *Departs 2:30 p.m.
Tuesdays. **Sun.: Early Sept.-mid-Oct.: Lv. North Haven** 8 a.m., 3 p.m.;
lv. Rockland 9:20 a.m., 4:20 p.m. **Late Oct.-Feb.: Lv. North Haven** 2
p.m.; **lv. Rockland** 3:20 p.m. **Early Mar.-mid-May: Lv. North Haven** 3
p.m.; **lv. Rockland** 4:20 p.m.

RESTRICTIONS: Trailers, pickup-campers, and RVs permitted.
                         Load limit 30 tons. Overhead clearance 13 ft.
                         9 in.

North Haven

FACILITIES: Restrooms

FARE: Fares collected in one direction only; round-trip good for 30 days, Mid-June-mid-Sept.: Car or pickup-camper and driver $5.50; passengers $1.50; children (5-11) $1; trailers and RVs by length. Mid-Sept.-mid-June: Car or pickup-camper and driver $4.50 one way; passengers $1.25; children (5-11) $.75.

RESERVATIONS: No

DIRECTIONS: Take US 1 to the center of Rockland.

MAP LOCATION: P. 7, ME, 14

CONTACT: Maine State Ferry Service, Box 645, Rockland, ME 04841, (207)594-5543, or North Haven, ME 04853, (207)867-4441

STATE: Maine

PLACES SERVED: Rockland—Vinalhaven

BODY OF WATER: Penobscot Bay

FERRY SERVICE
HISTORY:
The vessel on this service, run by the Maine State Ferry Service, is the *Governor Curtis*, newest of the fleet. Captain Richard G. Spear, manager of the service, has vividly described the scenic route, with its views of "many small, spruce-covered, granite islands," in the magazine *Dirigo*. The channel into Carver's Harbor on Vinalhaven is so sinuous, according to Agatha Cabaniss, that the *Governor Curtis* does not easily travel after dark (and winter afternoons are dark on the Maine coast).

LOCAL POINTS
OF INTEREST:
[For notes about Rockland, please see entry under Rockland—Matinicus, p. 46].
Vinalhaven is an island with a population of more than 1250 with stores, gift shops, restaurants, picnic areas, taxi service, etc. There is an all-year motel, the Tidewater, and at least one all-year restaurant. The ferry docks in the village, and passengers can walk around town. Patricia Crossman, a fiction writer and daughter of Edwin Maddox, one of the founders of the Maine State Ferry Service, wrote an article about Vinalhaven for *Linking the D.O.T.s* (Feb. 1986). She states that the island has a growing number of retirees, "people of varied background, education and experience, who have worked diligently to preserve what is best in island life, while opening our eyes to new possibilities and satisfactions." The island has excellent summer concerts and is not so isolated as one might imagine; there is same-day delivery of many items ordered from the mainland and the island has well-stocked grocery and dry-goods stores.

CROSSING TIME: 1 hr. 25 mins.

FERRY TYPE: Vehicle

VESSEL CAPACITY: 17 vehicles and 175 passengers

OPERATING SEASON: All year

SCHEDULE:
Summer schedule: Mon.-Sat.: Late Mar.-early Nov.: Lv. Vinalhaven 7 a.m., 11:20, 3:05 p.m.; **lv. Rockland** 8:40 a.m., 1 p.m., 4:45. **Sun.: June-early Sept.: Lv. Vinalhaven** 7 a.m., 3:30 p.m.; **lv. Rockland** 8:40 a.m., 5:10 p.m. **Non-summer schedule: Early Nov.-mid-Feb.; Mon., Wed., Fri.: Lv. Vinalhaven** 7 a.m., 10:20, 1:40 p.m.; **lv. Rockland** 8:40 a.m., noon, 3:20 p.m. **Tues., Thurs., Sat.: Lv. Vinalhaven** 7:30 a.m., 1 p.m.; **lv. Rockland** 9 a.m., 2:45 p.m. **Mid-Feb.-late Mar.; Mon., Wed., Fri.: Lv. Vinalhaven** 7 a.m., 11:20, 2:40 p.m.; **lv. Rockland** 8:40 a.m., 1 p.m., 4:20 **Tues., Thurs., Sat.: Lv. Vinalhaven** 7:30 a.m., 1

Governor Curtis

p.m.; **lv. Rockland** 9 a.m., 2:45 p.m. **Sun.: Jan.-Mar.: Lv. Vinalhaven**
1:30 p.m.; **lv. Rockland** 3 p.m. **Apr.-May: Lv. Vinalhaven** 8:15 a.m., 1:30
p.m.; **lv. Rockland** 9:45 a.m., 3 p.m. **Mid-Sept.-Dec.: Lv. Vinalhaven** 8:15
a.m., 1:30 p.m.; **lv. Rockland** 9:45 a.m., 3 p.m.

RESTRICTIONS: Trailers, pickup-campers, and RVs permitted.
                        Load limit 66 tons. Truck limits 13 ft. high, 9
                        ft. wide, 60 ft. long

FACILITIES: Restrooms

FARE: Mid-June-mid-Sept.: Car or pickup-camper
                        and driver $7.75 ($13 round-trip); passengers
                        $2 ($3 30-day round-trip); children (5-11) $1
($1.75 round-trip). Trailers and RVs by length. Mid-Sept.-mid-June: Car or
pickup-camper and driver $6.50 ($10.75 30-day round-trip); adults $1.75
($2.50 round-trip); child (5-11) $.75 ($1.50 round-trip).

RESERVATIONS: Reservation fee $2.50 (4 cars, 2 trucks)

DIRECTIONS: Take US 1 to the center of Rockland

MAP LOCATION: P. 7, ME, 15

CONTACT: Maine State Ferry Service, Box 645, Rock-
                        land, ME 04841, (207)594-5543 or Vinal-
                        haven, ME 04863, (207)863-4421

STATE: Maine

PLACES SERVED: Stonington—Isle au Haut

BODY OF WATER: Atlantic Ocean

FERRY SERVICE HISTORY: Isle au Haut is served by the mail boat year-round. The landing at Duck Harbor in the section of the island that is part of the Acadia National Park is observed by the ferry boat during its open season. The two boats on this service are the *Miss Lizzie* and the *Mink*.

LOCAL POINTS OF INTEREST: Stonington, a picturesque fishing village at the southern tip of Deer Isle, has long attracted artists. Isle au Haut (the natives pronounce it "aisle a hoe" but some visitors say "eel a hoe") was first settled in 1792, but the island was too remote for permanent residents. It was eventually rediscovered by a group of bachelors from Boston, Philadelphia, and New York, who purchased land and formed the Point Lookout Club, which became a family affair as they married. Over the years, the group built roads and stocked half the lake with game fish. Most of the land was eventually given to the Acadia National Park.

The Isle au Haut lighthouse still stands, and each night its red light beams a warning to wayward ships. While most lighthouse properties are owned by the Federal government, a few, including the one on Isle au Haut, were sold during the 1930s. The house was resold in 1985 to Jeff and Judi Burke, who have remodeled it as a four-room inn unique on the East Coast, the Keeper's House, but who have also kept the way of life once led by the keeper intact (there are no telephones or electric lights, but there are wood stoves providing hot water and modern bathrooms). Ferry riders may well wish to reserve a room here; the inn is open June 1 through October 30. Rates include meals and ferry fare. Jeff Burke explains the reason for their project: "The lighthouse is symbolic of a whole era of American history. . . . The fact that they're threatened to some degree now strikes a chord in most people's hearts." (In many ways, he might have been speaking of ferries.) Valerie Nelson, co-director of the Lighthouse Preservation Society, based in Rockport, MA, believes this to be an ideal solution to the expense of restoring and maintaining lighthouses. There is a ferry landing at the lighthouse. There is no lodging in the town of Isle au Haut, though there is camping (call 207/288-3338).

Visitors may explore the island by hiking; wild deer, seal, and porpoise are also visible. Visitors often go over to the Park on the mail boat and spend several hours; if you do this, make sure you have food and drink and warm raingear, as there is little shelter if it rains.

CROSSING TIME: 45 mins.

FERRY TYPE: Pedestrian

VESSEL CAPACITY: 50 passengers

OPERATING SEASON: All year town of Isle au Haut; summer only
                          Acadia National Park.

SCHEDULE: **Summer (Late June-Sept. 14): Lv. Stoning-
                          ton** 7 a.m., *11, *4:30 p.m.; **lv. Isle au Haut** 8
                          a.m., noon, 6:30 p.m. *These trips extended to
Duck Harbor, in the Acadia National Park. No service Sun. and Postal
Holidays, but in summer Sun. afternoon service is available by advance
reservation only.* **Late Sept.-mid-Oct.: Lv. Stonington** 7 a.m., 11, 5 p.m.;
lv. Isle au Haut 8 a.m., noon, 5:50 p.m. **Late Oct.-late Mar.: Lv.
Stonington** 7 a.m., 11, *3 p.m.; **lv. Isle au Haut** 8 a.m.; noon; *3:50 p.m.
*Tues. & Fri. only.** **Late Mar.-mid-June: Lv. Stonington** 7 a.m., 11, *5
p.m.; **lv. Isle au Haut** 8 a.m., noon, *5:50 p.m. *Tues. & Fri. only.

RESTRICTIONS: No dogs allowed in park.

FACILITIES: None

FARE: Adult $5; child (under 12) $3; late Oct.-May
                          adult $4; child $2.

RESERVATIONS: No

DIRECTIONS: Boats depart from Atlantic Ave. in Stonington.

MAP LOCATION: P. 7, ME, 16

CONTACT: Isle au Haut Company, Isle au Haut, ME
                          04645 (207)367-5193

STATE: Massachusetts

PLACES SERVED: Boston—Charlestown

BODY OF WATER: Boston Harbor/Mystic River

FERRY SERVICE   Since 1979, the Bay State Spray & Province-
HISTORY: town Steamship has provided regularly sched-
          uled cruises which tour Boston Harbor and
stop in the Charlestown Navy Yard.

LOCAL POINTS   On a hot August afternoon in 1850, two small
OF INTEREST: girls, daughters of subscribers to the Boston
          Athenaeum, sat reading in its newly completed
library. One was absorbed in an abstruse book on the science of navigation
and the other in *Vanity Fair* — titles noted with astonishment and recorded in
her journal by a visitor from England, the Hon. Victoria Alexandrina Maria
Wortley. "Neither of the young ladies could have been more than twelve, and
if one was to judge by their diminutiveness they looked between seven and
nine," she observed. The Hon. Victoria was herself only twelve, but her
elders could have told her that Boston had the reputation of being more
literate, more rational, more industrious, and more tolerant than most places
she would encounter in North America. Throughout the nineteenth century,
visitors from Britain and the Continent flocked to America; those who left
accounts of their travels were largely from the leisured or professional
classes, if not the nobility. Boston unfailingly served as a corrective to their
dim expectations of civilization in the New World. Charlestown, Bunker
Hill, and Harvard were staples of most sightseeing expeditions. Henry
James, in *The American Scene* (1906), termed Boston "the city of character
and genius," though he mourned the changes which threatened to obliterate
the "Boston of history, the Boston of Emerson, Thoreau, Hawthorne, Longfellow, Lowell, Holmes, Ticknor, Motley, Prescott, Parkman and the rest."
Today, one might mourn the passing of the Boston of 1906 — yet, somehow,
the quintessential city survives, where eccentricity is beloved and college
and graduate students cannot bring themselves, on graduation, to move more
than twenty miles away, where fashion and the weather are regarded as minor
impediments to higher concerns, where the *Boston Globe*'s "Confidential
Chat" column has fifteen readers' solutions for any dilemma, and where
twelve-year-olds are still likely to study anything from navigation to bell-
ringing to Homer.

From her earliest days, Boston was a maritime city. Massachusetts Bay

Bay State

and Boston Harbor were explored at length by Europeans, though the first permanent settlement was at Weymouth (in 1623). In 1625 an Anglican clergyman, William Blackstone, built his home on the west slope of Beacon Hill; others began settling in Charlestown and Chelsea. The marshy shoreline was gradually filled in; Dock Square and Faneuil Hall, now the site of Faneuil Hall Marketplace, consisting of Quincy Market, North Market, and South Market, were once close to the water. The Boston Tea Party took place in 1773, when a group of indignant colonists, disguised as Indians, threw tea from three ships into Boston Harbor. During the early part of the nineteenth century, the city was *de rigueur* on almost any self-respecting North American tour. Many visitors arrived on sailing packets, such as the *Amity* and the *Orbit*. In 1838, the *Sirius* and the *Great Western* became the first ships to cross from England to America with the unceasing aid of steam. Boston became particularly important when the North American Royal Mail Steam Packet Company (later the Cunard Line) chose it rather than New York, as its western terminus in 1840. Charles Dickens crossed from Liverpool to Boston in 1842 on the Cunard wooden side-wheel steamer *Britannia*, but, likening the interior to a hearse, he chose to return some months later in a sailing vessel.

The waterfront has adapted gracefully to change for over three hundred years and in its latest metamorphosis incorporates several new museums. Central Wharf is the site of the New England Aquarium, and sightseeing boats and airport shuttles depart from Rowes Wharf and Long Wharf. (A new Marriott hotel with atrium is also on Long Wharf). Restaurants and condominiums occupy other former wharves. *Sail* magazine is published on the old Commercial Wharf. The brig *Beaver II* is at the Congress Street Bridge; the original *Beaver* took part in the Boston Tea Party (a few blocks away from the dock). The Boston Children's Museum and the new Computer Museum are on Museum Wharf, 300 Congress Street.

Charlestown has been somewhat silted over with expressways and urban congestion but, underneath, pure history glitters. The frigate *USS Constitution,* "Old Ironsides," launched in 1797, which made history in the War with Tripoli and the War of 1812, is at the Boston National Historical Park, and the Bunker Hill Monument is on Monument Square, Charlestown, a few blocks from the *Constitution.* This is a granite obelisk, about 220 feet high, erected between 1825 and 1842; it commemorates the Battle of Bunker Hill, which took place June 17, 1775. The ferry trip has an option to visit the *Constitution* and the Charlestown Navy Yard.

CROSSING TIME:	55 mins.
FERRY TYPE:	Pedestrian
VESSEL CAPACITY:	Usually either the *Bostonian II,* 149 passengers, or the *Edward Rowe Snow,* 190 passengers.
OPERATING SEASON:	Early spring-late fall
SCHEDULE:	**Lv. Long Wharf** 10:30 a.m. and every hour on the half-hour until 5:30 p.m.; **lv. Charlestown Navy Yard** 11:15 a.m. and every hour on the quarter-hour until 4:15 p.m.
RESTRICTIONS:	The *USS Constitution* closes to the public at 3:45 p.m., so 2:30 p.m. is the last crossing allowing time to see her. Other sights at the Navy Yard are open later.
FACILITIES:	Restrooms; snack bar
FARE:	$1 from Navy Yard to Long Wharf. Round-trip: adults $3; children under 12 $2. Group rates available.
RESERVATIONS:	Not required except for groups of 75 or more
DIRECTIONS:	The boat leaves from Long Wharf in Boston, off Atlantic Ave. at the foot of State St., next to the New England Aquarium. The Red

Ticket Office is halfway down Long Wharf. Also, Pier 1, Charlestown Navy Yard.

MAP LOCATION: P. 7, MA, 1

CONTACT: Bay State Spray & Provincetown Steamship
                      Co., 20 Long Wharf, Boston, MA 02110,
                      (617)723-7800

STATE: Massachusetts

PLACES SERVED: Boston—George's Island

BODY OF WATER: Boston Harbor

FERRY SERVICE   Bay State Spray and Provincetown Steam-
HISTORY: ship, Inc., initiated public ferry service to
                      the Metropolitan District Commission's
island, George's Island, for special groups and on a regular schedule,
beginning in 1965. Also, the company initiated the first regular schedules
to Peddock's Island in Boston Harbor. The vessel on this run is usually
the *Bay State,* though other vessels may be used.

LOCAL POINTS   [For notes on Boston, please see entry under
OF INTEREST: Boston—Charlestown, p. 54.]
                     George's Island is the most popular island in
Boston Harbor, the site of the historic Fort Warren. From here, there is a
free water taxi to several other islands.

CROSSING TIME: 45 mins.

FERRY TYPE: Pedestrian

VESSEL CAPACITY: 500 passengers (if *Bay State)*

OPERATING SEASON: Early spring-late fall

SCHEDULE: **Weekdays: Lv. Long Wharf** 10 a.m., 1
                      p.m., 3; **lv. George's Island** 10:45 a.m., 1:45
                      p.m., 3:45. **Weekends: Lv. Long Wharf** 10
a.m., noon, 3 p.m., 5; **lv. George's Island** 10:45 a.m., 12:45 p.m., 3:45,
5:45.

RESTRICTIONS: No pets or alcohol are allowed on board or
                      on the island unless by special MDC permit

FACILITIES:	Restrooms; seasonal snack bar; no potable water
FARE:	Adults $3; children under 12 $2 (round-trip); group rates available
RESERVATIONS:	No, except for groups of 15 or more
DIRECTIONS:	Ferry leaves from Long Wharf in Boston, Red Ticket Office, halfway down Long Wharf, at the foot of State St., off Atlantic

Ave., next to the New England Aquarium.

MAP LOCATION:	P. 7, MA, 2
CONTACT:	See CONTACT, p. 57.

Virginia C. II

STATE:	Massachusetts
PLACES SERVED:	Boston—Gloucester
BODY OF WATER:	Massachusetts Bay
FERRY SERVICE HISTORY:	The vessel on this service is the *Virginia C. II*. She is an eighty-six-foot double-deck wooden boat, built in the mid-1960s; the

lower deck is enclosed with a counter for snacks and cocktails. Service was inaugurated in 1976. Many years ago this run was very popular, but it had not been in operation for quite some time; A. C. Cruise Lines decided to reinstate the service. The route is past the coasts of Winthrop, Nahant, and Swampscott; at Marblehead there may be sailboat races in progress. Hammond Castle is visible at the Reef of Norman's Woe, along with the Eastern Point Light, both of which signal the entrance to Gloucester Harbor. The *Virginia C. II* passes magnificent estates along Eastern Point before reaching the dock site at the Studio Restaurant at Rocky Neck.

LOCAL POINTS OF INTEREST: [For notes on Boston, please see entry under Boston—Charlestown, p. 54.]

Gloucester, on Cape Ann, has had a seafaring tradition for over three hundred years. Its busy harbor with its fishing fleet, the weathered houses and spires, and the narrow streets give it a special appeal. More lobsters are distributed from Gloucester than from anywhere else in the country. The Gloucester Fishermen statue commemorates Gloucestermen lost at sea. One can sense still, in Gloucester, the fierce pride of her fishermen, "who worked for such wage as the sea gave," in Kipling's words, and one can almost feel the presence of Disko Troop, Salters, Penn, Dan, and the other members of the *We're Here* crew, newly returned from the Grand Banks fishing season, heroes of Kipling's *Captains Courageous*. Rocky Neck, nearby, has for many years been a summer haven for artists, actors, and writers, with bungalows, sail lofts, and remodeled sheds. For serendipitous exploration, the small galleries, antique shops, and restaurants overlooking the water at Rocky Neck can hardly be surpassed. Rockport, north of Gloucester, is another charming small town; Bearskin Neck has a dense thicket of artists' studios, along with the picturesque lobster shack which has inspired so many artists it has been termed "Motif No. 1."

CROSSING TIME:	2 hrs. 45 mins.
FERRY TYPE:	Pedestrian
VESSEL CAPACITY:	200 passengers
OPERATING SEASON:	Memorial Day—Labor Day
SCHEDULE:	**Sun.—Fri.** (No Sat. sailings). **Lv. Boston** 10 a.m.; **lv. Gloucester** 3 p.m.
RESTRICTIONS:	No pets; smoking in restricted areas
FACILITIES:	Restrooms; snack bar

FARE:	Round-trip: Adult $16.50; children under 12 $9.
RESERVATIONS:	No
DIRECTIONS:	In Boston, the boat leaves from Pier One, Northern Ave. Bridge.
MAP LOCATION:	P. 7, MA, 3
CONTACT:	A. C. Cruise Lines, 28 Northern Ave., Boston, MA 02210, (617)426-8419

STATE:	Massachusetts
PLACES SERVED:	Boston—Hingham (Boston Harbor Commuter Service)
BODY OF WATER:	Boston Harbor

FERRY SERVICE HISTORY: The ferry is a commuting one, with several trips each way on weekdays. "We're spoiling the people on the South Shore,' says one of the executives at Boston Commuter Service, but anyone who has ever wrestled with the morass of potholes and bumper-to-bumper traffic on the Southeast Expressway will present himself for spoiling. Instantly. The service began under state subsidy in March 1984. Five high-speed aluminum commuter vessels are now in use, and there is ample parking at Hingham.

LOCAL POINTS OF INTEREST: [For notes on Boston, please see entry under Boston—Charlestown, p. 54.]
Hingham is an old town on the South Shore, settled about 1633, named for the former English home of many of its settlers. The Hingham Historical Society at 21 Lincoln St. is housed in the Old Ordinary, part of which was built in 1650. There are several historic houses open to the public. The Elizabethan gothic Old Ship Church has been in use since it was built in 1681. Of interest is the annual Cook's Tour of outstanding local kitchens, held each Sept.

CROSSING TIME:	30 mins.
FERRY TYPE:	Pedestrian

VESSEL CAPACITY:	150 passengers
OPERATING SEASON:	All year
SCHEDULE:	**Mon.-Fri. only: Lv. Hingham** (Shipyard Dock) 6 a.m., 6:50, 7:20, 7:40, 8, 8:10, 8:40, 11. **Lv. Boston** (Rowes Wharf) 2:30 p.m., 3:45, 4:20, 4:40, 5:30, 6, 7.
RESTRICTIONS:	None
FACILITIES:	Restrooms, full galley
FARE:	$3 (10-ride book $27.50)
RESERVATIONS:	No
DIRECTIONS:	In Boston, ferry leaves from Rowes Wharf, off Atlantic Ave., near the Aquarium. In Hingham, ferry leaves from Shipyard Dock.
MAP LOCATION:	P. 7, MA, 4
CONTACT:	Boston Harbor Commuter Service, 1 Range Rd., Nahant, MA 01908, (617)740-1253

STATE:	Massachusetts
PLACES SERVED:	Boston—Hingham (Mass Bay Lines)
BODY OF WATER:	Boston Harbor
FERRY SERVICE HISTORY:	Mass Bay Lines ran a ferry from Hull to Boston from 1963 until the late 1970s (tied to their service to Nantasket Beach); that ser-

vice was discontinued. The ferry service from Hingham began in the late 1970s; it is aboard crew boats and the *Gracious Lady,* a custom built vessel. Presently, according to William Spence, president of Mass Bay Lines, the company is transporting an average of two thousand passengers a day.

LOCAL POINTS OF INTEREST: [For notes on Boston, please see entry under Boston—Charlestown, p. 54. For notes on Hingham, please see entry under Boston—Hingham (Boston Harbor Commuter Service), p. 60.]

CROSSING TIME: 28 mins.

FERRY TYPE: Pedestrian

VESSEL CAPACITY: 149 passengers

OPERATING SEASON: All year

SCHEDULE: **Mon.-Fri. only: Summer schedule: Lv. Hingham** (Shipyard Dock) 6 a.m., 6:50, 7:10, 7:20, 7:40, 8, 8:10, 8:45, 11, noon, 3:30 p.m., 4:20, 5, 6:05. **Lv. Boston** (Rowes Wharf) 6:35 a.m., 7:25, 8, 9, 2:30 p.m., 3:45, 4:40, 5:10, 5:15, 5:30, 6, 7, 8. *Schedule slightly reduced in winter.*

RESTRICTIONS: None

FACILITIES: Restrooms, galley (coffee, snacks, cocktails in the afternoon)

FARE: $3.00 (10-ride book $27.50)

RESERVATIONS: No

DIRECTIONS: In Boston, ferry leaves from Rowes Wharf, off Atlantic Ave., near the Aquarium. In Hingham, ferry leaves from Shipyard Dock.

MAP LOCATION: P. 7, MA, 5

CONTACT: Mass Bay Lines Inc., Rowes Wharf, 344 Atlantic Ave., Boston, MA 02110, (617)749-4500

STATE: Massachusetts

PLACES SERVED: Boston—Hull

BODY OF WATER: Boston Harbor

FERRY SERVICE HISTORY: Nantasket Beach and Paragon Park have been served by steamers throughout the century. Bay State Cruises began the route in 1978-1979; it now includes commuter service. The vessel on this run is usually the *George's Island*.

LOCAL POINTS OF INTEREST: [For notes on Boston, please see entry under Boston—Charlestown, p. 54.]
Hull was first settled in 1624 and incorporated in 1647; it has a beach lined with summer cottages, and there are a number of historic buildings in the town.

CROSSING TIME: 50 mins.

FERRY TYPE: Pedestrian

VESSEL CAPACITY: 400 passengers

OPERATING SEASON: All year

SCHEDULE: **Commuter schedule: Mon.-Fri.: Lv. Hull** (Pemberton Pier) 7:20 a.m.; **lv. Boston** (Long Wharf) 5:30 p.m. **Beach and sightseeing trips leave Hull** at 10 a.m., 1 p.m., and 5:30 weekends, and at 10 a.m. and 2 p.m. weekdays.

RESTRICTIONS: Pets permitted at discretion of captain if well-behaved and leashed

FACILITIES: Restrooms; snack bar

FARE: $2.50 (commuter books available)

RESERVATIONS: No

DIRECTIONS: Landing in Hull is at Pemberton Pier, behind Hull High School

MAP LOCATION: P. 7, MA, 6

CONTACT: See CONTACT, p. 57.

STATE:	Massachusetts
PLACES SERVED:	Boston—Logan Airport
BODY OF WATER:	Boston Harbor

FERRY SERVICE HISTORY: Ferries of one sort or another have existed in Boston Harbor since about 1631. Ferry service to East Boston (where Logan International Airport is located) existed during the early part of the twentieth century but was discontinued in 1952. It has now been revived, in the form of the Airport Water Shuttle; anyone who has fidgeted frantically in the Callahan Tunnel will appreciate the logic and convenience of the service. The water taxi was launched on July 1, 1985, on an experimental basis, under an agreement between Massport (operating authority for Logan International Airport and a major landlord on Boston's waterfront) and two private boat operators with experience in Boston Harbor. The water shuttle picks up and drops off airport passengers at locations in downtown Boston; there is free shuttle-bus transfer between the new $2.5 million ferryboat dock and Logan air terminals. The vessels are large and comfortable, with such amenities as snack bars and newspapers. The shuttles make good connections with ferries from Quincy (Marina Bay) and Hingham at Rowes Wharf and connect with the Hull commuter boat at Long Wharf. There is ample parking at all three South Shore locations.

LOCAL POINTS OF INTEREST: [For notes on Boston, please see entry under Boston—Charlestown, p. 54.]

Logan Airport is the eleventh busiest in the world; in 1985, it handled a record 20.4 million passengers. It is the only international gateway in New England.

CROSSING TIME: 10-12 mins.

FERRY TYPE: Pedestrian

VESSEL CAPACITY: 138 passengers

OPERATING SEASON: Early May—early Dec.

SCHEDULE: **Mon.-Fri.: Lv. Rowes Wharf** every half hour, on the quarter-hour, 6:15 a.m.-8:15 p.m. **Lv. Logan Airport** every half hour, on the hour and half hour, 6:30 a.m.-8:30 p.m. **Other trips leave from**

Long Wharf at 8:15 a.m., 8:55, 5 p.m., and 5:55 p.m. **and from the Commonwealth Pier/World Trade Center** at 8:45 a.m. and 4:45 p.m. **Trips from Logan to Long Wharf via Commonwealth Pier** are at 8:25 a.m., 9:05, and 6:30 p.m. and **Logan direct to Long Wharf** at 5:10 p.m. **Logan to Commonwealth Pier:** 8:25 a.m., 8:55, 9:05, 4:55 p.m., 6:05. **Sun.: Service between Rowes Wharf and Logan** every half hour starting at 3:15 p.m. until 8:15 p.m. **and between Quincy and Logan** from 2:30 p.m. until 8:45 p.m.

RESTRICTIONS:	None
FACILITIES:	Restrooms, snack bar; newspapers available.
FARE:	$3 (discount books available)
RESERVATIONS:	No
DIRECTIONS:	Rowes Wharf and Long Wharf are on Atlantic Ave., and the Commonwealth Pier/World Trade Center is off Northern Ave. near the Boston Fish Pier.
MAP LOCATION:	P. 7, MA, 7
CONTACT:	Massport, Ten Park Plaza, Boston, MA 02116-3971, (800)23-LOGAN

STATE:	Massachusetts
PLACES SERVED:	Boston—Nantasket Beach
BODY OF WATER:	Boston Harbor
FERRY SERVICE HISTORY:	Ferry history on this route has many antecedents in the grand old schooners and steamers of the nineteenth and early twen-

tieth centuries. Bay State Spray & Provincetown, Inc. picked up the route in 1978-1979 after another operator ceased running.

**LOCAL POINTS
OF INTEREST:** [For notes on Boston, please see entry under Boston—Charlestown, p. 54.]

Nantasket Beach is a popular bathing beach in Hull. It is three miles long; opposite the beach is Paragon Park, an amusement park. Strawberry Hill, in Hull, affords a comprehensive view of the peninsula and bay. Legend has it that Thorwald, son of Eric the Red, was slain and buried in Point Allerton in Hull in 1004.

CROSSING TIME: Approx. 1½ hrs.

FERRY TYPE: Pedestrian

VESSEL CAPACITY: The ferry usually used on this run is the *George's Island,* which holds 400 passengers.

OPERATING SEASON: Early spring—late fall

SCHEDULE: **Weekends, Memorial Day weekend through late fall; Weekdays, mid-June— early Sept.: Weekdays: Lv. Long Wharf** 10 a.m., 2 p.m.; **lv. Nantasket Pier** noon, 3:45 p.m. **Weekends: Lv. Long Wharf** 10 a.m., 1 p.m., 5:30; **lv. Nantasket Pier** 11:30 a.m., 3:30 p.m., 7.

RESTRICTIONS: None

FACILITIES: Restrooms; snack bar

FARE: Adults $4 (round-trip $6); children under 12 $2 (round-trip $3); group rates available

RESERVATIONS: Not required except for groups of 15 or more

DIRECTIONS: Ferry leaves from Long Wharf Red Ticket Office, halfway down Long Wharf, Boston, at the foot of State St., off Atlantic Ave., next to the New England Aquarium.

MAP LOCATION: P. 7, MA, 8

CONTACT: See CONTACT, p. 57.

Provincetown II

STATE: Massachusetts

PLACES SERVED: Boston—Provincetown

BODY OF WATER: Massachusetts Bay

FERRY SERVICE   Bay State Spray & Provincetown Steamship,
HISTORY: Inc. reinstated this route after years of dormancy with the construction of the *Provincetown* in 1978. The vessel was renamed the *Commonwealth* in 1980 after the completion of the new 1100-passenger-capacity *Provincetown II*.

LOCAL POINTS   [For notes on Boston, please see entry under
OF INTEREST: Boston—Charlestown, p. 54.]
                          Provincetown, or P-town to Cape Codders, is one of the liveliest places on the Cape. After World War I writers such as Eugene O'Neill began coming here (the Provincetown Playhouse still performs his works). During the 1960s the town became a nucleus of counterculture, with artists, transient shops, and a casual lifestyle; it was called "Greenwich Village North." The atmosphere is a little more conventional now, but the town is still a hybrid mix of tourists, artists, picturesque old houses, boutiques, narrow streets, and many commercial fishermen, a number of them Portuguese. There is a bronze tablet marking the Pilgrims' first landing, the Provincetown Art Association and Museum of Art, with changing exhibits, and the Provincetown Heritage Museum with Victorian rooms and antique fire equipment.

CROSSING TIME: 3 hrs.

FERRY TYPE: Pedestrian

VESSEL CAPACITY: 1100 passengers (if, as is usually the case, the *Provincetown II* is used on this service)

OPERATING SEASON: Summer only

SCHEDULE: **Memorial Day—Mid-June and early Sept.—Columbus Day: weekends. Sept.— Mid-June—Labor Day: Daily: Lv. Boston** (Commonwealth Pier) 9:30 a.m.; **lv. Provincetown** 3:30 p.m. *Shuttle boat available from and to Long Wharf, Boston.*

RESTRICTIONS: Pets not encouraged but permitted with captain's approval, conditions permitting. No alcohol may be brought on board.

FACILITIES: Restrooms; snack bar; Dixieland band

FARE: Adults $12 (same-day round-trip $18); children under 12 $10 (same-day round-trip $13); bicycles $3. Group rates available.

RESERVATIONS: Not required except for groups of more than 15

DIRECTIONS: Boat leaves from Commonwealth Pier, off Northern Ave. (near Atlantic Ave.), Boston. Shuttle boat from Long Wharf ($1 each way) from Red Ticket Office halfway down Long Wharf, Boston, half-hour before scheduled departure.

MAP LOCATION: P. 7, MA, 9

CONTACT: See CONTACT, p. 57.

STATE: Massachusetts

PLACES SERVED: Boston—Quincy (Squantum section)

BODY OF WATER: Boston Harbor

FERRY SERVICE HISTORY: In 1984 the developers of Marina Bay, a residential waterfront community in the Squantum section of Quincy, began to offer seasonal commuter service to Boston for their residents. In July 1985, Marina Bay Commuter Company (MBCC) became one of the operators under contract to Massport for the Airport Water Shuttle. For the 1985 and 1986 seasons, MBCC has not only brought Quincy commuters into Boston points (Rowes Wharf, Commonwealth Pier, and the Logan dock), but has also utilized their boats to provide service between Rowes Wharf and Logan Airport. Two seventy-seven-foot high-speed aluminum vessels are in service, the *Independence* and the *Liberty*.

LOCAL POINTS OF INTEREST: [For notes on Boston, please see entry under Boston—Charlestown, p. 54.]

Quincy was settled in 1625, incorporated as a town in 1792, and became a city in 1888; it now has a population of about 100,000. It is known for granite quarries (the Bunker Hill Monument is made of Quincy granite) and for shipbuilding. It is unique in having the birthplaces, homes, and final resting-places of two US presidents, John Adams and his son, John Quincy Adams. The Adams National Historic Site, home of four generations of the Adams family, is well worth visiting.

CROSSING TIME: 30 mins.

FERRY TYPE: Pedestrian

VESSEL CAPACITY: 138 passengers

OPERATING SEASON: May—Dec. 1, weather permitting

SCHEDULE: *Schedule subject to change; check with company.* **Mon.-Fri.: To Rowes Wharf: Lv. Quincy** 5:45 a.m., 11:45, 6:15 p.m. **Lv. Rowes Wharf** 12:10 p.m., 6:40, 8:45. **To Logan Airport: Lv. Quincy** 7 a.m.; **lv. Logan** 7:25 a.m. **To Commonwealth Pier: Lv. Quincy** 7:50 a.m., 4:15 p.m.; **lv. Commonwealth Pier** 9:15 a.m., 5:45 p.m.

RESTRICTIONS: None

FACILITIES: Restrooms; snack bar

FARE: Adults $3 (commuter books available)

RESERVATIONS: No

DIRECTIONS: In Quincy, ferry terminal is at Marina Bay, 542 E. Squantum St. In Boston, Rowes Wharf is on Atlantic Ave.; Commonwealth Pier is off Northern Ave. near the Boston Fish Pier.

MAP LOCATION: P. 7, MA, 10

CONTACT: Marina Bay Commuter Co., 542 E. Squantum St., North Quincy, MA 02171, (617)328-0600; Also: Massport, Ten Park Plaza, Boston, MA 02116-3971; General information no.: (800)23-LOGAN

STATE: Massachusetts

PLACES SERVED: Falmouth—Martha's Vineyard (Oak Bluffs)

BODY OF WATER: Buzzards Bay, Vineyard and Nantucket Sounds

FERRY SERVICE   The vessel on this run is the *Island Queen,* a
HISTORY: steel-hulled 120-foot vessel with three decks. The Island Commuter Corporation has been in operation since 1960. The company runs a two and one-half hour bus tour of Martha's Vineyard, meeting all boats until 2 p.m. and connecting with several return trips.

LOCAL POINTS   In 1602, Bartholomew Gosnold sailed from
OF INTEREST: Falmouth, England, to the New World. He anchored off Provincetown and named the new land "Cape Cod" because of the great number of cod in the water. Falmouth itself was settled about 1660 by a group of Quakers led by Isaac Robinson. The town was named for the one from which Gosnold had sailed; at one time it was the home port for 148 sea captains. In 1779 and 1812 Falmouth was attacked by British ships. Places of interest in

Falmouth today include the home of Katharine Lee Bates, who wrote "America the Beautiful," the Model Farm at the New Alchemy Institute, the Congregational Church, whose bell was cast by Paul Revere, and the Falmouth Historical Society.

Oak Bluffs, on Martha's Vineyard, is across the harbor from Vineyard Haven, where most of the ferries dock. It was settled in the seventeenth century but, in the nineteenth century, became a center for Methodist camp meetings. Like Craigville, near Hyannis, the community of Victorian gingerbread cottages was built around a tabernacle; each summer, on Illumination Night, the cottages are festooned with Japanese paper lanterns. The best way to get around Martha's Vineyard, since car space is limited on the ferries, is to rent a bicycle. There is no camping. [For further notes on Martha's Vineyard, please see entry under Martha's Vineyard (Edgartown)—Chappaquiddick Island, p. 79.]

CROSSING TIME:	40 mins.
FERRY TYPE:	Pedestrian
VESSEL CAPACITY:	600 passengers
OPERATING SEASON:	Memorial Day—Columbus Day

SCHEDULE: **Mid-June—mid-Sept.: Lv. Falmouth** 9 a.m., 10:20, 11:45, 1:05 p.m., 2:50, 4:10, 5:30, *7, 8; **Lv. Oak Bluffs** 9:35 a.m., 11, 12:25 p.m., 2:10, 3:30, 4:50, 6:15, *7:45, 8:45. *Sunday only & Labor Day; Fridays and July 3 only. **Memorial Day—late June and Mid-Sept.—Columbus Day, Mon.—Thurs.: Lv. Falmouth** 9:15 a.m., 10:45; **lv. Oak Bluffs** 2:30 p.m., 4. **Fri.: Lv. Falmouth** 9:15 a.m., 10:45, 3:15 p.m., 6, 8.; **lv. Oak Bluffs** 10 a.m., 2:30 p.m., 4, 6:45, 8:45. **Sat., Sun., Memorial Day and Columbus Day: Lv. Falmouth** 9:15 a.m., 10:45, 12:10 p.m., 3:15, 4:45; **lv. Oak Bluffs** 10 a.m., 11:20, 2:30 p.m., 4, 5:30. *Check with company as schedule may change.*

RESTRICTIONS:	None; small pets accepted if controlled
FACILITIES:	Restrooms, snack bar
FARE:	Adults $4.00 (round-trip $7.50); children under 13 $2 (round-trip $4); bicycles $3 (round-trip $5).
RESERVATIONS:	No

DIRECTIONS:	The ferry leaves from Falmouth Heights Road, Falmouth Harbor, just below the eastern end of Main St.
MAP LOCATION:	P. 7, MA, 11
CONTACT:	Island Queen Corporation, Dillingham Ave., Falmouth, MA 02540, (617)548-4800

STATE:	Massachusetts
PLACES SERVED:	Hyannis (Ocean Street Dock)—Martha's Vineyard (Oak Bluffs)
BODY OF WATER:	Buzzards Bay, Vineyard and Nantucket Sounds

FERRY SERVICE HISTORY: In the early 1960s, brothers Richard and Robert Scudder, natives of Cape Code and graduates of the Massachusetts Maritime Academy, and Raymond Taylor went to sea on the *Prudence*. Their partnership developed from sightseeing tours on Lewis Bay into cruises to the islands. In 1972, Hyannis Harbor Tours purchased Nantucket Boat, a service which ran to Martha's Vineyard. Formed by a group of local merchants in 1946, Hy-Line is now one of the most successful boat lines in history and one of the largest passenger-carrying fleets on the East Coast. The *Prudence* is the oldest excursion boat in continuous service in the US. She is the Grand Dame of a fourteen-vessel fleet, which includes the *Becky Thatcher,* the *Brant Point,* the *Cross Rip,* the *East Chop,* the *Hyannisport,* the *Lady Fenwick,* the *Patience,* the *Point Gammon,* the *Prudence,* the *Sea Queen,* the *Silver Star,* and the *Viking.* The vessels on this run are the *Cross Rip* and the *East Chop.*

LOCAL POINTS OF INTEREST: The traditional charm of Hyannis is all but eclipsed by traffic in summer; it is a commercial center for tourism, a fashionable resort, and a transportation hub combined. Hyannis Port is famous for the Kennedy family compound, but not much of it is visible because of a high fence. Lewis Bay is a yachting mecca and the point of departure for ferries to Martha's Vineyard and Nantucket. An interesting oasis in Hyannis is Craigville, which, somewhat like Oak Bluffs on Martha's Vineyard, was once a conference site for the Christian churches of New

Prudence

England, settled in 1872. It is now a nineteenth-century hamlet of Victorian gingerbread cottages around an oval green, with the former tabernacle a focal point. There is a miniscule post office, an old inn, and the Craigville beach. The poet Henry Van Dyke and many New England clergymen and educators found inspiration here. Today, Craigville is a year-round conference site. Each August the Cape Cod Writers' Conference is held here, with nightly lectures by well-known writers and publishers; these are open to the public and well attended by Cape Cod residents and visitors. The Cape Cod Railroad, a scenic journey past cranberry bogs and dunes, and the Cape Cod Canal are other attractions in Hyannis.

[For notes on Martha's Vineyard, please see entry under Martha's Vineyard (Edgartown)—Chappaquiddick Island, p. 79.]

CROSSING TIME: 1 hr., 45 mins.

FERRY TYPE: Pedestrian

VESSEL CAPACITY: *Cross Rip:* 400 passengers; *East Chop:* 500 passengers

OPERATING SEASON: Late May—late October

SCHEDULE: **Late May—mid-June: Lv. Hyannis** 9:30 a.m., **lv. Oak Bluffs** 3:45 p.m. **Mid-June— late June: Lv. Hyannis** 9:15 a.m., 1:15 p.m., 5:15; **lv. Oak Bluffs** 11:15 a.m., 3:15 p.m., 7:15. **Late June—mid-Sept.: Lv. Hyannis** 9:15 a.m., 10:35, 1:15 p.m.; **lv. Oak Bluffs** 11:15 a.m., 4:15 p.m., 7. **Mid-Sept. through late Oct.: Lv. Hyannis** 9:30 a.m.; **lv. Oak Bluffs** 3:45 p.m.

RESTRICTIONS:	None; small pets allowed
FACILITIES:	Restrooms; snack bar
FARE:	Adult $9; child (under 12) $4.50
RESERVATIONS:	No
DIRECTIONS:	In Hyannis, go south on Ocean St. and look for the Hy-Line sign. At the Hy-Line sign (in front of the Mooring Restaurant), turn left into Hy-Line's dock area.
MAP LOCATION:	P. 7, MA, 12
CONTACT:	Hy-Line, Ocean St. Dock, Hyannis, MA 02601, (617)775-7185

STATE:	Massachusetts
PLACES SERVED:	Hyannis (Ocean Street Dock)—Nantucket
BODY OF WATER:	Buzzards Bay, Vineyard and Nantucket Sounds

FERRY SERVICE HISTORY: The first steamer to cross Nantucket Sound was the eighty-ton *Eagle,* in 1818; her twin copper boilers were heated by wood fires, and she was famed for her rescue of the whaler *George.* She began a long parade of vessels, such as the *Hamilton,* the *Marco Bozzaris,* the *Telegraph,* the *Massachusetts,* and, in 1854, the luxury steamer *Eagle's Wing.* The *Eagle's Wing* had a "Ladie's Cabin" with two staterooms and fourteen berths (in vain, female passengers tried to persuade Capt. James Barker to correct the spelling, but he replied that, not being a lady, he didn't care what it was and that the signmaker must know his trade.) Later vessels included the side-wheelers *Martha's Vineyard, Nantucket, Gay Head,* and *Uncatena.* The first propeller-driven steamer was the *Sunkaty* (1911); later ones included the *Islander,* the *Nobska,* and the *Naushon,* which boasted thirty-six staterooms. In 1886, the Nantucket Steamboat Company and the New Bedford, Martha's Vineyard and Nantucket Steamship Company, which had been operating independently between the islands, merged; the company was sold to the New York-New Haven & Hartford Railroad Co. in 1911. The ferry service continued under varying corporate management until the Woods Hole, Martha's

Brant Point

Vineyard and Nantucket Steamship Authority was formed in 1960. Falmouth, in her late seventeenth and early eighteenth century heyday, was home port for 148 sea captains. Summer residents began coming in 1852. Martha's Vineyard was also once the home of a whaling fleet but is today more of a playground for a summer colony.

[For notes on history of the Hy-Line ships, please see entry under Hyannis (Ocean St. Dock)—Martha's Vineyard (Oak Bluffs), p. 72.]

LOCAL POINTS OF INTEREST: Who could not love Nantucket? Wilder and more primitive than Martha's Vineyard, it was a long established whaling center when Melville's Ishmael made his way there: "For my mind was made up to sail in no other than a Nantucket craft, because there was a fine, boisterous something about everything connected with that famous old island which amazingly pleased me." The island was included in the royal grant to the Plymouth Company in 1621. The name is a corruption of the Indian word *Nanticut,* or "far-away land"; another Indian name for it is *Canopache,* "the place of peace." Because of the frequent mists, it has also been called "the gray lady." Initially, the inhabitants farmed and raised sheep, but they turned to whaling when the farms dwindled. By 1768 the town possessed 125 whaling ships.

Today, visitors flock to its cobbled lanes and bypaths, but there is still a sense of homespun, ships' chandlers, and oilskins. The Whaling Museum on Broad Street is a must; next-door is the Peter Foulger Museum. Other historic buildings are the Hadwen-Satler Memorial House, the Lightship *Nantucket,* and the Jethro Coffin House (built in 1686 and the oldest on the island). There is no camping allowed on Nantucket, and, unless you plan a long stay, it is best not to bring a car. There are sightseeing buses which meet morning arrivals, shuttles to the beach, and rental mopeds, bicycles, and cars.

~75~

CROSSING TIME:	2 hrs.
FERRY TYPE:	Pedestrian
VESSEL CAPACITY:	The two vessels usually on this run are the *Brant Point* (600 passengers) and the *Point Gammon* (450 passengers).
OPERATING SEASON:	Mid-May—late October

SCHEDULE: **Mid-May—mid-June: Lv. Hyannis** 9:15 a.m.; **lv. Nantucket** 3:45 p.m.; **Mid-June— late June: Lv. Hyannis** 9 a.m., 10:15, 1:30 p.m.; **lv. Nantucket** 11:15 a.m., 4:15 p.m., 7:30. **Late June—early Sept.: Lv. Hyannis** 9 a.m., 10:30, 1:30 p.m., *3:20, 6:10, **8:10; **lv. Nantucket** 11:15 a.m. *12:55 p.m., 3:50, 5:45, 8:25, **10:35. **Early Sept.—mid-Sept.: Lv. Hyannis** 9 a.m., 10:15, 1:30 p.m.; **lv. Nantucket** 11:15 a.m., 4:15 p.m., 7:30. **Late Sept.—late Oct.: Lv. Hyannis** 9:15 a.m.; **lv. Nantucket** 3:45 p.m. *No Fri. sailing. **Fridays only.

RESTRICTIONS:	None
FACILITIES:	Restrooms; snack bar
FARE:	Adult $9; child (under 12) $4.50
RESERVATIONS:	No
DIRECTIONS:	In Hyannis, go south on Ocean St. and look for the Hy-Line sign. At the Hy-Line sign (in front of the Mooring Restaurant), turn left into Hy-Line's dock area.
MAP LOCATION:	P. 7, MA, 13
CONTACT:	See CONTACT, p. 74.

STATE:	Massachusetts
PLACES SERVED:	Hyannis (South Street Dock)—Nantucket
BODY OF WATER:	Buzzards Bay, Vineyard and Nantucket Sounds

Nantucket

FERRY SERVICE
HISTORY:
The twin-screw steel-hull *Nantucket* is usually used on this run; she was built by the Bellinger Shipyard in 1974, has a crew of eighteen, and is 230 feet long, with a gross weight of 1,152 tons.

[For notes on the history of ferry service to the islands, please see entry under Hyannis (Ocean Street Dock)-Nantucket, p. 74.]

LOCAL POINTS
OF INTEREST:
[For notes on Hyannis, please see entry under Hyannis (Ocean Street Dock)-Martha's Vineyard (Oak Bluffs), p. 72. For notes on Martha's Vineyard, please see entry under Martha's Vineyard (Edgartown)-Chappaquiddick Island, p. 79.]

CROSSING TIME: 2 hrs. 30 mins.

FERRY TYPE: Vehicle

VESSEL CAPACITY: 48 cars; 1,000 people

OPERATING SEASON: All year

SCHEDULE: **Mid-Jan.-Mid-April: Lv. Hyannis** 9:20 a.m., 3 p.m., 8:40; **lv. Nantucket** 6:30 a.m., 12:10 p.m., 5:50 p.m. **Mid-April-mid-June: Lv. Hyannis** 9:30 a.m., 3:30 p.m., 9:30; **lv. Nantucket** 6:30 a.m., 12:30 p.m., 6:30. **Mid-June-Oct.: Lv. Hyannis** 9:30 a.m.; *1:45 p.m., 3:30, 9:30; **lv. Nantucket** 6:30 a.m., *10:55, 12:30 p.m., 6:30. *Operates mid-June-mid-Sept. only. *Consult company for Nov.-Dec. schedules.*

RESTRICTIONS: Trailers, pickup-campers, and RVs permitted. Overhead clearance 13 ft.

FACILITIES: Restrooms, snack bar

FARE: Mid-May-mid-Oct.: Car $66.50; adult $8.50; child (5-15) $4.25; bicycle $4. Mid-Oct.-mid-May: Car $43; adult $8; child $4; bicycle $4. There are higher rates for pick-up trucks and RVs; there are also one-day round-trip rates and special round-trip rates for trips originating from the islands.

RESERVATIONS: Absolutely essential if you plan to take your car. Reservations open at the end of January and are processed the first week in February. A week's head start is given to in-person and mail reservations to avoid telephone overload. See under "Contact" for address and telephone number. You must be at the dock 30 minutes prior to scheduled sailing or reservation will be released to stand-by traveller.

DIRECTIONS: To reach South Street Dock, cross the Sagamore Bridge to Cape Cod; take Rt. 6 E to Hyannis Rt. 132. Follow Rt. 132 to Airport Rotary, take second right onto Barnstable Road, and follow signs to South St. Dock.

MAP LOCATION: P. 7, MA, 14

CONTACT: For summer reservations, it is best to telephone or write before January 15 for the dates mail and telephone reservations will be accepted each year. Mail reservations: Steamship Authority, Box 284, Woods Hole, Massachusetts, 02543. For information and advance reservations: (617)540-2022. Day of sailing information only: Ticket offices—Woods Hole: (617)548-3788; Hyannis: (617)771-4000; Nantucket: (617)228-0262.

STATE: Massachusetts

PLACES SERVED: Martha's Vineyard (Edgartown)—Chappaquiddick Island

BODY OF WATER: Buzzards Bay, Vineyard and Nantucket Sounds, between Edgartown Harbor and Katama Bay

FERRY SERVICE HISTORY: Chappaquiddick is not always an island; sometimes the beach breaks through, and four-wheel drive vehicles can be used. Usually, though, it is separated form Martha's Vineyard by 450 feet of water. The history of the Chappaquiddick Ferry, according to Jerry Grant, present owner, goes back to the late 1800s and early 1900s. At this time, Jimmy Yates rowed people across and towed horses and cattle behind the rowboat. In the 1920s, Midgie Bettencourt built a small one-car ferry and put down planks on the beach so that cars could be driven on it; a push boat provided the power. About 1928 or 1929, he put an engine in the barge and, in the 1930s, lengthened it to accommodate two cars. The ferry was named *City of Chappaquiddick*. In 1948, Bettencourt lost the county contract to his nephew, Foster Silver, who built a new two-car ferry, the *On Time I*. In 1952, Silver sold it to George T. Silver, who owned it until about 1961, when he sold it to Lawrence Mercier. The latter sold it to Jerry Grant in May 1967, and Grant also bought the *City of Chappaquiddick*. In 1969, he built the *On Time II*, sold the *City of Chappaquiddick*, and kept both going until 1975, when he built the *On Time III*. Today, he uses both the *On Time II* and the *On Time III*. The *City of Chappaquiddick* sank in a hurricane and is at the bottom of Edgartown Harbor, and the *On Time I* is a floating fish market on the island. Grant says one of his most unusual cargoes is horses (on foot, not in trailers).

LOCAL POINTS OF INTEREST: Martha's Vineyard is a triangular island off Cape Cod, with an area of less than twenty miles from east to west and ten from north to south. Bartholomew Gosnold was the first white man known to have visited it, though Leif Ericson may have done so. This island has been summarized by Walter Prichard Eaton as "a land of old towns, new cottages, high cliffs, white sails, green fairway, salt water, wild fowl and the steady pull of an ocean breeze." It is so wholesome, with its shingled cottages, heath, surf-beaten beaches, scrubby oaks, and bustling harbors, it seems almost a composite of the perfect island; there is a balance between deserted and unspoiled places, nourishing to the intellect, and such sophisticated places as Edgartown. It is the most fashionable resort town on the island, with posh shops and good hotels and restaurants, along with handsome ship captains' houses with widows' walks and tree-lined streets. At the Dukes County Historical Society on Cooke Street in Edgartown there are relics of the Vineyard's whaling days, including scrimshaw and other whaling artifacts.

Chappaquiddick, well known as the scene of the accident involving

Senator Edward Kennedy, is also the home of the 489-acre Cape Pogue Wildlife Refuge, with dunes, salt marsh, tidal flats, and barrier beach.

CROSSING TIME: 2 mins.

FERRY TYPE: Vehicle

VESSEL CAPACITY: 3 cars

OPERATING SEASON: All year

SCHEDULE: **June 1-Oct. 15:** On signal, 7 a.m.-midnight. **Oct. 15-June 1:** On signal, 8 a.m.-6 p.m., plus night trips at 7 p.m., 9, and 11.

RESTRICTIONS: Trailers, pickup-campers, and RVs permitted. Load limit 56,000 gross lbs.

FACILITIES: None

FARE: Car and driver $1.75; passenger $.35; bicycle & rider $1.00; pickup-camper $2-$4; trailers $3 to $8; RVs $2 to $5.

RESERVATIONS: No

DIRECTIONS: Ferry runs from Edgartown Road to Chappaquiddick

MAP LOCATION: P. 7, MA, 15

CONTACT: The Chappaquiddick Ferry, Box 1330, Edgartown, MA 02539, (617)627-9794 (617)627-5391

Uncatena

STATE:	Massachusetts
PLACES SERVED:	Martha's Vineyard (Oak Bluffs)—Nantucket
BODY OF WATER:	Buzzards Bay, Vineyard and Nantucket Sounds

FERRY SERVICE HISTORY: The twin-screw steel-hull *Uncatena* is usually used on this run; she was built by Blount Marine in 1965, has a crew of ten, and is 202 feet long, with a weight of 439.5 gross tons. Note that *passengers only* may go on this service from Martha's Vineyard to Nantucket; there is ample time for sightseeing allowed in the schedule. [For notes on the history of ferry service to the island, please see entry under Hyannis (Ocean Street Dock)-Nantucket, p. 74.]

LOCAL POINTS OF INTEREST: [For notes on Martha's Vineyard, please see entry under Martha's Vineyard (Edgartown)— Chappaquiddick Island, p. 79. For notes on Nantucket, please see entry under Hyannis (Ocean Street Dock)-Nantucket, p. 75.]

CROSSING TIME: 2 hrs. 25 mins.

FERRY TYPE: Vehicle; however, cars are carried only from Woods Hole to Nantucket; you may not take your car from Martha's Vineyard to Nantucket, as only a passenger stop is made at Martha's Vineyard. To take your car to Nantucket, you must leave from Woods Hole or Hyannis.

VESSEL CAPACITY:　　28 cars; 528 passengers

OPERATING SEASON:　Summer only, mid-June-mid-Sept.

SCHEDULE:　　**Lv. Oak Bluffs** 8 a.m.; **lv. Nantucket** 4:30 p.m.

RESTRICTIONS:　Passengers only Martha's Vineyard to Nantucket.

FACILITIES:　Restrooms, snack bar

FARE:　Adults $8.30; child (5-15) $4.15; bicycle $4.

RESERVATIONS:　No

DIRECTIONS:　Ferry leaves from Oak Bluffs on Martha's Vineyard.

MAP LOCATION:　P. 7, MA, 16

CONTACT:　Steamship Authority, Box 284, Woods Hole, MA 02543, (617)540-2022; Day of sailing information only: Ticket offices: Woods Hole: (617)548-3788; Hyannis: (617)771-4000; Nantucket: (617)228-0262

STATE:　Massachusetts

PLACES SERVED:　New Bedford—Cuttyhunk Island

BODY OF WATER:　Buzzards Bay, Vineyard and Nantucket Sounds

FERRY SERVICE HISTORY:　This ferry service has been in operation since 1917. Since 1974 Richard Hopps has worked on the ferry, and he has owned it since 1983. The vessel is a sixty-five-foot wooden boat named the *Alert*.

LOCAL POINTS OF INTEREST: New Bedford was settled as early as 1640, mainly by Quakers from Rhode Island and Cape Cod. It was named by Joseph Russell in honor of the Duke of Bedford, a relative, and incorporated as a town in 1787; it became a city in 1847. The town has an enduring nautical flavor, reminiscent of the early nineteenth century, when it outstripped Nantucket as the leading whaling center. The New Bedford Whaling Museum is still a major sight in the town, as is the Seamen's Bethel, the chapel where Melville once sat. In *Moby Dick* he wrote of finding in New Bedford a startling mix of people, "wild specimens of the whaling-craft which unheeded reel about the streets," but also considered that "nowhere in all America will you find more patrician-like houses; parks and gardens more opulent, than in New Bedford. . . . all these brave houses and flowery gardens came from the Atlantic, Pacific, and Indian oceans. One and all, they were harpooned and dragged up hither from the bottom of the sea." The importance of whale oil declined after petroleum was discovered in Pennsylvania in 1857, and the city's fortunes went downhill. They were revived by the New England textile boom in the 1880s and by a short-lived glass industry now commemorated in the New Bedford Glass Museum. In the County Street Historic District many of the mansions built by sea captains survive today.

Cuttyhunk Island is the southernmost island in the Elizabeth Islands archipelago, between Martha's Vineyard and the mainland. For the two centuries prior to 1864 the Elizabeth Islands were tied to the town of Chilmark; they then became the Town of Gosnold. Walter Teller has described the islands, when not shrouded in fog: "Each link rises clean and abrupt like a chain of low mountains with watery rifts between. Rolling or hilly, some hillsides furrowed with valleys, the islands present sun-bleached concave faces, cliffs of pale yellow clay and sand. . . . Settlement never gained much of a hold on these islands." Today, about fifty families live on the island, many of them related. The island has a town hall, wooden church, general store, schoolhouse, and library. Cuttyhunk Island has public beaches and restaurants.

VESSEL CAPACITY: 49 passengers

OPERATING SEASON: All year

SCHEDULE: **June 15-Sept. 15: Mon.-Fri.: Lv. New Bedford 10 a.m.; lv. Cuttyhunk Island 3 p.m. Sat., Sun., and holidays: Lv. New Bedford** 9 a.m.; **lv. Cuttyhunk Island** 3 p.m. *During July and August, extra trip from New Bedford Sat. at 12:30 and extra trip from Cuttyhunk Island Sun. at 5:30.* **Memorial Day-June 15 and Sept. 15-Columbus Day:** Tues.,

Fri., Sat., Sun. only (same times as above). **Columbus Day-Memorial Day:** operates Tues. and Fri. only (same times as above).

RESTRICTIONS:	None
FACILITIES:	Restrooms; soda sold on boat
FARE:	Adults $5; children under 12 $2.50
RESERVATIONS:	No
DIRECTIONS:	Go to the bottom of Union St.; turn left; the ferry leaves from Pier 3, 300 yards ahead on the right.
MAP LOCATION:	P. 7, MA, 17
CONTACT:	Cuttyhunk Boat Lines, Inc., Pier 3, New Bedford, MA 02741, (617)992-1432

STATE:	Massachusetts
PLACES SERVED:	New Bedford—Martha's Vineyard (Vineyard Haven)
BODY OF WATER:	Buzzards Bay, Vineyard and Nantucket Sounds
FERRY SERVICE HISTORY:	The vessel on this run is the *Schamonchi*. She was invited to take part in the "Salute to Liberty," the nation's celebration and

rededication of the Statue of Liberty in New York City on July 3-4, 1986. This service, which has been in operation more than ten years, is run by Janet and Dick Thompson.

LOCAL POINTS OF INTEREST:	[For notes about New Bedford, please see entry under New Bedford-Cuttyhunk Island, p. 83. For notes on Martha's Vineyard,

please see entry under Martha's Vineyard (Edgartown)-Chappaquiddick Island, p. 79.]

CROSSING TIME:	1 hr. 15 mins.
FERRY TYPE:	Pedestrian

VESSEL CAPACITY: 450 passengers

OPERATING SEASON: Summer only

SCHEDULE: **Mid-May-late June and early Sept.-late Sept.: Lv. New Bedford** 9 a.m., *1 p.m., *5, ˜9; **lv. Vineyard Haven** *11 a.m., *3 p.m., ^4, *6:45, ˜10:45. **Late June-early Sept.: Lv. New Bedford** 9 a.m., 1 p.m., 5, ˜9; **lv. Vineyard Haven** 11 a.m., 3 p.m., 6:45, ˜10:45. *Additional holiday sailings; contact company for dates and times.* *Fri., Sat., and Sun. only. ˜Fri. only. ^Mon.-Thurs. only.

RESTRICTIONS: Small pets allowed if confined or on leash.

FACILITIES: Restrooms, snack bar

FARE: Adults $7 ($12 round-trip); child $4 ($6 round-trip); bicycles $2 ($4 round-trip).

RESERVATIONS: No

DIRECTIONS: From Rt. I-195 take Downtown Exit #15 (Rt. 18), then, for garage, take Downtown Exit from Route 18 (third right). Take first right on Elm St. Garage is 200 feet ahead.

MAP LOCATION: P. 7, MA, 18

CONTACT: Cape Island Express Lines, Box J-4095, New Bedford, MA 02741, (617)997-1688

STATE: Massachusetts

PLACES SERVED: Woods Hole—Martha's Vineyard (Oak Bluffs)

BODY OF WATER: Buzzards Bay, Vineyard and Nantucket Sounds

FERRY SERVICE HISTORY: The vessels on this run are usually the *Uncatena* or the *Naushon*. The twin-screw steel-hull *Uncatena* was built by Blount

Marine in 1965, has a crew of ten, and is 202 feet long, with a weight of 439.5 gross tons. The twin-screw steel-hull *Naushon* was built by John H. Mathis Company in 1956, has a crew of twenty-six, and is 229.6 feet long with a gross weight of 2,652 tons.

[For notes on the history of ferry service to the islands, please see entry under Hyannis (Ocean Street Dock)-Nantucket, p. 74.]

LOCAL POINTS OF INTEREST: Woods Hole is about five miles from Falmouth; it is a principal port and resort. There are boutiques and restaurants near the wharf, and varied accommodation here and in Falmouth and Falmouth Heights, ranging from early inns to elaborate modern hotels and motels. The Woods Hole Oceanographic Institution, founded in 1930, is a major marine reserach center, but it is closed to the public. Here also is the aquarium of the US Bureau of Commercial Fisheries.

[For notes on Martha's Vineyard, please see entry under Martha's Vineyard (Edgartown)-Chappaquiddick Island, p. 79].

CROSSING TIME: 45 mins.

FERRY TYPE: Vehicle

VESSEL CAPACITY: *Uncatena*: 28 cars; 663 passengers; *Naushon*: 48 cars; 1,278 passengers

OPERATING SEASON: All year

SCHEDULE: **Mid-June-mid-Sept.: Lv. Woods Hole** *7 a.m., 9:30, 12:15 p.m., 2:45; **lv. Oak Bluffs** 10:45 a.m., 1:30 p.m., 4, *7:10. *Passengers only on these trips. **Mid-Sept.-Oct.: Lv. Woods Hole** 9:45 a.m., 12:15 p.m., 2:45; **lv. Oak Bluffs** 11 a.m., 1:30 p.m., 4.

RESTRICTIONS: Trailers, pickup-campers, and RVs permitted. Overhead clearance for *Uncatena* 13 ft.; for *Naushon* 12 ft. 6 in.

FACILITIES: Restrooms, snack bar

FARE: Car mid-May-mid-Oct. $26.50; adults $3.75; children (5-15) $1.90; car mid-Oct.-mid-May $13.75; adult $3.50; child $1.75.

RESERVATIONS: See RESERVATIONS, p. 78.

DIRECTIONS:	In Woods Hole, cross the Bourne Bridge to Cape Cod. Follow Rt. 28 south to Falmouth and Woods Hole; follow signs.
MAP LOCATION:	P. 7, MA, 19
CONTACT:	See CONTACT, p. 78.

Islander

STATE:	Massachusetts
PLACES SERVED:	Woods Hole—Martha's Vineyard (Vineyard Haven)
BODY OF WATER:	Buzzards Bay, Vineyard and Nantucket Sounds

FERRY SERVICE HISTORY: The vessels on this run are usually the *Islander* or the *Uncatena*. The *Islander* is a double-end steel-hull ferry built at the Maryland Drydock in 1950; she has a crew of fifteen and is two hundred feet long, with a gross weight of 2,030 tons. The twin-screw steel-hull *Uncatena* was built by Blount Marine in 1965, has a crew of ten, and is 202 feet long, with a weight of 439.5 gross tons. [For notes on the history of ferry service to the islands, please see entry under Hyannis (Ocean Street Dock)-Nantucket, p. 74.]

LOCAL POINTS
OF INTEREST:
[For notes on Woods Hole, please see entry for Woods Hole-Martha's Vineyard (Oak Bluffs), p. 86. For notes on Martha's Vineyard, please see entry under Martha's Vineyard (Edgartown)-Chappaquiddick Island, p. 79.]

CROSSING TIME: 45 mins.

FERRY TYPE: Vehicle

VESSEL CAPACITY: *Islander* 48 cars; 788 passengers; *Uncatena* 28 cars; 528 passengers

OPERATING SEASON: All year

SCHEDULE: **Mid-Apr.-mid-June: Lv. Woods Hole** *7 a.m., 8:15, 9:30, 10:45, 11:45, 1 p.m., 2, 3:15, 4:30, 5:45, 6:30, 8, ˜8:45, **10. **Lv. Vineyard Haven** *5:45 a.m., 7, *8:15, 9:30, 10:45, noon, 1 p.m., 2, 3:15, 4:30, 5:30, 6:45, 7:30, **9:30. **Mid-June-mid-Sept.: Lv. Woods Hole** 7:05 a.m., 8, 10:45, 1:15 p.m., 3:45, 5:15, 6:15, ˜7:45, 8:15, 8:45, ˜˜10:45. **Lv. Vineyard Haven** 5:45 a.m., 6:45, 8:15, 9:15, noon, 2:30 p.m., 5, 6:30, 7:30, ˜8:45, ˜˜9:45. **Mid-Sept.-Oct.: Lv. Woods Hole** 7:15 a.m., 8:15, 10:45, 1:15 p.m., 3:45, 5:15, 6:15, 7:45, 8:45, 9:45, **10:45. **Lv. Vineyard Haven** 5:45 a.m., 7, 8:30, 9:30, noon, 2:30 p.m., 5, 6:30, 7:30, 8:45, **9:45. **Late Jan.-Feb.: Lv. Woods Hole** *8:15 a.m., 10:45, 1 p.m., 3:15, 5:45, ˜˜8. (8:30 Sun.) **Lv. Vineyard Haven** *7 a.m., 9:30, noon, 2 p.m., ˜˜4:15, 6:45. **Late Feb.-early April: Lv. Woods Hole** *8:15 a.m., 10:45, 1 p.m., 3:15, 5:45, 8, **10. **Lv. Vineyard Haven** *7 a.m., 9:30, noon, 2 p.m., 4:30, 6:45, **9. *Daily except Sundays. ˜Daily except Saturdays. **Will operate Fridays & Sundays. ˜˜Operates Fridays, Sundays, and holidays. **Memorial Day Weekend:** Additional service; contact Steamship Authority for schedule. *For other holidays and Nov.-Dec. schedules, contact Steamship Authority.*

RESTRICTIONS: Trailers, pickup-campers, and RVs permitted. Overhead clearance on *Uncatena* 13 ft.; on *Islander* 12 ft. 6 in.

FACILITIES: Restrooms, snack bar

FARE: Car mid-May-mid-Oct. $26.50; adults $3.75; children (5-15) $1.90; car mid-Oct.-mid-May $13.75; adult $3.50; child $1.75.

RESERVATIONS: See RESERVATIONS, p. 78.

DIRECTIONS: See DIRECTIONS, p. 87.

MAP LOCATION: P. 7, MA, 20

CONTACT: See CONTACT, p. 78.

STATE: Massachusetts

PLACES SERVED: Woods Hole—Nantucket

BODY OF WATER: Buzzards Bay, Vineyard and Nantucket Sounds

FERRY SERVICE HISTORY: The vessel on this run is usually the twin-screw steel-hull *Uncatena*, built by Blount Marine in 1965. She has a crew of ten, and is 202 feet long, with a weight of 439.5 gross tons.

[For notes on the history of ferry service to the islands, please see entry under Hyannis (Ocean Street Dock)-Nantucket, p. 74.]

LOCAL POINTS OF INTEREST: [For notes on Woods Hole, please see entry under Woods Hole-Martha's Vineyard (Oak Bluffs), p. 86. For notes on Nantucket, please see entry under Hyanis (Ocean Street Dock)-Nantucket, p. 74.]

CROSSING TIME: 3 hours, 25 mins.

FERRY TYPE: Vehicle

VESSEL CAPACITY: 28 automobiles; 663 passengers

OPERATING SEASON: Summer only, mid-June-mid-Sept.

SCHEDULE: **Lv. Woods Hole** 7 a.m.; **lv. Nantucket** 4:30 p.m.

RESTRICTIONS: Trailers, pickup-campers, and RVs permitted. Overhead clearance 13 ft.

FACILITIES:	Restrooms, snack bar
FARE:	Car $66.50; adults $8.50; child (5-15) $4.25.
RESERVATIONS:	See RESERVATIONS, p. 78.
DIRECTIONS:	See DIRECTIONS, p. 87.
MAP LOCATION:	P. 7, MA, 21
CONTACT:	See CONTACT, p. 78.

STATE:	New Hampshire
PLACES SERVED:	Portsmouth—Isles of Shoals
BODY OF WATER:	Piscataqua River and Atlantic Ocean
FERRY SERVICE HISTORY:	In 1962, Captain Arnold Whittaker took over the ferry service to Star Island, becoming one of many ferry-boat operators to the Isles

of Shoals since the mid-1900s. His first vessel was the sixty-five-foot wooden boat *Viking*. In 1967, the *Viking Star* was added, also sixty-five feet, with a capacity of one hundred passengers. In 1974, Captain Whittaker purchased the 109-foot, 385-passenger *Viking Queen,* followed in 1980 by the 130-foot *Viking Sun*. By 1986, the *Viking Sun* was paired with the seventy-one-foot *Oceanic* for whale-watching cruises. In 1987, the *Viking Sun* will be replaced by the Isles of Shoals Steamship Company's ninety-foot Coastal Steamship replica, the *Thomas Laighton,* built along the lines of a turn-of-the-century coastal steamship, which will carry 350 passengers. It is said that, before telegraph communication was established with the Isles of Shoals, boats transported carrier pigeons as well as passengers. Once the boat had left Portsmouth, passengers would state whether they expected to dine at one of the Isles of Shoals restaurants, and a pigeon would be dispatched with a note clipped to its leg to make the reservation. Today the island is a private one, and you may stay at the hotel only if you are attending a conference. There is no camping. The public may disembark on the island only by taking the 11 a.m. boat, spending three hours, and returning on the 3:30 p.m. boat [see schedule]. On the island, optional walking tours are offered, with a visit to the library, the museum, and the gift shop. You may take a picnic, buy a box lunch from Viking Cruises, or have lunch at the island snack bar. If stopover tickets are sold out, you may ride over and return immediately, without disembarking.

Thomas Laighton

LOCAL POINTS OF INTEREST: Portsmouth was named Strawbery Banke by the first settlers, who, arriving in 1630, discovered a strawberry-covered embankment. The name has now been given to the renovation and preservation program in the ten-acre historic waterfront neighborhood. Thirty-five buildings from 1695-1865 are undergoing restoration. One dwelling, the Thomas Bailey Aldrich house, was the boyhood home of the author, represented as the Nutter House in his *The Story of a Bad Boy*. The Theatre by the Sea is in a renovated brewery on the waterfront. Portsmouth was once a prosperous mercantile seaport, an era recalled in the many craft shops, restaurants, chandleries, and homes of the Strawbery Banke site and the Old Harbor area. The John Paul Jones house, owned by the Portsmouth Historical Society, contains valuable antiques, silver, and costumes; it was built by Capt. Gregory Purcell. Captain Jones stayed here, though he never owned the house.

"Isles of Shoals" means a place where fish are schooling or shoaling, literally the "Isles of Schooling Fish." The Isles consist of nine islands that, in the early 1600s, became the center of all colonial fishing industries and the economic hub of New England many years before that position was held by Boston. As many as six hundred British Isles fishermen and their families lived on the shoals in the 1600s and 1700s. It was considered the wealthiest settlement per capita at the time in the colonies. The Isles also developed during this era as the major trading center for English merchants and colonists. By the 1850s, the Isles had become known as one of the most sought-after health resorts along the East Coast. Thomas Laighton built the first grand summer-resort hotel, accommodating more than five hundred people, along the coast in 1848 on Appledore Island. His daughter, Celia Thaxter, became a famous poet and counted Hawthorne, Whittier, Longfellow, and Harriet Beecher Stowe among her literary friends; they all frequented the island. The Oceanic Hotel on Star Island was built in 1873 and stands today as a unique family center virtually unchanged in more than one hundred years. In recent years, Margaret Mead, the famous anthropologist, was a guest speaker at the Star Island Conference Center.

CROSSING TIME: 1 hour

FERRY TYPE: Pedestrian

VESSEL CAPACITY: *Thomas Laighton:* 350 passengers (handicapped accessible); *Oceanic:* 149 passengers

OPERATING SEASON: Regular ferry service mid-June-Labor Day. Special trips May 1-end of Oct.

SCHEDULE: **Daily: Lv. Portsmouth** 7:30 a.m., *11, 2 p.m., 6. **Lv. Isles of Shoals** 8:45 a.m., 12:30 p.m., 3:30, 7. *Disembarkation allowed on this trip only; 100 3-hr. stopover tickets sold, first-come, first serve, beginning 9 a.m. [Usually sold out; come early.]

RESTRICTIONS: No pets except seeing eye dogs

FACILITIES: Restrooms (*Thomas Laighton* has handicapped facilities); galley; full beverage service

FARE: All fares round-trip. Four fares: 7:30 a.m.: adult $6; child (6-12) $4; under 5 free. 11 a.m. and 2 p.m.: adult $10, child $6.50, but 3-hour stopover tickets (11 a.m. only) are adult $13.50, child $8.50. 5:30 p.m.: adult $7.50, child $5.50.

RESERVATIONS: Individual, no; groups, yes

DIRECTIONS: From I-95 S or N, take Exit 7 and go toward downtown Portsmouth Historic District on Market St. Extension. Isles of Shoals Steamship Co. is one mile on left. Parking is available dockside.

MAP LOCATION: P. 7, NH, 1

CONTACT: Isles of Shoals Steamship Co. (formerly Viking Cruises), Box 311, Portsmouth, NH 03801, (603)431-5500

Prudence Ferry

STATE:	Rhode Island
PLACES SERVED:	Bristol—Prudence Island—Hog Island
BODY OF WATER:	Narragansett Bay
FERRY SERVICE HISTORY:	In Rhode Island, located as it is on both shores of Narragansett Bay, ferries have played an important role since colonial days,

when the post roads ended on opposite shores with no means of communication between except ferries. Despite bridge construction today, they are still a vital component of the transportation system.

The first ferries were controlled by towns, which granted franchises to private owners and operators. Before they became profitable, grants of land were included as an inducement; such wealthy men as Benjamin Ellery of Newport and Deputy-Governor Abbott of Providence made efforts to secure ferry franchises. By 1690, post riders were rated as free passengers, and a 1747 act mandated that ferrymen be ready to transport passengers from March 10 through September 10 from 5 a.m. to 8 p.m., and from 6 a.m. to 7 p.m. the rest of the year "if the weather will permit boats passing." However, "Physicians, Surgeons, Midwives, and Persons going to fetch Physicians, Surgeons, or Midwives were to be carried at any Time of Night." Other rules covered maintenance and mandated that ferries be kept afloat and at the ferry landings when not being repaired.

Ferrymen often kept inns near their wharves, contriving to keep passengers overnight. Passengers were not above subterfuge, either, sometimes pretending to be fetching a physician. Since many ferries were sailboats, and dependent on winds, the inn or "House of Entertayne-ment" was a great convenience.

Bristol Ferry had a great deal of post traffic during the late eighteenth and early nineteenth centuries, and a Ferry Act of 1844 mentions rates for a "coach, barouche, wagon, four-wheel carriage, chaise or sulky, carryall or pleasure carriage, wagon hung on springs, or ox wagon or cart." In 1830, Bristol Ferry had two sailboats, and one horse-powered ferry. It did not have a steam ferry until 1905, though they did exist in other parts of the state. The original Bristol ferry route was displaced by the Mount Hope Bridge, but today the ferry to Prudence Island and Hog Island does a thriving business.

Prudence Ferry, Inc. took over the service in March 1986 from Prudence Island Navigation Company (which had established service about 1924) with a new ten-car, 149-passenger ferry built by Blount Marine of Warren and completed in March 1986. The new company is owned by Luther H. Blount of Warren, who originally was a part-owner of Prudence Island Navigation Company. The vessel is the *Prudence Ferry*; she is sixty-five feet long with a thirty-five-foot beam and a four and one-half-foot draft; she has a crew of two. Her most unusual cargo has been a trailer-truck loaded with parts for a house. Most of the riders come from Southern New England. The *Bay Queen,* also owned by Blount, offers a number of cruises (leaving from nearby Warren).

LOCAL POINTS OF INTEREST: Bristol is perhaps best known as the site of the Herreshoff Boatyard, where six defenders of the America's Cup were built between 1893 and 1934. Bristol's reign as a yacht-building center is recalled at the Herreshoff Marine Museum. King Philip's War (1675-76) began and ended on the Bristol Peninsula, and the rebel Indian King Philip was felled here. Once a trading port, Bristol is now a mecca for pleasure craft. Other attractions are the Blithewold Gardens and Arboretum (with exotic plants from China and Japan), the Haffenreffer Museum of Anthropology, and the Coggeshall Farm Museum in Colt State Park (a working eighteenth-century farm project).

Prudence Island was originally bought from the Indians by Roger Williams. He sold half of it to finance his trip to England to secure the charter for Rhode Island. The lower part of the island contains the Bay Island State Park; the remainder is not commercialized but does have two small stores, widely separated, an inn, a gift shop, and a winery. Homestead and Sandy Point landings are on the eastern shore. The Prudence Island Vineyards are here at Sunset Hill Farm, a four hundred-acre estate located one-third of a mile uphill from the Homestead Ferry Landing. The vineyard is owned by William Bacon. The farmhouse was built in 1783 and has been lived in by eight generations of Mrs. Bacon's family. The principal wines produced are Pinot Noir and Chardonnay (the latter has won a number of awards in wine competitions). Visitors are welcomed for informal tours May 30-Labor Day, daily 10-12 and 2-5; the rest of the year, visitors are encouraged to come on weekends from 10 a.m.-3:30 p.m.. Camping on Prudence Island is discouraged.

Hog Island is not commercial, but consists of a closely-knit community of farming people.

CROSSING TIME: 20 mins. (Bristol-Prudence Is.)

FERRY TYPE: Vehicle

VESSEL CAPACITY: 10 cars; 149 passengers

OPERATING SEASON: All year

SCHEDULE: **Mid-Mar.-mid-Apr.: Mon., Wed., Fri.: Lv. Bristol** 8 a.m., 3:30 p.m. **Lv. Homestead** 8:35 a.m., 4:05 p.m. **Lv. Sandy Point** 8:50 a.m. **Sat.: Lv. Bristol** 8 a.m., *10:30, 3:30 p.m. **Lv. Homestead** 8:35 a.m., 11:05, 4:05 p.m. **Lv. Sandy Point** 8:50 a.m., 11:15. **Lv. Hog Island** *10:45 a.m. **Sun.: Lv. Bristol** 10 a.m., 4 p.m. **Lv. Homestead** 10:35 a.m., 4:50 p.m. **Lv. Sandy Point** 10:45 a.m., 4:35 p.m. **Lv. Hog Island** *10:15 a.m., *5:10 p.m. *Starting about April 9. **Mid-Apr.-late May: Mon., Wed., Fri.: Lv. Bristol** 8 a.m., 3:30 p.m., 6. **Lv. Homestead 8:35 a.m., 4:05 p.m., *6:35. Lv. Sandy Point** 8:50 a.m., **4:15 p.m. *Fri. only. **Mon., Wed. only. **Sat.: Lv. Bristol** 8 a.m., 3:30 p.m., 6. **Lv. Homestead** 8:35 a.m., 10:40, 4:05 p.m. **Lv. Sandy Point** 8:50 a.m., 10:50, 4:15 p.m. **Lv. Hog Island** 10:15 a.m. **Sun.: Lv. Bristol** 10 a.m., 3:15 p.m., 5. **Lv. Homestead** 10:40 a.m., 4:05 p.m., 5:50. **Lv. Sandy Point** 10:50 a.m., 3:50 p.m., 5:35. **Lv. Hog Island** 10:15 a.m., 4:25 p.m. **Late May-mid-June: Mon. through Fri.: Lv. Bristol** 8 a.m., 10, 3:30 p.m., 5, 7. **Lv. Homestead** 8:35 a.m., 10:35, 4:05 p.m., 5:35, *7:35. **Lv. Sandy Point** 8:50 a.m., 10:45, **4:15 p.m. *5:45. *Fri. only. **Mon. through Thurs. **Sat.: Lv. Bristol** 8 a.m., 10, 5 p.m. **Lv. Homestead** 8:35 a.m., 10:40, 5:35 p.m. **Lv. Sandy Point** 8:50 a.m., 10:50, 5:45 p.m. **Lv. Hog Island** 10:15 a.m. **Sun. & Memorial Day: Lv. Bristol** 10 a.m., 3:15 p.m., 5. **Lv. Homestead** 10:40 a.m., 4:05 p.m. 5:50. **Lv. Sandy Point** 10:50 a.m., 3:50 p.m., 5:35. **Lv. Hog Island** 10:15 a.m., 4:25 p.m. **Mid-June-early Sept.: Mon.-Fri.: Lv. Bristol** *7 a.m., 10, 3:30 p.m., **7:30. **Lv. Homestead** *7:30 a.m., 10:40, 4 p.m., 6:40. **Lv. Sandy Point** 10:55 a.m., 4:15 p.m., 6:50. **Lv. Hog Island** 7:45 a.m., 10:15, 3:45 p.m., 6:15. *7 a.m. boat is replaced by 6 a.m. boat on Mon. **Fri. only (to Homestead only). **Sat.: Lv. Bristol** 8 a.m., 10, 3:30 p.m., 5:45. **Lv. Homestead** 8:45 a.m., 10:45, 4:10 p.m., 6:30. **Lv. Sandy Point** 8:30 a.m., 11, 4:25 p.m., 6:45. **Lv. Hog Island** 8:15 a.m.10:15, 6 p.m.

Sun., July 4, Aug. 13 (a RI holiday) & Labor Day: Lv. Bristol 8 a.m., 10, 3:30 p.m., 6, 7:10. **Lv. Homestead** 8:35 a.m., 10:40, 4:30 p.m., 8. **Lv. Sandy Point** 8:50 a.m., 10:55, 4:10 p.m., 7:45. **Lv. Hog Island** 10:15 a.m., 6:20 p.m. *In addition, there are Homestead and Hog Island express shuttles from mid-June to early Sept., consult company for schedules.*

RESTRICTIONS:	Trailers, pickup-campers and RVs permitted.
FACILITIES:	Restrooms; two cabins
FARE:	Cars $12.50; to Prudence Island adult $2.35; child $.90. To Hog Island adult $1.50; child $.90.
RESERVATIONS:	Essential for cars.
DIRECTIONS:	In Bristol, ferry leaves from the Church St. Wharf.
MAP LOCATION:	P. 7, RI, 1
CONTACT:	Prudence Ferry, Inc., % Blount Marine Corp., Box 368, Warren, RI 02885, (401)245-8303

STATE:	Rhode Island
PLACES SERVED:	Galilee (Point Judith)—Block Island
BODY OF WATER:	Block Island Sound
FERRY SERVICE HISTORY:	Service on this run began in the 1940s. The vessels on this run are the *Manitou,* built in 1970; *Carol Jean,* built in 1984, and the *Manisee,* built in 1971.
LOCAL POINTS OF INTEREST:	Block Island was named for the Dutch explorer Adriaen Block, who landed here in 1614.

Once frequented by pirates and smugglers, and plagued by shipwrecks, today, it attracts artists and summer visitors. Bird migrations cross over in the spring and fall. Mohegan Bluffs, two hundred feet high, affords excellent sea views. Settlers' Rock commemorates the first settlers (1661). There is swimming at Block

Manitou

Island State Beach and lodging at a few hotels, guesthouses, and rental cottages. Most of these are seasonal, only open from spring through early fall. Ballard's Inn, the Atlantic Inn, and the Harborside Inn all serve breakfast, lunch and dinner, as does the Samuel Peckham Tavern. For a list of accommodations, write the Tourism Division, RI Deptartment of Economic Development, 7 Jackson Walkway, Providence, RI 02903, as information about the island is not widely distributed.

Galilee is a community on Block Island Sound; the Roger W. Wheeler Memorial Beach is nearby, along with the Galilee Bird Sanctuary. Galilee can be reached from Wakefield, at the northern end of Point Judith Pond. The Point Judith Coast Guard Station is a few miles away.

CROSSING TIME: 1 hr. 15 mins.

FERRY TYPE: Vehicle

VESSEL CAPACITY: The *Manitou* and the *Manisee* take 16 cars. The *Carol Jean* takes 1300 passengers (no cars).

OPERATING SEASON: All year

SCHEDULE: *Dates may vary each year; check with company.* **Jan. 1-Mar. 3 & Nov. 30-Dec. 31: Mon., Wed., Sat. and Sun.: Lv. Galilee 11** a.m.; **lv. Block Island** 2:30 p.m. **Tues. & Thurs.: Lv. Galilee** 7 a.m., 11 and 4 p.m.; **lv. Block Island** 8:30 a.m., 2 p.m., 5:30. **Fri.: Lv. Galilee** 11 a.m., 4 p.m.; **lv. Block Island** 2 p.m., 5:30. **Mar. 4-Apr. 14 & Nov. 2-29: Mon., Tues., Thurs., Sat. & Sun.: Lv. Galilee** 10 a.m.; 2:45 p.m.; **lv. Block Island** noon, 5 p.m.; **Wed.: Lv. Galilee** 7 a.m., 11, 4 p.m.; **lv. Block Island** 8:30 a.m., 2 p.m., 5:30; **Fri.: Lv. Galilee** 7 a.m., 11, 6:30

p.m.; **lv. Block Island** 8:30 a.m., 2 p.m., 7:45. **Apr. 15-June 7 & Sept. 9-Nov. 1: Mon.-Fri.: Lv. Galilee** 9 a.m., 11, 3 p.m., 5 (except Fri.); 7 (Fri. only). **Sat. & Sun.: Lv. Galilee** 9 a.m., 11, 1 p.m., 6:30; **lv. Block Island** 8 a.m., 11, 3 p.m., 5. **June 8-Sept. 8: Mon.-Fri.: Lv. Galilee** 8 a.m., 9, 10:30, 11:30, 1 p.m., 3:30, 6, 7, **(except Fri.)**; 8 **(Fri. only)**. **Sat. & Sun.: Lv. Galilee** 8 a.m., 9, 10:30, 11:30, 1 p.m., 3, 5, 6:30, 9:30; **lv. Block Island** 8 a.m., 9:45, 11, 12:30 p.m., 3, 4, 5, 6:30. *No trip Dec. 25.*

RESTRICTIONS: Overhead clearance 9 ft.

FACILITIES: Restrooms, lunch counter

FARE: Car $16.20; adult $5 ($8 same-day round-trip); children under 12 $2.50 ($4 same-day round-trip); bicycle $1.40; motorcycle $9.50.

RESERVATIONS: Reservations for cars must be made in advance, in writing, accompanied with full payment for each one-way reservation. Cars must be at the dock ready to be loaded 30 mins. before scheduled sailing.

DIRECTIONS: From I-95 N: Take North Stonington-Westerly Exit (# 92). Bear right onto North Stonington Rd. Continue until Westerly bypass. Take right bypass Rt. 78. At end of bypass take left onto Rt. 1. Follow Rt. 1 to exit for Galilee, Rt. 108. Bear right to Pt. Judith Rd. Continue until right exit for B.I. Boat.

MAP LOCATION: P. 7, RI, 2

CONTACT: Interstate Navigation Co., Galilee State Pier, Point Judith, RI 02882, (401)789-3502

STATE: Rhode Island

PLACES SERVED: Portsmouth (Bend Boat Basin)—Prudence Island

BODY OF WATER: Narragansett Bay

FERRY SERVICE
HISTORY:
The name of the vessel on this service is the *Patriot,* a fiberglass motorboat with wood superstructure; she is thirty-seven feet long with a twelve-foot beam, and has a captain and one mate. Service was inaugurated in 1981. Most riders are naturalists, local residents, students, civic groups, and day trippers.

LOCAL POINTS
OF INTEREST:
Portsmouth was settled in 1638; it was, at one time, the most populous town in the state. It was founded by free-speech advocate Anne Hutchison, first woman to establish a town in the nation. A copy of the Portsmouth Compact, an instrument which organized the first truly democratic form of government in the world, is inscribed on a bronze and stone marker on Pudding Rock.

One of the leading attractions is the Green Animals Topiary Gardens, eighty sculptured trees and shrubs shaped in animal forms (giraffe, elephant, lion, etc.). Thomas E. Brayton, Treasurer of the Union Cotton Manufacturing Company in Fall River, Massachusetts, had long been fascinated with the topiary gardens created by ancient pharoahs and European kings. Topiary had reached the zenith of its popularity during the seventeenth century in Europe, and Brayton sought to emulate the form on his estate on the shore of Narragansett Bay. He and his Portuguese gardener, Joseph Carreiro, developed this rare garden, and the estate was preserved by his daughter, Alice Brayton. The New York Botanical Garden offered to transport the garden to the Bronx, but she refused, saying, "I couldn't bear the idea of seeing my giraffe leaving through the front gate." At her death (1972), the Preservation Society of Newport County took over the estate. There is also a small children's Victorian Toy Museum.

[For notes on Prudence Island, please see entry under Bristol—Prudence Island—Hog Island, p. 94.]

CROSSING TIME: 15 min.

FERRY TYPE: Pedestrian

VESSEL CAPACITY: 42 passengers

OPERATING SEASON: Mid-May-mid-Oct.

SCHEDULE: **Summer, late June-Aug.: Thurs., Fri., Sat., Sun., & Mon. holidays: Lv. Portsmouth 10 a.m., 12, 2 p.m., *3, 4, 6. Lv. South Prudence Island 10:30, **12:30 p.m., 2:30, *3:30, **4:30, 6:30.** *This trip does not operate Thurs. and Fri. **These trips return via North Prudence Island, leaving there at 1:15 p.m. and 5:15. **Spring and fall, mid-May-late June and early Sept.-mid-Oct.:** Ferry only operates Fri., Sat., Sun., & Mon. holidays (same schedule).

RESTRICTIONS: Small pets permitted.

FACILITIES: Porta Potti.

FARE: Round-trip: Adults $3.00; children under 12 $2.50; bicycles $1.50.

RESERVATIONS: Not required, but preferred for groups

DIRECTIONS: In Portsmouth, ferry leaves from Bend Boat Basin, Stringham Rd. On Prudence Island, ferry lands near Bay Island Park.

MAP LOCATION: P. 7, RI, 3

CONTACT: Oldport Marine Services, Inc., Box 141, Newport, RI 02840, (401)847-9109

STATE: Rhode Island

PLACES SERVED: Portsmouth (Melville)—Prudence Island (Sandy Point & Homestead Landing)

BODY OF WATER: Narragansett Bay

FERRY SERVICE HISTORY: This ferry service has existed since 1984; it is owned and operated by Harry Church. The boat is the sixty-four-foot *Island Transport,* a steel vessel unique in that it does not need docks; it is similar to a Navy landing craft with ramps.

LOCAL POINTS OF INTEREST: [For notes on Portsmouth, please see entry under Portsmouth—Prudence Island (Bend Boat Basin), p. 99; for notes on Prudence Island, please see entry under Bristol—Prudence Island—Hog Island, p. 94.]

CROSSING TIME: 20 mins.

FERRY TYPE: Vehicle

VESSEL CAPACITY: 5 cars, 149 passengers

OPERATING SEASON: All year

SCHEDULE: **Daily. Summer: Lv. Portsmouth** 6:10 a.m., 8, 9:30, 2:30 p.m., 4, 6. **Lv. Prudence Island** approx. 20 mins. later. *Check with company for off-season schedules.*

RESTRICTIONS: Trailers, pickup-campers, and RVs permitted. Load limit 25 tons.

FACILITIES: None

FARE: Car $15 ($25 round-trip); adults $2; children $1.50 (6-12; under 6 free)

RESERVATIONS: No

DIRECTIONS: In Portsmouth, ferry leaves from Melville. On Prudence Island, ferry leaves from Sandy Point and Homestead Landing.

MAP LOCATION: P. 7, RI, 4

CONTACT: Island Transport Co., 19 Maniton Dr., Portsmouth, RI 02781, (401)683-9681

STATE: Rhode Island

PLACES SERVED: Providence-Newport-Block Island

BODY OF WATER: Narragansett Bay

FERRY SERVICE HISTORY: The vessel is the *Nelseco*, built in 1981.

LOCAL POINTS OF INTEREST: Providence, the capital of Rhode Island, was founded in 1636 by Roger Williams, who fled Massachusetts to escape religious persecution. He named the city in gratitude "for God's merciful providence unto me in my distress." It has a long history as a shipping and shipbuilding town, for ships from Providence carried slaves, rum, and molasses in a "Triangle Trade" between Africa, the West Indies, and New England. The history of the city is intricately bound up with that of its preeminent Ivy League university, Brown, internationally known for its academic excellence and so competitive fewer than one-tenth of their applicants are admitted. Founded in 1764, it is the nation's seventh oldest university. On surrounding streets, such as Benefit and Cooke, there is an impressive concentration of colonial, federal, and early nineteenth-century architecture. John Quincy Adams said of the John Brown House on Power Street (1786) that it was "the most magnificent and elegant private mansion that I have ever seen on this continent." It was named for John Brown, who began the China trade in Providence.

"All that has been said of Newport you may safely set down as an understatement," wrote American critic James Huneker. This is still true of Newport today, whether you prefer eighteenth-century colonial simplicity, nineteenth-century Baroque opulence, or the contemporary ambience of a restored waterfront marketplace and marina, with hewn timber walks, seafood restaurants, ship's chandler shops, and a flotilla of yachts from far-flung ports. The vigilant Preservation Society of Newport has restored many eighteenth-century homes, such as the Hunter House, which has fine Rhode Island furniture. The "Gilded Age" when the opulent "cottages" were built (1880s, 1890s, and 1900s) is vividly alive today, as a number of the mansions are open to the public. (The Cliff Walk affords a good view of some of them). The age was one of extravagant spectacle and splendor (one hostess even invited one hundred dogs to a dinner party, all chauffeured, naturally), but it also attracted many *literati* such as Henry James, Julia Ward Howe, George Berkeley, Thornton Wilder, and Bret Harte. James deplored the excesses, but referred to Newport in *Daisy Miller* as an "American watering place." A good place to stay is the Treadway Inn, at the edge of the restored waterfront (reserve well ahead). From here you can admire the harbor and wander among the boutiques and restaurants on Bowen's Wharf and Bannister's Wharf; harbor tours leave from this area also. An excellent place to dine is the Inn at Castle Hill, high above the Bay (reserve here also). Thornton Wilder stayed here and wrote of a turret room in *Theophilus North:* "From that magical room I could see at night the beacons of six light houses and hear the booming and chiming of as many sea buoys."

[For notes on Block Island, please see entry under Galilee—Block Island, p. 96.]

CROSSING TIME:	Providence—Newport 2 hrs. Newport—Block Island 2 hrs. Providence—Block Island 4 hrs. 30 min.
FERRY TYPE:	Pedestrian *(Note that this service is now passengers only; cars may not be taken from Providence or Newport to Block Island.)*

VESSEL CAPACITY: 800 passengers

OPERATING SEASON: Late June-early Sept. *(Check with company for exact dates of operation.)*

SCHEDULE: **Daily: Lv. Providence** 9 a.m.; **lv. Newport** 11 a.m.; **lv. Block Island** 3:45 p.m.; **lv. Newport** 5:30 p.m.

RESTRICTIONS: None

FACILITIES: Restrooms; lunch counter

FARE: Providence to Newport: Adult $3.10 ($4.50 same-day round-trip); child $1.80 ($2.25 same-day round-trip). Providence to Block Island: Adult $5.25 ($7.75 same-day round-trip); child $2.75 ($4 same-day round-trip); Newport to Block Island: Adult $4.75 ($7 same-day round-trip); child $2.25 ($3.25 same-day round-trip).

RESERVATIONS: No

DIRECTIONS: In Providence, ferry leaves from India St., Providence Harbor. Boat leaves from Fort Adams in Newport.

MAP LOCATION: P. 7, RI, 5

CONTACT: Nelseco Navigation Co., Box 482, New London, CT 06320, (203)442-7891

STATE: Vermont/New York

PLACES SERVED: Burlington, VT—Port Kent, NY

BODY OF WATER: Lake Champlain

FERRY SERVICE HISTORY: In 1825 the Champlain Ferry Company began running the *General Greene*, a seventy-five-foot steam-driven ship with wood-burning boilers, between Burlington and Port Kent. A "four-wheel pleasure carriage on springs, drawn by two horses, including the driver," cost $2.00; a two-horse sleigh was $1.50. In 1825 the company absorbed all the others which had been running ferries on the lake and established its

Champlain

headquarters in Burlington, where it has been ever since. This crossing is the most direct route from northern Vermont to the heart of the Adirondacks, saving eighty-five miles between Burlington and Port Kent. Today, the vessels on this run are: the *Adirondack*, built in 1913 in Jacksonville, FL (length 130 feet, gross tonnage 333, crew of four); the *Champlain*, built in 1930 in Baltimore (length 148 feet, gross tonnage 440, crew of five); and the *Valcour*, built in 1947 in Shelburne, VT (length 177 feet, gross tonnage 446, crew of six).

LOCAL POINTS OF INTEREST: The Lake Champlain Valley has been called "New England's West Coast." Lake Champlain is the sixth largest lake in the US, 108 miles long and twelve miles across at its widest point. It flows north into Canada and empties into the St. Lawrence River. It is bordered by the lofty peaks of the Adirondacks to the west and the Green Mountains of Vermont to the east. Each year the lake is restocked with salmon, lake trout, and steelhead rainbow in order to attract anglers. Through October, the two-masted schooner *Homer W. Dixon* plies the lake on cruises out of Burlington, anchoring in coves at night. The *Spirit of Ethan Allen*, a 149-passenger replica of a Mississippi paddlewheeler, offers short cruises.

Burlington is the largest city in Vermont and also has the distinction of having the oldest university (the University of Vermont, site of the annual Champlain Shakespeare Festival) and the oldest daily newspaper in the state (the *Burlington Free Press*, established in 1848). The Shelburne Museum, nearby, has an interesting forty-five-acre reconstruction of three centuries of American life and has the old Lake Champlain side-wheel steamer *Ticonderoga* mounted outside. Other places of interest include the Green Mountain Audubon Nature Center and the Discovery

Museum. Burlington now has a paved jogging and bicycle path along the lake. There is good shopping in the pedestrian Church Street Marketplace; good restaurants include the Ice House and, in nearby Colchester, Gerard's. Middlebury has the Dog Team Tavern and, rich with atmosphere, the 150-year-old Middlebury Inn.

Port Kent is a resort town near the Ausable Chasm, a notable attraction for over one hundred years. It is a gorge about a mile and a half long, with many waterfalls and rapids cut by the Ausable River. In some places the walls are two hundred feet high. Combined foot and boat trips through the chasm are offered (wear comfortable walking shoes).

CROSSING TIME: 1 hr.

FERRY TYPE: Vehicle

VESSEL CAPACITY: *Adirondack:* 30 vehicles; 311 passengers
Champlain: 30 vehicles; 312 passengers
Valcour: 45 vehicles; 340 passengers

OPERATING SEASON: Mid-May-mid-Oct.

SCHEDULE: **Summer, mid-June-Sept. 1: Lv Burlington** 7:30 a.m., 8:35, 9:45, 12:55 p.m., 1:35, 2:45, 3:25, 4:05, 5:15, 6:55, 7:30. **Lv. Port Kent** 8:35 a.m., 9:50, 11, 11:40, 12:20 p.m., 1:30, 2:10, 2:50 4, 4:40, 5:20, 6:25, 7:10, 8:30. **Spring, mid-May-mid-June: Lv. Burlington** 8 a.m., 9:20, 10:40, noon, 1:20 p.m., 2:40, 4, 5:30; **lv. Port Kent** 9:20, 10:40, noon, 1:20 p.m., 2:40, 4, 5:20, 6:30. **Fall, Sept.-mid-Oct.: Lv. Burlington** 8 a.m., 9:20, *10, 10:40, noon, 12:40 p.m., 1:20, 2:40, 3:20, 4, 5:30. **Lv. Port Kent** 9:20 a.m., 10:40, *11:20, noon, 1:20 p.m., *2, 2:40, 4, *4:40, 5:20, 6:30. *Trips run Sept. 27-mid.-Oct.

RESTRICTIONS: Trailers, pickup-campers, and RVs permitted. Load limit 40 tons. Overhead clearance 13 ft.

FACILITIES: Restrooms, snack bar, gift shop on all vessels

FARE: Car & driver $10.50 (round-trip $21); adult $2.75 (round-trip $5.25); child (6-12) $1.00 (round-trip $1.50), child under 6 free; maximum car fare $18 (round-trip $26).

RESERVATIONS: No

DIRECTIONS:	From Vermont: I-89; Exit 14W; 2 miles to ferry. From New York: I-87; Exit 34 or 35; 6 miles to ferry.
MAP LOCATION:	P. 7, VT, 1
CONTACT:	Lake Champlain Transportation Co., King St. Dock, Burlington, VT 05401, (802) 864-9804

STATE:	Vermont/New York
PLACES SERVED:	Charlotte, VT—Essex, NY
BODY OF WATER:	Lake Champlain
FERRY SERVICE HISTORY:	There has been a ferry from Essex to Vermont since 1807. This crossing is the quick-

est route from northern Vermont to Adirondack Northway I-87. The vessels used are the *Essex*, built in 1981 in Warren, Rhode Island (with a length of eighty feet, gross tonnage of ninety-seven, and crew of two), and the *Mt. Marcy*, built in 1972 in Warren, Rhode Island (with a length of ninety-two feet, gross tonnage of seventy-eight, and crew of two). Cindy Davis is Captain of the *Essex*; she grew up on a farm in South Hero, Vermont, in a family which, she says, had little to do with boats. She obtained her one hundred-ton inland waters operator's license from the Coast Guard in 1979; she had to pass rigorous exams on the rules of the road, basic navigation, fire safety, sea and water conditions, and radar before qualifying. For some time another woman, April Bailey, was the deckhand working with Cindy (she has now left); they were proud of the fact that it had been fourteen years since the *Essex* last had a man working on the ferry (Larry Bliss).

LOCAL POINTS OF INTEREST:	Charlotte is a few miles south of Shelburne, noted for the Shelburne Museum. It is here that the paddle streamer *Ticonderoga* is

exhibited; she was towed overland after being retired from service on the lake.

On the National Register of Historic Places, Essex is a beautiful little village that could be the background for a folk art painting; in fact, it has been painted by artist S. Alberts and others. Among the historic buildings are the Beldon Noble Memorial Library, dating from 1805 (once a general store, built by Beldon Noble), Greystone, a Greek Revival mansion built by Noble in 1856, Dower House, built by Daniel Ross for his bride,

Elizabeth Gilliland, in 1786, and the 1790 inn first kept by General Daniel Wright of the Essex militia. The Marina is on the site where shipyards existed before the War of 1812. One of the last octagonal stone schoolhouses in New York State is two miles west of town on SR 22. The fishing shanties on Lake Champlain off Beggs' Point are particularly picturesque; they are built on the ice when the lake is frozen.

CROSSING TIME: 20 mins.

FERRY TYPE: Vehicle

VESSEL CAPACITY: *Essex*: 18 vehicles; 90 passengers
Mt. Marcy: 18 vehicles; 90 passengers

OPERATING SEASON: Apr. 1-Dec. 1

SCHEDULE: **Summer, mid-May-mid-Oct.: Lv. Charlotte** 6:30 a.m., 7:30, 8:30, and on the hour and half-hour until 7:30 p.m., 8:30. **Lv. Essex** 7 a.m., 8, 9, 9:30, and on the hour and half-hour until 7 p.m., 8, 9. **Spring & fall, Apr. 1-mid-May and mid-Oct.-Dec. 1: Lv. Charlotte** 7:30 a.m., and every hour on the half-hour until 5:30 p.m. **Lv. Essex** 8 a.m. and every hour on the hour until 6 p.m. *[Apr. 1 opening subject to ice conditions]*

RESTRICTIONS: Trailers, pickup-campers, and RVs permitted. Load limit 20 tons. Overhead clearance 13.6 ft.

FACILITIES: Restrooms only

FARE: Car & driver $6.25 (round-trip $10); adult $1.50 (round-trip $2.25); child (6-12) $.50 (round-trip $.75), child under 6 free, maximum car fare $10 (round-trip $15.50).

RESERVATIONS: No

DIRECTIONS: From Vermont: On US 7 take Rt. F-5 at Charlotte; 3 miles to ferry. From New York: I-87; Exit 32; 10 miles to ferry.

MAP LOCATION: P. 7, VT, 2

CONTACT: See CONTACT, p. 106.

STATE:	Vermont/New York
PLACES SERVED:	Grand Isle, VT—Plattsburgh, NY (via Cumberland Head, NY)
BODY OF WATER:	Lake Champlain
FERRY SERVICE HISTORY:	A number of crossings of Lake Champlain are thought to have been established in the eighteenth century. There were, in addition,

many other boats on the lake (six hundred vessels of all types were registered in 1868). Ralph Nading Hill sorted out the complex history of the Lake Champlain ferries in two articles for *Vermont Life*, later amended and republished by the Lake Champlain Transportation Company. The early ferries were cedar log floats, followed by oar-propelled, then sail-driven scows. The first documented ferry from Grand Isle to Cumberland Head was the schooner *Lion*, run by Benjamin Bell in the early nineteenth century; he charged eighty-three cents for a man and a horse, thirty-eight cents for a cow, and eight cents for a hog. Lake Champlain was the first lake in the world to have a regularly scheduled steamboat; the paddleboat *Vermont* entered service in 1809, the first of twenty-nine steamers on the lake (the last was the 220-foot side-wheel steamer *Ticonderoga*, built in 1906 and now on view at the Shelburne Museum.)

The ferries on this run are: the *Grand Isle*, built in 1953 in Tampa, Florida (length of 132 foot, gross tonnage of 265, crew of four); the *Plattsburgh*, built in 1984 in Panama City, Florida (length of 173 feet, gross tonnage of 268, crew of four), and the *Gov. George D. Aiken*, built in 1975 in Warren, Rhode Island (length of 132 feet, gross tonnage of 284, crew of four). Ice does not stop the Lake Champlain ferries; in fact, there is a bubbler in the slips to prevent ice from forming. One captain, Capt. Merritt Carpenter of the *Grand Isle*, has called the crossing the "Siberia Run"; sometimes the ferry breaks ice two to three inches thick. She has a strip of metal plating around the "iceline" (waterline in summer). Capt. David Geer, of South Hero, Vermont (a veteran of thirty years on the lake), says the company has been making winter crossings since the late 1970s. "One winter we tried it and we were surprised to find out we could do it. We have only lost two or three days of trips in several years, and that's not too bad. Spring is the hardest time of the year because of the ice floes."

LOCAL POINTS OF INTEREST:	Grand Isle is among the several picturesque islands in Lake Champlain that are rich in history. Of special interest here, on the main

road in Grand Isle, is the Hyde Log Cabin, America's oldest original log cabin, built in 1783 by Jedediah Hyde, Jr., a Revolutionary soldier and surveyor.

Plattsburgh figured in the struggle for United States independence. It was offshore here that the British won the Battle of Lake Champlain in 1776. In 1814, Commodore Thomas Macdonough defeated a British fleet from Canada by devising an arrangement to swivel his vessels around. The Kent-Delord House in Plattsburgh is linked with many significant events in history; it was built in 1797 and was once commandeered by the British (in 1814) as their headquarters. Fort Montgomery is nearby, and the art galleries of Plattsburgh State University College are well worth visiting. The Clinton County Historical Museum depicts the history of Clinton County with artifacts, paintings, domestic utensils, and military souvenirs. The Rockwell Kent Gallery in the Feinberg Library of Plattsburgh State University College contains an extensive collection of his paintings and other works. The *Juniper* offers excursions from Plattsburgh on the lake, passing sites of battles fought during the American Revolution and War of 1812.

CROSSING TIME: 12 mins.

FERRY TYPE: Vehicle

VESSEL CAPACITY: *Grand Isle*: 26 vehicles; 130 passengers; *Plattsburgh*: 40 vehicles; 200 passengers; *Gov. George D. Aiken*: 26 vehicles; 130 passengers

OPERATING SEASON: All year, subject to ice conditions

SCHEDULE: **Summer, mid-June-Sept. 1: Lv. Grand Isle** *6 a.m., *6:40, 7:20, every 20 mins. until 11:40 p.m.; **lv. Plattsburgh** (Cumberland Head) *6:20 a.m., *7, 7:40, every 20 mins until midnight. **Spring & fall, Apr. 1-mid-June and Sept.-early Dec.: Lv. Grand Isle** *6 a.m., *6:40, 7:20, every 20 mins. to 10:20 p.m.; **lv. Plattsburgh** (Cumberland Head) *6:20 a.m., *7, 7:40, every 20 mins to 10:40 p.m. **Winter, Dec. 1-Mar. 31: Lv. Grand Isle** *6 a.m., *6:40, 7:20, every 20 mins. until 10 p.m.; **lv. Plattsburgh** (Cumberland Head) *6:20 a.m., *7, 7:40, every 20 mins. until 10:20 p.m. *First departure Sun. 7:20 a.m. from Grand Isle; 7:40 from Plattsburgh. *40 mins. service Thanksgiving, Christmas Day, and New Year's Day.*

RESTRICTIONS: Trailers, pick-up campers, and RVs permitted. Load limit 40 tons. Overhead clearance 13.6 ft.

FACILITIES:	All vessels have restrooms only
FARE:	Car & driver $6.25 (round-trip $10); adult $1.50 (round-trip $2.25); child (6-12) $.50 (round-trip $.75), child under 6 free, maximum car fare $10 (round-trip $15.50).
RESERVATIONS:	No
DIRECTIONS:	From Vermont: I-89, use Exit 17, 12 miles to ferry. From New York: I-87, use Exit 39, 5 miles to ferry.
MAP LOCATION:	P. 7, VT, 3
CONTACT:	See CONTACT, p. 106.

STATE:	Vermont/New York
PLACES SERVED:	Larrabee's Point, Shoreham, VT—Fort Ticonderoga, NY [The "Fort Ti Ferry"]
BODY OF WATER:	Lake Champlain
FERRY SERVICE HISTORY:	The "Fort Ti Ferry" is one of the oldest continuously operating businesses in Vermont. At one time there were thirteen ferries

connecting New York and Vermont across the "Narrows" of Lake Champlain. This lower section of the lake is shallow and narrow, and looks more like a wide river than a lake. The "Fort Ti Ferry," the last survivor, dates back directly to 1799 and indirectly to the 1740s. As James R. Bullard, president of Shorewell Ferries, puts it in a history of the ferry, "This venerable enterprise owes its longevity to a good location, anciently for military and commercial purposes and presently for commercial and recreational purposes." The franchise was originally granted to John S. Larrabee, Jr., in 1799, but there are tales of earlier service provided in a dugout canoe by a certain Jake the Indian. Larrabee was succeeded by Henry Clay Holley, Almon C. Farr, Zeb Martin, Archie J. Cook, Flora D. Cunningham, Elisha Goodsell and Richard Botsford, William Rader, and by James Bullard, who purchased Shorewell Ferries, Inc., in 1977. From 1847 until it was destroyed by fire in 1919, a large summer hotel, the United States, was a popular gathering spot on Lar-

rabee's Point. Today, the service has a ninety-four-ton barge *Fort Ticonderoga* and a sixteen-ton diesel tugboat, *Addie B*.

In 1838, an English traveler named James B. Buckingham rode the ferry; he called it "little more than than an oblong trough or tray." Nathaniel Hawthorne also rode it in the 1840s; he revelled in the "continual succession of travelers" waiting for the ferry, which allowed him "just enough time to make their acquaintance, penetrate their mysteries, and be rid of them without the risk of tediousness on either side."

James Bullard reflects that, though the physical landscape has changed little since the ferry was established, the nature of the passengers has evolved considerably. "They are no longer westward-bound immigrants leaving Vermont for Indiana, Wisconsin, and California, but, in very many cases, are the descendants of those immigrants, responding to the need to explore New England for family roots and heritage." Today, he says, a summer season will bring passengers from all fifty states and fifty foreign countries as well.

LOCAL POINTS OF INTEREST: Shoreham, Vermont, is located in the Narrows of Lake Champlain in its southern portion. It is not too far from the old town of Middlebury, home of Middlebury College, founded in 1800. An interesting place to stay in Vergennes, to the north, is the Basin Harbor Club, a resort posh enough to offer boating, tennis, and its own airstrip, but homey enough to have a Blueberry Festival and a Red, White, and Blue Breakfast on July 4. For four generations it has been run by the Beach family, and grew out of an 1882 boarding house established by Ardelia Beach (the boarding house is still used as the Main Lodge). The non-profit Basin Harbor Maritime Museum opened in 1986, founded by Bob

Beach, Jr. This is Vermont's first historical collection devoted exclusively to Lake Champlain.

The French built Fort Ticonderoga in 1755; it was originally named Fort Carillon. It was in a strategic position to guard the water access route from Canada to the interior colonies. In 1758 the French defended it against the British. Ethan Allen and his Green Mountain Boys captured it in 1775, and in 1776 Benedict Arnold assembled the American fleet here. General Burgoyne captured it for the British in 1777, and they burned all the buildings. The fort has now been restored according to the original French plans. There are guided tours, cannon-firing demonstrations, and fife and drum music, as well as a museum with colonial weapons, uniforms, paintings, and other artifacts. The admission fee includes admission to Mount Defiance, which is a scenic overlook with a panoramic view of Lake Champlain (it may also be seen separately).

CROSSING TIME:	6 mins.
FERRY TYPE:	Vehicle
VESSEL CAPACITY:	18 cars
OPERATING SEASON:	May-October
SCHEDULE:	**Continuous crossings. May, Sept., Oct.:** 8 a.m.-6 p.m.; **June:** 8 a.m.-7 p.m.; **July-Aug.:** 8 a.m.-9 p.m.
RESTRICTIONS:	Trailers, pick-up campers, and RVs permitted. Load limit 15 tons. Overhead clearance 16 ft.
FACILITIES:	None
FARE:	Car $4 (round-trip $6); bicycle $1, pedestrians $.25-$.50 per head according to size; motorcycles $2; trailer $.75-$5; pickup-camper $4; RVs $5-$8.
RESERVATIONS:	No
DIRECTIONS:	Ferry connects SR 74 between Shoreham and Fort Ticonderoga.
MAP LOCATION:	P. 7, VT, 4
CONTACT:	Shorewell Ferries, Inc. Shoreham VT 05770 (802)897-7999

FERRIES
OF THE
MID-ATLANTIC

Ferries of the Mid-Atlantic States

DELAWARE

* [Lewes-Cape May, NJ; see NJ]

1. Laurel-Woodland

MARYLAND

1. Allen-SR 349 ("The Upper Ferry")
2. Crisfield-Ewell (Smith Island)
3. Crisfield-Tangier, VA
4. Oxford-Bellevue
5. Point Lookout State Park-
   Smith Island

* [Smith Island-Smith Point, VA;
   see VA]
6. Whitehaven-Widgeon
7. White's Ferry-Leesburg, VA

NEW JERSEY

1. Cape May-Lewes, DE
2. Fort Lee (Ross Dock)-Manhattan
   (Pier 11)

3. Highlands-Manhattan (Pier 11)
4. Weehawken and West New York-
   Manhattan (Pier 78)

NEW YORK

1. Bay Shore-Dunewood
2. Bay Shore-Fair Harbor
3. Bay Shore-Kismet
4. Bay Shore-Ocean Bay Park-Seaview
5. Bay Shore-Ocean Beach
6. Bay Shore-Point O'Woods
7. Bay Shore-Saltaire
8. Bemus Point-Stow
9. Cape Vincent-Wolfe
   Island, ON
10. City Island (the Bronx)-Potters
    Field (Hart Island, the Bronx)
* [Essex-Charlotte, VT; see VT]
* [Essex-Grand Isle, VT; see VT]
* [Fishers Island-New London, CT;
   see CT]
* [Fort Ticonderoga-Shoreham, VT;
   see VT]
11. Greenport-Shelter Island, LI
12. Manhattan (Battery Park)-
    Ellis Island
13. Manhattan (Battery Park)-Statue
    of Liberty National Monument
14. Manhattan (South St.)-Roosevelt
    Island

* [Manhattan (South St., Pier 11)-
   Fort Lee, NJ (Ross Dock); see NJ]
* [Manhattan (South St., Pier 11)-
   Highlands, NJ; see NJ]
* [Manhattan (Pier 78)-Weehawken and
   West New York, NJ; see NJ]
15. Manhattan (Whitehall St.)-
    Governors Island
16. Manhattan (Whitehall St.)-
    St.George,SI ("The Staten
    Island Ferry")
17. Montauk, LI-Block Island, RI
18. Montauk, LI-Groton, CT
19. North Haven-Shelter Island, LI
* [Orient Point, LI-Bridgeport, CT;
   see CT]
20. Patchogue-Davis Park
21. Patchogue-Watch Hill
22. Sayville-Barrett Beach
23. Sayville-Cherry Grove
24. Sayville-Fire Island Pines
25. Sayville-Sailors Haven (Sunken
    Forest)

PENNSYLVANIA

1. Erie-Presque Isle
2. Fredericktown-East bank of
   Monongahela River

3. Millersburg-Liverpool

WEST VIRGINIA

1. Parkersburg-Blennerhassett
   Island Historical Park

2. Sistersville-Fly, OH

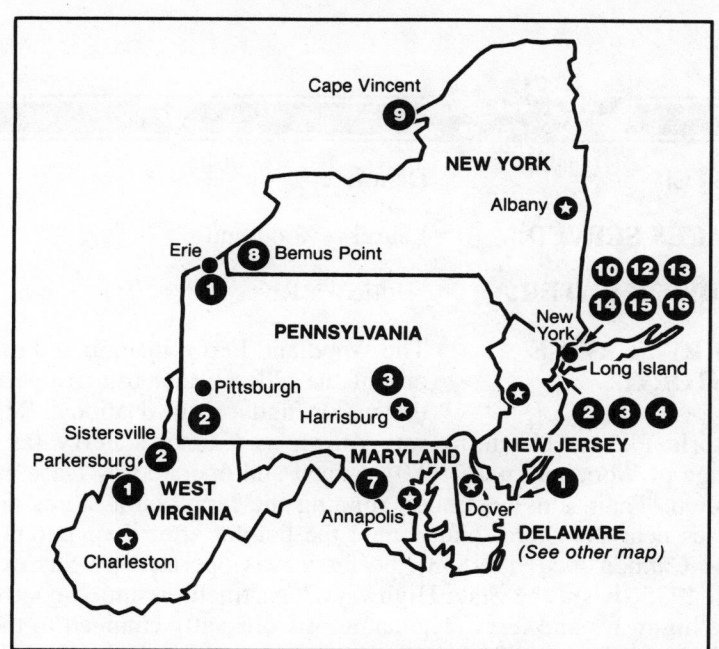

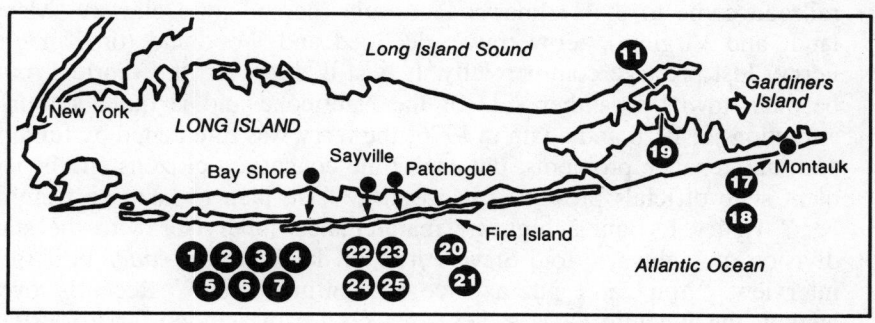

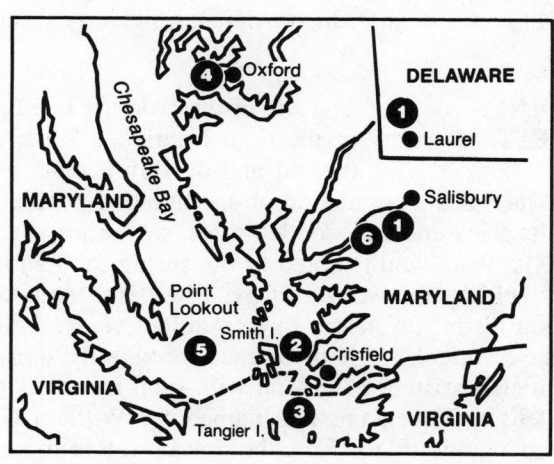

STATE:	Delaware
PLACES SERVED:	Laurel—Woodland
BODY OF WATER:	Nanticoke River

FERRY SERVICE HISTORY: The Woodland Ferry, inaugurated in 1793, is one of the oldest water transit operations in the nation and on the National Register of Historic Places. The ferry was known as Cannon's Ferry (as was the village of Woodland until 1880), owned and operated by Isaac and Betty Cannon. Their sons continued running the ferry, built stores and warehouses near the shore, and named the hamlet after their parents. When Isaac Cannon died, in 1843, the ferry was operated by Sussex County until 1935, when the State Highway Department assumed control of the state highways and ferry. The name was officially changed to the Woodland Ferry about 1880. It is the last river ferry in Delaware. When the railroad came to the Delmarva Peninsula (named for Delaware, Maryland, and Virginia), ferry traffic declined and Woodland (or Cannon's Ferry) lost prestige commercially. It is still, however, the shortest route between towns on either side of the Nanticoke and is quite a tourist attraction. In 1970 and again in 1976, the ferry was threatened by funding and maintenance problems, but each time concerned citizens and benevolent state officials prevented its demise. "We plan to keep on running her," Henry I. Banks, highway maintenance supervisor with the state division of highways, told Steve Parris of the *Seaford Leader* in a 1980 interview. "You can't put a price on sentimentality." Recently overhauled, the *Virginia C.* is a diesel-powered cable-guided ferry fourteen by thirty-eight feet. On an ordinary day, it transports seventy-five to 150 people.

LOCAL POINTS OF INTEREST: The site of the crossing is a beautiful stretch of the tidal Nanticoke River sweeping past the old and drowsy back-country village of Woodland, which has a population of one hundred people. The old ferry house, with its brick end and wooden sides, was originally constructed in the early 1700s. Woodland is noted for its spring shad and for the annual shad suppers held by the women of the Woodland Methodist Church.

Laurel has a history of nearly three hundred years, dating back to the days when the Nanticoke Indians roamed through the dense pine forests. European settlers christened the land with such names as Greenland and Bachelor's Delight; Greenland was named for William Green, who, in 1680, received a grant of land from the first Lord Baltimore. By 1711, Old

Virginia C.

World settlers had made their mark upon the land, driving out the Nanticoke Indians, who rejected an offer of three thousand acres along Broad Creek. Barkley Townsend bought most of the land upon which Laurel was built and, in 1802, plotted the present town. Much of Laurel burned in 1899 but was rebuilt. Five years later, the sailing ship *Golden Gate*, moving down Broad Creek, was struck by a mail train, thought to be the only recorded collision between a train and a sailing ship. Today Laurel is a quiet, peaceful community, with ponds and parks still providing a tranquil setting for one of the earliest of the US ferries.

CROSSING TIME: 6 mins.

FERRY TYPE: Vehicle

VESSEL CAPACITY: 3 cars

OPERATING SEASON: All year

SCHEDULE: On signal, daylight hours, weather permitting.

RESTRICTIONS: No combustible materials; no trailers, pickup-campers, or RVs.

FACILITIES: None

FARE: Free

RESERVATIONS: No

DIRECTIONS: Connects SR 78 from Laurel on the southeast and SR 78 and 538 on the northwest side.

MAP LOCATION: P. 115, DE, 1

CONTACT: Dept. of Transportation, Administration Center, Box 778, Dover, DE 19902; At the ferry: (302)629-7742

STATE: Maryland

PLACES SERVED: Allen—SR 349 ("The Upper Ferry")

BODY OF WATER: Wicomico River

FERRY SERVICE HISTORY: The ferry is an outboard motor-propelled cable ferry; it does not have a formal name, but is known just as "The Upper Ferry." Service on this crossing was inaugurated prior to 1897.

LOCAL POINTS OF INTEREST: Maryland's Eastern Shore has a benign simplicity about it that conceals its true flavor. Its quiet coves, bays, and rivers yield seafood delicacies prized all over the East Coast and make it a major yachting center; its protected marshes and barrier beaches attract rare species of waterfowl and other wildlife; its small ports and inland towns are livelier than many of their counterparts on the mainland. Whether you drive down the Eastern Shore or across it, you will probably go through Salisbury, a busy market town with Victorian buildings dating from the 1880s. River Walk Park is a meandering walk along the downtown section of the Wicomico River. The North American Wildfowl Art Museum has fine wildfowl carvings. Main Street has been transformed into a pedestrian mall and open-air plaza. Notable here also are the Salisbury Zoological Park, the Newtown Historic District with Poplar Hill Mansion (a Federal-style house with Palladian windows and finely carved woodwork), and a number of Victorian houses.

A bit further East is Maryland's only ocean resort, Ocean City, where trains run along a three-mile long, wide boardwalk, making it a popular destination for families. Just north of the ferry, at Mardela Springs, a small stone monument off SR 54 marks the Mason-Dixon line, laid out by English surveyors Charles Mason and Jeremiah Dixon.

CROSSING TIME:	3 mins.
FERRY TYPE:	Vehicle
VESSEL CAPACITY:	2 cars, 6 passengers
OPERATING SEASON:	All year, weather conditions and tides permitting.
SCHEDULE:	**On demand, Mon.-Fri.: Spring and summer, Mar.-early Sept.:** 7 a.m.-6 p.m. **Fall and winter, Oct.-Feb.:** 7 a.m.-5 p.m. **Sat.,**

all year: 7 a.m.-1 p.m. *No service Sundays, Independence, Labor, Thanksgiving, Christmas, New Year's Days.*

RESTRICTIONS:	Trailers permitted at driver's risk; prohibited during extremely high or low tides
FACILITIES:	None
FARE:	Free
RESERVATIONS:	No
DIRECTIONS:	Ferry is west of Salisbury; take SR 349 west about 5 miles and follow signs. Turn left on Upper Ferry Road.
MAP LOCATION:	P. 115, MD, 1
CONTACT:	Wicomico County Roads Division, Box 1897, Salisbury, MD 21801, (301)548-4872

STATE:	Maryland
PLACES SERVED:	Crisfield—Ewell (Smith Island, *Capt. Jason*)
BODY OF WATER:	Tangier Sound
FERRY SERVICE HISTORY:	The boats on this service are the *Capt. Jason* and the *Capt. Jason II*.

LOCAL POINTS OF INTEREST: Crisfield has been called the "Seafood Capital of the World." Said to be built almost entirely on oyster shells, it has a thriving seafood industry, with several packing plants. It is on an inlet of Tangier Sound and is also a pleasure-boating center. A number of wildfowl carvers also live here.

Ewell is the capital of Smith Island, which is actually a group of three islands that form an area about eight miles long by four miles wide. It was named for Capt. John Smith, who explored the Chesapeake Bay in 1608. It was settled in 1657 by English dissenters from Lord Baltimore's colony. The lifestyle here has changed slowly with the passing of time. Descendants of original English and Cornish settlers populate the island, depending on seafood as a livelihood. Some of the ancient modes of speech have survived here.

CROSSING TIME: 35 mins., weather permitting

FERRY TYPE: Pedestrian

VESSEL CAPACITY: 50 passengers each boat

OPERATING SEASON: All year

SCHEDULE: **Daily: Lv. Crisfield** 12:30 p.m., *5 p.m.; **lv. Ewell** at *4 p.m.; 8 a.m. *During Daylight Saving season, this trip leaves Crisfield at 4:30 p.m. and leaves Ewell at 3:30 p.m.

RESTRICTIONS: None

FACILITIES: No

FARE: Adults $3 ($5 round-trip); children (6-12) $2; under 6 free.

RESERVATIONS: No

DIRECTIONS: From SR 50, take SR 413 to Crisfield. Ferry leaves from the Public Dock in Crisfield.

MAP LOCATION: P. 115, MD, 2

CONTACT: Larry Laird, Box 205, Tylerton, MD 21866, (301)425-4471

Capt. Tyler II

STATE: Maryland

PLACES SERVED: Crisfield—Ewell (Smith Island, *Capt. Tyler II*)

BODY OF WATER: Tangier Sound

FERRY SERVICE HISTORY: The vessel on this run is the *Capt. Tyler II,* a sixty-five-foot riverboat-style paddlewheel. She was built in New York during World War II as a cargo vessel for the US military. Prior to use as a tour boat, she was used to haul oyster seed and shells on the Chesapeake Bay. In 1984-85, she was converted to a paddlewheel-style passenger ferry for use on this crossing.

LOCAL POINTS OF INTEREST: [For notes on Crisfield and Smith Island, please see entry under Crisfield-Smith Island (*Capt. Jason*), p. 120.]

CROSSING TIME: 1 hr. 10 mins.

FERRY TYPE: Pedestrian

VESSEL CAPACITY: 150 passengers

OPERATING SEASON: May-Oct.

SCHEDULE: **Daily: Lv. Crisfield** 12:30 p.m.; **lv. Ewell** 4 p.m. Fare includes bus trip to Rhodes Point.

RESTRICTIONS: No

FACILITIES: Restrooms, snack bar

FARE: Round-trip only. Adult $13; child (6-12) $6.50.

RESERVATIONS: No

DIRECTIONS: To Crisfield from SR 50, take SR 13 to SR 413. Boat leaves from Somers Cove Marina, Crisfield.

MAP LOCATION: P. 115, MD, 2

CONTACT: Capt. Alan Tyler, Tyler's Cruises, Rhodes Point, MD 21858, (301)425-2771

STATE: Maryland

PLACES SERVED: Crisfield—Ewell (Smith Island, *Island Bell II*)

BODY OF WATER: Tangier Sound

FERRY SERVICE HISTORY: The ship on this crossing is the *Island Belle II*. It is a mail boat, the only one in the state of Maryland. The freight boat *Darrell Dale* is also used on this run.

LOCAL POINTS OF INTEREST: [For notes on Crisfield and Smith Island, please see entry under Crisfield-Smith Island (*Capt. Jason*), p. 120.]

This crossing is a family enterprise, as Captain Tyler's mother, Eloise Tyler, owns the Harborside Restaurant in Ewell, at the dock, which specializes in excellent local seafood (nothing is frozen).

CROSSING TIME: 1 hr.

FERRY TYPE: Pedestrian

VESSEL CAPACITY:	42 passengers
OPERATING SEASON:	All year
SCHEDULE:	**Daily: Lv. Crisfield** 12:30 p.m., 5; **lv. Ewell** 4 p.m.; 8 a.m.
RESTRICTIONS:	None
FACILITIES:	No
FARE:	Adults $3 ($5 round-trip)
RESERVATIONS:	No
DIRECTIONS:	To reach Crisfield from SR 50, take SR 413.
MAP LOCATION:	P. 115, MD, 2
CONTACT:	Capt. Otis Ray Tyler, *Island Belle II,* Box 12, Ewell, MD 21824, (301)425-4271 or 425-2201

STATE:	Maryland
PLACES SERVED:	Crisfield—Ewell (Smith Island, *Teresa Ann Evans*)
BODY OF WATER:	Tangier Sound
FERRY SERVICE HISTORY:	The vessel on this crossing is the *Teresa Ann Evans,* built at Deltaville, Virginia, in 1955. She is sixty-three feet long and twenty-two

feet wide and has a crew of two. Service was inaugurated in 1984. Many riders come from Delaware, Baltimore, and New Jersey; there are often bike riders going to Smith Island to take the *Capt. Evans* to Smith Point, Virginia, and continue south.

LOCAL POINTS OF INTEREST:	[For notes on Crisfield and Smith Island, please see entry under Crisfield-Smith Island (*Capt. Jason*), p. 120.]
CROSSING TIME:	1 hr. 15 mins.

FERRY TYPE:	Pedestrian
VESSEL CAPACITY:	100 passengers
OPERATING SEASON:	May-Sept.
SCHEDULE:	**Daily: Lv. Crisfield** 12:15 p.m., **lv. Ewell** 5 p.m..
RESTRICTIONS:	Pets allowed
FACILITIES:	Restrooms; you may take a nap on the cushions in the lower house if desired
FARE:	Adults $8; children (3-12) $4
RESERVATIONS:	No, but nice to have
DIRECTIONS:	To Crisfield from SR 50, take SR 413. Follow signs after entering Crisfield.
MAP LOCATION:	P. 115, MD, 2
CONTACT:	Capt. Gordon Evans, *Teresa Ann Evans,* % Smith Island Skipjack Restaurant, Ewell, MD 21824, (301)425-5571 or 425-3221

STATE:	Maryland/Virginia
PLACES SERVED:	Crisfield, MD—Tangier Island, VA
BODY OF WATER:	Chesapeake Bay
FERRY SERVICE HISTORY:	Service on this crossing was inaugurated in 1958. The vessel is the *Steven Thomas,* a ninety-foot cruise boat (twenty-six feet

wide). The majority of passengers come from the northern states of New Jersey and Pennsylvania and from Washington, DC.

| **LOCAL POINTS OF INTEREST:** | [For notes on Crisfield, please see entry under Crisfield-Smith Island (*Capt. Jason*), p. 120.] |

Tangier Island was discovered in 1608 by that intrepid explorer Capt. John Smith. It was settled in 1686 by John Crockett; many of his descendants live here today. Since the 1800s, excellent crabs and oysters have been exported from Tangier Island. With its tidy little homes, picket fences, Elizabethan accents, and crab farms, it seems almost an island

Steven Thomas

where time has been arrested. There are fewer than a dozen cars and trucks here, and tourist trams take visitors along the island's two diminutive ten-foot-wide streets. Bicycles are available, and popular activities are duck hunting, fishing, and swimming.

CROSSING TIME: 1 hr. 15 mins.

FERRY TYPE: Pedestrian

VESSEL CAPACITY: 300 passengers

OPERATING SEASON: Memorial Day-Oct.

SCHEDULE: **Daily: Lv. Crisfield** 12:30 p.m.; **lv. Tangier** 4 p.m.

RESTRICTIONS: None

FACILITIES: Restrooms

FARE: Adults $6; children $4

RESERVATIONS: Individuals, no; groups, yes, definitely advisable.

DIRECTIONS: Ferry leaves from the Thomas Dock, end of Main St.

MAP LOCATION: P. 115, MD, 3

CONTACT: *Steven Thomas,* Crisfield, MD 21817, (301)968-2338

STATE:	Maryland
PLACES SERVED:	Oxford—Bellevue
BODY OF WATER:	Tred Avon River

FERRY SERVICE HISTORY: The Oxford-Bellevue ferry was established in 1683 and is thought to be the oldest "free-running" (not connected to a cable) privately-owned ferry in the country. It is as likely to carry pedestrians laden with shopping bags as cars, and there is no better approach to Oxford, especially at sunset, when fishing vessels, yachts, and sailboats will be silhouetted against the sky.

LOCAL POINTS OF INTEREST: Oxford existed as a town long before Baltimore and, with Annapolis, was one of the two leading Maryland settlements. Now a quiet little residential town on the Tred Avon River near its juncture with the Chesapeake Bay, it is still important in boatbuilding and provides a harbor for watermen who harvest oysters, crabs, clams, and fish. It is the scene each August of a three-day regatta sponsored jointly by the Tred Avon Yacht Club and the Chesapeake Bay Yacht Club of Easton. The Oxford Museum has maritime exhibits, and there is an excellent inn right by the ferry landing, the Robert Morris, former home of the father of Robert Morris, financier of the American Revolution. The inn is run by Ken and Wendy Gibson. Many rooms are restored, and the dining room murals are wallpaper samples dating from the early nineteenth century. At the desk you can buy bags of corn to feed the spoiled mallards waddling about the ferry landing beach.

Bellevue is hardly more than a pretty country road, but it leads to another vitally important Talbot County town, St. Michaels, also a mecca for boating people. It has an air of understated wealth, with whimsical boutiques and seafood restaurants in old mansions. The Chesapeake Bay Maritime Museum here is a must; it has five buildings on sixteen acres offering an unparalleled look at maritime history. It puts in visual perspective the terms which have usually been puzzling the visitor since he first arrived on the Eastern Shore: "bugeye" and "skipjack." He may have been under the vague apprehension that these are a variety of insects or ducks, but at the museum he will discover they are small craft used for dredging oysters and fishing. The museum has examples of both, as well as hand-carved decoys and the Victorian Tolchester Beach bandstand.

CROSSING TIME: 7 mins.

FERRY TYPE: Vehicle

VESSEL CAPACITY: 10 cars

OPERATING SEASON: All year

SCHEDULE: **Continuous crossings. May 1-Labor Day, Mon.-Fri.:** 7 a.m.-9 p.m. **Sat.-Sun.:** 9 a.m.-9 p.m. **Labor Day to May 1, Mon.-Fri.:** 7 a.m.-sunset. **Sat.-Sun.:** 9 a.m.-sunset.

RESTRICTIONS: Trailers, pickup-campers, and RVs permitted. Load limit 20 tons.

FACILITIES: None

FARE: Car $3.50; passengers $.25; trailer $1.50; pickup-camper $3.50.

RESERVATIONS: No

DIRECTIONS: To Oxford, from Easton or SR 50, take SR 33 and SR 333; to Bellevue, take SR 33 and 329 to Royal Oak and follow signs.

MAP LOCATION: P. 115, MD, 4

CONTACT: Oxford-Bellevue Ferry, Oxford, MD 21654, (301)226-5408

STATE: Maryland

PLACES SERVED: Point Lookout State Park—Smith Island

BODY OF WATER: Chesapeake Bay

FERRY SERVICE HISTORY: The vessel on this crossing is a sixty-five-foot cruiser, the *Captain Tyler*. Service was inaugurated in 1984.

LOCAL POINTS OF INTEREST: Smith Island, actually a group of three islands that form an area about eight miles long by four miles wide, was named for

Capt. John Smith, who explored the Chesapeake Bay in 1608. It was settled in 1657 by English dissenters from Lord Baltimore's colony. The lifestyle here has changed slowly with the passing of time. Descendants of original English and Cornish settlers populate the island, depending on seafood as a livelihood. Some of the ancient modes of speech have survived here. A delicious family-style seafood dinner is available at Tyler's Restaurant.

Point Lookout State Park is across the Chesapeake Bay at its juncture with the Potomac River in St. Mary's County; the area is generally known as Southern Maryland. This ferry service is more easily accessible from Washington than the one from Crisfield. Point Lookout played an important role in the Civil War. Fort Lincoln, here, was built by Confederate prisoners of war under Union supervision to deter attempts to free prisoners. St. Mary's City has an interesting outdoor history museum, Historic St. Mary's City, with exhibits on eight hundred acres of unspoiled tidewater landscape.

CROSSING TIME:	1 hr. 40 mins.
FERRY TYPE:	Pedestrian
VESSEL CAPACITY:	150 passengers
OPERATING SEASON:	June-Aug.
SCHEDULE:	**Lv. Point Lookout** 10 a.m. **lv. Smith Island** 2 p.m.
RESTRICTIONS:	None
FACILITIES:	Restrooms, snack bar
FARE:	Round-trip only. Adults $16; child (6-12) $8
RESERVATIONS:	No
DIRECTIONS:	Take SR 5 from Washington.
MAP LOCATION:	P. 115, MD, 5
CONTACT:	See CONTACT, p. 122.

STATE: Maryland

PLACES SERVED: Whitehaven—Widgeon,   connecting
                             Wicomico and Somerset Counties (the
                             "Whitehaven Ferry")

BODY OF WATER: Wicomico River

FERRY SERVICE   The Whitehaven ferry has operated here con-
HISTORY: tinuously since 1690. The cable-operated
                             boat is named the *Som-Wico*. Most pas-
sengers are local inhabitants, but occasionally bicyclists and other
unusual riders are to be found.

LOCAL POINTS   Whitehaven and Widgeon are tiny towns at
OF INTEREST: the mouth of the Wicomico River, near the
                             Chesapeake Bay. Whitehaven is the oldest
incorporated town on the river and was once an important deepwater port
and shipbuilding center. Old records suggest that George Washington's
grandmother lived here. It is just north of the Deal Island Wildlife
Management Area. The Eastern Shore is considered one of the prime
duck and goose hunting regions on the Atlantic Flyway. One can drive
out to Deal Island and see the herons delicately picking their way through
the water, along with egrets, ducks, and other waterfowl. Deal is a small
watermen's community where many Chesapeake Bay skipjacks can be
seen during the spring, summer, and early autumn. There is a free self-
guided driving tour brochure available.

CROSSING TIME: 5 mins.

FERRY TYPE: Vehicle

VESSEL CAPACITY: 3 cars, 6 passengers

OPERATING SEASON: All year, weather conditions and tides
                             permitting

SCHEDULE: **Daily, on demand. Mar. 1-mid-May and
                             mid-Sept.-end of Sept:** 7 a.m.-6 p.m. **Mid-
                             May-mid-Sept.:** 6 a.m.-7:30 p.m. **Oct. 1-
                             Feb.:** 7 a.m.-5:30 p.m.

RESTRICTIONS:	Trailers permitted unless extremely high or low tides. Pickup-campers and RVs permitted at operator's discretion.
FACILITIES:	None
FARE:	Free
RESERVATIONS:	No
DIRECTIONS:	Ferry is off SR 352 at Whitehaven.
MAP LOCATION:	P. 115, MD, 6
CONTACT:	C. K. Banks, Rd. Engineer, Wicomico County Roads Div., Box 1897, Salisbury, MD 21801, (301)548-4822 or (301)548-4873

STATE:	Maryland/Virginia
PLACES SERVED:	White's Ferry, MD—Leesburg, VA
BODY OF WATER:	Potomac River
FERRY SERVICE HISTORY:	White's Ferry is the only one remaining on the Potomac River and the only crossing between Cabin John and Point of Rocks. In

1828 it was known as Conrad's Ferry, named for Ernest Conrad, who poled the mail on a barge across the one thousand-yard stretch between Maryland and Virginia. At that time, rates were six and one-quarter cents one way for a man, horse or mule, and three cents for a head of cattle. Carriages and carts paid six and one-half cents. When a turnpike was built west of Leesburg in 1832, frugal travellers chose to cross the ferry on their journeys west rather than pay the toll. Local history holds that Conrad ran the ferry during the Civil War, after which the business was purchased by Elijah Veirs White, for whom the tiny settlement on the Maryland side of the river is named. The vessel, the *General Jubal Early,* is named for the Confederate leader who crossed here after a raid on Washington in August 1864. The ferry is cable-guided and propelled by a diesel tug (the main tug is *Early's Aid;* the back-up tug is the *General's Pusher*). The pivoting tug deftly whips around to propel the ferry in, in a graceful maneuver that surprises drivers. Riders include a corps of suburban loyalists who commute between Leesburg and such places as Rockville and Gaithersburg, Maryland, as well as truckers from a nearby sod

General Jubal Early

farm, tourists, and refugees from Beltway accidents. Malcolm E. D. Brown, part-owner and manager of the ferry, says he does not need a helicopter to tell him when there has been a wreck. Brown took over the ferry in 1972. He says he was a "reluctant recruit," but his father and some other men had purchased it in the 1940s, and his father insisted that he come for a year; he has never left. "It's different; it's a challenge," he says.

LOCAL POINTS OF INTEREST: The hills of Montgomery County once crossed by General Jubal Early seem now to be succumbing to another march: that of suburbia. Between the mushrooming shopping malls and office complexes of Rockville in Montgomery County (with one of the highest per capita incomes in the nation) and White's Ferry, the pseudo-Victorian and colonial houses, complete with Vanpool signs, are stealthily creeping. They haven't reached Poolesville, though, the town nearest the ferry. The ferry is still protected, reached by winding roads through fertile fields. "It's a tourist attraction, all right," says the Poolesville gas station attendant. "I'm amazed at the people who'll drive out from Washington or Rockville, twenty or twenty-five miles, just to ride White's Ferry."

Leesburg is a few miles from the Virginia landing, in Loudoun County, an affluent region with vast horse and cattle farms behind miles of white fences. Near Leesburg is Oatlands, a large estate with a Classical Revival mansion where races and horse shows are held. The American Work Horse Museum and Morven Park, which has a carriage museum and the International Equestrian Institute as well as a large manor house, are also of interest.

There are picnic tables and canoes available on the Maryland side and good fishing for smallmouth bass, carp, catfish, and bluegills.

CROSSING TIME:	3 mins.
FERRY TYPE:	Vehicle
VESSEL CAPACITY:	6 cars
OPERATING SEASON:	All year
SCHEDULE:	**Daily, on signal:** 6 a.m.-11 p.m.; **Dec. 21-Mar. 21** to 8 p.m., river permitting.
RESTRICTIONS:	Trailers, pickup-campers, and RVs permitted. Load limit 20 tons.
FACILITIES:	None
FARE:	Car $2 ($3.50 round-trip); pickup-camper $4 up.
RESERVATIONS:	No
DIRECTIONS:	From Rockville, take SR 28 to Dawsonville, SR 107 to Poolesville and ferry. From Leesburg, take SR 15 north 2 mi.; right on SR 655.
MAP LOCATION:	P. 115, MD, 7
CONTACT:	Malcolm Brown, White's Ferry, MD 20837, (301)394-5200

STATE:	New Jersey/Delaware
PLACES SERVED:	Cape May, NJ—Lewes, DE
BODY OF WATER:	Delaware Bay
FERRY SERVICE HISTORY:	"A ferry service does not begin in the drafting room of engineers nor in the swank offices of financiers. It begins, rather, in the

imagination of men who want to get from one land base to another, across a body of water, in as straight a line as possible—and as quickly as possible." This statement by William P. Frank, though it is from the

Twin Capes

program for the 1964 dedication ceremonies marking the opening of the Cape May-Lewes ferry, could serve as a text for all ferries. William J. Miller, Jr., Executive Director of the Delaware River and Bay Authority, has vividly described the history of the Cape May-Lewes service in *A Ferry Tale: Crossing the Delaware on the Cape May-Lewes Ferry.* The project was first conceived in 1953; many years of planning, building the approach roads, and acquiring the ferries were necessary before the first vessel left Lewes on July 1, 1964, at 6:47 a.m. (seven minutes later than planned). It carried eight vehicles and fifteen passengers. Today, it is an integral part of the New England-Florida "ocean highway" route, carrying thousands each year, the number augmented by the opening of the Atlantic City casinos. One passenger from Conneaut Lake, Pennsylvania, said the ferry ride, with its beautiful sunset, was the highlight of the trip he and his wife took to Florida. As Miller puts it, "The shrill whistle of the ferry vessel as it prepares to leave the terminal each day for its trip across the Delaware Bay quickens the pulse of adults and sends youngsters scurrying to their parents. Another ferry ride between Delaware and New Jersey is about to begin."

There are five vessels, the *Delaware*, the *New Jersey*, the *Twin Capes*, the *Cape Henlopen*, and the *Cape May*. They are two hundred feet long, sixty-eight feet wide, seventeen feet deep, and are driven by two 2,000 – horsepower main engines.

LOCAL POINTS OF INTEREST: If there were an American Victorian Resort Prize, Cape May would surely win hands down; it is to the nineteenth century what Williamsburg is to the eighteenth. With over six hundred Victorian buildings, it has served as a congenial meeting place for the Dickens Society, the Victorian Society in America, and other historic groups; the entire town has been designated a National Historic Landmark. At Christmas, the gingerbread architectural motifs are echoed in gingerbread house-making demonstrations, and there is a Christmas Lights Trolley Tour, all part of the annual Cape May Inns at Christmastime celebration. The town's recorded history as a resort goes back to an 1801 Philadelphia newspaper advertisement by Postmaster Ellis Hughes: "The subscriber has prepared himself for entertaining company who use sea bathing, and he is accommodated with extensive house room, with fish, oysters and crabs and good liquors." Presidents Lincoln, Grant, Pierce, Buchanan, and Harrison, as well as Horace Greeley and many congressmen vacationed here. The Cape was named for Cornelius Jacobsen Mey, who sailed past in 1623; his name was later changed to May. Today, there is a good beach, where "Cape May diamonds" (quartz rocks) abound, and many hotels, one of the more famous being the Chalfonte, built in 1876. Points of interest include the lighthouse at Cape May Point, the Washington Street Victorian Mall, historic Cold Spring Village, and a sunken concrete ship.

Lewes is smaller than Cape May, and, with its small weather-beaten, cypress-shingled dwellings and legends of Captain Kidd (who reportedly bargained away his treasure here), it has a more nautical flavor. The Zwaanendael Museum in Lewes, built in 1931 in the style of an ornate Amsterdam town house, is a tribute to the ill-fated Dutch whaling company of 1631. The company of twenty-eight Dutchmen, who planned to establish a farming and whaling settlement, mistook the bevies of wild geese for swans and named the town Zwaanendael, or "Valley of the Swans." They were massacred by the Indians. The Lewes Historical Society maintains several restored buildings, such as the Cannon Ball House (containing a marine museum), Plank House, Rabbit's Ferry House, Burton-Ingram House, Ellegood House, and others. The Cape Henlopen State Park is a mile away; here, there are a nature center, programs, and trails.

CROSSING TIME: 1 hr. 10 mins.

FERRY TYPE: Vehicle

VESSEL CAPACITY: Five vessels on the run, each holding 100 cars and 800 passengers.

OPERATING SEASON: All year

SCHEDULE: **Summer (late June-early Sept.): Lv. Cape May** 7 a.m., *8, 9, ˉ9:40, 10:20, 11:20, 12:20 p.m., ˉ1, 1:40, 2:40, 3:40, 5, 6, **8:30, ˉˉ10:20. **Lv. Lewes** 8:40 a.m., *9:40, 10:40, ˉ11:10, noon,

1 p.m., 2, ˜2:40, 3:20, 4:20, 5:20, 6:40, 8:40, *10:30,˜˜ midnight. *Sat. & Mon. only late June-Aug. ˜Thurs.-Mon. only mid-July-late Aug. **Fri. & Sun. only, late June-early Sept. ˜˜Wed. & Sat. only, early July-late Aug. *(Consult ferry authority on specific dates each year.)* **Spring/Fall (late Apr.-late June, weekends in April, and early Sept.-Oct.): Lv. Cape May** 7:30 a.m., 9:30, 11, 1 p.m., 3, 6:30; **lv. Lewes** 9:30 a.m., 11:30, 1 p.m., 3, 5, 8:30. **Winter (Nov.-Apr.): Lv. Cape May** 7:30 a.m., 11, 3 p.m., 6:30; **lv. Lewes** 9:30 a.m., 1 p.m., 5, 8:30.

RESTRICTIONS: Trailers, pickup-campers,and RVs permitted. Overhead clearance 13 ft. 6 in. No carry-on alcoholic beverages.

FACILITIES: Restrooms, snack bar

FARE: Cars and campers $24; adults $3.50 (same-day round-trip $6); children (before sixth birthday) $2.25; bus passengers, other than driver $3; other vehicles according to length $16.75 to $50.00; bicycles $6; motorcycle $12.00. Group rates.

RESERVATIONS: No

DIRECTIONS: From New Jersey: take Garden State Parkway to SR 9 and Cape May; from Maryland: take SR 9 to Lewes.

MAP LOCATION: P. 115, NJ, 1

CONTACT: Cape May-Lewes Ferry, Box 827, North Cape May, NJ 08204; Cape May Terminal—(609)886-2718, Lewes Terminal—(302) 645-6313

STATE: New Jersey/New York

PLACES SERVED: Fort Lee, NJ (Ross Dock)—Manhattan, NY (Pier 11)

BODY OF WATER: Hudson River

FERRY SERVICE HISTORY: The service was started in the fall of 1986 by Tradebase International, a firm headquartered in Totowa, New Jersey. The president

of Tradebase, Gene R. Wahl, says that the impetus for the service came from the overwhelming congestion on the bridges and tunnels leading to Manhattan. "Over 215,000 people come into the city each weekday from New Jersey, and there are basically only six ways to get across the river, all bridges and tunnels at maximum capacity," he observes. The service is a luxurious one, with coffee, Danish pastries, and newspapers available to morning commuters and, if all goes as planned, bar service at night. The vessel, a triple diesel named the *Black Whale II*, is eighty feet long and twenty-two feet wide with an aluminum hull.

It is anticipated that passengers will be from Bergen and lower Rockland Counties, as there are bus connections from these areas to Ross Dock.

LOCAL POINTS OF INTEREST: Fort Lee, New Jersey, is a historic city with many elements of drama in its past which make it more than just a commuting suburb and terminus for one of Manhattan's newest ferries. It was the center of the movie industry from 1907 until the late 1920s, its dramatic palisades overlooking the Hudson River providing the backdrop for films by Charlie Chaplin, Rudolph Valentino, Mary Pickford, and others. One of the perils of Pauline was shot on the cliffs at Fort Lee. The area played an important role earlier in American history, when George Washington built fortifications here to defend the city of New York and the river against the British. The Fort Lee Historic Park has campaign exhibits, with dioramas, films, and military artifacts.

[For notes on South Street, Manhattan, please see entry under Manhattan-St. George, p. 166.]

CROSSING TIME: 45 mins.

FERRY TYPE:	Pedestrian

VESSEL CAPACITY: 150 per boat; three boats are anticipated by Spring 1987 making six round trips a day per boat.

OPERATING SEASON: All year

SCHEDULE: **Mon.-Fri.: Lv. Fort Lee** every hour 5 a.m.-10; **lv. Pier 11** every hour 3 p.m.-8 p.m. Weekend service is a future possibility.

RESTRICTIONS: No pets; no smoking

FACILITIES: The service is a luxury one, offering morning coffee, pastries, and newspapers; in the afternoon, bar service is planned. Restrooms.

FARE: $12

RESERVATIONS: Desirable

DIRECTIONS: The ferry leaves from Ross Dock in Fort Lee. I-80 of the Palisades Interstate Parkway, Rtes. 4 and 46, and River Road all connect to the dock.

MAP LOCATION: P. 115, NJ, 2

CONTACT: Tradebase International, 755 Union Blvd., Totowa, NJ 07511, (201)256-7410

STATE: New Jersey/New York

PLACES SERVED: Highlands, NJ—Manhattan, NY (Pier 11)

BODY OF WATER: New York Bay, Sandy Hook Bay, Hudson River

Little M.

FERRY SERVICE
HISTORY:
Direct Line Commuter Service began running two boats on this luxury service in July 1986. One is a fifty-four-foot crew boat, the *Little M.*, which once carried men and materials to off-shore oil rigs in the Gulf of Mexico; it was acquired when it was no longer needed there. The *Catherine J.* is a one hundred-foot crew and passenger vessel. Direct Line has ordered seven other vessels, according to John E. Westlake, Executive Vice-President. Two are six hundred-passenger vessels and five are one hundred-foot vessels that will carry 108 passengers each. Mr. Westlake expects the service to be expanded into the New York metropolitan area and fares to be reduced once the additional ships are placed in service.

LOCAL POINTS
OF INTEREST:
Highlands, New Jersey, is a town located inside Sandy Hook on the Shrewsbury River. Many years ago it was a vacation and fishing community, but because of its location on the water and vistas of the Atlantic Ocean, Long Island and the New York skyline, it has become very popular.

[For notes on lower Manhattan, please see entry under Manhattan-St. George, p. 166.]

CROSSING TIME: 43-53 mins., depending on vessel

FERRY TYPE: Pedestrian

VESSEL CAPACITY: *Little M.*: 48 passengers; *Catherine J.*: 100 passengers (additional 100-ft. vessels will carry 108 passengers each)

OPERATING SEASON: All year

SCHEDULE: **Mon.-Fri: Lv. Highlands** 6:30 a.m., 7:40, 8:30, 10; **lv. Pier 11, Manhattan**, 3:30 p.m., 4:30, 5:40, 6:30. *[Additional service from Keyport and Keansburg, NJ, anticipated in the future.]*

RESTRICTIONS: No pets; no smoking; no bicycles

FACILITIES: Restrooms, air conditioning; luxury service includes juice, coffee, newspapers, and Danish pastries in the morning; company has applied for a liquor license and expects to provide bar service in the afternoon.

FARE: $10 (monthly commuter books available allowing round-trip fare of $19.50; fares expected to come down once larger boats are in service)

RESERVATIONS: Yes, especially Fridays and Mondays; again, this may change with larger vessels on the service.

DIRECTIONS: In Highlands, terminal is waterside at Conner's Hotel on Shore Drive

MAP LOCATION: P. 115, NJ, 3

CONTACT: Direct Line Commuter Service, 500 Highway 36, Middletown, NJ 07760, (201)872-0122; John E. Westlake, Executive Vice-President

STATE: New Jersey/New York

PLACES SERVED: Weehawken and West New York, NJ-Manhattan, NY (Pier 78 at 38th Street and 12th Avenue)

BODY OF WATER: Hudson River

FERRY SERVICE HISTORY: Until the era of the auto, the main access between New York and New Jersey had been by water. Regular ferry service from Hoboken began in 1774, and, at one time, there were eleven ferry crossing points below 24th Street alone. This crossing is the first new Trans-Hudson ferry service instituted in this century; it was begun as an answer to the congestion on existing Trans-Hudson crossings (over 200,000 commuters traverse the Hudson during rush hour, a number expected to increase). Until December 1986, when this ferry service was inaugurated, there had been no ferry service between New York and New Jersey for twenty years. The old Weehawken ferry stopped operations in 1957, though the Hoboken ferry to lower Manhattan ran until 1967. The crossing is an example of private sector initiative, according to Ralph L. Stanley of the US Department of Transportation, who supported the founding of the service. It is proving a boon to commuters. The name of the first vessel is the *Port Imperial*; she is an aluminum and fiberglass Blount Hitech, seventy-seven feet long, built by Blount Marine Corporation of Warren, Rhode Island. Other vessels are planned. There is parking for 500 vehicles on the Weehawken side. The monthly commuter book includes transfer on arrival in Manhattan on special buses; one goes to the World Trade Center and one makes a loop to Lexington Avenue via 42nd and 50th Streets.

LOCAL POINTS OF INTEREST: Weehawken is a town of about thirteen thousand. A 350-acre site along the waterfront is owned by the founder of the service, trucking magnate Arthur E. Imperatore. Called by *New York Magazine* "the Emperor of the West Bank," he has proposed to develop the derelict tract (bought from Penn Central) in several phases, including a "state-of-the-art city" modeled after Venice's St. Mark's Square, with offices, parks, homes, and an aquarium. The Palisades Cliffs would be scaled by elevators. For now, the development is on hold, pending permission, but the intitiation of the ferry service is the first phase of the overall transformation.

CROSSING TIME: 3-4 mins.

FERRY TYPE: Pedestrian

VESSEL CAPACITY: 144 passengers in warm weather; in winter 90 in enclosed lower deck.

Port Imperial

OPERATING SEASON: All year

SCHEDULE: **Mon.-Fri.:** Every 20 mins. 6:20 a.m.-9:20 and 4:10 p.m.-7:10. (Off-peak service up to 20 hours per day 7 days per week is planned.)

RESTRICTIONS: No smoking, no pets, no bicycles

FACILITIES: None

FARE: Monthly ferry/bus commuter books $130; daily passengers to be accommodated in the future.

RESERVATIONS: No

DIRECTIONS: To reach Weehawken slip, go north on Boulevard East from the Lincoln Tunnel for 1 mile. Turn right on Pershing Rd. Ferry slip is at foot of Pershing Rd.

MAP LOCATION: P. 115, NJ, 4

CONTACT: Allan C. Marcus, President, The Marcus Group, Inc., 60 Park Place, Suite 1500, Newark, NJ 07102, (201)622-4141

STATE:	New York

PLACES SERVED:	Bay Shore—Dunewood

BODY OF WATER:	Great South Bay

FERRY SERVICE HISTORY: Frank Mina, Vice-President and Treasurer of Fire Island Ferries, Inc., has compiled the history of early service to Fire Island. Formal ferry service actually dates back to the late 1800s, when the building of the first summer colonies and large ocean-front hotels began. Earlier settlements did not endure, and ferry service was generally by unscheduled sailboats. Converted yachts of the early 1900s gave way to converted rum-runners of the 1920s and later to Navy surplus rescue craft. Fire Island Ferries, Inc., was started in 1947 by Capt. Elmer Patterson. The popular wooden sixty-three-foot ASR, built in the 1940s, was for three decades the backbone of the fleet.

Today, Fire Island Ferries, Inc., is the largest of the operations which run from the three mainland villages of Bay Shore, Sayville, and Patchogue to a dozen cummunities, several public beaches, and two National Seashore park areas. In general, each area is served by a single operator. The Fire Island Ferries fleet of fifteen vessels (all under one hundred gross tons) services about sixty percent of the island's traffic, or approximately 800,000 passengers annually. The ships are these:

Capt. Patterson (1972), *Fire Island Miss* (1976), *Traveler* (1977) and *Fireball* (1981), four sister-ships. These are steel-hulled vessels with aluminum superstructure powered by three GM 12V-TI engines. All were built by Blount Marine of Warren, Rhode Island, and carry three hundred passengers;

Firebird, built by Blount in 1984, an enlarged eighty-five-foot version of this class; she is all-aluminum, with the same power plant as the four sister-ships and carries 374 passengers;

Vagabond (1979), a flexible vessel with removable seating (she can carry general cargo in the morning, passengers in the afternoon, and a moonlight cruise at night), powered by two GM 6-71s; her capacity is 227 passengers or sixty tons of cargo;

Stranger (1985), built by Gulf Craft of Patterson, Louisiana, is all-aluminum, powered by two GM 12V-71 diesel engines; she carries 149 passengers;

Fire Island Trader (1972), a converted all-steel shellfish dredge, now flat-decked with a small pilothouse and hydraulic crane. She is used for bulk cargo, vehicles, and garbage compactors;

Seven wooden vessels: *Fire Island Flyer* (1933), originally constructed

Traveler

to be a rum-runner, powered by three GM 6-71s with a capacity of 117 passengers;

Fire Islander (150 passengers) and *Isle of Fire* (160 passengers), both converted World War II Navy sixty-three-foot rescue craft. The *Isle of Fire* is powered by two GM 6-110s; the *Fire Islander* also uses two GM 6-110s but with an additional centerline 6-71;

Three vessels originally built for ferry service on the bay, currently powered by twin GM 12V-71 NA engines: *Fire Island Belle* (1948, 188 passengers); *Zee Lion* (1966, 150 passengers); *Zee Whiz* (1964, 150 passengers); the *Zee Whiz* also has a centerline 6-110;

Fire Island Queen, ninety-four feet long, a converted steam yacht that is the largest and slowest of all passenger ferries on the Bay. She carries 285 passengers and is equipped with restrooms and generators for day and evening charter cruises; she is powered by two GM 6-110s.

The vessels all require a crew of a captain and from one to three deckhands, depending on passenger load. Boats are switched to different runs according to need.

LOCAL POINTS OF INTEREST: The Fire Island National Seashore was created in 1964. Fire Island itself is a straight thirty-two mile sandbar lying parallel to the central one-third of Long Island's south (Atlantic) shore. The width of the island ranges from a few hundred feet to just under a half-mile, making it a fragile ribbon of sand, a barrier island protecting the Great South Bay. The Bay is a shallow sand-bottom salt-water bay flushed by the two inlets at either end of Fire Island, Fire Island Inlet on the west and Moriches Inlet on the east. The depth of water ranges from little more than a foot in many areas to depths of six to ten feet. The normal tide range is twelve to sixteen inches. There are seventeen separate communities on Fire Island, primarily for summer recreation. Within this area, the seven-mile stretch from Smith Point West to Watch Hill was designated a wilderness area in 1980. There are strict regulations governing litter, eating on beaches, and other matters, all aimed at preserving the island's beauty and atmosphere. Parts of Fire Island are much as they were when Isaac Stratford of Babylon, Long Island, set up a whaling station at Whalehouse Point in 1653. The island is rich in marine life, waterfowl, and other wildlife. Walt Whitman, a native of Long Island, once suggested, only half in jest, that Long Island secede from the state of New York and become a small principality called Paumanok (a word used in the aborginal deeds for the island). Whitman wrote of the "long stretching beaches and sand-islands" on the south side of Long Island; he would surely be grateful for the preservation efforts that have ensured that at least portions of Fire Island have remained intact.

Dunewood is a small residential community adjacent to Fair Harbor; there are no commercial facilities.

CROSSING TIME: 30 mins.

FERRY TYPE: Pedestrian

VESSEL CAPACITY: Varies according to vessel used; please see initial list [Dunewood, p. 142].

OPERATING SEASON: Mar.-early Sept.

SCHEDULE: **Summer, late June-early Sept: Mon.-Fri.: Lv. Bay Shore** 7:10 a.m., 10:10, 11:30, 1 p.m., 3:10, 5:20, *6:45, 8:15 (Fri. only), 9 (Fri. only). **Lv. Dunewood** 6:20 a.m. (Mon. only), 7:45, 10:45, 12:05 p.m., 1:35, 4:25, 5:55, 7:15, 8:40 (Fri. only). **Sat., + July 3: Lv. Bay Shore** 9:40 a.m., *11, 1 p.m., 2:50, 4:05, 5:55, 7:35, 9. **Lv. Dunewood** 10:10 a.m., 11:30, 1:35 p.m., 3:25, 4:40, 6:50, 8:10, 10:10. **Sun. + July 4 & Labor Day: Lv. Bay Shore** 9:40 a.m., 11, 1 p.m., 3:50, 6, 6:55. **Lv. Dunewood** 10:15 a.m., 11:35, 2:05 p.m., 3:20, 4:25, 5:30, 6:30, *7:35, 8:45. *Stops at Alantique only Fri., Sat., Sun. *Tickets sold on excursion service from Bay Shore Marina NOT honored. Consult company for spring schedule.*

RESTRICTIONS: No freight carried on passener boats. Such items as plants, furniture, bikes, and surfboards must be shipped on the regular freight boat. No smoking on boats.

FACILITIES: None

FARE:	Adult $4.25; children (under 12) $2.25. All dogs carried at child rate; must be under leash at all times on boats and terminal property.
RESERVATIONS:	No
DIRECTIONS:	From Long Island Expressway take Exit 53S (Sagtikos Parkway) to Southern State Parkway-Eastern Long Island (left fork). From

Southern State Parkway take Exit 421S (5th Ave. Bay Shore). Take Fifth Ave. to first traffic light after LIRR tracks. Turn left on Union Blvd. Turn right at 3rd light onto Fourth Ave.; Fourth Av. becomes Maple Ave. after next light (Main St.). Ferries leave from first parking lot on left, 1/3 mi. from Main St. The company has two terminals, the Ocean Beach and the Saltaire. Check schedules to make sure of the proper departure terminals.

MAP LOCATION:	P. 115, NY, 1
CONTACT:	Fire Island Ferries, Inc., Maple Ave., Bay Shore, LI, NY 11706, (516)665-3600

STATE:	New York
PLACES SERVED:	Bay Shore—Fair Harbor
BODY OF WATER:	Great South Bay
FERRY SERVICE HISTORY:	[See entry under Bay Shore—Dunewood p. 142.]
LOCAL POINTS OF INTEREST:	[For notes on the Fire Island National Seashore, please see entry under Bay Shore—Dunewood, p. 143.]

Fair Harbor is an attractive beach community with a restaurant, the Dock, and three small stores. If you come to Dunewood or Saltaire, you will need to walk to Fair Harbor for facilities.

CROSSING TIME:	30 mins.
FERRY TYPE:	Pedestrian
VESSEL CAPACITY:	Varies according to vessel used; please see list under Bay Shore—Dunewood, p. 142.

OPERATING SEASON: Mar.-early Sept.

SCHEDULE: **Summer, late June-early Sept.: Mon.-Fri.: Lv. Bay Shore** 7:10 a.m., 10:10, 11:30, 1 p.m., 3:10 5:20, 6:45, 7:50 (Fri. only), 9, 10:15 (Thurs. & Fri. only), 11:25 (Fri. only). **Lv. Fair Harbor** 6:15 a.m., 7:40, 10:40, noon, 1:30 p.m., 4:30, 5:50, 7:10, 8:15 (Fri. only), 10:40 (Mon.-Thurs. only), 10:50 (Fri. only). **Sat. + July 3: Lv. Bay Shore** 7:30 a.m., 9:40, 11, noon, 1 p.m., 2:50, 4:05, 5:55, 7:35, 9, 11:15. **Lv. Fair Harbor** 8:15 a.m., 10:10, 11:30, 12:30 p.m., 1:30, 3:20, 4:35, 6:55, 10:15, 12:25 a.m. **Sun. + July 4 & Labor Day: Lv. Bay Shore** 8:15 a.m., 9:40, 11, noon, 1 p.m., 2:35, 3:45, 4:45, 5:50, 6:55. **Lv. Fair Harbor** 8:55 a.m., 10:10, 11:30, 12:30 p.m., 2:10, 3:15, 4:20, 5:25, 6:30, 7:35, 8:40, 9:30. *Consult company for spring schedule.*

RESTRICTIONS: See RESTRICTIONS, p. 144.

FACILITIES: No

FARE: See FARE, p. 145.

RESERVATIONS: No

DIRECTIONS: See DIRECTIONS, p. 145.

MAP LOCATION: P. 115, NY, 2

CONTACT: See CONTACT, p. 145.

STATE: New York

PLACES SERVED: Bay Shore—Kismet

BODY OF WATER: Great South Bay

FERRY SERVICE HISTORY: [See entry under Bay Shore—Dunewood, p. 142.]

**LOCAL POINTS
OF INTEREST:** [For notes on the Fire Island National Seashore, please see entry under Bay Shore—Dunewood, p. 143.]

Kismet is where most of the townspeople across the Bay go after working hours; it has two motels, a marina, a grocery store, and two restaurants. There has also been an influx of singles here.

CROSSING TIME: 30 mins.

FERRY TYPE: Pedestrian

VESSEL CAPACITY: Varies according to vessel used; please see list under Bay Shore—Dunewood, p. 142.

OPERATING SEASON: Mar.-early Sept.

SCHEDULE: **Summer, late June-early Sept.: Mon.-Fri.: Lv. Bay Shore** *7:10 a.m., ˉ9:30, ˉˉ10:50, ˉˉ1 p.m., ˉˉ3:10, ˉˉ5:15, ˉˉ6:50, 7:50 (Fri. only), **9, *10:15 (Thurs. & Fri. only), *11:25 (Fri. only). **Lv. Kismet** ˉˉ6:25 a.m., ˉˉ7:35, ˉˉ9:55, ˉˉ11:15, ˉˉ2:15 p.m., ˉˉ4:30, 5:40 (Fri. only), ˉˉ6:20 (Mon.-Thurs. only), 7:15 (Fri. only), ˉˉ8:05 (Mon.-Thurs. only), 7:15 (Fri. only), ˉˉ8:05 (Mon.-Thurs. only), 8:20 (Fri. only), *10:40 (Fri. only), *10:50 (Mon.-Thurs. only), *11:50 (Fri. only). **Sat. + July 3 & Sun. before Labor Day: Lv. Bay Shore** *7:30 a.m., 9:35, 11, noon, 1 p.m., ˉˉ2:50, ˉˉ4, ˉˉ6, ˉˉ7:30, *9, *11:15. **Lv. Kismet** *8 a.m., 10, 11:25, 12:25 p.m., ˉˉ2:25, ˉˉ3:15, ˉ5:25, ˉˉ6:25, ˉˉ8:50, *10:30, *12:35 a.m. **Sun. + July 4 & Labor Day: Lv. Bay Shore** *8:15 a.m., ˉˉ9:45, 11, noon, 1 p.m., 2:35, 3:45, 5, 6:05, 8:05. **Lv. Kismet** *8:40 a.m., ˉˉ10:10, 11:25, 12:25 p.m., 2:05, 3:15, 4:30, 5:35, 6:35, 7:35, 8:45, *9:40. *To or from Ocean Beach terminal. **From Ocean Beach Terminal Mon.-Thurs.; from Saltaire terminal Fri. only. ˉFrom Saltaire terminal daily. ˉˉTo or from Saltaire terminal Mon.-Thurs., Sat., Sun.; to or from Maple Ave. dock Fri. only. *Consult company for spring schedule.*

RESTRICTIONS: See RESTRICTIONS, p. 144.

FACILITIES: No

FARE: See FARE, p. 145.

RESERVATIONS: No

DIRECTIONS: See DIRECTIONS, p. 145.

MAP LOCATION: P. 115, NY, 3

CONTACT: See CONTACT, p. 145.

STATE:	New York
PLACES SERVED:	Bay Shore—Ocean Bay Park—Seaview
BODY OF WATER:	Great South Bay
FERRY SERVICE HISTORY:	[See entry under Bay Shore—Dunewood, p. 142.]
LOCAL POINTS OF INTEREST:	[For notes on the Fire Island National Seashore, please see entry under Bay Shore—Dunewood, p. 143.]

Ocean Bay Park and Seaview are two of the smaller communities on Fire Island. Seaview has a grocery store and a ball field, and Ocean Bay Park has a restaurant with bar which is very popular with both tourists and townspeople. Ocean Bay Park has a reputation as a singles center, while Seaview is more family-oriented.

CROSSING TIME:	30 mins.
FERRY TYPE:	Pedestrian
VESSEL CAPACITY:	Varies according to vessel used; please see list under Bay Shore—Dunewood, p. 142.
OPERATING SEASON:	Mar.-early Sept.
SCHEDULE:	**Summer (late June through early Sept.): Mon.-Thurs.: Lv. Bay Shore** 7:30 a.m., 9:15, 10:20, 11:40, noon, 1:20 p.m., 2:50,

4:10, 5:50, 7:20 (Thurs. only), 8:50. **Fri.: Lv. Bay Shore** 7:30 a.m., 9:15, 10:40, noon, 1:20 p.m., 2:10, 3:10, 4:10, 5:10, 6:10, 6:50, 7:30, 8:10, 8:50, 9:30, 10:15. **Sat.: Lv. Bay Shore** 7:30 a.m., 9, 9:40, 10:30, 11:15, 11:50, 12:30 p.m., 1:10, 1:50, 2:50, 3:50, 4:40, 6, 7:25, 8:50, 10:10. **Sun.: Lv. Bay Shore** 9 a.m., 9:40, 10:20, 11:05, 11:45, 12:30 p.m., 1:10, 2:25, 3:35, 4:50, 6:05, 7:20, 8:50. **Mon.-Thurs.: Lv. Ocean Bay Park** 8:15 a.m., 9:55, 11:20, 12:40 p.m., 2, 3:30, 4:50, 6:30, 8, 9:30 (Thurs. only). **Fri.: Lv. Ocean Bay Park** 8:15 a.m., 9:55, 11:20, 12:40 p.m., 2, 2:50, 3:50, 4:50, 5:50, 6:50, 7:30, 8:10, 8:50, 9:40. **Sat.: Lv. Ocean Bay Park** 8:10 a.m., 9:40, 10:20, 11:10, 11:55, 12:30 p.m., 1:10, 1:50, 2:30, 3:30, 4:30, 5:20, 6:40, 8:05, 9:30, 10:50. **Sun.: Lv. Ocean Bay Park** 9:40 a.m., 10:20, 11, 11:45, 12:25 p.m., 1:10, 1:50, 3:10, 4:25, 5:40, 6:55, 8:15, 9:30. Lv. Seaview 10 mins. earlier. *Consult company for spring schedules.*

RESTRICTIONS:	See RESTRICTIONS, p. 144.
FACILITIES:	None
FARE:	See FARE, p. 145.
RESERVATIONS:	No
DIRECTIONS:	See DIRECTIONS, p. 145.
MAP LOCATION:	P. 115, NY, 4
CONTACT:	See CONTACT, p. 145.

STATE:	New York
PLACES SERVED:	Bay Shore—Ocean Beach
BODY OF WATER:	Great South Bay
FERRY SERVICE HISTORY:	[See entry under Bay Shore—Dunewood, p. 142.]
LOCAL POINTS OF INTEREST:	[For notes on the Fire Island National Seashore, please see entry under Bay Shore—Dunewood, p. 143.]

Ocean Beach is one of the largest and most popular communities on Fire Island. It is also one of the most strictly controlled, with a vigilant police department. Residents of Ocean Beach are extremely concerned about fire, so visitors are asked to take every precaution. No eating or drinking is allowed on beaches or public docks; there are no public restrooms or locker facilities; use of radios is regulated; and violators are subject to fines up to $250. The beach has a reputation for being family-oriented, with many teenagers. The beach itself is wide and appealing.

CROSSING TIME:	30 mins.
FERRY TYPE:	Pedestrian

VESSEL CAPACITY:	Varies according to vessel used; please see list under Bay Shore—Dunewood, p. 142.

OPERATING SEASON:	Mar.—early Sept.

SCHEDULE: **Summer, late June-early Sept.: Mon.-Fri.: Lv. Bay Shore** 7 a.m., 9:25, 10:45, noon, 1 p.m., 2 (Fri. only), 3:05, 4:10, 4:55 (Fri. only), 5:25 (Mon.-Thurs. only), 5:50 (Fri. only), 6:40, 7:25 (Fri. only), 7:50 (Mon.-Thurs. only), 8:15 (Fri. only), 9, 10:15 (Thurs.-Fri. only). **Lv. Ocean Beach** 6:25 a.m., 7:40, 10, 11:15, 12:30 p.m., 1:30, 2:30 (Fri. only), 3:40, 4:45, 5:25 (Fri. only), 6 (Mon.-Thurs. only), 6:20 (Fri. only), 7:10, 7:55 (Fri. only), 8:20 (Mon.-Thurs. only), 8:45 (Fri. only), 9:30 (Thurs.-Fri. only), 10:30 (Mon.- Thurs. only), 10:45 (Fri. only). **Sat. + July 3: Lv. Bay Shore** 7:30 a.m., 9, 9:40, 10:25, 11:05, 11:50, 12:50 p.m., 1:50, 2:50, 4, 5:10, 6:20, 7:30, 8:30. **Lv. Ocean Beach** 8:10 a.m., 9:30, 10:10, 10:55, 11:35, 12:20 p.m., 1:20, 2:20, 3:20, 4:30, 5:40, 6:50, 8, 9:15, 11. **Sun. + July 4 & Labor Day: Lv. Bay Shore** 7:40 a.m., 9, 9:50, 10:35, 11:10, 11:50, 12:50 p.m., 1:30, 2:30, 3:40, 4:50, 6, 7:10, 8:10. **Lv. Ocean Beach** 8:15 a.m., 9:30, 10:20, 11:05, 11:40, 12:20 p.m., 1:20, 2, 3:10, 4:20, 5:30, 6:40, 7:40, 8:50, 9:40, 10:45.

RESTRICTIONS:	See RESTRICTIONS, p. 144.

FACILITIES:	No

FARE:	See FARE, p. 145.

RESERVATIONS:	No

DIRECTIONS:	See DIRECTIONS, p. 145.

MAP LOCATION:	P. 115, NY, 5

CONTACT:	See CONTACT, p. 145.

STATE:	New York

PLACES SERVED:	Bay Shore—Point O'Woods, Fire Island, LI

BODY OF WATER: Great South Bay

FERRY SERVICE
HISTORY: This is a private ferry for the use of Point
                       O'Woods residents and their guests. Mem-
                       bers who wish information about the ferry
                       should call (516)583-5660.

STATE: New York

PLACES SERVED: Bay Shore—Saltaire

BODY OF WATER: Great South Bay

FERRY SERVICE   [See entry under Bay Shore—Dunewood,
HISTORY: p. 142.]

LOCAL POINTS   [For notes on the Fire Island National Sea-
OF INTEREST: shore, please see entry under Bay Shore—
                       Dunewood, p. 143.] Saltaire is a wealthy and
conservative residential community; if you come here, you will need to
walk to Fair Harbor for facilities.

CROSSING TIME: 30 min.

FERRY TYPE: Pedestrian

VESSEL CAPACITY: Varies according to vessel used; please see
                       list under Bay Shore—Dunewood, p. 142.

OPERATING SEASON: Mar.-early Sept.

SCHEDULE: **Summer, late June-early Sept.: Mon.-Fri.:**
                       Lv. Bay Shore *7:10 a.m., 9:30, 10:50, 1
                       p.m., 3:10, 5:15, 6:50, 7:50 (Fri. only), 9
(Thurs. & Fri. only; use Ocean Beach Terminal Thurs., Saltaire terminal
Fri.) **Lv. Saltaire** 6:30 a.m., 7:40, 10:05, 11:20, 2:10 p.m., 4:25, 5:40
(Fri. only), 6:15 (Mon.-Thurs. only), 7:15 (Fri. only), 8 (Mon.-Thurs.
only), 8:15 (Fri. only). **Sat. + July 3: Lv. Bay Shore** *7:30 a.m., 9:35,
11, 12:55 p.m., 2:50, 4, 6, 7:30. **Lv. Saltaire** *8:05 a.m., 10:05, 11:25,
1:25 p.m., 3:20, 5:20, 8:45, *10:25. **Sun. + July 4 & Labor Day: Lv.**
Bay Shore *8:15 a.m., 9:45, 11, 12:55 p.m., 2:40, 3:45, 6:05, 7:10. **Lv.**

Saltaire *8:45 a.m., 10:15, 11:30, 2:10 p.m., 3:15, 4:30, 5:35, 6:40, 7:40, 8:50. *Use Ocean Beach Terminal. *Consult company for spring schedule.*

RESTRICTIONS:	See RESTRICTIONS, p. 144.
FACILITIES:	No
FARE:	See FARE, p. 145.
RESERVATIONS:	No
DIRECTIONS:	See DIRECTIONS, p. 145.
MAP LOCATION:	P. 115, NY, 7
CONTACT:	See CONTACTS, p. 145.

STATE:	New York
PLACES SERVED:	Bemus Point—Stow
BODY OF WATER:	Lake Chautauqua

FERRY SERVICE HISTORY: The Bemus Point—Stow ferry is one of the most historic institutions on Lake Chautauqua. The present vessel, the *Chautauqua Belle,* is powered by an English Ford diesel with hydraulically propelled paddlewheels, guided by thousand-foot cables. The ferry's early history was gathered and recounted by David A. Fuscus of Jamestown, New York, in "A History of the Bemus Point—Stow Ferry," written for the opening of the Lake Chautauqua Bridge in 1982. According to Fuscus, the first ferry license was granted to Thomas Bemus in 1811, in the first judicial act to take place in Chautauqua County. Bemus was allowed to charge six and one-quarter cents for a single person, eighteen and three-quarter cents for a rider and horse, and thirty-seven and one-half cents for a wagon and horses or oxen. The fractions have remained a mystery to historians. This ferry was a log raft, later improved by a crude pulley system. A later operator, Philip Strong, tried to pull the ferry by horses and mules, but failed. The ferry changed hands many times in the ensuing years.

When steamboats (first introduced in 1828) became common in the 1860s and 1870s, their steel propellors cut the rope ferry cables; this problem was not solved until steel cables came into use in the early twentieth century. Steamboats were required to whistle, making sure the cables were not in use and the ferry was on one side or the other. Summoning the ferry was also a problem in times of light use; finally, metal horns, steam whistles, and electric bells were used (the two bells are still there, though they do not operate). Ralph and Alton Ball were prominent among the many owners of the ferry and introduced the first steam-powered engine in 1902; Alton Ball built a steel-hulled ferry in 1928. In 1921, Alton Ball incorporated the holdings into Bemus Point— Stow Ferry, Inc. In 1942, his son Gerald sold it to the County of Chautauqua which ran and maintained the ferry until the Chautauqua Lake Bridge was opened in 1982. One ferryman, Steve Torrey, was hailed by a fishing boat after a heavy day of traffic. The fisherman had found a wad of bills, secured with a rubber band, floating in the lake, and decided the ferryman was the only probable owner; the money had fallen from Torrey's shirt pocket when he leaned over.

The opening of the bridge might well have signalled the end of this historic ferry, as has happened in many places, except for the Sea Lion Project, Ltd. (named for Carl F. Lyon, a moving spirit behind the enterprise). This is a nonprofit corporation formed to lease the ferry from the County of Chautauqua and to staff and run it with volunteer crews. The crews undergo training and take a test prescribed by the New York State Department of Parks and Recreation, Marine Division; they are licensed to run the vessel and have kept it staffed for the past several years, operating it in four- or five-hour shifts (noon to five and five to nine or ten each day). Thanks to the Sea Lion Project's team of committed volunteers, such as the 1986 manager, Arthur Thomas, and energetic Executive Director, Linda E. Crook, the ferry celebrated its 175th year of service in 1986. Few tourists or local residents miss taking the little sidewheeler across the narrows of lake Chautauqua, now an institution cherished beyond the dreams of Thomas Bemus.

LOCAL POINTS OF INTEREST: Lake Chautauqua is a summer arts and education center; the population doubles in the summer to about ten thousand. The Chautauqua Institution, founded in 1874, offers cultural activities in music, lectures, drama, education, and religion from late June to late August. Many visitors come year after year to the hotels and cottages on the lake. The Chautauqua movement was an outgrowth of the nineteenth-century lyceum movement. The first "American Lyceum" was founded in Massachusetts by Josiah Holbrook (1826). Hundreds of lyceums were subsequently established, dedicated to providing educational opportunities for adults, teacher-training, and the founding of museums and libraries. At Lake Chautauqua, annual Methodist Episcopal camp meetings were held, becoming assemblies for religious study and incorporating other branches of study. The Chautauqua Institution offered correspondence courses, published books, and began the summer schools still held today. The community also provided a platform for political and literary speakers.

CROSSING TIME: 7-8 mins.

FERRY TYPE: Vehicle

VESSEL CAPACITY: 8 cars

OPERATING SEASON: Memorial Day-Labor Day

OPERATING SEASON: **June: Sat.-Sun.:** Noon-9 p.m. **July-Aug.:** Daily, noon-9 p.m. Extended hours possible if traffic warrants. **Memorial Day and Labor Day weekends: Fri.-Mon.** Noon-9 p.m.

RESTRICTIONS: Trailers, pickup-campers, and RVs to 20 ft. permitted. Load limit 10 tons.

FACILITIES: No

FARE: Cars $1.50; pedestrians $.25

RESERVATIONS: No

DIRECTIONS: In Stow, the ferry landing is off Rt. 394; in Bemus Point, it is at the end of village on Lakeside Dr.

MAP LOCATION: P. 115, NY, 8

CONTACT: Sea Lion Project, Ltd., R. D. One, Sea Lion Dr., Mayville, NY 14757, (716)753-2403

William Darrell

STATE:	New York/Ontario, Canada
PLACES SERVED:	Cape Vincent, NY—Wolfe Island, ON
BODY OF WATER:	St. Lawrence River
FERRY SERVICE HISTORY:	The Cape Vincent-Wolfe Island ferry is the last remaining passenger and vehicular ferry crossing the St. Lawrence River between the

US and Canada. There are ferries operating in the US which are older, but none of more royal lineage. According to a historical account written by Earle M. Cass for the *Bulletin* of the Jefferson County Historical Society, as early as 1820, Samuel Hinckley of Wolfe Island ferried passengers across the river. In 1829, King George IV of England formally leased the ferry to him; the original parchment document was handed down in the Hinckley family for many years. The Crown lease reads, in part: "GEORGE the FOURTH by the Grace of GOD of the United Kingdom of Great Britain and Ireland KING defender of the Faith & & & To all to whom these Presents shall come Greeting. KNOW YE that for and in consideration of the rents hereby reserved and of the conditions herein after contained . . . WE HAVE demised leased and let . . . unto the said Samuel Hinckley his Executors Administrators and assigns our ferry from Wolfe Island in the said Midland District to Cape Vincent, in the State of New York in the United States of America.'' The lease enjoined Hinckley to carry across Indians and Soldiers "without Fee tole or reward.'' Eventually, the ferry rights went to Samuel's son Coleman and his brother-in-law, Demetreus Spinning, whose daughter, Angeline, married Thomas D. Horne. Horne succeeded to the ferry business and was the great-grandfather of George and Bruce Horne, the brothers who presently run the ferry. The vessel on this run is the *William Darrell*.

The ferry makes good connections with one from Wolfe Island to Kingston on the Canadian mainland, the *Wolfe Islander III*, which is operated by the Ontario Ministry of Transportation & Communications; the two terminals are seven miles apart. [Space prohibits including full details for ferries without a US terminus; call (613)544-2231 for schedule.]

LOCAL POINTS OF INTEREST: Cape Vincent is located at the very eastern end of Lake Ontario where the St. Lawrence River begins. In the late 1700s, French missionaries settled in the area, and some examples of the limestone houses of that period remain. A French Festival takes place the second Saturday of each July with a parade, carts selling delectable French pastries and breads, and historical exhibits. Interesting sights include the remains of Fort Haldiman, dating back to the War of 1812, on nearby Carleton Island; Tibbett's Point Lighthouse (1827), where Lake Ontario meets the St. Lawrence on a rocky point of land jutting out into Lake Ontario; and the Cape Vincent Seaway Pilot Station, from which river pilots board ocean-going ships for their transit of the St. Lawrence and lake pilots board for their voyage across Lake Ontario. Cape Vincent is the gateway to the "Golden Crescent," the communities of Cape Vincent, Three Mile Bay, Chaumont, Texter, Watertown, Sackets Harbor and Henderson.

Wolfe Island, the largest of the Thousand Islands, is primarily agricultural; the main town is Marysville. Here, accommodation can be found at the General Wolfe Hotel and the Hitchcock House; the Wolfe Island Inn is also extremely pleasant. You can watch Jan carving and painting wooden duck decoys at Jan's Decoy Shop; there is also a small Kraft cheese factory on the island. The ice-fishing shanties on the frozen St. Lawrence are a colorful winter sight.

CROSSING TIME: 10 mins.

FERRY TYPE: Vehicle

VESSEL CAPACITY: 10 cars, 98 passengers

OPERATING SEASON: Mid-May-mid-Oct.

SCHEDULE: **Lv. Wolfe Island** 8 a.m., 9:15, 10:15, 11, 11:45, 12:15 p.m., 1:15, 2:45, 3:45, 4:45, 5:40, *7. **Lv. Cape Vincent** 8:15 a.m., 9:30, 10:30, 11:15, noon, 12:30 p.m., 2, 3, 4, 5, 6, *7:30. *No trip Mon.-Thurs. after mid-Sept.

RESTRICTIONS:	Trailers, pickup-campers, and RVs permitted. Load limit 20 tons.
FACILITIES:	No
FARE:	Car and driver $5; adults $1; trailers $6-$7
RESERVATIONS:	No
DIRECTIONS:	Take SR 12-E to Cape Vincent and turn north on James St. From Hornes Point, the drive to Marysville is 7 miles (this is where you wait for the Kingston ferry).
MAP LOCATION:	P. 115, NY, 9
CONTACT:	Horne's Ferry Ltd., Wolfe Island, ON, Canada KOH 2Y0, (613)385-2291 or (613)385-2262

STATE:	New York
PLACES SERVED:	City Island (the Bronx)—Potter's Field (Hart Island, the Bronx)
BODY OF WATER:	Long Island Sound
FERRY SERVICE HISTORY:	This ferry is definitely not for tourists. It takes the unclaimed bodies of people who

die in New York (presently one out of every twenty-nine) to Potter's Field for burial in small New England pine coffins. Chip Brown of the *Washington Post* wrote an extensive and informative article (9/12/86) about this ferry, calling the daily journey "an eerie scene, perhaps because the image of a journey over water is ingrained in the iconography of death. The ferryman Charon is a fixture of Greek legend, running his 'rust-hued vessel' across the river Styx, collecting his money from the mouths of the dead." The ferrymen, according to Brown, fry sausage and eggs, discuss politics, and pat the ferry dog, Brownie, in a small dockside shack while waiting for the truck from the morgue. Many have retired here from years aboard the city of New York's Staten Island ferries, and, despite the nature of the job, have come to prefer the more leisurely pace. They call the ferry destination simply "the other side." John Wetmore, who works on the Staten Island ferries, says drily it is at least "one ferry where the customers don't complain." (Wetmore shares the special affection many Staten Islanders have for ferries; he does oil paintings of ferry boats, some of which hang in a bar on Staten Island.) The vessel on the Potter's Field service is the *Michael Cosgrove*. Prison volunteers perform the burials.

The public is not admitted, except by special permission, which can be obtained by writing to the Department of Corrections. Tours are given for officials, students, professors, and others about once a month. The ferry runs four days a week.

Several of the ferry captains interviewed for this book, in various states, have told of passengers who wished to scatter the ashes of a deceased relative from the boat, implying, perhaps, that there is indeed an archetypal connection between the ferry, the journey, and the metaphor of death.

LOCAL POINTS OF INTEREST: New York has had potter's fields for over two centuries, at several locations, including Washington Square and the site of the New York Public Library. Hart Island was purchased in 1869.

STATE: New York

PLACES SERVED: Greenport—Shelter Island

BODY OF WATER: Shelter Island Sound

FERRY SERVICE HISTORY: It is thought that ferries of one sort or another have run at this location since the 1600s and early 1700s. Four eighty-eight foot double-ended boats are on the present service, the *Islander*, the *Shelter Island*, the *New Prospect*, and the *Greenport*.

LOCAL POINTS OF INTEREST: Shelter Island is one of the most charming parts of Long Island, rich with literary associations. While not ostentatious, it suggests that kindly philanthropists have restored themselves during summers here. Carson McCullers came out to Shelter Island in 1961 to meet with Edward Albee and discuss the stage adaptation of *The Ballad of the Sad Cafe*. (A year later, she was his guest at Water Island, a small community on Fire Island.) It has a rural atmosphere with woodlands, flowering meadows, sandy beaches, and abundant wildlife. The Pridwin at Crescent Beach is a delightful resort hotel that offers speedboat rides as well as Edwardian pursuits such as croquet. The Shelter Island Resort Motel is also pleasant, on a bluff overlooking the sound, with a well-known Sunday buffet.

Greenport, a part of Southold Town, is an old Long Island village, with inviting streets lined with historic houses, such as the Gingerbread House on Main Street (part of the Townsend Manor Inn), antique and specialty shops (if you like scrimshaw, you should be able to find it here), and interesting restaurants. It was settled by early colonists from New Haven, Connecticut Colony, shortly after 1640. Farming, fishing, and shipbuilding were the principal pursuits of settlers. From the 1830s through the 1850s, the Whaling Years, about fifteen vessels sailed from Greenport, and it is still the yachting center of Long Island's North Fork. The Windward Sailing Company charters sailboats and offers lessons, and S. T. Preston & Son, on the Main Street Wharf, has general marine supplies. The Museum of Childhood, with antique dolls and a Swiss village, will interest families, as well as the Blacksmith Shop (built in the 1800s and still in use) and the 1899 Greenport Railroad Station. The Stirling Historical Society has displays on local history. In Southold, a few miles from Greenport, the Indian Museum, the Southold Marine Museum, the Southold Historical Society and Museum, and the Horton's Point Lighthouse are of interest.

CROSSING TIME: 10 mins.

FERRY TYPE: Vehicle

VESSEL CAPACITY: 12 cars

OPERATING SEASON: All year

SCHEDULE: **Daily: Lv. Shelter Island** 5:40 a.m., 6:15, 6:45, and every 15-20 mins. from 7 a.m.-9:45 p.m.; 10:15, 10:45, 11:15, 11:45. **Lv. Greenport** (Railroad Dock) 5:55 a.m., 6:30, 7, every 15-20 mins. from 7:15 a.m.-10 p.m., 10:30, 11, 11:30, midnight.

RESTRICTIONS: Trailers, pickup-campers, and RVs permitted. Load limit 30 tons. Overhead clearance 14 ft.

FACILITIES: None

FARE: Car and driver $3.50 ($5.50 same-day round-trip); passengers $.50; larger vehicles by weight.

RESERVATIONS: No

DIRECTIONS: Ferry connects SR 114 on Shelter Island with SR 25 at Greenport — ferry is at 3rd St.

MAP LOCATION: P. 115, NY, 11

CONTACT: North Ferry Co., Inc., Shelter Island Heights, New York, NY 11965, (516)749-0139

STATE: New York

PLACES SERVED: Manhattan (Battery Park)—Ellis Island National Monument

BODY OF WATER: New York Harbor

FERRY SERVICE HISTORY: Ferry service to Ellis Island has been suspended pending completion of renovation. The vessels normally on this run are the *Miss Freedom* (121.6 feet long; capacity 450 passengers) and the *Miss Gateway* (120.9 feet long; capacity five hundred passengers). The service is operated by the Circle Line; for information call (212)269-5755.

STATE: New York

PLACES SERVED: Manhattan (Battery Park)—Statue of Liberty National Monument

BODY OF WATER: New York Harbor

FERRY SERVICE HISTORY: The vessels on this service are the *Miss Circle Line*, 139.7 feet long, and the *Miss Liberty*, 121.5 feet long. The crossing, sometimes called "America's Favorite Boat Ride," attracts riders from all over the world and has been for decades one of the top tourist activities in New York.

LOCAL POINTS OF INTEREST: Battery Park is the southernmost tip of Manhattan, where the Hudson and East Rivers meet and where European explorers first

Miss Circle Line

came ashore on the island. It is the oldest part of town.

The Statue of Liberty, by Frederic Bartholdi, was presented to the United States by France in 1884 in commemoration of the American-French alliance during the American Revolution. The statue is the tallest of modern times, with a height of 151 feet, standing on a pedestal of 156 feet. The framework was designed by Gustaf Eiffel, designer of the Eiffel Tower in Paris. The statue underwent an extensive renovation completed in 1986. She was unveiled during a spectacular four-day gala (July 3-6, 1986), celebrated with Operation Sail, a parade of Tall Ships from Verrazano Bridge up the Hudson River, a music festival, fireworks, and other ceremonies. In the base of the statue is the American Museum of Immigration, well worth a trip in itself, with photographs, mannequins, dioramas, and other artifacts documenting the immigrant struggle.

CROSSING TIME: 12 mins.

FERRY TYPE: Pedestrian

VESSEL CAPACITY: *Miss Circle Line*: 1035 passengers
Miss Liberty: 827 passengers

OPERATING SEASON: All year

SCHEDULE: **Daily, except Christmas Day. Memorial Day-Labor Day (Mon.-Sat.):** service every half-hr. 9 a.m.-5 p.m.; **Sun.** 9 a.m.-7 p.m.
Labor Day-Memorial Day: daily service every hr. 9 a.m.-4 p.m.

RESTRICTIONS: No

FACILITIES:	Snack bar
FARE:	Round-trip only: adults $3.25; children under 11 $1.50
RESERVATIONS:	No
DIRECTIONS:	Take the IRT Subway, 7th Ave. local, to South Ferry.
MAP LOCATION:	P. 115, NY, 13
CONTACT:	Circle Line Statue of Liberty Ferry, Battery Park, South Ferry, New York, NY 10004, (212)269-5755

STATE:	New York
PLACES SERVED:	Manhattan (South Street, Pier 11)—Roosevelt Island
BODY OF WATER:	East River

FERRY SERVICE HISTORY: "Think positively, or don't do it!" says Petros Kontaratos, who began this service in August 1986. Kontaratos has a passion for ships and for ferries in particular. He began the commuter run with the vessel *Island Adventure*, which he acquired from Casco Bay Lines in Maine. He hopes, in time, to add a hovercraft, which will make the trip in eight or nine minutes, as opposed to the present thirty minutes (both much better times than the tramway/subway combination of an hour). As James Brooke of the *New York Times*, who rode the ferry on one of her early runs and wrote an article about it for the *Times*, put it, "The line is part of a regional resurgence of private ferry operations, spurred by entrepreneurs who believe commuters can be lured from crowded subways and congested highways." The ferry bypasses the tramway from Roosevelt Island and the IRT Lexington Avenue line. Brooke interviewed passengers, such as Inge Fiori, a vice-president for Goldman, Sachs & Company, who told him, "It's so relaxing. I don't miss the anxiety that comes with the subway." Jeffrey D. Campbell was pleased, he said, to land right at the foot of his building on the Wall Street waterfront.

**LOCAL POINTS
OF INTEREST:**   [For notes on Pier 11 and the South Street
                        Seaport Area, please see entry under Man-
                        hattan-St. George, p. 166].

Roosevelt Island was once called Welfare Island. It has now been
turned into a residential community, New York City's only economically
integrated, planned community. It is connected by tramway (which offers
a scenic view of the city) to the Upper East Side of Manhattan. This area
of the city has been called "ultra-chic, subtle, sumptuous, recherche,
highly energetic, quasi-European, and quintessentially New York."

Few ferry rides offer such a unique cityscape, one invisible to subway
and bus riders and one unheeded by drivers mired in East River Drive
traffic, who are in no mood to admire anything except a traffic-free exit.
The boat passes such New York landmarks as the Delacorte Fountain, the
United Nations headquarters, and the Chrysler Building, all, as Brooke
puts it, "bathed in morning light."

CROSSING TIME: 30 mins.

FERRY TYPE: Pedestrian

VESSEL CAPACITY: 300 passengers

OPERATING SEASON: All year

SCHEDULE: **Lv. Roosevelt Island** 6:30 a.m., 6:50, and
                        7:15. **Lv. Pier 11** at 4 p.m., 5:40. Additional
                        trips planned if traffic justifies it.

RESTRICTIONS: None

FACILITIES: Restrooms, snack bar, color television.

FARE: $2.50

RESERVATIONS: No

DIRECTIONS: The ferry leaves from a point near the Roo-
                        sevelt Island terminus of the tramway; the
                        tramway station on Manhattan is at 2nd Ave.
                        and 59th St. Pier 11 is just below Wall St.

MAP LOCATION: P. 115, NY, 14

CONTACT: Petros Kontaratos, 51-17 Van Loon,
                        Elmhurst, Queens, NY 11373 (212)363-2828
                        or (718)204-2220

STATE: New York

PLACES SERVED: Manhattan (Whitehall Street)—Governors Island

BODY OF WATER: New York Harbor

FERRY SERVICE HISTORY: Governors Island is a Coast Guard facility, and only persons with passes are admitted, though the Coast Guard does have open houses in the fall and spring when the public is invited. For information, call (212)668-7114.

STATE: New York

PLACES SERVED: Manhattan (Whitehall Street)—St. George, Staten Island ("The Staten Island Ferry")

BODY OF WATER: New York Harbor

FERRY SERVICE HISTORY: Over twenty million people ride the Staten Island Ferries each year, disengaged from city turmoil, time-honored claimants to a maritime right-of-way through the world's largest port. The antecedents of the Staten Island Ferry stretch back to 1655, when Dutch explorers recorded viewing a kind of commercial enterprise among the Raritan and Aquehonga Indians, who ferried between Staten Island and what is now Perth Amboy and Bayonne, New Jersey. Shortly afterwards, the Dutch installed their own ferry system, linking their Staten Island settlements with the city of New Amsterdam across the bay. A variety of sailing craft and rowboats between Richmond and Manhattan appeared in the 1700s. During the Colonial period, ferries served as a key link in travel between New York and Philadelphia, and, as early as 1712, a charter was granted for Manhattan-Staten Island service.

One of the most colorful services was that founded by Cornelius Vanderbilt in 1810 from the foot of Whitehall Street to Clifton. In 1817, steamboats were introduced, with the advent of Vanderbilt's *Nautilus*, which started regular service between the Quarantine Station, Clifton and the foot of Whitehall Street, Manhattan (South Ferry). The single-ended steamboats with large sidewheels plied back and forth across the harbor, evoking images of Mark Twain's riverboats. Dickens, in 1842, wrote in *American Notes* of the scene as he sailed into New York on the packet *New York* and saw "a forest of ships' masts, cheery with flapping sails and

Samuel I. Newhouse

waving flags. Crossing from among them to the opposite shore, were steam ferry-boats laden with people, coaches, horses, waggons, baskets, boxes: crossed and recrossed by other ferry-boats: all travelling to and fro: and never idle.'' In 1853, Vanderbilt merged his operation with two rival lines; a few years later the Staten Island Railroad bought the ferry line. By 1898, Staten Island was incorporated into the city, and the aging fleet needed replacement. In 1905, New York City assumed ownership, paying $300,000 for five boats and ordering five new ones bearing the names of the five boroughs. The organization of a ferry system under municipal guidelines ended an era of competitive private ownership that had often come up short in meeting public standards. In 1946, the grand old ferry terminal at St. George was destroyed by fire; the new one was opened in 1951. The famous nickel fare endured from 1897 to 1975.

The Staten Island ferry was almost a metaphor for the variety, opportunity, diligence, and optimism of New Yorkers during the immigrant era and succeeding decades. Alfred Kazin, in *A Walker in the City*, writes of his many crossings during the 1920s, of the accordian man who paced back and forth on the ferry, of the Italian shoeshine men, and of "all those suddenly relaxed New Yorkers comfortably staring at each other in

~165~

the high wind on the top deck; a garbage scow burning in the upper bay just under Liberty's right arm; the minarets on Ellis Island, the old prison walls under the trees of Governor's Island, then, floating back in the cold dusk toward the diamond-lighted wall of Manhattan skyscrapers, the way we huddled in the great wooden varnish-smelling cabin inside as if we were all getting under the same quilt on a cold night.''

Night is still the best time to view Manhattan from the Staten Island ferry, but daytime has its compensations, as the ferries of the fleet, painted blue and orange, the colors of New York, ply the harbor among the freighters, yachts, and tugs (though there are fewer masts than in Dickens' day). The newest ferry is the *John A. Noble*, a 1300-seat passenger vessel named for the maritime artist John A. Noble; it will be used mainly at night. His lithographs of scenes in and around the harbors of New York and New Jersey decorate the boat; especially moving is the *Ghost of a Bygone Ferry*. His work may be seen in the John A. Noble Collection, 270 Richmond Terrace, Staten Island (call 718/447-6490). Erin Urban and Alice Ladziak, curators, have discovered a letter Noble once wrote to the *Staten Island Advance*, suggesting that, for once, a new ferry be named for "a poet — not a politician." He proposed that one be called the *Edna St. Vincent Millay*, for the poet who wrote in "Recuerdo" of the Staten Island Ferry. It seems fitting that the newest vessel be named for Noble, an outstanding seaman and marine artist, though one senses that he, modestly, would still defer to her. Music, dance, and art all have associations with the Staten Island ferry. There have been on-board concerts, and Marta Renzi, a contemporary choreographer, has performed on some of the vessels, pivoting on the supporting poles.

LOCAL POINTS OF INTEREST: The Staten Island Ferry leaves from the terminal on South Street, a few blocks from the South Street Seaport Museum at 16 Fulton Street, an eleven-block "living museum" in an area of the pier that has been carefully and tastefully restored to document the lifestyle of the nineteenth-century New York seaport. The "Seaport Experience" is a multi-media show explaining the port's early history, and the area has trendy shops and seafood restaurants. Here, you may board the 1907 lightship *Ambrose*, the 1893 Gloucester fishing schooner *Lettie G. Howard*, the 1885 sailing ship *Wavertree* and the German four-masted bark *Peking*. Other places of interest in the area are the Fraunces Tavern (54 Pearl Street), where Washington bade farewell to his officers in December 1783; the Beaux Arts US Customs House on Bowling Green; Trinity Church and Churchyard (at Broadway and Wall); the NY Stock Exchange (8 Broad Street); and Schermerhorn Row, a series of historic warehouses and counting-houses, also on Fulton Street.

Staten Island itself is well worth a voyage of discovery. Though the smallest of the five boroughs of New York, it offers astonishingly varied topography; within its wooded hilltops is Todt Hill, with an elevation of 409.8 feet. It is the highest peak between Maine and Florida. The island, discovered by Giovanni da Verrazano in 1524, was named "Staaten Eyelandt" in honor of the governing body of Holland when Henry Hudson first explored the area in the early seventeenth century. Today, it almost seems an anomaly, only a few miles from the skyscrapers of Wall Street and yet fiercely protective of open spaces. The Gateway National Recreation Area, managed by the National Park Service, occupies over twelve hundred acres of recreation area. The island has always had a nautical orientation. Its world-famous oyster and clamming industry sent products to the royal courts of Europe in the eighteenth and nineteenth centuries, and the turn of the century saw grand seashore hotels attracting yachtsmen and millionaires from all over the East Coast. Early on, Staten Island was cherished by photographers, including Matthew Brady, Timothy O'Sullivan, and Alice Austen, whose house is open to visitors. Snug Harbor, overlooking the Kill van Kull waterway, comprises twenty-six historic buildings, with gardens and sweeping views. It is a National Historic Landmark, celebrating Sailor's Snug Harbor, America's first home for retired sailors. Many cultural performances are given in the Greek Revival buildings here.

Also of interest on Staten Island are the Staten Island Children's Museum, the Staten Island Zoo, the Staten Island Botanical Garden, Fort Wadsworth, which guarded the Narrows, and the Richmondtown Restoration, a restored historic village and outdoor museum. Conference House (1675), open to visitors, is a restored stone manor house where the only peace conference of the Revolutionary War was held. Another unexpected treasure is the Jacques Marchais Center of Tibetan Art. The Staten Island Institute of Arts and Sciences administers several facilities, including a museum in St. George and the William T. Davis Wildlife Refuge. There is a small museum in the St. George Ferry Terminal with models and other artifacts of the ferry era, but at this writing it is closed; visitors should inquire at the terminal before planning a visit. Staten Island is twice the size of Manhattan with one-twenty-fourth the population. It has become more accessible with construction of the Verazzano-Narrows bridge, and conservationists are struggling to preserve its historic flavor against the demands of developers.

CROSSING TIME:	25 mins.
FERRY TYPE:	Vehicle (some trips passenger only)
VESSEL CAPACITY:	25-45 cars; some ships carry as many as 6,000 passengers
OPERATING SEASON:	All year

SCHEDULE: **Daily. Mon.-Fri.: Lv. Whitehall St.** 12:30 a.m., 1:30, 2:30, 3:30, 4:30, 5:30, 6:30, *7, *7:15, 7:30, 7:50, *8:10, *8:30, *8:45, 9, *9:15, *9:30, 10, *10:30, 11, *11:30, noon, *12:30 p.m., 1, *1:30, 2, *2:30, *3, *3:30, *4, 4:20, 4:40, *5, *5:15, 5:30, 5:45, *6, *6:15, 6:30, 6:45, *7, *7:20, 7:40, 8, *8:30, 9, 9:30, 10, 11, 11:30. **Lv. St. George** midnight, 1, 2, 3, 4, 5, 6, *6:30, *6:45, 7, 7:20, *7:40, *8, 8:15, 8:30, *8:45, *9, 9:30, *10, 10:30, *11, 11:30, *noon, 12:30 p.m., *1, 1:30, *2, *2:30, *3, *3:30, 3:50, *4:10, *4:30, 4:50, 5:10, *5:30, *5:45, 6, 6:15, *6:30, *6:45, 7, 7:30, *8, 8:30, 9, 9:30, 10, 10:30, 11. *Passengers only.* **Sat., Sun., holidays:** Hourly service 12:30 a.m.-9:30 a.m.; half-hour service 9:30 a.m.-9:30 p.m. Hourly service 9:30 p.m. to 12:30 a.m. *All Sat., Sun., and holiday boats carry vehicles.*

RESTRICTIONS: Trailers, pickup-campers, and RVs permitted. Load limit 10 gross tons on each axle. Overhead clearance of 12 ft. 6 in. Bottled gas not permitted.

FACILITIES: Restrooms, snack bar

FARE: Passengers $.25 round trip (to Staten Island only; free from Staten Island); car $3; trailers, pickup campers, RVs $3 up.

RESERVATIONS: No

DIRECTIONS: The ferry leaves from the South Ferry terminal at the foot of Battery Park.

MAP LOCATION: P. 115, NY, 16

CONTACT: Dept. of Transportation, City of New York, Battery Maritime Bldg., New York, NY 10004, (718)727-2508 (Area Code NOT 212)

STATE: New York/Rhode Island

PLACES SERVED: Montauk, LI, NY—Block Island, RI (Christman's Dock)

BODY OF WATER: Block Island Sound

FERRY SERVICE HISTORY: There has been service on this crossing for twenty years, at least. Capt. Howard Carroll has operated the present ferry since 1979. The boat on this run is the *Jigger III*, a sixty-five-foot wooden boat, formerly a fishing vessel.

LOCAL POINTS OF INTEREST: Montauk, once inhabited by the Montaukett Indians, is a lively resort on the south shore of the easternmost part of Long Island, beyond the Hamptons and Amagansett. East Hampton has been called "America's most beautiful village," with a Currier and Ives flavor. F. Scott Fitzgerald may well have had this stretch of Route 27 in mind, from East Hampton to Montauk, when he called Long Island "that slender riotous island." Montauk itself was once a sheep-grazing area, and two shepherds' houses may still be seen. Montauk Harbor is a mecca for fishermen, with many charter boats for hire; it is said that as many as one thousand boats, of every description, crowd the Harbor during the summer season. The Montauk Lighthouse, authorized in 1795 and completed in 1797 at a cost of $23,300, is a landmark of the Montauk Point State Park. Block Island, eighteen miles away, is visible in the distance. Excellent restaurants here are Gosman's, at the Harbor entrance, with a good water view, and Gurney's Inn, on the old Montauk Highway; it is also a health and beauty spa with a time-sharing plan. There are nearly eighty motels, but reservations are essential in summer.

[For notes on Block Island, see entry under Block Island-Galilee (Point Judith), p. 96]

CROSSING TIME: 2 hrs.

FERRY TYPE: Pedestrian

VESSEL CAPACITY: 75 passengers

OPERATING SEASON: Mid-June-late Sept., weather permitting

SCHEDULE: **Daily, mid-June-early Sept.: Lv. Montauk** 9:30 a.m.; **lv. Block Island** 4:30 p.m.

RESTRICTIONS: None

FACILITIES: Restrooms; beer and soda available

FARE: Adults $13 ($20 round-trip); child under 12 half-price; $1 discount with proof of AAA membership.

RESERVATIONS: No

DIRECTIONS: The ferry leaves from Christman's Dock in Montauk and from Payne's Dock, New Harbor, Block Island.

MAP LOCATION: P. 115, NY, 17

CONTACT: Captain Howard Carroll, Box 461, Montauk, NY 11954, (516)668-2214

STATE: New York/Rhode Island

PLACES SERVED: Montauk, LI, NY—Block Island, RI (Viking Dock)

BODY OF WATER: Block Island Sound

FERRY SERVICE HISTORY: This service has existed off and on for about fifteen years; in its present form it has been in operation since 1982. The ship is the 140-foot *Viking Starship*.

LOCAL POINTS OF INTEREST: [For notes on Montauk, please see entry under Montauk-Block Island (Christman's Dock), p. 169. For notes on Block Island, please see entry under Block Island-Galilee (Point Judith), p. 96.]

CROSSING TIME: 1 hr. 30 mins.

FERRY TYPE: Pedestrian

VESSEL CAPACITY: 300 passengers

OPERATING SEASON: June 1-Sept. 30

SCHEDULE:	**Daily. Lv. Montauk** 10 a.m.; **lv. Block Island** 4:30 p.m.
RESTRICTIONS:	Small pets permitted
FACILITIES:	Restrooms, restaurant, bar
FARE:	Adults $13 (same-day round-trip $20); children $7 (same-day round-trip $13)
RESERVATIONS:	Yes, advisable
DIRECTIONS:	In Montauk, ship leaves from the Viking Dock. On Block Island, she leaves from the Boat Basin.
MAP LOCATION:	P. 115, NY, 17
CONTACT:	Capt. Paul G. Forsberg, Box 730, Montauk, LI, NY 11954, (516)668-5709

STATE:	New York/Connecticut
PLACES SERVED:	Montauk, LI, NY—Groton, CT
BODY OF WATER:	Long Island Sound
FERRY SERVICE HISTORY:	The ship on this service is the 140-foot *Viking Starship*, owned by Capt. Paul G. Forsberg.
LOCAL POINTS OF INTEREST:	[For notes on Montauk, please see entry under Montauk-Block Island (Christman's Dock), p. 169.]

Groton is the home of a large US naval submarine base and is the site where the first diesel submarine was built in 1912 by the boat division of General Dynamics. An interesting river cruise is offered on the *River Queen*, a replica of the *African Queen* (of the Bogart-Hepburn film). Educational cruises are offered by Project Oceanology aboard a research vessel. There are guided tours of the World War II submarine *USS Croaker*. Gray Line offers bus tours which include visits to Japanese and

German midget subs captured in World War II. Fort Griswold State Park was the scene of a 1781 massacre when Benedict Arnold led British forces and New London and Groton were burned.

CROSSING TIME:	1 hr. 30 mins.
FERRY TYPE:	Pedestrian
VESSEL CAPACITY:	300 passengers
OPERATING SEASON:	June 1-Sept. 30
SCHEDULE:	**Daily. Lv. Montauk** 6 a.m., 6 p.m.; **lv. Groton** 8 a.m., 8 p.m.
RESTRICTIONS:	Small pets permitted
FACILITIES:	Restrooms, restaurant, bar
FARE:	Adults $13 (same-day round-trip $20); children $7 (same-day round-trip $13)
RESERVATIONS:	Yes, advisable
DIRECTIONS:	In Montauk, ship leaves from the Viking Dock. In Groton, ship leaves from the *USS Croaker* Submarine Memorial Dock, Thames St.
MAP LOCATION:	P. 115, NY, 18
CONTACT:	See CONTACT, p. 171.

STATE:	New York
PLACES SERVED:	North Haven—Shelter Island, LI
BODY OF WATER:	Shelter Island Sound
FERRY SERVICE HISTORY:	There has been a ferry at this crossing for over two hundred years. The ferry is run by Cliff Clark, who is the fifth generation of his

family to run it. The Clarks are another of the American ferry "dynasties," completely devoted to the ferry service which has long been a vital component of Long Island life.

LOCAL POINTS OF INTEREST:

[For notes on Shelter Island, please see entry under Greenport-Shelter Island, p. 158.]

The North Haven peninsula is reached by bridge from Sag Harbor. The ferry does not actually run from the town of North Haven, but from a point on the northern shore of the peninsula a little over three miles above it. The Old Whaler's Church is a short distance from Sag Harbor, and, just over the bridge on the peninsula, the Whaling Museum is of interest.

CROSSING TIME: 3 mins.

FERRY TYPE: Vehicle

VESSEL CAPACITY: 10-12 cars

OPERATING SEASON: All year

SCHEDULE: **Daily, continuous service** 6 a.m.-11:45 p.m.; **July and Aug.** to 1:45 a.m.

RESTRICTIONS: Trailers, pickup-campers, and RVs permitted. Load limit 60 tons.

FACILITIES: None

FARE: Car or pickup-camper and driver $4 ($5 same day round-trip); passengers $.50; trailers $2.75 to 18 ft. + $.25 each additional foot.

RESERVATIONS: No

DIRECTIONS: Ferry connects segments of SR 114

MAP LOCATION: P. 115, NY, 19

CONTACT: Mr. Cliff Clark, Box 614, Shelter Island, New York, NY 11964, (516)749-0007

STATE:	New York
PLACES SERVED:	Patchogue, LI—Davis Park, Fire Island, LI (also Leja Beach and Ocean Ridge)
BODY OF WATER:	Patchogue Bay
FERRY SERVICE HISTORY:	The ferry was founded by Fred Sherman in 1947; his sons Charles, Matthew, and Fred own it now. The vessels are the seventy-five-

foot *Kiki* (288 passengers), the sixty-five-foot *Quaiaten* (250 passengers), the sixty-five-foot *Highlander* (210 passengers), the sixty-three-foot *Bayberry Mist* (137 passengers), the forty-severn-foot *Leja Beach* (62 passengers), and the forty-five-foot *Meshomac* (49 passengers).

LOCAL POINTS OF INTEREST:	Patchogue is the location of the National Seashore headquarters (120 Laurel Street). Davis Park is a small community of about three hundred people.
CROSSING TIME:	20 mins.
FERRY TYPE:	Pedestrian
VESSEL CAPACITY:	See listings above.
OPERATING SEASON:	Mid-Mar.-Nov.
SCHEDULE:	**Summer (late June-day after Labor Day): Mon.-Thurs: Lv. Patchogue** 7:30 a.m., 10, 11:20, 1:30 p.m., 3:30, 5:15, 6:20, 8:15. **Lv.**

Davis Park 6:45 a.m., 8, 10:40, 12:45 p.m., 2:30, 4:20, 5:40, 7:40. *(Mon. and Tues. last trip at 8:45; Wed. & Thurs. at 9:30)* **Fri.: Lv. Patchogue** 7:30 a.m., 10, 11:20, 1:30 p.m., 3:30, 5:15, 6:20, 7:15, 8:15, 8:40, 9:20, 10:20. **Lv. Davis Park** 6:45 a.m., 8, 10:40, 12:45 p.m., 2:30, 4:20, 5:40, 6:45, 7:40, 8:40, 9:40, 10:45. **Sat.: Lv. Patchogue** 7:30 a.m., 9, 10, 11, noon, 1 p.m., 2, 3:40, 5, 6:15, 7:50, 9, 10, 11, 12:15. **Lv. Davis Park** 8 a.m., 9:20, 10:20, 11:20, 12:20 p.m. 1:20, 3, 4:20, 5:35, 7, 8:20, 9:30, 10:30, 11:30, 12:45 a.m. **Sun.: Lv. Patchogue** 7:30 a.m., 9, 10, 11, noon, 1 p.m., 2, 3:30, 4:25, 5:25, 6:25, 7:25, 8:25. **Lv. Davis Park** 8 a.m., 9:20, 10:20, 11:20, 12:20 p.m., 1:20, 3, 4, 5, 6, 7, 8, 9:15. **Fall: Early Sept.-mid-Sept.: Weekdays: Lv. Patchogue** 7:30 a.m., 10, 1:30 p.m., 3:30, 6:20. **Lv. Davis Park** 6:45 a.m. (Mon. only), 8, 10:40, 2:30 p.m., 4:20. **Fri. night only: Lv. Patchogue** 7:15 p.m., 8:15, 9:20. **Lv.**

Davis Park *7:40 p.m., 8:40. *Passengers may carry only 2 pieces of hand luggage. **Sat.: Lv. Patchogue** 10 a.m., 11:25, 12:30 p.m., 1:45, 3:40, 6:15, 7:45. **Lv. Davis Park** 10:40 a.m., 11:55, 1 p.m., 3, 4:20, 7, 8:15. **Sun.: Lv. Patchogue** 10 a.m., 11:25, 12:30 p.m., 1:45, 3:30, 5:25, 6:25, 7:25. **Lv. Davis Park** 10:40 a.m., 11:55, 1 p.m., 3, 4:20, 6, 7, 8, 9:15. **Mid-Sept.-mid-Oct.: Weekdays: Lv. Patchogue** 10 a.m., 3:30 p.m. **Fri. only: Lv. Patchogue** 6:40 p.m., 8:15. **Lv. Davis Park** 8 a.m. **(Mon. only.)**, 10 a.m., 4:20 p.m., 6:15. (Columbus Day only). **Sat. & Sun.: Lv. Patchogue** 10 a.m., 11:30, 1 p.m., 3:30. **Lv. Davis Park** 10:30 a.m., noon, 1:30 p.m., 4:20, **6:15. ** Sun. only. *Consult company for other schedules.*

RESTRICTIONS: No smoking on boats. Passengers may carry one normal-sized handbag (not exceeding 25 lbs.). Baggage, bikes, furniture, lumber, etc., are charged for and may be carried on passenger boat at discretion of captain. All excess freight will be carried on freight boats. Flammable liquids must be carried on freight boats.

FACILITIES: None

FARE: Adults $3.75; children (2-11) $2.25; senior citizens (65+) $3.50; dogs round-trip $2; commuter books available.

RESERVATIONS: No

DIRECTIONS: Ferries operate from the Brookhaven Town Recreation Park at the Sandspit, Brightwood St., Patchogue, NY.

MAP LOCATION: P. 115, NY, 20

CONTACT: Davis Park Ferry Co., Box 814, Patchogue, LI, NY 11772, (516)475-1665

STATE: New York

PLACES SERVED: Patchogue, LI—Watch Hill, Fire Island, LI

BODY OF WATER: Patchogue Bay

| **FERRY SERVICE HISTORY:** | Please see history under Patchogue, LI—Davis Park, Fire Island, LI, p. 174. The vessel on this run is usually the sixty-five-foot *Quaiaten*. |

LOCAL POINTS OF INTEREST: Patchogue is the location of the National Seashore headquarters (120 Laurel Street).

Watch Hill is one of the main National Park Service facilities, with a marina (158 slips), interpretive activities, summer lifeguards, visitor center, picnic tables, a nature trail with a guide leaflet, a dog-walk area, and family and group campgrounds. The campground has a four-night maximum (reservations required).

CROSSING TIME: 25 mins.

FERRY TYPE: Pedestrian

VESSEL CAPACITY: 250 passengers

OPERATING SEASON: May 15-Oct. 15

SCHEDULE: **Mid-May-late May: Daily: Lv. Patchogue** 10 a.m., 3:15 p.m. **Lv. Watch Hill** 10:45 a.m., 4 p.m.. **Late May-late June: Weekdays: Lv. Patchogue** 10 a.m., 3:15 p.m., *6:15. **Lv. Watch Hill** 10:45 a.m., 4 p.m., *7. *Friday only. **Sat & Sun.: Lv. Patchogue** 10 a.m., noon, 4:10 p.m. **Lv. Watch Hill** 10:45 a.m., 12:45 p.m., 4:45. **Late June-Sept. 1: Weekdays: Lv. Patchogue** 9:30 a.m., 11:15, 1:15 p.m., 3:30, 4:45, **6:15. **Lv. Watch Hill** 10:15 a.m., noon, 2:30 p.m., 4:15, 5:30, **8:30. **Wed. through Fri. only. **Sat. and Sun.: Lv. Patchogue** 8:30 a.m., 10, noon, 2 p.m., 3:30, 5:15, 7. **Lv. Watch Hill** 9 a.m., 10:45, 12:45 p.m., 2:45, 4:15, 6, 9:20. **Sept.-mid-Oct.: Weekdays: Lv. Patchogue** 10 a.m., 3:15 p.m., ˜6:15. **Lv. Watch Hill** 10:45 a.m., 4 p.m., ˜7. ˜Fri. only through late Sept. **Sat. & Sun.: Lv. Patchogue** 10 a.m., noon, 4:10 p.m. **Lv. Watch Hill** 10:45 a.m., 12:45 p.m., 4:45. *Consult company for holiday schedules.*

RESTRICTIONS: See RESTRICTIONS, p. 175.

FACILITIES: None

FARE: Adults $3.75; children (2-11) $2.25; senior citizens (65 +) and handicapped $3.50; dogs (round-trip) $2.

RESERVATIONS: No

DIRECTIONS: Ferries operate from the Brookhaven Town Recreation Park at the Sandspit, Brightwood St., Patchogue, NY

MAP LOCATION: P. 115, NY, 21

CONTACT: See CONTACT, p. 175.

STATE: New York

PLACES SERVED: Sayville, LI—Barrett Beach

BODY OF WATER: Great South Bay

FERRY SERVICE HISTORY: [For history of the Sayville Ferry Service, please see entry under Sayville-Cherry Grove, p. 178.]

LOCAL POINTS OF INTEREST: [For notes on Fire Island, see entry under Bay Shore-Dunewood, p. 143.]
Barrett Beach is a Town of Islip beach, with many private houses. It has beautiful views, a snack bar, and a marina, but is not a popular gathering spot for people coming to Fire Island for a short time in search of a variety of restaurants, bars, shops, and a more convivial scene. Riders are mostly Town of Islip residents.

CROSSING TIME: 30 mins.

FERRY TYPE: Pedestrian

VESSEL CAPACITY: Varies according to need [see vessel listing under Sayville-Cherry Grove, p. 179].

OPERATING SEASON: Late May-early Sept.

SCHEDULE: **Sat., Sun., and holidays only until June 30; then daily: Lv. Sayville *9:30 a.m., 10:45, noon. Lv. Barrett Beach 3 p.m., *4,** 5. Ferries depart when filled. *Rainy day schedule.

RESTRICTIONS: No freight carried on passenger boats. Such items as plants, furniture, bikes, and surf-boards must be shipped on the regular daily freight boat. Personal carry-on freight accepted. Pets accepted.

FACILITIES: None

FARE: Adults $2.25; children (under 19) $1.25.

RESERVATIONS: No

DIRECTIONS: In Sayville, ferry leaves from Browns River (off Foster Ave.). There are ample signs.

MAP LOCATION: P. 115, NY, 22

CONTACT: Sayville Ferry Service, Inc., River Road, Box 626, Sayville, LI, NY 11782 (516)589-0810

STATE: New York

PLACES SERVED: Sayville, LI—Cherry Grove, Fire Island, LI

BODY OF WATER: Great South Bay

FERRY SERVICE HISTORY: In 1898, German immigrant Charles Stein sailed passengers across the bay to Fire Island on weekends and holidays. Charles was one of many locals with boats who transported church groups, duck hunters, and holly pickers for a day's outing. In 1922, Stein charged his first known fare, forty cents for a round trip. Charles' son, Fred, took over the ferry in 1926 and had a boat specially built for the business in 1937. It was finished just months before the devastating 1938 hurricane, which washed away most of Fire Island. Fred sold her to the British as a hospital ship.

Fred's son, Ken, then operated the ferry business with one boat; during World War II, there were more customers, as mainlanders were unable to drive long distances because of gas rationing. After the war, city people discovered Fire Island, and Ken converted surplus warcraft into ferries. Since the 1950s, business has grown steadily; in 1977, Ken's son, Ken, Jr., took over, the fourth generation to operate ferry service to Fire Island,

and Ken III may well follow his father in the business, making the fifth generation of the ferry "dynasty."

Today, the company operates a fleet of boats to several locations on Fire Island. The boats are not assigned to any special run, but are changed around according to events, demand, groups, and other fluctuations in need. The passenger boats are:

Fire Island Clipper: built in 1979, aluminum, 75 feet long, capacity 350 passengers; *Monitor II*: built in 1963, wood, 51 feet long, capacity 105 passengers; *Merrimac II* : built in 1968, wood, 51 feet long, capacity 105 passengers; *Fire Island Duchess*: built in 1966, wood, 65 feet long, capacity 150 passengers; *Roamer II*: built in 1940, wood, 55 feet long, capacity 100 passengers; *Fire Island Empress*: built in 1963, wood, 63 feet long, capacity 150 passengers; *Wayfarer III*: built in 1973, steel, 64 feet long, capacity 200 passengers; *Pathfinder II*: built in 1977, steel, 68 feet long, capacity 180 passengers; *Typhoon Gwen*: built in 1962, wood, 30 feet long, capacity 6 passengers (used as a V.I.P. vessel and for private after-hours trips.)

The *Fire Island Maid* and the *Beachcomber IV* are used to carry freight to and from the island.

LOCAL POINTS OF INTEREST: [For notes on Fire Island, see entry under Bay Shore-Dunewood, p. 143.]

About 1946, the poet W. H. Auden, who had a genius for discovering unique habitations, purchased (with friends James and Tania Stern) a cottage covered with tarpaper at Cherry Grove, reached then, as now, by the ferry crossing from Sayville. The shack was in a sparsely settled area of the beach, owing to the 1938 hurricane, which washed away many houses, with an unimpeded view of the sea. In

"Pleasure Island" he described the island as "a huddle of huts related / By planks, a dock, a state / Of undress and improvised abandon . . . this outpost where nothing is wicked / But to be sorry or sick." He and Chester Kallman were visited at "Bective Poplars" (a takeoff on Stern's family home in Ireland) by Stephen Spender, Christopher Isherwood, and other *literati*. Today, "the Grove" is a lively community, especially in summer, with a large gay population and a relaxed, free-spirited ambiance. There is an assortment of stores and restaurants. The houses are still far apart, and the beach spacious and inviting.

CROSSING TIME: 30 mins.

FERRY TYPE: Pedestrian

VESSEL CAPACITY: Varies according to need [see initial vessel listing].

OPERATING SEASON: Late May.-Oct., but Sat. and Sun. only from late Mar.-early Apr. Early Apr.-late Apr.: Fri., Sat., and Sun. Late Apr.-Sept. Daily. Oct.: Fri., Sat., and Sun. only.

SCHEDULE: **Summer, mid-May-early Sept. Mon.-Thurs.: Lv. Sayville** *5:45 a.m., 7, **8:15, 10:15, 11:30, **12:30 p.m., 1:30, 3:30, 5:45, 7, 8:15, 9:15 (Thurs. only). **Lv. Cherry Grove** *6:10 a.m., 7:25, **8:40, 10:45, noon, **1 p.m., 2, 4, 6:15, 7:30, 8:40, 10 (Thurs. only). *Mon. only (but not holiday Mondays). **Late June-late Aug. only. **Fri. & July 3: Lv. Sayville** 7 a.m., ˜8:30, 10:15, 11:30, 12:30 p.m., 1:30, 2:30, 3:30, 4:30, 5:30, 6:30, 7:30, 8:30, 9:30, 10:30, 11:30, ˜˜12:30 a.m. **Lv. Cherry Grove** 7:25 a.m., ˜9, 10:45, noon, 1 p.m., 2, 3, 4, 5, 5:55, 6:55, 7:55, 8:55, 9:55, 10:55, 11:55, ˜˜1 a.m. ˜Starts late June. **Sat.: Lv. Sayville** 8:15 a.m., 9:30, 10:30, 11:30, 12:30 p.m., 1:30, 2:30, 3:45, 4:45, 5:45, 6:45, 7:45, 8:45, 9:45, 10:45, 11:45, 12:45, ˜˜1:45 a.m. **Lv. Cherry Grove** 8:45 a.m., 10, 11, noon, 1 p.m., 2, 3, 4:15, 5:15, 6:15, 7:15, 8:15, 9:15, 10:15, 11;15, 12:15, 1:15 a.m., ˜˜2:15 a.m. **Sun., Memorial Day, Labor Day: Lv. Sayville** 8:15 a.m., 9:30, 10:30, 11:30, 12:30 p.m., 1:30, 2:30, 3:40, 4:40, 5:40, 6:40, 7:40, 8:40, 9:40, ˜˜10:45. **Lv. Cherry Grove** 8:45 a.m., 10, 11, noon, 1 p.m., 2, 3, 4:15, 5:15, 6:15, 7:15, 8:15, 9:15, 10:15, ˜˜11:15. ˜˜Late June through late Aug. only. *Consult company for off-season schedules.*

RESTRICTIONS: See RESTRICTIONS, p. 178.

FACILITIES: None

FARE:	Adults $4.00; children (under 12) $2.00.
RESERVATIONS:	No
DIRECTIONS:	See DIRECTIONS, p. 178.
MAP LOCATION:	P. 115, NY, 23
CONTACT:	See CONTACT, p. 178.

STATE:	New York
PLACES SERVED:	Sayville, LI—Fire Island Pines, LI
BODY OF WATER:	Great South Bay
FERRY SERVICE HISTORY:	[For history of the Sayville Ferry Service, please see entry under Sayville-Cherry Grove, p. 178.]
LOCAL POINTS OF INTEREST:	[For notes on Fire Island, see entry under Bay Shore-Dunewood, p. 143.]

Fire Island Pines has made a quantum leap from the pup tents and shacks which characterized it as late as the 1940s. Many of the present homes, built to blend with and enhance the natural surroundings, have an understated elegance fully appreciated by design magazine editors. The area, once known as Lone Hill, was purchased in 1924 by Dr. Warren Smadbeck, and the metamorphosis slowly began. It is now considered by many people to be Fire Island's most glamorous community, with a Botel, hotel, and yachts moored along the Botel dock—as one writer put it, "like gleaming limos parked in front of a posh East Side nightspot." Some of the world's top designers, models, performing artists, and professional people come to Fire Island. The resort, like its sister community to the west, Cherry Grove, counts among its residents and visitors a large gay population. There are parties almost non-stop from Memorial Day through Labor Day, with some guests barefoot in evening clothes.

The Pines and Dunes Yacht Club, part of John White's Fire Island Pines Botel, overlooking the harbor, is a lovely spot to eat and gather, particulary recommended by Ken Stein of Sayville Ferries. Other interesting places are the Cultured Elephant and the Restaurant at the Pavilion. The Pines Pantry is an excellent gourmet food market. The Pavilion is a disco. If you survive the festivities, you might wander, the next day, along the famous roller coaster walks between the grove of wild cherry, holly, and pines that form leafy tunnels connecting the bay and ocean.

CROSSING TIME:	30 mins.
FERRY TYPE:	Pedestrian
VESSEL CAPACITY:	Varies according to need [see vessel listing under Sayville-Cherry Grove, p. 179].
OPERATING SEASON:	Year-round except for ice; weekends only Dec.-Mar. 15

SCHEDULE: **Summer, Mid-May-early Sept. Mon.-Thurs.: Lv. Sayville** *5:45 a.m., 7, **8:15, 10:15, 11:30, **12:30 p.m., 1:30, 3:30, 5:45, 7, 8;15, 9:15 (Thurs. only). **Lv. F.I. Pines** *6:10 a.m., 7:25, **9, 10:45, noon, **1 p.m., 2, 4:15, 6:15, 7:35, 8:40, 9:40 (Thurs. only). *Mon. only, but not holiday Mondays; will run Tues. after Memorial Day and Labor Day. **Late June-late Aug. only. **Fri. & July 3: Lv. Sayville** 7 a.m., ˜8:30, 10:15, 11:30, 12:30 p.m., 1:30, 2:30, 3:30, 4:30, shuttle service as needed between 5:30 and 10:30, midnight. **Lv. F.I. Pines** 7:25 a.m., ˜9, 10:45, noon, 1 p.m., 2, 3, ˜4, 5, shuttle service as needed between 5:30 and 10:30 p.m., 11, 12:30 a.m. ˜Starts late June; consult company for date. **Sat.: Lv. Sayville** 8:15 a.m., 9:30, 10:30, 11:30, 12:30 p.m., 1:30, 2:30, 3:45, 4:45, 5:45, 6:45, 7:45, 8:45, 9:45. **Lv. F.I. Pines** 8:40 a.m., 10, 11, noon, 1 p.m., 2, 3, 4:15, 5:15, 6:15, 7:15, 8:15, 9:15, 10:15. **Sun. & holidays Memorial Day, July 4, and Labor Day: Lv. Sayville** 8:15 a.m., 9:30, 10:30, 11:30, 12:30 p.m., 1:30, 2:30, 3:40, 4:40, 5:40, 6:40, 7:40, 8:40, 9:40. **Lv. F.I. Pines** 8:45 a.m., 10, 11, noon, 1 p.m., 2, 3, 4:15, 5:15, 6:15, 7:15, 8:15, 9:15, 10:15. *Consult company for off-season schedules.*

RESTRICTIONS:	See RESTRICTIONS, p. 178.
FACILITIES:	None
FARE:	Adults $4.00, children (5-12) $2.
RESERVATIONS:	No
DIRECTIONS:	See DIRECTIONS, p. 178.
MAP LOCATION:	P. 115, NY, 24
CONTACT:	See CONTACT, p. 178.

STATE: New York

PLACES SERVED: Sayville, LI—Sailors Haven (Sunken Forest), LI

BODY OF WATER: Great South Bay

FERRY SERVICE
HISTORY: [For history of the Sayville Ferry Service, please see entry under Sayville-Cherry Grove, p. 178.]

LOCAL POINTS
OF INTEREST: [For notes on Fire Island, see entry under Bay Shore-Dunewood, p. 143.]

Sailors Haven, a mile west of Cherry Grove, offers a marina with thirty-six slips, a visitor center, a guarded beach in the high tourist season, naturalist activities, picnicking, a snack bar, grocery stores, and a dog walk. It is a US National Seashore run by the Department of the Interior and the gateway to the Sunken Forest, which has a thick canopy of gnarled holly, sassafras, tupelo, and other vines climbing from the forest floor toward the sun. The trees are unable to grow above the level of the dunes because the high salt concentration kills thrusting twigs; the smooth canopy protects them from wind damage. The trail, which begins at the Sailor's Haven Visitor Center, is one and one-half miles and takes at least an hour for leisurely exploration. The National Park Service cautions visitors against going barefoot, straying from the boardwalk and touching poison ivy.

CROSSING TIME: 30 mins.

FERRY TYPE: Pedestrian

VESSEL CAPACITY: Varies according to need [see vessel listing under Sayville-Cherry Grove, p. 179].

OPERATING SEASON: May 1-Oct. 31

SCHEDULE: **Summer, late June-Sept. 1: Mon.-Fri.: Lv. Sayville *9:45 a.m., 11, noon, 1:30 p.m., *3:45, 5. Lv. Sailors Haven *10:15 a.m.,** 11:30, 12:45 p.m., 3, *4:20, 5:45. **Sat., Sun., Holidays: Lv. Sayville** *9 a.m., 10:15, 11:30, 1 p.m., 2:15, *3:40, 4:50, 6. **Lv. Sailors Haven** *9:30 a.m., 10:45, noon, 1:30 p.m., 3, *4:15, 5:30, 6:40. *Rainy day schedule. *Consult company for off-season schedules.*

RESTRICTIONS:	See RESTRICTIONS, p. 178.
FACILITIES:	None
FARE:	Adults $3.25, children (5-12) $1.75.
RESERVATIONS:	No
DIRECTIONS:	See DIRECTIONS, p. 178.
MAP LOCATION:	P. 115, NY, 25
CONTACT:	See CONTACT, p. 178.

STATE:	Pennsylvania
PLACES SERVED:	Erie—Presque Isle
BODY OF WATER:	Lake Erie

FERRY SERVICE HISTORY: This ferry service was inaugurated in 1950. The vessel is the *Little Toot*, a jaunty fifty-five-foot diesel-powered boat with a single-screw propeller. She has ornamental smokestacks and fretwork around the bridge and cheerful flags flying. Most of the riders come from the Greater Pittsburgh area. The most unusual cargo this ferry has carried is the ashes of a cremated person. There is free ferry service for senior citizens, provided by funds through the Pennsylvania Totto games. In addition to the ferry to Presque Isle, the company has dinner cruises and sightseeing cruises on Lake Erie, plus charter-boat fishing.

LOCAL POINTS OF INTEREST: Erie is Pennsylvania's Great Lakes port; it was named for the Eriez Indians. Erie has broad avenues lined with trees and many historic buildings, including Cashier's House, headquarters of the Erie County Historical Society. The Perry Memorial House and Dickson Tavern is one of Erie's oldest surviving buildings; it was built as a tavern about 1815 and later enlarged. Here, there is a diorama showing the construction of Commodore Perry's fleet (used in the Battle of Lake Erie, 1813). Also of interest is a replica of the flagship *Niagara*, of Perry's fleet.

Presque Isle is a peninsula, whose shores and waters protected Com-

Little Toot

modore Perry's fleet during construction until he sailed forth into Lake Erie in the War of 1812. It was acquired by Pennsylvania as a state park in 1921. It offers recreational opportunities such as boating and picnicking, hiking, ice skating and ice fishing in winter, and swimming (the sandy beaches provide the only surf swimming within the Commonwealth of Pennsylvania).

CROSSING TIME:	50 mins.
FERRY TYPE:	Pedestrian
VESSEL CAPACITY:	49 passengers
OPERATING SEASON:	Summer
SCHEDULE:	From 10:30 a.m.-9 p.m., service every 1½ hours.
RESTRICTIONS:	Small pets free
FACILITIES:	Restrooms; refreshments (beer, liquor)
FARE:	$3 round-trip
RESERVATIONS:	No

DIRECTIONS: Boat leaves from the Erie Public Dock, foot of State St.

MAP LOCATION: P. 115, PA, 1

CONTACT: Captains Tony and Ron Rugare, Owners and Operators, Rugare's Sightseeing Cruises and Ferry Service, Erie Public Dock, 4104 Pleasant View Drive, Erie, PA 16509, (814)455-5892 or (814)866-2830

STATE: Pennsylvania

PLACES SERVED: Fredericktown (Washington County)—East bank of Monongahela River (Fayette County)

BODY OF WATER: Monongahela River

FERRY SERVICE HISTORY: The ferry has been in operation since the turn of the century. Helen Dobrunick of Fredericktown has researched the early history of the ferry and discovered that the owners of the ferry in the beginning were the Ward family, followed by the Crouch family, then, until the time of the sale, Betty and Ed Bresovsky. In 1977 it was taken over by the commissioners of Fayette and Washington Counties. The jaunty red and white ferry is a contrast to the coal barges going from West Virginia to Pittsburgh; the wide, winding river is in a picturesque valley between hills. According to Jacob R. Wright, the pilot, the ferry was built by the Hillman Barge Company in Pennsylvania in 1948. It has cable propulsion, with a fifty horsepower diesel motor; its length is sixty-four feet and its width twenty-five feet.

LOCAL POINTS OF INTEREST: The Whiskey Rebellion took place in 1794 in these Western Pennsylvania counties to protest the excise tax imposed by Alexander Hamilton in 1791. Today, the area, though a depressed coal-mining region, is rich in history. There are so many covered bridges that the Covered Bridge Weekend Festival is held each September, with arts, crafts, and entertainment. Another special area event is the National Pike Festival in May. Fredericktown is between Washington, founded in 1781 and the county seat of Washington County, and Uniontown, founded in 1768, the county seat of Fayette County; it is situated not far from I-79 below Pittsburgh.

CROSSING TIME:	4 mins.
FERRY TYPE:	Vehicle
VESSEL CAPACITY:	6 cars
OPERATING SEASON:	All year
SCHEDULE:	Mon.-Fri., on signal, 6:30 a.m.-10 p.m.
RESTRICTIONS:	Trailers, pickup-campers, and RVs permitted. Load limit 10 tons.
FACILITIES:	None
FARE:	Cars $.75
RESERVATIONS:	No
DIRECTIONS:	Take SR 88 to Fredericktown; ferry landing is on the bottom road by the river.
MAP LOCATION:	P. 115, PA, 2
CONTACT:	Commissioner's Office, Fayette County Court House, Uniontown, PA 15401, (412)437-4525

STATE:	Pennsylvania
PLACES SERVED:	Millersburg—Liverpool
BODY OF WATER:	Susquehanna River
FERRY SERVICE HISTORY:	The Millersburg Ferry became a Registered Historic Landmark on January 1, 1971. The ferry service dates back to 1817 and beyond.

At first rowboats were used, when the river was high in the spring. In summer, when the river reached its usually shallow level, poleboats were used. Steam-powered boats such as the *Enterprise* were introduced in 1873; a dam covered with loose stones was erected across the river to insure adequate water for the paddlewheelers. Steam-driven sidewheelers

Roaring Bull and Falcon

were replaced by gasoline-powered boats which still had a paddlewheel, located at the stern, after World War I. They have been of the sternwheel configuration ever since. At one time four boats were needed (the *Monarch*, *Bluegoose*, *Falcon*, and *Roaring Bull*). Now only the *Falcon* and *Roaring Bull* remain. Passenger comfort is provided by cross-ventilation in the summer and wood stoves during cold weather. Certainly there are not many ferries which are such a cozy hybrid, with all the flavor of a diner mixed with a houseboat, laced with the glamor of a Mississippi sternwheel. Chris McDonnell, a furniture finisher from Pennsylvania and a recent rider, told Gary Rotstein of the Harrisburg *Post-Gazette* in an interview, "It's one of the most underrated, fascinating rides I can think of . . . something like this is going back in history at a speed that's just right."

The ferry has been featured in the *National Geographic* (March 1985) and on ABC-TV's "Good Morning, America." It is now owned by a Liverpool chicken farmer, Robert "Bon" Wallis, who bought it in 1968. Captain Jack Dillman works the ferry for him, running it twelve hours a day, seven days a week, carefully navigating it along Suicide Curve, past Flat Rock and Big Rock. He calls himself a "river rat," and says, "I'm the indispensable man. I'm keeping history alive by being here." On one memorable trip the ferry was caught in a thunderstorm and blown against the dam. Dillman had a cargo of Mennonite boys driving three buggies, two wagons, and seven horses. One horse was so frightened he left teeth marks on the ferry rails. He plans to retire in 1989 but is willing to train a replacement, if one can be found. Wallis hopes to sell the ferry to someone who will agree to keep its historical character intact.

LOCAL POINTS OF INTEREST: Peter Miller, writing in the *National Geographic,* has called the Susquehanna a "river of small towns and small cities. Of red-brick houses along the railroad tracks with six pairs of blue jeans on the line. Of pancake breakfasts at the American Legion on the first day of small-game season. Of cider mills and pumpkin patches."

CROSSING TIME: 10-20 mins.

FERRY TYPE: Vehicle

VESSEL CAPACITY: 4 cars

OPERATING SEASON: All year, except in winter when river freezes

SCHEDULE: Daily, on signal, 7 a.m. to dusk, river conditions permitting

RESTRICTIONS: Trailers, pickup-campers, and RVs permitted. Load limit 5 tons per vehicle; 15 tons in all.

FACILITIES: None

FARE: Car $2.50; foot passengers $.25; trailer (to 25 ft.) $1.50 to $2; pickup-camper $2.50 to $3.50; RVs (to 5 tons) $2.50 to $4.

RESERVATIONS: No

DIRECTIONS: Ferry is found on SR 15, south of Liverpool; at Millersburg it connects with SR 147, near SR 209 (to I-81) and SR 25.

MAP LOCATION: P. 115, PA, 3

CONTACT: Captain Jack Dillman, The Millersburg Ferry, Millersburg, PA 17045, (717)444-3200

Blennerhassett

STATE:	West Virginia
PLACES SERVED:	Parkersburg—Blennerhassett Island Historical Park
BODY OF WATER:	Ohio River

FERRY SERVICE HISTORY: Ruble's Sternwheelers has been operating a ferry service since 1980, when Blennerhassett Island was opened as a state historical park. For the two preceding years sightseeing trips were offered. The *Centennial* sternwheeler was built in 1976 by Everet Ruble, Jr.; it has tables and chairs on the upper deck and is covered by a canopy. The lower deck is enclosed. Ruble also built the *Blennerhassett* sternwheeler in 1982; it has five thousand square feet of floor space. Both boats are heated and are equipped with public address systems and tape players. They are festive vessels; the *Blennerhassett* has bright pennants strung over the deck, a red stern wheel, and flags flying.

LOCAL POINTS OF INTEREST: The Blennerhassett Mansion was originally built by Harman and Margaret Blennerhassett between 1798 and 1800, but was destroyed by fire in 1811. Historical and archaeological research at the mansion site enabled its reconstruction from 1984-1985; it is a Georgian mansion with curved porticoes connected to two dependencies or wing buildings. It was here that Aaron Burr allegedly wove his mysterious plans for an expedition or "conspiracy" to establish a southwest empire. Both Blennerhassett and Burr were arrested for treason; Burr was cleared and Blennerhassett released. Their lives were ruined, and Blennerhassett fled the island; he never returned. In better days, however, famous visitors to the Blennerhassett estate included Gen. James Wilkinson, King Charles I of France, and Henry Clay. George Rogers encamped on the site with his army at the close of the Revolutionary War. The island has a huge tulip poplar tree, twenty-four feet in diameter and 106 feet high, the second largest tulip poplar east of the Mississippi. You can take carriage rides around the island, and there are also walnut groves and an Indian village site.

Parkersburg, at the confluence of the Little Kanawha and Ohio Rivers, was once an Indian hunting ground. The town was founded in 1810 and soon had improved transportation, including steamboat traffic on the Ohio River. When oil was first drilled in West Virginia in the 1860s, much of the "black gold" was shipped from Parkersburg. The town is now the center of more than one hundred industries, including chemicals, metals, and glass. Among the city's attractions are the Centennial Cabin Museum (1804) in the city park and the Parkersburg Art Center. The Riverfest is held Memorial Day weekend and attracts many visiting houseboats and steamers. Sebastian's is an excellent restaurant. Marietta, Ohio, a small and charming college town, home of Marietta College, right across the river, draws many natives of Parkersburg for entertainment and sightseeing. A good place to stay, and eat, in Marietta is the Lafayette Hotel on the river. The Campus Martius Museum in Marietta has an entire frontier home and other excellent exhibits on pioneer life in the mid-Ohio Valley. The Ohio River Museum has a trove of river lore (scale models of river boats, whistles, and pictures, along with a multimedia presentation on America's river systems). One of the first all-metal steam-powered towboats, the *W. P. Snyder, Jr.*, is moored alongside. Ferry lovers will delight in a visit to the *Becky Thatcher Theatre*, a paddlewheel steamer which is a showboat.

CROSSING TIME: 20 mins.

FERRY TYPE: Pedestrian

VESSEL CAPACITY: *Centennial*: 125 passengers; *Blennerhassett* Stern Wheeler: 150 passengers (275 with its party flat addition)

OPERATING SEASON: May-Oct.

SCHEDULE: **May, Sept., and Oct.: Sat., Sun.:** noon-5 p.m. **June, July, and Aug.: Wed.-Sun., plus holidays:** noon-5 p.m.

RESTRICTIONS:	No pets
FACILITIES:	Restrooms, light refreshments (soda pop and potato chips)
FARE:	Adults $2.50; children under 12 $1.50
RESERVATIONS:	No
DIRECTIONS:	Boats leave from the foot of 2nd St. in Parkersburg
MAP LOCATION:	P. 115, WV, 1
CONTACT:	Ruble's Sternwheelers, No. 4 Fourth St., Belpre, OH 45714, (614)423-7268

STATE:	West Virginia/Ohio
PLACES SERVED:	Sistersville, WV—Fly, OH
BODY OF WATER:	Ohio River
FERRY SERVICE HISTORY:	A ferry operated continuously at this site for more than 160 years, from 1808 until 1978. The landing was the site of the riverboat

trading center. In 1978 the owner of the private operation decided to cease business. Sistersville businessmen felt both communities had lost a lifeline. Citing a loss in revenue from neighboring eastern Ohio and a drop in the patient count at the Sistersville General Hospital, they began an effort to restore ferry service and succeeded in obtaining a ferry formerly used in Tiptonville, Tennessee. Service began again in 1980.

The ferry is run by Capt. Gilbert "Dib" Harmon, assisted by his son. Captain Harmon has been with the ferry over fifteen years. The crossing is almost too short for conversation, but, if no one is waiting, Captain Harmon will chat over a cup of coffee at the Riverview Restaurant, overlooking the ferry on the Ohio side. He piloted ferries at New Martinsville and St. Marys before Sistersville. He says he never gets bored: "I'm outside. I meet people. And it tickles me to death when I see cars on the other side of the river." Who is in the vehicles? A variety of people, including commuters, tourists who come for the pleasure of riding Sistersville's star attraction, and parents and grandparents eager to entertain children. School buses and delivery trucks also use the ferry; it

saves a twelve-mile drive north to New Martinsville or one seventeen miles south to St. Marys.

LOCAL POINTS OF INTEREST: Sistersville is a tranquil village of about twenty-three hundred residents; it has been named as a Historic District by the National Register of Historic Places. It resembles a town on the Eastern seaboard in many ways, with stately American Gothic homes, wrought-iron fences, Tiffany leaded-glass windows, and paved-brick alleys. This affluence dates from the 1890s, when Sistersville became the seat of America's oil industry. As many as fifty companies operated in the Sistersville field, and an 1899 town map shows a derrick on every street corner. Farmers beat their plowshares into drilling equipment and became overnight millionaires. Hucksters and opportunists soon arrived, bringing all the boisterous rowdiness of an overnight boom town. When the oil tide ebbed in 1915, the houses and beveled glass remained. The Wells Inn is a noted survivor of that era. It was built in 1893 by Ephraim Wells, the grandson of Charles Wells, the town's first settler. (He is said to have moved his family down the Ohio River from Wellsburg on a flatboat in 1802.) With its white columns, jardinieres brimming with geraniums, wrought-iron street lamps, Gay Nineties lobby, and Wooden Derrick Saloon in the basement (open to guests only), it evokes the prosperous oil days perfectly. Other buildings of interest are the 1832 *Oil Review* office, the oil derrick (a landmark of the 1890s, now being restored), the 1897 City Hall, the Masonic Temple, and the Wiser Building. The Wiser Oil Company is one of the few oil companies maintaining offices in Sistersville today (in 1902 there were 192).

Fly is a small town where they used to drill for oil, but now, according to Margaret Harr, there is little left but the Riverview Restaurant (owned by Christine Harr), a post office, a filling station, and a few residences. Margaret Harr says, "You just pass through Fly," but that many people do relish stopping for meals, coffee, and a chat with Captain Harmon when he has time.

CROSSING TIME: 5 mins.

FERRY TYPE: Vehicle

VESSEL CAPACITY: 8 cars

OPERATING SEASON: All year

SCHEDULE: Daily, on signal, 6 a.m.-6:30 p.m.

RESTRICTIONS: Trailers, pickup-campers, and RVs permitted. Load limit 35 tons.

FACILITIES: No

FARE: Cars $1.50; other vehicles according to size.

RESERVATIONS: No

DIRECTIONS: The Sistersville landing is on Catherine St. near Riverside Dr.

MAP LOCATION: P. 115, WV, 2

CONTACT: Capt. Gilbert "Dib" Harmon, Sistersville Ferry, 200 Diamond St., Sistersville, WV 26175, (614)795-6361

FERRIES
OF THE
SOUTH

Ferries of the South

ALABAMA

1. Bridgeport (Jackson County)
2. Dauphin Island-Fort Morgan State Park ("The Mobile Bay Ferry")
3. Davis (Monroe County)

ARKANSAS

1. Doddridge-Walnut Hill ("The Spring Bank Ferry")
2. Guion (Stone and Izard Counties)
3. Moro Bay (Union and Bradley Counties)
4. Peel (Marion County)

FLORIDA

1. Carrabelle-Dog Island
2. Fort Gates-Welaka
3. Georgetown-Drayton Island
4. Honeymoon Island-Caladesi Island
5. Mayport-Fort George Island

GEORGIA

1. Marshallville-Garden Valley
2. St. Marys-Cumberland Island

KENTUCKY

1. Augusta-Boudes Ferry, OH ("Ole Augusta")
2. Constance-Cincinnati, OH ("The Anderson Ferry")
3. Green River at Rochester ("The Rochester Ferry")
4. Hickman-Dorena, MO
5. Mammoth Cave Ferry
6. Mammoth Cave National Park ("Houchins' Ferry")
* [Marion - Cave-in-Rock, IL; see IL]
7. Monroe County, SR 214 ("The Turkey Neck Bend Ferry")
8. Rabbit Hash-Rising Sun, IN
9. Valley View-SR 169

LOUISIANA

1. Angola
2. Belle Chasse-Scarsdale
3. Cameron-Cameron Ship Channel
4. Cameron-Monkey Island
5. Edgard-Reserve
6. Lutcher-Vacherie
7. New Orleans (Canal St.)-Algiers
8. New Orleans (Donald St., Algiers)-Chalmette
9. New Orleans (Jackson Ave.)-Gretna
10. Plaquemine-Plaquemine Point
11. Pointe-a-la-Hache - West Pointe-a-la-Hache
12. St. Francisville-New Roads
13. Vinton-Gum Cove Road ("Gum Cove Ferry")
14. White Castle-Carville

MISSISSIPPI

1. Kings Point (near Vicksburg)

NORTH CAROLINA

1. Atlantic-Portsmouth Island
2. Aurora-Bayview
3. Cherry Branch-Minnesott Beach
4. Currituck-Knotts Island
5. Elwell-Carver's Creek ("Elwell Ferry")
6. Harkers Island-Cape Lookout
7. Hatteras-Ocracoke Island
8. Ocracoke-Cedar Island
9. Ocracoke-Swan Quarter
10. Parker
11. Sans Souci
12. Southport-Bald Head Island
13. Southport-Fort Fisher

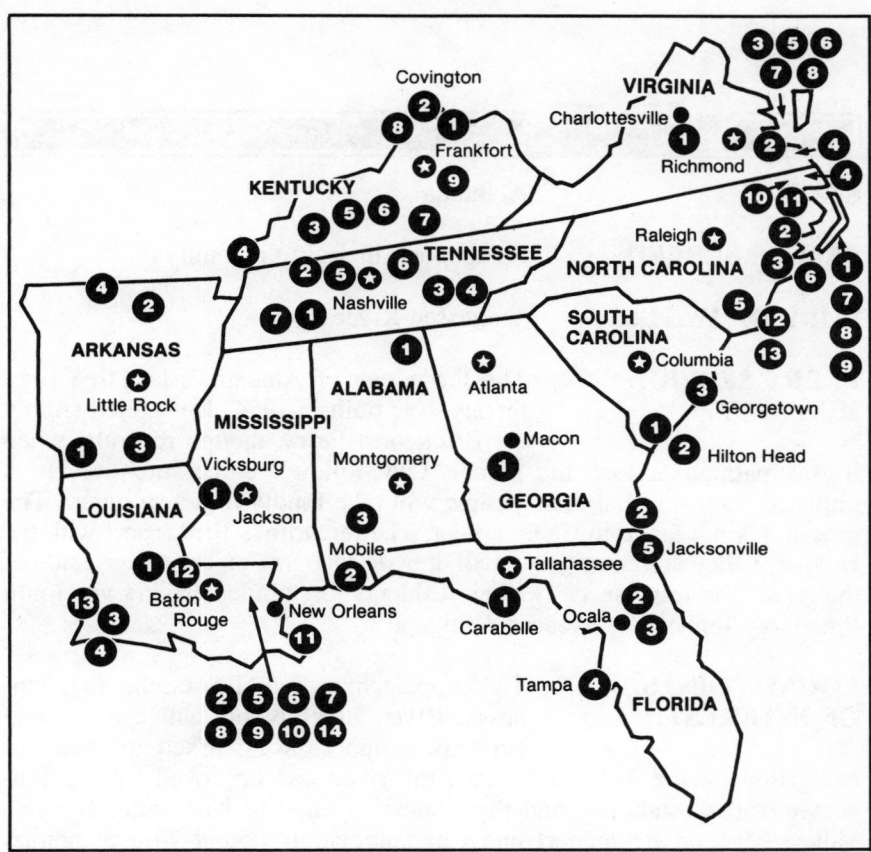

SOUTH CAROLINA

1. Hilton Head (Broad Creek Marina)-Daufuskie Island
2. Hilton Head (County Dock)-Daufuskie Island

3. South Island-SR 18

TENNESSEE

1. Clifton-Decaturville
2. Cumberland City-Throckmorton
3. Dayton-Cleveland ("The Blythe Ferry")
4. Decatur-Dayton ("The Washington Ferry")

5. Nashville-Scottsboro
6. Rome-Dixon Springs
7. Saltillo-SR 128

VIRGINIA

1. Hatton-SR 625 ("The Hatton Ferry")
2. Jamestown-Scotland
* [Leesburg-Whites Ferry, MD; see MD]
3. Merry Point-SR 604

4. Norfolk-Portsmouth
5. Onancock-Tangier
6. Reedville-Tangier
7. Smith Point-Smith Island, MD
8. Sunnybank-Ophelia
* [Tangier-Crisfield, MD; see MD]

STATE: Alabama

PLACES SERVED: Bridgeport, in Jackson County

BODY OF WATER: Tennessee River

FERRY SERVICE   The ferry, one of Alabama's last free river
HISTORY: ferries, was built in 1954. It is called simply
the Bridgeport Ferry, though recently, when
it was painted yellow, the name "Old Yellow" came into use. It is
unlikely, however, that local people will take fondly to a new name. The
crossing is not far from Chattanooga. The ferry links Bridgeport with the
Hogjaw Valley community, a small area of Alabama on the eastern side of
the river. The ferry saves Hogjaw residents forty miles driving via South
Pittsburg, Tennessee, to reach Bridgeport.

LOCAL POINTS   The Appalachian foothills cradle the Ten-
OF INTEREST: nessee River, which is split with canyons and
gaps. Bridgeport once marked the head of
navigation on the Tennessee, until the river was improved by the Tennessee Valley Authority and the channel opened to Knoxville. Brown's
Valley, between Bridgeport and Chattanooga, is dotted with plantation
homes. A country road left from US 72 at Bridgeport leads to Russell
Cave National Monument, site of the oldest human habitation discovered
in Alabama. The site is administered by the National Park Service.

CROSSING TIME: 15 mins.

FERRY TYPE: Vehicle

VESSEL CAPACITY: 6 cars, 24 passengers

OPERATING SEASON: All year, Mon.-Fri.; closed on state holidays.

SCHEDULE: On signal, 6 a.m.-4:30 p.m.

RESTRICTIONS: Trailers, pickup-campers, and RVs
permitted.

FACILITIES: None

FARE: Free

RESERVATIONS:	No
DIRECTIONS:	The ferry is reached from Jackson County Highway 91.
MAP LOCATION:	P. 197, AL, 1
CONTACT:	Mr. Floyd Lawrence, County Engineer, Rt. 4, Box 352, Scottsboro, AL 35768, (205)259-6037

STATE:	Alabama
PLACES SERVED:	Dauphin Island—Fort Morgan State Park ("The Mobile Bay Ferry")
BODY OF WATER:	Mobile Bay
FERRY SERVICE HISTORY:	The Mobile Bay Ferry began operation in 1979 after Hurricane Frederick destroyed the bridge connecting the mainland with

Dauphin Island. Since there were approximately two thousand residents living on Dauphin Island at that time, the State of Alabama contracted with Von Bergen, Ltd., to operate a ferry serving residents while a new bridge was under construction. Two vessels, the *Mount Marcy* and the *Mount Mansfield*, were leased from the Lake Champlain Transportation Company of Burlington, Vermont. At that time, only property owners could take vehicles to Dauphin Island. The new Dauphin Island Bridge was opened on July 16, 1982, and Von Bergen ceased ferry operations to Dauphin Island. Ed von Bergen, president of Von Bergen, then began a two-year attempt to obtain permits and leases to operate a ferry between Dauphin Island and Fort Morgan, a three-mile crossing saving 108 miles in driving distance. In June 1984 service began (at first excluding winter months) with the *Mount Mansfield*, the *Mount Marcy* having been returned to Lake Champlain Transportation in 1982. Service was suspended in 1984 owing to Hurricane Elena and the damage to Dauphin Island, and to access roads, but by July 1985 the service had become so busy a second ferry was needed. The *Charlotte*, again from Lake Champlain Transportation, was obtained, and year-round service began; the route has become a smashing success. In the past two years traffic has increased nearly 300 percent. The *Charlotte* runs daily (except

Christmas), and the *Mount Mansfield* is running as a secondary boat daily (except Tuesdays, Wednesdays, and Christmas).

LOCAL POINTS OF INTEREST: Dauphin Island was known to early explorers; the Spaniards surveyed it in the sixteenth century. In 1699, Pierre Le Moyne, Sieur d'Iberville, was sent by Louis XIV to establish a colony on the Gulf. He discovered Massacre, now Dauphin Island, and a colony was established there, though his expedition continued on to the flat beaches of Biloxi, building a stockade and cabins. The name "Dauphin" was given to honor the king's son. In the eighteenth century, French and British adventurers on the island traded gaudy trinkets to the Indians for fur. Today, Dauphin Island is a popular vacation retreat. Among the sights are the Indian Shell Mound, a prehistoric monument built by early Indians, Fort Gaines, a brick fortress commanding the entrance to Mobile Bay, and a sixty-acre Audubon Society Sanctuary.

Fort Morgan, a National Historic Landmark, is a group of weathered frame buildings, relics of the War of 1812 when it was named Fort Bowyer. It was renamed Fort Morgan in honor of the Mexican War hero Gen. John H. Morgan. Among the buildings are a museum, a powder magazine, and an old engineers' wharf. A buoy marks the resting place of the *Tecumseh* two hundred yards offshore. (Admiral Farragut shouted his famous command of "Damn the torpedoes! Full speed ahead!" when the Union ironclad sank at the beginning of the Battle of Mobile Bay in 1864. She hit a Confederate torpedo and went down with her captain and ninety-three crew members.) One can drive to Fort Morgan along the Gulf Islands National Seashore from the Florida Panhandle, along Perdido Key, then through Gulf State Park and Gulf Shores in Alabama. The Commandant's Quarters Restaurant at Fort Morgan Landing serves lunch, dinner, cocktails, beer, wine, and carry-outs. The ferry passes Bellingrath Gardens and Home (open to visitors); this is a magnificent riverfront estate with sixty-five acres of landscaped gardens and a noted exhibit of Boehm porcelain sculptures.

CROSSING TIME: 30 mins.

FERRY TYPE: Vehicle

VESSEL CAPACITY: *Charlotte*: 26 vehicles; 140 passengers
Mount Mansfield: 18-20 vehicles; 88 passengers

OPERATING SEASON: All year

SCHEDULE: **Lv. Dauphin Island** 8 a.m., *8:40, 9:20, *10, 10:40, *11:20, noon, *12:40 p.m., 1:20, *2, 2:40, *3:20, 4, *4:40, 5:20, *6, 6:40.
Lv. Fort Morgan 8:40 a.m., *9:20, 10, *10:40, 11:20, *noon, 12:40 p.m.,

*1:20, 2, *2:40, 3:20, *4, 4:40, *5:20, 6, *6:40, 7:20. *May 15-Sept. 15. *6:40 p.m. and 7:20 p.m. departures run daily except Nov., Dec., Jan., and Feb. During these months last departure times are 5:20 p.m. and 6 p.m.*

RESTRICTIONS: Trailers, pickup-campers, and RVs permitted. Load limit 20 tons.

FACILITIES: Restrooms

FARE: Car & driver $7; passengers $1; motorcycle and driver $5; trucks & motorhomes $9.00-$29.00 according to length; tow-behind vehicles up to 25 ft. $4.00; 25 ft. and over $9.

RESERVATIONS: No

DIRECTIONS: Take AL 163 (Dauphin Island Parkway) 30 mi. south from Mobile, then AL 193 (high-rise bridge and causeway) to Dauphin Island. Ferry operates from eastern tip of island.

MAP LOCATION: P. 197, AL, 2

CONTACT: Von Bergen Ltd., Box 745, Theodore, AL 36590, (205)973-2251

STATE: Alabama

PLACES SERVED: Davis, near Franklin, in Monroe County

BODY OF WATER: Alabama River

FERRY SERVICE HISTORY: The ferry was once owned by the State Highway Department, but now it is used by the county. The vessel has no name, but, according to the county engineer's office, is "just in place, the Davis ferry, without a name." The vessel is fifty feet long.

LOCAL POINTS OF INTEREST: The ferry is near Monroeville, which has been the seat of Monroe County since 1832; it was named for James Monroe when he was

Secretary of State. It is a trading center for the farmers nearby. The country is hilly and heavily wooded, with large pines. Of interest in Monroeville is the James Dellet House, built about 1816, which has a library with rare books and teakwood, rosewood, and mahogany furniture.

CROSSING TIME: 10 mins.

FERRY TYPE: Vehicle

VESSEL CAPACITY: 3 cars

OPERATING SEASON: All year, Mon.-Fri.

SCHEDULE: On signal as needed, daylight hours

RESTRICTIONS: Trailers, pickup-campers, and RVs permitted. Load limit 10 tons.

FACILITIES: None

FARE: Free

RESERVATIONS: No

DIRECTIONS: From Monroeville, take SR 41N, then County Road 17 west 3 miles, then go north on a dirt road (sign posted).

MAP LOCATION: P. 197, AL, 3

CONTACT: County Engineer's Office, Box 692, Monroeville, AL 36451, (205)743-3672

STATE: Arkansas

PLACES SERVED: Doddridge—Walnut Hill ["The Spring Bank Ferry"]

BODY OF WATER: Red River

Spring Bank Ferry

FERRY SERVICE HISTORY: In the southwest corner of Arkansas, seven miles from the Louisiana border, the Spring Bank Ferry crosses the Red River, connecting Lafayette and Miller counties. John Caffery was the first owner; it was then bought by William Richard Blanton, who came to Arkansas about 1836. His descendants operated the ferry until the death of the last Blanton owner, William Kelly Blanton, in 1952. His wife and daughter operated the ferry until it became a part of the state highway system. The ferry landing comes as a surprise to travellers who are not anticipating an abrupt end to SR 160. With its orange side structures, the ferry is a distinctive landmark as it plies between the flat shores of the Red River. It is one of the more historic of the four remaining Arkansas ferries, survivors of about two hundred "floating bridges." William E. Schmidt, writing in the *New York Times*, calls it "a pleasant surprise, a charming relic of another era." Schmidt has interviewed some of the commuters riding the ferry regularly, however, and discovered that a bridge would be a welcome replacement to such natives as H. T. Williams. Farmers often use it to move cotton to market, and, as William Tyler, District Engineer of southwestern Arkansas, puts it, "When it's down, they holler."

There are no tourist attractions as such nearby, but the bogs have given rise to the legend of the Fouk Monster; a film called *The Creature from Bogey Hollow* was made about it. Land use near the ferry is entirely farm acreage, with timber land to the southeast and southwest. Texarkana is the nearest large service center.

CROSSING TIME: 7 mins.

FERRY TYPE: Vehicle

VESSEL CAPACITY: 6 cars

OPERATING SEASON: All year

SCHEDULE: 5:30 a.m.-9:30 p.m.

RESTRICTIONS: Trailers, pick-up campers, and RVs permitted. Load limit 36 tons.

FACILITIES: None

FARE: Free

RESERVATIONS: No

DIRECTIONS: Located on Highway 160, 2 miles east of US 71, near Doddridge in Lafayette County.

MAP LOCATION: P. 197, AK, 1

CONTACT: B. K. Cooper, Chief Engineer, Arkansas State Highway and Transportation Dept., Box 2261, Little Rock, AK 72203, (501)569-2000

Guion Ferry

STATE: Arkansas

PLACES SERVED: At Guion, connecting Stone and Izard Counties ["Guion Ferry"]

BODY OF WATER: White River

FERRY SERVICE   Mertie A. Harris, a local historian in
HISTORY: Batesville, Arkansas, has undertaken research on the origins of the town of Guion
and the White River. The history of the town goes as far back as the
1800s, when Ozark pioneers arrived on rafts at Wild Haw Landing. By
the 1830s, steamboats were travelling up the White River, and, by 1877,
according to Mrs. Harris, there were fourteen boat landings between
Batesville and Calico Rock. Both Izard (where Guion is located) and
Stone Counties, on opposite sides of the river, increased in population. In
the early part of the century they were connected by a wooden ferry, but it
was destroyed by the 1929 tornado which demolished the town (with five
minutes warning, most people were saved by racing to mine tunnels and
storm cellars). There was apparently a second wooden ferry, in the 1940s,
which was discontinued. In 1962, citizens established a modern steel
ferry, which the local communities operated until 1970, when the state
took it over. It had been the last privately owned ferry on a major
Arkansas river. According to an Arkansas State Highway Department
survey conducted in October 1985, the majority of users at the time were
tourists. There is a silica plant on the east side of the river, but only three

plant workers said they used the ferry; other riders were local people visiting relatives. The ferry is a side-wheel and cable type.

LOCAL POINTS OF INTEREST: In an article called "Waiting for the Guion Ferry," published in *Ozarks Mountaineer*, Phyllis Rossiter describes her approach to the Guion ferry, in a jeep: "I love country roads . . . back roads that let me get close to the Ozarks: close to the trees and the streams, now running full of snowmelt, and the hills — the high country — awakening to the stirrings of an impatient Spring. And this gravel road snaking off into the hills is doubly attractive, for yet another sign reads, 'Guion Ferry Open.' " The approach has a hairpin curve. "We shift to second and tiptoe into the sunshine. Not much time for sightseeing, but there's a glimpse of a sheer bluff face dripping icicles like the bearded face of Old Man Winter who knows his days are numbered . . . rock outcroppings punctuate the hillsides . . . and over there a pyramid-steep hill crowned, incredibly, with a stock pond perched on the very summit like a Turkish turban, cows studding its sides like jewels." The town, situated in a deep valley with picturesque towering limestone bluffs, is a starting point for White River trout fishing. A nearby riverside park welcomes campers and offers a privately-owned trout dock. It is southeast of the Ozark National Forest and not far from Mountain View, home of the Ozark Folk Center, an Arkansas state park dedicated to preserving the folk songs and mountain ways of the Ozark pioneers, with craft demonstrations and music and dances in a 1,064-seat auditorium. The ferry is also near Calico Rock, whose Main Street has served as the setting for several films and television shows. A well-known ferry on Norfork Lake, midway between the Guion and Peel ferries, has been converted to sightseeing cruises, but is still of interest to those going west.

CROSSING TIME: 7 mins.

FERRY TYPE: Vehicle

VESSEL CAPACITY: 6 cars

OPERATING SEASON: All year

SCHEDULE: On signal, 6:30 a.m.-6:30 p.m.

RESTRICTIONS: Trailers, pick-up campers, RVs permitted. Load limit 15 tons.

FACILITIES: None

FARE: Free

RESERVATIONS: No

DIRECTIONS: Ferry is on State Highway 58, northwest of Batesville.

MAP LOCATION: P. 197, AK, 2

CONTACT: See CONTACT, p. 204.

STATE: Arkansas

PLACES SERVED: Moro Bay, in Union and Bradley Counties

BODY OF WATER: Ouachita River

FERRY SERVICE HISTORY: The vessel here is a flat-topped barge pushed by a pivoting tug; it is painted fiery orange, with cables laced around pulleys to raise and lower the ramps on each end. Randy Gates, who superintends the three two-man crews who maneuver the ferry, says that the summer is the most popular time of the year for tourists, especially July 4. Fall is slower. Winter is trickier, as far as maneuvering the boat goes, because of the current and the wind. The vehicles may range, on a given day, from timber trucks to Lincoln Continental sedans carrying poodles. Riders are often workers commuting to jobs in Bradley County or Union County (the ferry connects the two). Many campers bound for the state park also ride the ferry. The most unusual passenger, a few years ago, was a doe deer who often used the ferry to cross the river; the superintendent of the ferry at the time witnessed it.

LOCAL POINTS OF INTEREST: Moro Bay is a popular camping park; the one-quarter-mile Deer Run Hiking Trail provides a close-up look at the forest. El Dorado, once a hamlet, came to life when oil was discovered in 1921. A unique museum is the Arkansas Oil and Brine Museum north of El Dorado on Highway 7 at Smackover; the information center here resembles an early service station. Magnolia, about halfway betwen El Dorado and the Spring Bank Ferry, is a charming small southern town, the site of Southern Arkansas University.

CROSSING TIME:	7 mins.
FERRY TYPE:	Vehicle
VESSEL CAPACITY:	6 cars
OPERATING SEASON:	All year
SCHEDULE:	On signal, 5 a.m.-10 p.m.
RESTRICTIONS:	Trailers, pick-up campers, and RVs permitted. Load limit 32 tons.
FACILITIES:	None
FARE:	Free
RESERVATIONS:	No
DIRECTIONS:	Ferry is on State Highway 15, 21 miles northeast of El Dorado.
MAP LOCATION:	P. 197, AK, 3
CONTACT:	See CONTACT, p. 204.

STATE:	Arkansas
PLACES SERVED:	Peel, in Marion County
BODY OF WATER:	Bull Shoals Lake
FERRY SERVICE HISTORY:	The Peel ferry serves local farmers as well as tourists going and coming to and from Missouri. Some feed trucks use it to get to farms on the Missouri side.
LOCAL POINTS OF INTEREST:	Bull Shoals Lake, a 45,500-acre lake created by a dam, sprawls amid the Ozark Mountains; the resort communities of Lakeview

and Bull Shoals both have ample accommodations. Bull Shoals State Park offers good campsites. Mountain Village 1890, near the Bull Shoals community, has restored nineteenth-century buildings and, from spring to fall, craft demonstrations. The lake and river are a mecca for fishermen, with record-breaking mountain trout, bass, and bream. Houseboats are available for rental, and non-fishermen may float down the White River in a jonboat past high bluffs and green hillsides.

CROSSING TIME:	22 mins.
FERRY TYPE:	Vehicle
VESSEL CAPACITY:	6 cars
OPERATING SEASON:	All year
SCHEDULE:	On signal, daylight hours; non-operational in high winds.
RESTRICTIONS:	Trailers, pickup campers, and RV's permitted. Load limit 25 tons.
FACILITIES:	None
FARE:	Free
RESERVATIONS:	No
DIRECTIONS:	Ferry is on State Highway 125, at Bull Shoals Lake, 29 miles north of Yellville.
MAP LOCATION:	P. 197, AK, 4
CONTACT:	See CONTACT, p. 204.

Ruby B.

STATE:	Florida
PLACES SERVED:	Carrabelle—Dog Island
BODY OF WATER:	St. George Sound and Carrabelle River

FERRY SERVICE HISTORY: Dog Island was undeveloped until the late 1940s or early 1950s, when it was purchased by Jeff Lewis; he opened concessions and owned the island until about 1980. Ferry service was provided by the county (a car-and-passenger vessel), but it was discontinued in 1982. Since 1984, passenger-only service has been provided by Capt. Raymond Williams aboard the *Ruby B.*, a thirty-eight-foot fiberglass boat built in 1984. According to his wife, Ruth, wedding parties are among the more festive groups carried to Dog Island. Dogs and cats have also, on occasion, been passengers. Swimmers often take surfboards with sails. A military LCN is used to remove garbage from the island and take heavy freight, but the *Ruby B.* does sometimes carry light freight such as windows or doors.

LOCAL POINTS OF INTEREST: Carrabelle is the home of the world's smallest police station and the Crooked River Lighthouse, built in 1894-5. Franklin County is known for its seafood production; grouper, red snapper, speckled trout, oysters, and shellfish are caught here in the Gulf and in the Carrabelle River, Crooked River, and New River.

Apalachicola and Eastpoint are two other vital Bay communities nearby. From Eastpoint there is a bridge to St. George Island, where fishing and birdwatching are twin obsessions. The island has its own magazine, *St. George*, which publishes the work of island poets and brings visitors up to date on the galleries, restaurants, motels, shops, and other businesses in the area. Martha and Tom Edmonds of Richmond, Virginia, who owned a beach house on the island until it was destroyed by a hurricane, think of St. George as their Shangri-la. Martha says they never fail to stop in Carrabelle at "the" drugstore, a throwback to the 1940s and 1950s with a marble soda fountain and huge dips of ice cream.

Apalachicola Bay is, as Charles House, editor of the *Carrabelle Times*, puts it, "a haven for boat lovers." He wrote a picture story for the *Times* on representative boats; they ranged from brawny tugs to homebuilt barges, shrimpers and workboats to ketches, sportfishermen, yachts, and sloops. The area is very sea-oriented; the *Times* publishes the tide tables and a column on saltwater fishing by Linda Arnold.

Dog Island is a romantic, almost melancholy island with about one hundred private homes and approximately a dozen full-time residents. In the 1970s it was saved from luxury development (with a bridge and condominiums) by a determined group of Island residents who persuaded the Nature Conservancy to buy three-fourths of it as a preserve. The Conservancy, in turn, sold eleven hundred acres to a private, charitable trust that is funding research on the island. There is now nothing commercial, and it is said that the harbor is the only "grocery store." More than thirty endangered and threatened animals, plants, and birds inhabit the island. The terrain is marsh, forest, sand dunes, and beach, with live oaks and sand pines. The marshes on the bay side of the island serve as an interface between the sea and uplands, providing nutrient for the fish and crabs of the estuary (in turn, food for the birds and mammals). Island life is often studied by scientists, such as Sam Johnston of Florida's Department of Environmental Regulation, who recently discovered the northernmost location of the black mangrove, growing in bonsai form. Visitors may stay at the Pelican Inn, which has eight small apartments with kitchen facilities, private porches, and air-conditioning. Dan Tonsmeire, manager of the Pelican Inn, also helps guests with luggage and groceries and lends expert advice about casting for dinner fish and identifying rare bird species. The island is peaceful and pristine; the coin of the realm is shells, and the theater of lingering and uninterrupted sunsets is the prevailing pastime.

CROSSING TIME:	45 mins.
FERRY TYPE:	Pedestrian
VESSEL CAPACITY:	26 passengers
OPERATING SEASON:	All year

May 1-Sept. 30: Lv. Carrabelle Th.-Mon.:
11 a.m.; Fri.: 6 p.m.; Sat. & Sun.: 4 p.m.
Lv. Dog Island Th.-Mon.: noon; Fri.:
7 p.m.; **Sat. & Sun.: 5 p.m. Oct. 1-Apr. 30: Lv. Carrabelle Fri.: 4**
p.m.; **Sat., Sun., & Mon.: 10:30 a.m. Lv. Dog Island Fri.: 5 p.m.; Sat.**
& Sun.: 4 p.m.; Mon.: noon.

RESTRICTIONS: No pets allowed at Pelican Inn

FACILITIES: No

FARE: $8

FACILITIES: Yes

DIRECTIONS: From US 98 in Carrabelle, turn on Meridian
St. and follow to Marine St. South and ferry
dock.

MAP LOCATION: P. 197, FL, 1

CONTACT: Capt. Raymond Williams, Box 648, Carrabelle, FL 32322, (904)697-3434

STATE: Florida

PLACES SERVED: Fort Gates—Welaka

BODY OF WATER: St. Johns River

FERRY SERVICE   This ferry crossing has existed for over sev-
HISTORY: enty years. It is privately operated by the
Fort Gates Fish Camp. The barge and tug are
called the *Fort Gates Ferry*. Riders are usually commuters from Ocala
and tourists taking a short cut to Silver Springs, where glass-bottomed
boat rides are offered, and to and from Tampa; the ferry saves many miles
of driving.

LOCAL POINTS   The Ocala National Forest is near here, as
OF INTEREST: well as the Welaka Aquarium and Fish
Hatchery and Juniper Springs.

CROSSING TIME: 11 mins.

FERRY TYPE:	Vehicle
VESSEL CAPACITY:	4-5 cars
OPERATING SEASON:	All year
SCHEDULE:	Daily, except Tues., 7 a.m.-5:30 p.m.
RESTRICTIONS:	Trailers, pickup-campers, and RVs permitted.
FACILITIES:	None
FARE:	Cars $5; trucks, vans, trailers $10
RESERVATIONS:	No
DIRECTIONS:	Take SR 17 to SR 309 past Welaka towards Fruitland; follow signs to Fort Gates Ferry
MAP LOCATION:	P. 197, FL, 2
CONTACT:	Fort Gates Fish Camp, (904)467-2411

STATE:	Florida
PLACES SERVED:	Georgetown—Drayton Island
BODY OF WATER:	Lake George

FERRY SERVICE HISTORY: This ferry serves property owners on Drayton Island; there are fewer than twenty people living there in the summer, though there are more in the winter. The county owns the barge, and ferryman Eddie Babbitt pushes it with his own boat. "Island people are a little different," says Babbitt. "Those that like it stay for a long, long time and those that don't sell out and get out." He was born and raised in Georgetown ("and," he points out, "you can't say that about many people in Florida these days.") He ferries building supplies, groceries, and other necessary items as well as people, and has been operating the ferry off and on since the age of twelve.

LOCAL POINTS OF INTEREST: Drayton Island is largely private; there are no facilities on the island for the public. Georgetown is a small town with fishing camps. The nearest major tourist attractions are Disney World at Orlando, ninety miles away, and St. Augustine, fifty-five miles away.

CROSSING TIME:	5-6 mins.
FERRY TYPE:	Vehicle
VESSEL CAPACITY:	4 cars
OPERATING SEASON:	All year, exclusive of Wed., Christmas, and Thanksgiving.
SCHEDULE:	**Mon., Tues., Thurs., Fri., Sat.:** 7:30-9 a.m. and 3:30-5 p.m. **Sun.:** 3:30-5 p.m. only.
RESTRICTIONS:	Trailers, pickup-campers, and RVs permitted. Load limit 28 tons.
FACILITIES:	None
FARE:	Car $4; pickup-camper $6-8; two-axle trailer to $8; RV (over 21 ft.) to $24.
RESERVATIONS:	No
DIRECTIONS:	In Georgetown, take Ferry Rd. near the Methodist Church.
MAP LOCATION:	P. 197, FL, 3
CONTACT:	Eddie Babbitt, Box 5, Georgetown, FL 32039, (904)467-2194

STATE:	Florida
PLACES SERVED:	Honeymoon Island State Recreation Area— Caladesi Island
BODY OF WATER:	Gulf of Mexico
FERRY SERVICE HISTORY:	This ferry service was inaugurated in 1978. The present operator, the Captain Anderson Dinner Boat Company, took over the ferry in

May 1986, calling it the *Caladesi Connection*. The boats are two forty-foot catamarans.

LOCAL POINTS OF INTEREST: Honeymoon Island was once the home of the Tocobaga Indians; it was later named Sand Island and, by 1880, Hog Island. It was renamed Honeymoon Island by the New York developer who bought it in 1939. He constructed fifty palm-thatched bungalows; honeymoons were advertised in *Life* and in newsreels and used as contest prizes. During World War II, exhausted Cleveland defense plant workers were flown in for recuperation. The cottages were destroyed by storms and beach erosion, but Honeymoon Island began to be developed commercially in 1966. In 1970, the Department of Natural Resources acquired most of the island, and today it is a recreation area, managed to appear as it did when the first Europeans arrived. Rare osprey nest in the tall pines; the island has over 208 species of plants and a wide variety of shore birds.

Caladesi Island State Park is rich in dunes, sea oats, exotic shells and white sandy beaches; boardwalks have been built to protect the fragile ecology of the island. Nature study, cast-netting for mullet, and boating are permitted; interpretive programs and guided walks by Park rangers are provided according to seasonal demand. There are no overnight facilities, but there is a restaurant.

CROSSING TIME: 20 mins.

FERRY TYPE: Pedestrian

VESSEL CAPACITY: 69 passengers

OPERATING SEASON: All year, weather permitting

SCHEDULE: 8 a.m.-sunset; operates hourly, leaving Honeymoon Island on the hour

RESTRICTIONS: Pets not allowed on ferry.

FACILITIES: None

FARE: Round-trip only; adults $3.50; children (under 12) $2

RESERVATIONS: Optional (813/734-5263)

DIRECTIONS: From Dunedin take US 19A 2 mi. north; then FL 586W (Dunedin Causeway) to Honeymoon Island; ferry dock is on left.

MAP LOCATION: P. 197, FL. 4

CONTACT: Ferry concessionaire: (813)734-5263; Caladesi Island State Park, #1 Causeway Blvd., Dunedin, FL 33528, (813)443-5903

STATE:	Florida
PLACES SERVED:	Mayport—Fort George Island
BODY OF WATER:	St. Johns River
FERRY SERVICE HISTORY:	The Mayport ferry was established in 1950 with two small vessels, the *Jean Lafitte* and the *Monadnock.*

The present vessels are the closed-deck 773-ton *Buccaneer* (ex-*Norfolk County* of Virginia), and the open-deck 575-ton *Blackbeard* (ex-*Carquinez* of California), which was purchased in 1962. To some people, the service is a charming bit of nostalgia, a bulwark against modern preoccupation with size and speed. To others, it is an essential transportation link. The ferry is Florida's last state-operated crossing, shuttling riders along a watery stretch of the scenic Buccaneer Trail in northeastern Florida, so named because at one time piracy, smuggling, and slave-trading were the major industries along the coast. The state employs over thirty workers at the station (including ferry captains, toll collectors, mechanics, and others), and the ferries carry nearly 500,000 vehicles across each year. The whistle shrieks to let other river traffic know the ferry is moving out; a tape-recorded message warns travelers to brace just before the ferry glides back into the dock. The crossing saves a lengthy drive through Jacksonville. It has been used for burials (scattering of ashes), but riders are usually tourists. One man arrived on horseback, leading a second horse; the second one was charged the vehicle rate of fifty cents. The ferry is not a money-making proposition, but it still rouses strong affections in the hearts of Floridians. "You can't put this in the bank," said one man the last time the threat of a bridge loomed, "but a tremendous amount of nostalgia goes with riding the ferry." The average number of cars carried on a weekday is twelve hundred; on Sunday, twenty-one hundred.

LOCAL POINTS OF INTEREST:	Mayport is a fishing village north of Atlantic Beach; it is the home of shrimp and charter boats.

On Fort George Island is the Kingsley Plantation State Historic Site, the site of the oldest plantation house in the state, with slave quarters, carriage house, and guided tours. Amelia Island is an appealing seaside port with narrow historic streets; it is the only place in the US to have lived under eight different flags. It became a prominent resort soon after the Civil War, when Northern tourists began coming down on the Mallory Steamship Line. Fernandina Beach has fine old Victorian houses; the Palace Saloon is the second oldest in the state of Florida and advertises "refreshing libations" in a Victorian atmosphere.

CROSSING TIME: 5-9 mins.

FERRY TYPE: Vehicle

VESSEL CAPACITY: *Buccaneer:* 35 vehicles; 294 passengers
Blackbeard: 50 vehicles; 200 passengers

OPERATING SEASON: All year

SCHEDULE: Daily. 30 min. service from 6 a.m.-10:30 p.m. (Leaves Mayport on the hour and half-hour; leaves Fort George on the quarter hour.) Second ferry sometimes added during the summer and on special holidays.

RESTRICTIONS: Trailers, pickup-campers, and RVs permitted. Load limit: highway legal. Overhead clearance on *Buccaneer* 12 ft. 3 in. No flammable materials. Drivers of special cargoes should telephone ahead for clearance.

FACILITIES: None

FARE: Pedestrians $0.10; 2 & 3-axle vehicles $1.50; 4 axles $2; 5 axles $2.50

RESERVATIONS: No

DIRECTIONS: Take FL A1A at Fort George and A1A at Mayport.

MAP LOCATION: P. 197, FL, 5

CONTACT: St. Johns River Ferry Service, Richard W. Klebs, Marine Superintendent, 4610 Ocean St., Mayport, FL 32233, (904)246-2922

STATE: Georgia

PLACES SERVED: Marshallville—Garden Valley (SR 127)

BODY OF WATER: Flint River

FERRY SERVICE HISTORY: Johnny Brooks, who operates the Flint River ferry for the State of Georgia, has conducted research on its history and written a brief account of it called "Sound Horn for Ferry." Crossing the Flint River has always presented a challenge, according to Brooks, but, "shuttling slowly back and forth beneath the hanging Spanish moss" is Georgia's last free ferry. An early Macon County history states that the Flint was first crossed by a ferry at "Travelers Rest," on the original "Barnards Path." Barnard had come from Savannah about 1770; he built a trading post and operated a ferry, which was replaced by a bridge when Oglethorpe began to boom. A second ferry operated from Oglethorpe to Montezuma, and another at Lanier, operated by Little Clowsey Snow. Lanier was once the county seat but declined when the Central of Georgia Railroad announced plans to extend the tracks to Oglethorpe. When Marshallville began to rise, a ferry was built, variously known as Wannamaker's Ferry and Holinshed's Ferry; it was operated by an old Negro man and his wife, Uncle Lewis Fish and Aunt Sallie. In 1875, a law was passed to exempt the ferry operator from jury duty, because he was essential to transportation. The Marshallville ferry was later called Underwood's Ferry and renamed for subsequent owners. Mrs. Furlow Brown deeded a half-acre of land to Macon County, which operated the ferry until the Georgia Highway Department took over the roads and ferries in 1920. The number declined from about twenty in 1933 to one today (plus the private ferry to Cumberland Island National Seashore). As Brooks puts it, "The ferry's nostalgic lure is causing more and more wandering tourists to see it, to recapture a bit of the peace of yesteryear." Once powered by the operator, who wielded a long pole to take advantage of the river current, the ferry today is powered by a 1959 Chevy six-cylinder truck engine, which turns a large steel drum around which runs the drive cable. A second cable, strung higher, keeps the ferry on course by two short cables attached to movable pulleys. "As time marches on," says Brooks, "the Macon County ferry on Georgia State Route 127 links modern man with a whisper of the past." Jimmy Hogg and William English, two other operators, know the regular patrons by name (such as farmer C. T. Montford, welldigger Bennie Robinson, and Queenie McInvale, an employee of the Oaks Nursing Home in Marshallville). They often carry out-of-state cars, from as far away as Alaska. This historic ferry may be replaced by a bridge within a few years, so call before driving a great distance to ride it.

LOCAL POINTS OF INTEREST: Marshallville (a few miles east of the ferry), Garden Valley (just west of it), and Montezuma (eight miles south of it) are in the part of Georgia called Plains Country, southwest of Macon. Marshallville is the headquarters of the American Camellia Society; well worth visiting here are the Camellia Gardens (the blossoms peak January 15-March 15). A brochure outlining a historic driving tour of Oglethorpe, Montezuma, and Marshallville is available at the Macon County Chamber of Commerce and the Andersonville National Historic Site.

CROSSING TIME: 2 mins.

FERRY TYPE: Vehicle

VESSEL CAPACITY: 2 cars

OPERATING SEASON: All year

SCHEDULE: On signal 6 a.m.-10 p.m. daily

RESTRICTIONS: Trailers, RVs and loaded trucks not permitted. Load limit 3 tons.

FACILITIES: None

FARE: Free

RESERVATIONS: No

DIRECTIONS: Go west from Marshallville on SR 127 or east from Garden Valley; ferry connects sections of SR 127.

MAP LOCATION: P. 197, GA, 1

CONTACT: Department of Transportation, State of Georgia, No. 2 Capitol Sq., Atlanta, GA 30334-1002, (404)656-5267

STATE: Georgia

PLACES SERVED: St. Marys—Cumberland Island

BODY OF WATER: Intracoastal Waterway

FERRY SERVICE HISTORY: Until the Cumberland Island National Seashore was established in October 1972, Cumberland Island was privately owned. Until

the turn of the century, there was a hotel on the north end of the island, which operated its own ferry service. The Dungeness-Grayfield Inn's ferry operated up to the 1960s. In 1974, the ferry service began with a boat called the *Marineland,* which was used until the *Cumberland Queen* made her first trip in 1976. The *Cumberland Queen* was formerly the *Tangier Princess* from Crisfield, Maryland; she was built in Deltaville, Virginia, in 1975.

LOCAL POINTS OF INTEREST: Cumberland Island was inhabited by the Missoe Indians as early as four thousand years ago. In 1566, the Spanish governor of Florida ordered construction of a fort. In 1736, the island was renamed Cumberland by Gen. James Oglethorpe, founder of the English colony of Georgia; the English built a hunting lodge, Dungeness. In 1783, Gen. Nathanael Greene purchased a large acreage on the island; his widow married Phineas Miller and built Dungeness, a four-story mansion known as Greene Dungeness, which was destroyed by fire after the Civil War. Thomas Carnegie, brother of Andrew, purchased the Dungeness property and built another mansion, known as Carnegie Dungeness, now in ruins because of a fire during the 1950s (the ruins are unstable and closed).

Today, 85 percent of the island is part of the Seashore; visitors are asked to respect the rights of the private inhabitants. Present legislation, according to K. O. Morgan, Superintendent of the Cumberland Island National Seashore, precludes restoring the mansion as a hotel or commercial venture; it mandates preservation of the seashore in its primitive state and forbids any construction that would be incompatible with the preservation of the unique flora and fauna now on the island. Herds of horses graze in the marshes and loggerhead turtles come ashore to lay eggs. Day visitors should carry food, drinks, suntan lotion, insect repellent, walking shoes, rain gear, film, and sunglasses. There are sixteen miles of white sand beach and dunes as high as forty feet. Camping is allowed up to seven days at developed and primitive backcountry sites. In winter there are deer drives; participants are decided by lottery (consult the National Park Service).

At St. Marys, there is the Toonerville Trolley, featured in the 1930s Wash Tubbs cartoon, the 1788 Oak Grove Cemetery, and the antebellum Orange Hall.

CROSSING TIME:	45 mins.
FERRY TYPE:	Pedestrian
VESSEL CAPACITY:	146 passengers
OPERATING SEASON:	All year; mid-May-Labor Day daily; rest of year does not run Tuesdays and Wednesdays.
SCHEDULE:	**Lv. St. Marys 9 a.m., 11:45; Lv. Cumberland Island 10:15 a.m., 4:45 p.m. Extra sailing on Fri., Sat., and Sun.: Lv. Cumberland 2:45; Lv. St. Marys 3:40.**
RESTRICTIONS:	No bicycles
FACILITIES:	Restrooms, snack bar
FARE:	Round-trip only: Adults $7.50; senior citizens $6.25; children 12 & under $3.85.
RESERVATIONS:	Advisable.
DIRECTIONS:	Ferry dock in St. Marys is on the waterfront at the end of Osborne St.
MAP LOCATION:	P. 197, GA, 2
CONTACT:	National Park Service, Box 806, St. Marys, GA 31558, (912)882-4335

Ole Augusta

STATE: Kentucky/Ohio

PLACES SERVED: Augusta—Boudes Ferry, Ohio, connecting
                        Bracken County, Kentucky, and Brown
                        County, Ohio ["Ole Augusta"]

BODY OF WATER: Ohio River at Mile 427.2

FERRY SERVICE   The Augusta ferry has been an institution on
HISTORY: the Ohio River for eighty years, according to
                        Augusta Mayor Isaac Weldon; it has been in
existence since 1800. In 1986 it was threatened with extinction, but had a
reprieve when it was purchased by David Cartmell. What possessed
Cartmell to buy the *Ole Augusta*? "It was accidental," he says. "I was
down there one day, rode the ferry, found out it was for sale, put a bid in,
and, to my surprise, got it."

LOCAL POINTS   Augusta, founded in 1797, is a historic river
OF INTEREST: village eighteen miles west of Maysville.
                        Riverside Drive, a row of historic houses
sweeping down to the waterfront, is on the National Register of Historic
Places. The town is so picturesque it has been used in the TV miniseries
Centennial, as the setting for St. Louis in the 1880s, and for the PBS
production of *Huckleberry Finn.* Two noted buildings here are the residences of Senator Thornton F. Marshall, who cast the deciding vote to
keep Kentucky in the Union, and Dr. Joseph S. Tomlinson, first president

of Augusta College, the world's first Methodist college, founded in 1822. Tomlinson was the uncle of Stephen Foster, who often visited here; it is thought that Augusta may have inspired Foster's "My Old Kentucky Home." The Sternwheeler Regatta and Arts and Crafts Fair is held here the third weekend in June.

Boudes Ferry, Ohio, is between Utopia and Higginsport. It was named for John Boude, who established a ferry here in 1798. President Grant's birthplace is about twenty miles away, at Pt. Pleasant, and, at Ripley, there is the John Rankin House, named for a leader of the Underground Railroad.

CROSSING TIME:	10 mins.
FERRY TYPE:	Vehicle
VESSEL CAPACITY:	8 cars or 1 tractor-trailer
OPERATING SEASON:	All year
SCHEDULE:	Daily: On signal: Mon.-Fri.: 8 a.m.-6 p.m. Sat. & Sun.: 9 a.m.-6 p.m.
RESTRICTIONS:	Trailers, pickup-campers, and RVs permitted. Load limit 61 net tons.
FACILITIES:	No
FARE:	Car or pickup-camper $3.50; pedestrian $.50; trailer or RV $3.50-$5.50.
RESERVATIONS:	No
DIRECTIONS:	Ferry landing is on Riverside Dr. in Augusta; Boudes Ferry is 1 min. west of Higginsport, off SR 52. Ferry crosses the Ohio R. at Mile 427.2.
MAP LOCATION:	P. 197, KY, 1
CONTACT:	David Cartmell, 310 Market St., Maysville, KY 51056, (606)564-5688

The Anderson Ferry

STATE: Kentucky

PLACES SERVED: Constance—Cincinnati, OH ["The Anderson Ferry"]

BODY OF WATER: Ohio River

FERRY SERVICE HISTORY: The Anderson Ferry is a National Historic Landmark. In 1817, George Anderson purchased an existing ferry operation at this site. He and members of his family operated it until 1841; it then had various owners until 1864, when Charles Kottmyer purchased the ferry and landing sites. In 1867, he built *Boone 1,* a steam paddlewheel ferry boat, which replaced a horse-and-treadmill boat. *Boone 7,* built in 1937 and still operating today, is a diesel-powered boat with side paddlewheels; *Little Boone,* built in 1952, is propelled by a pivoting tug. From the beginning, the Kottmyers and a succession of Boone boats made history. *Boone 1* was the first double-ended ferry in western waters. *Boone 4* was the first with a rudder. *Boone 5* provided the first pilot house. Each boat to this day has been named for Daniel Boone. The ferry had remained in the Kottmyer family since its beginning, until 1986, when Richard Kottmyer sold it to one of his employees, Paul Anderson, who had worked for him about twenty-five years. "After 122 years of the family business of running ferries, since April 1864, when my great-grandfather bought ferries and nearby property, I hated to give up the ferries,'' says Kottmyer. "I am sixty-three years old and have stayed by the ferries for twenty-two years, and I believe I deserve a little time for myself and wife,'' he continues. Few people would deny that he deserves some leisure; it is, nevertheless, fortunate that this particular Historic Landmark, an institution, can continue in the future. The Anderson Ferry has long provided continuous conveyance of people, commodities, materials, and vehicles along the majestic Ohio.

LOCAL POINTS OF INTEREST: Northern Kentucky, while part of the metropolitan Cincinnati region, retains its own identity and charm. It has been called the "Rhineland of America,'' evocative of Germany to many settlers. The German influence may still be seen today in Covington's Main Strasse Village, which includes Goebel Park. Throughout the region there are Germanic-style houses. The waterfront is being restored, and BB Riverboats offers Ohio River cruises from Covington (606/261-8500). Cincinnati was called by Longfellow the "Queen City of the West.'' Today, the metropolis is known for its zoo, for the Taft Museum, and for the Public Landing, at the foot of Broadway, where the first settlers set foot ashore and built the first log cabin. Cincinnati also has river cruises on the *Delta Queen* and *Mississippi Queen* (800/543-1949).

CROSSING TIME: 3 mins.

FERRY TYPE: Vehicle

VESSEL CAPACITY: 8 cars

OPERATING SEASON: All year

SCHEDULE: On signal, daily. **May 1-Oct. 31: Weekdays:** 6 a.m.-9:30 p.m. **Sun. & holidays:** 7 a.m.-9:30 p.m. **Nov. 1-Apr. 30: Weekdays:** 6 a.m.-8 p.m. **Sun. & holidays:** 7 a.m.-8 p.m.

RESTRICTIONS: Load limit 58 tons. Trailers, pickup-campers, and RVs permitted.

FACILITIES: None

FARE: Car and driver $1.25; passengers $.10 each; pickup-camper $1.25-$2; trailer $1.50-$2.50; RV $2-$3.

RESERVATIONS: No

DIRECTIONS: Ferry is located at Ohio River Mile 477.6; in Kentucky it is reached by KY 8 and is near its interesection with Dry Creek; in Ohio it is reached by OH 50 (River Rd.) and is near its intersection with Anderson Ferry Rd. The ferry connects Constance in Boone County, KY and Hamilton County, OH.

MAP LOCATION: P. 197, KY, 2

CONTACT: Mr. Paul W. Anderson, 215 Boone St., Bromley, KY, 41016, (606)581-3607

STATE: Kentucky

PLACES SERVED: Green River at Rochester, connecting Butler and Ohio Counties ["The Rochester Ferry"]

BODY OF WATER: Green River

FERRY SERVICE HISTORY: There has been a ferry at this site since the early part of the century. The early history of the ferry has been researched by Myrtle Givens, whose husband, Wilma Nolan Givens, ran the ferry from 1957 to 1986. During the late eighteenth and early nineteenth centuries, the ferry was owned and operated by Bob Brown. Wallace Brown and his heirs operated the ferry from the early 1900s until 1954, when Henry C. Peay and Shelby Wester bought the ferry. In 1914, Wallace Brown had to petition the War Department Engineer's Office for permission to place a wire rope across the Green River to be used during seasons of low water. In his application, Brown said, "This ferry has been operated by means of a rope in the manner described, for the past forty years, and no damage has ever resulted from its use; in fact no craft other than a very small one could be stopped by it." He received permission to place the rope.

Brown sold the ferry to Givens in 1957. Jay Mather of the Louisville *Courier-Journal* interviewed Givens in July 1985 and asked what the strangest single item he had carried across had been. "I guess it would have to be an airplane," Givens replied. "The wings were all folded up and there wasn't any problem getting it or the flatbed truck it was on across. It was one of those spray planes." Givens admitted he had fallen

Rochester Ferry

in three times in twenty-eight years, but only once in winter. He said the job entailed "a lot of walkin' and talkin'." On a summer day, Givens would sit under a tree in the yard of his home above the bank where the ferry was docked, whittling and chatting with Rochester people; when customers came, he and his dog Blackjack would amble down to the ferry for yet another crossing. Givens and his wife sold the business in September 1986 to John and Bessie Speer and retired.

LOCAL POINTS OF INTEREST: In spring the Green River rises and falls with the rains and snow-melt, bringing driftwood and other debris downstream and sometimes making the crossing difficult. Fog and cold weather also hamper ferry operations. On a peaceful summer day, though, the river is cool and tranquil. According to Mrs. Givens, there is a two-story house at the former Lock No. 3 dam said to be haunted by the ghosts of two lock masters, Rendall Lytle and Thomas Buck. The locks are now closed.

CROSSING TIME: 6 mins.

FERRY TYPE: Vehicle

VESSEL CAPACITY: 6 full-sized cars

OPERATING SEASON: All year

SCHEDULE: On signal, 5 a.m.-8 p.m. daily except in winter; then 5 a.m.-6 p.m.

RESTRICTIONS:	Long trailers prohibited; low trailer hitches may drag if water level is too low. Load limit 22 tons.
FACILITIES:	None
FARE:	Car $1.25; trailer or pickup-camper $1.25-$2.00; RV $2-$2.50.
RESERVATIONS:	No
DIRECTIONS:	Ferry crosses the Green River at Mile 108.9, at Rochester, connecting Butler County and Ohio County. It is located on KY 369, 7 mi. south of Cool Springs.
MAP LOCATION:	P. 197, KY, 3
CONTACT:	John Speer, Rochester Ferry, Rochester, KY 42320, (502)934-3303

STATE:	Kentucky/Missouri
PLACES SERVED:	Hickman, KY—Dorena, MO
BODY OF WATER:	Mississippi River
FERRY SERVICE HISTORY:	The ferry has been owned since January 20, 1962, by Hugh Lattus of Hickman, whose uncle previously owned it; it has been in the

Lattus family over half a century. The ferry is in the southwest corner of Kentucky, just above the Tennessee border. The vessel is an eighty-foot steel-deck barge, the *Hickman,* pushed by a small towboat, the *Barbara Don* (named for the Lattuses' son and daughter.) The service is used by tourists, farmers, business people, and, frequently, by cyclists.

LOCAL POINTS OF INTEREST:	Hickman is a town of about three thousand with historic homes of the 1850s and 1860s and the oldest West Kentucky bank. It is

known for its Fourth of July celebration with a parade, the "Mississippi River Queen" beauty pageant, and its barbeque cookoff.

Dorena has a state park of about a thousand acres, with a man-made lake and picnic facilities.

CROSSING TIME:	10 mins.
FERRY TYPE:	Vehicle
VESSEL CAPACITY:	12 cars
OPERATING SEASON:	March-December
SCHEDULE:	Daily. On signal, 7 a.m.-6 p.m., weather permitting
RESTRICTIONS:	Trailers, pickup-campers, and RVs permitted. Load limit 60 tons.
FACILITIES:	None
FARE:	Car, pickup-camper $7; trailers & RVs according to size
RESERVATIONS:	No
DIRECTIONS:	Ferry is located on the Mississippi River at Mile 922.0; it runs between Hickman, in Fulton County, KY (SR 125) and New Madrid County, MO, near Dorena (SR 77).
MAP LOCATION:	P. 197, KY, 4
CONTACT:	Mr. Hugh Lattus, Hickman Ferry Co., Myron Cory Dr., Rt. 1, Hickman, KY 42050, (502)236-2013

STATE:	Kentucky
PLACES SERVED:	Mammoth Cave Ferry
BODY OF WATER:	Green River
FERRY SERVICE HISTORY:	This ferry serves the north section of the park and residents of the Forks community. It is owned and operated by the National

Park Service and is a self-propelled diesel-powered side-wheel cable ferry. Service at this site was inaugurated in 1941, but there was a

previous ferry a mile upstream dating back to the early 1900s at least. The vessel has no formal name, but is known simply as the "Mammoth Cave Ferry." It usually carries local traffic and nearby residents.

LOCAL POINTS OF INTEREST: Mammoth Cave, discovered in 1798 by a Mr. Houchins, who was chasing a bear, is the world's longest network of cavern corridors, over three hundred miles in length. It is located beneath picturesque hills and valleys. Of special note is the gypsum-clustered Snowball Room, 267 feet below, where you may dine. Several tours of varying length are offered.

CROSSING TIME: 5 mins.

FERRY TYPE: Vehicle

VESSEL CAPACITY: 3 cars

OPERATING SEASON: All year

SCHEDULE: On demand, daily 6 a.m.-10 p.m.

RESTRICTIONS: Not suitable for over 12′-wide load or trailers or large buses. Load limit 8 tons.

FACILITIES: None

FARE: Free

RESERVATIONS:	No
DIRECTIONS:	The ferry operates at Mile 197 over the Green River, 1½ miles from cave entrance.
MAP LOCATION:	P. 197, KY, 5
CONTACT:	Mammoth Cave National Park, Mammoth Cave, KY 42259, (502)758-2251

STATE:	Kentucky
PLACES SERVED:	Mammoth Cave National Park ["Houchins' Ferry"]
BODY OF WATER:	Green River

FERRY SERVICE HISTORY: Houchins' Ferry crosses the Green River at Mile 185 in Mammoth Cave National Park; it is owned and operated by the National Park Service. It is a self-propelled gasoline side-wheel cable ferry, but will soon be diesel-powered. It serves mainly northside residents and the Great Onyx Job Corps Center. Service was inaugurated in about 1906, but it became a Park Service facility in 1941. The vessel does not have a formal name, but is known as "Houchins' Ferry" after a local landowner who owned the land and established a ferry.

LOCAL POINTS OF INTEREST: The Mammoth Cave systems are the longest ever discovered; over three hundred miles have been charted on five levels. Several tours are available, including one for the physically handicapped. Near the ferry are a picnic area, campground, water, and chemical toilets.

CROSSING TIME:	5 mins.
FERRY TYPE:	Vehicle
VESSEL CAPACITY:	3 cars
OPERATING SEASON:	All year
SCHEDULE:	On demand, daily, 6 a.m.-10 p.m.

RESTRICTIONS:	Trailers, pickup-campers, and RVs permitted. Load limit 8 tons.
FACILITIES:	None
FARE:	Free
RESERVATIONS:	No
DIRECTIONS:	The ferry operates at Mile 185 over the Green River, near Brownsville, KY.
MAP LOCATION:	P. 197, KY, 6
CONTACT:	See CONTACT, p. 231.

STATE:	Kentucky
PLACES SERVED:	Monroe County, SR 214 ("The Turkey Neck Bend Ferry")
BODY OF WATER:	Cumberland River

FERRY SERVICE HISTORY: This service was inaugurated about 1948. The Kentucky Department of Highways bought it in 1968. Motorists save from twenty-five to thirty-seven miles depending on destination. In 1981, the ferry served forty-four residences, two churches, and a general store; it also served school buses and a mail carrier.

LOCAL POINTS OF INTEREST: The ferry is east of the Old Mulkey Meeting House State Shrine near Tompkinsville and west of the Lake Cumberland-Dale Hollow recreation area. Here, there are lakeside log cabins, houseboats, camping, and pontoon boats, as well as lake resorts. The Dale Hollow State Park, the closest part of the area to the ferry, is near Burkesville. Ferry devotees might make a loop from the three ferries in the northern part of the state, at Rabbit Hash, Constance, and Augusta, down to the Valley View ferry near Lexington, down to the Turkey Neck Bend ferry and up to the two at Mammoth Cave, continuing west to those at Rochester, Hickman, and Cave-in-Rock on the Illinois border.

CROSSING TIME:	5-10 mins. depending on load
FERRY TYPE:	Vehicle
VESSEL CAPACITY:	4 cars or 2 medium-size trucks; 17 passengers (+2 employees)
OPERATING SEASON:	All year
SCHEDULE:	On signal, 7 days a week, daylight hours
RESTRICTIONS:	Trailers, pickup-campers, and RVs permitted. Load limit 28 tons (2 medium trucks or 4 cars).
FACILITIES:	Small room to shelter passengers in bad weather
FARE:	Free
RESERVATIONS:	No
DIRECTIONS:	Ferry connects SR 214, southeast of Tompkinsville.
MAP LOCATION:	P. 197, KY, 7
CONTACT:	State Highway Engineer's Office, Kentucky Department of Highways, Transportation Cabinet, Frankfort, KY 40622, (502)564-3730

STATE:	Kentucky/Indiana
PLACES SERVED:	Rabbit Hash, KY—Rising Sun, IN
BODY OF WATER:	Ohio River
FERRY SERVICE HISTORY:	Ferry lovers will be heartened by the saga of the *Buckeye,* the Rabbit Hash ferry, inaugurated in 1983 by BB Riverboats at the request

of the citizens of Boone County, Kentucky, especially Rabbit Hash, and

Ohio County, Indiana, especially Rising Sun. Nancy C. Tretter, who with her husband was the moving spirit behind the enterprise, explains that she and her husband, Mayor Lowell Lee (Louie) Scott, a native of Rabbit Hash, purchased the General Store in town in 1978. The town had dwindled since the disastrous flood of 1937. He already owned the Iron Works building and the doctor's office, and later rebuilt an 1840s log cabin in which the Tretters live. The remainder of the town proper has a barn, a woodshed, a blacksmith shop, a chicken co-op, and two out-houses. The Tretters began a local craft co-op and then decided it would be nice to have a ferry so the people of Rabbit Hash could visit with the people of Rising Sun. (In fact, the entire population of Rabbit Hash could call on Rising Sun in one ferryload.) They approached Ben Bernstein, owner of BB Riverboats in Covington, managed by his son Alan; the company was already running river cruises from Covington. "A few minutes after he received the letter, Ben was on the phone with me saying he had a ferry and he would be very interested in bringing it to Rabbit Hash. I was completely unprepared for this," says Nancy Tretter; "I thought he might respond with suggestions, not an answer." Alan Bern-stein was bewildered also. "Rabbit Hash? I couldn't find Rabbit Hash," he said, at first; now, he is one of the ferry's most prominent enthusiasts. "It's crazy enough to work," he said of the idea. Nancy Tretter and her mother-in-law, Sally Scott, along with Lucille McDermott and Emily Sowle, two Rabbit Hash antique proprietors, then sounded out the people in Rising Sun, who were reluctant at first but agreed to give it a try, as their economy had declined also. The Bernsteins brought the Rabbit Transit Company to town in 1983, and it has been operating every summer since.

LOCAL POINTS OF INTEREST: Rabbit Hash is a hamlet of forty people first settled in 1789. At that time it was named Carlton, but the mail was often confused with that for nearby Carrollton. Legend has it that the present name commemorates a favorite local dish that was often served when river flooding forced rabbits from their warrens along the banks. Town life centers on the General Store, in business since 1831, where farmers talk around a wood stove in the back and visitors are invited to do the same. There are also a blacksmith shop, antique and crafts shops, a barn, the Iron Works, and a woodworking shop. It's worth a visit just to see the treasures in the antique shop and in the General Store such as pork chitterlings, Watch Dog cleanser, and Putnam Fadeless Dyes, let alone the ferry.

Rising Sun, the Indiana ferry terminus, dates from 1811 but in 1983 was suffering from a high unemployment rate. Of interest here are Greek revival homes as well as a log cabin; the grainery, restored by the Magic Crafters, who display their wares in shops here; and an active historical society.

CROSSING TIME:	10 mins.
FERRY TYPE:	Pedestrian
VESSEL CAPACITY:	40 passengers
OPERATING SEASON:	Memorial Day-Labor Day
SCHEDULE:	Weekends and holidays only, continuously, 11 a.m.-6 p.m.
RESTRICTIONS:	No
FACILITIES:	None
FARE:	$0.50
RESERVATIONS:	No
DIRECTIONS:	Rabbit Hash is reached from Covington or Lexington via I-75 and KY 18 through Burlington and Belleview; it turns into KY 338.

Take Rabbit Hash Hill Rd. right, follow it for ⁹/₁₀ of a mile; take unmarked left turn. It has been said it is "just around the bend and back a few years." Rising Sun is at the juncture of IN 56 and IN 262.

MAP LOCATION:	P. 197, KY, 8
CONTACT:	Alan Bernstein, General Manager, BB Riverboats, Box 1007, Covington, KY 41012, (606)261-8500

STATE:	Kentucky
PLACES SERVED:	Valley View—SR 169, connecting Jessamine and Madison Counties ["The Valley View Ferry"]
BODY OF WATER:	Kentucky River
FERRY SERVICE HISTORY:	The oldest ferry still operating on the state's primary system, and probably the oldest continuously operating business in

Kentucky, the Valley View Ferry operates under a ferry privilege granted by the Virginia Legislature in 1785, when Kentucky was a Virginia county: "Be it enacted by the general assembly, That public ferries shall be constantly kept at the following places . . . from the land of William Steele, in the county of Fayette, across Kentucky River, at the place called Stone Lick, to the land of John Craig, in the county of Lincoln." The ferry had various owners until 1950, when it was purchased by Claude C. Howard, who is currently President of the Valley View Ferry Company, Inc.

LOCAL POINTS OF INTEREST:	The Valley View trail, on the Kentucky River at Valley View, offers miles of hiking along the scenic river cliffs.
CROSSING TIME:	3 mins.
FERRY TYPE:	Vehicle
VESSEL CAPACITY:	3 cars
OPERATING SEASON:	All year
SCHEDULE:	On signal, daily, except Christmas and during high water, sunrise to sunset
RESTRICTIONS:	Trailers, pickup-campers, and RVs permitted. Load limit 16 tons. Overhead clearance 11 ft.
FACILITIES:	None
FARE:	Car or pickup-camper $1.50; trailer or RV under 25 ft. $1.50-$4.00
RESERVATIONS:	No
DIRECTIONS:	Ferry crosses the Kentucky River at Mile 157.8; it is on KY 169, at Tates Creek Pike. The ferry is not far from I-75, south of Lexington.
MAP LOCATION:	P. 197, KY, 9
CONTACT:	Mr. Claude C. Howard, President, Valley View Ferry Co., Inc., Route 4, Richmond, KY 40475, (606)623-2648

STATE:	Louisiana
PLACES SERVED:	Angola
BODY OF WATER:	Mississippi River
FERRY SERVICE HISTORY:	The ferry on this run is the *Iberville*, 104 feet by forty-eight feet. She carries a boatmaster, engineer, and two deckhands. All of the riders are employees of the State Penitentiary at Angola.
LOCAL POINTS OF INTEREST:	The state prison is located at Angola, and only state employees are authorized to ride this ferry.
CROSSING TIME:	15-30 mins., depending on river conditions
FERRY TYPE:	Vehicle
VESSEL CAPACITY:	18 cars
OPERATING SEASON:	All year
SCHEDULE:	Daily, split shift, 3:30 a.m.-11:30 a.m.; 2:30 p.m.-10:30 p.m.; on call 24 hrs. per day. Lv. west bank on hr. and half-hr.; lv. east bank on quarter hour.
RESTRICTIONS:	Load limit 10 tons. Trailers, pickup-campers, and RVs permitted.
FACILITIES:	None
FARE:	Free
RESERVATIONS:	No
MAP LOCATION:	P. 197, LA, 1
CONTACT:	Mississippi River Bridge Authority, Box 6297, New Orleans, LA 70174, (504)361-6555

STATE: Louisiana

PLACES SERVED: Belle Chasse—Scarsdale (Braithwaite)

BODY OF WATER: Mississippi River

FERRY SERVICE HISTORY: This ferry is administered by the Plaquemines Parish Commission Council, which also administers the crossing at Pointe-a-la-Hache. The Belle Chasse crossing has existed at least since the late 1950s, and probably long before. The 1941 Louisiana WPA *Guide* mentions the *Seatrain*, an ocean-going car train (railroad car) operated by the Missouri-Pacific and Texas & Pacific Railroads; the loaded freight cars were lifted by crane and placed on the tracks of the ship. There are two vessels now in service, the *Louisiana* and the *Belle Chasse*.

LOCAL POINTS OF INTEREST: Belle Chasse is French for "fine hunting," one explanation of the name. It is thought that the town may also have been named for J. D. deGoutin Bellechasse, who owned a great deal of property in New Orleans. Bellechasse commanded the troops at the transfer of Louisiana from Spain to France and from France to the United States in 1803. Not far from Belle Chasse is the Jean Lafitte National Historical Park. There is a museum at Fort Jackson, and, leaving from Venice, down past Pointe-a-la-Hache at the end of SR 23, there are deep delta riverboat trips leaving twice a month to view wildlife.

CROSSING TIME: 10 mins.

FERRY TYPE: Vehicle

VESSEL CAPACITY: 36-38 cars

OPERATING SEASON: All year

SCHEDULE: **Daily, 5:30 a.m.-11:30 p.m. Lv. Belle Chasse** 5:30-8:15 a.m. and 2:45-6:15 p.m. every 15 mins.; 8:15 a.m.-2:45 p.m. and 6:15-11:30 p.m. on the hr. and half-hr. **Lv. Scarsdale** 5:30-8:15 a.m. and 2:45-6:15 p.m. every 15 mins.; 8:15 a.m.-2:45 p.m. and 6:15-11:30 p.m. on the 1/4 hr. and 3/4 hr.

RESTRICTIONS:	Trailers, pickup-campers, and RVs permitted. Overhead clearance 15 ft. Maximum combined vehicle length 60 ft. Load limit 9 tons per axle.
FACILITIES:	None
FARE:	Free
RESERVATIONS:	No
DIRECTIONS:	The ferry connects SR 23 at Belle Chasse and SR 39 at Scarsdale.
MAP LOCATION:	P. 197, LA, 2
CONTACT:	Plaquemines Parish Commission Council, 106 Ave. G, Belle Chasse, LA 70037, (504)392-6690

STATE:	Louisiana
PLACES SERVED:	Cameron—Cameron Ship Channel
BODY OF WATER:	Calcasieu River
FERRY SERVICE HISTORY:	The vessel on this service is the *Cameron II* (204 feet by fifty feet). It is a double-ended barge with a captain, an engineer, and two

deckhands. Many of the riders are tourists going along SR 82 to and from Texas.

LOCAL POINTS OF INTEREST:	Cameron Parish was created in 1870 from portions of Calcasieu and Vermilion parishes; with over 900,000 acres, it has the

largest land area in the state. It is a mecca for birds, and regular bird-watchers' conventions are held here. Over one-quarter of the area is devoted to wildlife and game reserves. There are about seventy miles of beaches along the Gulf of Mexico, and Cameron is one of the hubs of saltwater fishing activity in southwest Louisiana, with charter yachts available for deep-sea trips and smaller day boats for rental. Outboard launching facilities are available near the ferry landing on the west side of the ship channel. The Southwest Louisiana Deep Sea and Inland Fishing Rodeo, held on the weekend closest to July 4, attracts hundreds of people, and the Louisiana Fur and Wildlife Festival attracts crowds in January. The Creole Nature Trail, off SR 82, routes visitors along SR 27 north, through Creole, to Chenier Perdu and Little Chenier, where you may view the massive, twisted moss-covered Chenier Oaks.

CROSSING TIME: 5 mins.

FERRY TYPE: Vehicle

VESSEL CAPACITY: 50 cars

OPERATING SEASON: ..ll year

SCHEDULE: Daily, 24 hrs., continuous as needed

RESTRICTIONS: Explosive cargo restricted. Trailers, pickup-campers, and RVs permitted. Load limit 10 tons.

FACILITIES: None

FARE: Free

RESERVATIONS: No

DIRECTIONS: Ferry is located 10 miles east of Holly Beach on SR 27 and 82.

MAP LOCATION: P. 197, LA, 3

CONTACT: See CONTACT, p. 237.

STATE: Louisiana

PLACES SERVED: Cameron—Monkey Island

BODY OF WATER: Calcasieu River

FERRY SERVICE HISTORY: The vessel on this service is the *George Bailey*, a barge with side-mounted tug (barge is sixty feet by thirty-two feet ; tug is forty-five feet by twelve feet, five inches). The boat is operated by a captain and one deckhand.

LOCAL POINTS
OF INTEREST: [For notes on Cameron, please see entry under Cameron—Cameron Ship Channel, p. 239.]

Monkey Island is a small island, about three miles square, where a US Coast Guard station once existed. The island is swampy, with a ridge along which about thirteen families live. There is a shrimp plant, but there are no restaurants or motels. This ferry runs all night; Mrs. Dorothy Gibson, a native of Monkey Island, says that most riders in the middle of the night are workers going home or local residents coming back from restaurants, football games, or other leisure activities.

CROSSING TIME: 3 mins.

FERRY TYPE: Vehicle

VESSEL CAPACITY: 6 cars

OPERATING SEASON: All year

SCHEDULE: Daily, 24 hrs., continuous as needed

RESTRICTIONS: Trailers, pickup-campers, and RVs permitted. Load limit 10 tons.

FACILITIES: None

FARE: Free

RESERVATIONS: No

DIRECTIONS: Ferry is on SR 1141.

MAP LOCATION: P. 197, LA, 4

CONTACT: See CONTACT, p. 237.

STATE:	Louisiana
PLACES SERVED:	Edgard—Reserve
BODY OF WATER:	Mississippi River

FERRY SERVICE HISTORY: The vessel on this run is the *Ascension* (150 feet by sixty feet); she has a Captain, an engineer, and two deckhands. Edgard was once known on Caire's Landing, and the old store owned by E. J. Caire was a landmark for steamboats.

LOCAL POINTS OF INTEREST: Edgard is the seat of St. John the Baptist Parish. The ferry is a few miles from the Lake des Allemands, where swamp tours are offered. It is also not far from Lafitte's Landing Restaurant (off River Road, SR 18, at the foot of Sunshine Bridge — LA 3089 Service Road). This huge raised cottage, built in 1797, was frequented by the pirate Jean Lafitte.

CROSSING TIME:	10 mins.
FERRY TYPE:	Vehicle
VESSEL CAPACITY:	40 cars
OPERATING SEASON:	All year
SCHEDULE:	Daily, 5 a.m.-9:45 p.m.
RESTRICTIONS:	Trailers, pickup-campers, and RVs permitted. Load limit 10 tons.
FACILITIES:	None
FARE:	Free
RESERVATIONS:	No
DIRECTIONS:	The ferry connects SR 44, along the river below Reserve, and SR 18 at Edgard.
MAP LOCATION:	P. 197, LA, 5
CONTACT:	See CONTACT, p. 237.

STATE: Louisiana

PLACES SERVED: Lutcher—Vacherie

BODY OF WATER: Mississippi River

FERRY SERVICE   This ferry is administered by the St. James
HISTORY: Parish Council. The vessel is the *Saint
                        James*, in service since 1957. From time to
time the ferry has been plagued by the problem of large barges and tugs
anchored too close during the Mississippi's seasonal rise, but, on its
twentieth anniversary, the local newspaper reported that it had "served
the citizens of this parish well throughout the years." The crossing had
been established long before the St. James Parish Council took over
operation; the 1941 WPA *Guide* to Louisiana mentions the ferry crossing
between Lutcher and Vacherie. At that time the toll was thirty cents for a
five-passenger car.

LOCAL POINTS   Vacherie, in French, means "a place where
OF INTEREST: cows are kept." It is a pleasant town on
                        scenic SR 18 on the south bank of the Mis-
sissippi River. Swamp tours of the Lake des Allemands, nearby, are
offered.
    Also close by is Oak Alley Plantation (on SR 18), built between 1837
and 1839 by Jacques Telesphore Roman, a French sugar planter. The
Greek Revival mansion is painted a delicate pink, with a quarter-mile
alley of sheltering live oaks over 250 years old, sugar cane fields, and an
impressive colonnade with twenty-eight Doric columns. It could serve as
a setting for a story by Kate Chopin, the turn-of-the-century writer who
is known for her portrayal of Creole life in Louisiana. The new governor's
mansion in Baton Rouge was modeled after Oak Alley.

CROSSING TIME: 15 mins.

FERRY TYPE: Vehicle

VESSEL CAPACITY: 32 cars

OPERATING SEASON: All year

SCHEDULE: Daily. **Lv. Vacherie** every half-hr. 5:30 a.m.-10 p.m.; then 10:45, 11:15, 11:45, 12:30 a.m. **Lv. Lutcher** every half-hr. 5:45 a.m.-10:15 p.m.; then 11 p.m., 11:30, midnight, 12:30 a.m.

RESTRICTIONS: Trailers, pickup-campers, and RVs permitted. Load limit 20 tons. Explosive or flammable bottled gas not permitted.

FACILITIES: None

FARE: Free

RESERVATIONS: No

DIRECTIONS: The ferry is about ¼-mi. downstream from Vacherie. It connects SR 18 on the Vacherie side with SR 44 on the Lutcher side.

MAP LOCATION: P. 197, LA, 6

CONTACT: St. James Parish Council, Convent Courthouse, Convent, LA 70723, (504)562-2260

STATE: Louisiana

PLACES SERVED: New Orleans (Canal St.)—Algiers

BODY OF WATER: Mississippi River

FERRY SERVICE HISTORY: The ferries *Stumpf* (two hundred feet by seventy-three feet) and *Col. Frank X. Armiger* (ninety-five feet by thirty-two feet) are on this run. This crossing goes back many years; one elderly New Orleans taxi driver confessed that in the 1920s he used to "shoot hooky on ferry boats; my mama never knew where I was." (At that time, there was a daytime curfew for school children.) The ferry leaves from the foot of Canal Street and affords a good view of the busy river, where as many as eleven thousand steamboats once ran. They had decorated wedding cakes, bars, barber shops, their own newspaper, and dining rooms. They rivalled hotels on land. The *Creole Queen*, which offers excursions from Riverwalk, near the Canal Street terminal, is modeled after the old pad-

dlewheels. The *Natchez* is a steam sternwheeler offering cruises also; it leaves from the Jax Brewery. The Canal Street ferries once advertised that one could ride all day for a nickel. One of the earliest was the *Louisa*, which ran between 1867 and 1879. Edwin L. Jewell reported in his 1873 *Cresent City Illustrated* that the *Louisa* carried twenty-five carriages or vehicles, with ample accommodations for passengers: "The cabins and decks of the boats and the ferry passages and platforms are kept in scrupulous order and the officers are noted for urbanity." The tug pro-peller *Little Jerry* served foot passengers at night. The atmosphere was evidently extremely convivial: "In warm summer, by invitation of the liberal proprietors, the boats are thronged with citizens who remain on board for several hours enjoying the breezes of the river, making several trips for a single fare." The ferry was owned by the firm of John Kouns & Company. Another interesting ship was the Texas and Pacific Railroad transfer boat, the *Gouldsboro*, originally built in 1863 as the *Chickasaw*; she began service in 1881 and ran until the Huey P. Long Bridge was built. It is said that, about 1870, teams of Spanish mules were used to haul freight cars off the ferry transfer boats. During the 1930s, six ferries crossed the Mississippi from New Orleans. Today, the Canal Street ferry is used mainly by residents who work in New Orleans and live in Algiers (or vice versa) and who want to avoid the heavy bridge congestion, by tourists, and sometimes by film crews making television commercials and movies.

LOCAL POINTS OF INTEREST: New Orleans is a city of intense personality, where the air of Mardi Gras hovers all year in the masks hanging in shop windows and there is a *joie de vivre* mixed with sophistication. Founded as a European outpost, rather than a frontier town, it is in some ways more Gallic than France; many of the women have flashing black eyes and dark hair, dress in bright silks, and talk animatedly. The aristocratic French and Spanish settlers called themselves Creole, but the term has now been extended to include the French-speaking population. Food is paramount, and the top restaurants do not, as in some places, cater principally to tourists but have a dedicated local following. Some establishments, such as K-Paul's and Galatoire's, take no reservations. The daily lunch line at Galatoire's is a special New Orleans experience; paper towels are wedged behind a pipe against the wall to help those afflicted with the humidity, whose enthusiasm holds up better than their shirt collars as they compare notes: "Did you come last week?" "No, but twice the week before." "It's worth the wait," uncertain visitors are told, and certainly it is. (Here, as in several of the famous restaurants, the decor is surprisingly plain, with tile floors, ceiling fans, and coathooks lining the walls.) The French Quarter, while shabby in parts, still invites exploration at leisure, with street musicians and trolley tours. Jackson Square and St. Louis Cathedral (1724) are a must for visitors. The Cafe du Monde, just off the Square, in the old French Market, is open twenty-four hours a day; it has irresistible beignets (a form of doughnuts without holes, which are good at any hour, and, with a glass of milk, make a fine lunch if you are dining more lavishly). Here, you will see a cross section of New Orleans, from tourists to revelers in black tie to truck drivers. The Roman Candy Man still makes his way through the streets with a white cart pulled by a mule (as he has since 1915). Not far from Jackson Square is the Beauregard-Keys house, where Frances Parkinson Keyes lived and wrote many of her novels, including *Dinner at Antoine's*. (The novel also begins with a line, at Antoine's.) Other good restaurants are Brennan's, which has a very pleasant ambiance, and the Commander's Palace. A pleasant hotel, just across Canal Street from the French Quarter and insulated from its merrymaking, is the Meridien, owned by a French chain; it has a European decor with vaulted marble arches and does not cater to huge conventions.

The streetcar system was founded in 1835; Tennessee Williams's streetcar named Desire ran along Desire Street. One of the Desire Street cars is now on display at the Louisiana State Museum in the French Quarter. The St. Charles streetcar is a tourist bargain; it runs through the Garden District, rolling beneath huge arching oaks on St. Charles Avenue. Riverwalk, opened in 1986, is a waterfront development built around and beneath the New Orleans Hilton Riverside and Towers, with a landscaped promenade, speciality shops, produce markets, and cafes. Canal Place is also of interest, with fashionable shops and an interesting bookstore-coffeehouse, Upstart Crow and Company.

Algiers is a historic community, but seems more like a bayou or upriver town; it is less interesting for walking. It was part of the Crown property granted in 1717 to the Company of the West and was called King's Plantation. One explanation of the name is that it enjoys the same relation to New Orleans as Algiers to France; another is the association with piracy, as the pirate Jean Lafitte made use of the Verret Canal enroute to Barataria. There are two well-known restaurants, Hilary's Landing and the Algiers Landing; both are near the ferry.

CROSSING TIME:	15 mins.
FERRY TYPE:	Vehicle
VESSEL CAPACITY:	*Stumpf:* 60 cars, 1000 pedestrians; *Col. Frank X. Armiger:* 400 pedestrians
OPERATING SEASON:	All year
SCHEDULE:	Daily, 5:45 a.m.-9:30 p.m.; lv. west bank on $1/4$ hr. and $3/4$ hr.; lv. east bank on the hr. and half-hour.
RESTRICTIONS:	Trailers, pickup-campers, and RVs permitted. Load limit 10 tons. Overhead clearance 12 ft.
FACILITIES:	None
FARE:	Cars $1 (round-trip); pedestrians $0.25.
RESERVATIONS:	No
DIRECTIONS:	Ferry landing is at the foot of Canal St., next to Riverwalk.
MAP LOCATION:	P. 197, LA, 7
CONTACT:	See CONTACT, p. 237.

STATE:	Louisiana
PLACES SERVED:	New Orleans (Donald Street, Algiers)— Chalmette (Paris Road)
BODY OF WATER:	Mississippi River

FERRY SERVICE HISTORY:	The vessel in use most of the time is the *Neville Levy*.
LOCAL POINTS OF INTEREST:	[For notes on Algiers, please see entry under New Orleans (Canal St.)—Algiers, p. 246.]

Chalmette is a settlement along the river from New Orleans; it is a deep-water shipping terminal (unfortunately, several fine old homes were demolished to build the slip). It was at Chalmette Plantation in 1815 that General Andrew Jackson scored a stunning victory over crack British troops, the last battle of the last war fought between England and the US. The victory preserved America's claim to the Louisiana Purchase and prompted a wave of migration and settlement along the Mississippi River. The site is now under National Park Service management, with a visitor center in the Beauregard House (a fine example of French-Louisiana architecture), the imposing Chalmette Monument, and the Chalmette National Cemetery. The *Creole Queen* boat cruise from Riverwalk stops here, if the ferry schedule is not convenient.

CROSSING TIME:	15 mins.
FERRY TYPE:	Vehicle
VESSEL CAPACITY:	60 cars; 1,000 pedestrians
OPERATING SEASON:	All year
SCHEDULE:	Daily, 5:45 a.m.-9:30 p.m.
RESTRICTIONS:	Trailers, pickup-campers, and RVs permitted. Load limit 10 tons. Overhead clearance 12 ft.
FACILITIES:	None
FARE:	Cars $1 (round-trip); pedestrians $0.25
RESERVATIONS:	No
DIRECTIONS:	The ferry leaves from the Donald St. landing in Lower Algiers (west bank) and goes to the Chalmette landing, Paris Road, on the east bank of the Mississippi.
MAP LOCATION:	P. 197, LA, 8
CONTACT:	See CONTACT, p. 237.

STATE: Louisiana

PLACES SERVED: New Orleans (Jackson Avenue)—Gretna

BODY OF WATER: Mississippi River

FERRY SERVICE   The ferry on this run is the *Westside* (149 feet
HISTORY: by sixty-six feet). She carries a boatmaster,
an engineer, an oiler, and two deckhands.
Ferry riders are usually local people going to and from work. The 1941
WPA *Guide* to Louisiana mentions the New Orleans ferry; at that time
pedestrians paid five cents, two-passenger cars thirteen cents, and five-
passenger cars twenty-five cents; there was twenty-four-hour service.

LOCAL POINTS   [For notes on New Orleans, please see entry
OF INTEREST: under New Orleans (Canal St.)—Algiers,
p. 245.]
  Gretna sprawls on the shore across from New Orleans, with industrial
plants and dockside-shipping terminals dominating the scene. The town
was founded in the early nineteenth century by Nicholas Noel Destrehan,
who granted villagers perpetual rights to the riverfront. Since 1884,
Gretna has been the seat of government of Jefferson Parish. Of interest
here is the Memorial Arch at the foot of Huey P. Long Boulevard,
dedicated in 1923 to the "Jefferson Parish dead of all wars." An avenue
of palms leads from the arch to the courthouse.

CROSSING TIME: 15 mins.

FERRY TYPE: Vehicle

VESSEL CAPACITY: 35 cars; 800 pedestrians

OPERATING SEASON: All year

SCHEDULE: Daily, 5:30 a.m.-9:30 p.m. Lv. west bank on
hr. and half-hr.; lv. east bank on $^1/_4$ hr. and $^3/_4$
hr.

RESTRICTIONS: Trailers, pickup-campers, and RVs permitted. Load limit 10 tons. Overhead clearance
12 ft.

FACILITIES: None

FARE:	Cars $1 (round-trip); pedestrians $0.25
RESERVATIONS:	No
DIRECTIONS:	The ferry crosses from Gretna on the west bank to Jackson Ave. in New Orleans.
MAP LOCATION:	P. 197, LA, 9
CONTACT:	See CONTACT, p. 237.

STATE:	Louisiana
PLACES SERVED:	Plaquemine—Plaquemine Point
BODY OF WATER:	Mississippi River

FERRY SERVICE HISTORY: The vessel on this run is the *Acadia* (150 feet by sixty feet). The crew consists of a captain, an engineer, and two deckhands. Most riders are local residents. In 1941, the Plaquemine ferry, according to the Louisiana WPA *Guide*, operated on call; a five-passenger car was fifty cents.

LOCAL POINTS OF INTEREST: Plaquemine (plak-meń) is named for the bayou nearby, which in turn was named for the bread (pliakmine) that local Indians made from the fruit of the persimmon trees. The Plaquemine Locks State Commemorative Area, overlooking the Mississippi River in downtown Plaquemine, is a five-acre site overlooking the original 1909 locks that once provided the only link to waterways west of the Mississippi River. There are a pavilion and a viewing tower. The diminutive Chapel of the Madonna, between Point Pleasant and Bayou Goula on SR 168, is six feet by eight feet with five chairs and an altar; it has been called the smallest church in the world.

CROSSING TIME:	10 mins.
FERRY TYPE:	Vehicle
VESSEL CAPACITY:	35 cars

OPERATING SEASON: All year

SCHEDULE: Daily, 5 a.m.-9:45 p.m. Lv. west bank on hr. and half-hr.; lv. east bank on ¹/₄ hr. and ³/₄ hr.

RESTRICTIONS: Trailers, pickup-campers, and RVs permitted. Overhead clearance 12 ft. 6 in. Load limit 10 tons.

FACILITIES: None

FARE: Free

RESERVATIONS: No

DIRECTIONS: Ferry is on Rt. 75.

MAP LOCATION: P. 197, LA, 10

CONTACT: See CONTACT, p. 237.

STATE: Louisiana

PLACES SERVED: Pointe-a-la-Hache—West Pointe-a-la-Hache

BODY OF WATER: Mississippi River

FERRY SERVICE HISTORY: This ferry is administered by the Plaquemines Parish Commission Council. The boat is the 150-foot *Pointe-a-la-Hache*. The 1941 WPA *Guide* to Louisiana mentions the Pointe-a-la-Hache ferry, which was twenty-five cents for a car and two passengers; additional passengers were five cents each.

LOCAL POINTS OF INTEREST: The ferry is located near a wildlife management area. It is the southernmost settlement of any size on the Mississippi River. The botanist-priest, Father A. B. Langlois, who collected more than five thousand rare plants and new species of Louisiana, lived here from 1857-1887; in 1892 his catalogue of twelve hundred varieties of fungi of the region was issued. Today, the area is peopled by fishermen and hunters; it has been called a "sportsman's paradise." There is excellent fishing and crabbing in the bayous. Fort Jackson, on the west bank of the Mississippi near the town of Buras, was begun in 1822 to protect the approach to New Orleans by river. It was named for General Andrew Jackson. In 1862, Confederate forces at Fort Jackson endeavored to block Admiral Farragut's Union fleet from entering the channel; the battle lasted more than a week, but ultimately the fleet reached and captured New Orleans. There is a museum here. Bayou boat tours leave from Venice twice a month. Sig's at Port Sulphur is a good restaurant.

CROSSING TIME: 5 mins.

FERRY TYPE: Vehicle

VESSEL CAPACITY: 35 cars

OPERATING SEASON: All year

SCHEDULE: **Daily. Lv. Pointe-a-la-Hache** every half-hr. 8 a.m.-5 p.m.; hourly 6 a.m.-8 a.m. and 5 p.m.-11 p.m. **Lv. West Pointe-a-la-Hache** every half-hr. 8:15 a.m. to 5:10 p.m.; hourly, 6:30, 7:30 a.m. and 5:30 p.m.-11:30 p.m.

RESTRICTIONS: Trailers, pickup-campers, and RVs permitted. Load limit 9 tons per axle. Maximum combined vehicle length 55 ft.

FACILITIES: None

FARE: Free

RESERVATIONS: No

DIRECTIONS: Ferry connects SR 39 on the east bank and SR 23 on the west bank.

MAP LOCATION: P. 197, LA, 11

CONTACT: Plaquemine Parish Commission Council, 106 Ave. G, Belle Chasse, LA 70037, (504)392-6690

New Roads

STATE: Louisiana

PLACES SERVED: St. Francisville—New Roads

BODY OF WATER: Mississippi River

FERRY SERVICE HISTORY: The vessel on this run is the *New Roads* (150 feet by sixty feet). She carries a captain, an engineer, and two deckhands. Service at this crossing goes back well into the early nineteenth century. In 1832, Stephen Vanwickle of Pointe Coupee was granted a ten-year ferry privilege between Bayou Sarah landing and a point "opposite to the courthouse in the parish of Pointe Coupee." Vanwickle was to provide a steam or horsepower ferry able to transport two four-wheel carriages and six horses, with a cabin for twelve passengers. The St. Francisville Ferry is also listed in the 1941 WPA *Guide* to Louisiana; a car and driver cost fifty cents, with additional passengers five cents. There was twenty-four-hour service.

LOCAL POINTS OF INTEREST: St. Francisville was founded near the site of a 1785 Capuchine monastery built on land granted by the King of Spain and later destroyed by fire. The town was in territory retained by Spain after the 1803 Louisiana Purchase. For seven years the United States debated whether the purchase included this section; the planters did not want Spanish rule. In 1810 they set up their own government, and St. Francisville became the capital of the Free and Independent Republic of West Florida. After 74 days, the US Army declared West Florida a part of the

Louisiana Purchase. Built on a narrow ridge above Mississippi floodwaters, the town has been called "two miles wide and two yards long."

The town has such interesting buildings as the 1819 Town Hall, built as an open-air market, Propinquity, reflecting the Spanish colonial days, and Barrow House, an 1811 saltbox. St. Francisville is a good base for touring some of the notable plantations in the area. The artist and naturalist James Audubon visited Oakley Plantation (built in 1799) in 1821 and produced thirty-two bird paintings here (over eighty of the *Birds of America* series were painted while he lived in West Feliciana Parish.) He recorded his impressions of the estate in his journal: "The rich magnolias covered with fragrant blossoms, the holly, the beech, the tall yellow poplar, the hilly ground and even the red clay, all excited my admiration. Such an entire change in the fall of nature in so short a time seems almost supernatural, and surrounded once more by numberless warblers and thrushes, I enjoyed the scene."

In March, during the West Feliciana Historical Society's annual Audubon Pilgrimage, many private homes are open to the public. Rosedown, built in 1835, has French Renaissance-style gardens and furniture made by Prudent Mallard of New Orleans. Greenwood, though the original mansion burned, has been restored to its original Greek revival state; it is a twelve thousand-acre working plantation.

CROSSING TIME:	15 mins.
FERRY TYPE:	Vehicle
VESSEL CAPACITY:	35 cars
OPERATING SEASON:	All year
SCHEDULE:	**Daily. 4 a.m.-midnight:** Lv. west bank on ¼ hr. and ¾ hr. Lv. east bank on hr. and half-hr. **Midnight—4 a.m.:** Lv. west bank on half-hr.; lv. east bank on hr.
RESTRICTIONS:	Trailers, pickup-campers, and RVs permitted. Overhead clearance 13 ft. 6 in. Load limit 10 tons.
FACILITIES:	None
FARE:	Free
RESERVATIONS:	No

DIRECTIONS:	Ferry connects SR 10; from St. Francisville, go west on Ferdinand St., which becomes SR 10.

MAP LOCATION: P. 197, LA, 12

CONTACT: See CONTACT, p. 237.

STATE: Louisiana

PLACES SERVED: Vinton—Gum Cove Road off SR 108 ("Gum Cove Ferry")

BODY OF WATER: Intracoastal Waterway

FERRY SERVICE HISTORY: The Gum Cove ferry, sometimes called the "Gum Cove Navy," has been operating since 1902. It is used mainly by hunters to reach the wild game of the area's marshes and woodlands and by residents on the south side of the Intracoastal Waterway. The Shell and Amoco oil companies also use the ferry to move their oil-rig equipment in and out of the area. L. Breman Baker, an area historian, has researched the history of the ferry and found that the first ferry was built about 1920, made of wood, thirty feet long and twelve feet wide, to carry sacks of rough rice from the bayou across the Intracoastal Canal to the rice mills of Vinton and Edgerly. The original ferry was built at a small local shipyard, according to Dorothy Carnahan, whose husband, J. B., operated it for many years. Baker says groups of ten or more little boys, taking the ferry to school during the 1920s, would run from side to side, until the ferry rocked and tilted. When the operator became angry, they would dive overboard and swim to shore, with time to dry off before school. A larger ferry was then built to carry a loaded wagon, a team, and a light buggy at the same time; this one was poled. A later one was pulled by the passengers and operator, who had to grasp the tout rope and walk with it, pulling at the same time. In 1925, a small gasoline-powered boat was put in service; this ran until the late 1930s, when the canal was re-dug and widened from Brownsville, Texas, to Florida and up the East Coast. Today, the ferry crosses a three hundred-foot canal; it is eighty feet long and forty feet wide, powered by a 371-horsepower Detroit engine; she can carry a huge rice combine and a heavy oil-loaded eighteen-wheeler. The ferry is under the jurisdiction of Calcasieu Parish; the present operator is Fred Grisby. Birdwatchers also use the ferry, according to deckhand

David Simoneaux of Sulphur, to observe the Black Francolin (introduced from Pakistan), the Crested Caracara, and other rare birds. There was a very old ferry crossing near here, used long before the twentieth century, as the Old Spanish Trail crossed the Sabine River by ferry near what is now Orange, Texas. This was the only trail between Texas and New Orleans; huge herds of cattle were taken along it to market hundreds of miles away.

LOCAL POINTS OF INTEREST: Vinton was founded about 1888 by settlers from Iowa, who named it for Vinton, Iowa. The discovery of oil here in 1911 has been largely responsible for the growth of the town. From Vinton, you can follow the West Calcasieu Old Spanish Trail which has scenic stops such as Niblett's Bluff and the Archway of the Oaks. The I-10 Eastbound Information Center is an excellent place to stop for material about the area, as they have as part of the Rest Area a Nature Walk across the swamp with look-out points for Lake Bienvienu. The Sabine National Wildlife Refuge is south of the ferry. Sulphur, nearby, has the famed Paragon Drug Store (1891).

CROSSING TIME: 10 mins.

FERRY TYPE: Vehicle

VESSEL CAPACITY: 9 cars

OPERATING SEASON: All year

SCHEDULE: Daily, on signal, 6 a.m.-10 p.m.

RESTRICTIONS: Trailers, pickup-campers, and RVs permitted. Load limit 80 tons.

FACILITIES: None

FARE: Free

RESERVATIONS: No

DIRECTIONS: From I-10 at Sulphur, head south on SR 27. At SR 108 (west), turn right for 9 miles to the Gum Cove Rd. Turn south; the ferry leads to a dead-end road traversing an agricultural area.

MAP LOCATION: P. 197, LA, 13

CONTACT: Overall management: Police Jury of Calcasieu Parish, Box 1583, Lake Charles, LA
70602, (318)437-3500. Operator: Fred
Grisby, (318)583-2554.

STATE: Louisiana

PLACES SERVED: White Castle—Carville

BODY OF WATER: Mississippi River

FERRY SERVICE   The vessel on this service is the *Feliciana*
HISTORY: (97.3 feet by thirty-six feet). Ferry service
was first proposed in 1951 at a meeting of the
Town Council in White Castle, since at that time there was no vehicular
ferry crossing the Mississippi between Donaldson and Baton Rouge. It
was stated at the meeting that many residents on the east side of the River
at Carville would use the ferry and that from twelve to twenty residents of
White Castle were employed at the Leprosarium at Carville and would
make at least one daily round trip on the ferry. By 1954, the ferry was in
place; it was owned by a Mr. Hernandez. It later came under state
management, but was threatened with extinction in 1985. A concerted
appeal was launched by county officials, Dr. John R. Trautman, Director
of the National Hansen's Disease Center, and others. There were, in 1985,
sixteen Center employees using the ferry, as well as staff from the Hunt
Correctional Institute. Dr. Trautman pointed out that, in case of a chemical spill at one of the chemical plants in the area (including Goodyear,
Shell, Ciba Geigy, and others), the ferry offered the only resource for an
emergency evacuation of the Center. At peak work hours, he observed,
the ferry was filled to capacity. The state agreed to continue the ferry for
the present.

LOCAL POINTS   White Castle was named for a gabled nine-
OF INTEREST: teenth-century mansion with columns and
galleries, approached by a quarter-mile drive
with weeping willows; Gov. Paul O. Hebert once resided here. Unfortunately, the manor house fell victim to erosion; it was moved four times to
escape the advancing river and ultimately was destroyed. Visitors will
find Nottoway Plantation here well worth seeing. With sixty-four rooms,
it was once the largest house in Louisiana; it represents a blend of the
Greek Revival and Italianate styles. Accommodations are available here
(ten bedrooms, with champagne and a guided tour).

Carville is best known as the location of the National Hansen's Disease Center, the only facility in the country for the research and treatment of Hansen's disease; it was once known as the Louisiana State Leprosarium. The administration building is housed in the ante-bellum manor house of the Indian Camp Plantation. An average of 350 patients are hospitalized here at any given time. The professional staff includes members of the Daughters of Charity, St. Vincent de Paul, and officers of the US Public Health Service. Tours are given (visitors under sixteen not admitted). The book *Miracle at Carville*, by Betty Martin (1950), was written about the facility.

CROSSING TIME:	8 mins.
FERRY TYPE:	Vehicle
VESSEL CAPACITY:	18 cars
OPERATING SEASON:	All year
SCHEDULE:	Daily service, 5 a.m.-7:45 a.m. and 4 p.m.-8:45 p.m. Lv. west bank on the hr. and half-hr.; lv. east bank on 1/4 hr. and 3/4 hr.
RESTRICTIONS:	Trailers, pickup-campers, and RVs permitted. Load limit 10 tons.
FACILITIES:	None
FARE:	Free
RESERVATIONS:	No
DIRECTIONS:	The ferry is on SR 3075.
MAP LOCATION:	P. 197, LA, 14
CONTACT:	See CONTACT, p. 237.

Kings Point Ferry

STATE: Mississippi

PLACES SERVED: Kings Point (near Vicksburg)

BODY OF WATER: Yazoo Diversion Canal

FERRY SERVICE   The Yazoo Diversion Canal was cut, accord-
HISTORY: ing to Ed Blake, writing in the *Vicksburg
                              Evening Post* (5/14/86), about 1900 to restore
water traffic in and out of the port of Vicksburg, which had been cut off
from the Mississippi River. The canal, however, isolated the area known
by some people as King's Point Island (it is also called Belle Isle). Four-
wheeled drive vehicles are all but mandatory for going on the narrow dirt
and gravel road. The ferry making the two hundred-yard crossing is a
ninety-six-foot by twenty-three-and-a-half-foot steel barge pushed by a
side-hitched nineteen-foot Morrison Fiberglass boat driven by a seventy
horsepower outboard motor. The ferry has been in service for approximately thirty years. It is owned by the County, but is contracted out each
year. It is operated by young Wesley Vickers, a third-generation ferry
operator, whose father, Jim Vickers, a deep-sea diver who does professional underwater salvage and repair jobs, has turned it over to him. The
canal is forty to forty-five feet deep at midstream. Sometimes Vickers
makes as many as two hundred trips a day in winter (in summer, he
usually makes twenty or thirty crossings).

LOCAL POINTS OF INTEREST: The area is thickly forested, the deep, dark, dense woodland set amid productive farms.

Typical ferry patrons are fishermen, hunters, farmers, and local citizens, usually in four-wheel drive vehicles. In winter, during deer season, the ferry is busy with hunters going to deer camps. As Ed Blake puts it, "You have the feeling that deer are everywhere—just out of sight . . . deer stands rise in the middle of cotton fields as permanent fixtures. Camphouses run the gamut from old rusting buses and campers to no-frills bedrooms on creosote stilts."

CROSSING TIME: 3-4 minutes

FERRY TYPE: Vehicle

VESSEL CAPACITY: 6 cars

OPERATING SEASON: All year

SCHEDULE: Daily, 24 hrs. per day

RESTRICTIONS: Trailers, pickup-campers, and RVs permitted. Load limit 20 tons.

FACILITIES: None

FARE: Free

RESERVATIONS: No

DIRECTIONS: From Vicksburg, take Chickasaw Rd. north to the Yazoo River.

MAP LOCATION: P. 197, MS, 1

CONTACT: Warren County Board of Supervisors, Vicksburg, MS 39180, (601)636-1431

Green Grass

STATE:	North Carolina
PLACES SERVED:	Atlantic—Portsmouth Island
BODY OF WATER:	Core Sound
FERRY SERVICE HISTORY:	Don Morris of Atlantic has been operating ferry service to Portsmouth Island for forty years, following in his father's footsteps. The

vessel used is the forty-eight-foot *Green Grass*. Don and his wife, Katie, who helps with the service, have had guests from all over the US and foreign countries; the summer of 1986 brought groups from Italy, England, Vietnam, and Japan.

LOCAL POINTS OF INTEREST:	Atlantic is a small fishing village on Cedar Island, across Core Sound from Portsmouth Island.

Portsmouth Island is on the National Register of Historic Places, the national honor roll which recognizes outstanding historic buildings and districts throughout the US. It is also part of the Cape Lookout National Seashore, administered by the National Park Service. It was once well-populated; today, the only resident is a Park Service caretaker for Portsmouth Village. The village is now a ghost town, though it was established in 1753 and by 1770 was the largest settlement on the Outer Banks. Ocracoke Inlet was the major trade route through the Outer Banks to such ports as Wilmington, but heavily laden ships could not sail through the shallow inlet and transferred their cargo to shallow draft boats at Portsmouth. In 1846, a deeper inlet was opened at Hatteras by a storm, and shipping shifted north. After the Civil War, many people left Portsmouth, never to return. In 1976, new life came to Portsmouth with the establishment of the Cape Lookout National Seashore. Today, over twenty buildings in the 250-acre site are open, including houses, the school house, the post office and general store, and the Methodist Church. There is a visitor center in the Dixon/Salter House. Other activities on the island include excellent shelling, fishing, and swimming. There are no roads on the island, so only four-wheel drive vehicles are transported. Bring insect repellent in the summer, along with suntan lotion, a hat, and sturdy walking shoes; the beach is a one-mile hike from the Village, over a hot and dry sand flat (sometimes, though, it is cold and wet). Beware of strong currents and rip tides on the shoreline.

Accommodation is available in seventeen rustic older cabins and eight new ones through the Morrises, who are concessionaires for the National Park Service.

[*NOTE:* There is unscheduled boat service to Portsmouth Island from Ocracoke also. In Ocracoke, call Rudy Austin, 919/928-4361 or Dave Harless, Box 381, Ocracoke, NC 27960, 919/928-1951, to make arrangements.]

CROSSING TIME: 38 mins.

FERRY TYPE: Vehicle [only 4-wheel drive, as there are no roads on the island]

VESSEL CAPACITY: 4 vehicles, 49 passengers

OPERATING SEASON: Apr.-Nov.

SCHEDULE: **Daily: Lv. Atlantic** 7 a.m., 11, 3 p.m. (4 daylight-saving time). **Lv. Portsmouth Island** 8 a.m., noon, 4 p.m. (5 daylight-saving time).

RESTRICTIONS: No gasoline transported with passengers; special supply runs made. Extra trips when needed.

FACILITIES: No

FARE: Adults $10 round-trip; children (7-12) $5; free under 6; ATV $20; larger vehicles $50; cabins $30-$90 per night.

RESERVATIONS:	Needed for cabins, groups, extra trips.
DIRECTIONS:	SR 70-E comes to Atlantic.
MAP LOCATION:	P. 197, NC, 1
CONTACT:	Don L. Morris, Morris Marina Ferry, Star Route 76J, Atlantic, NC 28511, (919)225-4261

STATE:	North Carolina
PLACES SERVED:	Aurora—Bayview
BODY OF WATER:	Pamlico River

FERRY SERVICE HISTORY: This ferry operation began, in 1966, to accommodate North Shore residents who were employees of the phosphate mining company near Aurora. The vessel name is the *Beaufort* (129.5 feet long).

LOCAL POINTS OF INTEREST: The ferry is near the Bath State Historic Site (SR 92), the oldest incorporated town in North Carolina (1705), where Blackbeard (Edward Teach) lived when not engaged in piracy. (In the present town of Bath, an outdoor musical drama, *Blackbeard—Knight of the Black Flag*, is presented late June-mid-August.) Several restored homes are open here, including the Palmer-Marsh House (c. 1744). Washington, founded in 1776, about eleven miles away, was the first American town named for the first President. The town was burned during the Civil War and rebuilt, but a devastating fire in 1900 destroyed most of it again. Much of the city's late Victorian architecture dates from the rebuilding effort following this fire; there are also some buildings which survived both fires, such as the Myers House (c. 1760).

CROSSING TIME:	25 mins.
FERRY TYPE:	Vehicle
VESSEL CAPACITY:	18 cars, 304 pasengers
OPERATING SEASON:	All year

SCHEDULE: Daily: Lv. Bayview (North Shore) 5:30 a.m., 7, 9:15, 11, 1 p.m., 3, 5:30, 7, 9, 11. Lv. Aurora (South Shore) 6:15 a.m., 8:30, 10, noon, 2 p.m., 4:45, 6:15, 8, 10, 12:30 a.m.

RESTRICTIONS: Trailers, pickup-campers, and RVs permitted. Load limit 16 tons. Overhead clearance 13 ft. 6 in.

FACILITIES: Restrooms

FARE: Free

RESERVATIONS: No

DIRECTIONS: Ferry connects SR 306.

MAP LOCATION: P. 197, NC, 2

CONTACT: Director, Ferry Division, Room 116, Maritime Bldg., 113 Arendell St., Morehead City, NC 28557, (919)726-6446 or (919) 726-6413

STATE: North Carolina

PLACES SERVED: Cherry Branch—Minnesott Beach

BODY OF WATER: Neuse River

FERRY SERVICE HISTORY: This ferry began operation in 1972 for the purpose of providing a more direct access to the Cherry Point Marine Base for employees from Pamlico County. The vessels are the *Governor Cherry* and the spare, the *Emmett Winslow*.

LOCAL POINTS OF INTEREST: The Neuse River merges with the calm, shallow waters of Pamlico Sound near the ferry. The area north of the landing has few commercial establishments other than the occasional filling station or country store; it is a popular spot for children's camps and for boaters (especially

Oriental, which has a well-known marina). Visitors to Oriental find that a fascinating pastime is wandering through the marina, seeing the posh yachts and sailboats, discovering what famous people are moored for the night. The main facility south of the ferry is the Cherry Point Marine Base. The Croatan National Forest is also at the southern terminus of the ferry; this is over 150,000 acres with estuaries and waterways and is the northernmost territory for alligators. Activities on the Neuse River are swimming, picnicking, boating, fishing, and, in season, hunting for deer, bear, turkey, quail, and waterfowl. New Bern is inland on the river; this is one of North Carolina's earliest towns, settled by Germans and Swiss and named for Berne, Switzerland. Of special interest here is Tryon Palace and Gardens, the first state capitol (burned in 1798, but restored in the 1950s). At Morehead City there is an excellent restaurant, the Sanitary Fish Market, overlooking the water, famous for many years for its simple, fresh seafood.

CROSSING TIME: 20 mins.

FERRY TYPE: Vehicle

VESSEL CAPACITY: 20 cars, 156 passengers

OPERATING SEASON: All year

SCHEDULE: **Daily. Lv. Cherry Branch** 5:45 a.m., 6:45, 7:45, 8:45, 9:45, 10:45, 11:45, 1:30 p.m., 2:30, 3:45, 4:45, 5:45, 6:45, 7:45, 8:45, 9:45, 11:30, 12:45 a.m. **Lv. Minnesott Beach** 6:15 a.m., 7:15, 8:15, 9:15, 10:15, 11:15, 12:15 p.m., 2, 3, 4:15, 5:15, 6:15, 7:15, 8:15, 9:15, 10:30, 12:15 a.m., 1:15.

RESTRICTIONS: Trailers, pickup-campers, and RVs permitted. Load limit 18 tons.

FACILITIES: No

FARE: Free

RESERVATIONS: No

DIRECTIONS: Ferry connects SR 306.

MAP LOCATION: P. 197, NC, 3

CONTACT: Cherry Branch Ferry Terminal, Cherry Branch, NC 28532, (919)447-1055

STATE:	North Carolina
PLACES SERVED:	Currituck—Knotts Island
BODY OF WATER:	Intracoastal Waterway

FERRY SERVICE HISTORY: The ferry *Knotts Island* was placed in operation between Currituck Courthouse on the Currituck County mainland and Knotts Island during the fall of 1962. The primary reason for this operation was to transport school children from Knotts Island to Currituck to attend the Currituck County schools. The trip by school bus took one and one-half hours, and the ferry reduced the time to fifty minutes. Residents of Knotts Island who need to transact courthouse business are also able to use the ferry, as both the school and the courthouse are located near the ferry terminal. The present vessel is the *Governor James Baxter Hunt, Jr.*

LOCAL POINTS OF INTEREST: Currituck is a small town, the county seat of Currituck County, just below the North Carolina-Virginia border. Knotts Island is quite near the lower part of Virginia's Back Bay, close to Virginia Beach. The ferry serves many riders from the Hampton Roads area bound for the Outer Banks, and, in the words of Joe Owens of the ferry division, it is a "nice little ferry ride."

CROSSING TIME:	50 mins.
FERRY TYPE:	Vehicle
VESSEL CAPACITY:	20 cars, 150 passengers & crew
OPERATING SEASON:	All year
SCHEDULE:	**Daily. Lv. Currituck** 6:15 a.m., 9, 11, 1 p.m., 3:45, 5:45. **Lv. Knotts Island** 7:15 a.m., 10, noon, 2 p.m., 4:45, 6:45.
RESTRICTIONS:	Trailers, pickup-campers, and RVs permitted. Load limit 18 tons.
FACILITIES:	Restrooms

FARE:	Free
RESERVATIONS:	No
DIRECTIONS:	The ferry connects SR 615 on Knotts Island with SR 168 at Currituck.
MAP LOCATION:	P. 197, NC, 4
CONTACT:	Currituck Ferry Terminal, Currituck, NC 27929, (919)232-2683

STATE:	North Carolina
PLACES SERVED:	Elwell—Carver's Creek ("The Elwell Ferry")
BODY OF WATER:	Cape Fear River

FERRY SERVICE HISTORY: The ferry has been operating since 1905 or 1906, when there was no bridge across the Cape Fear River in Bladen County. A bridge was built at Elizabethtown about 1930, but the Elwell Ferry has remained, moving from an oar-driven barge to the modern single-vehicle barge driven by an outboard motor. Walter Russ ran the ferry when it was oar-driven, and legend has it that he was so skillful he could row backward and hit the ramp every time. The present operator is Paul Campbell. He is used to strangers who drive down the narrow road between SR 87 and SR 53 and scratch their heads, reaching for a road map. The official state map shows an unbroken line, but, in fact, the ferry is part of the line. It prevents drivers from going twenty miles round-trip to the nearest bridge. Commuters in Kelly can reach the other side in four miles, rather than twenty. Campbell has worked at the ferry for several years, after working in the county tax supervisor's office. "It took some getting use to," he says. "There's some times down here when you don't have much traffic and it can get a little lonesome." The ferry is busiest in summer when tourists are going to the beaches.

LOCAL POINTS OF INTEREST: Carvers is a small town, as is Kelly, on the Elwell side; there are no restaurants or motels. The Moores Creek National Battleground is on SR 210, not far from the ferry. It was established in 1926 to commemorate an important battle of the American Revolution. White Lake and Lake Waccamaw, both pleasant recreation areas, are also nearby.

CROSSING TIME: 5 mins.

FERRY TYPE: Vehicle

VESSEL CAPACITY: 2 cars; 25 passengers

OPERATING SEASON: All year

SCHEDULE: **Daily, on signal. Summer (Mar. 15-Sept. 16):** 6:30 a.m.-6 p.m. **Winter (Sept. 16-Mar. 15):** 6:45 a.m.-5 p.m.

RESTRICTIONS: Trailers, pickup-campers,and RVs permitted. Load limit 9 tons.

FACILITIES: None

FARE: Free

RESERVATIONS: No

DIRECTIONS: Ferry connects segments of 1537, a rural road running between SR 53 near Kelly and SR 87 at Carvers in Bladen County, northwest of Wilmington; the road is clearly marked on state highway maps as an unbroken line.

MAP LOCATION: P. 197, NC, 5

CONTACT: See CONTACT, p. 264.

STATE: North Carolina

PLACES SERVED: Harkers Island—Cape Lookout

BODY OF WATER: Back Sound

FERRY SERVICE HISTORY: The Harkers Island-Cape Lookout ferry began service in 1978; the vessel is the *Jan D.*

LOCAL POINTS OF INTEREST: Harkers Island is a fishing village noted for its skilled boatwrights. A good place to stay here is the Harkers Island Fishing Center, a motel/marina with a tackle shop and ship's store (919/728-3907). The ferry leaves from the Fishing Center. This entire area of Carteret County is known as the Crystal Coast, and you will find it less commercialized than the Outer Banks. At Swansboro, in the Crystal Coast Amphitheatre, an outdoor pageant, *Blackbeard's Revenge*, is presently nightly from mid-June through late August. At Morehead City, an excellent restaurant, the Sanitary Fish Market, overlooking the water, has been known for many years for its fresh, simple seafood. The Spouter Inn, at Beaufort, also offers waterfront dining, continental specialities, and seafood.

Cape Lookout is a wilderness area, and ferry passengers are almost exclusively surf-fishers or beachcombers. This part of the Cape Lookout National Seashore has only the lighthouse and two abandoned Coast Guard stations, but a jitney (trailer pulled by an all-terrain vehicle) is available for a five-dollar fee to those who want to ride to Cape Point, a favorite fishing location one and one-half miles from Cape Lookout landing. The island has an intriguing history, however. Early map makers could not distinguish between Cape Fear and Cape Lookout, so that, on the De Bry engraving of White's 1585 map, Cape Lookout is shown as the "Promontorium Tremendum" and on the 1611 Velasco map as "Cape Feare." There were suggestions, as early as 1755, that a fort be built on the harbor formed by the "hook," and Spanish privateers used it as a hiding place.

The first lighthouse was authorized by Congress in 1804 and put into service about 1812 (now in ruins); it was considered ineffective, as it was not high enough to be seen. One skipper said bluntly that the lighthouses at Cape Hatteras, Cape Lookout, and Cape Florida should be dispensed with as "the navigator is apt to run ashore looking for them." A second one, built in 1859, with a light 156 feet above sea level, is still in use; an unmanned automatic beacon has been used since 1950. The distinctive diagonal checkers date from 1873.

[NOTE: There is unscheduled boat service from Davis, N.C., on Cedar Island, to Cape Lookout. The landing is at Shingle Point, above the lighthouse. Write or call Alger Willis Fishing Camps, Inc., Box 234, Davis, N.C., 28524 (919/225-2791), to make arrangements.]

CROSSING TIME: 45 mins.

FERRY TYPE: Pedestrian

VESSEL CAPACITY: 60 passengers and crew

OPERATING SEASON: All year, but regular trips only from early April through mid-Oct. For service at other times, call or write.

SCHEDULE: **First Sat. in Apr.-Thurs. of Memorial Day weekend (weekends): Lv. Harkers Island** 9 a.m., 1 p.m. **Lv. Cape Lookout** noon, 4 p.m. **First Mon. in Apr.-Thurs. of Memorial Day weekend *(week-days):** 11 a.m. **Lv. Cape Lookout** 4 p.m. **Fri. of Memorial Day week-end-Labor Day: Daily: Lv. Harkers Island** 9 a.m., 1 p.m. **Lv. Cape Lookout** noon, 4 p.m. **After Labor Day-2nd weekend in Oct. (weekends): Lv. Harkers Island** 9 a.m., 1 p.m. **Lv. Cape Lookout** noon, 4 p.m. **(Weekdays): Lv. Harkers Island** 11 a.m. **Lv. Cape Lookout** 4 p.m. **Beginning first Mon. after the 2nd weekend in Oct.: Daily: Lv. Harkers Island** 6 a.m. **Lv. Cape Lookout** 4 p.m. *Reservations required one day in advance.

RESTRICTIONS: None

FACILITIES: No

FARE: Round-trip. Adults $10; children (6-10) $5; under 5 accompanied by parent free.

RESERVATIONS: Required one day in advance.

DIRECTIONS: Ferry leaves from Harkers Island Fishing Center, Harkers Island.

MAP LOCATION: P. 197, NC, 6

CONTACT: Carteret Boat Tours, Inc., Harkers Island Fishing Co., Box 275, Harkers Island, NC 28531, (919)728-3907

STATE: North Carolina

PLACES SERVED: Hatteras—Ocracoke Island

BODY OF WATER: Hatteras Inlet

FERRY SERVICE HISTORY: This ferry route is actually one of the oldest on the Outer Banks. As early as April 1953, Frazier Peele instituted service between Hatteras and the northern end of Ocracoke Island. The ferry used was a small wooden craft with a capacity for four standard-sized automobiles, or one five-ton truck with a light load and two automobiles. This service was continued by Peele as a toll operation until August, 1957, when the ferry franchise and equipment were purchased by the State Highway Commission and the operation made toll-free. Six ships are assigned to this run: the *Herbert C. Bonner*, the *Ocracoke*, the *Lindsey Warren*, the *R. B. Etheridge*, the *Alpheus W. Drinkwater*, and the *Conrad Wirth*. They are sister ships, all 122 feet long with a gross tonnage of 199. The first ferry service between the Outer Banks and the outside world was begun by J. B. Tillett in 1932 (Wanchese, Roanoke Island, to Rodanthe, Hatteras). The operation was moved to Oregon Inlet in 1934, sold to the Highway Commission in 1950, and made obsolete by the H.C. Bonner Bridge, opened in 1963.

LOCAL POINTS OF INTEREST: Hatteras village is a small resort town and fishing village. It lies on the south end of Hatteras Island beside the Hatteras Inlet. Nearby is a famous landmark, the candy-striped Cape Hatteras Lighthouse, at 208 feet the tallest lighthouse in America. The balcony is closed to the public, but there is a small visitor center in the former keeper's quarters. The shoreline is at the heart of the "graveyard of the Atlantic," where more than six hundred ships have been lost. Many Outer Banks cottages are decorated with ships' nameplates, such as *Peconic*, *Emma C. Cotton*, *Mary Lee*, and *William H. Macy*, grim reminders of the dangers of the turbulent, shifting shoals. As early as 1870, villagers served as members of the US Life Saving Service, attempting to save survivors; others manned the lighthouses built to guide mariners.

The disposition of the Outer Banks to attract tourists was an established fact before 1970, when the centennial of the illumination of the present lighthouse was celebrated. The souvenir booklet was dedicated "to the highly adaptable citizens of Dare who have been stockmen, lifesavers, fishermen and now entrepreneurs. The dramatic surge of tourism is merely a new blessing from the sea." If it were not for the Park Service, however, the "surge of tourism" might threaten to topple the lighthouse itself. Hatteras Island, in fact, seems to be almost everybody's idea of a wilderness beach. It has been protected from overdevelopment because the island is part of the Cape Hatteras National Seashore Recreational Area and under the strict control of the National Park Service. The Seashore area covers about forty-five square miles on the Outer Banks, including part of Ocracoke Island and the southern portion of Bodie Island. Along Route 12 there are a few tiny settlements, such as Rodanthe, Avon, and Buxton, some with decoy carvers and other small shops. It is a rare visitor to Nags Head or Hatteras who does not schedule a trip to Ocracoke Island from Hatteras Island, ostensibly, perhaps, to see

Blackbeard's Hideaway or the British Cemetery, but secretly to ride the ferry across Hatteras Inlet.

Lodging, restaurants, gift shops, and activities are available at Nags Head, Kitty Hawk, and Manteo, to the north. The Nags Head dunes are famous for hang gliding, and Manteo is famous as the home of the first of Paul Green's outdoor pageants, *The Lost Colony*, another must for visitors; the Elizabethan Gardens are also well worth visiting. The Wright Brothers National Monument is at Kill Devils Hill and has an interesting information center with aviation exhibits.

CROSSING TIME: 40 mins.

FERRY TYPE: Vehicle

VESSEL CAPACITY: 22 cars; 154 passengers

OPERATING SEASON: All year

SCHEDULE: **Daily: Summer, Apr. 15-Oct. 31: Lv. Hatteras** 5 a.m., 6:10, 6:50, 7:30, 8:10, 8:50, 9:30, 10:10, 10:50, 11:30, 12:10 p.m., 12:50, 1:30, 2:10, 2:50, 3:30, 4:10, 4:50, 5:30, 6:10, 7, 9, 11. **Lv. Ocracoke** 6 a.m., 7:10, 7:50, 8:30, 9:10, 9:50, 10:30, 11:10, 11:50, 12:30 p.m., 1:10, 1:50, 2:30, 3:10, 3:50, 4:30, 5:10, 5:50, 6:30, 7:10, 8, 10. **Winter, Nov. 1-Apr. 14: Lv. Hatteras** every hour on the hour, 5 a.m.-5 p.m. and 7, 9, and 11. **Lv. Ocracoke** every hour on the hour, 6 a.m.-6 p.m., 8, 10.

RESTRICTIONS: Trailers, pickup-campers, and RVs permitted. Load limit 18 tons. Overhead clearance 12 ft. 6 in.

FACILITIES: Restrooms

FARE: Free

RESERVATIONS: No

DIRECTIONS: Ferry connects segments of SR 12.

MAP LOCATION: P. 197, NC, 7

CONTACT: This is a free ferry, which shuttles back and forth between Hatteras Island and Ocracoke Island. You do not need reservations on it; you only need reservations on the Swan Quarter-Ocracoke and Cedar Island-Ocracoke ferries. For local information: Hatteras Ferry Terminal, Hatteras, NC 27943, (919)986-2136.

Pamlico

STATE:	North Carolina
PLACES SERVED:	Ocracoke—Cedar Island
BODY OF WATER:	Pamlico Sound

FERRY SERVICE HISTORY: The vessels on this service are the *Pamlico* (221 feet long), which has now been "stretched" to add sixty feet to its length and the *Silver Lake* (161 feet long), its sister ship. Plans are now being developed to undertake similar renovations for the *Silver Lake*. The ferries have an appealing rotund shape from a distance, like floating tops, which, somehow, contributes to the holiday mood which prevails on the Outer Banks. The first ferry to operate between the village of Ocracoke and the mainland (Atlantic) was the toll ferry *Sea Level* in April 1960; it was operated by the Taylor Brothers of Atlantic. The State Highway Commission purchased this vessel from the Taylor Brothers on Feb. 9, 1961, and it began operating on May 1, 1961, from Atlantic to Ocracoke, making one trip daily. When the Cedar Island ferry terminal was built in May 1964, it became feasible to make two trips per day.

LOCAL POINTS OF INTEREST: Ocracoke Island is one of the barrier islands forming the Outer Banks; it is part of the Cape Hatteras National Seashore, established in 1953. The town of Ocracoke is a small resort which retains most of its

~273~

old charm, thanks to its remoteness. Built around Silver Lake, it is a fishing village with roots dating back to before the days when Blackbeard made the island one of his favorite retreats; he was killed in Ocracoke Inlet in 1718, in an engagement with two sloops of the British Navy. The sandy streets wind below mossy live oaks and give the town a remote, tranquil flavor, with hedges and pleasant shingled houses.

The Ocracoke Lighthouse, built in 1823, is one of the oldest still in use on the Eastern seaboard. The Ocracoke Trolley tours the area, stopping at Blackbeard's Hideaway.

[NOTE: From Ocracoke, at least two private boat operators offer unscheduled ferry service to Portsmouth Village, the historic ghost town at the tip of Portsmouth Island. For details, please see entry under Atlantic-Portsmouth Island, p. 261.]

Cedar Island has several small fishing villages, such as Atlantic (which has a ferry to Cape Lookout). A good place to stay here or to have a meal while waiting for the ferry is the Driftwood Motel.

CROSSING TIME: 2 hrs. 15 mins.

FERRY TYPE: Vehicle

VESSEL CAPACITY: *Pamlico:* 50 vehicles; *Silver Lake:* 30 vehicles

OPERATING SEASON: All year

SCHEDULE: **Summer, Apr. 15-Oct. 15: Lv. Ocracoke** 7 a.m., 9:30, noon, 3 p.m., 6, 8:30. **Lv. Cedar Island** 7 a.m., 9:30, noon, 3 p.m., 6, 8:30. **Winter, Oct. 16-Apr. 14: Lv. Ocracoke** 10 a.m., 4 p.m. **Lv. Cedar Island** 7 a.m., 1 p.m.

RESTRICTIONS: Trailers, pickup-campers, and RVs permitted. Load limit 18 tons. Overhead clearance 13 ft. 6 in. Maximum width 8 ft.

FACILITIES: Restrooms; soft drink and candy machines

FARE: Pedestrians $1; bicycle & rider $2; single vehicle or combination 20′ or less in length & motorcycles $10; vehicles or combinations 20′-40′ in length $20; vehicles or combinations 50′-60′ $30.

RESERVATIONS: Recommended, and essential in summer; reservation is void if not claimed 30 minutes before scheduled sailing.

DIRECTIONS: Ferry connects segments of SR 12.

MAP LOCATION: P. 197, NC, 8

CONTACT: Reservations: Departures from Ocracoke: call (919)928-3841; departures from Cedar Island: call (919)225-3551. (Office hours 6 a.m.-6 p.m.). General information (further size limitations, etc.): Director, Ferry Division, Room 116, Maritime Bldg., 113 Arendell St., Morehead City, NC 28557, (919)726-6446 or (919)726-6413.

STATE: North Carolina

PLACES SERVED: Ocracoke-Swan Quarter

BODY OF WATER: Pamlico Sound

FERRY SERVICE HISTORY: This ferry route is one of the newer ones on the Outer Banks; it was established in June, 1977, at the direction of the North Carolina General Assembly. Prior to the opening of this service, residents of Ocracoke had to drive a round trip of close to four hundred miles to register a deed, serve on a jury, or make use of any of the services available at Swan Quarter, the Hyde County seat. The vessel is the *Governor Edward Hyde*.

LOCAL POINTS OF INTEREST: [For notes on Ocracoke, please see entry under Ocracoke-Cedar Island, p. 273.]
Swan Quarter is a typical small North Carolina fishing village. Located near Lake Mattemuskeet and the Swan Quarter National Wildlife Refuge, it is a favorite gathering place for naturalists and sportsmen.

CROSSING TIME: 2 hrs. 30 mins.

FERRY TYPE: Vehicle

VESSEL CAPACITY: 30 cars, 306 passengers & crew

OPERATING SEASON: All year

SCHEDULE: **Daily. Lv. Ocracoke** 6:30 a.m., 12:30 p.m.
Lv. Swan Quarter 9:30 a.m., 4 p.m.

RESTRICTIONS: Trailers, pickup-campers, and RVs permitted. Overhead clearance 13 ft. 6 in.

FACILITIES: Restrooms; soft drink and candy machines

FARE: See FARE, p. 274.

RESERVATIONS: Required in order to ensure space; void if not claimed 30 minutes before scheduled sailing.

DIRECTIONS: Ferry goes from the Ocracoke Harbor to SR 45 at Swan Quarter.

MAP LOCATION: P. 197, NC, 9

CONTACT: Reservations: Departures from Ocracoke: call (919)928-3841; departures from Swan Quarter: call (919)926-1111. (Office hours 6 a.m.-6 p.m.). General information (further size limitations, etc.): Director, Ferry Division, Room 116, Maritime Bldg., 113 Arendell St., Morehead City, NC 28557, (919)726-6446 or (919)726-6413.

STATE: North Carolina

PLACES SERVED: Parker (connecting rural routes 1306 and 1175), near Murfreesboro

BODY OF WATER: Meherrin River

FERRY SERVICE HISTORY: The ferry has been operating for over twenty years. It was designed with the local residents and farmers in mind. Because the river is narrow, the ferry can be cable-operated; when the ferry tender sees a vehicle on the opposite bank, he runs the boat to the waiting traveler and ferries him back across.

LOCAL POINTS OF INTEREST: The ferry is in Hertford County, in the historic Albemarle region of North Carolina. It is not far from Murfreesboro, a Meherrin River port dating from 1747. Here, there are over ninety original eighteenth- and nineteenth-century brick and frame structures, many of which have been restored. The 1790 Roberts-Vaughan Village Center, the Rea

Museum, the Winborne Country Store, and the Wheeler House are open to the public. The Museum of the Albemarle at Elizabeth City is a history center interpreting the heritage of ten northeastern North Carolina counties; the exhibits are about hunting, lumbering, farming, rural society, and maritime commerce, with displays of decoys and other artifacts.

CROSSING TIME: 5 mins.

FERRY TYPE: Vehicle

VESSEL CAPACITY: 2 cars; 25 passsengers

OPERATING SEASON: All year

SCHEDULE: **Daily, on signal. Summer (Mar. 15-Sept. 16):** 6:30 a.m.-6 p.m. **Winter (Sept. 16-Mar. 15):** 6:45 a.m.-5 p.m.

RESTRICTIONS: Trailers, pickup-campers, and RVs permitted. Load limit 9 tons.

FACILITIES: None

FARE: Free

RESERVATIONS: No

DIRECTIONS: The ferry is located just west of the mouth of the Meherrin River, where the Meherrin flows into the Chowan River. From Winton, take SR 158 west toward Murfreesboro. About .7 of a mile from Winton, take secondary road 1175 north. After 1.7 miles, it forks; do not take the paved section, 1321, to the right, but keep on the unpaved section straight ahead, which is still 1175. The ferry is 1.7 miles ahead. From Murfreesboro, take SR 258 to Barretts Crossroads. After about 2.5 miles, take SR 1306, a paved road, which changes to an unpaved road after 1.5 miles. Keep on 1306, and the ferry is another 3.5 miles.

MAP LOCATION: P. 197, NC, 10

CONTACT: See CONTACT, p. 264.

STATE: North Carolina

PLACES SERVED: Sans Souci

BODY OF WATER: Cashie River

FERRY SERVICE HISTORY: The ferry at Sans Souci has been operating for more than twenty years; it is a motorized, cable-drawn ferry.

LOCAL POINTS OF INTEREST: If you have a picnic hamper or a fishing pole, Sans Souci is the ferry for you. You will not find it on the map, but for many years it has been a favorite riverfront place for visiting, fishing, and ferry-riding. In summer, there is an abundance of wildflowers (cardinal flowers, duck potatoes—a swamp flower with white flowers—pickerel weed, and cow lilies), all framed by towering cypress trees from which Spanish moss hangs in long tendrils. Nearby is the unused Woodard school. West of the ferry site, the Cashie River curves north, then west. On the east, it widens before joining the Albemarle Sound, about three miles distant. If you must begin your journey from civilization, Williamston, Plymouth, or Windsor would be the places—it is not too far from the Highway 17 Bypass around Williamston. From here, the road to Woodard is paved; beyond, it is gravel, winding through an area of corn, peanut, and soybean farms. The farm homes are vivid with colors.

CROSSING TIME: 5 mins.

FERRY TYPE: Vehicle

VESSEL CAPACITY: 2 cars; 25 passengers

OPERATING SEASON: All year

SCHEDULE: **Daily, on signal. Summer (Mar. 15-Sept. 16):** 6:30 a.m.-6 p.m. **Winter (Sept. 16-Mar. 15):** 6:45 a.m.-5 p.m.

RESTRICTIONS: Trailers, pickup-campers, and RVs permitted. Load limit 9 tons.

FACILITIES: None

FARE: Free

RESERVATIONS: No

DIRECTIONS: From the 17 Bypass around Williamston: 4 miles north of the Roanoke River, turn right on the first paved road. Where the road comes to a T, turn right for Woodard. The last 3 miles of the road from Woodard to Sans Souci is a well-maintained dirt road covered with gravel. (Woodard is on the map, but has only a Methodist church now.)

MAP LOCATION: P. 197, NC, 11

CONTACT: See CONTACT, p. 264.

STATE: North Carolina

PLACES SERVED: Southport—Bald Head Island

BODY OF WATER: Cape Fear River

FERRY SERVICE
HISTORY: Ferry service to Bald Head Island began in 1976, with the *Bald Head I*, designed and built by Capt. Herman Sellers (a long-time ship pilot) from the hull of an old LCM-6. The *Adventure* began operation in 1983; she was constructed as a transportation boat to offshore oil wells.

LOCAL POINTS
OF INTEREST: The Southport area has been formally described as the "northernmost subtropical region on the East Coast," but, locally, Southport is thought of as an unspoiled fishing village and small resort town. It was originally named Smithville and began with the establishment of Fort Johnston, built in 1764 at the mouth of the Cape Fear River. In 1792, Smithville was created, named for North Carolina governor Benjamin Smith. During the Civil War, Fort Johnston and nearby Fort Caswell protected blockade runners, but in 1865 Union troops occupied Fort Johnston and Smithville surrendered. During the 1880s northern businessmen moved into Smithville, with the idea of developing a leading port; the town was changed to Southport in 1887. Today, it is undergoing another renaissance, with art galleries, shops, restaurants, and hotels. The film *Crimes of the Heart* was shot on location here in a house purposely

antiqued from white to gray; it has become a tourist attraction. Good restaurants are the Pharmacy on Moore Street, the Ship's Chandler, and Port Charlie's; the latter two overlook the water.

Bald Head is a unique residential-resort community, with amenities possessed by other resorts, plus many added dimensions. Unlike some resorts, all homes and condominiums are designed to blend in with the natural growth on the Island and reflect its history. The island is the home of "Old Baldy," built in 1817, the oldest lighthouse on the North Carolina coast. (Funds to complete a lighthouse already begun were appropriated by Congress in 1792, according to historian David Stick, who has written a history of Bald Head Island.) It was decommissioned in 1935, but visitors may still climb the dark, narrow steps to the top for a panoramic view of the Atlantic Ocean, the Cape Fear River, and nearby islands. Bald Head has many miles of uncrowded beaches; East Beach is reached by the winding Federal Road. The marina has dock space for yachts also, attracting many local sailors as well as transient yachtsmen making their way along the Inland Waterway. Complete lunch and dinner packages are available, including the ferry ticket, a tour, and a meal at the Bald Head Island Inn; golf packages including the ferry ticket are also offered. Electric vehicles for touring the island, bicycles, canoes, beach equipment, and charter fishing boats are available for rental.

The development of the island was carefully planned to be consonant with wildlife preservation. The Bald Head Conservancy was founded in 1983 with the special aim of conserving the natural resources of Bald Head Island, particularly the loggerhead sea turtle nests. Every summer, giant loggerhead sea turtles return to Bald Head Island to lay their eggs. Fifty percent of the nests laid, mostly those threatened by erosion or overwash, are transferred to the turtle hatchery on East Beach to promote the safety of the eggs and hatchlings. In 1986 alone, approximately eighteen thousand hatchlings were released from the hatchery. None of these turtles would have survived had the nests not been relocated.

CROSSING TIME: *Adventure* 15 mins.; *Bald Head I* 25 mins.

FERRY TYPE: Pedestrian

VESSEL CAPACITY: 45 passengers

OPERATING SEASON: All year

SCHEDULE: **Daily. Lv. Southport** 7 a.m., 8, 9, 10, 11, 1 p.m., 2, 3, 4, 5, 6, 7, 9. **Lv. Bald head** 7:30 a.m., 8:30, 9:30, 10:30, 12:30 p.m., 1:30, 2:30, 3:30, 4:30, 5:30, 6:30, 7:30, 9:30.

RESTRICTIONS: None

FACILITIES: None

FARE: Round-trip only: day guests $15; overnight guests $10; property owners $8-$10.

RESERVATIONS: Required

DIRECTIONS: Enter Southport on Highway 211; turn left on E. Moore St.; Bald Head Island ferry departure is from dock at 704 E. Moore St.

MAP LOCATION: P. 197, NC, 12

CONTACT: Bald Head Island Management, Inc., P.O. Drawer 10999, Southport, NC 28461, (919)457-6763 or (800)722-6450 (NC only)

STATE: North Carolina

PLACES SERVED: Southport—Fort Fisher

BODY OF WATER: Cape Fear River

FERRY SERVICE HISTORY: Service began operation in 1965; vessels are the *Lauch Faircloth* and the *Sandy Graham* (spare vessel). Summer traffic has increased to the point that a second vessel was added during summer 1986 and will be continued during the summer season. Harry Sell has been one of the ferry captains for ten years. He recalls some unusual cargoes, including an antique cannon being taken to Fort Fisher for the battle reenactment, floats for a July 4 celebration, army trucks, clowns, and bicycles for a race. He chuckles especially when he remembers the tourists from inland regions who cannot bring themselves to drive on a boat. "One man, barefooted and in bib overalls, crouched down and watched the boat come and go for four hours. Finally he bought a ticket. He rode back and forth twice, then talked his family into riding; by the end of the day they had really enjoyed themselves. Another man drove his car half on, then changed his mind. We had to back all the traffic up to get him off." Shannon Grant was another bewildered recent rider. A fluffy white little dog belonging to Jane and Oscar Grant of Wrightsville Beach, she eagerly hopped out of the car, but then stopped and looked around, puzzled. She was clearly thinking, said Oscar, "I've been in a boat. I've been in a car. But I have never been in a car on a boat."

LOCAL POINTS OF INTEREST: [For notes on Southport, please see entry under Southport-Bald Head Island, p. 279.]
Fort Fisher is the site of the largest earth-work fortification in the South during the Civil War. Its beaches are largely underdeveloped and unspoiled. It is named for the Confederate fort that was built to guard the entrance to the Cape Fear River during the Civil War. A Civil War museum is at the site of the fort now. The North Carolina Marine Resources Center is also in Fort Fisher; it has an aquarium, exhibits, educational programs, touch tables, films, workshops, and a bookstore. It was established for the purpose of coastal education and research.

A circle tour may be made from here through Pleasure Island (Kure Beach and Carolina Beach) up to Wilmington, one of North Carolina's most historic port cities (settled in 1732). Here, visitors will enjoy Greenfield Lake (with ancient cypress trees), the *USS North Carolina* Battleship Memorial, the renovated downtown area, which includes the Cotton Exchange and Chandler's Wharf, departure point for river cruises, and such family-oriented (and very posh) beaches as Wrightsville (ten miles east). Historic buildings include the Burgin-Wright House (1771) and the Governor Dudley Mansion. Continuing the circle tour back down toward Southport, one comes to Orton Plantation (a historic rice plantation with beautiful gardens, house not open) and the ruins of Brunswick Town, burned by the British in 1776.

CROSSING TIME: 30 mins.

FERRY TYPE: Vehicle

VESSEL CAPACITY: 20 cars, 256 passengers

OPERATING SEASON: Year round

SCHEDULE: **Daily: Lv. Southport** at 8 a.m., 9:40, 11:20, 1 p.m., 2:40, 4:20, 6. **Lv. Fort Fisher** at 8:50 a.m., 10:30, 12:10 p.m., 1:50, 3:30, 5:10, 6:50. [Additional crossings on a second ferry are added during the summer.]

RESTRICTIONS: Trailers, pickup-campers, and RVs permitted. Maximum length 35′ (because of limited turning radius on boat). Drivers of large vehicles should telephone Southport Ferry Terminal to determine whether crossing is possible.

FACILITIES: Restrooms

FARE: Pedestrian $.50; Bicycle & rider $1; single vehicle or combination 20′ or less in length & motorcycles $3; single vehicle or combination 20′-35′ $6.

RESERVATIONS: None

DIRECTIONS: From Southport take E. Moore St. and turn right on Ferry Road. The ferry connects with SR 421 at Fort Fisher.

MAP LOCATION: P. 197, NC, 13

CONTACT: Southport Ferry Terminal, Southport, NC 28461, (919)457-6942

STATE:	South Carolina
PLACES SERVED:	Hilton Head (Broad Creek Marina)— Daufuskie Island
BODY OF WATER:	Intracoastal Waterway

FERRY SERVICE HISTORY: Ferry service in the Hilton Head area has existed at various times. From 1953-1956, there was service from Buckingham Landing to Hilton Head, which was discontinued after the May 1956 opening of the James Byrnes Bridge. In 1975, when an errant barge knocked out the Skull Creek Bridge, helicopters from Savannah ferried over champagne, filet mignons, and caviar, to sustain Hilton Head inslanders.

There are now two services to the island, one public, subsidized by Beaufort County, and this one, which is a private one instituted in 1986. The vessel is the *Caliboque* (pron. "Calley-bogie.")

LOCAL POINTS OF INTEREST: Hilton Head Island, twelve miles long and in places five miles wide, is the largest sea island between New Jersey and Florida. The island was named for an Englishman, Capt. William Hilton, who discovered it in 1663 when he sailed into Port Royal Sound. As early as 1526, Spanish, French, and English colonists had tried to settle on the island but were prevented from doing so by Indian raids and pirates. Before the Civil War, prosperous English rice and indigo plantations were established, only to be left in ruins after the war (some may still be seen). The freed slave ("Gullah") population then subsisted on the island by hunting, fishing, and farming.

The bridge to the island from the mainland, over SR 278, was completed in 1956, and the island was then developed as an all-year affluent resort, with over sixteen hundred hotel rooms, golf courses, riding stables, tennis courts, restaurants, and marinas. Hilton Head is bordered by one of the few surviving unspoiled marine estuaries on the East Coast. The Audubon Newhall Preserve, the Sea Pines Forest Preserve, and Hilton Head Plantation's Whooping Crane Conservancy attest to the fact that the island has not been completely exploited commercially.

Daufuskie is an isolated barrier island with a recorded history dating from the 1700s. The name of the island is said to be a corruption of the answer the Hilton Head Gullahs gave early visitors, when asked what the island in the distance was: "Da Fus Key" (the first key). According to the Rev. Dr. Robert E. H. Peeples, President of the Hilton Head Island Historical Society, Daufuskie Island has always been an agriculturally oriented island. Many of the old Gullah traditions are preserved here. Most of the island has been held since *ante bellum* years in five substantial plantations: Haig's Point, Melrose, Oak Ridge (also known as Ingleside), Webb, and Bloody Point. The southwest corner, formerly the Bland-Martinangele-Chaplin property, was sold off in small tracts suitable for subsistence-type living (fishing, crabbing, oystering), and had a population of several thousand, but the population declined to fewer than seventy-five residents when the Savannah River became too polluted for these activities. Since then, a two-room elementary schoolhouse has been sufficient for the island's needs.

Several residential, resort, and recreational projects are now underway, however, which may well change the character of the island to some extent (though such developments will probably remain private). One project is Melrose, on the site of a plantation whose history dates back to the early 1800s. Land on Daufuskie Island was acquired by David John "Money" Mongin, one of a long line of Mongins (mostly named David John and John David) who were originally of French Huguenot descent. His son, William Henry Mongin, and his wife, Isabella, built the original huge home, destroyed by fire in 1912. The Melrose development will include a fifty-room replica of the original, along with beach cottages, a golf course, and other resort amenities.

CROSSING TIME: 1 hr.

FERRY TYPE: Pedestrian

VESSEL CAPACITY: 42 passengers

OPERATING SEASON: All year

SCHEDULE: **Apr.-Sept.: Mon.-Fri.: Lv. Broad Creek Marina** 7 a.m., 9:20, 1:30 p.m. **Lv. Daufuskie Island** 9:10 a.m., 1:10 p.m., 6:15. **Oct.-March: Mon.-Fri.: Lv. Broad Creek Marina** 7 a.m. **Lv. Daufuskie Island** 5 p.m.

RESTRICTIONS: None

FACILITIES: Restrooms; soda and beer sold on board

FARE: $5 adults; children under 12 $2.50

RESERVATIONS: No

DIRECTIONS: Ferry leaves from the Broad Creek Marina on Hilton Head Island.

MAP LOCATION:	P. 197, SC, 1
CONTACT:	Mr. William Scurry, Broad Creek Marina, Box 1584, Hilton Head, SC 29925, (803)681-7335

STATE: South Carolina

PLACES SERVED: Hilton Head (County Dock at Outdoor Resorts)—Daufuskie Island

BODY OF WATER: Intracoastal Waterway

FERRY SERVICE HISTORY: This service, one of two to Daufuskie Island, is subsidized by Beaufort County; its primary objective is to transport high-school students to the mainland. Permanent residents may take passage at a reduced fare. The ferry schedule is tailored to the school bus schedule and to other needs of the permanent residents. The vessel is the sixty-five-foot *William Hilton,* built in Maine.

LOCAL POINTS OF INTEREST: Daufuskie Island is the scene of much development at present (see notes on the island and on Hilton Head under Hilton Head/Broad Creek Marina, p. 284). Jeep tours of the island are offered.

CROSSING TIME: 1 hr.

FERRY TYPE: Pedestrian

VESSEL CAPACITY: 65 passengers

OPERATING SEASON: All year

SCHEDULE: **Mon. and Fri.: Lv. Public Dock, next to Outdoor Resorts (Hilton Head)** 6 a.m., 4 p.m. **Lv. Daufuskie Island** 7:15 a.m., 5:15 p.m. **First Wed. each month: Lv. Public Dock** 10 a.m. **Lv. Daufuskie Island** 4 p.m.

RESTRICTIONS: None

FACILITIES: Restrooms, full galley (sandwiches, drinks)

FARE: $1.50

RESERVATIONS: No

DIRECTIONS: Ferry leaves from the County Dock, next to Outdoor Resorts at Hilton Head

MAP LOCATION: P. 197, SC, 2

CONTACT: Mr. Jim Creegan, Outdoor Resorts, Hilton Head Island, SC 29925, (803)681-8324

South Island

STATE: South Carolina

PLACES SERVED: South Island—SR 18 (near Georgetown)

BODY OF WATER: Intracoastal Waterway

FERRY SERVICE HISTORY: Prior to 1900, as part of the construction of the Intracoastal Waterway, the US Corps of Engineers dug a canal in Georgetown County, South Carolina, from Winyah Bay to the Santee Delta. This canal, known as the Estherville-Minim Canal, separates South Island on the east from the remainder of Georgetown County on the west. As part of the agreement, the US Government agreed to provide one steel bridge or two wooden ones for the right to cut the waterway; authorities also agreed to maintain these bridges and approaches in exchange for the channel-cutting permit. Residents chose two wooden bridges, which were built but which were later destroyed by fire. Two ferries then provided access and were eventually succeeded by a single ferry which leads onto Cat Island at the juncture owned by the Tom Yawkey Wildlife Center. After the villagers dwindled and plantations changed hands, the island became more or less a private affair.

From 1947 to 1978, a cable ferry was in use but was discontinued because of problems with waterway traffic. (Approximately five thousand vessels, mostly pleasure boats, use the canal each year, sometimes going as fast as thirty-five miles per hour through the canal.) Since 1978, a self-propelled ferry has been in operation at the site. The forty-six-foot boat is named the *South Island*. "I have spent many long cold hours at the South Island ferry since 1947," says Simon B. Forbes, Resident Maintenance Engineer of the SC Department of Highways and Public Transportation in Georgetown, who provided the history of the ferry. It embodies the slow and stately ways of the Low Country, replete with marsh grass and tall pines. As it threads its way among the sleek sailboats, often with dinghies in tow, and the high-bridged trawlers endlessly cruising up and down the waterway hinting of marinas and anchorages still to come, the South Island ferry seems, somehow, a stable link to the past. You may ride the ferry and take a car on it, but must turn around and come back unless you have an appointment on the island at the Tom Yawkey Wildlife Center.

LOCAL POINTS OF INTEREST: South Island is principally known as the home of the Tom Yawkey Wildlife Center. This tract of land embraces North and South Islands, and most of Cat Island, three coastal islands located at the mouth of Winyah Bay in Georgetown County. It was considered one of the most outstanding gifts to wildlife conservation in North America when it was willed to the SC Wildlife and Marine Resources Department in 1976 by the late Tom Yawkey. The area had been settled first by Indians (the Pee Dees, Santees, Sampits, See Wees, Waccamaws, and Winyahs), and later by rice planters. After the Civil War, many of the plantation homes were bought by Northern industrialists who, from 1890-1930, enjoyed golden years of prosperity. President Grover Cleveland often hunted on South Island. Gen. Elliot Porter Alexander bought plantation properties on the islands and in 1911 sold part of his land to William H. Yawkey, a wealthy industrialist and owner of the Detroit Tigers. His estate went to his nephew, Tom Yawkey (whom he adopted after both Tom's parents died), who said, "I hope I'll be able to do some good with it." Yawkey bought the Boston Red Sox in 1933 and entertained many famous players on South Island. An avid outdoorsman and ornithologist, Yawkey became interested in new techniques of waterfowl and game management. The

Wildlife Center was dedicated to him "in honor of the man who always gave more than just money or things."

Visitors to the Center must apply in advance, submitting proposals for study to the Executive Director, SC Wildlife and Marine Resources Dept., Box 167, Columbia, SC 29202.

Georgetown County has much of interest to visitors. Founded in 1730 and the third oldest city in South Carolina, Georgetown was declared a Colonial Port of Entry in 1732 by King George II and was the scene of many Revolutionary War conflicts. Long before, however, the Low County swamplands of Winyah Bay had proved a fertile region for growing rice, which, with indigo and lumber, made Georgetown County wealthy (it produced over half the rice grown in the US during the 1840s.) More than 150 plantations flourished in the county during the mid-1800s. The rice culture, however, was eliminated in the early twentieth century by a series of violent hurricanes. Georgetown has a rare Rice Museum in the Old Market Building (on the National Register of Historic Places) with diroramas depicting production of the crop. Today, there is a resurgence of ship traffic following a deepening of the city channel and the building of a new cargo dock.

Of special interest north of Georgetown is Brookgreen Gardens, on the site of a former rice and indigo plantation; more than 420 pieces of American sculpture are in the garden. Also of interest in the area are the pre-Revolutionary Harold Kaminski House (c. 1760); Hampton Plantation (1735); Hobcaw Barony, site of the home of Bernard Baruch; the Hermitage at Murrells Inlet; Hopsewee Plantation, birthplace of Thomas Lynch, Jr., one of the signers of the Declaration of Independence; and Pawleys Island, one of the oldest of the South Carolina beach resorts.

CROSSING TIME: 2 mins.

FERRY TYPE: Vehicle

VESSEL CAPACITY: 2 cars, 6 passengers

OPERATING SEASON: All year

SCHEDULE: Daily, on signal, 7 a.m.- 11 p.m.

RESTRICTIONS: Large vehicles not permitted. Load limit 10 tons. The ferry is public and anyone may ride it, turn around, and come back; only those with appointments at the Wildlife Center may continue further on the island.

FACILITIES: None

FARE: Free

RESERVATIONS:	No
DIRECTIONS:	From Georgetown take the South Island Road (SR18).
MAP LOCATION:	P. 197, SC, 3
CONTACT:	SC Dept. of Highways and Public Transportation, Box 593, Georgetown, SC 29440, (803)546-2405

STATE:	Tennessee
PLACES SERVED:	Clifton—Decaturville
BODY OF WATER:	Tennessee River
FERRY SERVICE HISTORY:	The ferry is run by the Tennessee Department of Transportation; it connects SR 114.

The ferry consists of a barge, the *Bern-eudine,* pushed by a tugboat, the *Decatur II*. The master here is Mitchell Reynolds, who has had extensive experience on riverboats.

| LOCAL POINTS OF INTEREST: | The ferry is not far from Kentucky Lake and is northwest of Waynesboro. Ten miles east of Waynesboro is Natural Bridge Park, |

believed to be the world's only double-span natural bridge, under which Cherokee Indians are said to have smoked their peace pipes. The ferry is northeast of the Shiloh National Military Park, of interest to Civil War historians.

CROSSING TIME:	4 mins.
FERRY TYPE:	Vehicle
VESSEL CAPACITY:	4-6 cars
OPERATING SEASON:	All year
SCHEDULE:	Daily, on demand, 6 a.m.-6 p.m.
RESTRICTIONS:	Trailers, pickup-campers, and RVs permitted. Load limit 28 tons.

FACILITIES:	None
FARE:	Cars $1; trucks $1.50; trailer trucks $1.50
RESERVATIONS:	No
DIRECTIONS:	Ferry connects SR 114 northwest of Waynesboro and northeast of Savannah.
MAP LOCATION:	P. 197, TN, 1
CONTACT:	Tennessee Dept. of Highways, Tennessee Dept. of Transportation, 2200 Charlotte Ave., Nashville, TN 37203, (615)320-8330

STATE: Tennessee

PLACES SERVED: Cumberland City—Throckmorton

BODY OF WATER: Cumberland River

FERRY SERVICE HISTORY: The ferry on this crossing is a forty-eight foot steel-deck barge, the *Cumberland,* pushed by a small tugboat named the *Lucille II*. It is operated by the Tennessee Department of Transportation. The ferryboat operator used to be a riverboat pilot and is an expert at easing the boat right up to the dock. This ferry is often involved in assisting with military maneuvers at nearby Fort Campbell, Kentucky.

LOCAL POINTS OF INTEREST: The ferry is southwest of Clarksville, a historic old city. Much of the downtown is on the National Register of Historic Places. The Clarksville-Montgomery County Historical Museum was originally constructed as a US Post Office and Customs House in 1898; the eclectic architecture makes this one of the most unique buildings in Tennessee. The Dunbar Cave State Natural Area, a 110-acre park, associated with many legends, is not far from the ferry.

CROSSING TIME: 4 mins.

FERRY TYPE: Vehicle

VESSEL CAPACITY:	4 cars or 2 trucks
OPERATING SEASON:	All year
SCHEDULE:	Daily, on demand, 6 a.m.-6 p.m.
RESTRICTIONS:	Trailers, pickup-campers, and RVs permitted. Load limit 15 tons.
FACILITIES:	None
FARE:	Cars $1, trucks $1.50
RESERVATIONS:	No
DIRECTIONS:	Ferry crosses the Cumberland River at Mile 104, 10 miles south of Indian Mound; it is on Rt. FAS-351 (off SR 46).
MAP LOCATION:	P. 197, TN, 2
CONTACT:	See CONTACT, p. 291.

STATE:	Tennessee
PLACES SERVED:	Dayton—Cleveland ("The Blythe Ferry")
BODY OF WATER:	Tennessee River
FERRY SERVICE HISTORY:	The Blythe Ferry connects Dayton and Cleveland along SR 60. It, along with the Washington Ferry, is listed on the National

Register of Historic Places and became a National Landmark in 1983. It was established by William Blythe, a Cherokee Indian, in 1809. In 1819 he signed a treaty which gave him a 640-acre reservation, including the ferry, in exchange for his renunciation of allegiance to the Cherokee Nation. When the Cherokees were removed to Oklahoma in 1838 on the "Trail of Tears," the Blythes were put in charge of transporting them across the river. The director of the removal, Dr. John Powell, complained that the Blythes were slow and uncooperative in the execution of this duty. The Blythe Ferry consists of a barge pushed by a tugboat, the *Jean Marie*. The present owner is Wilford Caraway; he has been working this stretch of the water for over twenty years, beginning as a deckhand, and has owned the ferry since 1973. He is assisted now by his brother, Bo, and Oland Robinson. At peak times, during the summer, the ferry will make as many as two hundred trips per day across the four-tenths of a mile width of the river.

LOCAL POINTS OF INTEREST: On one side of the ferry is Hiwassee Wildlife Refuge, with an abundance of water birds and other animals. The ferry owner, Wilford Caraway, reports sightings of geese, ducks, bald eagles, cranes, blue herons, seagulls, deer, and snakes. Once, he recalls, a snake decided it wanted a free ride across the river, which unnerved not a few passengers. The Blythe and Washington ferries are in close proximity to each other in the towns of Dayton and Decatur. The Rhea County Courthouse in Dayton was the scene of the famous "Scopes Monkey Trial" (1925). The Red Clay State Historic Area, twelve miles south of Cleveland, has a replica of an Indian farm and council house.

CROSSING TIME: 5 mins.

FERRY TYPE: Vehicle

VESSEL CAPACITY: 4-6 vehicles

OPERATING SEASON: All year

SCHEDULE: **Mon.-Sat.** from 6 a.m. and **Sun.** from 7 a.m.; in summer the ferry closes at 8:45 p.m. and in winter it closes at dark.

RESTRICTIONS: Trailers, pickup-campers, and RVs permitted. Load limit 20 tons.

FACILITIES: None

FARE: Cars $2; trucks $2-$7

RESERVATIONS: No

DIRECTIONS: The ferry is located 6 miles southeast of Dayton on SR 60.

MAP LOCATION: P. 197, TN, 3

CONTACT: Wilford Caraway, Rt. 2, Box 641, Dayton, TN 37321, (615)775-1601

STATE:	Tennessee
PLACES SERVED:	Decatur—Dayton ("The Washington Ferry")
BODY OF WATER:	Tennessee River

FERRY SERVICE HISTORY: The Washington Ferry is eloquent testimony to the failure of bridges to kill off ferries. After winding through Rhea County's peaceful, green farm country, SR 30 climbs a final hill and plunges into the Tennessee River about ten miles northeast of Dayton. The road is, it seems, bridgeless, a fact which fails to register on the six or eight people per year who drive right on, into the river. The *cognoscenti,* however, prepare to ride on one of the most venerable institutions in Tennessee, its oldest ferry crossing. The Washington Ferry is listed on the National Register of Historic Places and was named a National Historic Landmark in 1983. The barge is pushed by the pivoting tug *J.P. Hagler II.* As one newspaper reporter, Mary M. Mahoney, put it in the *Chattanooga Times,* "It's not quite the captain's bridge of the *Queen Mary,* but the Old Washington ferry tow boat has an air of distinction about it." The tow boat was bought in 1948, as was the barge (which was built by Sherman and Reilly, Inc., of Chattanooga.) The ferry is owned by Charles Smith, who purchased it when the previous owner, G. K. Aikman, died. Smith grew up within three miles of the ferry, and has operated the ferry since 1958; he is now aided by his son, Dean. He says the most troublesome cargos are large trucks and funeral processions. Because the river divides Rhea and Meigs counties, where people have intermarried, they are often buried away from the county where they have lived. The ferry once transported a fleet of twenty antique Rolls-Royces whose owners shipped them from Great Britain to tour the United States.

The original ferry was established in 1807 by Conley Hastings and was important in the development of transportation in the newly opened territories of Southeast Tennessee. It is estimated the ferry was taken over by the Locke family about 1820; it was later owned by Solomon Henry and Sons. The ferry is also called the Hastings-Locke Ferry, after its two early owners. One operator, since retired, was W. C. (Cleo) Jenkins; he says he was "raised up in ferrying." He used to ferry horses and buggies; when he retired in 1972, he had carried dignitaries such as the governor and entertainers such as Roy Acuff and the late Tex Ritter.

LOCAL POINTS OF INTEREST:	The ferry is in an ideal location for tourists, situated between Knoxville and Chattanooga. The Jack Daniel's Distillery, in Lynchburg, is quite close also.
CROSSING TIME:	3 mins.
FERRY TYPE:	Vehicle
VESSEL CAPACITY:	6-8 cars
OPERATING SEASON:	All year
SCHEDULE:	**Weekdays:** 6 a.m. to dark; **Sat.:** 7 a.m. to dark; **Sun.:** 8 a.m. to dark.
RESTRICTIONS:	Trailers, pick-up campers, and RVs permitted. Load limit 30 tons.
FACILITIES:	None
FARE:	Cars $1.50; trucks and trailer trucks higher ($2-$5, according to weight)
RESERVATIONS:	No
DIRECTIONS:	The ferry is located 6.5 miles west of Decatur on SR 30.
MAP LOCATION:	P. 197, TN, 4
CONTACT:	Charles Smith, Rt. 4, Box 280, Dayton, TN 37321, (615)775-3857

STATE:	Tennessee
PLACES SERVED:	Nashville—Scottsboro
BODY OF WATER:	Cumberland River
FERRY SERVICE HISTORY:	James Jennings has been operating the ferry at this crossing for over twenty-five years; he says there has been a ferry at this site for

over one hundred years. Today, the ferry is run by the metropolitan government of Nashville. It is a single boat, the *Judge Hickman* (named for the Davison County judge at the time it was built, in 1952). The boat has been at this location since 1965. "I've had just about everything in Nashville on the ferry at one time or another," says Jennings. There have been weddings on the ferry, and he has carried monkeys, dogs, and a lynx, as well as fire engines, ambulances, and police cars ("They're hauled by themselves," says Jennings. "Nothing else is put on with them.") He has carried Johnny Cash, Waylon Jennings, and other country music stars also. Jennings lives in a house just above the ferry (part of his remuneration). "It gets a little aggravating at times, but it's never boring," he says.

LOCAL POINTS OF INTEREST: There is something about Nashville which seems to call for epithets, everything from the "Wall Street of the South" to the "Athens of the South," the "Protestant Vatican," and the "Buckle on the Bible Belt." It may come as a surprise to visitors to learn that the music industry is secondary to the city's banking and insurance interests. Nevertheless, most visitors will want to see the Country Music Hall of Fame, the Country Music Wax Museum and Shopping Mall, Opryland USA, Minnie Pearl's Museum, the Grand Ole Opry, and the many other attractions centered on the world of country music. In addition, the Belle Carol Riverboat Company offers cruises on the Cumberland River; some of the boats carry up to four hundred passengers. Both the Belle Meade Mansion and the Belmont Mansion are well worth seeing, as is the Hermitage, home of Andrew Jackson. The Loveless Motel is one of the better known Southern-style eateries (serving breakfast any time), and Julian's is famous for its French food.

CROSSING TIME: 5 min.

FERRY TYPE: Vehicle

VESSEL CAPACITY: 8 cars

OPERATING SEASON: All year

SCHEDULE: Daily, on demand, 6 a.m.-midnight; closed holidays.

RESTRICTIONS: Trailers, pickup-campers, and RVs permitted. Load limit 8 tons.

FACILITIES: None

FARE: Free

RESERVATIONS: No

DIRECTIONS: The ferry is on Old Hickory Blvd. in West Nashville.

MAP LOCATION: P. 197, TN, 5

CONTACT: James Jennings, 1099 Cleeces Ferry Road, Nashville, TN 37209, (615)352-6701

STATE: Tennessee

PLACES SERVED: Rome—Dixon Springs

BODY OF WATER: Cumberland River

FERRY SERVICE HISTORY: The Rome ferry is pushed by the tugboat *Jere Mitchell*. The ferry is operated by the government of Smith County.

LOCAL POINTS OF INTEREST: The Cumberland Plateau is one of the oldest mountain ranges in America. It rises like a gigantic wall spanning the width of the state, forming the western boundary of the vast Tennessee Valley. The terrain is marked by deep river gorges, lofty cliffs, natural bridges and majestic waterfalls. The ferry is near Carthage and the Cordell Hull Lake, above I-40. Dixona, built in the 1700s, was the home of Maj. Dixon Tilman and is on the National Register of Historic Places.

CROSSING TIME: 5 min.

FERRY TYPE: Vehicle

VESSEL CAPACITY: 3 cars

OPERATING SEASON: All year

SCHEDULE: Daily, on demand, 7 a.m.-4 p.m.

RESTRICTIONS: Trailers, pickup-campers, and RVs permitted. Load limit 5 tons.

FACILITIES: None

FARE: Free

RESERVATIONS: No

DIRECTIONS: The ferry is on FAS-1085, not far from SR 25 at Dixon Springs.

MAP LOCATION: P. 197, TN, 6

CONTACT: Smith County Highway Dept., 200 Upper Ferry Rd., Carthage, TN 37030, (615)735-9413

STATE: Tennessee

PLACES SERVED: Saltillo—SR 128 (Hardin County)

BODY OF WATER: Tennessee River

FERRY SERVICE HISTORY: The Saltillo ferry is pushed by the tugboat *Carolyn* and is operated by Hardin County.

LOCAL POINTS OF INTEREST: The ferry is west of the Clifton-Decaturville ferry, above Savannah and south of Kentucky Lake.

CROSSING TIME: 3 mins.

FERRY TYPE: Vehicle

VESSEL CAPACITY: 6 cars

OPERATING SEASON: All year

SCHEDULE: Daily, on demand, 6:30 a.m.-4 p.m.; closed Sun.

RESTRICTIONS: Trailers, pickup-campers, and RVs permitted. Load limit 15 tons.

FACILITIES: None

FARE: Car $.50; trucks $1; trailer trucks $1.50

RESERVATIONS: No

DIRECTIONS: The ferry is on a local county road at Saltillo, which is on SR 69.

MAP LOCATION: P. 197, TN, 7

CONTACT: Hardin County Highway Dept., Court Square, Savannah, TN 38372, (901)925-4993

STATE: Virginia

PLACES SERVED: Hatton—SR 625 ("The Hatton Ferry")

BODY OF WATER: James River

FERRY SERVICE HISTORY: Early ferries in Virginia developed in a somewhat haphazard fashion, across waterways used for centuries by Indians, with boat owners furnishing transportation for friends and, later, as a commercial venture. By 1647, ferriage rates were set by the General Assembly, but some ferrymen felt the fees to be unreasonably low. In 1696, an investigation of ferry keepers disclosed some who denied that they were in such a business, though they admitted they did "sometimes sett over ye River By Chance some footman or horse." Today, Virginia's three small cable ferries are free, retained as much for their historical value as for their role in transportation. In 1982 the Hatton Ferry (operated by the state since 1940) was threatened with extinction by the state, which decided it had outlived its usefulness as a means of transportation. The Albermarle County Historical Society protested and established a Standing Committee under the chairmanship of Joseph Jenkins, a retired Piedmont Community College dean. Jenkins and his committee commissioned a history of Albermarle County ferries, written by John Hammond Moore ("The Ferries of Albermarle," *The Magazine of Albermarle County History*, Vol. 42, 1984). The Highway Department agreed to divert maintenance funds, the season and schedule were curtailed, and the ferry was saved. The ferry is the youngest in Albermarle County, but the last one surviving. It reportedly began operating in the 1840s though it has been completely documented only from the mid-1870s. Charles E. "Chic" Moran, a member of the committee, has conducted research and found that it was not named until 1881, when a local merchant named Brown purchased the property and requested a post office. "Hatton," says Moran, "was the name of the postal officials who signed the papers for the post office." The tender's cottage was originally wooden; the cinderblock replacement was built some time before World War II. The cottage was recently refurbished with the assistance of the Historical Society.

The Hatton ferry is called a pole ferry, but is actually, says Moran, hand-powered across the river with winches and cables, assisted by the river current, which carries the boat across the river. Two cross bars on either side of the river support a main cable. Other cables run from the bow and stern and are attached to winches and linked to the overhead cable. The angle of the ferry is directed to the flow of the river, and the pole is used only as a push. When the water is low, additional poling by the ferryman may be needed. For over ten years, until his retirement in 1981, Ned Hocker worked the state's last pole ferry, though before that he operated other ferries and grain mills along the James. "I learned to have respect for that river. It ain't nothing to play with," he once said. "When that water starts jumping over the front end, you got to act." The ferry has become quite a tourist attraction. "Most of 'em look at a thing like this and can't believe how it could ever work. I just load 'em up and take 'em on over," he told a reporter for the Norfolk *Virginian-Pilot*. Both high and low water prevent operation of the ferry. This and the Los Ebanos ferry in Texas are thought to be the only two public non-powered ferries in the US.

In 1972, tropical storm Agnes demolished the ferry, but it was restored to service in July 1973. A September 22 dedication ceremony featured Richard Thomas, John-Boy in the television series *The Waltons*. That ferry sank in a 1985 flood, but another small ferry, built in 1972, was acquired and dedicated in August 1986. Joseph Jenkins and his committee proudly participated in the christening. "It would have been intolerable to let this important Albermarle County institution go down the drain," says Jenkins.

LOCAL POINTS OF INTEREST: Hatton is a very small hamlet; Scottsville is a pleasant litle town about twenty miles from Charlottesville. The Scottsville Museum on Main Street has an interesting regional history collection. Charlottesville is best known as the home of Thomas Jefferson, who founded the University of Virginia. Monticello is an imposing estate, as remarkable for the ingenious devices installed by Jefferson as for its beauty. A good place to have lunch or dinner nearby is the historic Michie Tavern Museum, which offers a colonial-style buffet and a look at many household inventions. The town of Charlottesville is dominated by the sprawling University. Tours begin in the Rotunda, modeled after the Pantheon in Rome. Major sights are the serpentine walls, the Pavilions housing distinguished faculty, and the Range (Poe lived in Room 13, West Range). The rolling Albemarle County countryside is the home of many affluent retirees. For a look at some of the famous estates and their equally famous stables, try to visit Virginia during Garden Week, the last of April, when many private homes and gardens are open to the public. Ash Lawn, home of President James Monroe, is also in Albemarle County.

CROSSING TIME: 5 mins.

FERRY TYPE: Vehicle

VESSEL CAPACITY: 2 cars

OPERATING SEASON: Mid-Apr.-mid-Oct. river permitting; check to see whether it is running

SCHEDULE: **Fri.-Sun.:** 9 a.m.-5 p.m.

RESTRICTIONS: Pickup-campers only; no trailers or RVs permitted.

FACILITIES: None

FARE: Free

RESERVATIONS: No

DIRECTIONS: The ferry is just off SR 20, southwest of Scottsville (south of Charlottesville). From the north: from SR 20, before you reach Scottsville, take SR 726 west, then SR 625 south. From the south: from SR 20, before you reach Scottsville, take 695 west, then 625 north.

MAP LOCATION: P. 197, VA, 1

CONTACT: Charlottesville Residency, Box 2013, Charlottesville, VA 22902-0013, (804)296-5102

Jamestown

STATE:	Virginia
PLACES SERVED:	Jamestown—Scotland
BODY OF WATER:	James River
FERRY SERVICE HISTORY:	Service began in 1925; vessels are the *Williamsburg*, the *Surry,* the *Jamestown,* and the *Virginia*.

The first automobile ferry was the *Captain John Smith,* which toiled across from Scotland Wharf to Jamestown on February 26, 1925, greeted by a stalwart delegation of Williamsburg and Newport News residents who braved the weather. Earlier, of course, ferries were as common in Virginia as elsewhere. In 1748, the General Assembly listed forty-one separate ferries on the James River and its tributaries alone. Among the more memorable moments on the Jamestown Ferry was the time in 1974 when an Indiana man appeared at the tollbooth on horseback, leading a pack horse. The purser and the pilot were at a loss, as there was no published toll for a horse, so he was not charged for crossing. One newspaper reporter wondered, however, if he had been charged a toll based on the number of axles or horsepower. In 1960, severe winter weather immobilized operations; a frustrated commuter complained that John Smith and company "came over and settled this country some three hundred years ago, traveling three thousand miles, and you can't even get across this three-mile-wide river!" He was right for several long hours. Local historian Parke S. Rouse has written of the feeling he always has, going from Williamsburg on "romantic forays" to Surry, Isle of Wight, and Smithfield: "I'm struck by the contrast between Southside and the rest of Virginia. The southern counties seem to be a survival of the nineteenth century, where people still live the rural, slow-paced life of tobacco-planting days." Many county residents fear a bridge would urbanize their county, "like Gloucester." One Surry commuter told Rouse, "The ferry gives me time to read the paper and catch my breath."

Marion Line, Richmond folk artist, has also perceived the ferry as an icon of simpler days. She has painted the *Surry* with its center tower looking rather medieval, with colorful toy-sized cars and people ranged along the railings, surrounded by a cloud of pigeons (one small girl is depicted staring from the back of a van, too frightened by the pigeons to get out). The voyage is both an attraction in itself and, to a large extent, a reenactment of the approach Capt. John Smith and his band of settlers first made to historic Jamestown Island.

LOCAL POINTS OF INTEREST: Jamestown Island is the site of the first permanent English-speaking colony in America; it was settled in 1607. Replicas of the three ships that brought the first settlers (the *Susan Constant,* the *Godspeed,* and the *Discovery*) may be seen at the Jamestown Festival Park, which also houses the Old World and New World pavilions (the ferry glides past the ships entering and leaving the landing at Jamestown). Williamsburg, the restored colonial capital, is a few miles from Jamestown; this is the most extensive eighteenth-century town in the United States, voted by US travel writers one of the ten foremost destinations for visitors to America. It is a reincarnation of the eighteenth-century era, with stately architecture, fife and drum music, topiary boxwood, authentic colonial eating places, and more than five hundred buildings and residences evoking the heyday of Williamsburg as the colonial capital. Yorktown, where the decisive battle of the American Revolution was fought in October 1781, is accessible from Jamestown via the Colonial Parkway. Several historic plantations may be visited on both sides of the river not far from the ferry. Near the Scotland terminus of the ferry is the Rolfe-Warren House, former home of the Indian princess Pocahontas and her English husband, John Rolfe. The grounds include a replica of a small English garden planted by the Garden Club of Virginia. For excellent regional Virginia cookery, try the Surrey House on Route 10 (hush puppies, crab cakes, delicately smoked razor-thin Virginia ham, apple fritters, and peanut raisin pie). And if you cross to Surry County, dine at the Surrey House (they retain the old spelling), and miss your evening ferry, what then? You can walk along the little beach by the landing and watch the small rowboats swinging at anchor, silhouetted against the sunset. There are decidedly worse ways to spend an hour.

CROSSING TIME: 20 mins.

FERRY TYPE: Vehicle

VESSEL CAPACITY: *Williamsburg:* 50 vehicles; *Surry:* 50 vehicles; *Jamestown:* 40 vehicles; *Virginia:* 28 vehicles

OPERATING SEASON: All year

SCHEDULE: **Sept. 16-May 31: Mon.-Thurs.: Lv. Scotland Wharf** *5 a.m., 5:40, 6:30, *6:50, 7:15, *7:35, then every hour on the hour until 2 p.m.; then every half-hour 2:30-6; then every hour on the hour 7-midnight; **lv. Jamestown** *5:20 a.m., 6:05, 6:50, *7:15, 7:35, *8, then every hour on the half-hour 8:30-2:30 p.m., then every half hour 3-6:30, then every hour on the half-hour 7:30 p.m.-12:30 a.m. **Sept. 16-May 31: (Fri., Sat, Sun.) and June 1-Sept. 15 daily: Lv. Scotland** *5 a.m.; 5:40, 6:30, *6:50, 7:15, *7:35, 8, 9, 10, then every half-hour 10:30-7 p.m., 8, 9, 10, 11, midnight; **lv. Jamestown** *5:20 a.m., 6:05, 6:50, *7:15, 7:30, *8, 8:30, 9:30, then every half-hour 10:30-7:30 p.m., 8:30, 9:30, 10:30, 11:30, 12:30 a.m. *Mon.-Fri. only.

RESTRICTIONS: Trailers, pickup-campers, and RVs permitted. Load limit 16 tons. Overhead clearance 12'6".

FACILITIES: Restrooms

FARE: Car, pick-up camper $2; with trailer to $6; pedestrian or bicycle $0.15.

RESERVATIONS: None

DIRECTIONS: From Williamsburg or Jamestown, take Rt. 31 west; ferry crosses at Jamestown. From Surry take Rt. 31 east to Scotland, 6 mi.

MAP LOCATION: P. 197, VA, 2

CONTACT: Ferry Wharf, (804)294-3354; also Waverly Residency, Virginia Dept. of Highways and Transportation, Box 45, Waverly, VA 23890, (804)834-2333

Lancaster

STATE: Virginia

PLACES SERVED: Merry Point—SR 604

BODY OF WATER: Corrotoman River

FERRY SERVICE   Lancaster County records indicate that the
HISTORY: Merry Point ferry may have started as early
                            as 1668, though service was apparently not
always continuous. During the 1700s, planters brought tobacco to the
warehouse here (simply called "The Point") for shipping. On the
opposite side was "The Ferry Point" (now Ottoman), also a tobacco
warehouse site. In 1790, Gavin Lowry stipulated in his will that the ferry
and his warehouses were to be rented out for five years, the proceeds to
be used to repair the ferry. About 1820, Addison Hall, a Baptist minister,
ran the ferry, then known as Hall's Ferry. Until recently, the vessel used
was the much loved *Arminta,* the workboat that pushed the barge; she has
been replaced by the *Lancaster,* an "iron-clad" with self-contained
motor. In 1847, the General Assembly authorized a public ferry here and
gave the circuit court judge authority to close the ferry if need for it
ceased to exist. A number of years ago, the Virginia State Highway
Department did request discontinuation of the ferry, but there was such an
uproar no request has found its way to the circuit court since. Ferryman
Norman "Pat" Patterson has worked the Merry Point ferry for ten years
and has enjoyed the variety of travellers; in one day recently, he had cars
from California, Tennessee, and Indiana. The ferry now carries about
twelve thousand vehicles a year.

LOCAL POINTS OF INTEREST: Merry Point has been called a "kind of memory" on SR 604. The ferry is named from the community that used to live here; the number has now dwindled to ten people. The village was once known as Mary's Mount, settled by Daniel Dockin, Jr., before 1630. As early as 1748, it had become Merry Point. The approach to the ferry along SR 604 is extremely scenic, with valleys bordering the winding highway. Just before the ferry, on the left, the restored Merry Point House is visible, once the home of a Presbyterian minister, the Rev. James Waddell. The Corrotoman River has a tranquil beauty, with wild shrubs and trees matting the bank near a soft sand beach.

The considerable charms of Lancaster County are now being discovered by affluent retirees from other states as well as Virginia. A number came to know of it by visiting Tide's Inn, an elegant resort at Irvington, or its sister facility, the Tides Lodge. The inn opened in 1947; it was founded by E. A. Stephens. With its water setting, European furnishings, yacht *Miss Ann* (rates include cruises), breakfast menus in the form of homey letters from Bob Lee Stephens, one of Stephens's sons, marina, and excellent golfing, the inn attracts yachtsmen and guests nationwide. Also near Irvington is historic Christ Church (1732).

CROSSING TIME: 10 mins.

FERRY TYPE: Vehicle

VESSEL CAPACITY: 2 cars

OPERATING SEASON: All year

SCHEDULE: Mon.-Sat., on demand, 7 a.m.-7 p.m.

RESTRICTIONS: Trailers to 22 ft., pickup-campers, and RVs permitted. Load limit 8 tons. Max. comb. vehicle length 45 ft.

FACILITIES: None

FARE: Free

RESERVATIONS: No

DIRECTIONS: From Richmond: take US 360 to Warsaw, SR 3 to Lancaster County, SR 354 to Ottoman, and SR 604 to the ferry. From Irvington, take SR 3 to SR 604. Ferry connects 2 segments of SR 604.

MAP LOCATION: P. 197, VA, 3

CONTACT: Warsaw Residency, Box 38, Warsaw, VA 22572, (804)333-3696

Elizabeth River Ferry

STATE: Virginia

PLACES SERVED: Norfolk-Portsmouth

BODY OF WATER: Elizabeth River

FERRY SERVICE HISTORY: This ferry service across the Elizabeth River began after Waterside, Norfolk's festival waterplace, opened in 1983. At first a temporary vessel was used, but then the blue and white *Elizabeth River Ferry* was acquired. She has a stern paddlewheel and is seventy-seven feet long, with two decks and a sixty-foot-long cabin; the lower deck is enclosed and heated. She had been operating on the Mississippi River and in Florida before being purchased for use in Virginia. As she sails across the river, she is dwarfed by the giant Navy ships at anchor in Norfolk Harbor. A sister ship, the *Elizabeth River Ferry II,* has now been added.

The harbor has had a long history of ferries, beginning as early as 1636, when Adam Thoroughgood operated a crude, hand-rowed skiff (replacing an Indian log canoe) and charged a bale of tobacco or sixpence for a man and his horse. Later, there were paddlewheel boats driven by horses on treadmills. Beginning in 1832, the *Gosport,* a steam ferry, established a tradition of regular service. One popular side-wheeler was the *Manahassett,* known as the "Mammy Ferry." The upper deck was enclosed in latticework, making it safe for children, and on sunny summer afternoons her upper deck was reserved for Norfolk area nursemaids. Once the gate leading to the upper deck had been locked by a deckhand, they were able to gossip at leisure in the checkered sunlight. Eventually, car ferries came into use; one well-known one was the *City of Portsmouth.* The Norfolk-Portsmouth Bridge Tunnel (1952) sounded the death knell for the large old ferries, and the last one ran in 1955. The cycle has come full circle now, though, with ferry travel gaining popularity because of the revitalization of the waterfront and the crowding on bridges and in tunnels.

LOCAL POINTS OF INTEREST: Norfolk, settled in 1682, is a major seaport, part of Hampton Roads, one of the largest natural harbors in the world. The famous *Merrimac-Monitor* battle was fought here in 1862. The Norfolk Naval Shipyard in Portsmouth and the Naval Station and Naval Air Station in Norfolk constitute a major naval complex. It was in Norfolk in 1907 that President Teddy Roosevelt launched the Great White Fleet, which symbolized the naval power of the United States. It is the Atlantic NATO headquarters. Today, the city is the home of the Chrysler Museum, the Norfolk Botanical Gardens, the Adam Thoroughgood House (built in 1636 and believed to be the oldest brick house in America), and many other historic buildings; the city operates a trolley sightseeing tour. It is adjacent to such resort areas as Virginia Beach and is the gateway to Virginia's Eastern Shore (via the Chesapeake Bay Bridge-Tunnel). The city is undergoing renewal in several areas, most notably the waterfront. Here, over 120 ships and dining places are housed in the Waterside complex, patterned after Norfolk's original ferry terminal. The Omni International Hotel is also here. Harbour tours in the *Carrie B.,* a replica of a nineteenth-century riverboat, leave from Norfolk and Portsmouth, and tours aboard the *New Spirit* leave from Waterside.

Portsmouth was founded in 1752 and is also part of the port of Hampton Roads. Portside is Portsmouth's waterfront complement to Norfolk's Waterside; it features the Olde Harbour Market and an Olde Towne Trolley Tour. Portsmouth has many interesting museums, such as the Portsmouth Naval Shipyard Museum, the Portsmouth Lightship Museum, and a children's museum.

Both cities are near the Mariners' Museum in Newport News, which has a major maritime collection, and about an hour from Williamsburg.

CROSSING TIME: 5 mins.

FERRY TYPE: Pedestrian

VESSEL CAPACITY: 150 passengers

OPERATING SEASON: All year

SCHEDULE: **Summer: Mon.-Fri.:** 7 a.m.-midnight; **Sat. and Sun.:** 10 a.m.-midnight. **After Sept. 1: Mon-Fri.:** 7 a.m.-10 p.m.; **Fri. and Sat.:** 10 a.m.-midnight. Leaves Portside on the hr. and half-hr. and Waterside 15 mins. and 45 mins. after the hr.

RESTRICTIONS: Small pets permitted

FACILITIES: No

FARE: Adults $0.50; children under 12, senior citizens, and handicapped persons $0.25

RESERVATIONS: No

DIRECTIONS: In Norfolk, leaves from Waterside; in Portsmouth, leaves from Portside.

MAP LOCATION: P. 197, VA, 4

CONTACT: Norfolk By Boat, Inc., 1034 Naval Ave., Portsmouth, VA 23704, (804)393-4735

STATE: Virginia

PLACES SERVED: Onancock—Tangier

BODY OF WATER: Chesapeake Bay

FERRY SERVICE HISTORY: Ferry service to Tangier is provided aboard the *Captain Eulice,* a sixty-five-foot cruise ship which was the former mail boat to Tangier. A unique feature of this service is the five-mile trip each way down Onancock Creek, a narrated cruise past beautiful waterside homes. It is quite feasible for bicyclists to cross from Onancock (pronounced OhNANcock), spend some time on Tangier, and take the *Capt. Thomas* to Reedville; the two services can thus be combined to form a cross-bay ferry, though neither ship carries cars.

LOCAL POINTS OF INTEREST: Onancock is a tranquil harbor town located at the head of Onancock Creek, five miles from Chesapeake Bay. Its large, deep harbor is three blocks from the main downtown area. Few ferry offices have the ambiance of the one at Onancock, and even fewer are museums and historic landmarks in their own right. The Hopkins and Bro. general store, however, is an APVA property and National Historic Landmark, one of the oldest stores on the East Coast, built by Capt. Stephen Hopkins in 1842. Today, Miriam and Steven King lease the Hopkins Wharf Museum from the APVA, satisfying a longstanding desire to become involved in their own museum (Steven King was a history major at Old Dominion University and says they came to it by a "long circuitous path"). The Kings have adapted it as a general store, selling marine supplies and fishing tackle, but are proudest of continuing the building's maritime tradition as a historic steamboat ticket office. A dock existed here as early as 1838, and the Hopkins brothers sold steamship tickets from the same ticket window after the Civil War, beginning in 1866. The store's original office has been unchanged; century-old transactions are recorded in yellowing ledgers. The cash register was installed in 1906. One side of the building is a restaurant, also run by the Kings, featuring local seafood. Onancock is also noted for Kerr Place, dating from 1799, the home of the Eastern Shore Historical Society.

Virginia's Tangier Island welcomes visitors. With its tidy little homes, picket fences, lingering Elizabethan accents, and crab farms, it seems an island where time has almost been arrested. Residents cherish the Tangier lifestyle, and most have no desire to live on the mainland; the way of living has been passed down through many generations as something worth preserving. There are few motor vehicles here, and tourist trams take visitors along the island's diminutive ten-foot wide streets. You may eat a traditional seafood dinner at one of the Island's well-known restaurants or eat a picnic lunch aboard ship or at tables overlooking the harbor. It has been called the "soft-shell crab capital of the nation." Hilda Crockett's Chesapeake House is a famous restaurant with regional specialties.

CROSSING TIME: 1 hr. 30 mins.

FERRY TYPE: Pedestrian

VESSEL CAPACITY: 100 passengers

OPERATING SEASON: June-Sept.

SCHEDULE: **Mon.-Sat. (no sailings Sun.): Lv. Onancock** 10 a.m. **Lv. Tangier** 1:30 p.m.

RESTRICTIONS: Small pets accepted

FACILITIES: Restrooms, snack bar

FARE: Adults $8 (round-trip $14); children (6-12) half-fare; under 6 free; bicycles $1.

RESERVATIONS: Available

DIRECTIONS: The wharf is 3 blocks from downtown.

MAP LOCATION: P. 197, VA, 5

CONTACT: Hopkins & Bro. Store, #2 Market St., Onancock, VA 23417, (804)787-8220

Capt. Thomas

STATE: Virginia

PLACES SERVED: Reedville—Tangier

BODY OF WATER: Chesapeake Bay

FERRY SERVICE HISTORY: Two vessels are used on this run, the seventy-five-foot cruiser *Capt. Thomas* and the one-hundred-foot cruiser *Chesapeake Breeze*. Both boats are usually used on busy Saturdays. Service was inaugurated in 1970. Bicyclists often take the *Captain Eulice* on to Onancock, Virginia, forming a cross-bay ferry of the two services.

LOCAL POINTS OF INTEREST: Reedville is located at the tip of Virginia's Northern Neck, in Northumberland County. It is a busy fishing port with a seafaring atmosphere, as well as a historic town with a mixture of New England style homes and Victorian mansions. The heritage of Reedville, as well as the county, is nicely captured in the Northumberland Preservation logo, designed by artist Jane Stouffer, a sampler depicting a brick Georgian manor house with a fish above it representing the fishing industry which helped develop and maintain the community. People come to admire the architecture and to watch watermen unload their catch at Reedville's bustling docks.

[For notes on Tangier, please see entry under Onancock-Tangier, p. 311.]

CROSSING TIME: 1 hr. 45 mins.

FERRY TYPE: Pedestrian

VESSEL CAPACITY: *Capt. Thomas:* 150 passengers; *Chesapeake Breeze:* 150 passengers

OPERATING SEASON: May 1-Sept. 30

SCHEDULE: Daily. Lv. Reedville 10 a.m.; return to Reedville 4:15 p.m.

RESTRICTIONS: No pets

FACILITIES: Restrooms, snack bar

FARE: Adults $16 round-trip; children (4-13) $8.

RESERVATIONS: Necessary

DIRECTIONS: Reedville is on US 360, approx. 3 hrs. from Washington, 2 hrs. from Richmond, and 2½ hrs. from Norfolk.

MAP LOCATION: P. 197, VA, 6

CONTACT: Tangier and Chesapeake Cruises, Inc., Warsaw, VA 22572, (804)333-4656

STATE:	Virginia/Maryland
PLACES SERVED:	Smith Point, VA—Smith Island, MD
BODY OF WATER:	Chesapeake Bay
FERRY SERVICE HISTORY:	Service on this crossing is aboard the *Capt. Evans.* Service was inaugurated June 14, 1980; the *Capt. Evans* was commissioned in

1983. She is a sightseeing and excursion boat sixty-five feet long with two decks and a crew of three. Most riders come from nearby metropolitan areas, but there are many out-of-state tourists as well. Northbound bicyclists often cross on this boat, then take the *Teresa Ann Evans,* the *Island Belle II,* the *Capt. Jason,* or the *Capt. Jason II,* on to Crisfield, Maryland.

LOCAL POINTS OF INTEREST:	Smith Point is on the tip of Virginia's Northern Neck, not far from Reedville. There are pretty bays and coves here; the boat leaves

from the Smith Point/Reedville KOA Campground.

Ewell is the "capital" of Smith Island, which is actually an archipelago of three islands with interlacing creeks and canals that connect the three fishing villages of Ewell, Tylerton, and Rhodes Point. The area, about eight miles long by four miles wide, was named for Capt. John Smith, who explored the Chesapeake Bay in 1608. It was settled in 1657 by English dissenters from Lord Baltimore's colony. The lifestyle here has changed slowly with the passing of time. Descendants of original English and Cornish settlers populate the island, depending on seafood as a livelihood. Some of the ancient modes of speech have survived here.

CROSSING TIME:	1 hr. 30 mins.
FERRY TYPE:	Pedestrian
VESSEL CAPACITY:	150 passengers
OPERATING SEASON:	All year
SCHEDULE:	Daily: Lv. Smith Point at 10 a.m.; lv. Smith Island at 2:15. The boat docks at Ewell.
RESTRICTIONS:	Pets not permitted
FACILITIES:	Restrooms, snacks, sodas
FARE:	$8

RESERVATIONS:	Yes
DIRECTIONS:	Campground is 2½ miles northeast of junction of US 360 and SR 652.
MAP LOCATION:	P. 197, VA, 7
CONTACT:	Capt. Gordon Evans, Island & Bay Cruises, Inc., Rt. 1, Box 289-R, Reedville, VA 22539, (804)453-3430

Northumberland

STATE:	Virginia
PLACES SERVED:	Sunnybank—Ophelia
BODY OF WATER:	Little Wicomico River
FERRY SERVICE HISTORY:	The Sunnybank ferry reportedly began operating in 1906, according to a senior citizen of Sunnybank, Tennyson Evans Hammack,

whose father owned the Sunnybank Ferry landing. Hammack says that the Northumberland County Board of Supervisors approved establishment of the ferry at that time. The ferry was pulled by hand before the advent of the motorboat. Recently the old wooden *Hazel* was replaced by the *Northumberland,* a single-unit, all-steel, motor-driven barge, an "ironclad" built in Deltaville. It still operates on a cable, however. John M. Dodson, who has been operating the ferry for twenty-one years, has ferried vehicles from all over the country across the river; riding the ferry round trip is a popular recreation for families exposing their children to a treasured bit of Americana. This ferry, along with the Merry Point ferry in Lancaster County, has been retained by Virginia because of its historic value and as an example of the river transportation used many years ago.

LOCAL POINTS OF INTEREST: Driving through Northumberland County, one has to have faith in directions, as the agricultural countryside seems at first unlikely to harbor a ferry. Suddenly, signs appear and the wide and beautiful Little Wicomico River comes into view. At the Sunnybank landing, there was once the crab house of the late Capt. Curtis Smith, but today the wooden crab shedding floats are piled onshore, along with derelict boats. The Hack's Neck (or Ophelia) side is even more rural, with a few houses nestled beneath the pines. The ferry is close to Reedville and Smith Point, departure points for ferries to Tangier and Smith Island. More of the Little Wicomico can be seen aboard the *Kit II*, which makes river cruises from Smith Point (call Capt. Danny Crabbe of Heathsville, 804/453-3251). One of Heathsville's historic homes, Belleville, is now a bed-and-breakfast inn (call Jane H. Blackwell, 804/580-5293).

CROSSING TIME: 10 mins.

FERRY TYPE: Vehicle

VESSEL CAPACITY: 2 cars

OPERATING SEASON: All year

SCHEDULE: Mon.-Sat., on demand, 7 a.m.-7 p.m.

RESTRICTIONS: Trailers to 22 ft., pickup-campers, and RVs permitted. Load limit 8 tons. Max. comb. vehicle length 45 ft.

FACILITIES: None

FARE: Free

RESERVATIONS: No

DIRECTIONS: Ferry connects SR 651 and SR 644 near Smith Point, on Virginia's Northern Neck, in Northumberland County

MAP LOCATION: P. 197, VA, 8

CONTACT: See CONTACT, p. 308.

FERRIES
OF THE
GREAT LAKES
AND MIDWEST

Ferries of the Great Lakes and Midwest

ILLINOIS

1. Batchtown-Winfield, MO
2. Brussels-Grafton
3. Cave-in-Rock - Marion, KY
4. Darwin-Vigo, IN
5. Golden Eagle-St. Charles, MO
6. Kampsville-Eldred
* [Meyer-Canton, MO; see MO]

INDIANA

* [Rising Sun-Rabbit Hash, KY; see KY]
* [Vigo-Darwin, IL; see IL]

MICHIGAN

1. Algonac-Harsens Island
2. Algonac-Walpole Island, ON
3. Barbeau-Oak Ridge Park, Neebish Island
4. Boblo Island-Detroit, Gibraltar, and Amherstburg, ON
5. Charlevoix-St. James, Beaver Island
6. Cheboygan-Pointe Aux Pins, Bois Blanc Island
7. Copper Harbor-Isle Royale National Park
8. De Tour-Drummond Island
9. Houghton-Isle Royale National Park
* [Isle Royale National Park-Grand Portage, MN; see MN]
10. Ironton-Boyne City (10 mi. W.)
11. Leland-South Manitou Island
12. Ludington-Kewaunee, WI
13. Mackinaw City-Mackinac Island
14. Marine City-Sombra, ON
15. St. Ignace-Mackinac Island
16. Sault Ste. Marie (Mission Point)-Sugar Island

MINNESOTA

1. Grand Portage-Isle Royale National Park, MI

MISSOURI

1. Akers-Highways "K" and "KK" (Shannon County)
2. Canton-Meyer, IL
* [Dorena-Hickman; see KY]
3. Route "J" (Osage and Gasconade Counties)
* [St. Charles-Golden Eagle, IL; see IL]
* [Winfield-Batchtown, IL; see IL]

OHIO

* [Boudes Ferry-Augusta, KY; see KY]
1. Catawba Point - Put-in-Bay (South Bass Island)
2. Marblehead-Kelleys Island
3. Port Clinton - Put-in-Bay (South Bass Island)
4. Put-in-Bay (South Bass Island)-Middle Bass Island
5. Sandusky-Kelleys Island
6. Sandusky-Pelee Island, ON
7. Toledo - Put-in-Bay (South Bass Island)

WISCONSIN

1. Bayfield-LaPointe (Madeline Island)
* [Kewaunee-Ludington, MI; see MI]
2. Merrimac-Okee
3. Northport (Gills Rock)-Washington Island
4. Washington Island-Rock Island State Park

Isle Royale
Grand Portage
MINNESOTA
Lake Superior
Bayfield
CANADA
MICHIGAN
WISCONSIN
(See other map)
Minneapolis
St. Paul
Lake Michigan
Merrimac
MICHIGAN
(See other map)
Madison
Milwaukee
Lansing
Detroit
Bass
Islands
Lake Erie
Chicago
Toledo
Cleveland
Sandusky
ILLINOIS
Canton
Springfield
OHIO
INDIANA
Hannibal
Columbus
Terre
Haute
Cincinnati
Jefferson
City
St. Louis
MISSOURI

Lake Superior
CANADA
Sault Ste. Marie
MICHIGAN
Georgian Bay
Mackinac
Island
Beaver
Island
Rock
Island
Lake Huron
Washington
Island
Green Bay
Kewaunee
CANADA
WISCONSIN
Ludington
Lake
Michigan
MICHIGAN
Algonac
Detroit
Lake Erie

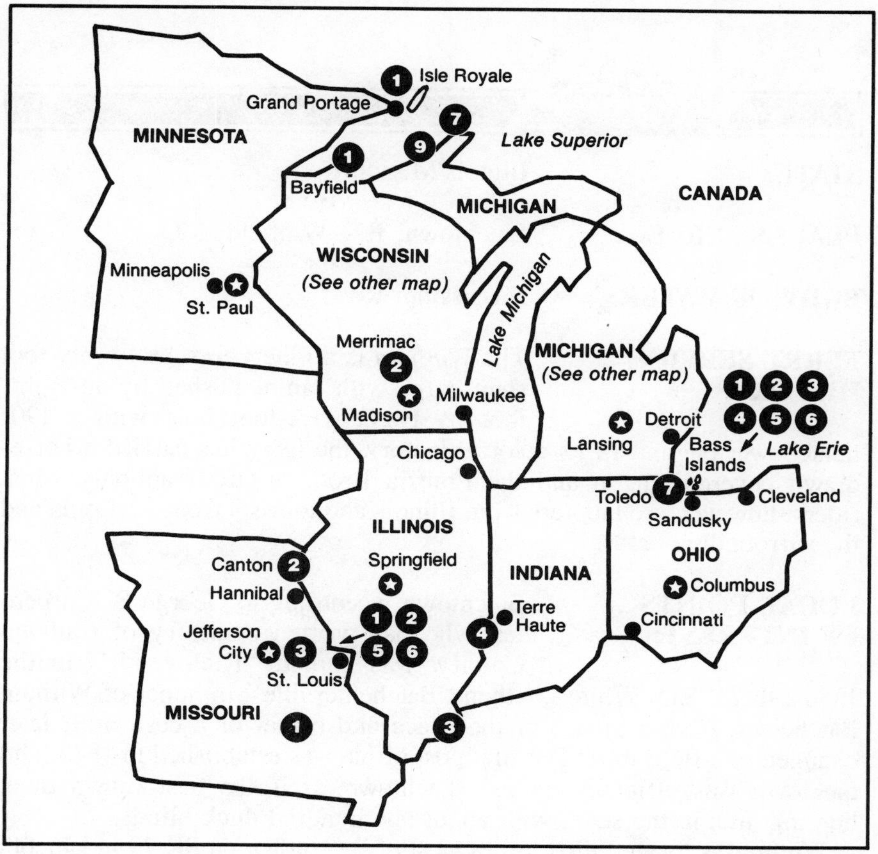

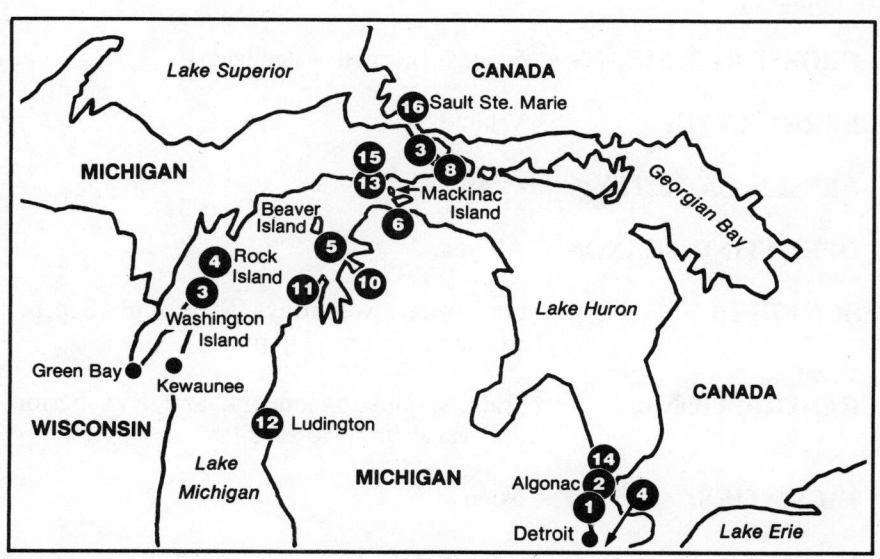

STATE: Illinois/Missouri

PLACES SERVED: Batchtown, IL—Winfield, MO

BODY OF WATER: Mississippi River

FERRY SERVICE   The *Winfield* is a ninety-foot by twenty-foot
HISTORY: steel barge with ramps pushed by an eight-
foot by twenty-five-foot boat with a 190-
horsepower engine. In its colorful history, the ferry has carried a horse-
drawn covered wagon and the Franzia Brothers circus animals. Most
riders, however, are laborers from Illinois and tourists from St. Louis and
the surrounding areas.

LOCAL POINTS   Batchtown, according to George B. Carpen-
OF INTEREST: ter, who has written a history of Calhoun
County, was named "Richwoods" in the
1850s, then "Sam White's," then "Batchelderville" in honor of William
Batchelder, once a justice of the peace and owner of a corn mill, later
changed to a flour mill. The first post office was established in 1879, and
the town was officially named Batchtown. It is the best-known duck
hunting area in the state, with about one hundred duck blinds.

Winfield is located three miles west of Batchtown on SR 79 in Lincoln
County.

CROSSING TIME: 5 mins. (normal water level)

FERRY TYPE: Vehicle

VESSEL CAPACITY: 8 cars

OPERATING SEASON: All year

SCHEDULE: On signal, weekdays 5:30 a.m.-8 p.m.;
weekends 8 a.m.-8 p.m.

RESTRICTIONS: Trailers, pickup-campers, and RVs permitted. Load limit 30 tons.

FACILITIES: None

FARE: Cars $3.50

RESERVATIONS: No

DIRECTIONS: From St. Louis, take Highway 70 west to Highway 79 and go north 15 miles to Winfield. Turn right on Highway N and go 3 miles to ferry landing. From Batchtown, take west side road 1¹/₂ miles to ferry road. Ferry is located on IL and MO maps.

MAP LOCATION: P. 319, IL, 1

CONTACT: Mr. Vincent Baalman, Mr. Steve Baalman, Box 8, Batchtown, IL 62006-0008, (618)396-2447

STATE: Illinois

PLACES SERVED: Brussels—Grafton

BODY OF WATER: Illinois River

FERRY SERVICE HISTORY: The earliest known licenses for ferries in Calhoun County were issued in 1825. Ferry service was privately run and restricted to daylight hours until 1961, when Carl Wittmond of Brussels, publisher of the *Calhoun Herald,* proprietor of the Wittmond Hotel, and a former state legislator, introduced a bill to get state-provided ferry service; the ferry runs twenty-four hours per day, weather permitting. The ferry runs twenty-four hours a day to serve commuters in St. Louis and Alton who are on shift work and returning at midnight and later. The current vessels are the *Brussels* and the *Brussels II.*

LOCAL POINTS OF INTEREST: To many people from St. Louis, Calhoun County is a delicious blend of apple orchards, fall color, and the Wittmond Hotel in Brussels. The hotel contains the Brussels Post Office, a tavern, a general store, an antique shop, and a restaurant which draws crowds from several counties, especially at apple-picking time, and, in fact, spring and summer also. The Mark Twain Wildlife Refuge is in the southern part of the county. On the Grafton side is the Pere Marquette State Park, Illinois' largest state park. It was named in honor of Father Jacques Marquette, the French Jesuit missionary priest who, in 1673, explored the area with Louis Jolliet. They were the first Europeans to enter what is now the state

of Illinois. Long popular and much used is the massive Pere Marquette Lodge, built of colorful native stone and rustic timbers. The Lodge has what is believed to be the world's largest chess set, twelve feet square with figures as large as a six-year-old child.

CROSSING TIME:	5 mins.
FERRY TYPE:	Vehicle
VESSEL CAPACITY:	12 cars [additional 12-car barge during peak hours on weekends in spring, summer, and early fall]
OPERATING SEASON:	All year, weather permitting [may be frozen in winter]
SCHEDULE:	On signal, 24 hrs. per day
RESTRICTIONS:	Trailers, pickup-campers, and RVs permitted. Load limit 15 tons.
FACILITIES:	None
FARE:	Free
RESERVATIONS:	No
DIRECTIONS:	The ferry is located on IL 100, approx. 3 miles west of Grafton.

MAP LOCATION: P. 319, IL, 2

CONTACT: Illinois Dept. of Transportation, Division of Highways, 9300 St. Clair Ave., Fairview Heights, IL 62208, (618)786-3636

STATE: Illinois/Kentucky

PLACES SERVED: Cave-in-Rock, IL—SR 91, near Marion, KY

BODY OF WATER: Ohio River

FERRY SERVICE HISTORY: James Ford inaugurated ferry service at Cave-in-Rock in 1823, attracting travellers by maintaining roads on either side of the crossing totalling twenty miles, a considerable enticement in a roadless region. He also cut his rates to twenty-five cents for a horse, twelve and one-half cents for a man. Unfortunately, he recouped his losses by hiring pirate outlaws and by counterfeiting; Ford was not driven from his stronghold until 1831. Since 1974, the Cave-in-Rock ferry has been owned by Tom Patton and his son, Bill. The Cave-in-Rock ferry uses either the *Danny L,* a ninety-foot steel-deck barge, or the eighty-five-foot steel-deck barge, the *David Z.,* pushed by a pivoting tug. The *Kathy Z.* and the *Becky D.* are tugboats still in use.

LOCAL POINTS OF INTEREST: Cave-in-Rock is a massive hole within a limestone bluff along the Illinois shoreline, just beyond the jurisdiction of Kentucky. The cave is 150 to two hundred feet long, and the entrance is twenty-five feet wide and fifteen feet high. There are heiroglyphics thought to be pre-historic. The cave was notorious from 1797-1810 as the headquarters of gangs of bloodthirsty pirates such as "Big" Micajah Harpe and "Little" Wiley Harpe, as well as the river pirate Sam Mason, counterfeiters William Hall and John Duff, and outlaw Jim Wilson. In 1797, cutthroat Samuel Mason is said to have placed a sign on the river bank, "Liquor Vault and House for Entertainment," a successful lure for travellers, who were then robbed and coerced into joining the thieves or murdered. In 1810 John Waller of Maysville destroyed the gang, returning the severed head of its leader, Jim Wilson, to Pittsburgh authorities.

CROSSING TIME: 5 mins.

FERRY TYPE:	Vehicle
VESSEL CAPACITY:	15 cars
OPERATING SEASON:	All year
SCHEDULE:	On signal, 6 a.m.-6 p.m., weather and river conditions permitting
RESTRICTIONS:	Trailers, pickup-campers, and RVs permitted. Load limit 100 tons.
FACILITIES:	None
FARE:	Car, pickup camper $4, with 1-axle trailer $5; additional axles $.50.
RESERVATIONS:	No
DIRECTIONS:	Ferry is located on the Ohio River at Mile 881. It connects KY 91, 11 miles northwest of Marion, to IL 1 at Cave-in-Rock. The

ferry connects Hardin County, Illinois, with Crittenden County, Kentucky.

MAP LOCATION:	P. 319, IL, 3
CONTACT:	Mr. Thomas A. Patton, Pres., Mr. James W. Patton, Vice-President & Manager, Cave-in-Rock Ferry Co., Inc., Box 36, Elizabethtown, IL 62931, (618)289-4599

STATE:	Illinois/Indiana
PLACES SERVED:	Darwin, IL (Clark County)—Vigo, IN (Vigo County) ("The Darwin Ferry")
BODY OF WATER:	Wabash River
FERRY SERVICE HISTORY:	This ferry was started in 1818 by John McClure and has been running ever since. At present it is owned by the Darwin Ferry

Association, a group of eight Illinois farmers who also own and farm land in Indiana (at one time there were eighteen farmers). Frank Gard of West Union, Illinois, who with his family farms several hundred acres in Indiana, calls the ferry "a necessary evil," as some of the farm equipment is not allowed on I-70. The ferry, carrying trucks, tractors, combines, and other equipment, along with grain, saves Association farmers a drive of forty to forty-four miles. In November 1986, a mishap occurred. The ferry was carrying a heavy load of grain, not centered, which shifted and toppled over, sinking the boat. A new boat has been ordered. "It will be just what we need," says Gard; "it will be eighty feet long, including aprons, with sealed compartments, making it unsinkable. Some of the newer farm machinery folds up now, so it will be fine for our purposes." The ferry is guided by an overhead cable and pushed by a pivoting side boat. This is the only ferry remaining on the Wabash River, and it attracts many riders from the Terre Haute area, as well as tourists en route from Chicago to Florida along Route 1.

LOCAL POINTS OF INTEREST: Darwin is an old river town. The Lincoln Trail State Park is north of Darwin.

Terre Haute (named "high land" by the French) has many sites of interest, including the Historical Museum of the Wabash Valley, the Sheldon Swope Art Gallery, the Early Wheels Museum, and the Eugene V. Debs Home. The Vigo-Terre Haute area has many quaint covered bridges.

CROSSING TIME: 4 mins.

FERRY TYPE: Vehicle

VESSEL CAPACITY: 3 cars

OPERATING SEASON: All year, weather permitting (river sometimes iced over or too high in winter or there is debris); once crops are in, however, there is less call for ferry; check before making special trip.

SCHEDULE: 6 a.m.-dark

RESTRICTIONS: Trailers, pickup-campers, and RVs permitted. Load limit 10 tons (old boat).

FACILITIES: None

FARE: Car or pickup truck $2; larger vehicles $2.50-$4.50; combines $10

RESERVATIONS: No

DIRECTIONS: The Illinois road to the ferry is paved. The Indiana road to the ferry runs off SR 63 outside Prairieton, south of Terre Haute. Dawrin is just off Rt. 1.

MAP LOCATION: P. 319, IL, 4

CONTACT: Frank Gard, Rt. 2, Box 114, West Union, IL 62477, (217)826-2626

STATE: Illinois/Missouri

PLACES SERVED: Golden Eagle, IL—St. Charles County, MO

BODY OF WATER: Mississippi River

FERRY SERVICE HISTORY: According to George Carpenter of Hardin, Illinois, author of *Calhoun is My Kingdom,* a history of Calhoun County, the first license for a crossing near the site of the present ferry was issued to John Bolter in 1825. Present service was inaugurated in 1923. The *Golden Eagle* is the only paddlewheel ferry on the Mississippi; it is self-contained and side-loading (the cars are loaded from the side and not from the end). It has become quite a tourist attraction and has been featured in articles and on televison. During the winter, the ferries are sometimes iced in and cut off. Many natives of Calhoun County commute to jobs in St. Louis over the ferries; if the ferries close, they have to drive many miles out of their way.

LOCAL POINTS OF INTEREST: Calhoun County is known for its apples and is also one of the leading duck hunting areas in the Midwest. Many visitors from St. Louis come over on the Golden Eagle ferry to such excellent restaurants as the Wittmond Hotel in Brussels.

CROSSING TIME: 10 mins.

FERRY TYPE: Vehicle

VESSEL CAPACITY: 16 cars

OPERATING SEASON: Early Mar.-mid-Dec., weather permitting

SCHEDULE: Daylight hours; service to 9 p.m. during summer months

RESTRICTIONS: Trailers, pickup-campers, and RVs permitted. Load limit 80 tons. Maximum vehicle length 46 ft.

FACILITIES: None

FARE: Car $4.00; trailer or pickup camper $4.50 up depending on size.

RESERVATIONS: No

DIRECTIONS:	From St. Louis, take 70 West to 94 North, then Highway B; the ferry is signposted.
MAP LOCATION:	P. 319, IL, 5
CONTACT:	Mr. Fred Pohlman, Calhoun-St. Charles Ferry Co., Box 30, Golden Eagle, IL 62036, (618)883-2217

STATE:	Illinois
PLACES SERVED:	Kampsville—Eldred
BODY OF WATER:	Illinois River
FERRY SERVICE HISTORY:	Kampsville was one of the early villages settled in Calhoun County. According to historian George Carpenter, Jacob Crader and

Salmon Bushnell were two of the first settlers, and Bushnell operated a ferry. The place was known as "Bushnell's Ferry." In 1847, the town was known as "Farrowtown," for Stephen Farrow, who also obtained a ferry license. By 1863, Capt. M. A. Kamp was the leading merchant, and the name was changed once again to honor him. The Kampsville Ferry, according to Carpenter, was purchased by the State of Illinois in late 1941 or early 1942. The vessels are the *Kampsville I* and the *Kampsville II*.

LOCAL POINTS OF INTEREST:	[For more on Calhoun County, see p. 321.] The Kampsville ferry landing in winter, with the trees silhouetted against the clear sky and

the river a snowy plain, would be a suitable subject for an artist. The ferry office is a blue and white barge perched on a bank, a cozy sight with flags flying.

Eldred is a small town in Greene County not far from Carrollton. It is an easy drive from Illinois' largest state park, the Pere Marquette.

CROSSING TIME:	5 mins.
FERRY TYPE:	Vehicle
VESSEL CAPACITY:	12 cars
OPERATING SEASON:	All year, weather permitting

SCHEDULE: On signal, 24 hours per day, weather permitting (often frozen in winter)

RESTRICTIONS: Trailers, pickup-campers, and RVs permitted. Load limit 15 tons.

FACILITIES: None

FARE: Free

RESERVATIONS: No

DIRECTIONS: The Kampsville Ferry landing is located on IL 108.

MAP LOCATION: P. 319, IL, 6

CONTACT: See CONTACT, p. 323.

STATE: Michigan

PLACES SERVED: Algonac—Harsens Island

BODY OF WATER: St. Clair River

FERRY SERVICE HISTORY: This ferry was founded in 1937 by the grandfather of the current president, J. Arthur Bryson. Four eighty-foot double-ended ferries are currently in use, the *South Channel*, the *North Channel*, the *St. Clair Flats*, and the *Champion*. The ferry carries shift workers, as well as employees and patrons of the bars and restaurants on Harsens Island.

LOCAL POINTS OF INTEREST: Algonac has been a shipbuilding center for more than a century; the name, in Indian, means "land of the Algonquin." It has pretty parks and water sports on the river.

Harsens Island is the largest American island in the group forming St. Clair Flats. (South and west of Algonac, where the St. Clair River enters Lake St. Clair, a delta, known as the Flats, is created by sediment washed down from the upper lakes.) About two thousand people live on the island, which offers golfing and water sports (no camping).

CROSSING TIME:	5 mins.
FERRY TYPE:	Vehicle
VESSEL CAPACITY:	12 cars
OPERATING SEASON:	All year
SCHEDULE:	**Summer and early fall:** Continuous service on signal, 24 hrs. daily. **Spring, late fall, and winter:** Service every 20 mins., 24 hrs. daily.
RESTRICTIONS:	Trailers, pickup-campers, and RVs permitted. Load limit 25 tons.
FACILITIES:	None
FARE:	Car, including passengers $1.75 ($3 round-trip); pickup-campers $1.50 to $4.25; trailers $2.25 to $2.65; RVs $1.75 to $4.25.
RESERVATIONS:	No
DIRECTIONS:	The ferry leaves from 23 Mile Rd. in Algonac and SR 154 on Harsens Island.
MAP LOCATION:	P. 319, MI, 1
CONTACT:	Champion's Auto Ferry, Inc., 3647 Pte. Tremble Rd., Algonac, MI 48001, (313)748-3757

STATE:	Michigan/Ontario, Canada
PLACES SERVED:	Algonac, MI—Walpole Island, ON
BODY OF WATER:	St. Clair River
FERRY SERVICE HISTORY:	The vessel on this service is the *Lowell D.* Ferry service on this crossing goes back many years; the 1941 WPA *Guide* to Michi-

gan gives the ferry rate as fifty cents for automobiles, ten cents for passengers, and states that there are guides on the island.

LOCAL POINTS OF INTEREST: The Algonac State Park is near Algonac, a small town on the St. Clair River. Walpole Island is really a group of five small islands, with nineteen acres of stately oak trees. It is a native American reservation that includes the Chippewa, Pottawatomie, and Ottawa Indians. Visitors will want to sample the native delicacies, such as corn soup and bannock. At the Kinomaagew-Gamig Cultural Centre, there is an assortment of native handicrafts. The annual Indian Pow-Wow in late July features dances, crafts, and canoe racing. The Tecumseh Monument marks the grave of the great Shawnee Chief who was killed in the War of 1812.

CROSSING TIME: 5 mins.

FERRY TYPE: Vehicle

VESSEL CAPACITY: 6 cars

OPERATING SEASON: All year

SCHEDULE: On signal, continuous service, river permitting. **Mon.-Sat.: Lv. Walpole** 6:20 a.m., **last return trip from Algonac** at 10 p.m. **Sun. and US holidays: Lv. Walpole** 6:50 a.m.; **last return trip from Algonac** 11 p.m.

RESTRICTIONS: Trailers, pickup-campers, and RVs permitted. Load limit 15 tons.

FACILITIES: None

FARE: Car $3; foot passengers $.50; pickup-campers $3-$4; trailers $2.50 up; RV $3.50.

RESERVATIONS: No

DIRECTIONS: Algonac: ferry dock
Walpole: 3 mi. south of Port Lambton

MAP LOCATION: P. 319, MI, 2

CONTACT: Walpole-Algonac Ferry Line, Ltd., 101 River Dr. N, Port Lambton, ON, Canada N0P 2B0, (519)677-5679

STATE: Michigan

PLACES SERVED: Barbeau—Oak Ridge Park, Neebish Island

BODY OF WATER: St. Marys River

FERRY SERVICE   The operator of the present Neebish Island
HISTORY: ferry is Clifford Tyner; he and Fred Miller,
father of his wife, Dorothy, bought the company from a Mr. Cardinal in 1952 or 1953. The vessel is the fifty-foot *Neebish Islander*; she is made of steel and is twenty-two feet wide. The crossing existed long before the 1950s. In the 1941 WPA *Guide* to Michigan, a ferry is mentioned; the cost at that time was forty-five cents for a car and driver, and ten cents for passengers.

LOCAL POINTS   Neebish Island is where water boils, the site
OF INTEREST: of former rapids in St. Marys River below
Sault Ste. Marie, where large vessels now pass through a scenic rock cut. The island was settled in 1887, but has never had a large population. There is camping at Franklin's Fishing Resort.

CROSSING TIME: 5 mins.

FERRY TYPE: Vehicle

VESSEL CAPACITY: 5 cars

OPERATING SEASON: April 15-Dec. 15

SCHEDULE: Daily, every hour, 8 a.m.-7 p.m.

RESTRICTIONS: Trailers, pickup-campers, and RVs permitted. Load limit 20 tons. Overhead clearance 15 ft. Max. comb. vehicle length 54 ft.

FACILITIES: No

FARE: Car and driver \$3.00; passengers \$.75; larger vehicles \$3 up.

RESERVATIONS: No

DIRECTIONS:	The ferry leaves Barbeau from the head of the rock cut. On Neebish Island, the landing is at Oak Ridge Park.
MAP LOCATION:	P. 319, MI, 3
CONTACT:	Clifford Tyner, Box 303, Barbeau, MI 49710, (906)635-0209

STATE:	Michigan/Ontario
PLACES SERVED:	Boblo Island—Detroit, Gibraltar, and Amherstburg, ON
BODY OF WATER:	Detroit River
FERRY SERVICE HISTORY:	Detroit children may not quite believe that they are riding the same ships to the same amusement park their great-grandparents

and great-great-grandparents rode, but it is true. The *Columbia* (built in 1902) and her sister ship the *Ste. Claire* (built in 1910) are a triumphant rebuttal to anyone who holds that steamships have had their day. Carrying twenty-five hundred passengers each, they are the last pair of large ships remaining on a North American excursion line. In 1979 they were declared National Historic Monuments by the Heritage Conservation and Recreation Service, Department of the Interior. They ferry passengers to the venerable Boblo Island amusement park, which is even older than the ships, dating from 1901.

Detroit has a long history of ferries. A canoe ferry was known as early as 1802, followed by the *Olive Branch* (1825-1832), or "Horse Boat" Ferry (driven by horses treading a turnstile), which carried stagecoaches as well as passengers. The *Argo* was the first steam ferry. In 1881 the Detroit River Ferry Company and the Detroit and Windsor Ferry Company merged, forming the Detroit, Belle Isle and Windsor Ferry Company, which operated ferries to Belle Isle, an early city park. Once bridges were built to Belle Isle, the company leased Bois Blanc Island and operated its own park. The first ferries were *Pleasure* and *Promise*, followed by the *Columbia* and the *Ste. Claire*, which went into service in 1911. The company became "The Bob-Lo Excursion Company" and then "The Bob-Lo Company." After the 1948 season the excursion ships were almost discontinued, but were purchased, along with the island, by the Ralph Browning family; in 1979 the present Island of Boblo Company came into being.

The *Columbia* is 216 feet long, with a Triple Expansion Steam engine; it was built by the Detroit Shipbuilding Company. The *Ste. Claire* is 198 feet long, with the same engine, built by the Toledo Shipbuilding Company. Each year the much-cherished ships are painstakingly scraped, revarnished and overhauled, an enduring legacy of Detroit's maritime past. (The ferry from Amherstburg is the smaller vessel *Papoose*.)

LOCAL POINTS OF INTEREST: The Boblo Island park covers 272 acres; it opens daily at eleven during the season. There are seventy-five rides, shows, and attractions, with three roller coasters, several theaters, and a British blockhouse; one of the first lighthouses on the Great Lakes is also here.

Detroit, founded in 1701, is synonymous with the growth of the automobile, but has much else of cultural and commercial interest. The Detroit Institute of Arts, Orchestra Hall (1920), the Detroit Science Center, the splendid new Civic Center and the Renaissance Center, along with Fort Wayne and the famed Detroit Zoological Park, are all of interest.

Gibraltar is a small community on the banks of the Detroit River with a marina next to the ferry dock.

Amherstburg, a small town with beautiful waterfront parks, is about thirty miles south of Windsor. Fort Malden National Historic Park is here.

CROSSING TIME: From Detroit 90 mins.; from Gibraltar 40 mins.; from Amherstburg 6 mins.

FERRY TYPE: Pedestrian

VESSEL CAPACITY: *Columbia:* 2500
Ste. Claire: 2500 passengers
Papoose: 275 passengers

OPERATING SEASON: Early May-Sept.

SCHEDULE: *Consult company for exact dates season begins and ends; varies annually.* **From Detroit: Daily: Lv. Detroit** 9:30 a.m., 10:30, 1:30 p.m., 3:30, 6:30, *8:30 (weekends only) **From Boblo Island** first departure is at 9:30 a.m.; others intermittently throughout the day, according to hour of park closing. **From Gibraltar and Amherstburg: Sat. and Sun. only 2nd and 3rd wks. in May and after Labor Day; otherwise daily: Lv. Gibraltar** hourly from 10:30 a.m.-park closing. **Lv. Amherstburg** 11 a.m.-park closing (continuous service). Ferries **leave Boblo island** hourly 3:30-park closing.

RESTRICTIONS: No pets; smoking allowed

FACILITIES: Restrooms, snack bars, gift shops

FARE: All fares include round-trip ferry and unlimited access to rides, games and attractions on the island. From Detroit: adults $15.95, children (3-6) $9.95; from Gibraltar: adults $12.95; children $7.95; from Amherstburg: adults $10.50, children $6.50 (*US funds*).

RESERVATIONS: Not permitted (large groups may make arrangements for priority boarding)

DIRECTIONS: In Detroit, ferry dock is off Atwater behind the Joe Lewis Areana. In Gibraltar, take Exit 29-A off I-75 near Flat Rock; go east on Gibraltar Rd. 3 mi. In Amherstburg, 30 mins. south of Windsor, dock is off Highway 18; follow signs.

MAP LOCATION: P. 319, MI, 4

CONTACT: Island of Boblo Company (headquarters Veterans Memorial Building, 151 W. Jefferson, Detroit, MI 48226); for park information call (313)259-7500 or (313)259-9500.

Beaver Islander

STATE:	Michigan
PLACES SERVED:	Charlevoix—St. James, Beaver Island
BODY OF WATER:	Lake Michigan
FERRY SERVICE HISTORY:	Ferry service to Beaver Island has existed since the late nineteenth century, when various ship captains carried mail and freight

between Beaver and other locations. The *Erie L. Hackley* was one of the early ferries, built in 1882 for Capt. Seth Lee's Muskegon Lake Ferry Line; she foundered off Menominee in 1903. Later vessels included the *Beaver* (nicknamed the "Oral Agitator"), the *Columbia*, the *Bruce*, the *Sanford*, the *Ossian Bedell*, and the *Marold II* (the ultimate in private yachts, 145 feet long), and the *Mary Margaret*. The Beaver Island Boat Company was established in 1955 by a group of Island businessmen who purchased the *Emerald Isle* and, in 1962, added the *Beaver Islander*. The company was sold in 1981 to John P. McGoff, a Williamston publisher and travel entrepreneur; he then merged the company with his Waters Edge Corporation of Charlevoix. A group of seven Beaver Island businessmen bought the company back in 1984 and again named it the Beaver Island Boat Company, amid rejoicing on the island which was reported in a number of newspapers. Only residents and property owners on the island, registered voters on the island, their children and grandchildren, regular summer visitors, and certain other categories of people may own stock in the company. The president of the company is Edward B. Wojan, a real-estate broker and developer. He said at the time of the purchase, "As island businessmen and residents we would like to have control over our own ferry company. It is our lifeline to the mainland."

The present vessels are the *Beaver Islander* (one hundred feet) and the *South Shore* (sixty feet). The company has built corrals on deck to transport herds of cattle, held wedding receptions on the car deck, transported mobile homes, and met the entire needs of the community. Riders come from all over the US but, predominantly, are from Michigan, Illinois, and Indiana.

LOCAL POINTS OF INTEREST: Charlevoix is a picturesque resort on the shore of Lake Michigan. The attractions here include the *Star of Charlevoix*, a 114-foot restaurant cruise ship which serves lunch, dinner, and Sunday brunch during the summer and fall. This section of the Michigan coast has been called the "Land of the Million Dollar Sunset"; the beaches and parks of Charlevoix offer perfect spots from which to enjoy the spectacular sunsets.

One feels it might have been the view from Charlevoix that Willa Cather had in mind when, in *The Professor's House*, she wrote of Lake Michigan: "The sun rose out of it, the day began there; it was like an open door that nobody could shut. . . . It was the first thing one saw in the morning . . . and it ran through the days like the weather, not a thing thought about, but a part of consciousness itself. When the ice chunks came in of a winter morning, crumbly and white, throwing off gold and rose-coloured reflections from a copper-colored sea behind the grey clouds, he [Professor St. Peter] didn't observe the details or know what it was that made him happy; but now, forty years later, he could recall all its aspects perfectly."

Beaver Island was first colonized by the French, who abandoned their settlement in 1603. Since the nineteenth century it has had a troubled yet fascinating history, its fortunes linked early on to the Mormons who came to Beaver seeking refuge in 1847. They declared it a monarchy, and their leader, Jesse Strang, reigned for ten years as the only "king" in North American history. He caused resentment on the mainland, which led to the forced dissolution of the colony in 1856. With its miles of coastline, inland lakes, and historic monuments, Beaver Island is a small, quiet resort which features natural splendor at its finest. Michigan newspaper columnist Bob Clock once wrote that, when people consulted him about whether they would like Beaver Island, he would reply that, if visitors were seeking "crowds, traffic congestion, a plethora of bright lights, posh cocktail lounges, strings of fudge shops, battalions of ritzy clothing stores, and ankle deep carpeting in your hotel — forget it." He would suggest instead that the prospective tourist spend one night "overseas," because, "It is not until the last boat leaves for the day that the visitor can begin to experience Beaver Island's splendid isolation in the misty reaches of Northern Lake Michigan."

CROSSING TIME:	2 hrs. 15 mins.
FERRY TYPE:	Vehicle
VESSEL CAPACITY:	*Beaver Islander:* 12 vehicles, 200 passengers; *South Shore:* 6 vehicles, 120 passengers
OPERATING SEASON:	Mid-Apr.-Dec., weather permitting

SCHEDULE: **Schedule A: Lv. Beaver Island** 8:30 a.m.; **lv. Charlevoix** 12:30 p.m. **Schedule B: Lv. Beaver Island** 10 a.m.; **lv. Charlevoix** 1 p.m. **Schedule C: Lv. Beaver Island** 2:30 p.m.; **lv. Charlevoix** 8:30 a.m. **Schedule D: Lv. Beaver Island** 9 a.m., 3 p.m.; **lv. Charlevoix** 8:30 a.m., 1 p.m. **Schedule E: Lv. Beaver Island** 9 a.m., 11:30, 5:30 p.m.; **lv. Charlevoix** 8:30 a.m.; 1 p.m., 2:30. *This schedule is approximate only; boat does not sail certain days; check with company for exact schedule, which changes each year.* **Apr.: Mon., Wed., Fri. only:** Schedule A. **May:** No Tues. or Thurs. sailings in May; no Sun. sailings before mid-May. **Mon., Wed., Fri., Sat:** Schedule A. **Sun.:** Schedule B. **June:** In general, Schedule A. **July: Daily except Sat.:** Schedule D; **Sat.** Schedule E. **Aug.: Daily except Sat.:** Schedule D; **Sat.:** Schedule E; **last of month daily:** Schedule C. **Sept.:** No Tues. & Thurs. sailings in Sept.; in general, Schedule A. **Oct.:** No Tues. and Thurs. sailings in Oct.; in general, Schedule A. **Nov.:** In general, Schedule A. **Dec.:** In general, Schedule A.

RESTRICTIONS:	Trailers permitted; RVs not permitted. Clearance 9 ft. *Beaver Islander* (high spot); 6 ft. 4 in. remaining spaces. Maximum vehicle length 24 ft.
FACILITIES:	Restrooms
FARE:	Car $32; adult $9 ($16 round-trip); child (5-11) $4 ($8 round-trip); trailers according to size; RVs not permitted.
RESERVATIONS:	Absolutely necessary for cars, which must be at dock 1 hour before sailing.
DIRECTIONS:	In Charlevoix, the office and dock are located next to the drawbridge on Round Lake.

MAP LOCATION: P. 319, MI, 5

CONTACT: Beaver Island Boat Co., 102 Bridge St., Charlevoix, MI 49720, (616)547-2311

STATE: Michigan

PLACES SERVED: Cheboygan—Pointe Aux Pins, Bois Blanc Island

BODY OF WATER: Lake Huron

FERRY SERVICE HISTORY: This ferry has been operated by the Plaunt family for over fifty years; three generations of Plaunts have now owned Plaunt Transportation. The company delivers the mail all year round to Bois Blanc Island, taking it by boat, then by snowmobile once the ice has made. If neither boat nor snowmobile is possible because of ice conditions, the Plaunts hire a commercial plane to fly the mail over. The present vessel is the sixty-five-foot *Chee-maun-nes*.

LOCAL POINTS OF INTEREST: Cheboygan, settled in the 1840s, was once a busy lumber port. It is now the home of other industries, as well as the US Coast Guard cutter *Mackinaw*, one of the world's largest icebreakers, which welcomes visitors when in port. There are several lakes nearby; Mullet Lake and Bass Lake are part of the historic inland waterway. The Cheboygan Opera House has performances of many kinds.

Bois Blanc Island is not far from Mackinac Island; the Mackinaw State Forest is here. In summer the island has about 350 residents, but only a few dozen in winter.

CROSSING TIME: 35 mins.

FERRY TYPE: Vehicle

VESSEL CAPACITY: 3 vehicles

OPERATING SEASON: Apr.-Nov.

SCHEDULE: **May, Oct., Nov.: Lv. Bois Blanc Island Mon., Wed., Fri.:** 9:30 a.m.; **Fri.:** also 6 p.m.; **Sun.:** 4 p.m. **Lv. Cheboygan Mon., Wed., Fri.:** 12:30 p.m.; **Fri.:** also 10 p.m. **July-Labor Day: Lv. Bois**

Blanc Island Mon.-Sat.: 8 a.m., 12:30 p.m., 6; **Fri.:** also 8 p.m.; **Sun.:** 2 p.m., 4. **Lv. Cheboygan Mon.-Sat.:** 9:30 a.m., 3:30 p.m., 7; **Fri.:** also 10 p.m.; **Sun.:** 3 p.m., 5.

RESTRICTIONS: Trailers, pickup-campers, and RVs permitted. Maximum combined vehicle length 28 ft.

FACILITIES: No

FARE: Car $15 ($25 round-trip, good for 1 week); adult $3.25; child $2.25; camper trailer $7.50; RVs permitted.

RESERVATIONS: Yes, for vehicles

DIRECTIONS: The ferry leaves from 406 Water St. in Cheboygan, 1 block east of Main St. Look for BBI Ferry signs.

MAP LOCATION: P. 319, MI, 6

CONTACT: Plaunt Transportation Co., Cheboygan, MI 49721, (616)634-5800 (or 634-5531 or 627-2354)

STATE: Michigan

PLACES SERVED: Copper Harbor—Isle Royale National Park

BODY OF WATER: Lake Superior

FERRY SERVICE HISTORY: The vessel on this service is the *Isle Royale Queen II*, a US Coast Guard-approved sixty-five-foot all-steel twin diesel-powered boat; she lands at Rock Harbor. Service was inaugurated in the 1930s.

LOCAL POINTS OF INTEREST: Copper Harbor is now a resort, though in 1843 the Michigan copper boom opened the western Upper Peninsula to white settlement. Copper Harbor was a rendezvous and supply point for early prospectors, situated as it is on the tip of the Keweenaw. Its lighthouse (1866) is the oldest working one on Lake Superior. At the peak of the mining era, in the 1840s, townsmen spent their leisure time hunting in the wilderness, much as people do now, enjoying a pollution-free sky and the spectacular northern lights. The Astor House Museum, at the Astor House-Minnetonka Resort, has a large antique doll and toy collection and pine-panelled cottages overlooking the harbor. There is a lighthouse boat tour and, in winter, snowmobiling along special trails. At Fort Wilkins State Park, the stockade has been restored, preserving the frontier post atmosphere.

Isle Royale, a National Park, is a primitive archipelago without roads but with over 166 miles of foot trails, roaming moose, wildflowers, and magnificent scenery. A boat circumnavigates Isle Royale and will drop off and pick up passengers at various points. At Rock Harbor there is accommodation, boat rental, and an information center. At Windigo, the other end of the island, there is also an information center and grocery, but no accommodation. (For lodging, write National Park Concessions, Box 405, Houghton, MI 49931.) The park is open April 16 to October 31, with full services offered mid-June to August 31.

CROSSING TIME:	4 hrs. 30 mins.
FERRY TYPE:	Pedestrian
VESSEL CAPACITY:	57 passengers
OPERATING SEASON:	Mid-May-Sept.
SCHEDULE:	**Mid-May-mid-June and Sept., Mon. and Fri. only: Lv. Copper Harbor** 8 a.m. **Lv. Isle Royale** 2 p.m. **Mid-June-Labor Day: Lv. Copper Harbor** 8 a.m. **Lv. Isle Royale** 3:30 p.m.
RESTRICTIONS:	No gas in outboard motors. No pets allowed on island.
FACILITIES:	Restrooms
FARE:	Round-trip rates: adults $40; child (12 and under) $20; canoes $12; outboard motors $5.
RESERVATIONS:	Definitely advisable.
DIRECTIONS:	Take US 41 to Copper Harbor and continue straight past Gratiot St. and Bernard St.; ferry dock and parking are on Brockway Ave.

MAP LOCATION:	P. 319, MI, 7
CONTACT:	Isle Royale Passenger Ferry, Copper Harbor, MI 49918, (906)289-4437 in season, (906)482-4950 off season

STATE:	Michigan
PLACES SERVED:	De Tour—Drummond Island
BODY OF WATER:	St. Marys River

FERRY SERVICE HISTORY: This ferry crossing goes back many years. The 1941 WPA *Guide* to Michigan lists a ferry with extra trips during the summer and deer-hunting season; it cost one dollar "up," with trailers one dollar extra. The ferry is now under the jurisdiction of the Eastern Upper Peninsula Transportation Authority. From April through January, there is service twenty-four hours a day. The vessel is the *Drummond Islander*.

LOCAL POINTS OF INTEREST: De Tour Village is in Chippewa County at the edge of the passage separating Lake Huron from the North Channel, at the tip of the Upper Peninsula at the mouth of the St. Marys River; it was a major Indian campsite at one time. It was so named because of the sharp turn ships had to make in order to enter St. Marys River. According to the 1941 WPA *Guide* to Michigan, in 1907, 120 boats were stopped opposite De Tour by an ice blockade; their lights at night created the illusion of a large industrial center. The village is a fueling station for vessels of all kinds during the river's open season.

Drummond Island, "gem of the Huron," is part of the Manitoulin archipelago, an island noted for its high rocky cliffs facing the richly colored waters of many bays and coves; the air is scented with pine and balsam. The earliest permanent settler, about 1857, was a Mormon minister named Seaman. The first stone quarry was opened in the late 1870s. The largest community is Drummond, on Potagannissing Bay. Wildlife includes grouse, ducks, northern pike, walleye, yellow perch, and deer. At one time islanders were afflicted with cabin fever in the winter, but the invention of the snowmobile all but eliminated this malady; it has replaced the propeller-driven snowsleds that once carried islanders to winter fishing grounds and made the island increasingly attractive to visitors, with hundreds of miles of snowmobile country on the island. There are moonlight snowmobile safaris attracting as many as eighty-five snowmobiles; volunteers stack firewood in the afternoon for campfires and participants cook an outdoor dinner before setting out. The British made an attempt, when ousted from Mackinac Island, to establish a garrison here, but failed; it had been called the "Gibraltar of the Great Lakes." The remains of Fort Drummond are still visible.

CROSSING TIME: 12 mins.

FERRY TYPE: Vehicle

VESSEL CAPACITY: 12 cars

OPERATING SEASON: All year

SCHEDULE: **Daily service all year. Jan., Feb., and Mar.: Lv. Drummond** 6:10 a.m., 7:30, 8:30, 10, noon, 2 p.m., 3:10, 4:10, 5, 6, 7:10, 9:10, 11:10. **Lv. De Tour** 6:40 a.m., 7:45, 9, 10:30, 12:30 p.m., 2:30, 3:45, 4:30, 5:30, 6:30, 7:30, 9:40, 11:30. **Apr.-Dec.: Lv. Drummond** 6:10 a.m., 7:10, 7:30, 8:30, 10, 11, noon, 1:10 p.m., 2:10, 3:10, 4:10, 5, 6, 7:10, 8, 9:10, 10:10, 11:10, midnight, 1 a.m., 3:10, 5. **Lv. De Tour** 6:40 a.m., 7:20, 7:45, 9, 10:30, 11:30, 12:30 p.m., 1:40, 2:40, 3:45, 4:30, 5:30, 6:30, 7:30, 8:30, 9:40, 10:40, 11:30, 12:30 a.m., 1:30, 3:30, 5:40.

RESTRICTIONS: Trailers, pickup-campers, and RVs permitted. Load limit 80 tons. Overhead clearance 16 ft.

FACILITIES: No

FARE: Car and driver $3.25; passengers $.80; pickup-camper $4.55; trailer $3.25 to $6.50; RV $7.80.

RESERVATIONS: No

DIRECTIONS: On Drummond Island, ferry leaves from the ferry dock near Duck Lake.

MAP LOCATION: P. 319, MI, 8

CONTACT: Don Myers, Drummond Island Chamber of Commerce, Drummond Island, MI 49726, (906)493-5245

Ranger III

STATE:	Michigan
PLACES SERVED:	Houghton—Isle Royale National Park
BODY OF WATER:	Lake Superior

FERRY SERVICE HISTORY: The vessel on this service is the *Ranger III*, a package freighter 165 feet long with a crew of seven. She lands at Rock Harbor. Most riders are tourists, who come from all over the nation.

LOCAL POINTS OF INTEREST: Houghton and its sister city, Hancock, are situated across Portage Lake at its narrowest point. This is the scene of the first great mineral strike in the western hemisphere, which brought a great mining rush to the area beginning in 1843. Many were Cornishmen, who came from the mines in Cornwall; others were Finns. Descendants of both groups survive today. Actually, there had been prehistoric copper mining, as evidenced by the pits and relics discovered by the early white miners. Of interest is the A. E. Seaman Mineralogical Museum at Michigan Technological University, which displays copper and silver specimens from the region. The University has an annual winter carnival. Houghton was incorporated as a village in 1861; Hancock was platted in 1859 and organized into a township in 1861. Unfortunately, fire nearly destroyed Hancock in 1869. By 1882, however, Hancock was thriving along with Houghton; both had schools, fire departments, newspapers, and benevolent and literary societies. Hancock currently has a population of just over five thousand, with good restaurants and recreational facilities.

[For notes on Isle Royale, please see entry under Copper Harbor-Isle Royale National Park, p. 341.]

CROSSING TIME: 6 hrs.

FERRY TYPE: Pedestrian

VESSEL CAPACITY: 123 passengers

OPERATING SEASON: Early June-early Sept.

SCHEDULE: **Tues. and Fri.: Lv. Houghton** 9 a.m.; **Wed. and Sat.: Lv. Isle Royale (Rock Harbor)** 9 a.m.

RESTRICTIONS: No gas in outboard motors. No pets.

FACILITIES: Restrooms; snack bar; audio-visual programs in the lounge

FARE: Adults $28 ($48 round-trip); child (under 12) $14 (round-trip $24); canoes $20; outboard motors $10; boats to 16' $40 round-trip; 17' and over $90 round-trip; baggage 100 lbs. per person included in ticket.

RESERVATIONS: Required in advance with full payment (remittance payable to National Park Service); cancellation notice: 24 hrs. for full refund.

DIRECTIONS: The ferry leaves from the Houghton waterfront, adjacent to the Isle Royale National Park Headquarters Office.

MAP LOCATION: P. 319, MI, 9

CONTACT: Isle Royale National Park, 87 N. Ripley St., Houghton, MI 49931, (906)482-3310

STATE: Michigan

PLACES SERVED: Ironton—Local road 10 miles west of Boyne City

BODY OF WATER: Lake Charlevoix

FERRY SERVICE HISTORY: A cable-guided ferry has been in operation at Ironton since 1876. It was made famous by an entry in *Ripley's Believe It or Not:* "Captain Sam Alexander travelled 15,000 miles and was never more than 1,000 feet from his home." The ferry saves twenty miles in circling the lake. The vessel is the *Charlevoix*; it is a fifty-foot cable-guided car ferry built in 1926 in Ferrysburg, Michigan. There is one crew member per eight-hour shift. Most of the riders come from the city of Charlevoix and Boyne City, though there are many tourists from June through August.

LOCAL POINTS OF INTEREST: Lake Charlevoix is the third largest inland lake in Michigan, with facilities for boating and bathing; it covers 17,260 acres and has sixty miles of shoreland.

CROSSING TIME: 5 mins.

FERRY TYPE: Vehicle

VESSEL CAPACITY: 4 cars; 27 passengers

OPERATING SEASON: May 1-Nov. 30

SCHEDULE: Daily, on signal, 6:30 a.m.-10:30 p.m. (Beginning and end of operating season depends on ice conditions.)

RESTRICTIONS: Trailers, pickup-campers, and RVs permitted. No motor homes. Load limit 2.5 tons. Maximum vehicle length 21 ft. Overhead clearance 18 ft.

FACILITIES: None

FARE: Car $1.25; pedestrian $.25

RESERVATIONS:	No
DIRECTIONS:	Ironton is on MR 66.
MAP LOCATION:	P. 319, MI, 10
CONTACT:	Mr. Richard W. Stangis, Ferry Manager, Box 39, Boyne City, MI 49727; Telephone contact: Charlevoix County Clerk's Office, (616)547-7200

STATE:	Michigan
PLACES SERVED:	Leland—South Manitou Island
BODY OF WATER:	Lake Michigan
FERRY SERVICE HISTORY:	Service on this crossing was inaugurated in 1918. Manitou Island Transit now has two vessels on this run, the sixty-five-foot steel

diesel craft *Mishe-Mokwa*, which has a crew of three, and the fifty-two-foot steel diesel craft *Manitou Isle*, which has a crew of two. Years ago, this line carried freight, including cows. Today, most of the riders come from Michigan, Ohio, Illinois, and Indiana.

LOCAL POINTS OF INTEREST:	Leland is a quaint fishing village, with fish for sale at Fishtown on the wide planks of the dock; it is also well known for its art studios, galleries, and restaurants.

South Manitou Island, along with North Manitou Island, is part of the Sleeping Bear Dunes National Lake Shore. North Manitou Island is open for primitive camping; Manitou Island Transit runs a limited schedule into North. South Manitou has sand fine enough for egg timers, the tallest lighthouse on the Great Lakes, and twelve miles of shoreland. It was formed from glacial moraines. The first settlers were Europeans. Today, it is used by campers and day visitors. The Valley of the Giants is a grove of virgin white cedar trees more than five hundred years old. A Chippewa Indian legend has it that a mother bear and two cubs once tried to swim from Wisconsin to Michigan. The exhausted cubs fell behind as they neared the Michigan shore and never made it. The mother bear climbed to the top of a bluff to wait for them, in vain. The cubs are the North and South Manitou islands.

CROSSING TIME:	1 hr. 25 mins. on the *Mishe Mokwa*; about 45 mins. on the *Manitou Isle*
FERRY TYPE:	Pedestrian
VESSEL CAPACITY:	*Mishe Mowka*: 136 passengers; *Manitou Isle*: 66 passengers
OPERATING SEASON:	May-Oct.
SCHEDULE:	**June, July, Aug. (daily); May, Sept., Oct. (Mon., Wed., Fri., Sat., Sun.) Lv. Leland** 10 a.m. (check in by 9:30). **Lv. South Manitou** 3:30 p.m.
RESTRICTIONS:	None
FACILITIES:	Restrooms; snack bar
FARE:	Round-trip only; adults $10; children $2
RESERVATIONS:	Reservations definitely advisable.
DIRECTIONS:	Leland is 25 miles northwest of Traverse City.
MAP LOCATION:	P. 319, MI, 11
CONTACT:	George and Mike Grosvenor, Manitou Island Transit, Box 591, Leland, MI 49654, (616)256-9061 or (616)256-9116

STATE:	Michigan/Wisconsin
PLACES SERVED:	Ludington, MI—Kewaunee, WI
BODY OF WATER:	Lake Michigan
FERRY SERVICE HISTORY:	Carferries, that is, ferries which moved railroad cars, have had a long history on the Great Lakes, and on Lake Michigan in particular. As early as 1849 railroads leased ships to carry people and

Badger

commodities between railroad terminals in several cities on both shores of
Lake Michigan, most notably Milwaukee and Muskegon. By the 1870s,
many railroads were in the steamship business, carrying grain eastbound
and lumber westbound. Carferries transporting railroad cars on the Great
Lakes included the *John Counter* (1853), the Buffalo and Lake Huron's
International of 1857, the *St. Ignace* of 1888, and the leviathan steamer
Ann Arbor No. 1. Lake Michigan traffic increased, from 1874, when the
Flint and Pere Marquette Railroad reached Ludington, through 1900,
when the Pere Marquette Railroad was formed. The PM merged with the
Chesapeake & Ohio Railroad in the 1920s, and tourist traffic from
Chicago and Milwaukee to Michigan resort areas began to increase. By
the 1960s, over 150,000 passengers were carried annually. Interstate
highway travel cut into the ferry service, however, during and after the
1960s. When the C&O, later the Chessie System, was displaced by
Amtrak, it became a freight-only railroad, accommodating passengers
only as a courtesy on the ferries. In an unfortunate cycle, declining
service led to declining business, and all but three of the boats were sold.
The Ludington-Kewaunee route was nearly discontinued, but in July of
1983 two Ludington businessmen, Glen Bowden and George Towns,
formed the Michigan-Wisconsin Transportation Company to revitalize the
Kewaunee run. Rail freight is still carried on the ferries, but the primary
emphasis is now on passengers and automobiles.

The vessel used on this service is the triple-tiered *City of Midland*,
built in 1941 for the Pere Marquette Railway Company. She is 406 feet
long, fifty-eight feet wide, and has a draft of eighteen feet; in summer she
has a crew of sixty (in winter, forty-nine). She is air-conditioned and
equipped with many safety devices; in addition, the bow is reinforced to
serve as an ice breaker during the winter months. In 1985, she carried
eighty thousand people. She can carry twenty-five railroad cars or 150
automobiles, along with 509 passengers. The company owns the *Badger*,
built in 1952, and the *Spartan*, built in 1953, but at present is operating
only the *City of Midland*.

LOCAL POINTS OF INTEREST: Ludington is an important port at the mouth of the Pere Marquette River. The spot where Pere Marquette, the missionary-explorer, died in 1675 is marked by the Marquette Memorial Cross, a huge illuminated cross overlooking the harbor. The city was first named Pere Marquette, but was later renamed for the lumber baron James Ludington. Ludington attracts vacationers with its beaches, forest lakes, and dunes, and has fine marina facilities for pleasure boats in the harbor. The Ludington State Park is a few miles away on Lakes Michigan and Hamlin and the Big Sable River. White Pine Village is of interest, with a complex of restored nineteenth-century buildings, including the first courthouse, town hall, barn, country farmhouse, and general store. Here, one can almost hear the thud and swish of lumberjacks felling the trees that built the Midwest.

Kewaunee has been called the "Gem of Lake Michigan" because of its beautiful harbor; it is also one of the oldest carferry ports in the world. The Historical Jail-Museum is well worth seeing; it has nine rooms of displays, including a signed letter by George Washington and hand-carved statues recreating Father Marquette's landing at Kewaunee. The county offers public hunting areas, good fishing, campgrounds, the Ahnapee trail for bikers and hikers, and a special rustic road in Montpelier known for its pastoral beauty past distinctive old barns.

CROSSING TIME: 4 hrs.

FERRY TYPE: Vehicle

VESSEL CAPACITY: 150 cars; 25 railroad cars; 509 passengers

OPERATING SEASON: All year

SCHEDULE: *Check with company for schedule; no sailings certain days during summer.* **Early Jan.-mid-June; mid-Sept.-mid-June (no holiday sailings): Mon.-Fri.: Lv. Ludington** 9:30 p.m. Eastern time; **Tues.-Sat.: Lv. Kewaunee** 2:30 a.m. Central Time. **Mid-June-mid-Sept., daily: Lv. Ludington** 9:30 a.m., 9:30 p.m.; **lv. Kewaunee** 2:30 p.m.; 2:30 a.m.

RESTRICTIONS: Trailers, pickup-campers, and RVs permitted. Overhead clearance 16 ft., 8 in.

FACILITIES: Restrooms, vending machines

FARE: Cars or light truck (including driver) $50 (round-trip $92); bicycle $5; trailers from $18 to $36 according to length (round-trip $36 to $72); consult brochure for other vehicles. Adults: $19 ($30 round-trip); children (5-15) $9.50 (round-trip $15); under 5 free. Accommodations are additional, in 2 classes. First (parlor with ¾-size bed, twin bunk, shower, chair): day sailing $16; night sailing $22. Second (stateroom with twin bunks & sink): day sailing $11; night sailing $16.

RESERVATIONS: Two weeks advance reservation recommended for all passengers and/or cars.

DIRECTIONS: In Ludington, dock is on William St., SR 10, near Lake Shore Dr. In Kewaunee, dock is on SR 29, near Main St.

MAP LOCATION: P. 319, MI, 12

CONTACT: Michigan-Wisconsin Ferry Service, Passenger Information Dept., Box 0279, Ludington, MI 49431-0279, (616)843-2521; Information recording: June 5, 1986 (800)632-0064 (MI) or (800)253-0094 (elsewhere in US)

STATE: Michigan

PLACES SERVED: Mackinaw City—Mackinac Island (Arnold Transit Company)

BODY OF WATER: Straits of Mackinac

FERRY SERVICE HISTORY: Nine large cruise ships on Arnold's line provide service to Mackinac Island. They are the *Mackinac Islander* (400 passengers), the *Huron* (400), the *Mohawk* (400), the *Algomah* (600), the *Chippewa* (600), the *Ottawa* (600), the *Straits of Mackinac II* (525—used for dinner cruises), the *Island Queen* (350), and the *Island Princess* (200). The company was founded by George Arnold over a century ago.

LOCAL POINTS OF INTEREST: Mackinaw City (the British spelling) and Mackinac Island (the French spelling) are both pronounced "Mak-i-naw"; the names derive from the Indian name for the island, "Michilimackinac," or "great turtle." Mackinaw City is the single place in the US where the sun rises on one Great Lake (Huron) and sets on another (Michigan). The original trading post built by the French became Fort Michilimackinac about 1715; the British took it over in 1761, and two years later it was captured by Indians. The British reoccupied the fort in 1764. In 1780-81, the British moved the fort to Mackinac Island, a more strategic location. One major sight here is the Mackinac Bridge going to St. Ignace, the world's longest suspension bridge. The restored Fort Michilimackinac is in a state park at the southern end of the bridge. The Mackinac Maritime Museum in the Old Mackinac Point Lighthouse contains dioramas recreating the story of Great Lakes transportation.

Lawrence Durrell once wrote of the universal yearning people have toward islands: "The mere knowledge they are on an island, a little world surrounded by the sea, fills them with indescribable intoxication." Mackinac Island invokes such feelings, if any island does. It is splendidly anachronistic (automobiles have been banned since 1904), with a turn-of-the-century atmosphere rare today. Since the 1800s it has been a resort; it was visited throughout the nineteenth century by antebellum planters and such notable figures as Susan B. Anthony, Mark Twain, and William Cullen Bryant. It is three miles long by two miles wide, with ravines, cliffs, caves, and many strange rock formations. With its horses and carriages and its Grand Hotel, Mackinac Island would be right at home in a novel by Mary Shelley or Thackeray. The majestic Grand Hotel dominates the white clapboard buildings of Mackinac Island. W. Stewart Woodfill of Indiana, the owner, has been largely responsible for its air of old-world grace; the hotel is now presided over by his nephew, R. Daniel Musser. Guests may play golf and tennis and then enjoy high tea and rocking on the porch. It was built in the late 1800s on the bluffs overlooking the Straits, looking from afar like a layer of transplanted white cliffs, in contrast to the simpler white clapboard buildings of the town. It has the longest porch in the world (880 feet) and has been the setting for such films as *This Time for Keeps* and *Somewhere in Time*. Carriage tours of the island are offered. Sights of interest include the reconstructed Jesuit chapel in Marquette Park and Old Fort Mackinac, with fourteen original buildings, now preserved as a museum with costumed guides and cannon firings. The Stuart House Museum of the American Fur Company Trading Post, formed in 1810 by John Jacob Astor, is well worth seeing; it recaptures the fur trading era with the agent's house and warehouse entrance on view.

CROSSING TIME: 30 mins.

FERRY TYPE: Pedestrian

VESSEL CAPACITY:	Varies according to vessel used; see initial list.

OPERATING SEASON:	Early May-mid-Oct.; inquire locally about winter service.

SCHEDULE: **Early-late May: Lv. Mackinaw City** 8:45 a.m., 10:45, 12:30 p.m., 2:30, 4:15. **Lv. Mackinac Island** 9:30 a.m., 11:45, 1:30 p.m., 3:30, 5:15. **Late May-late June: Lv. Mackinaw City** 8:30 a.m., 9:30, 10:30, 11:30, 1 p.m., 2, 3, 4, 5. **Lv. Mackinac Island** 9:30 a.m., 10:30, 11:30, 12:30 p.m., 2, 3, 4, 5, 6. **Late June-Aug.: Lv. Mackinaw City** 8 a.m., 9, 9:45, 10:30, 11:15, 11:45, 12:30 p.m., 1:15, 2, 2:45, 3:30, 4:15, 5, 5:45, 7, *9:15; **Lv. Mackinac Island** 9 a.m., 10:15, 11, 11:45, 12:30 p.m., 1:15, 2, 2:45, 3:30, 4:15, 5, 5:45, 6:15, 7, 8, *11. *Night boat lands at Arnold boat dock only. **Early Sept.-mid-Sept.: Lv. Mackinaw City** 8:30 a.m., 9:30, 10:30, 11:30, 1 p.m., 2:30, 3:30, 4:30, 5:30; **lv. Mackinac Island** 9:30 a.m., 10:30, 11:30, 12:30 p.m., 2, 3:30, 4:30, 5:30, 6:30. **Mid-Sept.-mid-Oct.: Lv. Mackinaw City** 9 a.m., 11, 12:45, 2:30, 4:15; **lv. Mackinac Island** 9:45, 11:45, 1:30 p.m., 3:30, 5:15.

RESTRICTIONS:	None

FACILITIES:	Restrooms, snack bar

FARE:	Adult $6.75 (round-trip; no one-way fare); child (5-12) $4; under 5 free.

RESERVATIONS:	No

DIRECTIONS:	The terminal is on Huron St. in Mackinaw City.

MAP LOCATION:	P. 319, MI, 13

CONTACT:	Arnold Transit Co., Mackinac Island, MI 49757, (906)643-8275

Wyandot

STATE:	Michigan

PLACES SERVED: Mackinaw City—Mackinac Island
(Shepler's)

BODY OF WATER: Straits of Mackinac

FERRY SERVICE   Nancy Campbell and Judy Ranville have
HISTORY: compiled a valuable history of Mackinaw,
called *Memories of Mackinaw*, for which
they taped interviews with the members of many old families and
gathered photographs which might otherwise have been lost. Included in
the book are photographs of several generations of Schepler ship captains,
one of the nautical dynasties which mark the history of American ferryboats: Capt. William (Bill) Schepler, Sr., Captain of the *Algomah*,
Captain William Schepler II, and Captain William Schepler III. The
present service was begun in 1945 with a charter boat company using two
thirty-foot "Hacker" speed boats holding ten persons each; this service
gave way to a scheduled ferry service in 1967. Capt. William R. Shepler
is president of the company at present.

There are four high-speed hydroplaning passenger boats on this service, all of special design and all constructed of aluminum and stainless
steel with diesel power. They are named after famous sailing vessels that
sailed the Straits and Great Lakes in the late 1700s, each playing an
important role in the nation's history. Each was designed by J. B.
Hargrave, Naval Architect, of West Palm Beach, Florida. They are:
Welcome: Length 60'; beam 16'9"; draft 3'; power 2-12V71TI-Detroit

diesel; capacity 120 passengers; speed 35 mph; built in 1969 by Camcraft in Louisiana; *Felicity*: Length 65'; beam 18'9"; draft 3'; power 2-12V74TI TI-Detroit diesel; capacity 150 passengers; speed 30 mph; built in 1972 by Camcraft in Louisiana; *Hope*: Length 65'; beam 18'9"; draft 3'; power 2-12V75TI-Detroit diesel; capacity 150 passengers; speed 30 mph; built 1975 by Bergeron in Louisiana; *Wyandot*: Length 77'; beam 20'9"; draft 3'; power 3-12V71TI-Detroit diesel; capacity 267 passengers; speed 32 mph; built 1979 by Bergeron in Louisiana. Each vessel has a crew of three (one captain and two deckhands). Over the years, the company has carried many dignitaries to the island, including actors, actresses, and Lady Bird Johnson.

LOCAL POINTS OF INTEREST:	[For notes on Mackinaw City and Mackinac Island, please see entries under Mackinaw City-Mackinac Island (Arnold Transit Co.), p. 351.]
CROSSING TIME:	18 mins.
FERRY TYPE:	Pedestrian
VESSEL CAPACITY:	Noted in vessel descriptions.
OPERATING SEASON:	Early May-early Nov.

SCHEDULE: **Early May-mid-May: Lv. Mackinaw City** 9 a.m., 10:30, noon, 1 p.m., 2:30, 4:30. **Lv. Mackinac Island** 9:30 a.m., 11, 12:30 p.m., 1:30, 3, 5. **Mid-May-early June: Lv. Mackinaw City** 8:30 a.m., 9:30, 10:30, 11:30, 12:30 p.m., 1:30, 2:30, 3:30, 4:30, 5:30. **Lv. Mackinac Island** 9 a.m., 10, 11, noon, 1 p.m., 2, 3, 4, 5, 6. **Early June-Aug.: Lv. Mackinaw City** 8 a.m., 8:30, 9, 9:30, 10, 10:30, 11, 11:30, noon, 12:30 p.m., 1, 1:30, 2, 2:30, 3, 3:30, 4, 4:30, 5, 5:30, 6, 6:30, 7. **Lv. Mackinac Island** 8:30 a.m., 9, 9:30, 10, 10:30, 11, 11:30, noon, 12:30 p.m., 1, 1:30, 2, 2:30, 3, 3:30, 4, 4:30, 5, 5:30, 6, 6:30, 7, 7:30. **Early-mid-Sept.: Lv. Mackinaw City** 8 a.m., 10, 11, noon, 1 p.m., 2, 3, 4, 5. **Lv. Mackinac Island** 9:30 a.m., 10:30, 11:30, 12:30 p.m., 1:30, 2:30, 3:30, 4:30, 5:30. **Mid-Sept.-early Oct.: Lv. Mackinaw City** 9 a.m., 10:30, noon, 1 p.m., 2:30, 4:30. **Lv. Mackinac Island** 9:30 a.m., 11, 12:30 p.m., 1:30, 3, 5. **Early Oct.-early Nov.: Lv. Mackinaw City** 9 a.m., 10:30, 12:30 p.m., 2:30, 4:30. **Lv. Mackinac Island** 9:30 a.m., 11, 1 p.m., 3, 5.

RESTRICTIONS:	Aft deck ramps are 6½ ft. high and 6 to 7 feet wide.
FACILITIES:	No

FARE:	Adults (round-trip only) $6.75; child $4. Bicycles $2.75. AAA members receive $.25 discount.
RESERVATIONS:	Strongly recommended for tour groups
DIRECTIONS:	Dock facilities are located in downtown Mackinaw City at the foot of the main street (Central Ave.), one block south of the city water tower at the city public marina.
MAP LOCATION:	P. 319, MI, 13
CONTACT:	Shepler's, Mackinaw City, MI 49701, (616)436-5023

STATE:	Michigan/Ontario, Canada
PLACES SERVED:	Marine City, MI—Sombra, ON
BODY OF WATER:	St. Clair River
FERRY SERVICE HISTORY:	Lowell Dalgety of the Blue Water Ferry, Ltd., in Sombra, Ontario, has undertaken considerable research and written a history

of the ferry service. Before 1880, he has found, Samuel Whitely started the first ferry from Sombra Village across the St. Clair River with a sailboat called the *Silent*. When there was no wind, he used a rowboat. He charged ten cents a round trip. In winter, he used a boat with iron runners on the ice; when they came to open water, they all got in and rowed across. After Samuel's death in 1888, his son, Tom, took over, using the same boats, until he got a small steam ferry called the *Comfort*. Sombra, at this time, was a village with a population of 280. William Ball also ran a ferry at the same time, starting about 1884; he ferried for over thirty years, using a sailboat named the *Marian* (it was later converted to a gasoline-powered motor, which exploded at the dock in 1912, burning the boat). This ferry was eventually sold to Joe Miller of Marine City, an American. The two ferries were in competition for some time, even going so far as to force passengers to change boats in mid-stream, as each ferry was only allowed to go to the middle of the river. They finally agreed to run on alternate days. Ultimately, Whitely bought out Joe Miller and carried on the ferry business in a converted yawl named the *Whitely*.

Whitely built his first towscow about 1912, then built another one to carry two cars. In the 1920s, he ran both launches and tow scows. Tom Whitely put the famous life-sized lion on top of the customs office, a landmark for many years. The ferry business was eventually sold to Morgan Dalgety and George Dean in 1948; the *Daldean* was built in 1951. A new customs house was built in 1986. Customs officers alternate between Walpole Island and offices in Sombra. The present vessels are the *Daldean*, an all-steel double-ended boat seventy-five feet by thirty-six feet, with a crew of three, and the *Ontamich* (formerly at Roberts Landing). The most unusual passengers carried on the ferry were mourners wishing to sprinkle the ashes of a deceased aunt. Normally, in summer, there are tourists from all states; in winter, the traffic is mostly from local businesses. Service at Roberts Landing-Port Lambton has been discontinued and incorporated into this ferry, which has taken over the boat once used at Roberts Landing.

LOCAL POINTS OF INTEREST: Sombra is known as the location of the first ferry to the US south of Sarnia. The Sombra Museum is well worth visiting; it is a pioneer home with a special Marine Room. Cathcart Park, just north of Sombra, is a beautiful site with fully serviced campsites, children's play area, and pleasant scenery.

Marine City is a small river town on the Belle and the St. Clair Rivers. It has a marina, several motels, and restaurants.

CROSSING TIME: 4 mins.

FERRY TYPE: Vehicle

VESSEL CAPACITY: Both boats: 12 cars

OPERATING SEASON: All year

SCHEDULE: Daily: frequent crossings; 16-hr. service, 6:30 a.m.-10:30 p.m.

RESTRICTIONS: Trailers, pickup-campers, and RVs permitted. Load limit 50 tons. Max. combined vehicle length 75 ft.

FACILITIES: None

FARE: Car $3; pickup-camper $3; trailer or RV $3-$5.

RESERVATIONS: No

| **DIRECTIONS:** | The ferry landing is signposted locally. |

| **MAP LOCATION:** | P. 319, MI, 14 |

CONTACT: Mr. Lowell Dalgety, Blue Water Ferry, Ltd., Box 171, St. Clair Parkway, Sombra, ON NOP 2HO Canada, (313)765-3343; Canada (519)677-5651 or Canadian Customs, Box 239, Port Lambton, ON NOP 2BO Canada, (519)677-5651

STATE: Michigan

PLACES SERVED: St. Ignace—Mackinac Island (Arnold Transit Company)

BODY OF WATER: Straits of Mackinac

FERRY SERVICE HISTORY: Nine large cruise ships on Arnold's line provide service to Mackinac Island. The 1940 WPA *Guide* to Michigan mentions the Arnold steamers from St. Ignace to Mackinac Island and gives a vivid description of St. Ignace as seen from a ferry: "Point St. Ignace appears first, jutting southward into the Straits, the dark green of thickly growing pines and cedars softened by lighter touches of greensward. Small homes are visible through the trees. Within the harbor, with its fishing boats and loading docks, the aspect changes. To the north along the shore are the unpretentious homes of fishermen in the French section, and along the highway, tourist homes." [For history of Arnold's and list of ships and capacities, please see entry under Mackinaw City-Mackinac Island (Arnold Transit Co.), p. 351.]

LOCAL POINTS OF INTEREST: St. Ignace, Michigan's second-oldest community, was founded in 1671 by the Explorer Fr. Marquette, who established a mission here. A fortress was then built, but in 1701 it was moved to Detroit. The city is the home of one of the world's largest icebreakers, the *Chief Wawatam*; on Labor Day there is the annual Mackinac Bridge Walk over the bridge here from Mackinaw City, which is one of the world's longest suspension bridges. It has been said that in winter it is like an "outpost of former day," with the snow blanketing the town.

[For notes on Mackinac Island, please see entry under Mackinaw City-Mackinac Island (Arnold Transit Co.), p. 351.]

CROSSING TIME:	30 mins.
FERRY TYPE:	Pedestrian
VESSEL CAPACITY:	Varies according to vessel used; please see list of ships under Mackinaw City-Mackinac Island (Arnold Transit Co.), p. 350.
OPERATING SEASON:	Mid-Apr.-early Nov.; inquire about winter service.

SCHEDULE: *Schedule dates vary from year to year; consult annual schedule; there may also be seasonal aberrations.* **Mid-Apr.-Apr. 20 (approx.) (no Sunday service): Lv. St. Ignace** 7:45 a.m., 10, 1:30 p.m., 3:30; **lv. Mackinac Island** 8:30 a.m., 11, 2:30 p.m., 4:15. **Late Apr.-late May: Lv. St. Ignace** 7:30 a.m., 9:30, 11:30, 2 p.m., 4; **lv. Mackinac Island** 8:30 a.m., 10:30, 12:30 p.m., 3, 5. **Late May-late June: Lv. St. Ignace** 7:30 a.m., 8:30, 9:30, 10:30, 11:30, 1 p.m., 2, 3, 4, 5; **lv. Mackinac Island** 8:30 a.m., 9:30, 10:30, 11:30, 12:30 p.m., 2, 3, 4, 5, 6. **Late June-Aug.: Lv. St. Ignace** 7:30 a.m., 8:30, 9:15, 10, 10:45, 11:30, 12:15 p.m., 1, 2, 2:45, 3:30, 4:15, 5, 6, 7, 10:30; **lv. Mackinac Island** 8:15 a.m., 9:30, 10:15, 11, 11:45, 12:45 p.m., 1:30, 2:15, 3, 3:45, 4:30, 5, 6, 7, 8, 10. **Early Sept.-mid-Sept.: Lv. St. Ignace** 7:30 a.m., 9, 10, 11, 12:30 p.m., 2, 3, 4:15, 5:30; **lv. Mackinac Island** 8:30 a.m., 9:45, 11, 12:30 p.m., 2, 3, 4, 5, 6. **Mid-Sept.-Nov. 3: Lv. St. Ignace** 7:30 a.m., 9:30, 11:30, 2 p.m., 4; **lv. Mackinac Island** 8:30 a.m., 10:30, 12:30 p.m., 3, 5.

RESTRICTIONS:	None
FACILITIES:	Restrooms, snack bar
FARE:	Adult $6.75 (round-trip; no one-way fare); child (5-12) $4; under 5 free.
RESERVATIONS:	No
DIRECTIONS:	Terminal is on State St. in St. Ignace.
MAP LOCATION:	P. 319, MI, 15
CONTACT:	See CONTACT, p. 353.

STATE: Michigan

PLACES SERVED: St. Ignace—Mackinac Island (Star Line)

BODY OF WATER: Straits of Mackinac

FERRY SERVICE HISTORY: The Star Line has existed since 1979; the company took over an existing boat line at that time. There are three vessels on this service, all hydroplanes, blue and white with red trim, with seating both inside and on an open deck. They are the *Nicolet*, the *Marquette*, and the *LaSalle*.

LOCAL POINTS OF INTEREST: [For notes on St. Ignace, please see entry under St. Ignace-Mackinac Island (Arnold Transit Co., p. 358; for notes on Mackinac Island, please see notes on Mackinaw City-Mackinac Island (Arnold Transit Co.), p. 351.]

CROSSING TIME: 18 mins.

FERRY TYPE: Pedestrian

VESSEL CAPACITY: 150 passengers

OPERATING SEASON: Mid-May-Oct.

SCHEDULE: **Mid-May-late May: Lv. St. Ignace** 7:30 a.m., 9, 10:20, noon, 3 p.m., 4:30. **Lv. Mackinac Island** 8 a.m., 9:30, 11, 12:30 p.m., 2:30, 5. **Early June-mid-June: Lv. St. Ignace** 7:30 a.m., 9, 10, 11, 12, 1 p.m., 3, 5. **Lv. Mackinac Island** 8 a.m., 9:30, 10:30, 11:30, 12:30 p.m., 1:30, 3:30, 5:30. **Mid-June-late June: Lv. St. Ignace** 7:30 a.m., 9, 10, 11, noon, 1 p.m., 2, 3, 4, 5, 6, 7. **Lv. Mackinac Island** 8 a.m., 9:30, 10:30, noon, 1 p.m., 2, 3, 4, 5, 6, 7, 8. **Late June-July: Lv. St. Ignace** 7:30 a.m., 8:30, and on the hour and half-hour until 6 p.m., 7. **Lv. Mackinac Island** 8 a.m. and on the hour until 3:30 p.m., 4, 4:30, 5, 5:30, 6, 7, 8. **Sept.: Lv. St. Ignace** 7:30 a.m., 9, 10, 11, noon, 1 p.m., 2, 3, 5. **Lv. Mackinac Island** 8 a.m., 9:30, 10:30, 11:30, 12:30 p.m., 1:30, 2:30, 4, 5:30. **Early Oct.-late Oct.: Lv. St. Ignace** 7:30 a.m., 9, 10, 11, noon, 2 p.m., 4:30. **Lv. Mackinac Island** 8 a.m., 9:30, 10:30, 11:30, 12:30 p.m., 3, 5. **Late Oct.: Lv. St. Ignace** 7:30 a.m., 4:30 p.m. **Lv. Mackinac Island** 8 a.m., 5 p.m.

RESTRICTIONS: None

FACILITIES: Restrooms on the *Marquette* and *LaSalle*

FARE: Round-trip: adult $7.25; child (5-12) $4.25

RESERVATIONS: No

DIRECTIONS: Main dock is at the north end of St. Ignace; railroad dock is at south end of town. Boats run from both locations; customers at hotels in south end may find these boats more convenient.

MAP LOCATION: P. 319, MI, 15

CONTACT: Star Line, 590 N. State St., St. Ignace, MI 59781, (906)643-7635

STATE: Michigan

PLACES SERVED: Sault Ste. Marie (Mission Point)—Sugar Island

BODY OF WATER: St. Marys River

FERRY SERVICE HISTORY: The current ferry service between Sugar Island and Sault Ste. Marie started in 1946. The boat, the *Sugar Islander*, is a double-ended ferry, eighty-nine feet long, with a crew of two per shift. The *Sugar Islander* has carried, among other things, pigs and bears. Fortunately, the bears were in traps. Usually, the ferry riders are commuters who live on the island and work in town and, in summer, tourists. The crossing goes back for some time before the current service; the 1941 WPA *Guide* to Michigan lists a Sugar Island ferry.

LOCAL POINTS OF INTEREST: Sault Ste. Marie is the oldest town in Michigan; it was once described by Henry Clay as "the remotest settlement in the United States, if not in the moon." In 1620 the French explorer Etienne Brule went through the area en route to Lake Superior. He was followed by Jesuit missionaries. The city is noted for its great engineering accomplishment, the locks of St. Marys River, which lower or raise lake and

ocean vessels twenty-one feet between Lake Superior and Lake Huron. The locks are necessitated because of the river cascades. It is said that the Jesuit priests, when they first gazed upon the spot, said "Sault!" (cascades), and then "Sainte Marie," feeling that only the name of the Blessed Virgin was suitable to grace such a beautiful place. This is the only entrance into Canada for almost three hundred miles. The locks may be toured by train (the Soo Locks Tour Trains) or by boat (the Soo Locks Boat Tours).

Sugar Island was the historic home of the Chippewa Indians. It is now a popular tourist destination; among the island's resorts are Gil Nelson's, Mountain View, Lookout Point, and Hay Point Hideaway.

CROSSING TIME: 3-5 mins.

FERRY TYPE: Vehicle

VESSEL CAPACITY: 15 cars

OPERATING SEASON: All year

SCHEDULE: **Daily: Lv. Sugar Island** on the hour and half hour 6 a.m.-midnight; **Fri. and Sat.** to 2 a.m.; **Lv. Mission Point** on the quarter-hour and three-quarters-hour 6:15 a.m.-12:15 a.m.; **Fri. & Sat.** to 1:45 a.m.

RESTRICTIONS: Trailers, pickup-campers, and RVs permitted. Load limit 60 gross tons. Overhead clearance 11'6" (unlimited with turnaround).

FACILITIES: None

FARE:	Car and driver $1.25; passengers $.50; children (5-12) $.15 (under 5 free); trailers $1.25-$1.75; pickup-campers and RVs $2.50.
RESERVATIONS:	No
DIRECTIONS:	Ferry leaves from E. Portage Ave. at Sault Ste. Marie across from the Room Golf Course.
MAP LOCATION:	P. 319, MI, 16
CONTACT:	Sugar Island Ferry, E. Portage Ave., Sault Ste. Marie, Michigan, 49783, (906) 635-5421

STATE:	Minnesota/Michigan
PLACES SERVED:	Grand Portage, MN—Isle Royale National Park, MI
BODY OF WATER:	Lake Superior
FERRY SERVICE HISTORY:	The Grand Portage-Isle Royale Transportation Line, Inc., has carried passengers to Isle Royale from Grand Portage since 1938.

Previous ships on the run were the *Rita Marie*, the *Disturbance*, the *Voyageur I*, and the *Nee Gee* ("good friend"). The most recent vessels are the sixty-three-foot twin-engine *Voyageur II*, built in 1973, and the sixty-five-foot cruiser *Wenonah*, built in 1964 (named for the mother of Hiawatha). Both ships pass over the site in the North Gap of Isle Royale, off Washington Harbor, where the steamer *America* struck a reef during the pre-dawn hours of June 7, 1928 (all aboard were able to get safely to shore). The bow and one-third of the boat are still visible. The parents of Captain Stanley S. Sivertson of the *Wenonah* were aboard; he tells the story of the fresh grapefruit, oranges, cherries, lemons, and other fruit, salvaged from the wreck, which sustained families living out at the Island all summer. Captain Stanley has run the *Wenonah* since 1967. "There are so many stories, so much history," he told Peter Oikarinen, who interviewed him for *Island Folk, the People of Isle Royale*. Oikarinen describes him as "unassuming and steady," habitually watching the surrounding water

even while the ship is docked. Captain Roy Oberg, who has been piloting passengers and cargo vessels since 1937, also has many stories to tell. He knows every rock and island and, when they first installed radar on the old *Voyageur*, he had to interpret the water to Peter Finch, the technician sent from England. "That's the first time I was ever on a boat where I had somebody explain what I was seeing," said Finch. Oikarinen likens the thrice weekly arrival of the *Voyageur II* at McCargoe Cove to the loading dock of a busy truck terminal, with ice, groceries, and mail offloaded along with passengers. Captain Roy says that, even when he retires, he will "make one or two trips a year. . . . It gets in your blood, just like anything else."

LOCAL POINTS OF INTEREST: Grand Portage, or "kitchi onigum," "the great carrying place," is a quiet village on the north shore of Lake Superior, with a past rich in historical significance. To early Indians, it was a summer village site; from here, they travelled in birchbark canoes on the network of lakes and rivers that lace the region. They used the Grand Portage trail to link the Great Lakes with the border country waterways. Early explorers and fur traders followed these waterways to the Northwest, and in 1778 the British fur traders of the Northwest Company established their inland headquarters at Grand Portage. For the ensuing twenty-five years Grand Portage served as the central depot and meeting place for the trade. For several months every summer, hundreds of Northwest Company voyageurs concentrated on reaching Grand Portage and the great rendezvous, shedding the weariness of their portages and participating with hundreds of trappers, guides, and the local Ojibway people for many days of revelry. The August Grand Portage Rendezvous still brings people here, helping to preserve Ojibway traditions and to recreate the era of the voyageur. Events include a pow-wow, log sawing, canoe packing, and races. The Grand Portage National Monument is administered by the National Park Service; it includes a partially reconstructed fur-trading post and stockade, kitchen, and warehouse.

Isle Royale, a National Park since 1940, is a primitive archipelago with over two hundred islands, no roads, and over 166 miles of foot trails. There are roaming moose, wildflowers, miles of thickly wooded coast, and magnificent scenery. The Windigo area was a prehistoric copper mining area. The modern Minong mine, which in 1875 employed seventy men and their families, closed in 1894. After that, according to Captain Stanley, some real estate people in Duluth, Omaha, and Chicago established the Washington Club. He says they came out to the island for two things: "one, a hay fever haven; two, a place to fish speckled and lake trout." The island was popular for summer homes and as a wilderness retreat; the homes were eradicated after the National Park was established in 1940. Some buildings remain: Pete Edison's fishery, the Rock Harbor Lighthouse, and the Minong Mine have been listed as historic sites. Detroit journalist Albert Stoll has led the fight for the park.

Today, the *Voyageur II* circumnavigates Isle Royale three times weekly and will drop off and pick up passengers at various points. At Rock Harbor there is boat rental, an information center, and accommodation at the Rock Harbor Lodge. This is Park Service wholesome without television sets; there are also some housekeeping cottages. At Windigo (Washington Harbor), the other end of the island, there is also an information center and grocery, but no accommodation. (For lodging, write National Park Concessions, Box 405, Houghton, MI 49931.) The park is open mid-May through mid-October, with full services offered mid-June through August. The lodge is open mid-May through September.

CROSSING TIME:	*Wenonah:* 3 hrs.; *Voyageur II:* 3 hrs.
FERRY TYPE:	Pedestrian
VESSEL CAPACITY:	*Wenonah:* 150 passengers; *Voyageur II:* 49 passengers
OPERATING SEASON:	*Wenonah:* Mid-June-Labor Day (begins 2nd Sat. of June); *Voyageur II:* May-Oct.
SCHEDULE:	*Wenonah:* **Daily. Lv. Grand Portage** 9:30 a.m. CDT for Windigo (Washington Harbor); **Lv. Isle Royale (Windigo)** 3 p.m.

CDT. *Voyageur II:* **Service to Isle Royale Mon., Wed., Sat.: lv. Grand Portage** 9:30 a.m. CDT, arriving Windigo (Washington Harbor) at noon;

after a brief stop, cruises north side of Isle Royale, arriving at Rock Harbor 5 p.m. CDT. **Service to Grand Portage Tues., Thurs., Sun.: Lv. Isle Royale (Rock Harbor)** for trip along south side of island 8 a.m. CDT; after making brief stops along the way, arrives Washington Harbor about 1 p.m. CDT, departs immediately, and arrives at Grand Portage about 4 p.m. CDT.

RESTRICTIONS: No gas in outboard motors (may be purchased at Rock Harbor and Windigo; Mott Island during off-season) on Isle Royale. No pets.

FACILITIES: Restrooms. Limited choice of sandwiches and soft drinks on *Wenonah*. No food service on *Voyageur II*. Box lunches available in Grand Portage.

FARE: *Wenonah:* Adults $20 (same-day round-trip $25), children 3-12 half fare, children under 3 free. Car-top boats $15; canoes $10; outboard motors according to size ($5-$10). Baggage: 75 lbs. per adult ticket fare; excess charge $7.50 per 100 lbs. *Voyageur II:* Adult fares: between Grand Portage and Washington Harbor $25; between Grand Portage and McCargoe Cove, Belle Isle, Rock Harbor $30, (round-trip; 2 days; overnight accommodation at Rock Harbor only — LODGE NOT INCLUDED — $50). Between Washington Harbor and McCargoe Cove, Belle Isle, and Rock Harbor $30. Between Rock Harbor and Daisy Farm, Chippewa Harbor, Malone Bay, and Washington Harbor $30. Children's fares: under 12 any trip $25, Rock Harbor 2-day round-trip $40. Baggage, boats, canoes, and motors same as *Wenonah* listing. Wheeled vehicles (bicycles, small motorbikes) $10.

RESERVATIONS: Advisable on *Wenonah*. Required on *Voyageur II* with full remittance in advance; cancellation notice 72 hours for full refund.

DIRECTIONS: Docks in Grand Portage are approx. 1 mile apart on a gravel and paved road. *Wenonah* leaves from the stockade; *Voyageur II* leaves from the Voyageur Gateway to Adventure Marina on Hat Point. Both are off SR 61 from Duluth.

MAP LOCATION: P. 319, MN, 1

CONTACT: Sivertson GPIR, Box 754, Duluth, MN 55801, (218)728-1237

Akers Ferry

STATE:	Missouri
PLACES SERVED:	Akers (at junction of highways "K" and "KK," Shannon County)
BODY OF WATER:	Current River

FERRY SERVICE HISTORY: Prior to the era of the automobile, many small shallow Ozark rivers were crossed by fords, which presented no difficulty to horses. With the widespread use of the automobile, however, which bogged down in gravel or mud bottoms, ferries became the common method of crossing such rivers as the Current, St. Francis, White, Gasconade, Eleven Point, and Niangua. The ferry had to be on a road with sufficient traffic to make it profitable, and the approach and banks on either side had to be suitable for automobiles and landing points. Something permanent, such as a tree or a post, was needed to anchor the cable, and the river needed to be at least three or four feet deep to float a loaded ferry. Many of these ferries were actually powered by the current itself. A cable was run across the river and a wire cable attached to the front and back of the ferry with a pulley to the big cable. The flatboat was then nosed into the current and, slowly, the boat moved out and crossed the river. On the return trip, the other end of the boat was pointed into the current to cross. The ferryman was on duty twenty-four hours a day, year round, only getting time off if he could find a substitute. Some ferrymen slept on the ferry, and often their families were involved with other small businesses, such as country stores, mills, or blacksmith shops. Many of these ferries have disappeared, but the one at Akers is still operating; it is part of the Ozark National Scenic Riverway and operated by a park concessioner, Akers Ferry Canoe Rental. Arnold Smith was one of the first ferry operators; he used the self-propelled method around 1949. G. E. Maggard bought the ferry in 1959 and added a motor; he then built a two-car ferry, which he still operates. To cross the ferry, the motorist rings a bell. Maggard says the most unusual cargo he has carried has been an antique car tour. The boat is named the *Akers Ferry*; it is fifty-five feet by eighteen feet, steel, with a wooden top.

LOCAL POINTS OF INTEREST: The first settlers in Akers were Indians; arrowheads and burial mounds have been found indicating that there were campgrounds in the area thousands of years ago. The French were in the area in the 1700s, but, when John Lewis brought his family to the mouth of the creek in the early 1830s, there was no permanent settlement. The first post office was granted in 1871, and the first store was opened about 1885. Akers is just southeast of the Montauk State Park and northwest of the area of the Current River, which has been designated a member of the Ozark Scenic Riverways. The access point to the river at Akers is a popular one with floaters; between Akers and Pulltite is Cave Spring (big enough to paddle a canoe in for one hundred feet) and Troublesome Hollow, once crossed by narrow-gauge logging trains. If starting a float trip, however, you should check with the ranger about river conditions and get a copy of the Ozark Riverways strip map. Mild winters allow floating almost year-round, but spring is recommended, as the water is up. Canoes and jon boats can be rented.

CROSSING TIME: 5 mins.

FERRY TYPE: Vehicle

VESSEL CAPACITY: 2 cars

OPERATING SEASON: All year, river and weather permitting

SCHEDULE: **Daily, on signal. Summer (Apr.-Sept.):** 7 a.m.-7 p.m. **Winter (Oct.-Mar.):** 8 a.m.-5 p.m.

RESTRICTIONS: Trailers, pickup-campers, and RVs permitted. Max. combined vehicle length 40 ft.

FACILITIES: None

FARE:	Car $1.50; with trailer $2; truck $1.75
RESERVATIONS:	No
DIRECTIONS:	Ferry connects Rts. "K" and "KK" between Hartshorn and Jadwin, in Shannon County, near Summersville.
MAP LOCATION:	P. 319, MO, 1
CONTACT:	George Eugene Maggard, Akers Ferry Canoe Rental, Cedargrove Route, Box 90, Salem, MO 65560, (314)858-3224

STATE:	Missouri/Illinois
PLACES SERVED:	Canton, MO—Meyer, IL
BODY OF WATER:	Mississippi River
FERRY SERVICE HISTORY:	This ferry service was inaugurated in 1853 and has operated each year since that time.

The original ferry was called the *Lewis-Adams,* and the first charter stated the fares to be charged: footmen, ten cents; team and wagon, fifty cents. Early boats included the *Rosa Lee* and the *Cantonia.* The Canton ferry is the oldest continuously operated one on the Mississippi, connecting Illinois and Missouri from March 15 to December 15. It is the modern counterpart of the old Mississippi ferry boats that have served the people of Missouri and Illinois since 1843. Canton is located where the Mississippi River makes its widest sweep westward. Riding the boat, one can almost sense the excitement Mark Twain felt as the entire town waited for the steamboat to come, expressed in *Life on the Mississippi.* Twain describes the town as almost asleep by "the great Mississippi, the majestic, the magnificent Mississippi, rolling its mile-wide tide along, shining in the sun." A puff of smoke appears, and the people gather; they "fasten their eyes upon the coming boat. . . . long and sharp and trim and pretty; she has two tall, fancy-topped chimneys, with a gilded device of some kind swung between them; a fanciful pilot-house, all glass and 'gingerbread,' perched on top of the "texas" deck behind them; the paddleboxes are gorgeous with a picture or with gilded rays above the boat's name . . . the captain stands by the big bell, calm, imposing . . . great volumes of the blackest smoke are rolling and tumbling out of the chimneys . . . a husbanded grandeur created with a bit of pitch-pine just before arriving at a town." A mad scramble ensues to unload and load cargo and passengers, and the ship

leaves. "After ten more minutes the town is dead again."

The vessel, called the *Canton Ferry,* is a double-ended ferry barge with a push boat; it is twenty feet by sixty feet with a three-foot draft. It is owned and operated by Wallace and Clara Kizer, who purchased it in 1985 from Mrs. John S. Froman, who had operated it since 1977. Before that, it was owned for thirty-six years by Allen Blackmore. The ferry is a lifeline for farmers who lack the time and money to drive fifty miles out of their way to cross bridges at Quincy, Illinois, or Keokuk, Iowa. Sometimes Kizer keeps the ferry running long after the river has ice on it; he claims he is the only ferry pilot crazy enough to haul grain trucks across the river in December. Among the unusual cargoes the Kizers have carried (Clara Kizer works with her husband on board) were two small barns taken in half at the center, each half transported separately, and a double-wide house trailer, carried in the same fashion. Kizer also recalls transporting "loads of livestock which had been coaxed and pushed into the hayloft of several barns when the Meyer levee broke and flooded thousands of acres of low ground behind the levee." Their passengers come from all over the US and from many foreign countries.

LOCAL POINTS OF INTEREST: Canton is a small college town, the home of Culver-Stockton College, founded in 1853 and the oldest college west of the Mississippi to be chartered for co-education. Ferry enthusiasts will enjoy the Golden Eagle Riverboat Dinner Theatre, a replica of a Mississippi riverboat; also of interest are Wakonda State Park and Canton's North Riverfront Park. The town is near Hannibal, birthplace of Mark Twain, and the Mark Twain Lake.

CROSSING TIME: 6 mins.

FERRY TYPE:	Vehicle
VESSEL CAPACITY:	6 cars
OPERATING SEASON:	Mid-Mar.-mid-Dec.
SCHEDULE:	**Daily. Mid-Mar.-mid-May and mid-Sept.-mid-Dec.:** 7 a.m.-6 p.m. **Mid-May-mid-Sept.:** 7 a.m.-8 p.m.
RESTRICTIONS:	Trailers, pickup-campers, and RVs permitted. Load limit 30 tons. Maximum vehicle length 60 ft.
FACILITIES:	None
FARE:	Car $3; pickup-camper $3-$6; RVs permitted; trailers permitted.
RESERVATIONS:	No
DIRECTIONS:	The ferry is located in the northeast corner of Missouri, in Lewis County, near the Federal Locks and Dam No. 20.
MAP LOCATION:	P. 319, MO, 2
CONTACT:	Wallace L. Kizer, 604 Grant St., Canton, MO 63435, (314)288-3823

STATE:	Missouri
PLACES SERVED:	Route "J," between Osage and Gasconade Counties
BODY OF WATER:	Gasconade River
FERRY SERVICE HISTORY:	This ferry crossing was established before 1880. Anna Hesse of Hermann, Missouri, has written two local histories of Hermann

and Gasconade County and says that the Gasconade River was one of the main sources of travel and transportation of lumber and other goods during the early years of the county. Roland "Whitey" Meyer has owned the ferry since 1959. "I carry anything I can carry within my license," he says. He has carried antique cars and horses for parades in Hermann. The ferry is an all-steel sixty-five-foot vessel called the *Roy J.*; it is all-electric, running from an overhead trolley. The crossing is four hundred feet wide.

LOCAL POINTS OF INTEREST: Hermann is known as the "Rhine City on the Missouri River," with its hills and valleys.

Anna Hesse has described the city: "Cupped against the background of three hundred-foot hills and early houses set against the sidewalk, the neat lawns and flower gardens give the city an old world charm." One of the first surveyors was Daniel M. Boone, the son of Daniel Boone. Highway J cuts across the hills and valleys of the northern part of the county.

CROSSING TIME: 2 mins.

FERRY TYPE: Vehicle

VESSEL CAPACITY: 2-3 cars

OPERATING SEASON: Mar.-Nov. usually; Dec.-Mar. also if river conditions permit

SCHEDULE: Daily, daylight hours, river conditions permitting

RESTRICTIONS: Trailers, pickup-campers, and RVs permitted. Load limit 8 tons.

FACILITIES: None

FARE: Car $2 ($3 round-trip for pedestrian groups)

RESERVATIONS: No

DIRECTIONS: The ferry connects Osage and Gasconade counties over Route "J," southwest of Hermann.

MAP LOCATION: P. 319, MO, 3

CONTACT: Roland "Whitey" Meyer, Rt. 1, Morrison, MO 65061, (314)294-7203

Islander

STATE: Ohio

PLACES SERVED: Catawba Point—Put-in-Bay (South Bass Island)

BODY OF WATER: Lake Erie (West End)

FERRY SERVICE HISTORY: The history of the Miller Boat Lines has been written by Thomas A. (Andy) Sykora of Rocky River, Ohio, for the *Inland Seas,* published by the Great Lakes Historical Society. The founder of the company, William M. Miller, started his business in 1912 with a few old rowboats, later progressing to an eighteen-foot flat-bottomed rig, the *Livery,* powered by a one-cylinder, two-cycle, three horsepower Relacco gas engine. He later acquired a fleet of thirty-five-foot vessels designed as head boats, which became a familiar sight for years around the Bass Islands. When William Miller retired, his son, Lee, took over, and expanded the service to transport the mail year-round (before the advent of the airplane). In 1945, the Catawba Dock facility had been secured by Miller, and the *South Shore* was put into service; it was later sold to the Beaver Island Ferry Company in Beaver Island, Michigan. In 1947, construction of the *West Shore* began, and in 1954 Lee Miller contracted again with Sturgeon Bay Shipbuilding for construction of the *Wm. M. Miller.* In 1959, the *Put-in-Bay* was acquired. In 1973, Lee Miller's son Bill, 29, lost his life in a boating accident. In 1978, William E. Market III, an employee of the company, and his wife, Mary Ann, purchased the

Miller Boat Line, Inc. from Mrs. Mary Miller. The Markets have continued to operate the fleet of ferries, adding the *Islander* and offering more facilities on Catawba Island. As Sykora puts its, Market "has the unbelievable clear vision of his predecessors . . . to cast the line and make the thing go!" The present vessels, all steel-welded, are: *West Shore:* 65 ft. long; built 1947; single screw; 300 hp.; 10 cars; 250 passengers; *Wm. M. Miller:* 65 ft. long; built 1954; single screw; 380 hp.; 10 cars; 250 passengers; *Put-in-Bay:* 65 ft. long; built 1959; twin screw; 400 hp.; 10 autos; 150 passengers; *Islander:* 90 ft. long; built 1983; twin screw; 700 hp.; 16 autos; 700 passengers.

The 1940 WPA *Guide* to Ohio mentions that from June to September there was service three times a day from Catawba Island to Middle and South Bass Island on the *Erie Isle* (passengers were fifty cents and autos $1.50). Today, most passengers come from Cleveland, Columbus, and Toledo, Ohio, and from Detroit, Michigan.

LOCAL POINTS OF INTEREST: Put-in-Bay: "Its real name is South Bass Island but no one but a mapmaker would call it anything but Put-in-Bay," says George Cantor in his *Great Lakes Guidebook*. Put-in-Bay has a natural harbor, which has attracted generations of boating people. The island, with a population of only four hundred, is well set up for fishing and family touring. The spring smallmouth black bass fishing, the walleye fishing in summer, and the perch and walleye fishing in winter are well known. The Put-in-Bay tour train operates from a depot near the ferryboat, offering a fifty-minute tour of the island. Other attractions are Perry's Victory and International Peace Memorial, commemorating Commodore Oliver Hazard Perry's victory over the British at the Battle of Lake Erie in 1813, Perry's Cave, where he is supposed to have stored ammunition, and Crystal Cave, with deposits of strontium sulphate crystals. You may also tour the Heineman winery. The August boat regatta draws big crowds. The Park Hotel, c. 1880, offers accommodation.

Catawba Point is a community on the shore of Lake Erie above the Catawba Island State Park. Here, there are boat ramps and a fishing pier; the waters abound in perch and catfish. In winter there is excellent ice fishing.

CROSSING TIME: 18 mins.

FERRY TYPE: Vehicle

VESSEL CAPACITY: See listing of vessels under Ferry History section.

OPERATING SEASON: Early Apr.-Sept.

SCHEDULE: **Early Apr.-mid-Apr., daily: Lv. Put-in-Bay** *8, 9:15, 10:30, 1:15 p.m., 2:45, 4:30. **Lv. Catawba** *8:30, 9:45, 11, 1:45 p.m., 3:30, 5. *No Sun. trip. **Mid-Apr.-mid-May, daily: Lv. Put-in-Bay** *7:15, 8:30, 9:45, 11, **noon, 1:30 p.m., 2:30, 3:45, 5, **6:15. **Lv. Catawba** *7:45, 9, 10:30, 11:30, **12:30 p.m., 2, 3:15, 4:30, 5:30, **6:45. *No Sun. Trip. **Fri., Sat., Sun. only. **Mid-May-mid-June, daily: Lv. Put-in-Bay** *7, 8, 9, 10, 11, noon, 1:15 p.m., 2:15, 3, 4, 5, 6, **7. **Lv. Catawba** *7:45, 8:45, 9:45, 10:45, 11:30, 12:30 p.m., 1:45, 2:45, 3:45, 4:45, 5:45, 6:30, **7:30. *No Sun. trip. **Fri., Sat., Sun., holidays only. **Mid-June-late June, + certain days in late Aug. & early Sept., daily: Lv. Put-in-Bay** 7, 8, 9, 10, 11, 11:30, noon, 12:30 p.m., 1, 1:30, 2, 3, 4, 4:30, 5, 5:30, 6, 7, *8. **Lv. Catawba** 7:30 a.m., 8:30, 9:30, 10:30, 11:30, noon, 12:30 p.m., 1, 1:30, 2, 2:30, 3:30, 4:30, 5, 5:30, 6, 6:30, 7:30, *8:30. *Fri., Sat., Sun., holidays only. **Late June-late Aug., plus certain days in late Aug. and early Sept., daily: Lv. Put-in-Bay** every half hour 7 a.m.-7 p.m. *7:30 p.m., *8. **Lv. Catawba** every half hour 7:30 a.m.-7:30 p.m.; *8 p.m., *8:30. *Fri., Sat., Sun., holidays only. *Additional special weekend service; consult company schedules.*

RESTRICTIONS: Trailers, pickup-campers, and RVs permitted. Load limit 30 tons (truck and load). Semi-tractor-trailers 60′ OAL.

FACILITIES: Restrooms

FARE: Cars $6, adults $3, children (6-11) $1; trailer or pickup-camper $7 up; RVs $14 up.

RESERVATIONS: None. Cars must be in line 15 mins. before departure. No round-trip cars from Catawba on Saturdays, Sundays, or holidays.

DIRECTIONS: From Rt. 2, take Rt. 53 north to dock.

MAP LOCATION: P. 319, OH, 1

CONTACT: Miller Boat Line, Inc., Put-in-Bay, Ohio 43456, (419)285-2421

STATE: Ohio

PLACES SERVED: Marblehead—Kelleys Island

BODY OF WATER: Lake Erie

FERRY SERVICE HISTORY: The Neuman Boat Line has been in operation since 1907. Its regular service to the islands dates from 1921, and service on this run from 1955. The present vessels are the *Kelley Islander,* one hundred feet long (captain and two deckhands), the *Corsair,* sixty-five feet long (captain and one deckhand), and the *Commuter,* sixty-five feet long (captain and one deckhand). All three boats are flat-topped, partially decked over auto and passenger ferries. When the B. F. Goodrich Company tested emergency rapid-exit chutes for the airline industry, which were later put on airplanes, the electrical lines to the island were laid from the boats. Most riders come from Ohio, Michigan, West Virginia, Kentucky, Indiana, Illinois, and Pennsylvania. Passenger and freight boats have a long history on this crossing. Dwight Boyer, in *Ships and Men of the Great Lakes,* recounts the sad tale of the loss of the *Margaret Olwill,* a lake steamer regularly carrying limestone from Kelleys Island to Cleveland, in a sudden storm in 1899 and mentions a ferry dock at that time on the south side of the island. The 1940 WPA *Guide* to Ohio states that the *Lakeside III* ran twice a week to Kelleys Island and also to South Bass Island.

LOCAL POINTS OF INTEREST: Marblehead, a summer resort and fishing center, is on the tip of the Marblehead peninsula. It is the site of the oldest lighthouse in continuous service on the lake, the Marblehead Lighthouse. It was built in 1821-22 and is a favorite spot from which to view the lake and Kelleys Island.

Kelleys Island, with twenty-eight hundred acres, is the largest one on the American side of Lake Erie. It has been said, "Scratch Ohio and you find a success story." This is surely true of the Kelley brothers, who founded a general store in Cleveland, the Commercial Bank of Lake Erie, and the Cleveland Pier Company. Irad and Datus Kelley bought Kelleys Island in 1833 and began quarrying its limestone and selling its cedar. The island was called a "little city-state" by the 1940 WPA *Guide* to Ohio, self-sufficient in winter, with rich resources such as quarrying and fishing. The Erie Indian prehistoric pictographs at Inscription Rock State Memorial are one of the more famous sights. At the Kelleys Island State Park, dramatic evidence of glaciation is visible at the Glacial Grooves

State Memorial, embodying fossilized marine life in limestone bedrock, among the finest glacial carvings in North America.

CROSSING TIME: 20 mins.

FERRY TYPE: Vehicle

VESSEL CAPACITY: *Kelley Islander:* 15 cars, 150 passengers; *Corsair* and *Commuter:* 9 cars, 150 passengers

OPERATING SEASON: Early Apr.-late Nov.

SCHEDULE: **Early Apr.-late May: Mon-Fri.: Lv. Marblehead** 8:30 a.m., 10:30, 1:30 p.m., 4:30. **Lv. Kelleys Island** 8 a.m., 10, 1 p.m., 4. **Fri. only: Lv. Marblehead** 5:30 p.m., 6:30, 7:30. **Lv. Kelleys Island** 5 p.m., 6, 7. **Sat.: Lv. Marblehead** 7:30 a.m., 8:30, 9:30, 10:30, 11:30, 1:30 p.m., 4:30, 6:30. **Lv. Kelleys Island** 8 a.m., 9, 10, 11, 1 p.m., 4, 6. **Sun.: Lv. Marblehead** 8:30 a.m., 10:30, noon, 1:30 p.m., 2:30, 3:30, 4:30, 5:30, 6:30. **Lv. Kelleys Island** 8 a.m., 10, 11:30, 1 p.m., 2, 3, 4, 5, 6, 7. **Late May-early June: Mon.-Thurs.: Lv. Marblehead** *7:30 a.m., 8:30, 10:30, 11:30, 1:30 p.m., 2:30, 4:30, 5:30, 6:30. **Lv. Kelleys Island** *7 a.m., 8, 10, 11, 1 p.m., 2, 4, 5, 6. *Mon. only. **Fri.: Hourly service. Lv. Marblehead** 7:30 a.m.-9:30 p.m. **Lv. Kelleys Island** 8 a.m.-9 p.m. **Sat.: Hourly service. Lv. Marblehead** 7:30 a.m.-7:30 p.m. **Lv. Kelleys Island** 7 a.m.-7 p.m. **Sun.: Hourly service. Lv. Marblehead** 8:30 a.m.-9:30 p.m. **Lv. Kelleys Island** 8 a.m.-9 p.m. **Memorial Day schedule same as Sun. Early June-early Sept.: Hourly service every day. Lv. Marblehead** **7:30 a.m., 8:30, 9:30, 10:30, 11:30, 12:30 p.m., 1:30, 2:30, 3:30, 4:30, 5:30, 6:30, ˜7:30, ˜8:30, ˜˜9:30. **Lv. Kelleys Island** **7 a.m., 8, 9, 10, 11, noon, 1 p.m., 2, 3, 4, 5, 6, ˜7, ˜8, ˜˜9. **Mon., Fri., Sat. only. ˜Fri., Sat., Sun. only. ˜˜Fri., Sun. only. *For additional weekend service, consult company schedule.* **Early Sept.-late Nov.: Mon.-Fri.: Lv. Marblehead** *8:30 a.m., **9:30, *10:30, 1:30 p.m., 4:30, ˜*5:30, ˜*6:30, ˜*7:30. **Lv. Kelleys Island** 8 a.m., **9, *10, 1 p.m., 4, ˜*5, ˜*6, ˜*7. **Sat.: Lv. Marblehead** *7:30 a.m., 8:30, 9:30, 10:30, *11:30, 1:30 p.m., 4:30, *6:30. **Lv. Kelleys Island** *8 a.m., 9, 10, *11, 1 p.m., 4, *6. **Sun.: Lv. Marblehead** *8:30 a.m., **9:30, ˜˜10:20, ˜˜noon, 1:30 p.m., 2:30, 3:30, 4:30, *5:30, *6:30. **Lv. Kelleys Island** *8 a.m., **9, ˜˜10, ˜˜11:30, 1 p.m., 2, 3, 4, 5, *6, *7. *Through mid-Oct. or third week in Oct.; *consult company schedule for dates.* **Beginning mid-Oct. or third week in Oct.; *consult company schedule for dates.* ˜Fri. only. ˜˜Beginning late Oct.

RESTRICTIONS: Trailers, pickup-campers, and RVs permitted. Maximum width 12 ft.

FACILITIES: Restrooms

FARE: Cars $6, adults $3.25, children (6-11) $2; trailer $5.50 up; pickup-camper $7.25-$9.25; RV $9.50 up; bicycle $1; motorcycle $4.25.

RESERVATIONS: Not necessary

DIRECTIONS: The Marblehead office is at the foot of Francis St.; the Kelleys Island office is on Lake Shore Dr.

MAP LOCATION: P. 319, OH, 2

CONTACT: Neuman Boat Line, 101 E. Shoreline Dr., Box 604, Sandusky, OH 44870, (419) 626-5557; Marblehead office: (419) 798-5800; Kelleys Island office: (419)746-2261

STATE: Ohio

PLACES SERVED: Port Clinton—Put-in-Bay (South Bass Island)

BODY OF WATER: Lake Erie

FERRY SERVICE HISTORY: This service began in 1953 as the Erie Isle Ferry Company. Boats on this service are the sixty-five-foot *Erie Isle* and the ninety-five-foot *Yankee Clipper*. The *Yankee Clipper* was once in service in Florida, running to Sanibel Island, until the bridge was built there; she was then brought to Ohio and extended to her present length.

LOCAL POINTS OF INTEREST: Port Clinton is at the western end of the thirty-five miles of pleasant towns and resorts known as Lake Erie's Vacationland. The circular drive from Port Clinton to Marblehead and back through Gypsum has been designated by the American Automobile Association as a scenic highway. The area around Sandusky Bay was the scene of battles between the colonial French and British governments, both of whom claimed it. Commodore Perry's victory during the War of 1812 ended British ambitions. Port Clinton itself had a dramatic beginning in 1827, when a group of westbound immigrants was shipwrecked at the mouth of the Portage River and decided to settle here instead of pushing westward. Today, visitors enjoy the Enchanted Lake Park and also the African Lion Safari, through which visitors drive to view wild animals roaming free in a natural setting.

[For notes on Put-in-Bay, please see entry under Catawba Point—Put-in-Bay (South Bass Island), p. 374.]

CROSSING TIME:	1 hr. 15 mins.
FERRY TYPE:	Vehicle
VESSEL CAPACITY:	*Erie Isle:* 186 passengers or 6 cars and 136 passengers; *Yankee Clipper:* 300 passengers or 18-19 cars and 200 passengers
OPERATING SEASON:	April-mid-Nov.

SCHEDULE: **Early Apr.-late Apr., daily: Lv. Port Clinton** 8 a.m., 11:30, 3 p.m. **Lv. Put-in-Bay** 9:45 a.m., 1:15 p.m., 4:45. (**Fri. only: Lv. Port Clinton** 7 p.m.; **lv. Put-in-Bay** 8:30 p.m.) **May-late June, daily: Lv. Port Clinton** 7 a.m., 9, 11, 12:45 p.m., 2:30, 6. **Lv. Put-in-Bay** 7 a.m., 9, 11, 12:45 p.m., 4:30, 5:15. (**Fri. only: Lv. Port Clinton** 7 p.m.; **lv. Put-in-Bay** 8:30 p.m.) **Late June-early Sept., daily: Lv. Port Clinton** 7 a.m., 9, 11, 1 p.m., 2:45, 4:30, 6, 7:30. **Lv. Put-in-Bay** 7 a.m., 9, 11, 1 p.m., 2:45, 4:30, 6, 7:30. **Early Sept.-late Sept., Mon.-Fri.: Lv. Port Clinton** 7:30 a.m., 10:45, 2:15 p.m. **Lv. Put-in-Bay** 9 a.m., 12:30 p.m., 4:30. (**Fri. only: Lv. Port Clinton** 6:30 p.m.; **lv. Put-in-Bay** 8 p.m.; **Sat. only: Lv. Port Clinton** 7:30 a.m.; **lv. Put-in-Bay** 7:30 a.m. **Sat. and Sun.: Lv. Port Clinton** 9:15 a.m., 11, 1 p.m., 2:30; **lv. Put-in-Bay** 9:15 a.m., 11, 1 p.m., 4:30.) **Late Sept.-mid-Nov., Mon.-Fri.: Lv. Port Clinton** 8:30 a.m., 1 p.m. **Lv. Put-in-Bay** 10 a.m., 3:30 p.m. (**Sat. only: Lv. Port Clinton** 8:30 a.m., 11:30, 2:45 p.m.; **Lv. Put-in-Bay** 10 a.m., 1:15 p.m., 4:15. **Sun. only: Lv. Port Clinton** 9:30 a.m., 1:30 p.m.; **lv. Put-in-Bay** 11 a.m., 4 p.m.) *Memorial Day weekend: consult company schedule.* NOTE: *Ferry stops at Middle Bass by appointment only.*

RESTRICTIONS:	Trailers, pickup-campers, and RVs permitted. Load limit 18 tons.

FACILITIES: Restrooms

FARE: Cars $6, adults $3.50, children (6-11) $1.50; trailer or pickup-camper from $6; RVs permitted.

RESERVATIONS: Advisable going to Put-in-Bay; leaving the islands, reservations MUST be confirmed to the Put-in-Bay office when vehicle arrives at either island. All vehicles over ½ ton carried by reservation. Vehicles for ferry must be in line 15 mins. before departure.

DIRECTIONS: Port Clinton dock is at the foot of Jefferson St. in downtown Port Clinton. Put-in-Bay landing is at downtown dock. Parking is free at Port Clinton.

MAP LOCATION: P. 319, OH, 3

CONTACT: Parker Boat Line, Inc., Put-in-Bay, Ohio, 43456, Port Clinton: (419)732-2800; Put-in-Bay: (419)285-3491

STATE: Ohio

PLACES SERVED: Put-in-Bay (South Bass Island)—Middle Bass Island

BODY OF WATER: Lake Erie

FERRY SERVICE HISTORY: The vessel on this run is the fifty-foot *Sonny S.*, a former fishing tug. Charles Schneider and his wife Carol have operated this ferry off and on since 1961.

LOCAL POINTS OF INTEREST: At Middle Bass Island there is camping, boating, and the Lonz Winery. This historic winery has been a tradition on Middle Bass Island since the 1800s; it was first opened during the Civil War as the Golden Eagle Winery, and by 1875 it was the largest wine producer in the US. Peter Lonz founded the winery, and his son, George, designed the magnificent Gothic architectural structure that houses it today. Many dignitaries, including five US presidents, have been guests on the island. The Lonz Marina has dockage for over 150 boats (no electrical or water connections).

[For notes on Put-in-Bay, see entry under Catawba—Put-in-Bay (South Bass Island), p. 374.]

CROSSING TIME: 8-10 mins.

FERRY TYPE: Pedestrian

VESSEL CAPACITY: 45 passengers

OPERATING SEASON: May-Sept.

SCHEDULE: **Weekends only May & June: daily July 1-Labor Day; weekends through Sept. Mon.-Fri. and Sun.: Lv. Put-in-Bay** every hour on the hour, noon-6 p.m.; **lv. Middle Bass Island** at quarter past every hour, 12:15 p.m.-6:15 p.m. **Fri.:** runs until 10 p.m. **Sat.: Lv. Put-in-Bay** every hour on the hour noon-midnight; **lv. MIB** at quarter past every hour 12:15 p.m.-12:30 a.m.

RESTRICTIONS: No

FACILITIES: No

FARE: Adult $2.50 ($4 round-trip); children 10-12 half price; under 10 free.

RESERVATIONS: No

DIRECTIONS: Ferry leaves PIB from foot of Dollars St.

MAP LOCATION: P. 319, OH, 4

CONTACT: Water Taxi, P.I.B., Middle Bass, OH 43446, (419)285-8774 or (419)285-4631

STATE:	Ohio
PLACES SERVED:	Sandusky—Kelleys Island
BODY OF WATER:	Lake Erie

FERRY SERVICE HISTORY: The Neuman Boat Line has been in operation since 1907; it has had regular service into the island since 1921. The present vessel is the seventy-foot *Challenger*. The vessel was new and began service into Kelleys Island in 1947. It is a two-deck boat (decked over), single-screw auto and passenger ferry; the crew consists of a captain and two deckhands. The ferry passengers are often camp children attending the two main camps on the island. The Neuman Boat Line also offers a number of cruises aboard the vessel, including a Kelleys Island cruise and island tour, sunset dinner cruise, Lonz Winery cruise, and a lunch break mini-cruise. The 1940 WPA *Guide* to Ohio mentions the *Mascot* and the *Messenger* as serving Kelleys Island and Middle Bass and South Bass Islands from Sandusky.

LOCAL POINTS OF INTEREST: Sandusky stretches along the Sandusky Bay waterfront for over six miles; it is a large coal-shipping port and, since 1882, has been a tourist center. Of interest is the Blue Hole, an artesian spring; Battery Park, Ohio's first wave-action swimming pool; and Cedar Point, a mile-long swimming beach with a marina and campground.

[For notes on Kelleys Island, please see entry under Marblehead-Kelleys Island, p. 376.]

CROSSING TIME:	1 hr.
FERRY TYPE:	Vehicle
VESSEL CAPACITY:	9 cars
OPERATING SEASON:	Early July-late Aug. (Freight runs as necessary early Apr.-early July and early Sept.-late Nov.; limited service in Mar. & Dec., weather permitting; no service Jan. & Feb.)
SCHEDULE:	**Daily: Lv. Sandusky** 9 a.m.; **lv. Kelleys Island** 10:30 a.m.

RESTRICTIONS:	Trailers, pickup-campers, and RVs not permitted. Load limit 6 tons. Overhead clearance 6 ft.
FACILITIES:	Restrooms
FARE:	Car and driver $9.25; adults $3.25; children (6-12) $2.
RESERVATIONS:	Yes, necessary for vehicles
RESERVATIONS:	Landing is in downtown Sandusky. Take Rt. 250 north, go left onto Perkins Ave., right onto Columbus Ave. to Sandusky Point.
MAP LOCATION:	P. 319, OH, 5
CONTACT:	See CONTACT, p. 378.

STATE:	Ohio/Ontario, Canada
PLACES SERVED:	Sandusky, OH—Pelee Island, ON—Leamington/Kingsville, ON
BODY OF WATER:	Lake Erie
FERRY SERVICE HISTORY:	Service on this run was inaugurated in 1978. The present vessels are the *Pelee Island* (135 feet long) and the *Upper Canada* (100 feet

long), side-loading auto-passenger ferries. The most unusual cargo these boats have carried is coffins.

LOCAL POINTS OF INTEREST:	[For notes on Sandusky, please see entry under Sandusky-Kelleys Island, p. 382.]

Pelee Island has miles of sandy beaches and many interesting Indian ruins, including quarries. It is famous for sport fishing and for its October and November pheasant hunts (you must have a Province of Ontario Small Game Gun License, available on the island).

Kingsville is the most southerly town in Canada; it is the site of Jack Miner's sanctuary for Canada Geese which earned him the Order of the British Empire in 1943. Thousands of geese fly over the sanctuary each year, and there is a "Migration Festival" weekend and parade in mid-

October. The Pelee Island Winery, with its Austrian atmosphere, attracts many visitors also.

Leamington is the home of the world's largest tomato-processing plant. It also has convenient parks (Mersea and Seacliff).

CROSSING TIME: From Sandusky to Pelee Island 2 hrs. 15 mins.; from Pelee Island to Leamington or Kingsville 1 hr. 30 mins.; from Sandusky to Leamington or Kingsville 4 hrs. 30 mins.

FERRY TYPE: Vehicle

VESSEL CAPACITY: *Pelee Islander:* 15 vehicles; 268 passengers; *Upper Canada:* 10 vehicles; 100 passengers.

OPERATING SEASON: Mid-June-early Sept.

SCHEDULE: *For schedule between Pelee Island and Kingsville/Leamington, please consult company brochures.* **Between Sandusky and Pelee Island/Kingsville: Early May-late June: Lv. Kingsville** 4 p.m.; **lv. Pelee Island** 6 p.m.; **lv. Sandusky** 9 p.m. **Late June-early Sept., Mon., Sat., Sun.: Lv. Sandusky** 8:30 a.m.; **lv. Pelee Island** 11 a.m.; **lv. Kingsville** 3:15 p.m.; **lv. Pelee Island** 6 p.m. **Between Sandusky and Pelee Island/Leamington: Early May-late June: Lv. Leamington Fridays** 4 p.m.; **lv. Pelee Island** 6 p.m.; **lv. Sandusky** 9 p.m. **Lv. Pelee Island Saturdays** 7 a.m. **Between Pelee Island and Sandusky: Early May-late June: Sundays: Lv Pelee Island** 6 p.m.; **lv. Sandusky** 8 p.m. **Late June-early Sept.: Lv. Pelee Island** daily 6 p.m., **Fridays** 6 a.m. and 6 p.m.; **lv. Sandusky daily** 8:30 a.m.; **Fridays** 8:30 a.m., 9 p.m. **Early Sept.-late Sept.: Lv. Pelee Island Fridays and Sundays** 6 p.m.; **lv. Sandusky Fridays** 9 p.m.; **Sundays** 8 p.m.

RESTRICTIONS: Trailers, pickup-campers, and RVs permitted. Load limit 46,000 lbs. Overhead clearance 9 ft. 6 in. (higher vehicles can be accommodated; notify operator in advance); max. vehicle length 31 ft., max. width 9 ft. 6 in.

FACILITIES: Restrooms; snack bars; licensed lounge

FARE: Sandusky-Pelee Island: Cars and trailers $11; adults $5.50; children (6-12) $2.75 (under 6 free); seniors (65+) $2.75; bicycles $2.75; motorcycles $5; large vehicles $22 up. Sandusky-Leamington/Kingsville:

Cars and trailers $18; adults $9; children (6-12) $4.50 (under 6 free); seniors (65 +) $4.50; bicycles $4.50; motorcycles $8; large vehicles $36 up.

RESERVATIONS: Necessary for cars and passengers. Cars must be at dock half-hour before sailing time; tickets must be purchased before boarding.

DIRECTIONS: At Sandusky, ferry leaves from municipal dock at the foot of Jackson St. From Pelee Island, ferry leaves from West Dock. From Leamington and Kingsville, ferry leaves from government docks.

MAP LOCATION: P. 319, OH, 6

CONTACT: Pelee Island Transportation Services, Pelee Island, ON, Canada NOR 1MO, (519)724-2115

STATE: Ohio

PLACES SERVED: Toledo—Put-in-Bay (South Bass Island)

BODY OF WATER: Lake Erie

FERRY SERVICE HISTORY: The Toledo River Cruise Lines has been operating boats on the Maumee River since 1932. In addition to the ferry/cruise service to Put-in-Bay, the company offers sightseeing cruises on the *Arawanna II* and the *Arawanna Princess*. The *Arawanna Queen* makes the run to Put-in-Bay, with an on-board breakfast as the boat glides past the busy Port of Toledo facilities. On the return trip, a buffet is offered.

LOCAL POINTS OF INTEREST: Toledo, located at the mouth of the Maumee River, the largest one flowing into the Great Lakes, is the third-busiest port on the Great Lakes. It was first explored by the French in 1615, and was probably named after Toledo, Spain. Fort Industry, dating from 1794, once occupied the city site. Both Michigan and Ohio claimed it in the Toledo War of 1835; it was given to Ohio and, in compensation, the Northern Peninsula went to Michigan. The Metroparks focus on special features, such as Promenade Park, port-of-call of the *Arawanna Princess* and a good spot from which to view Maumee River traffic. In the Old West End are restored Victorian homes (closed to the public). Of interest also are the Toledo Museum of Art, with more than seven hundred paintings; the Toledo Zoological Park, an extensive zoo; and the Crosby Gardens, which has a children's garden. The ferry leaves from the Moorings at Toledo's Portside. The Moorings is an attraction in itself, with Chief Turkey Foot's Floating Pub, gift shop, and restaurant. Portside is a festival marketplace with ninety-seven shops.

[For notes on Put-in-Bay, please see entry under Catawba Point—Put-in-Bay (South Bass Island), p. 374.]

CROSSING TIME:	3 hrs. 30 mins.
FERRY TYPE:	Pedestrian
VESSEL CAPACITY:	425 passengers
OPERATING SEASON:	Early June-Sept. 1
SCHEDULE:	**Mon., Tue., Wed., and Sun. Lv. Toledo** 9 a.m.; **lv. Put-in-Bay** 5 p.m.
RESTRICTIONS:	No
FACILITIES:	Restrooms, dining room, lounge
FARE:	Adult $21.75 (round-trip $49.75); children round-trip only $34.75; rates include breakfast, dinner, and live entertainment on both decks.
RESERVATIONS:	Required, plus advance payment in full
DIRECTIONS:	The boat leaves from The Moorings at Portside Boat Basin on the Toledo waterfront, at the intersection of Summit and Adams Sts.

next to Owens-Illinois (a tall, green glass building).

MAP LOCATION:	P. 319, OH, 7
CONTACT:	Toledo River Cruise Lines, 615 Front St., Toledo, OH 43605, In Ohio: (800)824-1124 Outside Ohio: (419)693-Boat

STATE:	Wisconsin
PLACES SERVED:	Bayfield—La Pointe (Madeline Island)
BODY OF WATER:	Lake Superior

FERRY SERVICE HISTORY: This route, approximately 2.6 miles, is very scenic. Leaving from the small commercial fishing village of Bayfield, the ferry crosses a channel busy with racing sailboats, yachts, and fishing vessels, to the historical and picturesque village of La Pointe on the south end of Madeline Island. Madeline Island Ferry Line operates three ferries, the *Madeline*, the *Island Queen*, and the *Nichevo II*. The ninety-foot *Madeline* was launched in 1984, designed by Timothy Graul Marine Design and built by the owners. She carries twenty cars and up to 150 passengers. The *Island Queen* was built by Fraser Shipyards at Superior, Wisconsin, in 1966. She carries fifteen cars and 150 passengers. The *Nichevo II* (preceded by two other *Nichevos*, one wooden and one steel) was built in 1962 by Fraser Shipyards of Superior, Wisconsin for Harry Nelson. She carries ten cars and 150 passengers. All three can transport motorcoaches and have passenger cabins and sufficient upper-deck seating. The company also transports passengers, mail, freight, cars, trucks, and many camper vehicles. Ferry service normally begins about April 1 with spring ice break-up and ends about January 1 after freeze-up. During the busy months of May through October, up to twenty-four trips are scheduled daily with a trip every half-hour during July and August. Because of the shelter afforded by the Apostle Islands, rough weather is not normally a problem. It is a rare occurrence to have trips cancelled because of bad weather. The grandfather of Gary W. Russell, the current president of the Madeline Island Ferry Line, began the ferry service in the 1880s.

LOCAL POINTS OF INTEREST: Bayfield was once the shipping point of locally quarried brownstone; the town still has mansions of this material. It is a popular summer resort and offers good hunting, fishing, and boating. Sightseeing cruises of the Apostle Islands depart from here.

Madeline Island is the largest of Wisconsin's Apostle Islands and supports 150-165 year-round residents (increased to about two thousand during the summer season). Early trading and missionary activity centered on Madeline Island; Etienne Brule visited the area as early as 1662 in his search for the fabled "Northwest Passage" to China and the East Indies. Radisson and Groseillers, the French explorers, came to the island in 1659, and La Pointe was headquarters for a post of the American Fur Company in 1816.

Of interest here is the Madeline Island Historical Museum, a fur-company building surrounded by a log stockade; exhibits depict the life of the American Indian, the arrival of the fur trader, and the development of the fishing industry in the Chequamegon region. Madeline has a mile of sandy beach on its east side.

The Apostle Islands National Lakeshore, with dark forests, high sandstone cliffs, gull rookeries, sea caves, and five lighthouses, is an area well worth visiting. There are twenty-two islands, ranging from less than an acre to fourteen thousand acres.

CROSSING TIME: 15 mins.

FERRY TYPE: Vehicle

VESSEL CAPACITY: 15 cars

OPERATING SEASON: Apr.-Dec., depending on weather conditions

SCHEDULE: **Summer schedule, daily: Lv. Madeline Island** 7 a.m., 8, 9, 10, 10:30, 11, 11:30, noon, 12:30 p.m., 1:15, 1:45, 2:15, 2:45, 3:15, 3:45, 4:15, 4:45, 5:15, 5:45, 6:30, 7:30, *8:30, **9, *9:30, 10:30, *11:30, **12:30 a.m. **Lv. Bayfield** 7:30 a.m., 8:30, 9:30, 10, 10:30, 11, 11:30, noon, 12:45 p.m., 1:15, 1:45, 2:15, 2:45, 3:15, 3:45, 4:15, 4:45, 5:15, 5:45, 6:10, 7, 8, *9, **9:30, *10, 11, *midnight, *1 a.m. *Fri. & Sat. only. **Except Fri. & Sat.

RESTRICTIONS: Trailers, pickup-campers, and RVs permitted. Load limit 50 tons. Overhead clearance 26 ft.

FACILITIES: None

FARE: Car $4.25; adult $1.75; child (6-11) $1; trailer $0.25 per foot; pickup-camper $5; bicycle $1; motorcycle $2. RV to 18 ft. $5.25 ($0.25 each additional ft.)

RESERVATIONS: No, except for motorcoaches

DIRECTIONS: Go to City Dock, South Highway 13, in Bayfield.

MAP LOCATION:	P. 319, WI, 1
CONTACT:	Mr. Gary Russell, Madeline Island Ferry Line, Box 66C, La Pointe, WI 54850, (715)747-2051

Colsac II

STATE:	Wisconsin
PLACES SERVED:	Merrimac—Okee
BODY OF WATER:	Wisconsin River

FERRY SERVICE HISTORY: Ferry service has been provided in this area for more than a century. In 1844, four years before Wisconsin became a state, Chester Mattson, the second settler on the site of the Village of Merrimac, obtained charters to provide ferry service at this location. The ferry was operated long before the development of a regular roadway. Mattson charged either thirty-five cents or one dollar to ferry a team and wagon across the river (the toll has been variously reported). Even at one dollar, however, the ferryman earned it, for he pulled it himself until a gasoline engine was added around the turn of the century. W. P. Flanders, a private investor, took over the ferry in 1849 for $700, and for many years it continued as a private operation. Various methods were used over the years to propel the ferry. Area residents recall stories of a "scow being pulled across the river by horses harnessed to a long cable," but later it was current-propelled.

The first modern vessel, *Colsac I* (a phonetic combination of the two county names, Columbia and Sauk), was built in 1924 in Dubuque, Iowa. It was operated as a toll ferry until 1933, when the state of Wisconsin took over the service. *Colsac I* was purchased by the Village of Merrimac for $300, and for many years it resided in the city park. *Colsac II*, the present vessel, was built by Marinette Marine Corporation in Marinette, Wisconsin; she was christened on April 6, 1963.

The Merrimac ferry has become such an institution that tourists flock by the thousands each summer to take the mile-long boat trip, despite the presence of the interstate system bridge twelve miles away. It is now benevolently operated by the state of Wisconsin as a free tourist attraction, curiosity, and convenience. The ferry runs twenty-four hours per day; in the middle of the night, riders are mostly locals going to and from their cottages or summer homes and nearby eating places.

LOCAL POINTS OF INTEREST: The ferry crossing is about thirty miles from the Wisconsin Dells, a major tourist attraction. These are the scenic dells of the Wisconsin River, where the river has cut the soft sandstone into fantastic forms. From the Wisconsin Dells you can take amphibious boat tours (Wisconsin Ducks and Dells Ducks) along the river. Merrimac is also near the Devil's Lake State Park; Devil's Lake is bounded on three sides by quartzite cliffs. Going north from Merrimac to the Dells, you might stop at Baraboo, original home of Ringling Brothers and Barnum & Bailey Circus; there is a Circus World Museum. The ferry is about thirty miles from Madison, and the beautiful rural drive from Madison to Baraboo to the Dells is very scenic and well worth taking.

CROSSING TIME: 4-5 mins.

FERRY TYPE: Vehicle

VESSEL CAPACITY: 12 cars

OPERATING SEASON: Spring until ice forms or "from thaw to freeze" (about mid-Apr.-Nov.)

SCHEDULE: 24 hours daily

RESTRICTIONS: Trailers, pickup-campers, and RVs permitted. Load limit 8 tons.

FACILITIES:	None
FARE:	Free
RESERVATIONS:	No
DIRECTIONS:	The ferry is west of I-90/I-94, above Madison. It crosses SR 113.
MAP LOCATION:	P. 319, WI, 2
CONTACT:	Mr. Don Flottmeyer, Wisconsin Dept. of Transportation, Box 7916, Madison, WI 53707, (608)266-3722

STATE:	Wisconsin
PLACES SERVED:	Northport (Gills Rock)—Washington Island
BODY OF WATER:	Green Bay
FERRY SERVICE HISTORY:	Mary C. Richter of Washington Island, a local historian and wife of Capt. Arni Richter of the Washington Island Ferry Line,

wrote a history of the island ferries in 1970. She states that the first mail service (by boat from Green Bay) was in 1854. During the late 1800s and early 1900s, many steamboats plied the waters of Green Bay and Lake Michigan, carrying freight and passengers between Escanaba, Marinette, Green Bay, Milwaukee, Chicago, and other places, and stopping at Washington Island. In the late 1800s, Nels Jepson, Capt. William Jepson's father, carried mail and supplies on a sailboat called the *Razor Back*. The *Georgia*, in 1900, and later, in 1928, the *Carolina*, both of the Goodrich Line, provided regular service, which led to the development of the summer resort business. Other sea captains were Carl Christiansen (*Sea Queen*, and Chris Anderson (*Wisconsin*); people would stock up for the winter with salt-pork, corned beef, kegs of syrup, and barrels of flour and sugar. Carl G. Richter and his son, Arni, bought the ferry line from Capt. William Jepson in 1940; they had the *North Shore* and the *Welcome* and later built the *C. G. Richter*. (The *North Shore* was sold in 1946 to become the ferry between Beaver Island and Charlevoix, Michigan, and in 1950 the *Welcome* was sold to become the ferry between Sandusky, Ohio and Kelleys Island in Lake Erie.) In 1953, Arni Richter became the

sole owner and operator of the Washington Island Ferry Line, Inc., operating the *Griffin* and the *C. G. Richter*. The all-steel ferry *Voyageur* was built in 1960 by Sturgeon Bay Shipbuilding and Dry Dock Company.

The year 1970 marked the hundredth year since the Icelandic immigration to Washington Island began; this was the year in which the *Eyrarbakki* was built (named for the town in Iceland from which the first Icelanders came). She was christened at the Icelandic Immigration celebration in July 1970 by Gertrude Anderson, the first Icelandic child born on Washington Island in 1872 (the christening water was flown over from a well in Eyrarbakki by Icelandic Airlines). The white, red-trimmed *Robert Noble* was christened in 1979; she was named for the man who established one of the first ferries in the area, a steam ferry across Sturgeon Bay in 1874. He was a legendary figure, who had lost both legs and all his fingers in a disastrous attempt to go from Washington Island to the mainland in December 1864. He was trapped on Plum Island (now a Coast Guard station), fell below the ice, and barely survived; his limbs were then mistakenly immersed in kerosene instead of ice water. Undaunted, and outfitted with wooden legs, he began the ferry service.

Dick Purinton, manager of the ferry line, recalls an icy night several years ago, December 23, when the temperature was + 10 F and a mother-to-be was on the ferry in the Island ambulance. Because of the weather, the crew could not drive the ambulance off the ferry at the Northport Pier, but had to pass her, in a stretcher, over the ice bank onto the dock, where a mainland ambulance awaited her. She delivered ten minutes later, en route to the hospital fifty-five miles to the south. The ambulance attendants and ferry crew would have had the honors had the baby arrived a bit earlier, as there was no Island doctor at that time. The ferries have had weddings on board (Purinton always wonders whether there is any correlation between the weather and the future of the marriage). The ferries often participate in DNR fish plantings, when the hatchery trucks are transported directly to area reefs or shoals to plant chinook salmon and trout, making Door County's fishing some of the best in the nation. In fall 1985, the Great Lakes Lighthouse Keepers Association met on board the *C. G. Richter* to view lighthouses from the water.

LOCAL POINTS OF INTEREST: The Northport Pier ferry facility is just east of Gills Rock, in Door County, above Sturgeon Bay; it is called the "Top of the Thumb" (that is, the thumb of mitten-shaped Wisconsin).

Washington Island, twenty-three square miles of glaciated rock, is Lake Michigan's Icelandic outpost, with the largest extant community of Icelanders outside Iceland. It was settled in 1870; the original community was joined by other Scandinavian settlers (Norwegians, Swedes, and Danes). The telephone book still gives evidence of the island heritage, with its preponderance of Scandinavian names: Hannes Anderson, Jacob Ellefson, Russ Jorgenson and Jack Hagen. The Town Chairperson is Arbutus Greenfeldt. The ferry service has been called "Washington Island's umbilical cord to the outside world." The president of the company, Arni Richter (often referred to as "Mr. Washington Island") is of partial Icelandic heritage. He says that, in winter, it sometimes takes four or five hours to make the journey through ice. Passengers bring their knitting, and teenagers bring guitars and sing. If the ferry becomes totally trapped, friends and relatives come out in a convoy of snow-mobiles to retrieve the travellers. Mildred Gunnlaugsson captured the ambiance of the ferry in her poem "Ferry Ride to Washington Island": "The population figures tell the story just in part, / For many living far away are Islanders at heart. / There is a bond between them all that cannot be denied, / And it's nurtured by the visits on this friendly Ferry ride."

The scenery on the island varies dramatically from place to place and season to season. The north coast has one hundred-foot limestone bluffs. In winter, the coast is fringed with stiletto ice sculptures jutting into the boulders; spring brings wildflowers; summer inviting sandy shores, especially on the south coast; and fall brilliant foliage. There is sport fishing for giant salmon, trout, bass, whitefish, and northern pike.

The trip to the island passes Plum Island (so named because it lies "plum" in the center of the water passage from Lake Michigan to Green Bay) and Pilot Island, whose sentinel lighthouse guards the treacherous strait known as Death's Door. The US Lake Survey office *Bulletin* of 1924 described the *Porte des Morts* passage: "Known as Death's Door owing to the numerous detached reefs and shoals obstructing its navigation . . . almost certain destruction to craft going ashore." Here there are one-hundred foot piles of limestone, deep waters, and, in winter, unstable ice floes.

Present-day ferry riders will find, at the Northport Pier ferry facility, a special island hostess to greet passengers, distribute maps, and explain the attractions of Washington Island. Sightseeing on the island is beautifully simple: you board the Cherry Train, for which you can get a combination boat/train ticket if you wish. The trip is noteworthy for what you will not see: billboards, neon signs, and strip development. You will see Mann's General Store, the Jacobsen Museum, Little Lake (the lake within an island within a lake), Jackson Harbor, home of the commercial fishing fleet and the Fishing Museum, Mountain Lookout Tower, with its panoramic view, and other sights. And, if you still yearn for a ferry ride, the good news is that the *Karfi* runs from Jackson Harbor to Rock Island State Park.

CROSSING TIME: 30 mins.

FERRY TYPE: Vehicle

VESSEL CAPACITY: 3 boats, 50 cars

OPERATING SEASON: All year

SCHEDULE: **Daily service all year.** *Consult company schedules for exact dates, as they change annually.* **May 1-late May, Fri., Sat., Mon., Tues. only: Lv. Washington Island** *7 a.m.; **lv. Northport** *8 a.m. **Daily: Lv. Washington Island** 9:15 a.m., 1:15 p.m., 4. **Lv. Northport** 10:30 a.m., 2:15 p.m., 5. *This trip daily after mid-May. **Late May-early July: Daily: Lv. Washington Island** 7 a.m., 8:30, 9:30, 11, 1:15 p.m., 3, 4, 5; **lv. Northport** 8 a.m., 10, 10:45, noon, 2:15 p.m., 4, 5, 6. **Early July-early Sept.: Daily: Lv. Washington Island** 7 a.m., *7:30, 8, 8:30, 9, 9:30, 10, 10:30, 11, 11:30, 12:15 p.m., 12:45, 1:30, *2, 2:30, 3:15, 3:45, 4:15, 5, 5:30. **Lv. Northport** 7:45 a.m., *8:15, 8:45, 9:15, 9:45, 10:15, 10:45,11:30, noon, 12:30 p.m., 1, 1:45, 2:15, *2:45, 3:15, 4, 4:30, 5, 6, 6:30. *Not after late Aug. **Early Sept.-Oct.: Daily: Lv. Washington Island** 7 a.m., 9, 9:30, 10:45, *11:30, 1:15 p.m., 3, 4, *5. **Lv. Northport** 8 a.m., 10, 10:45, 11:45, *12:30 p.m., 2:15, 4, 5, *6. *Not after mid-Oct. *Consult company for off-season schedules; also for special Friday night and sunset trips.*

RESTRICTIONS: Trailers, pickup-campers, and RVs permitted. Load limit 40 tons. Overhead clearance 7 ft. under deck; unlimited in gangway.

FACILITIES: Restrooms

FARE: Cars $6; adults $2.25; children $1; bicycles $.50; motorcycles $2.

RESERVATIONS: Essential in winter for cars.

DIRECTIONS:	Northport is 2 miles east of Gills Rock on SR 42.
MAP LOCATION:	P. 319, WI, 3
CONTACT:	Washington Island Ferry Line, Inc., Detroit Harbor, Washington Island, Wisconsin 54246, (414)847-2546

STATE:	Wisconsin
PLACES SERVED:	Washington Island (Jackson Harbor)—Rock Island State Park
BODY OF WATER:	Green Bay
FERRY SERVICE HISTORY:	The *Karfi* (an Icelandic term meaning "seaworthy ship") makes this run.
LOCAL POINTS OF INTEREST:	[For notes on Washington Island, see entry under Northport (Gills Rock)-Washington Island, p. 393.]

Both Washington Island and Rock Island describe themselves as located "North of the Tension Line," and if a ride on a Washington Ferry ship, amid the knitting needles and guitar music hasn't convinced visitors, a ride on the *Karfi* to Rock Island should do it. The Rock Island State Park, a nine hundred-acre island across from Jackson Harbor on Washington Island, was once the home of Icelander Chester Hjortur Thordarson. He bought the island in 1910 for $6,000 and employed dozens of stonemasons to complete his Great Hall. The Thordarson Boathouse on Rock Island is open to the public; it housed a library worth several million dollars until the State of Wisconsin acquired the island as a state park. The books now belong to the University of Wisconsin at Madison. The Potawatomi Lighthouse on Rock Island was built in 1836-37. The island was always a haven for Indians. After Jean Nicolet visited it, it became an important spot, for the cargo canoes of the first traders were repacked here. Some went down the east side of the island headed to the villages that later became Chicago and Milwaukee. Others went down the west side and headed for New Orleans. The US Census of 1836 recorded one Rock Island couple, a Lowis Labute and his wife; by 1850 the island had two hundred people, but the population had dwindled again before it was bought by Thordarson. There is camping on the island, as well as hiking. David Kennison, the last surviving member of the Boston Tea Party and a veteran of the Battle of Bunker Hill, lived here.

CROSSING TIME: 10 mins.

FERRY TYPE: Pedestrian

VESSEL CAPACITY: 49 passengers

OPERATING SEASON: Late May-mid.-Oct.

SCHEDULE: **Late May-late June and early Sept.-mid-Oct.: Daily. Lv. Washington Island** 10 a.m., 1 p.m., 3:30; **added trips Sat., Sun., and Memorial Day** at 11 a.m., noon, 2 p.m. **Late June-early Sept.: Daily.** Lv. every hour on the hour 10 a.m.-4 p.m. **Lv. Rock Island** approx. 15 mins. after leaving Washington Island.

RESTRICTIONS: None

FACILITIES: None

FARE: Adults $4 round-trip; children $3 round-trip; campers with gear $5 round-trip; bicycles $2 round-trip.

RESERVATIONS: No

DIRECTIONS: The *Karfi* leaves from Jackson Harbor on Washington Island.

MAP LOCATION: P. 319, WI, 4

CONTACT: Mr. Jack Cornell, *Karfi* Ferry to Rock Island, Washington Island, WI 54246, (414)847-2425

FERRIES
OF THE
ROCKY MOUNTAIN
STATES AND
SOUTHWEST

Ferries of the Rocky Mountain States and Southwest

ARIZONA

* [Bullhead City-Laughlin, NV; see NV]
1. Lake Havasu City-Havasu Landing Resort

CALIFORNIA

1. Avalon (Santa Catalina Island)-Long Beach
2. Avalon (Santa Catalina Island)-Newport (Balboa Pavilion)
3. Avalon-San Pedro
4. Balboa Island-Balboa Peninsula
5. Bradford Island-Jersey Island-Webb Tract
6. Empire Tract-Venice Island
7. Grand Island-Ryer Island
8. Long Beach-Queen Mary-Queensway Bay Hilton
9. Princeton-Afton
10. Rio Vista-Ryer Island
11. San Francisco-Alcatraz Island
12. San Francisco-Angel Island
13. San Francisco-Larkspur
14. San Francisco-Sausalito
15. San Francisco-Tiburon
16. San Francisco-Vallejo
17. Tiburon-Angel Island
18. Two Harbors (Santa Catalina Island)-San Pedro
19. Upper Jones Tract-Woodward Island
20. Vallejo-Angel Island

MONTANA

1. Carter
2. Chinook-Winifred (The "McLelland Ferry" or "The Stafford Ferry")
3. Loma
4. Virgelle

NEVADA

1. Laughlin-Bullhead City, AZ

TEXAS

1. Galveston-Port Bolivar
2. Harbor Island-Port Aransas
3. Los Ebanos-Mission
4. Port Aransas-San Jose Island

UTAH

1. Bullfrog Marina (Glen Canyon)-Hall's Crossing Marina
2. Syracuse Landing-Antelope Island

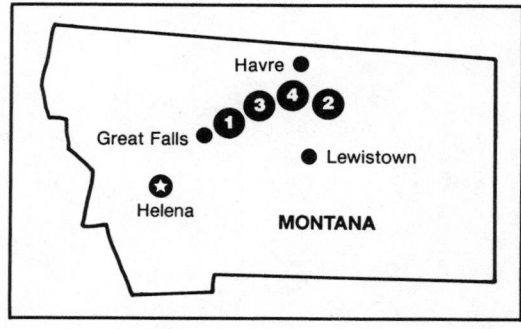

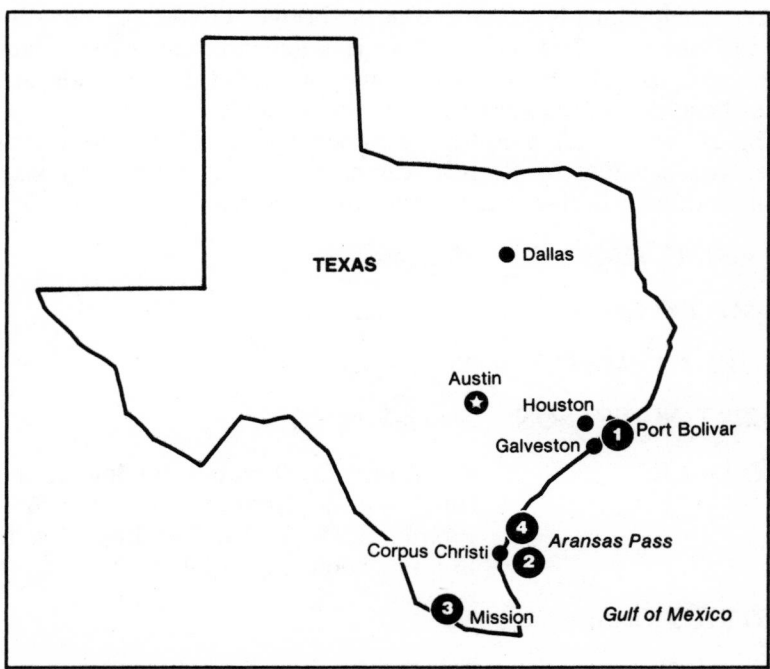

STATE:	Arizona
PLACES SERVED:	Lake Havasu City—Havasu Landing Resort
BODY OF WATER:	Lake Havasu
FERRY SERVICE HISTORY:	The ferry goes from Lake Havasu City (London Bridge Area) to the Chemehuevi Indians' Havasu Landing Resort; service

began in 1983. The vessel is the *Pan Coyer*, an Indian name.

LOCAL POINTS OF INTEREST:	Lake Havasu City is the center of a resort area on the shores of Lake Havasu. John McPhee has described the chain of deep,

cold pools in Havasu Canyon: "The pools were as much as fifteen feet deep, and the water in them was white where it plunged and foamed, then blue in a wide circle around the plunge point, and pale green in the outer peripheries." The centerpiece attraction on the lake is London Bridge, brought from England and reassembled here (it was designed by John Rennie and built between 1824 and 1831). It spanned the Thames until 1968. An authentic English village, complete with pub and a double-decker London bus, is at one end of the bridge. From Lake Havasu City you can take a two and one-half-hour jeep tour over the desert mountains to the east of Lake Havasu City, bumping along desert roads to gold mines hand-dug in the late 1800s and early 1900s.

The Havasu Landing Resort is owned by the Chemehuevi Indians. Here, you can rent boats, fish, camp, or dine at the resort's lakeside restaurant; there is also a new para-sailing service.

CROSSING TIME:	30 mins.
FERRY TYPE:	Pedestrian
VESSEL CAPACITY:	48 passengers
OPERATING SEASON:	March-Sept.
SCHEDULE:	**Fri.-Sun.: Lv. London Bridge area** (AZ time—no daylight saving) 9 a.m., 11, 1 p.m., 3, 5, 7. **Lv. Landing** (CA time) 10 a.m., noon, 2 p.m., 4, 6, 8.
RESTRICTIONS:	No
FACILITIES:	Restrooms

FARE: Adults $1; children under 12 free

RESERVATIONS: No

DIRECTIONS: Ferry leaves from London Bridge area, Lake Havasu City.

MAP LOCATION: P. 399, AZ, 1

CONTACT: Havasu Landing Resort, Lake Havasu, AZ 86403, (619)858-4593

STATE: California

PLACES SERVED: Avalon (Santa Catalina Island)-Long Beach

BODY OF WATER: San Pedro Channel

FERRY SERVICE HISTORY: Catalina Cruises operates a fleet of five spacious triple-decked seven-hundred-passenger vessels, the *Catalina King*, the *Catalina Monarch*, the *Catalina Empress*, the *Catalina Countess*, and the *Catalina Prince*. They are all 134 feet long and one hundred tons, with a crew of up to seven. They have spacious open decks, glass-enclosed lower decks with picture windows, and walking space on the decks.

LOCAL POINTS OF INTEREST: [For notes on Avalon, please see entry under Avalon-Newport, p. 404.]

Long Beach was founded by Briton W. E. Willmore as the "American Colony" of Willmore City; it was a popular seaside resort in the nineteenth century. Today, it is also a busy shipping center and convention mecca. The Terrace Theater and Center Theater are noted for their productions, and the Long Beach Museum of Art has an excellent collection specializing in art from the nineteenth century to the present day. The El Dorado Nature Center is an eighty-acre semiwilderness with gardens, trails, and plant and animal displays. The *Queen Mary*, one of the largest passenger liners ever built, is moored at Pier J, as is Howard Hughes' *Spruce Goose*, the largest airplane ever built. Londontowne, next to the *Queen Mary*, is a replica of an old English seaport village. All three may be reached by the Bay Shuttle Water Taxi [see p. 414].

CROSSING TIME: 1 hr. 50 mins.

FERRY TYPE: Pedestrian

VESSEL CAPACITY: 700 passengers

OPERATING SEASON: All year

SCHEDULE: *Schedules change frequently; call for current one.* **Mid-June-mid-Sept.: Daily. Lv. Long Beach** 8 a.m., 9, 12:30 p.m., 1:45, 5:45. **Extra trip at 7:30 p.m. Fri., Sat., and Sun. Lv. Avalon** 10 a.m., 11:15, 3:15 p.m., 4:30, 8. **Extra trip 9:45 p.m. Fri., Sat., and Sun. Rest of year: Daily. Lv. Long Beach** 9 a.m., 1:45 p.m. **Extra trip 7:30 p.m. Fri. Lv. Avalon** 11:15 a.m., 4 p.m. **Extra trip 9:45 p.m. Fri.**

RESTRICTIONS: Domestic pets, such as dogs, cats, and birds, may be brought on board; dogs must be properly leashed and muzzled or carried in a pet container. Cats and birds must be in a cage or pet carrier. If pet is not housebroken, cleaning material will be supplied. Bicycles carried as space permits; both wheels must be removed and secured to frame. Dangerous commodities such as camp stoves, lanterns, fuel, firewood, charcoal, flammable or combustible materials, construction material, internal combustion engines prohibited.

FACILITIES: Restrooms, snack bar, gift shop

FARE: Oct.-May: adults $9.95; children (2-11) $5.30; children under 2 $0.60; senior citizens (55+) weekday round-trip of $17.72. Rates June-Sept.: adults $10.95; children $5.85; children under 2 $0.60; senior citizens weekday round-trip of $19.60.

RESERVATIONS: Recommended.

DIRECTIONS: The Long Beach boat terminal, Catalina Landing, is on Golden Shore Blvd. Take the Long Beach Freeway (7) south; take downtown exit (DO NOT TAKE "Port of Long Beach-Queen Mary exit"); stay to right; exit Golden Shore.

MAP LOCATION: P. 399, CA, 1

CONTACT: Catalina Cruises, Box 1948, San Pedro, CA 90733; Long Beach (213)514-3838; Los Angeles (213)775-6111; Orange County (714)527-7111.

Catalina Holiday

STATE:	California
PLACES SERVED:	Avalon (Santa Catalina Island)—Newport (Balboa Pavilion)
BODY OF WATER:	San Pedro Channel

FERRY SERVICE HISTORY: The vessel on this service is the *Catalina Holiday*, with three decks and enclosed areas as well as topside seating. Service was inaugurated in 1965. The *Catalina Holiday* is 315 feet long, with a crew of six. The most unusual cargo she has carried is a sea lion.

LOCAL POINTS OF INTEREST: The Balboa Pavilion was built in 1905 by the Newport Bay Investment Company to coincide with the Pacific Electric Red Car Line completion in 1906. It is a classic example of a waterfront pavilion at the turn of the century and is a California Historical Landmark; it is also listed in the National Register of Historic Places. A succession of owners have fought valiantly to preserve the structure. Roy Gronsky undertook the Herculean task of replacing the old wooden pilings in 1947, when the building threatened to slide into the bay. Major restoration was begun in 1962, when A. Ducommun refurbished the exterior, including the original blue-shingled roof, the grey-paneled walls, and the distinctive cupola. Over one thousand lights, outlining the roof, were 1963 additions that still etch the Balboa Pavilion on the night sky. In 1969, the building was purchased by Davey's Locker, Inc., now known as the Balboa Pavilion Company. Led by Phil Tozer, the company is committed to a program of authentic restoration. Newport Harbor is one of the largest small craft harbors in the world and may be seen on a narrated cruise aboard the *Pavilion Queen*, run by the Balboa Pavilion Company.

Santa Catalina Island, twenty-two miles from the mainland, is twenty-one by eight miles. It was discovered in 1542 by Juan Rodriguez Cabrillo, a Portugese navigator who had set out from Baja California in search of the mythical Strait of Anian, thought to connect the Atlantic and Pacific oceans. The island was first named San Salvador. Santa Catalina, now a leading resort in the Los Angeles area, has had a colorful and quixotic history. It has served as a refuge from pirates, the seat of the Indian worship of the sun god Chiningchinich (a vast temple is believed to have been buried by a landslide), the center of a thriving sea otter fur trade, a smuggling headquarters, and a mining center. William Wrigley acquired the island in 1919, which marked its beginning as a playground. In 1974 Los Angeles County acquired much of the island for park, conservation and recreation uses. The Santa Catalina Island Conservancy was founded in 1975 and controls about 86 percent of the island.

Today, rugged and serene, with blue mountains, rocky shores, and azure waters, the island is what one naturalist has called "Southern California about two hundred years ago." The two main towns are Avalon and Two Harbors. One would not be surprised to find Avalon the principal settlement on a Greek island, with its red-tiled rooftops juxtaposed on the hillside and serpentine wall and promenade, perfect for bicycling. The pillared Catalina Casino, a half-century old, is one of the town's many outstanding buildings. Two Harbors is foreseen as a future year-round residential and boating resort; it is the site of the UCLA Marine Science Center.

If you arrive by ferry, you can tour the island by sightseeing bus or taxi; alternatives are hiring a golf cart (Avalon only) or horse, or hiking on your own. The Naturalist Catalina Conservancy (Box 2739, Avalon 90704) will arrange for you to join a group nature safari, overnight hike, bird-watching expedition, tide-pooling excursion, or other trip accompanied by their naturalists. Other expeditions can be arranged from Two Harbors. There is ample lodging, and excellent restaurants abound. In Avalon, you may stay at the Zane Grey Pueblo Hotel, former home of the novelist Zane Grey.

CROSSING TIME: 2 hrs. 30 mins.

FERRY TYPE: Pedestrian

VESSEL CAPACITY: 500 passengers

OPERATING SEASON: Late Dec.-Oct.

SCHEDULE:	**Easter-Oct. and Dec. 26-Jan 4: Daily. Lv. Newport** 9 a.m.; **lv. Avalon** 4:30 p.m. **Jan. 4-Easter, Fri., Sat., Sun. only** (same schedule).
RESTRICTIONS:	No
FACILITIES:	Snack bar, cocktail lounge, electronic games, color television
FARE:	Adults $9.75; children (12 and under) $5; senior citizens weekday round-trip $18.50
RESERVATIONS:	Advance reservations are necessary; also, advance reservations on the island are required for accommodations and camping.

[Contact Catalina Island Chamber of Commerce, Box 217, Avalon, CA 90704 (213)510-1520.]

DIRECTIONS:	Take Pacific Coast Highway 1 to Balboa Blvd. in Newport, and Balboa Blvd. to Balboa Pavilion.
MAP LOCATION:	P. 399, CA, 2
CONTACT:	Catalina Passenger Service, Balboa Pavilion, 400 Main St., Balboa, CA 92661, (213) 510-1520

STATE:	California
PLACES SERVED:	Avalon—San Pedro (Catalina Channel Express)
BODY OF WATER:	San Pedro Channel
FERRY SERVICE HISTORY:	This service was founded in July 1981 by three residents of Santa Catalina Island, Doug Bombard, now President of the com-

pany, his son, Greg (Vice-President and General Manager), and Tom Rutter, Vice-President, Operations. The company began as a commuter service with the *Channel Express*, a sixty-passenger vessel. The service has now been expanded to include the *Avalon Express*, the *Catalina*

Express, and the *Two Harbors Express*, all of which hold 149 passengers. The boats are fully stabilized, with the latest in technical sophistication. A videotape of highlights of things to see and do on the island is shown as passengers cross over, and the ships have airline-style seats (indoor and outdoor seating) and cellular telephones. The three larger boats have private staterooms for eight to ten people with complimentary bottles of champagne, a wet bar, and a private restroom. The ships are also used for whale-watching trips and cruises.

There was extensive excursion service to Santa Catalina during the late nineteenth century. In *Early Excursion Ships to Santa Catalina Island*, John M. Houston describes some of the steamers that once sailed out of San Pedro Bay for Santa Catalina. When the Southern Pacific Railroad was completed as far as the San Pedro docks from Los Angeles and Wilmington in 1882, hundreds of city people began arriving, hoping to visit the "Magic" Isle twenty miles off the coast. According to Houston, a visit to the island was considered "sporting." William, Joseph, and Hancock Banning, sons of General Phineas Banning, had established Banning Shipbuilding Company on Morman Island in the Inner Harbor of the bay in 1869, and they began a sailboat ferry service to the island in 1881. There was competition from Capt. Martin Lindskow, who rented his sloop *Louise* to weekend parties wishing to visit the island and from Capt. A. W. Timmons, who offered his schooner *Rosita* to take people over. Ladies, in particular, were doubtful about the sailing ships, but when the Bannings procured a Sacramento river side-wheeler, the *Amelia*, to make the run, they had more confidence. The Bannings later added the *Falcon*, built in 1886, and ordered a larger steamer, the *Hermosa*, to be built in San Francisco, laying aside a whole case of champagne for the christening of future Banning ships. The *Hermosa* made her maiden voyage to Santa Catalina in April 1889. For the next fourteen years, the Banning steamers, which also included the *Warrior* and the *Catalina (I)*, ran to the island, which the Banning Company purchased in 1892. By summer 1899, two ships ran to Avalon daily; on weekends three trips were needed. The bargain round-trip fare from Los Angeles, which included train and ship, was $2.75. In 1902 the *Hermosa (II)*, built by William Muller, a German shipbuilder hired by the Bannings, was launched; she carried six to seven hundred passengers. She was immediately popular, and by 1903 the company needed an even larger ship; this was the 194-foot *Cabrillo*, also built by Muller for the Bannings. The last of the grand old wooden excursion ships, she became known as the "Queen of the South Coast." As Houston puts it, "Her decks and rooms were host to thousands of parties, romances, and escapes from the humdrum." She was painted in 1911 by the noted ship painter Antonio Jacobsen. During World Wars I and II she was a troop ship in San Francisco Bay. She flew the flag of the Wrigley Corporation after 1918; the chewing-gum company had bought out the rights to the island and the ships serving it. The *Cabrillo* was eventually supplanted by the steel-hulled *Avalon* and the *Catalina (II)*, built in 1924, also called the "Great White Steamer" (she carried two thousand passengers). Of this ship, it has been said that she carried more people than any other ship in history. The last of the large excursion steamers, she was not retired until 1976.

There was also ferry service from San Pedro to Terminal Island, across a narrow channel, where there were a number of canneries. William Olesen of the Los Angeles Maritime Museum has carried out research on the ferries which once served this island, such as the *Blanche*, the *Dora*, the *Canso* (built in 1906), the *Peer*, the *Real*, and, later, the *Neleh*, the *Ace*, and others. In 1941 the *Islander* was secured. The Vincent Thomas Bridge, built in 1963, ended the era of these San Pedro ferries, though there has been discussion of reviving the foot ferry.

LOCAL POINTS OF INTEREST: [For notes on Avalon, please see listing under Avalon-Newport, p. 404.]

San Pedro, part of the Port of Los Angeles, is a major deepwater port in the country. Fort MacArthur overlooks the harbor; it was once a major coastal defense. The Cabrillo Marine Museum has extensive marine life displays, painting collections, and an aquarium; the name-board of the *Cabrillo* was removed from the ship (who was, sadly, in the graveyard of old ships near the Napa River) and given to the museum. San Pedro, though technically part of Los Angeles, is considered a separate community by many residents.

CROSSING TIME: 90 mins.

FERRY TYPE: Pedestrian

VESSEL CAPACITY: 60-149 passengers, according to vessel used

OPERATING SEASON: All year

SCHEDULE: *Schedule subject to change; please check with company.* **Mid-June-mid-Sept.: Daily: Lv. San Pedro** 7 a.m., 9, 11, 3 p.m., 5:45, *7:30. **Lv. Avalon** 9 a.m., **11, 3 p.m., 5, 7:30, *9:15. *Fri., Sat., Sun. only. **Mon.-Fri. only. *For off-season and holiday departures, consult company.*

RESTRICTIONS: See RESTRICTIONS, p. 402.

FACILITIES: Cocktail and refreshment service, color TV, deckhands to help with luggage; private stateroom available on the three larger ships

FARE: Adults $12.50; children (2-11) $7.50; children under 2 $0.50; senior citizens (55+) $10.50.

RESERVATIONS: Recommended for boat. Advance reservations for accommodation in Avalon needed (contact Catalina Island Chamber of Commerce, Box 217, Avalon, CA 90704; (213)510-1520).

DIRECTIONS: Take Harbor Freeway (Rt. 110) south to San Pedro. Take Harbor Blvd. off ramp. Follow Catalina signs across Harbor Blvd. From Long Beach, drive Ocean Blvd. west over Vincent Thomas Bridge and take first off ramp at San Pedro end to Berth 95.

MAP LOCATION: P. 399, CA, 3

CONTACT: Catalina Channel Express, Box 1391, San Pedro, CA 90733; San Pedro: (213)519-1212 Avalon: (213)510-1212

STATE: California

PLACES SERVED: Avalon—San Pedro (Catalina Cruises)

BODY OF WATER: San Pedro Channel

FERRY SERVICE HISTORY: Catalina Cruises operates a fleet of five spacious triple-decked seven hundred-passenger vessels [for brief description, please see entry under Avalon (Santa Catalina Island)-Long Beach, p. 401.] Service on this crossing began in 1970. If there is bad weather, shutting down airports, the ferries carry the US mail.

LOCAL POINTS OF INTEREST: [For notes on Avalon, please see listing under Avalon-Newport, p. 404. For notes on San Pedro, please see listing under Avalon-San Pedro (Catalina Channel Express), p. 407].

CROSSING TIME: 1 hr. 50 mins.

FERRY TYPE: Pedestrian

VESSEL CAPACITY: 700 passengers

OPERATING SEASON: All year

SCHEDULE: *Schedule changes frequently; consult company for current schedule.* **Lv. San Pedro** 9:45 a.m. **Lv. Avalon** 4:30 p.m. Extra trips mid-June-mid-Sept.

RESTRICTIONS: See RESTRICTIONS, p. 402.

FACILITIES: Restrooms, snack bar, gift shop

FARE: Adults $9.50; children (2-11) $5.05; children under 2 $0.60; senior citizens (55+) weekday round-trip $16.90 (holidays excluded).

RESERVATIONS: Required; advance reservations for accommodation in Avalon (contact Catalina Island Chamber of Commerce, Box 217, Avalon, CA 90704; 213/510-1520).

DIRECTIONS: To the Catalina Air-Sea Terminal in San Pedro, go to south end of Harbor Freeway (11), take Harbor Blvd. turn-off, continue 1 mi. Follow signs to Catalina Terminal entrance. Terminal is under the Vincent Thomas Bridge.

MAP LOCATION: P. 399, CA, 3

CONTACT: See CONTACT, p. 402.

STATE: California

PLACES SERVED: Balboa Island—Balboa Peninsula

BODY OF WATER: Balboa Reach Area in Newport Harbor

FERRY SERVICE HISTORY: This ferry service was founded in 1904 by Joseph Allan Beek, who was also Secretary of the California State Senate for over fifty years. He died in 1969, and the operation was taken over by his son, H. Seymour Beek, who is now the company president. Three flat-bottomed barges, built in-house, are used: the *Captain*, the *Admiral*, and the *Commodore*. The ferry has been designated a Historical Sight by the Newport Beach Historical Society.

LOCAL POINTS OF INTEREST: The Balboa Peninsula, containing Newport Beach and Balboa, is a long sandspit almost encircling Newport Bay. Balboa is the home of a dory fishing fleet that has been designated as a National Historic Landmark (it is based near McFadden's Pier). Old Town (or Cannery Village), in front of the fishing pier, is an area with buildings dating from the turn of the century. Balboa Pavilion, at Newport Beach, has been a local fixture since 1905 [see description under Avalon (Santa Catalina Island)—Newport (Balboa Pavilion), p. 403.]

Balboa Island itself has luxurious homes and yachts. The beaches here and on Balboa Peninsula are public, but parking is very limited.

CROSSING TIME: 5 mins.

FERRY TYPE: Vehicle

VESSEL CAPACITY: 3 cars; 75 passengers

OPERATING SEASON: All year

SCHEDULE: **Sun. through Thurs.** 6:30 a.m.-12 a.m.; **Fri. and Sat.** 6:30 a.m.-2 a.m.

RESTRICTIONS: Pickup truck with camper shell is maximum vehicle; no RVs permitted. Load limit 5 tons. Overhead clearance 9 ft. 10 in.

FACILITIES: None

FARE: Car and driver $0.55; additional adults $0.20; child $0.10

RESERVATIONS: No

DIRECTIONS: The Balboa Peninsula landing is at Palm St. and East Bay Ave. On Balboa Island, the landing is at Agate St. and South Bay Front.

MAP LOCATION: P. 399, CA, 4

CONTACT: Balboa Island Ferry, 410 So. Bay Front, Balboa Island, CA 92662, (714)673-1070

STATE: California

PLACES SERVED: Bradford Island-Jersey Island-Webb Tract

BODY OF WATER: False River

FERRY SERVICE HISTORY: The *Victory II*, built in 1949, operates on this route. Based overnight at Bradford Island, she is an appealing and sturdy vessel with gleaming white railings and a tower bridge beneath a large US flag. She serves hunters and property owners as well as truckers transporting grain and produce through the area during harvests. The service has been in operation for forty years.

LOCAL POINTS OF INTEREST: This region is known as the Sacramento-San Joaquin Delta. The three islands, with peat levees, were reclaimed over a century ago by the government, using Chinese coolie labor that became available once the Transcontinental Railroad was completed. The rich peat soil, though disaster-prone from flooding, is excellent for agriculture. Many cyclists come here to ride along the levees and view the wildlife, and there is good hunting for pheasant. Portions of the islands are game reserves. There are also underground gas reserves.

CROSSING TIME: Approx. 15-20 mins. between islands

FERRY TYPE: Vehicle

VESSEL CAPACITY: 6-10 cars

OPERATING SEASON: All year

SCHEDULE: **Mon.-Sat.:** Boat makes an hourly loop between the three islands, hourly from 8 a.m.-5 p.m., beginning at Jersey Island. **Sun. & holidays:** Loops at 8 a.m., 10, 4 p.m., 5.

RESTRICTIONS: Trailers, pickup-campers, and RVs permitted. Load limit highway legal.

FACILITIES: None

FARE: Free

RESERVATIONS: No

DIRECTIONS: From San Francisco take Highway 80 toward Sacramento; then SR 4E to Stockton. Take Cypress Rd., then left on Jersey Island Road; ferry is at the end.

MAP LOCATION: P. 399, CA, 5

CONTACT: Mr. Don Freitas, The Delta Ferry Authority, 255 Glacier Dr., Martinez, CA 94553, (415)372-4480.

STATE: California

PLACES SERVED: Empire Tract—Venice Island

BODY OF WATER: Little Connection Slough

FERRY SERVICE HISTORY: Service on this crossing has existed since 1932. The vessel has no formal name, but is a steel-hulled cable-propelled boat, twenty-two feet by fifty feet, operated by a crew of one. Most of the riders come from Stockton, California. The ferry is administered by the San Joaquin County Department of Public Works.

LOCAL POINTS OF INTEREST: The area in which this ferry operates is known as the San Joaquin River Delta. [For more complete notes on the Delta, please see entry under Grand Island-Ryer Island, p. 413.]

CROSSING TIME: 5 mins.

FERRY TYPE: Vehicle

VESSEL CAPACITY: 6 cars

OPERATING SEASON: All year

SCHEDULE: Daily, on signal, 8 a.m.-noon and 1 p.m.-5.

RESTRICTIONS: Trailers, pickup-campers, and RVs permitted. Load limit 30 tons.

FACILITIES: None

FARE: Free

RESERVATIONS: No

DIRECTIONS: Ferry is at the west end of an eight-mile road approximately seven miles west of I-5.

MAP LOCATION: P. 399, CA, 6

CONTACT: San Joaquin County Dept. of Public Works, Box 1810, Stockton, CA 95201, (209)944-2291

STATE: California

PLACES SERVED: Grand Island—Ryer Island (Steamboat Slough) (*J-Mack*)

BODY OF WATER: Sacramento River

FERRY SERVICE HISTORY: There has been a ferry at this location since the late 1800s. The service was taken over from the county by the State of California in 1925. The original ferry was a wooden vessel with sheep gates used to haul animals more often than vehicles; originally, it was run along cables and pulled by hand across the channels. The ferry on this run is the *J-Mack*; it was first used in 1969. It is self-powered along a cable that stretches across the slough. The vessel is ninety-two feet long, including a fifteen-foot auto ramp at either end, and has a steel hull.

Traffic consists of farmers, schoolchildren, mail carriers, construction workers, delivery vans, and also boaters, fishermen, and tourists. Fall brings visiting duck and pheasant hunters who double the traffic (ordinarily several hundred vehicles a day). The *J-Mack*, like *The Real McCoy* at Rio Vista, runs twenty-four hours a day. According to ferry crews, the late night riders are usually night-shift commuters or locals coming to and from restaurants or other social life.

LOCAL POINTS OF INTEREST: The area in which this ferry and *The Real McCoy* operate is known as the Delta. The Sacramento, San Joaquin, Cosumnes, and Mokelumne Rivers drain into the basin, forming a network of channels and sloughs that weave their way first to Grizzly Bay, then San Pablo and San Francisco Bays before reaching the Pacific Ocean at the Golden Gate. Delta soil is rich and supports a very healthy agricultural community. Some farming is done on tracts of land created by an extensive levee system. Local waterways are a route for commerce and a first-class recreation area. There are numerous boat clubs and marinas with lots of fishing, water skiing, and houseboating. Local towns such as Ryde, Locke, Courtland, Rio Vista and Walnut Grove have what Daniel Parker calls a "comfortable, rumpled character," with excellent restaurants and nice shops.

CROSSING TIME: 3 mins.

FERRY TYPE: Vehicle

VESSEL CAPACITY: 6 vehicles

OPERATING SEASON: All year

SCHEDULE: Daily, on signal, 24 hr. service

RESTRICTIONS: Pickup-campers, small trailers, and RVs permitted. Load limit 15 tons.

FACILITIES: None

FARE: Free

RESERVATIONS: No

DIRECTIONS: The ferry is located 3 miles west of Ryde on SR 220 (near Walnut Grove).

MAP LOCATION: P. 399, CA, 7

CONTACT: Caltrans District 10 Regional Office, Box 8, Fairfield, CA 94533, (707)428-2032

STATE: California

PLACES SERVED: Long Beach (Shoreline Village)—Queen Mary—Queensway Bay Hilton (Bay Shuttle Water Taxi)

BODY OF WATER: Queensway Bay

FERRY SERVICE HISTORY: The vessel on this service is the *Bay Queen*, an open-air water taxi. Service was inaugurated May 27, 1985.

LOCAL POINTS OF INTEREST: [For further notes on Long Beach, please see entry under Avalon-Long Beach, p. 401.]
The *Queen Mary*, one of the largest passenger liners ever built, is permanently moored at Pier J in Long Beach Harbor. It is a combination restaurant, hotel, and convention center, and a

self-guided tour of the engine room, bridge, Captain's quarters, and other areas of the ship is offered. The Hughes Flying Boat Exhibit, featuring Howard Hughes' *Spruce Goose*, the largest airplane ever built, is housed in a dome at Pier J near the *Queen Mary*; a self-guided tour of the cockpit, flight deck, and cargo area is available. Londontowne, next to the *Queen Mary*, is a replica of an old English seaport village.

CROSSING TIME: 5 mins.

FERRY TYPE: Pedestrian

VESSEL CAPACITY: 49 passengers

OPERATING SEASON: All year

SCHEDULE: **Daily: Sun.-Thurs.:** 11:30 a.m.-7 p.m.; Fri., Sat., and holidays 11:30 a.m.-11:00 p.m. Crosses Bay twice each hour. **Shoreline Village (Long Beach) to Queen Mary:** Lv. on the hr. and 40 mins. past the hr. **Queen Mary to Queensway Bay Hilton:** Lv. 10 mins. past the hour. **Queensway Bay Hilton to Queen Mary:** Lv. 20 mins. past the hr. **Queen Mary to Shoreline Village:** Lv. on the half-hr. and 50 mins. past the hr.

RESTRICTIONS: Carry-on hand luggage only.

FACILITIES: None

FARE: Adults $1; children (2-11) $0.50; children under 2 with adult free (maximum 2 children per adult). Passengers boarding the shuttle must disembark at one of the route stops before boarding for a return trip.

RESERVATIONS: No

DIRECTIONS: Take Long Beach Freeway South; it turns into Shoreline Dr. Turn rt. on Pine Ave. and continue to Shoreline Village.

MAP LOCATION: P. 399, CA, 8

CONTACT: See CONTACT, p. 402.

STATE:	California
PLACES SERVED:	Princeton—Afton (a point 3 miles west of the settlement)
BODY OF WATER:	Sacramento River
FERRY SERVICE HISTORY:	The Princeton ferry is registered with the State of California as a historic landmark.

The service, connecting Glenn and Colusa Counties, is one of the last on the Sacramento River, which once had numerous ferries crossing the main channel. It was established by Dr. A. Lull, who was instrumental in getting the first post office opened at Princeton. The present boat was built in 1950 at the crossing site and draws power from an overhead electric cable. It has been said that it "looks like a collection of spare parts," with an automobile torque converter used as part of the engine and worn tanks on the barge-like structure. On board is a plaque reading "Marriages performed by the captain of the vessel are good for the duration of this voyage only." The trip lasts just over two minutes.

In 1978 the ferry was almost discontinued, a casualty of Proposition 13, but a petition signed by over twelve hundred people stayed its execution. At that time, Glenn Huffman, a Colusa County farmer who resides in Glenn County, said he took the ferry at least four times a day, saving him many miles driving around via SR 45. Eldon Nation, the pilot, said, "I wish I had a license plate for every car that has come aboard. We get visitors from Alaska, Pennsylvania, Kentucky, and other states. They come off I-5 just on purpose to see this." It is presently administered by Colusa County.

At the time of writing, the ferry was undergoing repair. Please check with Colusa County before making a special trip to ride this historic ferry.

LOCAL POINTS OF INTEREST:	Princeton, a town on the Sacramento River about twenty miles north of Colusa, dates back to the days of the mining and agri-

cultural boom in the 1800s. It became a stagecoach terminus and a wheat-shipping port; mule-powered road trains with as many as seven wagons used to bring wheat from Willows for shipping at Princeton. Slowly, sidewalks were laid, and granaries and banks opened, but then the town experienced a decline.

Afton is just off the river. A pleasant drive or bike tour can be made from the small scenic town of Colusa, through the Colusa Sacramento

River State Recreation Area. Bike tours can be arranged by Sutter Butte Tours of Colusa (916)451-4385.

CROSSING TIME: 2 mins.

FERRY TYPE: Vehicle

VESSEL CAPACITY: 4 cars

OPERATING SEASON: All year

SCHEDULE: 24 hrs. per day, 6 a.m.-midnight, weather permitting

RESTRICTIONS: Trailers, tractor-campers and RVs permitted. Load limit 10 tons.

FACILITIES: None

FARE: Free

RESERVATIONS: No

DIRECTIONS: Princeton is on SR 45 east of I-5; the ferry runs from Princeton to a point 3 miles west of Afton.

MAP LOCATION: P. 399, CA, 9

CONTACT: County Clerk, Colusa County Dept. of Public Works, 1215 Market St., Colusa, CA 95932, (916)458-5186

STATE: California

PLACES SERVED: Rio Vista (2.5 miles north)—Ryer Island (SR 84) (Cache Slough) (*The Real McCoy*)

BODY OF WATER: Sacramento River

FERRY SERVICE HISTORY: This location has had ferries in service since the late 1800s. California took over responsibility for the service from the county in

1925. Originally the ferry was a wooden vessel with sheep gates used to haul animals more often than vehicles; it was run along cables and pulled by hand across the channels. In 1961 *The Real McCoy* was converted from a power-driven cable ferry to a free-floating vessel. The present *Real McCoy* was put into service in 1962. It has a steel hull and is 103 feet long, including loading ramps. It is propelled and steered by two diesel engines and manned by a Caltrans ferry boat operator and a deck hand.

Daniel L. Parker of the California Department of Transportation says that "among ferry boat buffs, *The Real McCoy* is known as a dandy vessel. Cache Slough is part of the Sacramento-Yolo Port District Deep Water channel. Large freighters from around the world use the channel to reach the Port of Sacramento. *The Real McCoy* deftly maneuvers this tricky crossing many, many times each day." *The Real McCoy* maneuvers all night as well, offering twenty-four-hour service. Riders, like those on the *J-Mack* at Grand Island (also in the Delta), are mostly farmers, business people, tourists, sportsmen, and residents.

LOCAL POINTS OF INTEREST:	[For notes on the Delta area and Ryer Island, please see entry under Grand Isle-Ryer Island, p. 413.]

Rio Vista, once a port-of-call for riverboats travelling between San Francisco and Sacramento, is a town of just over three thousand. Here, you might visit the California Railway Museum, which has a two-mile ride on antique streetcars and steam trains; there is a vintage collection of railroad cars here. At the foot of Main Street a charming monument has been erected to Humphrey the Whale, who captured the hearts of millions when he strayed from his migration route into the Sacramento delta. State Highway 160 runs north/south through the area and is a designated California Scenic Highway. Just south of Rio Vista on Route 160 is Brannan Island State Recreation Area and the visitor center of the Delta National Historic Association.

CROSSING TIME:	3 mins.
FERRY TYPE:	Vehicle
VESSEL CAPACITY:	6 vehicles
OPERATING SEASON:	All year
SCHEDULE:	Daily, on signal, 24 hr. service
RESTRICTIONS:	Pickup-campers, small trailers and RVs permitted. Load limit 25 tons. Maximum vehicle width 8 ft.
FACILITIES:	None
FARE:	Free

RESERVATIONS:	No
DIRECTIONS:	The ferry is located 1.5 miles north of Rio Vista on SR 84.
MAP LOCATION:	P. 399, CA, 10
CONTACT:	See CONTACT, p. 414.

STATE:	California
PLACES SERVED:	San Francisco—Alcatraz Island
BODY OF WATER:	San Francisco Bay
FERRY SERVICE HISTORY:	This service is operated by the Red and White Fleet, a division of Crowley Maritime Corporation. Crowley was established in

1892; at that time it used long-boats to ferry crew and supplies between the sailing ships anchored along San Francisco's waterfront. Then it began to offer tours of the Bay, and from this enterprise the present Bay cruises arose. There are presently nine vessels used by the Red and White Fleet; they are used interchangeably on the six services, according to need. There are two catamarans: *CataMarin* (405 passengers) and *Dolphin* (405 passengers). The others are monohull vessels: *Royal Star:* (500 passengers); *Royal Prince:* (450 passengers); *Royal Knight:* (150 passengers); *Harbor Emperor:* (450 passengers); *Harbor Queen:* (350 passengers); *Harbor Princess:* (350 passengers); and *Harbor King:* (250 passengers).

LOCAL POINTS OF INTEREST:	There are few cities about which visitors feel as proprietary as the natives, but San Francisco is such a place. As colorful as Hong

Kong, as friendly as Atlanta, as exotic in cuisine as New York, as compact as Edinburgh, as impassioned as Paris — the only possible flaws are that the city is over-loved and over-sunbeamed. "We hope to have a fog for you before you leave," the natives tell the tourists, which mystifies those newly arrived in Paradise. Once foggy wisps arrive, though, one understands their siren charm, for can one appreciate the city's Graces without at least minimal Furies?

Robert Louis Stevenson described his arrival in the city (1879): "The day was breaking as we crossed the ferry; the fog was rising over the citied hills of San Francisco; the bay was perfect—not a ripple, scarce a stain, upon its blue expanse; everything was waiting, breathless, for the sun. A spot of cloudy gold lit first upon the head of Tamalpais, and then widened downward on its shapely shoulder; the air seemed to awaken, and began to sparkle; and suddenly 'The tall hills Titan discovered,' and the city of San Francisco, and the bay of gold and corn, were lit from end to end with summer daylight.'' (In May 1880 he and Fanny Osbourne crossed by ferry from Oakland to San Francisco and were married.)

The very streets of the city, such as Lombard, the "Crooked Street," seem to have preservation orders, not to mention the surrounding hills, cable cars, piers, and many neighborhoods. Most people, on first arriving, find their way to Fisherman's Wharf. This is no longer quite what it once was, with fishermen mending their nets, and, for many people, there are too many neon lights and souvenir shops, but the area is still a mecca for ferry-lovers. Both ferries and boat cruises leave from the piers scattered up and down the historic waterfront from the 1898 Ferry Building. Margot Patterson Doss has called it "that mellow colossus of Colusa sandstone that is still our most romantic city gate." Here, if there is time before the ferry leaves, you might enjoy a meal or a drink at Sindbad's Restaurant, across a small bridge to the next platform, a festive establishment with blue and white umbrellas. Pier 39 has been recast into a waterfront showcase with boutiques, restaurants, and the *San Francisco Experience* audio-visual theater (with a mesmerizing re-enactment of the 1906 earthquake and fire).

Among the myriad attractions of San Francisco are Ghiardelli Square, a converted nineteenth-century chocolate factory with shops and restaurants; the Cannery, a shopping-dining complex fashioned from the old Del Monte cannery; the National Maritime Museum; Coit Tower on Telegraph Hill — a tribute to Lillie Hitchcock with noted PWAP murals, the Golden Gate Promenade, the Japan Center, the Presidio, the Museum of Modern Art, and the Mission Dolores.

Alcatraz Island (one-quarter mile from shore) is now part of the Golden Gate Recreation Area of the National Park Service. It was named by the Spanish explorer de Ayala in 1775 ("Isla de los Alcatraces," or Island of the Pelicans). Under the Americans, it became a fortress, then an army prison, then, in 1934, a grim bastion, the dreaded federal penitentiary. It was thought to be completely secure, amid freezing, swirling water. Inmates of "The Rock" included Al Capone, Machine-Gun Kelly, Doc Barker, Creepy Karpis, and many others; no one is thought to have escaped alive, though three criminals may have done so in 1963 (or they may have drowned). It was almost a tomb, like something out of Poe, with no talking, no newspapers, and no rewards for good behavior. Because everything, even drinking water, had to be ferried across, the cost of maintaining Alcatraz was immense, and in 1963 the prison was closed. For ten years the island was in limbo, serving occasionally as a movie set. The tours began in the 1970s and include a look at the main block of cells (with an optional locking in) and the fortifications.

CROSSING TIME: 10-12 mins.

FERRY TYPE: Pedestrian

VESSEL CAPACITY: See initial listing.

OPERATING SEASON: All year, weather permitting (no service Christmas and New Year's).

SCHEDULE: **Summer: Lv. Pier 41** 15 mins. after the hour 8:15 a.m.-5:15 p.m. **Lv. Alcatraz** 9:35 a.m., 10:40, 11:40, 12:45 p.m., 1:45, 2:45, 3:45, 4:45, 5:45, 6:15, 7:05. **Winter: Lv. Pier 41** quarter to every hour 8:45 a.m.-2:45 p.m. **Lv. Alcatraz** 10:05 a.m., 11:10, 12:15 p.m., 1:15, 2:15, 3:15, 3:55, 4:40.

RESTRICTIONS: On catamarans, smoking on outer decks only

FACILITIES: Restrooms, snack bars including full beverage service

FARE: Adults $4.25; child (5-11) $2.75; under 5 free; senior citizen $3.75. Tickets must be purchased through local Ticketron outlet or at the ticket booth at Pier 41.

RESERVATIONS: Reservations are essential for the 1½-hour National Park Tour of Alcatraz, which only takes 150 people. Otherwise, you will face an interminable wait in the stand-by line on the pier. In summer you need to make these as much as 3 weeks in advance for a specific date and time; you can then make the boat reservation on Ticketron. Call (415)546-2805. Dress warmly and wear sturdy walking shoes.

DIRECTIONS: Ferry leaves from Pier 41 on Fisherman's Wharf.

MAP LOCATION: P. 399, CA, 11

CONTACT: Red and White Fleet, Pier 41, San Francisco, CA 94133, (415)546-2815

STATE:	California
PLACES SERVED:	San Francisco—Angel Island
BODY OF WATER:	San Francisco Bay
FERRY SERVICE HISTORY:	[For notes on the history of the Red and White Fleet, please see entry under San Francisco-Alcatraz, p. 419. For notes on the

history of San Francisco ferries, please see entry under San Francisco—Sausalito (Golden Gate Ferry), p. 426.]

| LOCAL POINTS OF INTEREST: | Angel Island (population two hundred or so deer, four resident rangers and eight care-takers) has been called a pocket-sized Cor- |

sica. The largest island (740 acres) in the Bay, it is a state park open for hiking and picnics; a five-mile hike takes you around the island. The Bay is constantly in view, from the ferry, trails, and beaches. It has a cove leading to a grassy rise with picnic tables and twelve miles of roads.

It is thought that Indian use of the island began over two thousand years ago. The Coast Miwok Indians reached the island by means of boats made of tule reeds. They established camps or villages at Ayala Cove, West, East, and North Garrisons. In 1775, Lt. Juan Manuel de Ayala brought his sailing ship, the *San Carlos,* into San Francisco Bay and anchored it in what is now Ayala Cove; at this time he named the island "Isla de Los Angeles." In the early nineteenth century, the island was uninhabited, as the Indians had been drawn into the Mission San Francisco de Asis (Mission Dolores in San Francisco) or driven away, though Russian hunters did visit the island. Richard Henry Dana mentioned the island in *Two Years Before the Mast* (1835); his landing place is thought to be the present Quarry Beach. Antonio Maria Osio was later granted part of the island for cattle farming, but his claim was disputed after the 1846 war with Mexico. The island was given over to military use during the late nineteenth and early twentieth centuries (during World War II, Japanese prisoners of war were detained here). The state of California acquired it in segments from 1954 to 1962 for use as a State Park (Point Blunt is still, however, reserved as a Coast Guard Station). A small museum and partially restored immigration station contain relics of its past as a military post and quarantine station.

[For notes on San Francisco, see entry under San Francisco-Alcatraz, p. 419.]

CROSSING TIME:	15 mins. catamaran; 30 mins. monohull
FERRY TYPE:	Pedestrian

VESSEL CAPACITY: [For notes on capacity of the ships in the Red and White Fleet, please see entry under San Francisco-Alcatraz, p. 419.]

OPERATING SEASON: All year

SCHEDULE: **Weekdays: Lv. Fisherman's Wharf** (Pier 43½) **10 a.m. Lv. Angel Island** 2:40 p.m. **Weekends: Lv. Fisherman's Wharf** 10:50 a.m. **Lv. Angel Island** 3:50 p.m. **Additional trips Sat. Sun., and holidays, Memorial Weekend through Labor Day Weekend: Lv. Fisherman's Wharf** 10:50 a.m., 12:20 p.m., 1:50, 3:15, 4:50 **Lv. Angel Island** 11:25 a.m., 12:55 p.m., 2:25, 3:50, 5:25. *No service Thanksgiving, Christmas, New Year's.*

RESTRICTIONS: On catamarans, smoking on outer decks only

FACILITIES: Restrooms, snack bar including full beverage service

FARE: Round-trip fares only. Adults $6.05; child (5-11) $3.30; under 5 free. Fare includes admission to Angel Island.

RESERVATIONS: No

DIRECTIONS: The ferry leaves from Pier 43½ at Fisherman's Wharf.

MAP LOCATION: P. 399, CA, 12

CONTACT: See CONTACT, p. 421.

STATE: California

PLACES SERVED: San Francisco—Larkspur

BODY OF WATER: San Francisco Bay

FERRY SERVICE HISTORY: The Golden Gate Ferry System is part of the Golden Gate Bridge, Highway and Transportation District; it operates a four-vessel fleet

Marin

between Marin County and San Francisco. Three are used between
Larkspur and San Francisco; the fourth is dedicated to the Sausalito-San
Francisco route. The ferries augment the District's commuter bus service
between Northern California counties and San Francisco, reducing automobile traffic congestion on the Golden Gate Bridge.

The vessels on this run have two diesel engines; they are the *Marin,* the
Sonoma, and the *San Francisco.* Each boat has a different historical
display, depending on the county for which it is named. The length is 165
feet; they are made of aluminum, and the net tonnage for each is fifty-six.
They were designed by Philip F. Spaulding & Associates, Inc., in Seattle,
Washington, and built by Campbell Industries, Inc., in San Diego. They
were delivered in 1976 and 1977. Mick Beattie, one of the ferry captains,
became a hero in April 1986 when he rescued a yachtsman being swept to
sea near the Richmond Bridge; he had gone overboard near the Brothers
Islands before Beattie came to his aid.

Visitors can have all the benefits of a low-cost cruise with none of the
hassles of commuting. The ferries have the luxurious space of a steamship salon, with blue and purple airline-type seats and two refreshment
counter/bars, providing convivial passage and a pleasant interlude,
especially in the mid-day hours.

Service was inaugurated December 11, 1976. In January 1982, the
Golden Gate Bridge was closed due to rain and wind, which caused mud
slides. The ferry was the only way to get to San Francisco from Marin
County — capacity crossings were the rule for the duration. Over 70
percent of the riders come from within a five-mile radius of the Larkspur
Terminal in Marin County.

LOCAL POINTS OF INTEREST: The Larkspur terminal is near Point San Quentin, about fifteen miles from San Francisco. A pedestrian bridge links the terminal to Larkspur Landing Shopping Center, encompassing about fifty shops and restaurants. Among the shops are A Clean Well-Lighted Place (a Hemingway-inspired bookstore) and For Paws, a restaurant which features a doggie brunch. An appealing wood carving of two fishermen, perched atop poles, dominates the plaza at Larkspur Landing. Except for the shopping center, the area near the terminal is not too walkable, but the ride provides an enticing look at Alcatraz and Angel Island from the east. Landmarks as you near Larkspur are Muzzi Marsh, Heerdt Marsh (a California game preserve), and Corte Madera Slough, a channel lined with houseboats.

CROSSING TIME: 45 mins.

FERRY TYPE: Pedestrian

VESSEL CAPACITY: 725 passengers

OPERATING SEASON: All year

SCHEDULE: **Weekdays (except holidays): Lv. San Francisco** 7 a.m., 7:45, 8:50, 10:45, 12:45 p.m., 2:45, 3:40, 4:20, 4:50, 5:20, 6, 6:45, 8:25. **Lv. Larkspur** 6 a.m., 7, 7:30, 8, 8:40, 9:45, 11:45, 1:45 p.m., 3:45, 4:25, 5:05, 5:40, 7:35. **Sat. Sun., Holidays: Lv. San Francisco** 10:45 a.m., 12:45 p.m., 2:45, 4:45, 6:45. **Lv. Larkspur** 9:45 a.m., 11:45, 1:45 p.m., 3:45, 5:45. *Holiday schedule: Washington's Birthday, Memorial Day, Independence Day, Labor Day. No service New Year's, Thanksgiving, or Christmas Day.*

RESTRICTIONS: No hazardous liquids (i.e., no motor bikes); no pets except Seeing Eye dogs.

FACILITIES: Refreshment counter; restrooms, forward observation lounge.

FARE: Mon.-Fri.: Adults $2.20; child (6-12) $1.65 (free when accompanied by adult); 5 and under free; senior citizens (over 65) and handicapped persons $1.10 with Medicare card. **Weekend and holidays:** Adults $3; senior and handicapped $1.50; child (6-12) $2.25. On weekends and holidays, a "Family Fare" is in effect whereby up to two children per adult (1-12) ride free when accompanied by the adult. Commuter books available.

RESERVATIONS: No

DIRECTIONS:	In San Francisco, ferry leaves from San Francisco Ferry Building. In Larkspur the terminal is located on the road to San Quentin (Sir Francis Drake Blvd.).
MAP LOCATION:	P. 399, CA, 13
CONTACT:	Golden Gate Ferry, 101 E. Sir Francis Drake Blvd., Larkspur, CA 94939, (415)982-8834 or (415)982-8835

STATE:	California
PLACES SERVED:	San Francisco—Sausalito (Golden Gate)
BODY OF WATER:	San Francisco Bay
FERRY SERVICE HISTORY:	This service to Sausalito is run by the Golden Gate Ferry System, part of the Golden Gate Bridge, Highway and Transpor-

tation District, for the purpose of augmenting the District's commuter bus service between Northern California counties and San Francisco, reducing automobile traffic on the Golden Gate Bridge. The *Golden Gate* is 113 feet, 10$^{1}/_{2}$ inches long and made of steel, with a net tonnage of thirty-eight; she was delivered in 1969, designed and built by the San Diego Marine Construction Company of San Diego. She is powered by two Caterpillar D-348 TA diesel engines, each delivering 650 SHP; her speed is fourteen knots, and she carries a crew of six. Service was inaugurated August 15, 1970.

The San Francisco-Sausalito route has existed throughout the glorious ferry boat era on San Francisco Bay, beginning as early as 1841. The Bay is thought to have been discovered by Jose de Ortega about 1769; in 1775 Manuel de Ayala sailed his ship *San Carlos* into the harbor, the first recorded vessel to enter the Golden Gate. In 1822, the country of Alta California came under Mexican rule, and many foreign nationals obtained Mexican citizenship in order to obtain land grants in the Bay area. One Mexican grantee, John Reed, of Britain, operated a sailboat on the Bay as early as 1826. After 1841, William Richardson, another British sailor grantee, operated a boat between his Rancho Saucelito (as it was then spelled) and San Francisco.

Mexico ceded California to the US in 1848, an event quickly succeeded by the Gold Rush, which brought countless wooden sailing vessels to the Bay. The first recorded Bay ferry operation was in 1850; Thomas Gray placed his ship *Kangaroo* in service between San Francisco and what is now Oakland Estuary. Soon many rivercraft were operating as ferries, ushering in the great era of the San Francisco ferries. Ultimately, there were nearly thirty major routes, and in their heyday they carried over fifty million passengers annually to and from the 1898 Ferry Building. The famous clock in the tower was stopped at 5:16 a.m. on April 18, 1906, by the earthquake, and remained so for over a year. The first wharf was built here in 1850 and the first ferry sheds in 1877. The Rancho Sausalito came under the ownership of Samuel R. Throckmorton, who sold twelve hundred acres on Richardson Bay to the Sausalito Land and Ferry Company, which began selling off lots. Customers were ferried over to look at lots on the steamer *Princess*.

Such famous ferries as the *San Rafael* and the *Petaluma* (later *Tamalpais*) were on this run. The grand old "White Arks" were spacious, seating up to twenty-five hundred passengers, and gracious, offering such amenities as restaurants, bars, buffet counters, newsstands, shoeshines, and secluded ladies' parlors with cabin attendants. Shipboard appointments included fine wood paneling, ornate glasswork and stately staircases with hand-carved balustrades. Some were owned by railroad companies, some catered to foot passengers, and others to automobiles and foot passengers. Ferries were such an integral part of San Francisco life that hotels used to keep packets of pajamas and toothbrushes at the ready for passengers who missed the last ferry home.

One example of an early ferry is on view today as part of the National Maritime Museum collection at the Hyde Street Pier, the *Eureka*, last of the walking beam ferries, built in 1890. Originally built as the railroad car float *Ukiah*, she was rebuilt as a passenger ferry in 1923 and in 1941 was the largest passenger ferry in the world. She was retired in 1957.

LOCAL POINTS OF INTEREST: [For notes on San Francisco, please see entry under San Francisco-Alcatraz, p. 419.]

If time permits only one ferry trip in San Francisco, Sausalito (a corruption of the Spanish name for Little Willow) is the ideal destination (avoid the crowds, if possible, by going mid-week or off-season). It is situated on the Mediterranean side of the Golden Gate, eight miles north of San Francisco. Nestled by the waterfront are boutiques and open-deck restaurants; winding, wooded streets disappear into staircases; beautifully stituated hillside houses, some cantilevered, afford circumspect views of the Bay. The town has a long-established reputation as an artists' colony, but only the affluent can afford such property now. In any case, you can enjoy the view by climbing to the Alta Mira Hotel and having lunch or dinner on the lovely terrace. Craftspeople can be seen at work at the Village Fair, once a Chinese gambling hall, opium den, and distillery. The Sausalito Art Festival is held Labor Day Weekend.

At Gate Five in Sausalito you can see an intriguing colony of over three hundred houseboats, representing a litany of lifestyles. There is remarkable architectural diversity, ranging from Tudor Gothic to tugboat simple. The boats are built on anything bouyant, from skiffs to aircraft balloon barges. Gate Five was once the spiritual focal point in the hip scene. Alan Watts lived here with painter Jean Varda on the converted ferry *Vallejo;* artist Piro Caro lived on another converted ferry, *The Issaquah.* Allen Ginsberg and Aldous and Laura Huxley were frequent visitors. The *Vallejo* remains headquarters for the Alan Watts Society for Comparative Philosophy. The community has been, in recent years, less colorful than it once was owing to increasing county regulation of sewage and building codes, but it is still well worth seeing.

The San Francisco Bay Delta and Hydraulic Model, at the Bay Model Visitor Center, is a two-acre scale model of San Francisco Bay; here, you can see the tidal action of the Bay (the model operates only when an experiment is in progress).

CROSSING TIME: 30 mins.

FERRY TYPE: Pedestrian

VESSEL CAPACITY: 575 passengers

OPERATING SEASON: All year

SCHEDULE: **Mon.-Fri., except holidays: Lv. San Francisco Ferry Building** 7:50 a.m., *9:15, 10:25, 11:45, 1:10 p.m., 2:35, 4:10, 5:30, 6:40, 8. **Lv. Sausalito** 7:15 a.m., 8:25, *9:50, 11:05, 12:25 p.m., 1:55, 3:20, 4:45, 6:05, 7:20. *Early May-late Sept. only. **Sat., Sun., and holidays: Lv. San Francisco Ferry Building** 11:30 a.m., 1 p.m., 2:30, 4, 5:30, 6:55. **Lv. Sausalito** 10:50 a.m., 12:15 p.m., 1:45, 3:15, 4:45, 6:10. *Holiday schedule: Washington's Birthday, Memorial Day, Independence Day, Labor Day. No service Thanksgiving, Christmas Day, or New Year's Day.*

RESTRICTIONS: No flammable liquids; no pets except Seeing Eye dogs.

FACILITIES: Refreshment counter, restrooms.

FARE: Mon.-Fri. adult $2.75; children 6-12 $2.05; 5 and under free; senior citizens (65 +) and handicapped persons $1.35. Saturdays, Sundays, and holidays there is a special "Family Fare" whereby up to two children per adult ride free when accompanied by the adult. Sat., Sun., holidays: Adults $3, children (6-12) $2.25; senior citizens and handicapped persons $1.50. Commuter books available.

RESERVATIONS: No

DIRECTIONS: The San Francisco Ferry Terminal is situated behind the south wing of the San Francisco Ferry Building (foot of Market St.). Look for the blue and white Golden Gate Ferry awning at the entrance. The Sausalito terminal is in the center of town.

MAP LOCATION: P. 399, CA, 14

CONTACT: Golden Gate Bridge, Highway and Transportation District, 101 E. Sir Francis Drake Blvd., Larkspur, CA 94939, San Francisco: (415)332-6600, Marin City: (415)453-2100

STATE: California

PLACES SERVED: San Francisco—Sausalito (Red and White)

BODY OF WATER: San Francisco Bay

FERRY SERVICE HISTORY: [For notes on the history of the Red and White Fleet, please see entry under San Francisco-Alcatraz, p. 419. For notes on the history of San Francisco ferries, please see entry under San Francisco-Sausalito (Golden Gate Ferry), p. 426].

LOCAL POINTS OF INTEREST: [For notes on San Francisco, please see entry under San Francisco-Alcatraz, p. 419. For notes on Sausalito, please see entry under San Francisco-Sausalito (Golden Gate Ferry), p. 427.]

CROSSING TIME: 15 mins. catamaran; 30 mins. monohull

FERRY TYPE: Pedestrian

VESSEL CAPACITY: [For notes on capacity of the ships in the Red and White Fleet, please see entry under San Francisco-Alcatraz, p. 419.]

OPERATING SEASON: All year

SCHEDULE: **Mon.-Fri. (except holidays): Lv. San Francisco (Pier 41)** 11:20 a.m., 12:40 p.m., 2, 3:15, 4:50. **Lv. Sausalito** 11:45 a.m., 1:05

p.m., 2:20, 3:40, 5:30. **Sat., Sun., and holidays: Lv. Pier 41** 11:05 a.m., 12:30 p.m., 2, 3:30, 5, *6:20. **Lv. Sausalito** 11:30 a.m., 12:55 p.m., 2:25, 3:55, 5:25, 6:45. *Operates April 1-Sept. 30 only. *Holidays: Washington's Birthday, Memorial, Independence, and Labor Day. No service Thanksgiving, Christmas, and New Year's Day.*

RESTRICTIONS: On catamarans, smoking on outer decks only

FACILITIES: Restrooms, snack bar including full beverage service

FARE: Adults $3.50; children (5-11) $1.75; under 5 free.

RESERVATIONS: No

DIRECTIONS: Fisherman's Wharf, Pier 41, is reached by cable car (Powell and Mason, 3 blks.; Powell & Hyde, 3 blks.) or from the Ferry Building (Muni Bus #32).

MAP LOCATION: P. 399, CA, 14

CONTACT: Red and White Fleet, Pier 41, San Francisco, CA 94133, Sausalito (415)788-1880, Tiburon (415)546-2815

STATE: California

PLACES SERVED: San Francisco—Tiburon

BODY OF WATER: San Francisco Bay

FERRY SERVICE HISTORY: Ferry service to Tiburon has a long history, for the scenic cove was a crossroads for ferry and train travelers until the last train pulled out in 1967. The San Francisco and North Pacific Railroad was completed to Tiburon in 1884, and the single-ender *James M. Donahue* (built 1875) began service to San Francisco, with passengers and cargo transferred from trains. The ferry steamer *Tiburon* also served on this run. Another ship was the *Antelope,* made immortal on April 15, 1860, when she carried the first pouch of Pony Express mail on the last western segment of the initial pony run from Sacramento to San Francisco.

The Red and White fleet has a high-speed *CataMarin* on this run. The

company began a special "Tiburon Evening Express" (weekends and holidays only) service in July 1986. This was a cooperative effort with five Tiburon restaurants (the Caprice, Christopher's, The Dock, Guaymas, and Sam's Anchor Cafe) to make the town more accessible to San Francisco visitors and residents during the evening hours.

[For further notes on the history of the Red and White Fleet, please see entry under San Francisco-Alcatraz, p. 419. For further notes on the history of San Francisco ferries, please see entry under San Francisco-Sausalito (Golden Gate Ferry), p. 426.]

LOCAL POINTS OF INTEREST: [For notes on San Francisco, please see entry under San Francisco-Alcatraz, p. 419.]

If Sausalito has been discovered and restrained, Tiburon seems to be rather on the verge of disclosure — but still in a state of naive charm. The diminutive Main Street does, it is true, have boutiques and restaurants, but just a half-block away, Upper Main Street becomes Ark Row. The parking lot in back of it was once a lagoon, where Victorian houseboats floated placidly, inhabited by fishermen. They have come to rest on shore as converted dwellings and shops. Amid trees and little foot bridges, there is an unhurried atmosphere; one can browse at will in such shops as the Piping Frog. Recently, a developer was given permission to build small condominiums on the waterfront, a condition being the paving and renovation of the promenade, which is now pleasant for walking. Good restaurants are the Caprice, with tables directly over the water (at the far end of the promenade, away from the ferry landing), and Sam's Anchor Cafe. Sam's is the "in" place for seafood; it is entered through an unpretentious bar that suddenly gives way to a deck with pretty umbrella tables. Tiburon once furnished the workmen and mechanics for Belvedere, just above, an elite little mountain community wrapped in narrow roads and posh cottages and villas in a variety of styles, some contemporary and others looking as though they are straight out of "Hansel and Gretel."

CROSSING TIME: 20 mins. (commuting ferry from Ferry Bldg.); 35 mins. (with Sausalito stop)

FERRY TYPE: Pedestrian

VESSEL CAPACITY: [For notes on capacity of the ships in the Red and White Fleet, please see entry under San Francisco-Alcatraz, p. 419.]

OPERATING SEASON: All year

SCHEDULE: *San Francisco departures are from the Ferry Bldg., north side, weekday mornings and evenings; from Pier 41, Fisherman's Wharf, weekday mid-day hours and weekends.* **Mon.-Fri. mornings (excluding holidays): Lv. Ferry Bldg.** 7:10 a.m., 8. **Lv. Tiburon** 6:45 a.m., 7:35, 8:25. **Mon.-Fri. evenings (excluding holidays): Lv. Ferry Bldg.** 4:25 p.m., 5:15, 6:05, 7:10. **Lv. Tiburon** 5:05 p.m., 5:40, 6:30, *8. **Mon.-Fri. (excluding holidays), mid-day (ferry also stops at Sausalito): Lv. Pier 41** 11:20 a.m., 12:40 p.m., 2; **Lv. Sausalito** 11:45 a.m., 1:05 p.m., 2:20. **Lv. Tiburon** 12:05 p.m., 1:25 p.m., 2:30. **Sat.-Sun. & holidays: Lv. Pier 41** 10:50 a.m., 12:20 p.m., 1:50, 3:15, 4:50. **Lv. Sausalito** 11:20 a.m., 12:50 p.m., 2:20, 3:50, 5:20. **Lv. Tiburon** 11:40 a.m., 1:10 p.m., 2:40, 4:10, 5:40. **Tiburon Evening Express (Weekends and holidays only): Lv. Pier 41** 5 p.m., 6:45, 8:25, 10:10. **Lv. Ferry Bldg.** 5:25 p.m., 7:05, 8:50, 10:35, 11:55. **Lv. Tiburon** 6:05 p.m., 7:45, 9:30, 11:15. *Operates March 1-Sept. 30. *No service Thanksgiving, Christmas, or New Year's.*

RESTRICTIONS: On catamarans, smoking on outer decks only

FACILITIES: Restrooms, snack bar including full beverage service

FARE: Adults $3.05, child under 5 free; special commuter books available. Tiburon Evening Express fares: $7 round-trip ($2 refund when validated by one of the participating restaurants).

RESERVATIONS: No

DIRECTIONS: The Ferry Bldg. is at the foot of Market St. Fisherman's Wharf, Pier 41, is reached by cable car (Powell and Mason, 3 blks.; Powell & Hyde, 3 blks.) or from the Ferry Building (Muni Bus #32).

MAP LOCATION: P. 399, CA, 15

CONTACT: See CONTACT, p. 430.

STATE: California

PLACES SERVED: San Francisco—Vallejo

BODY OF WATER: San Francisco Bay

FERRY SERVICE HISTORY: The vessel used on this newly established service is the *CataMarin,* designed in Australia. She has two hulls, fastened together with a space between them and was built by the Nichols Boat Builders of Freeland, Washington; she is eighty-six feet long. The ship's thin hulls encounter little friction while gliding through the water and can reach a speed of thirty knots. She is furnished with upholstered chairs, complimenting tables, a full bar, and snack counter. Commuters are expected to save eighty to ninety minutes per day over driving. The company had been running trips to Vallejo since the Marine World Africa USA theme park opened in early 1986, but the commuter service did not begin until September 1986, after the new boat was delivered.

It was near Vallejo that two of the largest ferries ever to operate within the Golden Gate, the *Solano* and *Contra Costa,* were used to carry whole trains between Benicia and Port Costa. They were over four hundred feet long, with four parallel tracks on which the cars were loaded. The service was inaugurated in 1879 by the Central Pacific and shortened the Sacramento/Oakland rail distance by more than fifty miles. In 1930 the ferries were replaced by a steel lift-span bridge. The "Six-Minute Ferry" was also near Vallejo; it operated from Morrow Cove to Crockett. The new service brings a reminder of the old Monticello Steamship Company service using the *Calistoga* (ex-*Florida*).

LOCAL POINTS OF INTEREST: [For notes on San Francisco, see entry under San Francisco-Alcatraz, p. 419.]
Vallejo lies at the junction of the Carquinez

Straits and the Napa River; it was founded by Gen. Mariano Guadalupe Vallejo, a citizen of California under both the Mexican and US governments. The town was California's capital in 1852 and again in 1853. It is now flourishing once more, with a large Hilton hotel and convention facility in the planning stage, new condos, and other development. The city manager, Michael Lynch, said at the opening of the new service, "We have never been recognized as part of the Bay Area. Now we have a sixty-minute connection to the San Francisco Financial District. It ties us in directly. . . . Vallejo is the hub of the North Bay." With water, freeways, and land, the city seems decidedly destined for expansion.

Sadly, the new ferry came just four days after the oldest continuously operating ferry on the West Coast, from Vallejo to the Mare Island, suspended operations because of a dispute with the Navy over its floating docks. The Mare Island Ferry had been established in 1854 by Capt. David Farragut and had been operated by the Raahauge family for sixty-two years. The Mare Island Shipyard is a twenty-three hundred-acre facility, the Navy's main Pacific Coast base.

CROSSING TIME: 60 mins.

FERRY TYPE: Pedestrian

VESSEL CAPACITY: 406 passengers

OPERATING SEASON: All year

SCHEDULE: **Vallejo-Ferry Building, San Francisco: Weekdays: Lv. Vallejo** 6:05 a.m., 7, **6:25 p.m., 8. Lv. Ferry Building, San Francisco** 5:15 p.m., 6:15, 7:55, 9:25. **Vallejo (Marine World Africa USA)-Fisherman's Wharf (Pier 41), San Francisco: Weekdays: Lv. Pier 41** 9:10 a.m., 11:50, 2:10 p.m. **Lv. Vallejo** 10:20 a.m., 1 p.m., 3:40, 6:25. **Sat., Sun. and holidays: Lv. Pier 41** 9 a.m., 11:45, 2:15 p.m., 5, 6:25, 7:50, 10:15. **Lv. Vallejo** 7:30 a.m., 9, 10:15, 1 p.m., 3:45, 6:35, 9:05.

RESTRICTIONS: On catamarans, smoking on outer decks only

FACILITIES: Restrooms, snack bar including full beverage service

FARE: Adults $5.95; children $3; senior citizens $5.45. Commuter books available.

RESERVATIONS: No

DIRECTIONS:	In San Francisco, the ferry leaves from the Ferry Building or Pier 41, according to the time of day and destination.
MAP LOCATION:	P. 399, CA, 16
CONTACT:	See CONTACT, p. 421.

STATE:	California
PLACES SERVED:	Tiburon—Angel Island
BODY OF WATER:	San Francisco Bay
FERRY SERVICE HISTORY:	This service was begun in 1957 by Milt McDonogh, who is the present owner. There are two vessels, the wooden-hulled *Gaycin* and the steel-hulled *Angel Island*.
LOCAL POINTS OF INTEREST:	[For notes on Tiburon, please see entry under San Francisco-Tiburon, p. 431. For notes on Angel Island, please see entry under San Francisco-Angel Island, p. 422.]
CROSSING TIME:	15 mins.
FERRY TYPE:	Pedestrian
VESSEL CAPACITY:	*Gaycin:* 49 passengers; *Angel Island:* 400 passengers
OPERATING SEASON:	All year, weather permitting
SCHEDULE:	**Weekends: Lv. Tiburon** every hour on the hour, 10 a.m.-6 p.m.; **lv. Angel Island** 15 mins. after the hour. **Weekdays: Lv.**

Tiburon every two hours, 10 a.m.-4 p.m.; **lv. Angel Island** every two hours 15 mins. after the hour.

RESTRICTIONS:	No dogs
FACILITIES:	Snack bar (restrooms available for longer trips; boats may also be chartered)

FARE:	Round-trip: adults $3; children $2 (5-11); children free under 5 if accompanied by an adult; bicycles $0.50
RESERVATIONS:	No
DIRECTIONS:	Ferry leaves from 21 Main St., Tiburon and from the Ayala Cove Dock on Angel Island.
MAP LOCATION:	P. 399, CA, 17
CONTACT:	Milt McDonogh, Tiburon-Angel Island Ferry, 21 Main St., Tiburon, CA 94920, (415)435-2131

STATE:	California
PLACES SERVED:	Two Harbors (Santa Catalina Island)—San Pedro (Catalina Channel Express)
BODY OF WATER:	San Pedro Channel
FERRY SERVICE HISTORY:	[For description of vessels and notes on ferry service history, please see entry under Avalon-San Pedro (Catalina Channel Express), p. 405.]
LOCAL POINTS OF INTEREST:	Two Harbors is foreseen as a future year-round residential and boating resort; it is the site of the UCLA Marine Science Center.

Several land and sea safari tours are offered, as well as a nature hike. [For futher notes on Santa Catalina and Avalon, please see entry under Avalon-Newport, p. 404. For notes on San Pedro, please see listing under Avalon-San Pedro (Catalina Channel Express), p. 407.]

CROSSING TIME:	90 mins.
FERRY TYPE:	Pedestrian
VESSEL CAPACITY:	60-149 passengers, according to vessel used
OPERATING SEASON:	All year

SCHEDULE: Lv. Two Harbors Wed.-Mon.: 2 p.m. Also Sun.: 6:30 Fri.: 8:15 Lv. San Pedro Wed.-Mon.: noon. Also Sun.: 4:30 Fri.: 6:30. *Additional holiday departures; call company.*

RESTRICTIONS: See RESTRICTIONS, p. 402.

FACILITIES: Cocktail and refreshment service, color TV, deckhands to help with luggage; private stateroom available on the three larger ships.

FARE: Adults $12.50; children (2-11) $7.50; children under 2 $0.50; senior citizens (55 +) $10.50.

RESERVATIONS: Recommended for boat. Advance reservations for accommodation in Avalon needed (contact Catalina Island Chamber of Commerce, Box 217, Avalon, CA 90704; 213/510-1520).

DIRECTIONS: Take Harbor Freeway (Rt. 110) south to San Pedro. Take Harbor Blvd. off ramp. Follow Catalina signs across Harbor Blvd. From Long Beach, drive Ocean Blvd. west over Vincent Thomas Bridge and take first off ramp at San Pedro end. Ship is at Berth 95.

MAP LOCATION: P. 399, CA, 18

CONTACT: Catalina Channel Express, Box 1391, San Pedro, CA 90733, San Pedro: (213)519-1212, On the Island: (213)510-1212

STATE: California

PLACES SERVED: Upper Jones Tract—Woodward Island

BODY OF WATER: Middle River

FERRY SERVICE HISTORY: Service on this crossing has existed since 1934. The vessel has no formal name, but is a steel-hulled, cable-propelled boat, twenty feet by fifty feet, operated by a crew of one. Like the one connecting

Empire Tract with Venice Island, it is administered by the San Joaquin County Department of Public Works. Most riders come from Stockton, California.

LOCAL POINTS OF INTEREST: The surrounding area is known as the San Joaquin River Delta; a more complete description of the Delta may be found in the entry under Grand Island-Ryer Island, p. 413.

CROSSING TIME: 5 mins.

FERRY TYPE: Vehicle

VESSEL CAPACITY: 6 cars

OPERATING SEASON: All year

SCHEDULE: Daily, on signal, 8 a.m.-noon and 1 p.m.-5.

RESTRICTIONS: Trailers, pickup-campers, and RVs permitted. Load limit 30 tons.

FACILITIES: None

FARE: Free

RESERVATIONS: No

DIRECTIONS: Take Bacon Island Road to the ferry, approximately 4 miles west of SR 4.

MAP LOCATION: P. 399, CA, 19

CONTACT: See CONTACT, p. 412.

STATE: California

PLACES SERVED: Vallejo—Angel Island

BODY OF WATER: San Francisco Bay

FERRY SERVICE HISTORY: This service was established in 1986.

LOCAL POINTS OF INTEREST: [For notes on Angel Island, please see entry under San Francisco-Angel Island, p. 422. For notes on Vallejo, please see entry under San Francisco-Vallejo, p. 433.]

CROSSING TIME: 50 mins.

FERRY TYPE: Pedestrian

VESSEL CAPACITY: [For notes on capacity of the ships in the Red and White Fleet, please see entry under San Francisco-Alcatraz, p. 419.]

OPERATING SEASON: All year

SCHEDULE: **Weekdays: Lv. Vallejo** 10 a.m. **Lv. Angel Island** 2:40 p.m. **Sat., Sun., Holidays: Lv. Vallejo** 9 a.m. **Lv. Angel Island** 2:25 p.m.

RESTRICTIONS: On catamarans, smoking on outer decks only

FACILITIES: Restrooms, snack bar including full beverage service

FARE: Adults $5.95 (round-trip $8.95); children 4-11 $3 (round-trip $4.95); commuter books and group rates available

RESERVATIONS: No

DIRECTIONS: Ferry leaves Vallejo at Georgia Street Wharf, Mare Island Way between Florida and Maine Sts.

MAP LOCATION: P. 399, CA, 20

CONTACT: See CONTACT, p. 421.

STATE:	Montana
PLACES SERVED:	Carter (5 miles south)—Secondary state road
BODY OF WATER:	Missouri River

FERRY SERVICE HISTORY: As early as 1832, steamboats appeared on the Missouri River, but they were not built with a sufficiently shallow draft to reach Fort Benton until 1859. Even so, the channel was torturous, filled with snags, sand bars, and rapidly changing water levels because of storms high up in the mountains. A steamboat might anchor in sufficient water, only to be on dry land by morning. Nevertheless, the river was the major waterway route to the Rocky Mountains west from the time of Lewis and Clark until the coming of the railroads in the 1800s. The topography is still extremely varied.

The Carter and Loma ferries, as well as the one at Virgelle, are under the jurisdiction of Chouteau County. The Carter and Loma ferries are 50.8 feet long by sixteen feet wide, powered by a 1945 vintage four-cylinder water-cooled International "F-Cub" ten-horsepower gas engine. The motor is mounted on a skid frame so that it can be slid into place and bolted down. The right hand wheel is removed and the axle drive blocked off, then a thirty-inch concave-surfaced steel wheel is mounted to the left side for the transmission of power. A three-eighths-inch steel cable goes around the wheel, pulling into the cable, which is anchored on each side of the river and suspended across it; in effect, there is a power winch pulling the boat across the river. The amount of water released by the electric power dams at Canyon Ferry and Great Falls causes variations in water level of as much as eighteen inches in twenty-four hours. The earlier ferries did not have a power cable, but were angled by the operators to take advantage of the river current. Each day the ferry operators must check the bottom of the boat to make sure it has not hit a rock and sprung a leak. The operators sign a twenty-four hour per day obligation contract; a house and utilities are furnished. The Carter and Loma ferries haul more grain trucks than the Virgelle ferry.

LOCAL POINTS OF INTEREST: Carter is a small town between Great Falls and Fort Benton. Of interest nearby are Great Falls and Giant Springs State Park. The Great Falls of the Missouri River were first seen by Capt. Meriwether Lewis on June 13, 1805; the following day, exploring alone, he was chased by a grizzly bear but escaped by plunging into the river and wielding his espontoon, a spearlike weapon. Lewis discovered the Giant Springs on June 19 of the same year. They discharge, every twenty-four hours, over 300 million gallons of water at a constant temperature of fifty-two degrees F. (Indians believed the spring gushed from a lake in the skies where the Sun had his tepee.) The works of Charles M. Russell, the cowboy artist, may be seen at the Charles M. Russell Museum and Original Studio in Great Falls. To the south is the Lewis and Clark National Forest.

CROSSING TIME:	3-5 mins.
FERRY TYPE:	Vehicle
VESSEL CAPACITY:	2 cars
OPERATING SEASON:	Mid-Mar.-mid-Nov.
SCHEDULE:	On signal, 24 hours per day
RESTRICTIONS:	Trailers, pickup-campers, and RVs permitted. Load limit 10-15 tons. Car/trailer combined length 36 ft.
FACILITIES:	None
FARE:	Free Mon.-Sat. 7 a.m.-7 p.m. and Sun. 9 a.m.-5 p.m. $2 Mon.-Sat. 7 p.m.-7 a.m. and 5 p.m.-9 a.m. Sun.
RESERVATIONS:	No
DIRECTIONS:	The ferry is 5 mile south of Carter. From Great Falls the ferry is just off I-87.
MAP LOCATION:	P. 399, MT, 1
CONTACT:	Chouteau County Clerk and Recorder, Box 459, Fort Benton, MT 59442, (406)622-5151

STATE:	Montana
PLACES SERVED:	Chinook (60 miles south)—Winifred (15 miles north of town) ("The McLelland Ferry," also called "The Stafford Ferry")

BODY OF WATER: Missouri River

FERRY SERVICE HISTORY: This ferry crossing has existed since 1916, though it was, at first, located one and one-half miles upriver from its present location. On the north side of the river, it is known as "The McLelland Ferry," and on the south side it is called "The Stafford Ferry." It is registered with the Coast Guard as "The McLelland Ferry." The ferry was privately run until 1939, when the county took over the operation. For twenty years Leona and Kenneth Gilmore have operated it (for the last seven years, Leona has run it as well as her husband). They live at the ferry during the season, and, though technically the hours are from 7 a.m. through 7 p.m., they are on call twenty-four hours a day. Leona Gilmore says one of the most unusual cargoes carried was a mule pack train going from Mexico to Canada. An Alaskan on horseback, following the Nez Perce trail, also crossed on the ferry. The location is marked on boating and floating maps of the river as The Stafford Ferry. It is on the Lewis and Clark Trail and has boat launching facilities and toilets. It has two low cables, and boaters are asked to beware of them. The Virgelle and Loma ferries also have low cables. The ferry is now administered by Blaine County.

LOCAL POINTS OF INTEREST: Chinook, founded in 1888, was named for the Indian word for the January and February winds that whip through the area, melting the snow and exposing the grass for cattle grazing. The Blaine County Museum contains exhibits on Chief Joseph Battleground, honoring the leader of the Nez Perce Indians, who surrendered to Gen. Nelson Miles in 1877 after a seventeen hundred-mile retreat through some of the most rugged territory in the West. The Chief Joseph Battleground of the Bear's Paw State Monument is the site of the surrender, marked by his famous and poignant speech: "From where the sun now stands, I will fight no more forever."

This ferry is between the White Rocks area of the Missouri River and the Badlands. The Missouri River was the major waterway route to the Rocky Mountains west from the time of Lewis and Clark until the coming of the railroads in the late 1800s. Lewis and Clark camped at several places along the river near here, including a spot quite near the ferry on May 27, 1805. Boating and floating down the river are popular activities here, and maps are available from the Bureau of Land Management in Lewiston (406/538-7461) with important information about clothing, water, etc. The Lewis and Clark Trail is well marked on these maps.

CROSSING TIME: 10 mins.

FERRY TYPE: Vehicle

VESSEL CAPACITY: 2 cars

OPERATING SEASON: Apr.-Oct.

SCHEDULE: On signal, 7 a.m.-7 p.m.

RESTRICTIONS: Trailers, pickup-campers, and RVs permitted. Load limit 18 tons. Car/trailer combined length maximum 36 ft.

FACILITIES: None

FARE: Free

RESERVATIONS: No

DIRECTIONS: The ferry is 60 miles south of Chinook and 15 miles north of Winifred. From Chinook, take SR 240 south, and then the secondary road through Lloyd. From Winifred, take the secondary road toward Lloyd.

MAP LOCATION: P. 399, MT, 2

CONTACT: Blaine County Road Dept., Chinook, MT 59523, (406)357-2840. (At the ferry, when operating): Mr. and Mrs. Kenneth Gilmore, (406)462-5513

STATE: Montana

PLACES SERVED: Loma (1 mile east)—Secondary state road

BODY OF WATER: Missouri River

FERRY SERVICE HISTORY: Material about the early history of the ferries on the Missouri near Fort Benton has been gathered by Joel F. Overholser of the *River Press* in Fort Benton; Henry O. Pope of the Earth Science Museum in Loma has also delved into the subject. At Fort Benton, according to Overholser, there was an ancient Indian ford. Employees of Fort Benton and Fort Campbell used to cross the river here to reach the Highwood Mountains to cut and transport lumber. In 1875, Ed Smith launched a ferry at the crossing, presumably large enough to transport a wagon and horses; he sold the ferry in 1883. After the Indian wars, more settlers arrived, and by 1881, according to the *Benton Record*, there was a second ferry operating a block away. The opening of the bridge in 1888 ended the Fort Benton ferry business. There were also ferries across the Sun River.

On the Marias River, a short distance above present Loma, Moses Solomon operated a ferry in the 1880s and 1890s; at least one man thought the tolls too high and swam his horse across. The Loma ferry is thought to have been two and one-half miles downriver from its present location. A retired rancher, Walt Wesche, took over the operation of the Loma ferry in 1973. In 1979, he was interviewed by Marcia Bumann for the *Great Falls Tribune*. The ferry is run by Chouteau County, which provides a small house on the south side of the river for the operator to stay in during the week-long shifts. "It's real comfortable," Wesche said. "It's got groceries, a bed, and even a good stove." Usually, the ferry can operate only from April to November because of ice. In summer, traffic consists of farmers and custom cutters hauling grain, as well as passengers from all over the western states and "as far east as New York." Thick cables connect the ferry to supports on either bank, and it is powered by an engine. Wesche said he talked with hunters and river floaters between trips. "I'm a happy man, doing something I like," he added. [For further information about the Loma ferry, see description under the Carter ferry, p. 440.]

LOCAL POINTS OF INTEREST: Loma is at the confluence of the Missouri and Marias Rivers. The Indians called the Marias "the River that scolds all others," but Capt. Meriwether Lewis renamed it in honor of his cousin Maria Wood (it was originally "Maria's River"). The Lewis and Clark party camped here nine days here in June 1805, and the water level was so high they were unable to determine which was the Missouri. They made the correct choice, fortunately, and continued westward. The Earth Science Museum in Loma displays many mineral specimens, fossils, and rare Indian artifacts.

Fort Benton is one of the oldest communities in Montana. It was a campsite in 1805 for Capt. William Clark, and in 1846 it was founded as a fur trading post. It continues as a trading center today. Of interest here is the Museum of the Upper Missouri River, which has dioramas and exhibits of early trading and river steamers.

CROSSING TIME: 3-5 mins.

FERRY TYPE: Vehicle

VESSEL CAPACITY: 2 cars

OPERATING SEASON: Mid-Mar.-mid-Nov.

SCHEDULE:	On signal, 24 hours per day.
RESTRICTIONS:	Trailers, pickup-campers, and RVs permitted. Load limit 10-15 tons. Car/trailer combined length 36 ft.
FACILITIES:	None
FARE:	See FARE, p. 441.
RESERVATIONS:	No
DIRECTIONS:	The ferry is 1 mi. east of Loma. From Fort Benton the ferry is just off US 87. Going north, there is a large sign just before you

cross the Marias River bridge, indicating that the Loma Ferry is 1 mile away.

MAP LOCATION:	P. 399, MT, 3
CONTACT:	See CONTACT, p. 441.

STATE:	Montana
PLACES SERVED:	Virgelle—secondary state road
BODY OF WATER:	Missouri River
FERRY SERVICE HISTORY:	Joel F. Overholser of the Fort Benton *River Press* has done research on the history of the Virgelle ferry in the early issues of the news-

paper. He found a mention on April 16, 1913, that a ferry was to be placed at Virgelle. On July 9, 1913, it was announced that J. C. Meyers was to build the ferry for $1050 and that V. F. Blackenbaker and others were to operate it. It is possible this ferry was a replacement for one lost to ice. According to the Chouteau County Clerk's Office, on April 4, 1917, a Mr. Joe Plutt was appointed ferryman and had to post a $500 bond. The present vessel is 50.8 feet long and eighteen feet wide. Today, the ferry is operated by Chouteau County, as are the Carter and Loma ferries.

LOCAL POINTS OF INTEREST:	Virgelle had a post office which operated from 1902 until 1961, with Edward Stehley as postmaster. The name of the town is a

combination of Virgil and Ella Blackenbaker, a prominent sheep rancher and former state senator. The Virgelle Ferry, along with the Loma and McLelland (at Winifred) ferries, are within the 149-mile stretch of the Upper Missouri designated the Upper Missouri National Wild and Scenic River. This area was designated a member of the National Wild and Scenic River System in 1976 because of its rich wildlife, scenic, historic and recreation values. A priceless remnant of primitive America, the upper Missouri remains much the same as it was when Lewis and Clark explored it in 1805. The designated route stretches from Fort Benton to the James Kipp Recreation Area on the west end of the Charles M. Russell National Wildlife Refuge. The Virgelle Mercantile, an old general store with antiques, gives visitors a look at homesteading days in Montana.

CROSSING TIME: 3-5 mins.

FERRY TYPE: Vehicle

VESSEL CAPACITY: 2 cars

OPERATING SEASON: Mid-Mar.-mid-Nov.

SCHEDULE: On signal, 24 hours per day.

RESTRICTIONS: See RESTRICTIONS, p. 441.

FACILITIES: None

FARE: See FARE, p. 441.

RESERVATIONS: No

DIRECTIONS: The ferry is at Virgelle, east of Loma and just south of the Rocky Boys Indian Reservation.

MAP LOCATION: P. 399, MT, 4

CONTACT: See CONTACT, p. 441.

Edgewater Casino

STATE:	Nevada/Arizona
PLACES SERVED:	Laughlin, NV—Bullhead City, AZ
BODY OF WATER:	Colorado River

FERRY SERVICE HISTORY: The five major casinos in Laughlin operate a fleet over about twenty-five small ferries to bring people from Bullhead City, where there is a parking facility, to Laughlin. The alternative is a drive over about twenty-five miles of twisting road across Davis Dam. The casinos all have a full complement of slot machines, keno, roulette, craps, and other games.

Among the casinos are:

The Edgewater Hotel & Casino. In 1986, the Edgewater finished construction of the newest dock on the river, constructed by United McGill (which builds offshore oil platforms). The Edgewater has five ferries in service, running twenty-four hours a day. Among the offerings at Edgewater are 602 rooms, a snack bar with sixteen flavors of ice cream, and a bowling center.

The Riverside Resort and Casino. This casino began using ferries in 1969; these early boats served the River Queen Motel Landing in Arizona and were eight foot by twenty-four foot pontoon boats powered by eighty-five horsepower motors, with a capacity of ten to twelve people. Since 1979, the Riverside has had a parking lot at Bullhead City, allowing transportation to the Bullhead City airport plus the River Queen Motel. The casino built the first ten foot by thirty foot pontoons, transporting thirty-two people, and now has seven in use. Three run to the River Queen (fifteen minutes), one to the airport dock (seven minutes), and the others to the parking lot. In 1985, the Riverside boats transported nearly a million and a half people to the Riverside Casino, which has 352 rooms, movie theaters, and twenty-four hour restaurants. The service is also used by employees, who are saved twelve miles a day driving. The boats are not named, but go by numbers.

Sam's Town Gold River, which has four boats, named for its restaurants (*Smokey Joe*, *Sutter's Mill*, *Vanderbilt*, and *River Ratt*). They are Starlite pontoon boats equipped with 150 horsepower outboard motors; they carry thirty people per boat. Sam's Town has 225 rooms, the all-night Vanderbilt's Dance Hall, and Smokey Joe's, a twenty-four hour cafe.

LOCAL POINTS OF INTEREST: Laughlin has been called a "mini-Baghdad-by-the-Colorado River." Not long ago, the site was a dusty speck across from the drowsy little hamlet of Bullhead City. Today, Laughlin has mushroomed as fast as any town in the bonanza mining era. In the late 1960s, Don Laughlin, an enterprising ex-Minnesotan, piloted his private plane over this remote spot across the Colorado River and speculated that residents of Kingman, Bullhead City, and Lake Havasu City, as well as Needles in California, might be willing to cross the Colorado to gamble. He bought a small club, which eventually became the Riverside. Another developer, Robert Bilbray, a Las Vegas lawyer, has been astonished at the growth of Laughlin: "Every projection I've made about Laughlin since I bought my land here in 1978 has taken half the [predicted] time to happen," he says. The present casinos are expanding, and new ones are in the planning stages. The town is just below popular Lake Mohave and not far from Lake Havasu, each a mecca for fishermen and water sportsmen. Much of Laughlin is federal property, but, even so, the infusion of gambling money ensures phenomenal growth.

CROSSING TIME: 2 mins. to Bullhead City; 7 mins. to airport dock; 15 mins. to River Queen Motel

FERRY TYPE: Pedestrian

VESSEL CAPACITY: 32 passengers

OPERATING SEASON: All year

SCHEDULE: Continuously, 24 hrs. per day

RESTRICTIONS: No

FACILITIES: None

FARE: Free

RESERVATIONS: No

DIRECTIONS: Ferries leave from casino docks

MAP LOCATION: P. 399, NV, 1

CONTACT: Edgewater Hotel & Casino (800)634-6154; Sam's Town Gold River Hotel & Casino (800)835-7903; Riverside Resort Hotel & Casino (800)227-3849—All in Laughlin, NV 89046

STATE: Texas

PLACES SERVED: Galveston—Port Bolivar

BODY OF WATER: Galveston Bay

FERRY SERVICE HISTORY: Proud ferrymen say that the Galveston-Bolivar ferry is the safest link in the Texas highway system, as well as the most picturesque. On its three-mile route extending Highway 87 to Galveston, the free ferry passes the city skyline, the swaying palm trees, and an occasional ocean-going freighter; the ride, it is said, has all of the excitement of a Caribbean cruise and none of the expense. Service was inaugurated in 1930, after discussion for fifteen years; Galveston had not, previously, had highway connections with the rapidly developing areas of Southeast Texas and Louisiana. In April of that year a private ferry began service; the *Galveston News* recorded the event: "With the inauguration of regular ferry service between Galveston and Bolivar today, Treasure Island's long-cherished desire for a highway connection with the outside world, independent of Houston, is fulfilled." The Highway Department soon took over the service, putting the *R. S. Sterling* and *Cone Johnson* into use. Fred Wemple, Chairman of the State Highway Commission, stated that they would become a vital part of the highway system, as Highway 87 "is one of the most important in the state, connecting the rich Texas industrial areas with the ports and refineries." At that time an average of 790 cars used the ferries, and the new boats were expected to speed up the traffic by 50 percent.

The *E. H. Thornton*, built by Burton Shipyard in Port Authur, Texas, joined the fleet in 1959. All three were 185 feet long and fifty-five feet wide, powered by two Cooper Bessemer diesel 865-horsepower engines. In 1977, the boats were lengthened sixty feet and widened eleven feet; they are now 245 feet long and sixty-six feet wide. The *Gibb Gilchrist*, the newest ship, was built in Jefferson, Indiana, by Jeffboat, Inc., in 1979. All were named for former highway commissioners. The service operates continuously. Since they were introduced, the ferries have endeared themselves to natives and visitors alike. "I've ridden the ferry five times this week. I love it," a Tennessee tourist told a reporter for *Texas Highways*. "This is something different. And there's not a soul on the beaches for miles." Bill Manes, former ferry manager, once told of an inebriated man who approached the crossing, stopped, then exclaimed, "There's a hole in the road and it's full of water!" "That's Galveston Bay and this is the ferry crossing," he was told. Capt. Robert F. Ewels is now the ferry manager. He says the most dramatic crossings are when babies are born aboard (this has happened numerous times). Riders include tourists, schoolchildren (who sometimes draw pictures of the experience and send them back), shift workers, and local residents. The trip is a 2.3 mile extension of SR 87. The ride is particularly beautiful at night.

LOCAL POINTS OF INTEREST: Few cities have had more dramatic origins than Galveston. The first European to discover Texas, Cabeza de Vaca, was shipwrecked on Galveston Island in 1528. Don Luis Aury arrived in 1816 with a fleet of fifteen vessels; he claimed the island for Mexico, but while on a raid against Spanish vessels was displaced by the pirate Jean Lafitte, who was lord of Galveston from 1817 until 1821. At this time, the city was rife with slave traders, saloon keepers, gamblers, smugglers, and pirates. In the late 1800s, Galveston was known as the "Queen City of the Gulf." It had an opera house, electric lights, and a country club, and a downtown called by the *New York Times* "The Wall Street of the Southwest.'' The hurricane of September 1900 devastated the city (six thousand people were killed and a four thousand-ton vessel was washed twenty-two miles away), but Galveston citizens rebuilt, raising the level of land with fill and constructing a seventeen-foot high seawall, topped by a boulevard, which has withstood subsequent storms. Today, preservation is rampant, gracefully co-existing with new development. Forty blocks of the East End Historical District have been protected. The Strand National Historic District is a fine concentration of Victorian commercial buildings, restored to its mid-1800s appearance and occupied by shops, restaurants, art galleries, and fashionable apartments.

Attractions today include the *Elissa* (a restored Scottish barque built in 1877), performances at the Grand Opera House, Seawolf Park, the Railroad Museum, and thirty-two miles of sandy beach, with several fishing piers. The Treasure Isle Tour Train makes a seventeen-mile trip around the city. A hand-painted trolley, the *Galveston Flyer*, also makes a tour circuit. *The Colonel*, a three-deck paddlewheeler, offers two-hour narrated cruises of Galveston Bay.

The Bolivar Peninsula has unfenced beaches, summer houses on stilts, fishing jetties, and a century-old lighthouse.

CROSSING TIME: 13 mins.

FERRY TYPE: Vehicle

VESSEL CAPACITY: *R. S. Sterling*: 65 cars; *Cone Johnson*: 65 cars; *E. H. Thornton*: 70 cars; *Gibb Gilchrist*: 70 cars.

OPERATING SEASON: All year

SCHEDULE: **24 hrs. a day: Lv. Galveston** approximately every 20 mins. 6 a.m.-9:20 p.m.; every hour 11 p.m.-6 a.m.; **Lv. Bolivar** approximately every 20 mins. 6:20 a.m. to 10:40 p.m.; every hour 11:30 p.m. to 5:30 a.m. *During rush periods boats leave when loaded.*

RESTRICTIONS: Trailers, pickup-campers, and RVs permitted. Load limit 80,000 lbs. Maximum combined length 65 ft. No flammable or explosive material.

FACILITIES: None

FARE: Free

RESERVATIONS: No

DIRECTIONS: The ferry crosses to Galveston from SR 87 (coming in from the east).

MAP LOCATION: P. 399, TX, 1

CONTACT: State Dept. of Highways & Public Transpor-
                     tation, Galveston-Bolivar Ferry Operations,
                     Box 381, Galveston, TX 77553,
                     (713)763-2386

STATE: Texas

PLACES SERVED: Harbor Island—Port Aransas

BODY OF WATER: Aransas Pass

FERRY SERVICE   The ferry goes from Harbor Island to Port
HISTORY: Aransas, on Mustang Island. The six vessels
                     are the *Jack Kultgen*, the *D. C. Greer*,
the *H. C. Petry*, the *Hal Woodward*, the *Garrett Morriss* (all named for
Highway Commissioners), and the *Janie Brisico* (named for the wife of
Governor Brisico). The crossing goes back at least to the 1930s. For some
riders, the ride is all the more convivial for the camaraderie of the line to
get aboard the ferry. June Thedford of Corpus Christi says that her
teenagers will willingly wait in line for several hours, though they could
drive around to Port Aransas over the bridge; it is "the" place to meet
people.

LOCAL POINTS   Port Aransas is a picturesque fishing village
OF INTEREST: of about two thousand on Mustang Island,
                     between the Gulf of Mexico and Corpus
Christi Bay, about thirty minutes from Corpus Christi. Once populated by
the Karankawa Indians, who first roamed Mustang Island and called it
home, the island was settled in 1855 by English colonists; the original
name was Tarpon. In 1880 Confederate soldiers pirated the lighthouse
lens to prevent Union troops from using the light. Port Aransas is on the
Texas Tropical Trail, with excellent views of the tropical marshlands and
vistas of the Gulf. Various fishing tournaments are held here, and the full-
facility marina and Gulf and Channel Piers attract both yachtsmen and
fishermen. The University of Texas Marine Science Lab displays local
marine plants and animals. Port Aransas has been called "the place where
the fish bite every day." The famous Tarpon Inn, which opened in 1886,
has tarpon scales on the lobby wall. Many celebrities have stayed here,
including Franklin D. Roosevelt. Harbor Island is an industrial island,
with fuel tanks; there are no beaches or recreational facilities.

CROSSING TIME:	5 mins.
FERRY TYPE:	Vehicle
VESSEL CAPACITY:	9 cars
OPERATING SEASON:	All year
SCHEDULE:	On signal, 24 hrs. a day
RESTRICTIONS:	Trailers, pickup-campers, and RVs permitted. Load limit 20 tons. Flammable materials prohibited. Overhead clearance 12 ft.
FACILITIES:	None
FARE:	Free
RESERVATIONS:	No
DIRECTIONS:	The ferry connects segments of SR 361.
MAP LOCATION:	P. 399, TX, 2
CONTACT:	State Dept. of Highways, Box 447, Port Aransas, TX 78373, (512)749-5494.

STATE:	Texas
PLACES SERVED:	Los Ebanos—Mission ("The Los Ebanos Ferry")
BODY OF WATER:	Rio Grande River
FERRY SERVICE HISTORY:	The Los Ebanos ferry is the last hand-operated ferry on the US-Mexican border. It dates from 1950, but it is already legendary.

The first recorded crossing here was in 1740 by the Spanish explorer Jose De Escandon. In 1846 Gen. Zachary Taylor moved his army up river from Fort Brown and invaded Mexico from this spot. On December 8, 1950, Los Ebanos became a legal port of entry and the ferry was established. Prior to that time, the crossing, officially named the Cuevas Crossing, was notorious for smuggling, cattle rustling, and bootlegging.

Today, Mexican men pull the ferry, called a *chalan* (from the Indian *chala* or "small boat") across the river some 120 times a day. One of them, Rene Garcia Gutierrez, 40, has been pulling it for eighteen years. He was interviewed in 1985 by Leslie Pound for the *Dallas Morning News*. "Am I strong? . . . It's all muscle and a lot of *frijoles*," he told

Pound. The river at this point is twelve to fifteen feet deep and about one hundred yards across. Two men may be enough to pull the ferry to Mexico, but it may take up to five men to pull it back to the United States, depending on the river current.

The thick steel ferry cable is anchored to the historic Las Cuevas Ebony, a tree thought to be more than two hundred years old; a ribbed corset of staves keeps the cable from damaging the tree. The famous ebony, which has a historic plaque marking it and is listed in *Famous Trees of Texas*, towers over comfortable benches and offers shade to ferry patrons. As Maurine Duncan puts it in the *Upper Valley Progress,* it "seems to give testament to the privilege of giving protection to neighborly people crossing the river." The ferry is closed about four days a year when the water level is too high or too low. Today, the ferry is used mainly by local residents going to school, commuting to work, visiting relatives and shopping (for liquor, tortillas, sugar, and baskets in Ciudad Diaz Ordaz, Mexico; for groceries, clothing, appliances, and mechanical parts in Mission, Texas). It is also used by "Winter Texans" (the name natives give to Northerners who spend the winter in South Texas) who enjoy the novelty. There is talk of an international bridge. "It would be very bad to close the ferry," says the ferry manager, Albert Simo; it is co-owned by his sister-in-law, Sara Reyna of Mission and Armando Garza de la Garza, former mayor of Ciudad Diaz Ordaz. "The ferry needs to stay open for pedestrians and school kids," says Simo. "This is history."

LOCAL POINTS OF INTEREST: Mission is a friendly city located on the Texas-Mexico border amid citrus orchards and rich farmlands. Among the sites of interest here are the La Lomita Mission erected by the Oblate Fathers in 1849, on the Rio Grande, and, a mile beyond, Anzalduas Park, with more than one hundred acres of shade trees. Bentzen-Rio Grande State Park is five miles southwest of Mission; this is a bird-watcher's paradise. The South Texas Wildlife Museum and Restaurant serves excellent Texas barbecued beef.

Ciudad Diaz Ordaz has a population of about twenty thousand and is a quiet border town with a few shops and a noncommercial flavor.

CROSSING TIME:	5 mins.
FERRY TYPE:	Vehicle
VESSEL CAPACITY:	3 vehicles (cars, trucks, buses)
OPERATING SEASON:	All year
SCHEDULE:	Daily, 9 a.m.-4 p.m.
RESTRICTIONS:	Trailers, pickup-campers, and RVs permitted. Load limit 10 tons.
FACILITIES:	None
FARE:	Cars $1; passengers & pedestrians $.25
RESERVATIONS:	No
DIRECTIONS:	Los Ebanos is 14 miles west of Mission on US 83 and 3 miles south on FM 886. From the town, drive south to the river.
MAP LOCATION:	P. 399, TX, 3
CONTACT:	Albert Simo, PO Drawer A, Los Ebanos, TX 78565, (512)485-2721

STATE:	Texas
PLACES SERVED:	Port Aransas—San Jose Island
BODY OF WATER:	Corpus Christi Ship Channel
FERRY SERVICE HISTORY:	Service on this crossing is on a forty-foot iron jetty boat, which has been operated by Edward Sheppard for over fifteen years. (It is

thought the crossing goes back to the 1930s and beyond). "Most people like San Jose because it's isolated," says Sheppard. "I think it's one of the best beaches on the Texas Coast. There's no access by car, so you don't have to worry about traffic. And there are no cars to run over the shells." No motorized vehicles are allowed.

LOCAL POINTS OF INTEREST: [For notes on Port Aransas, please see entry under Harbor Island—Port Aransas, p. 452.] It is thought by historians that San Jose Island may have been discovered by the Spanish explorer Alvar Nunez Cabeza de Vaca, as the island's rolling dunes and white sand beach correlate with his description of the island where he was marooned for two years before reaching the mainland in 1530 and setting out on his cross-continental odyssey. It is tempting now to want to be marooned on San Jose Island, a twenty-one-mile-long strip of sand paralleling the Texas coast near Corpus Christi. The shelling is marvelous, including moon snails, sand dollars, clams, murex, and giant tulip; banded cockle are also found. Bring food and water, as there are no amenities on the island. The fishing off the North Jetty is superb. Fishermen try their luck for trout, redfish, flounder, and even shark.

CROSSING TIME: 15 mins.

FERRY TYPE: Pedestrian

VESSEL CAPACITY: 48 passengers

OPERATING SEASON: All year

SCHEDULE: **Daily. Lv. Port Aransas** 6:30 a.m., 7, then hourly until noon and again at 2 p.m., 4, and 6. **Lv. San Jose** 10:15 a.m., 12:15 p.m., 2:15, 4:15, 6:15 (also earlier trips if passengers have requested service over to the island). No service Christmas Day.

RESTRICTIONS: Small pets allowed

FACILITIES: None

FARE: Round-trip only; adults $7; children $4

RESERVATIONS: No

DIRECTIONS: Boat leaves from Woody's Boat Basin in Port Aransas

MAP LOCATION:	P. 399, TX, 4
CONTACT:	Mr. Edward Sheppard, Woody's Boat Basin, Box 27, Port Aransas, Texas 78373, (512)749-5271

John Atlantic Burr

STATE:	Utah
PLACES SERVED:	Bullfrog Marina (Glen Canyon)—Hall's Crossing Marina (connecting SR 276)
BODY OF WATER:	Lake Powell
FERRY SERVICE HISTORY:	Utah claims that this is the highest operating ferry in the country; it is thirty-seven hundred feet high. The crossing is a historic

one. For centuries, explorers such as Father Escalante had found the Colorado River to be a formidable barrier to further western exploration. Early settlers used the impractical and dangerous route through Hole-in-the-Rock. Scouts from Escalante, Utah, found that a more feasible crossing place was at the mouth of Hall's Creek, and the Hall brothers, who had been running a ferry at Hole-in-the-Rock, moved their operations to the new site. Gradually, more northerly routes were developed, and by 1885, travel through Hall's Crossing had diminished to only a few wagons a year; eventually, this ferry site was abandoned. In the 1950s, however, when Glen Canyon Dam was being constructed, a group of southeastern Utah citizens led an effort to upgrade the roads in the area. Calvin Black, one of the leaders, conceived the idea of a ferry as a means of integrating the lake into the transportation system and showing off the magnificence of the rock scenery. Stewart Udall, then Secretary of the Interior, supported the idea, and a concession contract was negotiated with the National Park Service and Lake Powell Ferry Service, Inc., which was allowed to build Hall's Crossing Marina; later the Bullfrog Marina was built on the opposite shore. In 1963 a one-vehicle ferry, operated by Frank Wright and Company, began operations between Bullfrog and Hall's Crossing. In 1975, the ferry was shut down because of the adverse effects of the energy crisis.

Charles V. Anderson, at that time Utah's Chief Engineer, was instrumental in obtaining the present boat. Anderson began working on the project in 1982 and was able to secure a $900,000 grant from the state Community Impact Board to build the ferry. He canvassed the West Coast, searching for a vessel that would accommodate heavy passenger travel, yet survive daily use with minimal maintenance. The search led to Vancouver, British Columbia, and the nautical design company of Alexander Love. A model similar to the ferries operating in the Queen Charlotte Islands, off the coast of upper British Columbia, Canada, was chosen, scaled down from 150 feet to one hundred feet. The ferry was designed by Alexander Love and Company, Ltd., of Victoria, British Columbia, and was built by Mark Steel of Salt Lake City in Salt Lake City; she was then hauled three hundred miles and assembled at Lake Powell. She is sturdy enough to be an ocean-going ship, with a length of one hundred feet and a width of forty-two feet; she is powered by two 8V-71 Detroit diesel engines.

Anderson also named the boat the *John Atlantic Burr*; it was dedicated May 4, 1985. John Atlantic Burr, actually Anderson's great-grandfather, was a pioneer Utah rancher. Burr was born aboard the *SS Brooklyn* on February 24, 1846, somewhere in the Atlantic Ocean. The Burr family settled in Utah in 1848, eventually establishing the community of Burrville in Grass Valley. John Atlantic blazed what is known as the Burr Trail to solve the problem he faced of how to get his cattle from winter to summer range and to and from market. The Burr Trail led through rough and twisted land, meeting the mighty Colorado River at what is now known as Hall's Crossing; it is now an unpaved sixty-nine-mile wilderness route between Boulder, Utah, and Bullfrog Marina. The boat is regarded as an extension of the Burr Trail. Paving of the Burr Trail would further tourism in the area, saving Los Angeles area tourists 110 miles. As it is, the ferry saves 130 road miles and has opened up tourism in Southern Utah.

LOCAL POINTS OF INTEREST: Lake Powell is in an area so rugged it was the last part of the United States to be officially mapped; the shoreline is 1,960 miles, longer than the entire West Coast of the US. The lake was created when Glen Canyon was flooded and Glen Canyon Dam completed in 1963. It seems, in some ways, a surrealistic juxtaposition of emerald high desert waters and corrugated textured rock, in brilliant variegated tones of white and red. Parts of the lake have been used as settings for Biblical scenes in films. Commercial development has been carefully controlled; there are only four marinas on the lake (the other two are Hite to the north and Wahweap to the south, near Page, Arizona). Del E. Webb Recreational Properties is the concessionaire. Al Earley, company president, praised the new ferry, stating it would allow vacationers "to see more of this scenic, beautiful part of Utah" and "increase traffic to what we call the 'Grand Circle' of National Parks and Recreation Areas." The company offers lodging at Bullfrog and Wahweap marinas, as well as rental house-boats and powerboats. All marinas are open twelve months per year.

CROSSING TIME: 20 mins.

FERRY TYPE: Vehicle

VESSEL CAPACITY: 8 cars; 2 buses; 150 passengers

OPERATING SEASON: All year, weather permitting

SCHEDULE: **Daily. May 15-Oct. 15: Lv. Bullfrog Marina** odd hours 7 a.m.-5 p.m.; **lv. Hall's Crossing** even hours 8 a.m.-6 p.m. **Oct. 16-May 14: Lv. Bullfrog Marina** 9 a.m., 11, 1 p.m., 3. **Lv. Hall's Crossing** 10 a.m., noon, 2 p.m., 4.

RESTRICTIONS: Trailers, pickup-campers, and RVs permitted. Load limit approx. 100,000 tons.

FACILITIES: Restrooms; no food on ferry, though food available at both marinas

FARE: Cars, trucks, and campers up to 3/4-ton $7; foot passengers $2 (ages 13-64); $1 (5-12 and anyone with a bicycle); free for young children and seniors; motorhomes $15; add $10 for trailered boats.

RESERVATIONS: No

DIRECTIONS: Ferry connects SR 276 across Lake Powell

MAP LOCATION: P. 399, UT, 1

CONTACT: Del E. Webb Properties, Hall's Crossing Marina, Blanding, UT 84511, (800) 528-6154, (801)684-2261 (In AZ (602) 278-8888)

STATE: Utah

PLACES SERVED: Syracuse Landing—Antelope Island

BODY OF WATER: Great Salt Lake

FERRY SERVICE   The ferry service to Antelope Island was
HISTORY: begun in July 1985, replacing a seven-mile-
                               long causeway that was flooded in 1984.
Three J-boats are used, specially designed thirty-seven-foot neoprene
rubber boats with twenty separate flotation chambers and bimini shade
tops. The ferry fare includes shuttlebus tours of the northern end of the
island, including Buffalo Point. Hikers may take a shuttle to Buffalo
Point and return on a later shuttle. A complete scenic tour is offered for
$19.50, which includes the ferry, a twelve-mile tour along the east side of
Antelope Island, snacks, and cold drinks.

LOCAL POINTS   Antelope Island is the largest of eight islands
OF INTEREST: in the Great Salt Lake; it is fifteen miles
                               long, five and one-half miles wide, and
approximately twelve hundred acres in area. Kit Carson and John Fremont were shown to the island by Indians in 1843; herds of antelope
helped feed the survey party, and Fremont named it Antelope Island. In
1847, Mormon pioneers arrived and set the island aside as a grazing site
for cattle and sheep. Brigham Young, the Mormon leader, helped intro-
duce horses to the island, and by 1860 about a thousand wild horses
roamed over the grasslands. Today, about 350 head of buffalo inhabit the
island. Rocky slopes punctuated by mountain peaks are surrounded by
juniper and sagebrush, giving the island a haunting loveliness mixed with
a quality of desolation. Prominent points of interest include Buffalo
Point, White Rock Bay, Camera Flats, Elephant Head, Frary Peak (6,585
feet) and the Old Ranch House and Brigham Young Retreat. Part of the
mystique of Antelope Island is that it is in the Great Salt Lake, which
covers an area larger than Delaware. Since 1843, its maximum depth has
ranged between twenty-four and twenty-five feet. Annually, the lake sees
water rise as spring runoff raises the level; later, it falls as the summer sun
evaporates the water. Near the coast are saline and fresh water marshes as
well as sand dunes. In 1968, the State of Utah purchased two thousand
acres at the northern end of the island and, in 1980, acquired the
remainder of the island, which became Antelope Island State Park. There
are overnight camping facilities, food services, pavilions, aqua bikes and
canoes for rent, and open-air shower facilities.

CROSSING TIME: 1 hr.

FERRY TYPE: Pedestrian

VESSEL CAPACITY: 36 passengers

OPERATING SEASON: Easter to Labor Day

SCHEDULE: **Daily, Mon.-Fri.: Lv. Syracuse Landing** noon, 2 p.m., 4; **Lv. Antelope Island** 1 p.m., 3, 5. **Sat., Sun., and holidays: Lv. Syracuse Landing** 10 a.m., noon, 2 p.m., 4, 6; **Lv. Antelope Island** 11 a.m., 1 p.m., 3, 5, 7.

RESTRICTIONS: None

FACILITIES: Available on the ferries are cold water, soda pop, and light snacks.

FARE: Round-trip fares only; includes park admission and shuttlebus tour to Buffalo Point. Adults $5.50; children (3-12) $3.50; under 3 free.

RESERVATIONS: No

DIRECTIONS: From Salt Lake City go north on I-15; take 335 off ramp. It is an additional 7 miles from this point. Ferries are a total of 25 miles from Salt Lake City and 15 miles from downtown Ogden.

MAP LOCATION: P. 399, UT, 2

CONTACT: Western River Expeditions, 7758 Racquet Club Dr., Salt Lake City, UT 84121, (801)942-6669

FERRIES
OF THE
NORTHWEST

Ferries of the Northwest

ALASKA

1. Alaska Marine Highway (Southwest Route): Cordova-Valdez-Whittier
2. Alaska Marine Highway (Southern Panhandle Access Route): Ketchikan-Metlakatla-Hollis-Hyder-Prince Rupert, BC
3. Alaska Marine Highway (Southeast Route): Seattle, WA-Prince Rupert, BC-Ketchikan-Hollis-Wrangell-Petersburg-Kake-Sitka-Angoon-Tenakee Springs-Hoonah-Juneau-Auke Bay-Haines-Skagway
4. Alaska Marine Highway (Southwest Route): Seward-Kodiak-Homer Seldovia-Chignik-Sand Point-King Cove-Cold Bay-Dutch Harbor
5. Alaska Marine Highway (South Central Route): Seward-Port Lions-Kodiak-Homer-Seldovia

OREGON

1. Buena Vista-Talbot
2. Canby-Wilsonville
3. Wheatland
* [Westport-Puget Island, WA; see WA]

WASHINGTON

1. Aberdeen-Hoquiam-Westport
2. Anacortes-Guemes Island
3. Anacortes-San Juan Islands
4. Anacortes-Sidney (Victoria, BC)
5. Bellingham-Lummi Island
6. Chelan-Lucerne-Stehekin
7. Edmonds-Kingston
8. Fauntleroy (Seattle)-Vashon Island-Southworth
9. Inchelium-Gifford
10. Keller-Republic
11. Mukilteo-Clinton
12. Port Angeles-Victoria, BC
13. Port Orchard-Bremerton
14. Port Townsend-Keystone
15. Puget Island-Westport, OR
16. Seattle-Bremerton
* [Seattle-Prince Rupert, BC-Skagway, AK; see AK]
17. Seattle-Victoria, BC
18. Seattle-Winslow
19. Steilacoom-Ketron and Anderson Islands
20. Tacoma-Tahlequah (Vashon Island)

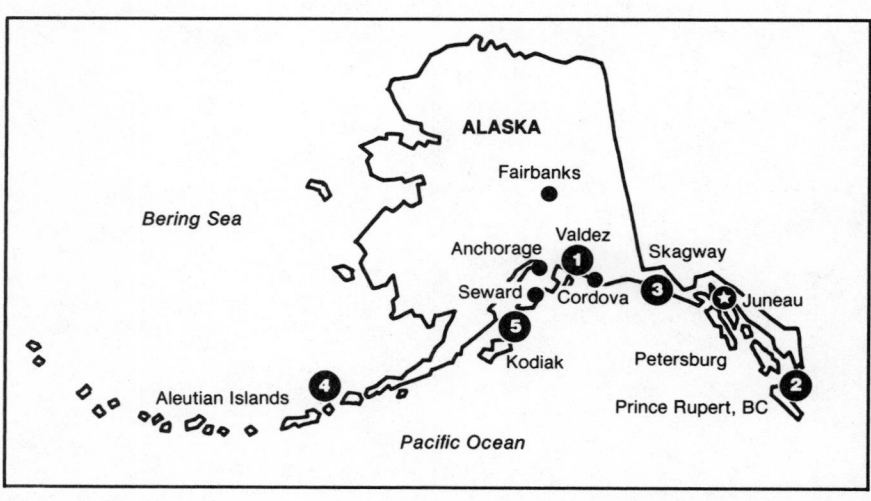

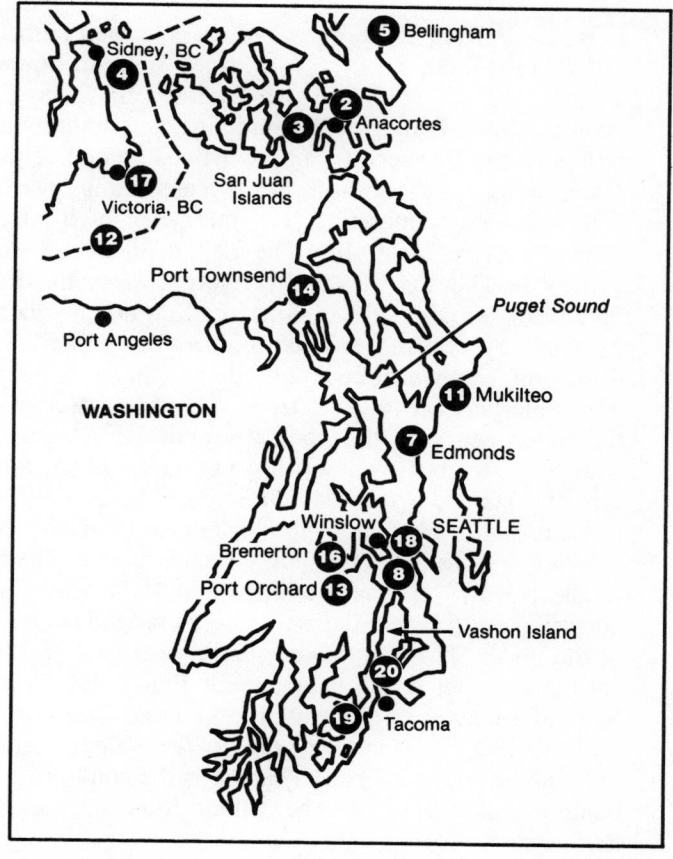

STATE:	Alaska

PLACES SERVED: Alaska Marine Highway (Southwest Route), serving Cordova—Valdez (pron. *deez*)—Whittier

BODY OF WATER: Prince William Sound

FERRY SERVICE HISTORY: The vessel on this service is the *Bartlett* (see description under Seattle-Skagway, Alaska Marine Highway, p. 00). Trips Valdez-Whittier and Whittier-Valdez are via the Columbia Glacier. Whittier is twelve and one-half miles from Portage and accessible only by rail. Ferry reservations guarantee space on the railroad, but rail fares are separate and must be paid to the Alaska Railroad.

LOCAL POINTS OF INTEREST: Cordova is located in the Copper River delta, on Prince William Sound. Named by Spanish explorer Salvador Fidalgo, it has long been a salmon-fishing center and big-game hunting area. It was once the rail port for Kennecott Copper Mines (which closed down in 1938). Cordova answers cabin fever by celebrating the Iceworm Festival in February, commemorating the emergence of the legendary iceworm of Robert Service fame. In "The Ballad of the Ice-Worm Cocktail," the natives of Dawson Town effectively correct the London dandy Major Percy Brown, who "called himself a Sourdough when he'd just been here a week" by offering to make him a *"bony-feed"* Sourdough, one who drinks an "ice-worm cocktail" down (made of the fabled "ice-worms" who emerge once a year from the "Mountain of Blue Snow"). The bartender concocts the cocktails and the Alaskans gulp them down; Brown chokes but swallows his and leaves town, too horrified to recognize the stained spaghetti. Of interest here is the Cordova Centennial Museum, with exhibits of the history and industry of the area.

Valdez, surrounded by snowy peaks, has been called the "Switzerland of the North." It was established in 1873 when miners used it as an outfitting point before departing over the Valdez Glacier to the gold fields of the north. The city was virtually destroyed by the 1964 Good Friday earthquake, but it has been rebuilt four miles west on the site of Port Valdez. It now has a convention center and a number of scenic drives and cruises. One popular tour goes to the Valdez terminal of the Alyeska Pipeline Service Company (Valdez is the southern terminus for the eight hundred-mile pipeline). The Valdez Museum has artifacts of the Gold Rush era.

Whittier is nestled between glacier-capped mountains and Prince William Sound and offers beautiful alpine scenery. Of special interest, according to Ruth Doumlele of Virginia, a recent traveller on the ferry, were the baby dolphins, bird rookeries, seals, and the fact that the glaciers were very close to the ship. Many backpackers visiting state parks cross here rather than take the one highway to Anchorage or Seward (Valdez-Seward is about 325 miles through mountainous terrain); tourists, hunters, fishermen, and business people also abound on this crossing. The Whittier Historical Society and Fine Arts Museum displays St. Lawrence Island artifacts and relics from the area's old fishing villages and canneries. Whittier is connected by ferry to Valdez and by "rail-ferry" aboard the Alaska Railroad to Portage on the Anchorage-Seward land highway.

CROSSING TIME: Cordova-Valdez approx. 6 hrs.; Valdez-Whittier approx. 8 hrs.

FERRY TYPE: Vehicle

VESSEL CAPACITY: 38 standard vehicles, 170 passengers

OPERATING SEASON: Mid-May-mid-Mar. (Does not operate Mar. 15-May 15).

SCHEDULE: *Space limitations prevent reproducing the complete schedule on this service; please contact Alaska Marine Highway for detailed schedule. A representative 2-week schedule between May 15 and Sept. 18, however, is this:* **Thurs. lv. Cordova** 11:45 p.m.; **Fri. lv. Valdez** 7:30 a.m.; **Fri. arr. Whittier** 2:15 p.m.; **Fri. lv. Whittier** 3 p.m.; **Fri. arr. Valdez** 10 p.m.; **Sat. lv. Valdez** 7:30 a.m.; **Sat. arr. Whittier** 2:15 p.m.; **Sat. lv. Whittier** 3 p.m.; **Sat. arr. Valdez** 10 p.m., **Sun. lv. Valdez** 7:30 a.m.; **Sun. arr. Whittier** 2:15 p.m.; **Sun. lv. Whittier** 3 p.m.; **Sat. arr. Valdez** 10 p.m.; **Mon. lv. Valdez** 7:30 a.m.; **Mon. arr. Whittier** 2:15 p.m.; **Mon. lv. Whittier** 3 p.m.; **Mon. lv. Valdez** 11:45 p.m., **Tue. arr. Cordova** 5:30 a.m.; **Tues. lv. Cordova** 11:45 p.m.; **Wed. lv. Valdez** 7:30 a.m.; **Wed. arr. Whittier** 2:15 p.m.; **Wed. lv. Whittier** 3 p.m.; **Wed. lv. Valdez** 11:45 p.m.; **Thurs. arr. Cordova** 5:30 a.m. *NOTE: Whittier is not included in the winter.*

RESTRICTIONS: No hazardous materials permitted. Bottled gas containers must be turned off and sealed by a Marine Highway employee before being transported. Pets must remain on the vehicle deck in a vehicle or other appropriate container. Maximum vehicle length 60 ft. Maximum vehicle weight 35 tons.

FACILITIES: Restrooms, food service

FARE: Because of space limitations, full tariff tables cannot be reproduced. Representative fares: Cordova-Valdez: Adults over 12 (meals not included) $22; children 6-11 $12; vehicles to 10 feet (driver not included) $23; Valdez-Whittier: Adults over 12 (meals not included); $50; children 6-11; $26; vehicles to 10 feet (driver not included) $28; full payment is required 45 days prior to sailing date.

RESERVATIONS: Advance reservations are required. You may write at any time, well in advance, listing alternate dates. Summer season reservations are processed beginning the first working day in January, in the order in which they are received.

DIRECTIONS: In most cases the ferry terminal is adjacent to the downtown community, but you need not worry if the ferry terminal is some distance away. In all cases, shuttlebuses or other transportation is provided. The Cordova ferry terminal is 100 yards from the Municipal Dock, 1/2-3/4 miles from downtown.

MAP LOCATION: P. 465 AK, 1

CONTACT: Alaska Marine Highway, Pouch R, Juneau, AK 99811, (907)465-3941

STATE: Alaska

PLACES SERVED: Alaska Marine Highway (Southern Panhandle Access Route): Ketchikan—Metlakatla—Hollis—Hyder—Prince Rupert, BC

BODY OF WATER: Inside Passage

FERRY SERVICE HISTORY: The vessels on this feeder service are the *Aurora* and the *Chilkat* (see entry under Seattle-Skagway, Alaska Marine Highway, p. 470).

LOCAL POINTS OF INTEREST: [For notes on Ketchikan, Prince Rupert, and Hollis, please see entry under Seattle-Skagway, p. 473.]

Metlakatla is a well-planned community on Alaska's only Indian Reservation. Here, visitors can visit the Duncan Cottage Museum, home of

Father Duncan, founder of Metlakatla; there are also historic walking tours, Indian dances, and tours of the Annette Island salmon cannery.

Hyder is located at the head of Portland Canal on the fringe of Misty Fjords National Monument. It was originally settled by Yukon gold prospectors and, in 1919, the gold and silver Premier Mine was opened. Now the population has shrunk to forty people, and Hyder is known as the "Friendliest Ghost Town in Alaska."

CROSSING TIME: Ketchikan-Metlakatla 1 hr. 35 mins.; Ketchikan-Hollis 3 hrs. 40 mins.; Ketchikan-Prince Rupert 7 hrs.; Hollis-Prince Rupert (via Ketchikan) approx. 11 hrs.

FERRY TYPE: Vehicle

VESSEL CAPACITY: *Chilkat:* 15 standard vehicles, 75 passengers; *Aurora:* 47 standard vehicles, 250 passengers

OPERATING SEASON: All year, but check schedules; the *Chilkat* is out of service May 1-13.

SCHEDULE: *Space limitations prevent reproducing the complete schedule on this service; please contact Alaska Marine Highway for detailed schedule. A representative summer schedule for Ketchikan-Metlakatla is:* **Wed., Thurs., Fri., Sat.: Lv. Ketchikan** 8 a.m.; **arr. Metlakatla** 9:35 a.m.; **lv. Metlakatla** 9:45 a.m.; **arr. Ketchikan** 11:20 a.m. **Hollis-Prince Rupert: Thurs. lv. Hollis** 6:15 a.m.; **Thurs. arr. Ketchikan** 9 a.m.; **Thurs. lv. Ketchikan** 9:30 a.m.; **Thurs. arr. Hollis** 12:15 p.m.; **Thurs. lv. Hollis** 5:15 p.m.; **Thurs. lv. Ketchikan** 8:45 p.m.; **Fri. arr. Hyder** 7:30 a.m.; **Fri. lv. Hyder** 10:30 a.m.; **Fri. lv. Ketchikan** 8:15 p.m.; **Fri. arr. Hollis** 11 p.m.; **Sat. lv. Hollis** 7 a.m.; **Sat. arr. Ketchikan** 9:45 a.m.; **Sat. lv. Ketchican** 5 p.m.; **Sat. arr. Hollis** 7:45 p.m.; **Sat. lv. Hollis** 8:45 p.m. **Sun. lv. Ketchikan** 12:15 a.m.; **Sun. arr. Prince Rupert** 7:30 a.m. **Sun. lv. Prince Rupert** 9:30 a.m.; **Sun. lv. Ketchikan** 3:45 p.m.; **Sun. arr. Hollis** 6:30 p.m.; **Mon. lv. Hollis** 7 a.m.; **Mon. arr. Ketchikan** 9:45 a.m.; **Mon. lv. Ketchikan** 6:45 p.m.; **Mon. arr. Hollis** 9:30 p.m.; **Tues. lv. Hollis** 7 a.m.; **Tues. arr. Ketchikan** 9:45 a.m.; **Tues. lv. Ketchikan** 11:45 a.m.; **Tues. arr. Hollis** 2:30 p.m.; **Tues. lv. Hollis** 7 p.m.; **Tues. lv. Ketchikan** 10:45 p.m.; **Wed. arr. Prince Rupert** 6:15 a.m.; **Wed. lv. Prince Rupert** 10:45 a.m.; **Wed. lv. Ketchikan** 5 p.m.; **Wed. arr. Hollis** 7:45 p.m.

RESTRICTIONS: No hazardous materials permitted. Bottled gas containers must be turned off and sealed by a Marine Highway employee before being transported. Pets must remain on the vehicle deck in a vehicle, or other appropriate container.

FACILITIES: Restrooms, food service

FARE: Because of space limitations, full tariff tables cannot be reproduced. Representative fares: **Ketchikan-Metlakatla:** Adults over 12 (meals not included) $10; children 6-11 $6; vehicles to 10 feet (driver not included) $12; **Hollis—Ketchikan:** Adults over 12 (meals not included) $14; children 6-11 $8; vehicles to 10 feet (driver not included) $16. Full payment is required 45 days prior to sailing date.

RESERVATIONS: See RESERVATIONS, p. 468.

DIRECTIONS: In most cases the ferry terminal is adjacent to the downtown community, but you need not worry if the ferry terminal is some distance away. In all cases, shuttlebuses or other transportation is provided. The Alaska State Ferry Terminal in Ketchikan is just off Tongass Avenue; walking time is about 20 mins. to the Westend Commercial District and about 40 mins. downtown.

MAP LOCATION: P. 465, AK, 2

CONTACT: See CONTACT, p. 468.

STATE: Alaska/British Columbia, Canada/Washington

PLACES SERVED: Alaska Marine Highway (Southeast Route), serving Seattle, WA; Prince Rupert, BC; Ketchikan, AK; Hollis, AK; Wrangell, AK; Petersburg, AK; Kake, AK; Sitka, AK; Angoon, AK; Tenakee Springs, AK; Hoonah, AK; Juneau/Auke Bay, AK; Haines, AK; Skagway, AK.

BODY OF WATER: Inside Passage

FERRY SERVICE HISTORY: Alaska has more coastline than the rest of the United States combined, and more than half of its largest cities are unreachable by conventional roads. In 1960, Alaskans voted the necessary bonding to establish the state's waterborne highway system. It started with one vessel, the *Chilkat*; by 1963, four ships served the fleet, and now there are nine, which provide feeder service in Southeastern Alaska from the Kenai Peninsula to the island city of Kodiak and to the communities on Prince William Sound. Today, an average of 400,000 passengers and 100,000 vehicles travel along thirty-four hundred miles of coastline each year. These ferryliners are less formal and more economical than cruise ships and afford more opportunities to meet Alaskans. While the Marine Highway ships do not have the type of nightlife and entertainment one finds on luxury cruise ships, they have National Park Service rangers who conduct programs on the wildlife and natural history seen along the route. They do not go into certain places such as Glacier Bay, Tracy Arm Fjord, or Misty Fjords, but they do enter the narrow, winding channels such as the Wrangell Narrows and Peril Strait, which larger cruise ships do not enter. Note that they call only long enough to load and unload passengers and vehicles; if you want sightseeing time, you need to disembark and take another ferry. It is strongly suggested by the Alaska Marine Highway office that you consider departing from Prince Rupert, rather than Seattle, as the sailings from Seattle are more crowded. You may have more choice of reservations between September and May than in the summer months, but some attractions are open in the summer only, and, of course, the summer solstice brings the famous Midnight Sun. *See important notes under reservations.*

The ships presently in use are these: the *Aurora:* The newest ship, built by Peterson Shipbuilders in Sturgeon Bay, Wisconsin, she began service in 1977. She is 235 feet long and transports forty-seven standard vehicles and 250 passengers. Used on short runs, she has no staterooms but has food service, a cocktail lounge, and solarium; the *Bartlett*: Launched in 1968 at Jeffersonville, Indiana, she began service at Cordova in 1969. She is 193 feet long and holds thirty-eight vehicles and 170 passengers. She also has no staterooms, but has food service and a solarium; the *Chilkat:* The first ship of the fleet, she now runs between Ketchikan, Metlakatla, and Hollis. She is just under one hundred feet long and holds fifteen vehicles and seventy-five passengers; the *Columbia:* The largest ferry, she is the flagship of the Marine Highway fleet. She was launched by Lockheed Shipbuilding in Seattle in 1973, is 418 feet long and has a capacity for 180 standard vehicles and one thousand passengers. She has twenty two-berth cabins and seventy-one four-berth cabins, plus five deluxe units with sitting rooms. Food service, a cocktail lounge, and a solarium are provided; the *LeConte:* Launched in late 1973, also built by Peterson Shipbuilders in Sturgeon Bay, Wisconsin, she joined the fleet in 1974. She is 235 feet long and holds forty-seven standard vehicles and 250 passengers. She has food service, a cocktail lounge, and a solarium; the *Malaspina:* Built by Lockheed in Seattle in 1963, she was lengthened in

Columbia

1972 and now is 408 feet long, holding 120 vehicles. She has fifty-six four-berth cabins and thirty two-berth cabins, with food service, a cocktail lounge, and a solarium; the *Matanuska:* Built in Seattle by Puget Sound Bridge & Dry Dock Company, she began service in 1963. Lengthened in 1978, she now holds 120 standard vehicles and 750 passengers. She has eighty-four two-berth cabins, twenty-four three-berth ones, and four four-berth ones, plus food service, cocktail lounge, and solarium; the *Taku:* Built by the Puget Sound Bridge & Dry Dock Company in Seattle in 1963, she is 352 feet long and holds 105 standard vehicles plus five hundred passengers. She has thirty-five two-berth cabins and nine four-berth ones, plus food service, a cocktail lounge, and a solarium; the *Tustumena:* She was built at Sturgeon Bay, Wisconsin in 1964 and was renovated in 1969. She holds fifty vehicles and 220 passengers, with twenty-five two-berth cabins and two four-berth ones. Food service, a cocktail lounge, and a solarium are provided. *A note about schedules:* Space limitations prevent our reproducing the complete Alaska Marine Highway schedule. For every month and every ship, there are separate schedules northbound and southbound. However, representative schedules from Seattle-Skagway for the largest ship in the fleet, the *Columbia,* and from Prince Rupert-Skagway for the *Malaspina* are provided. *Advance reservations required.* See details under reservations.

LOCAL POINTS OF INTEREST: Alaska has been called a "light-struck wilderness," and there are few better ways to view the massive thick-ribbed glaciers, foaming waterfalls, ice-topped dark mountains, and icebergs starkly jutting from the gray water than to ride the state's unique ferry system. In summer, the pale midnight sun glimmers for weeks before and after the summer solstice. One comes to comprehend the lines from "Alaska Is an Eagle" by Robert Black and Richard Nowels: "She is the mystery that I will never tame. She is Alaska. Alaska is her name."

Only Skagway and Haines have highway connections to the rest of Alaska. Ports on the Seattle-Skagway run are Prince Rupert, Ketchikan, Hollis, Wrangell, Petersburg, Kake, Sitka, Angoon, Tenakee, Hoonah, Juneau, and Haines (not all are visited on each trip; study schedule carefully).

[For notes on Seattle, see entry under Seattle/Bremerton, p. 521.]

Prince Rupert, British Columbia: "Such a land," said Rudyard Kipling of British Columbia in 1908, "is good for an energetic man. It is also not bad for a loafer." Prince Rupert can certainly accommodate both. It was founded as the western terminus of the Grand Trunk Pacific Railroad (reached in 1912). The northern terminus of the British Columbia Ferry Corporation (transfers can sometimes be made between systems), it is Canada's third-largest ice-free deep sea harbor. The harbor itself, against a backdrop of mountains, has a lively mix of trawlers, pleasure yachts, and freighters. A good view can be had from Franklin D. Roosevelt Park. The city is a focal point for Indian art, with totem poles and beautifully wrought black argillite carvings of totemic animals; you can see these in the Museum of Northern British Columbia.

Ketchikan, according to its residents, is "five miles long, four blocks wide, and two blocks up Deer Mountain." In Tlingit (pron. "KLINK-it") Indian, the name means "Thundering Wings of the Eagle." The town is also called the "King Salmon Capital of the World." Creek Street, once the red-light district in mining days, is one of the main sights here. Its houses are on pilings over the water, with a boardwalk running alongside; there are craft shops and restaurants. Dolly's House, complete with a scarlet satin-covered four-poster brass bed, is open to the public (in summer). The Totem Heritage Cultural Centre exhibits totem poles, and the Saxman Totem Park is two miles south of the town. Bring a raincoat; the summer rainfall is above average and measured in a large "liquid sunshine" gauge in town. You may, of course, be fortunate and join the locals in being "sun-shocked."

Hollis is located on the eastern shore of Prince of Wales Island, where there were substantial gold finds which helped the growth of Ketchikan. The village is connected by land highway to Craig and Klawock on the western coast. The area is noted for good hunting and fishing along the roadways and for the good examples of local Indian art.

Wrangell began as a fur-trading post in 1834 and has been under the Russian, English, and American flags. The harbor is thronged with charter fishing boats and sightseeing boats bound for Chief Shakes Island, with its tribal house and Tlingit totem collection. The Wrangell museum has historic petroglyphs; others are on display on a beach north of town.

Petersburg, or "Little Norway," has a beautiful situation with both near and distant mountains looming over the harbor. Its Norwegian heritage is evident in the brightly painted houses and storefronts decorated with rosemaling. The Little Norway festival is held in mid-May. The life of pioneer Petersburg families is depicted at the Clausen Memorial Museum.

Kake is a Tlingit community on the northwest corner of Kupreanof Island and is the home of the world's tallest totem pole. Fishing and logging are the main sources of income.

Sitka is exceptionally beautiful, even in a land of magnificent scenery. The route here, through the Peril Strait and Sergius Narrows, is especially scenic. The town is on lake-dotted Baranof Island and was one of the earliest Russian settlements in Alaska; it was founded by the Russian-American Company's general manager, Alexander Baranov, in 1799 to establish trading in otter fur. Unfortunately, the village of the Tlingit Indians was razed in order to build the town. Sitka's Russian heritage is still evident in the Russian Orthodox Church of St. Michael, with its onion dome, the Bishop's House, and the costumed New Archangel Dancers, who perform when ships are in port (in summer). The town is below the cone of Mt. Edgecumbe, often called the "Mt. Fuji of the Western Hemisphere." Other attractions are the Sitka National Historical Park (with totems from the 1904 St. Louis World's Fair), the Jackson Museum, and Castle Hill, where the Russians handed over Alaska to the Americans in 1867. Ferry passengers can take a Sitka Busline tour of the city. *Note that not every ferry calls at Sitka.*

Angoon is the sole permanent community on Admiralty Island. The village remains a stronghold of Tlingit culture. The Admiralty Island National Monument is here, as well as brown bear, eagles, and sitka deer.

Tenakee Springs, a small logging and fishing center, was a spa where prospectors once came to "take the waters." It takes its name from the hot sulphur springs, where temperatures range from 106 to 108 degrees. Many Alaskan Southeasterners retire here; the 120 permanent residents are joined, in summer, by visitors who have discovered the excellent saltwater fishing.

Hoonah (population, 1000) is the largest Tlingit community in Southeast Alaska. Logging and fishing are the main sources of income, and the Hoonah Indian Association Cultural Center is a treasure house of Tlingit exhibits passed down from generation to generation among local families. It is on the north shore of Chichagof Island on the canoe route to Tenakee Springs. The Spasski Trail, three and one-half miles, is well worth hiking. Fishing for Dolly Varden is good from the point, and the beach north of the picturesque old cannery has a variety of banded pebbles and rocks.

The tall government buildings attest to Juneau's status as Alaska's capital, but even these buildings are dwarfed by the splendor of Juneau's natural setting. Surrounding it are Mount Juneau, Mount Robert, the peaks of the Juneau Icefield, and the frosty striated Mendenhall Glacier (two hundred feet high), Taku, Eagle, and Herbert Glaciers. You can take a two and one-half-hour Mendenhall Glacier tour. The approach to Juneau through the Stephens Passage is strewn with icebergs. The Alaska State Museum has excellent Indian artifacts. You may want to sample the summer salmon bake at the Last Chance Basin (a mining company mess hall) and the beer at the swinging-door Red Dog Saloon. Not far away is the Tongass National Forest, a wilderness area where American bald eagles nest in treetops and whales splash in waters. The Forest, with sixteen million acres, is the largest National Forest in the US and covers 99 percent of Southeastern Alaska. It was named for the Tongass Clan of the Native Tlingits, who lived on a small island near the southern end of the Forest. It was created in 1907 and encompasses five Wilderness Study Areas: Russell Fjord, Tracy Arms-Ford's Terror, Granite Fjords, Petersburg Creek, and King Salmon Capes.

Haines is a jumping-off point for highway travel to the Yukon and interior Alaska. Dominated by glaciers, fjords, and spiralling white-capped mountain peaks, the town is the ancestral home of the Chilkat Tlingit Indians, though it grew up around a trading post and Presbyterian mission school established in 1879. The American bald eagle is highly visible from October through January at the Chilkat Bald Eagle Preserve. In August Haines hosts the Alaska State Fair. Of special interest here are Fort William H. Seward, the first Army post in Alaska (known to locals as Port Chilkoot), and the Sheldon Museum, with an excellent pioneer and Indian history collection.

Skagway embodies the spirit of the Klondike gold rush, which survives here among the boardwalks, saloons, horse-drawn carriages, and false-fronted buildings. The "Days of '98 Show" reenacts those days in the evenings, and the Trail of '98 Museum contains many relics. All the melodrama and color of the "Last Great Adventure" of the 1898 gold rush and its 1899 collapse in favor of Nome is highly visible today in Skagway. The town is situated on the alluvial plain of the Skagway River; nearby mountain peaks reach a majestic seven thousand feet. There are "flightseeing" tours of Glacier Bay and the Juneau Ice Fields. The White Pass and Yukon Route narrow-gauge railroad, engineered through rock cliffs and mountains before the turn of the century, is still a working train, but it is also a popular tourist excursion. You can go to the top of the Pass and back, or, if you have a vehicle, ship it to Whitehorse and drive from there on the Alaska Highway.

CROSSING TIME: Sailing times: Seattle-Skagway approx. 3½ days (round-trip takes a week); Seattle-Ketchikan 38 hrs.; Prince Rupbert-Skagway 32 hours (44 for sailings via Sitka); Prince Rupbert-Ketchikan 5½ hrs.; Ketchikan-Wrangell 5 hrs.; Wrangell-Petersburg 3 hrs.; Petersburg-Juneau 7 hrs.; Petersburg-Sitka 9 hrs.; Juneau-Sitka 8 hrs.; Juneau-Haines 4 hrs.; Haines-Skagway 1 hr.

| **FERRY TYPE:** | Vehicle |

| **VESSEL CAPACITY:** | See notes above. |

| **OPERATING SEASON:** | All year |

SCHEDULE: **Seattle-Skagway,** *Columbia,* **representative July schedule: Lv. Seattle Fri.** 8 p.m., **Lv. Ketchikan Sun.** 11 a.m. **Lv. Wrangell Sun.** 6:30 p.m. **Lv. Petersburg Sun.** 10:30 p.m. **Lv. Juneau/Auke Bay Mon.** 8:30 a.m. **Lv. Haines Mon.** 1:30 p.m. **Arr. Skagway Mon.** 2:30 p.m. **Lv. Skagway Mon.** 7:30 p.m. **Lv. Haines Mon.** 11 p.m. **Lv. Juneau/Auke Bay Tues.** 5 a.m. **Arr. Sitka Tues.** 1:45 p.m. **Lv. Petersburg Wed.** 5:15 a.m. **Lv. Wrangell Wed.** 8:45 a.m. **Lv. Ketchikan Wed.** 3:30 p.m. **Arr. Seattle Fri.** 7 a.m. **Prince Rupert-Skagway,** *Malaspina,* **representative July schedule: Lv. Prince Rupert Thurs.** 9:30 a.m. **Lv. Ketchikan Thurs.** 4 p.m. **Lv. Wrangell Thurs.** 11 p.m. **Lv. Petersburg Fri.** 3 a.m. **Lv. Juneau/Auke Bay Fri.** 12:30 p.m. **Lv. Haines Fri.** 5:45 p.m. **Arr. Skagway Fri.** 6:45 p.m. **Lv. Skagway Fri.** 11:15 p.m. **Lv. Haines Sat.** 2 a.m. **Lv. Juneau/Auke Bay Sat.** 8 a.m. **Arr. Sitka Sat.** 5:30 p.m. **Lv. Petersburg Sun.** 7:15 a.m. **Lv. Wrangell Sun.** 1 p.m. **Lv. Ketchikan Sun.** 10:45 p.m. **Arr. Prince Rupert Mon.** 5:45 a.m.

RESTRICTIONS: No hazardous materials permitted. Bottled gas containers must be turned off and sealed by a Marine Highway employee before being transported. No animals may be transported into the state unless the animal's owner or attendant possesses a valid health certificate for the animal. Dogs, cats, and household pets are charged $10 to/from Seattle and $5 to/from Prince Rupert. They are transported on car deck only in owners' vehicles or kennels. For transport of larger animals ask Alaska Marine Highway office.

FACILITIES: See notes above.

FARE: Because of space limitations, full tariff tables cannot be reproduced. Representative fares: **Seattle-Skagway:** Adults over 12 (meals and cabins not included) $208; children 6-11 $104; vehicles to 10 feet (driver not included) $218; 2-berth outside cabin (complete facilities) $171; dormitory cabin (per berth) $86. **Prince Rupert-Skagway:** Adults over 12 (meals and cabins not included) $102; children 6-11 $50; vehicles to 10 feet (driver not included) $104; 2-berth outside cabin (complete facilities) $81; dormitory cabin (per berth) $41. Full payment is required 45 days prior to sailing date.

RESERVATIONS: Advance reservations are required. You may write at any time, well in advance, listing alternate dates. Summer season reservations are processed beginning the first working day in January, in the order in which they are received, and within two or three days all Seattle-Skagway stateroom space is sold out. One way to obtain stateroom space after the early January "sold out" sign goes up is to book a package tour offered by an Alaska wholesaler: among these are Knightly Travel and Trav-Alaska Tours of Seattle and AlaskaBound of Ketchikan. Space from Prince Rupert to Skagway is also more likely to be available. Alternatively, connections can be made via the BC ferry system from Port Hardy on Vancouver Island. [See contact section to make reservations.]

DIRECTIONS: Ferry leaves from Pier 48 in Seattle, near the Washington State Ferries. It is 2½ miles from downtown in Prince Rupert. In most cases the ferry terminal is adjacent to the downtown community, but you need not worry if the ferry terminal is some distance away. In all cases, shuttlebuses or other transportation is provided. The Sitka dock is 8 miles from downtown, and the Haines dock is 3 miles.

MAP LOCATION: P. 465, AK, 3

CONTACT: See CONTACT, p. 468.

STATE: Alaska

PLACES SERVED: Alaska Marine Highway (Southwest Route): Seward—Dutch Harbor (with intermediate stops at Kodiak, Homer, Seldovia, Chignik, Sand Point, King Cove, and Cold Bay)

BODY OF WATER: Gulf of Alaska

FERRY SERVICE HISTORY: The vessel on this route is the *Tustumena* (see entry under Seattle-Skagway, Alaska Marine Highway, p. 472).

LOCAL POINTS OF INTEREST: *NOTE:* Trips from Seward to Dutch Harbor, on the Aleutian Chain, are only made about five times during the summer months; consult current schedule. The ship makes several intermediate stops and may be boarded in other places, such as Homer or Kodiak.

The Aleutians tend to be foggy, wet, and windy, yet the scenery is ruggedly beautiful, and the islands are fascinating in many ways. The

Aleuts, along with the Eskimos and Indians, are generally conceded by anthropologists to have been the earliest people in Alaska, having crossed over the Bering Sea from Asia. During World War II, the Aleutians were invaded by the Japanese, and several tours are offered of major World War II sites, including one by six-wheel-drive troop carrier. Sights include Bunker Hill, Ballyhoo, a Japanese POW camp, Fort Mears, and the hulk of the *SS Northwestern*. Alaska's oldest Russian Orthodox church is in the Aleutians. The industry here is primarily fishing and fish processing.

CROSSING TIME: 5 days (Sun. through Thurs.)

FERRY TYPE: Vehicle

VESSEL CAPACITY: 50 standard vehicles, 220 passengers

OPERATING SEASON: Summer only

SCHEDULE: *Note that these trips occur only 5 times during the summer & early fall; check schedule for dates. In 1986, Sun. dates for leaving Seward were May 12, June 9, July 7, Aug. 18, and Sept. 15.* Representative schedule: **Sun. lv. Seward** 1:30 p.m.; **Mon. lv. Port Lions** 3 a.m.; **Mon. lv. Kodiak** 6:30 a.m.; **Mon. lv. Homer** 6 p.m.; **Mon. arr. Seldovia** 7:30 p.m.; **Mon. lv. Seldovia** 8:15 p.m.; **Mon. lv. Homer** 11:45 p.m.; **Tues. lv. Kodiak** 12:45 p.m.; **Wed. lv. Chignik** 7:45 a.m.; **Wed. lv. Sand Point** 6:15 p.m.; **Thurs. lv. King Cove** 1:30 a.m.; **Thurs. lv. Cold Bay** 4 a.m.; **Thurs. arr. Dutch Harbor** 6:45 p.m.; **Thurs. lv. Dutch Harbor** 9 p.m.; **Fri. lv. Cold Bay** 12:45 p.m.; **Fri. lv. King Cove** 3:15 p.m.; **Fri. lv. Sand Point** 10 p.m.; **Sat. lv. Chignik** 8 a.m.; **Sun. lv. Kodiak** 4:15 a.m.; **Sun. arr. Seward** 5:30 p.m.

RESTRICTIONS: No hazardous materials permitted. Bottled gas containers must be turned off and sealed by a Marine Highway employee before being transported. Pets are not allowed in cabins; they must remain on the vehicle deck in a vehicle or other appropriate container. Maximum vehicle length 40 ft. Maximum vehicle weight 30 tons.

FACILITIES: Restrooms, food service, cabins

FARE: Because of space limitations, full tariff tables cannot be reproduced. Representative fares: **Seward-Dutch Harbor:** Adults over 12 (meals and berths not included) $186; children 6-11 $94; vehicles to 10 feet (driver not included) $187; 2-berth cabin, shower & toilet $206. Full payment is required 45 days prior to sailing date.

RESERVATIONS: See RESERVATIONS, p. 468.

DIRECTIONS: In most cases the ferry terminal is adjacent to the downtown community, but you need not worry if the ferry terminal is some distance away. In all cases, shuttlebuses or other transportation is provided.

MAP LOCATION: P. 465, AK, 4

CONTACT: See CONTACT, p. 468.

STATE: Alaska

PLACES SERVED: Alaska Marine Highway (South Central Route): Seward, Port Lions, Kodiak, Homer, Seldovia

BODY OF WATER: Gulf of Alaska and Cook Inlet

FERRY SERVICE HISTORY: The vessel on this route is the *Tustumena* (see entry under Seattle-Skagway, Alaska Marine Highway, p. 472).

LOCAL POINTS OF INTEREST: Seward was named after William H. Seward, Lincoln's Secretary of State and the man who negotiated with the Russians for the purchase of Alaska in 1867. Many people felt the purchase was "Seward's Folly" and called Alaska "Seward's Icebox." They had obviously not seen Seward, with its crescent shoreline, stand of rich pine trees, and Resurrection Bay, teeming with salmon and sea bass (local firms will can, smoke, or freeze your catch for a small fee). The harbor is filled with pleasure craft and, in August, is the scene of the eight-day Silver Salmon Derby. Sightseeing in Seward includes Bear Glacier, part of the Harding Icefield (third largest in the world; charter flights can be arranged to see it), and Rugged Island, home of several hundred sea lions. Kenai Fjords boat tours (eight and one-half hours), run by the National Park Service, depart from the wharf across from the fish house. The Resurrection Bay Historical Society Museum features baleen and Attu baskets and other Alaskan artifacts. Films and slides of the devastating 1964 earthquake are shown at the Seward Community Library.

Kodiak and Port Lions are on Kodiak Island. Kodiak, Alaska's oldest community, dates from 1792, when Alexander Baranof relocated his original settlement and administered the Russian Empire of the North Pacific from here. It is world famous among hunters, as the island is the natural habitat of the brown bear. It is the nation's third largest commercial fishing center and is known as the "King Crab Capital of the World."

The city has many vestiges of its Russian suzerainty, especially the Russian Orthodox churches with their onion domes and the Baranof Museum, with artifacts from the Russian fur trade era. "Cry of the Wild Ram" is an outdoor drama (given in August) depicting the Baranof era.

Homer is located on the tip of the Kenai Peninsula, the most western point to which it is possible to drive via interconnected roads on the North American continent. It is known for its wild berry products. There is a thriving artists' colony, along with galleries, cruises to the Gull Island bird rookery, and the Pratt Museum with a botanical garden and over four thousand Alaskan artifacts. Skyline Drive offers a panoramic view of Kachemak Bay.

Seldovia is situated across the bay from Homer; it is a quiet community of about five hundred people, who derive their livelihood from commercial fishing and logging. Seldovia was also founded by the Russians, and an old Russian Orthodox church overlooks Kachemak Bay. No roads lead here; it must be reached by plane or ferry. The 1964 earthquake forced the village to move to higher ground.

CROSSING TIME: Seward-Port Lions: approx. 13 hrs.; Port Lions-Kodiak: approx. 2 hrs. 30 mins.; Kodiak-Homer: approx. 9 hrs.; Homer-Seldovia: approx. 1 hr. 30 mins.; Kodiak-Seward: approx. 13 hrs.

FERRY TYPE: Vehicle

VESSEL CAPACITY: 50 standard vehicles, 220 passengers

OPERATING SEASON: Mar.-Dec. (does not operate in Jan. and Feb.)

SCHEDULE: *Space limitations prevent reproducing the complete schedule on this service; please contact Alaska Marine Highway for detailed schedule. A representative late July schedule is this:* **Sun. lv. Seward** 8:30 p.m.; **Mon. lv. Port Lions** 10:15 a.m.; **Mon. lv. Kodiak** 3 p.m.; **Tues. lv. Homer** 2:30 a.m.; **Tues. arr. Seldovia** 4 a.m.; **Tues. lv. Seldovia** 5:15 a.m.; **Tues. lv. Homer** 8:30 a.m.; **Tues. arr. Kodiak** 6:15 p.m.; **Tues. lv. Kodiak** 9 p.m.; **Tues. lv. Port Lions** 11:30 p.m.; **Wed. lv. Homer** 11:45 a.m.; **Wed. arr. Seldovia** 1:15 p.m.; **Wed. lv. Seldovia** 4:30 p.m.; **Wed. lv. Homer** 8:15 p.m.; **Thurs. lv. Kodiak** 8:15 a.m.; **Thurs. arr. Seward** 9:30 p.m.

RESTRICTIONS: See RESTRICTIONS, p. 476.

FACILITIES: Restrooms, food service, cabins

FARE: Because of space limitations, full tariff tables cannot be reproduced. Representative fares: **Seward-Kodiak:** Adults over 12 (meals and berths not included) $42; children 6-11 $22; vehicles to 10 feet (driver not included) $43; 2-berth cabin, shower & toilet $58; **Port Lions-Seldovia:** Adults over 12 (meals and cabins not included) $36; children 6-11 $18; vehicles to 10 feet (driver not included) $38; 2-berth cabin, shower & toilet $53. Full payment is required 45 days prior to sailing date.

RESERVATIONS: See RESERVATIONS, p. 468.

DIRECTIONS: See DIRECTIONS, p. 479.

MAP LOCATION: P. 465, AK, 5

CONTACT: See CONTACT, p. 468.

Buena Vista Ferry

STATE: Oregon

PLACES SERVED: Buena Vista—Talbot

BODY OF WATER: Willamette River

FERRY SERVICE HISTORY: Almost a century ago, you could take a sheep on the Buena Vista ferry for five cents. Ferries were essential to transportation in early Oregon to counteract the rainy season, when dry creek beds were flooded. There were a number on the Willamette River (as Oregonians say, "Wil-*lam*-it, dammit"). The first known Buena Vista ferry was begun by Reason B. Hall (the date is in dispute, but it was 1851, 1852, or 1853). He proposed that Buena Vista be made the capital of Oregon. The town was an important grain-shipping point and commercial center and the location of one of the first pottery works in the Northwest, but the honor went to Salem, about fifteen miles north. In 1893, the Marion County Court set the ferry rates at twenty-five cents for two-horse vehicles or a horse and rider, ten cents for a footman and each head of cattle or horses, and five cents for sheep. The boat in use is a forty-eight-foot steel ferry built in Portland in 1955 that replaced a wooden barge; it is powered by two electric motors. There is one full-time operator, one part-time operator, and one alternate; one present-day skipper is Oscar Frederic, who says he loves the idyllic life of running a ferry. For many years, twin ferrymen Willard Edgar Lawrence and Willie (Bill) Edwin Lawrence were the ferrymen; they logged a total of seventy-three years of crossing the river for a livelihood. The service is used by farmers and tourists.

LOCAL POINTS OF INTEREST: Today, it is hard to imagine the town as a commercial center; it is a quiet pastoral spot near many fruit orchards, but Hall's original description, in his proposal to make Buena Vista the state capital, is still valid: "The ground is high and dry, ascending from the river bank, and a more healthful situation cannot be found in the country—no swamp or low wet land about the place, and [it] is backed by as beautiful and as rich a country as there is in Oregon."

Salem is a good base from which to explore all three Willamette River ferries. The state capitol building (1938) is the nation's fourth newest, in modern Greek style with Vermont white marble facing the exterior. Two massive sculptures flank the main entrance, both by Leo Friedlander, *The Covered Wagon* and *Lewis and Clark Led by Sacajawea*. The striking statue of the Oregon pioneer atop the building is cast in bronze and finished in gold leaf; it was sculpted by Ulric Ellerhusen. Salem is an extremely pleasant small city, both drivable and walkable. The downtown area has excellent large department stores and easy parking. Among the notable acts of preservation in Salem are Mission Mill Village, in a former textile factory, with shops and tours of the former factory, and the Elsinore Theater, restored to its 1926 glory with frescoes, medieval arches, and quotations from Shakespeare.

CROSSING TIME: 5 mins.

FERRY TYPE: Vehicle

VESSEL CAPACITY: 4 cars

OPERATING SEASON: Mar.-Nov.

SCHEDULE: Mon.-Fri. only: 7 a.m.-6 p.m.

RESTRICTIONS: Trailers, pickup-campers, and RVs permitted. Load limit 10 tons. Maximum combined vehicle length 48 ft.

FACILITIES: None

FARE: All vehicles $1.50

RESERVATIONS: No

DIRECTIONS: Take I-5 south from Salem and exit at Talbot Road (Exit 242) and follow signs to Buena Vista. The landing is 5 miles from the freeway. You can also take SR 51 from Independence and then SR 17; follow it about 7 miles.

MAP LOCATION: P. 465, OR, 1

CONTACT: Polk County Commissioner's Office, Courthouse 104, Dallas, OR 97338, (503) 623-8173

STATE: Oregon

PLACES SERVED: Canby (2 miles north)—Wilsonville (4 miles east)

BODY OF WATER: Willamette River

FERRY SERVICE HISTORY: "The Clackamas Navy" is what local riders call the Canby Ferry, the *M. J. Lee*. Named for Millard Jerome Lee, an early Canby pioneer who was instrumental in procuring the river-crossing craft, it has been hauling people and cars back and forth across the Willamette River in Clackamas County since 1953. Service here was begun in 1914 by the Canby Business Men's Club, which bought a wooden boat; a new wooden ferry was built in 1917 (at a cost of $250) by Frank Dodge of Canby. In 1946 that boat was washed downstream in a disastrous flood. The present boat is powered by electric motors from an overhead trolley, with a cable guideline at water level; it is fifty-one feet by eighteen feet. A pleasant memento of your ride of the Canby Ferry is the oversized blue

ticket, which has a picture of the ferry on the front and a brief history of it on the back.

Miller Mays, a Canby ferrymen for thirty years, says his most unusual cargo has been livestock to the Clackamas County Fair; crossing the river to come to the fair is a ritual for many people (the ferry sees its greatest use during Fair week). The Willamette River here is wide and serene, at least in summer. One agrees with "Only in Oregon" columnist Ralph Friedman, who wrote over a decade ago: "It comes as a surprise to some people that in this day of advanced technology . . . ferries still operate in Oregon. . . . You don't really see and hear and feel a river from a bridge: you do from a ferry, and Oregon's ferries are small enough to have an intimate, folksy quality. You could probably put all of Oregon's ferries into one Staten Island ferry, but who would want that?" No sensible person, especially if he could ride the "Clackamas Navy" instead.

LOCAL POINTS
OF INTEREST:
Canby is a tranquil little town, with houses set in wooded grounds; it is more of a rural center than Wilsonville. On the Wilsonville side of the river, a pretty pastoral road, lined with fruit orchards, leads over rolling hills to the ferry landing. Canby has a historic railroad depot, built in 1873, open to the public on weekends. The William Barlow House, one mile south of Canby, is a National Historic Site, with Italian- ate architecture; it was built in 1844 and is open by appointment. Guided tours by appointment are offered of the Canby Forest Nursery, with fir, ponderosa pine, sitka spruce, etc., all of which are grown for reforesta- tion. The Champoeg State Park is nearby on the east bank of the river, with a Visitor Center featuring displays on early life in Oregon.

From mid-July to mid-August, Thursday through Sunday nights, the Champoeg Historical Pageant, a musical drama relating Oregon's early history, is presented in the amphitheater on the river; it is well worth attending.

CROSSING TIME: 5 mins.

FERRY TYPE: Vehicle

VESSEL CAPACITY: 5 cars

OPERATING SEASON: All year, weather permitting

SCHEDULE: Daily, except holidays, 6:30 a.m.-9 p.m., river and weather conditions permitting. (High water prevents the ferry from operating.)

RESTRICTIONS: Trailers, pickup-campers, and RVs permitted. Load limit 10 tons.

FACILITIES: None

FARE: Cars $1.

RESERVATIONS: No

DIRECTIONS: Take Oregon City-Interstate 205 exit from I-5 and go toward Oregon City. Take the Stafford Road exit. In ½ mile, go left on Mountain Road and stay on it about 3 miles to the crossing. From Salem take 99-E to Canby and follow signs.

MAP LOCATION: P. 465, OR, 2

CONTACT: Ardis Stevenson or Gordon Knutson, Clackamas County Dept. of Public Affairs, 902 Abernethy Rd., Oregon City, OR 97045, (503)655-8521

STATE: Oregon

PLACES SERVED: Wheatland

BODY OF WATER: Willamette River

FERRY SERVICE HISTORY: The oldest of the Willamette River ferries, the Wheatland Ferry was inaugurated in 1844 by a homesteader named Daniel Math-

Daniel Matheny IV

eny, who had come to Oregon in the great wagon trail migration of 1843. He settled on the west side of the river in the community known as Atchinson. Later, the name was changed to Wheatland, since it was a major shipping point for wheat.The Wheatland ferry had a long history of private owners until 1936, when Marion and Yamhill Counties took over joint operation. The *Daniel Matheny II* (1937) and the *Daniel Matheny III* (both wooden) preceded the present all-steel *Daniel Matheny IV*, put into service Oregon's Centennial year, 1959. It is twenty-four feet by sixty feet with eighteen-foot landing aprons. The earliest ferry was a current-powered drift ferry; later ones were rope-pulled and gas-powered. The Buena Vista, Canby, and Wheatland ferries have been called the "cable cars of the Willamette River," because at one time all three were powered by overhead electric trolley systems. Today, while electricity and diesel provide the power, the Wheatland ferry is tethered to an underwater cable. Irvin Hersha, chief operator, is the third generation of his family to operate the state's busiest ferry. Among the principal users are farmers bringing corn to canneries (sometimes in autumn the ferry will operate twenty-four hours a day to help them out), commuting farm laborers, students travelling from Yamhill County to Chemeketa Community College in Salem, commuters from the bucolic hamlets of Yamhill County who work in Salem-Keizer, and tourists. Terrie Justice of Salem says a favorite pastime of teenagers and young people is drifting downstream on rafts and inner tubes to Wheatland and coming back by car. Floating rafts and logs, as well as water-skiers, pose hazards for the ferry. Forrest Jones, Marion County Road Department Director, has called the crossing, which handles an average of seven hundred vehicles per day, "the most expensive six hundred feet of highway in Marion County," but, he adds, "Every time the rumor starts that ferry service will be ended, there's an outcry." Oregonians could hardly do without this and the other two

Willamette River ferries, among their most cherished institutions.

LOCAL POINTS OF INTEREST: The town of Wheatland no longer exists; its site is covered by a peach orchard. The state parks on the west side of the river, though, attract many people. On a summer weekend, there are dirt bikes scooting along, and on the river there are pleasure boats and water-skiers.

[For notes on Salem, see entry under Buena Vista-Talbot, p. 482.]

CROSSING TIME: 5 mins.

FERRY TYPE: Vehicle

VESSEL CAPACITY: 6 cars

OPERATING SEASON: All year, weather permitting

SCHEDULE: Daily, as traffic demands, 6 a.m.-9:45 p.m. (No service Thanksgiving or Christmas Day.)

RESTRICTIONS: Trailers, pickup-campers, and RVs permitted. Load limit 10 tons. Maximum trailer length 18 ft.

FACILITIES: None

FARE: Car, pickup-camper $0.50; 1-axle trailer $1; motorcycle $0.25, vehicle using entire ferry $2.

RESERVATIONS: No

DIRECTIONS: From Salem, go north on Front St. and River Rd. to Keizer, left on Wheatland Rd., and follow signs to ferry (about 6 mi.). On the west side, the ferry landing is just off SR 221 south of Dayton, between the Maud Williamson State Park and the Willamette Mission State Park.

MAP LOCATION: P. 465, OR, 3

CONTACT: Marion County Road Dept., 5155 Silverton Rd. NE, Salem, OR 97305-3899

A Note on Ferries in Washington State

Washington State has an enduring history of ferries, owing to its densely wooded coast, two thousand miles of coastline, large number of islands, and the often turbulent, deep, swirling waters that make bridge-building a formidable task. The history of ferries on Puget Sound has been extensively documented by M. S. Kline and G. A. Bayless in *Ferryboats: A Legend on Puget Sound.* The book was based on the maritime archives initially assembled by William O. Thorniley and augmented with further research. Kline and Bayless trace the ancestry of today's ferries, the early steamers and steam scows and freight barges, all of which serve the same purpose, as they put it: "to bring the residents and businesses of the state closer together over the water highways of Puget Sound." The first steamboat on the Pacific Coast was the *Beaver*, launched on the Thames by King William IV in 1835; she plied between Fort Vancouver and Fort Nisqually on Puget Sound and later served on the Victoria-New Westminster run. Another vessel was the first American-built steamer on the Sound, the side-wheeler *Fairy*, which arrived in 1853 and ran between Olympia and Fort Steilacoom. (She displaced Moxie's Canoe Express.) The Mosquito Fleet was the nation's first marine highway system, a collection of small steamboats carrying passengers, mail, and cargo and connecting scores of outlying towns to each other. It spanned a century, declining in the 1930s. Competition on the rugged fleet was fierce and heavy, with hard-working captains cutting deals and trying to outfox each other. The first ferryboat in Seattle was the steam-driven sidewheeler *City of Seattle,* which entered service New Year's Eve, 1888. Earl Clark has also chronicled ferry history in Washington State for *American West* and states that the automobile sounded the death-knell for the Mosquito Fleet. The last steam-powered ferry was the *San Mateo*, which ran until Labor Day, 1969. The complex history of ferries on Puget Sound spans a century and a half, with hundreds of vessels travelling over forty routes, few of which were ever replaced by bridges. Most of these early routes, as Kline and Bayless point out, were incorporated into the modern system of ferries.

Despite these early ships, however, few people at the turn of the century could have envisioned the number of ferries presently running. Washington State entered the ferry business June 1, 1951, when it acquired the Puget Sound Navigation Company, known as the Black Ball Line. Today, Washington State Ferries operates the largest ferry system in the United States, with twenty-two vessels on eight routes, serving twenty terminals; the system carries seven million vehicles and seventeen million passengers each year. It also operates a small free ferry on Lake Roosevelt. In addition, there are at least thirteen other ferries in the state run by private companies and counties. The Washington State ferries criss-cross the lives of the people of Puget Sound, forging such links that they become almost extensions of the communities they serve. At one time the clinic lobby in the Children's Orthopedic Hospital and Medical Center in Seattle had a ferryboat large enough for preschoolers to stand in; such an icon seems perfectly natural in a state where ferries have served as delivery rooms for over five hundred babies. All crews receive obstetrical training as a matter of course, in addition to first aid and CPR. The ferries are such a source of nurture that some passengers forget they are not in bed at home, fall asleep, and forget to deboard; others forget they have driven aboard and wander off (calling down the Coast Guard and a full sea search upon their absent-minded heads). There are, of course, complaints from time to time about various aspects of the service, such as fares and schedules. Riders have been known to tire of the cafeteria fare aboard and to bring tablecloths, candles, and Chinese take-out food for a relaxing cruise. But, on the whole, the ships have amenities which astonish outsiders used to more mundane forms of mass transit. There are video games; wine and beer; elevators on newer ships; long padded seats for stretching out; large tables for work and conversation; panoramic windows; duty-free shops on international sailings; sheltered and sunny seats on the top decks; and restrooms equipped with oversized gilt mirrors and outlets for electric razors, blow-dryers, and curlers.

The scenery on many routes is strikingly beautiful, with mountains edging the sea or towering above the horizon with snowy peaks. Passengers are so generally coddled, in short, that it is no wonder disembarking seems singularly unappealing.

STATE: Washington

PLACES SERVED: Aberdeen—Hoquiam—Westport

BODY OF WATER: Grays Harbor

FERRY SERVICE HISTORY: The vessel on the Grays Harbor Passenger Ferry service is the 149-passenger *Ed's Girl*. She makes three round trips a day, linking Aberdeen, Hoquiam, and Westport. En route you may see Caspian terns and colonies of harbor seals lazing on the long sand bar.

LOCAL POINTS OF INTEREST: Aberdeen and Hoquiam are twin cities at Grays Harbor and are closely linked geographically, Hoquiam being the senior community. Aberdeen was named for the city in Scotland; it was first the location of a cannery and later a lumber town, with the largest stand of Douglas fir ever found in the Northwest. Many present-day citizens are descended from Scandinavians of the Midwest who came here as lumbermen. Both towns have busy ports, with salmon fishing, seafood, and canning industries. Activities include deep-sea fishing, crabbing at the dock area, and surf and jetty fishing. Winter is a favorite time for residents because of the prizes brought in from the ocean by winter storms. Noted places of interest are the Westport Lighthouse (1898), Hoquiam Castle, a twenty-room mansion built in 1897 by Robert Lytle, a lumber baron, and Polson Park. The park contains the home of another lumber baron, Alex Polson, as well as a museum with a pictorial history of the Grays Harbor communities. The Takeland Hotel on Willapa Bay is on the National Historic Register; it has "Sherlock Holmes" annual events.

Westport, separated from Grays Harbor by a sandy strip of land, is home to one of the largest sports-fishing fleets in the world. It has an eighteen-mile-long beach. The Westport Viewing Tower offers scenic views of the sea, and historical bus tours leave from its base. Whale-watching and harbor and tidewater tours are also offered from Westport. Cranberry bogs may be viewed in June (full bloom) and October (harvest) south of the town. There are good restaurants on the Westport dock where you may eat during layovers.

CROSSING TIME: Aberdeen-Hoquiam 30 mins. Hoquiam-Westport 1 hr. 15 mins. (Note in planning there are 1-hr. layovers at Westport.)

FERRY TYPE: Pedestrian

VESSEL CAPACITY: 149 passengers

OPERATING SEASON: Apr.-mid-Oct.

SCHEDULE: **Weekend service only Apr., May, Sept.-mid-Oct. Daily service Memorial Day-Labor Day. Lv. Aberdeen** 9:15 a.m. for Hoquiam. **Lv. Hoquiam** 9:45 a.m. for Westport (1 hr. layover at Westport). **Lv. Westport** 12:15 p.m. for Hoquiam. **Lv. Hoquiam** 1:30 p.m. for Aberdeen. **Lv. Aberdeen** 2:15 p.m. for Hoquiam. **Lv. Hoquiam** 2:45 p.m. for Westport. (1 hr. layover at Westport). **Lv. Westport** 5 p.m. for Hoquiam. **Lv. Hoquiam** 6:15 p.m. for Aberdeen.

RESTRICTIONS: None

FACILITIES: Restrooms

FARE: Aberdeen to Westport: Adults $5 ($9 round-trip) (senior citizens 65 +) $4.50 ($8 round-trip); children (under 6) free. Hoquiam to Westport: Adults $5 ($8 round-trip) (senior citizens $4, $7 round-trip). Aberdeen to Hoquiam: Adults and senior citizens $3 ($5 round-trip).

RESERVATIONS: Some reserved tickets available; otherwise, tickets available at the dock in Aberdeen and Hoquiam 15 mins. before departure.

DIRECTIONS: Ferry is on Float 8, Marina, Westhaven Dr., in Westport

MAP LOCATION: P. 465, WA, 1

CONTACT: Ed's Charters, Box 461, Westport, WA 98595, (206)268-0047 or (800)562-0107

STATE: Washington

PLACES SERVED: Anacortes—Guemes Island

BODY OF WATER: Puget Sound

FERRY SERVICE HISTORY: The ferry on this run is the *Guemes*. Skagit County is one of three Washington counties that operate a ferry system owned by the county. The *Guemes*, put in operation in 1979, is a 124-foot double-ended 700-horsepower vessel. She was designed by Nickum & Spaulding Associates of Seattle and built by Gladding-Hearn Shipbuilding Corp. in Somerset, Massachusetts. She was launched in December 1978 and came to Anacortes via the Panama Canal to replace the *Almar*, which had been in service since 1956.

LOCAL POINTS OF INTEREST: Anacortes is a small community perched at the tip of Fidalgo Island (named for the Spanish explorer Salvador Fidalgo). The town itself was named for Anna Curtis Bowman, wife of pioneer Amos Bowman. It is the port of embarkation for the San Juan Islands. It also has chemical and plywood plants. The Anacortes Museum has excellent local history exhibits, including a doctor's office, a dentist's office, and a cannery office. Washington Park (220 acres) offers beaches, picnic areas, and boat-launching ramps. Mt. Erie is five miles away; from the top one has a good view of the San Juans and the Cascade Range. The refurbished US Army Corps of Engineers sternwheeler workboat *W. T. Preston* is on blocks ashore near the marina. Everywhere there are reminders of the area's Norwegian heritage, with names like "Gustavson," "Tollefson," and "Olafson." A landmark by the harbor is the Seafarer's Monument.

Guemes Island, nine-tenths of a mile away, is almost all privately owned. As a rule, local people use the ferry along with necessary service vehicles. Bus and taxi service are not available on Guemes.

CROSSING TIME: 7 mins.

FERRY TYPE: Vehicle

VESSEL CAPACITY: 19 cars; 100 passengers

OPERATING SEASON: All year

SCHEDULE: **Daily service. Mon.-Fri.: Lv. Anacortes** 6:30 a.m., 7, 7:30, 8, 9, 10, 11, 1 p.m., 2:30, 3:30, 4, 5:05, 5:30, 6. *Lv. Guemes Island 10 mins. later than Anacortes scheduled sailings.* **Additional Friday sailings: Lv. Anacortes** 7 p.m., 8, 10, 11, midnight. **Sat.: Lv. Anacortes** *6:30, then every hour on the hour 7 to 11 a.m. and 1 to 9 p.m., 10:30 p.m., midnight. **Sun. & holidays (except Fri. and Sat.): Lv. Anacortes** 9, 10:15, 11:30, 12:30 p.m., 1, 2:30, 3, 4, 5, 6, 7, *8:30. *Lv. Guemes Island 10 mins. later than Anacortes scheduled sailings.* *June 1-Labor Day only.

RESTRICTIONS: Trailers, pickup-campers, and RVs permitted. Load limit 36 tons.

FACILITIES: None

FARE: Round-trip fares. Car, pickup-camper or RV (under 20 ft.), incl. driver, $4.20; adult $2; child (6-high school) 35 cents (under 6 free); trailer (under 12 ft.) $2.40 (12-20 ft. $3.60); trailer or RV over 20 ft. $0.40 per ft.

RESERVATIONS: No

DIRECTIONS: The terminal is on 6th Ave., off Commercial St. in Anacortes.

MAP LOCATION: P. 465, WA, 2

CONTACT: Skagit County Dept. of Public Works, Mount Vernon, WA 98273 (206)336-9400

Hiyu

STATE:	Washington
PLACES SERVED:	Anacortes—San Juan Islands (Lopez, Shaw, Orcas, & Friday Harbor)
BODY OF WATER:	Puget Sound
FERRY SERVICE HISTORY:	Vessels used on this service are usually the *Elwha* (meaning "elk"), the *Kaleetan*

("arrow"), the *Hyak* (meaning "fast" or "speedy"), and the *Kittitas* (derived from the K'tatas Indian tribe of "shoal people"). Sometimes the smallest of the fleet, the *Hiyu* ("plenty"), is used; this is in a class by itself, built in Portland in 1967 and 150 feet long. Service was inaugurated by Washington State Ferries in 1951. Most riders in summer are tourists, usually from the Seattle area, but often from Oregon and California, as well as many other states.

Ferries are to the San Juan Islanders a means of transport *par excellence* through the maritime labyrinth of the San Juan archipelago; they have the drama of a medieval pageant wagon and the rich fabric of a caravan. They are a lifeline as well as a conduit for necessities and luxuries. Visitors may little realize the full role played by the ferries in the domestic life of the islands.

Once a year, for instance, islanders gather aboard the *Elwha* for the annual meeting of the San Juan County electric co-op as the ferry makes its daily run of the islands. The floating meeting, at which financial matters are decided and board members elected, is a festive social occasion as well, with a band and buffet; many islanders see each other only once a year at this event.

Visitors flock to the islands, especially in summers, glad to be free of shopping malls, expressways, and neon lights and basking in the tranquility and slow rhythm of the San Juans, even more marked after the ferries stop running and night settles in. To avoid summer lines, consider leaving your car on the mainland.

In 1783, James Boswell and Samuel Johnson made a celebrated tour of Scotland, sailing through the Hebrides. Boswell expressed a desire to buy the island of Inchkenneth and said his brother had always talked of acquiring an island. "Sir," said Dr. Johnson, "so does almost every man, till he knows what it is." But Johnson, of course, did not know the San Juans or possess a ferry, the better to reach them.

LOCAL POINTS OF INTEREST:

[For notes on Anacortes, see Anacortes-Guemes Island, p. 491.]

The San Juan islands were formed by glaciers that once blanketed Northwest Washington. They offer striking scenery, with fir-clad mountains, secluded coves, waterfalls, lakes, and giant trees. There are 172 islands, of which nineteen are inhabited.

Lopez has flat terrain and is popular with cyclists. It has a pastoral charm and one resort, the Islander, which provides van service from the ferry.

When approaching Shaw, you may be surprised to see the ferry received at the dock by nuns wearing habits. A landowner left the Franciscan Sisters of the Eucharist a large compound, where they have a retreat; when ferry service began, it seemed logical to Washington State Ferries to use the nuns as terminal agents.

Orcas Island, largest in the chain, has more resorts than the others and is hillier. A popular spot is Moran State Park, with its lovely Cascade Falls. The island has fifty-seven square miles of bays and forested ridges. The Orcas Island Historical Museum, in Eastsound, has Indian artifacts and relics of pioneer days. The grand old Rosario Resort gives a glimpse of the magnificent era of the philanthropic shipbuilding tycoon Robert Moran, who has been called "The Andrew Carnegie of the Northwest" and the "Fairy Godfather of the San Juans." Christopher Peacock has written an excellent history of Rosario and the heritage of Orcas, *Rosario Yesterdays*. The resort provides van service to and from the ferry terminal, as does the Deer Harbor Resort.

San Juan Island is the second largest and last of the ferry stops westbound; its lively waterfront town of Friday Harbor is the islands' largest town and commercial center. The harbor marina is busy with many private yachts (there are boat rentals available). The San Juan Island National Historical Park commemorates the dispute between the rival claimants, Britain and America, which resulted in the "Pig War" of 1859 (a British pig uprooted an American potato patch and was shot; it was the only war casualty). The old English and American camps are landmarks now. Of interest in Friday Harbor is the Whale Museum three blocks from the ferry landing with a variety of exhibits related to whales. (Watch, as you ride the ferry, for the pods of orca, or killer whales, which are supposed to ply the waters; they can be sighted during migrations.) Friday Harbor serves as headquarters for a salmon fleet.

A noted resort here is the 1880s settlement of Roche Harbor. Teddy Roosevelt once slept at the Hotel de Haro, a stately old gingerbread style building.

CROSSING TIME: Anacortes-Lopez 35 mins.; Lopez-Shaw 10 mins.; Shaw-Orcas 10 mins.; Orcas-Friday Harbor 40 mins.; Anacortes-Friday Harbor 1 hr. express, approx. 2 hrs. with full island stops.

FERRY TYPE: Vehicle

VESSEL CAPACITY: *Kittitas* 100 cars; others 160 cars

OPERATING SEASON: All year

SCHEDULE: **Daily.** *In winter ferries are less frequent; check with Washington State Ferries; this is the summer schedule. Note that some ferries are inter-island only and others are express. If island is not listed, ferry does not stop there on that trip.* **Westbound: Lv. Anacortes** 6:30 a.m., **Lopez** 7:10, **Shaw** 7:25, **Orcas** 7:40, **arr. Friday Harbor** 8:25. **Lv. Shaw** 8:45 a.m., ***Orcas** 8:35, **arr. Friday Harbor** 9:40. **Lv. Anacortes** 8:45 a.m., **Lopez** 9:25, **Shaw** 9:40, **Orcas** 9:55. **Lv. Anacortes** 10 a.m., **arr. Friday Harbor** 11:05. **Lv. Anacortes** 11:40 a.m., **Shaw** 12:30 p.m., **Orcas** 12:40. **Lv. Anacortes** 12:40 p.m., **Lopez** 1:20, **arr. Friday Harbor** 1:55. **Lv. Lopez** 12:55 p.m., **Shaw** 1:40, **Orcas** 1:20, **arr. Friday Harbor** 2:30. **Lv. Anacortes** 2:25 p.m., **Lopez** 3:05, **Shaw** 3:20, **Orcas** 3:35. **Lv. Anacortes** 3:50 p.m., **arr. Friday Harbor** 4:55. **Lv. Lopez** 3:55 p.m., **Shaw** 4:20, **Orcas** 4:35, **arr. Friday Harbor** 5:25. **Lv. Anacortes** 5:30 p.m., **Lopez** 6:10, **Shaw** 6:25, **Orcas** 6:40. **Lv. Anacortes** 6:35 p.m., **Lopez** 7:15, **arr. Friday Harbor** 7:50. **Lv. Lopez** 7:30 p.m., **Shaw** *6:55, **Orcas** 7:55, **arr. Friday Harbor** 8:45. **Lv. Anacortes** 8:15 p.m., **Lopez** 8:55, **Shaw** 9:10, **arr. Friday Harbor** 9:50. **Lv. Anacortes** 8:45 p.m., **Orcas** 9:45 p.m. **Lv. Lopez** 9:45 p.m., **Orcas** 10:05, ****arr. Friday Harbor** 10:50. **Lv. Anacortes** **11 p.m., **Lopez** **11:40, **Shaw** **11:55, **Orcas** **12:05 a.m., **arr. Friday Harbor** ** 12:50 a.m. *Load westbound on eastbound sailing. **Friday only. **Eastbound: Lv. Friday Harbor** 6:20 a.m., **Orcas** 7:10, **Shaw** 7:20, **Lopez** 7:35, **arr. Anacortes** 8:15. **Lv. Friday Harbor** 7:40 a.m., **Orcas** 8:35, **Shaw** 8:45.

Lv. Friday Harbor 8:40 a.m., **arr. Anacortes** 9:45. **Lv. Orcas** 10:10 a.m., ˜**Shaw** 9:40, **Lopez** 10:30, **arr. Anacortes** 11:10. **Lv. Friday Harbor** 9:50 a.m., **Orcas** 10:40. **Lv. Friday Harbor** 11:20 a.m., **arr. Anacortes** 12:25 p.m. **Lv. Orcas** 12:55 p.m., **Shaw** ˜12:30, **Lopez** 1:15, **arr. Anacortes** 1:55. ˜˜**Lv. Friday Harbor** 11:55 a.m., **Orcas** 1:20, **Shaw** 1:40, **Lopez** 12:50. **Lv. Friday Harbor** 2:10 p.m., **Lopez** 2:45, **arr. Anacortes** 3:25. + +**Lv. Friday Harbor** 2:55 p.m., **Orcas** 4:35, **Shaw** 4:20, **Lopez** 3:50. **Lv. Orcas** 3:50 p.m., ˜**Shaw** 3:20. **Lv. Friday Harbor** 5:05 p.m., **Lopez** 5:45, **arr. Anacortes** 6:20. **Lv. Friday Harbor** 5:40 p.m., **Orcas** 6:40, **Shaw** 6:55, **Lopez** 7:20. **Lv. Orcas** 6:55 p.m., ˜**Shaw** 6:25, **arr. Anacortes** 7:45. **Lv. Friday Harbor** 8:05 p.m., **Orcas** 8:50, **Shaw** 9, **Lopez** 9:15, **arr. Anacortes** 10. ˜˜**Lv. Friday Harbor** 8:55 p.m., **Orcas** 10:10, **Lopez** 9:45. **Lv. Friday Harbor** + +1:10 a.m., **arr. Anacortes** + +2:15 a.m. ˜Load eastbound on westbound sailing. ˜˜Trip operates to Lopez then Orcas and Shaw. + Trip operates to Lopez, then Shaw and Orcas. + +Friday only.

RESTRICTIONS:	Trailers, pickup-campers, and RVs permitted. Auto deck clearance 16 ft.
FACILITIES:	Restrooms, cafeteria.
FARE:	Round-trip fares. Car and driver: Anacortes-Lopez $11.25 (*$13.50), to Shaw, Orcas $13.45 (*$16.15), to Friday Harbor $15.40

(*$18.50); inter-island $6.50 (*$7.80). Passengers in vehicles or foot passengers: $4.50 from Anacortes; no charge inter-island. Bicycle and rider from Anacortes $6.05; inter-island $2.25. Vehicle/trailer to 28 ft. from Anacortes $19.85; inter-island $10.75. Varying rates for larger vehicles. Children (5-11) and senior citizens (65+) half fare. *Summer surcharge.

RESERVATIONS:	Vehicle customers should arrive early, with one-hour advance arrival recommended. Coffee shop available.
DIRECTIONS:	In Anacortes, landing is 4 miles west of town at the terminus of SR 20.
MAP LOCATION:	P. 465, WA, 3
CONTACT:	Washington State Ferries, Pier 52, Coleman Dock, Seattle, WA 98104, Seattle (206)464-6400; Washington state toll free: (800)542-7052 or (800)542-0810

STATE:	Washington/Victoria, BC
PLACES SERVED:	Anacortes—Sidney (Victoria, BC) (via San Juan Islands)
BODY OF WATER:	Puget Sound
FERRY SERVICE HISTORY:	The ferries used on this service are the *Elwha* and the *Kaleetan*. Both are super-

class car ferries, 382 feet long, carrying 160 vehicles and twenty-five hundred passengers, with a crew of fourteen. Washington State Ferries instituted this service in 1951. Sidney is seventeen miles north of Victoria; bus service is provided between the two. In both Sidney and Anacortes, passengers are subject to customs inspection; you need proper identification. San Juan passengers boarding boats originating in Sidney will also be subject to customs inspections.

LOCAL POINTS OF INTEREST:	[For notes on Anacortes, please see entry under Anacortes/Guemes Island, p. 491. For notes on San Juans, please see notes under

Anacortes/San Juan Islands, p. 494.]

Victoria, on the southeast tip of Vancouver Island, was established in 1843 as the Hudson Bay Company's main fur-trading post. It is like a reenactment of London by wistful colonials who have forgotten its congestion and frenetic pace. There are stately Parliament Buildings (illuminated at night), double-decker buses (you can ride them to the famous Butchart Gardens north of town), import shops, horse-drawn carriages, and Victorian lampposts decorated, in summer, with flower baskets. Victoria is moderate in climate, even in winter. Other attractions include the British Columbia Provincial Museum (with dioramas on the natural history of British Columbia) and Thunderbird Park, with a superb collection of totem poles, a wax museum, and the Pacific Undersea Gardens and Miniature World, with dioramas and dollhouses. If possible, take High Tea at the venerable 1908 Empress Hotel (reservations are a must) or, to avoid a succession of scheduled groups at the Empress, at the quiet Crystal Gardens behind the Empress Hotel, a tropical garden with exotic birds and plants.

CROSSING TIME:	Anacortes-Sidney 2 hrs. 30 mins. to 3 hrs.
FERRY TYPE:	Vehicle
VESSEL CAPACITY:	160 cars
OPERATING SEASON:	All year

SCHEDULE: *Schedule may vary in winter; please consult Washington State Ferries. This is the summer schedule.* **Westbound: Lv. Anacortes** 8:25 a.m., **lv. Orcas** 9:25, **arr. Sidney** 11:05. **Lv. Anacortes** 10:45 a.m., **lv. Lopez** 11:25, **lv. Friday Harbor** 12:10 p.m., **arr. Sidney** 1:30. **Lv. Anacortes** 3:30 p.m., **lv. Friday Harbor** 4:40, **arr. Sidney** 6. **Lv. Anacortes** 8:45 p.m., **lv. Orcas** 9:45, **arr. Sidney** 11:15. *See Anacortes/San Juan Islands schedule for best connecting trips.* **Eastbound: Lv. Sidney** 7:45 a.m., **arr. Anacortes** 10:05. **Lv. Sidney** 11:55 a.m., **lv. Friday Harbor** 1:25 p.m., **lv. Lopez** 2, **arr. Anacortes** 2:40. **Lv. Sidney** 2:15 p.m., **lv. Orcas** 4:05, **arr. Anacortes** 5. **Lv. Sidney** 6:55 p.m., **lv. Friday Harbor** 8:25 p.m., **arr. Anacortes** 9:30.

RESTRICTIONS: Trailers, pickup-campers, and RVs permitted. Auto deck clearance 16 ft.

FACILITIES: Restrooms, cafeteria. Coffee shop available.

FARE: Car and driver from $12.75 (*$15.30) from islands; $25.30 (*$30.35) from Anacortes. Passengers in vehicles or foot passengers: $2.25 from islands; $5.85 from Anacortes. Bicycle & rider $3.25 from islands; $8.30 from Anacortes. Vehicle/trailer to 28 ft. from islands $17.75; from Anacortes $32.15. Varying rates for larger vehicles. Children (5-11) and senior citizens (65 +) half-fare. *Summer surcharge.

RESERVATIONS: Advisable summers only. One-hour advance arrival recommended.

DIRECTIONS: Anacortes landing is 4 miles west of town at the terminus of SR 20. Sidney landing is 17 miles north of Victoria via SR 17; it is located at 2599 Ocean Ave. in Sidney.

MAP LOCATION: P. 465, WA, 4

CONTACT: See CONTACT, p. 496.

Whatcom Chief

STATE: Washington

PLACES SERVED: Bellingham (16 miles west at Gooseberry
                        Point)—Lummi Island

BODY OF WATER: Puget Sound (Hales Passage)

FERRY SERVICE   Ferry service to Lummi Island was inaugu-
HISTORY: rated in the late 1920s. The present vessel is
                        the *Whatcom Chief*; it is a steel double-ended
vessel, ninety-nine feet long, and carries a crew of two. The ferry has
carried equipment and camera crews making television commercials and
movies at times, but the most usual riders are island residents and others
from Whatcom County and British Columbia.

LOCAL POINTS   Bellingham was discovered in 1792 by the
OF INTEREST: English explorer Capt. George Vancouver;
                        he named it in honor of Sir William Bell-
ingham. The city is the last major settlement before the Canadian border;
traditionally a lumbermill town, its main industries are fishing, paper
processing, and boat building. The city has fine Victorian buildings,
especially the imposing old City Hall, which is now the Whatcom
Museum of History and Art, focusing on regional history. The Sehome

~499~

Hill Arboreton overlooks Bellingham Bay and the San Juan Islands. The Mount Baker Recreation Area is within easy reach; beyond it is often-photographed Mount Shuksan in the North Cascades. The Georgia-Pacific Corporation offers tours. A beautiful tour is Chuckanut Drive, south along the Samish Bay coastline; you can also drive to Vancouver (the Sumas and Blaine border crossings are open twenty-four hours daily).

Lummi Island is reached through the Lummi Indian Reservation; there is bed and breakfast accommodation on the island.

CROSSING TIME: 5 mins.

FERRY TYPE: Vehicle

VESSEL CAPACITY: 18-20 cars

OPERATING SEASON: All year

SCHEDULE: **Lv. Gooseberry Point** every hour 7:10 a.m.-12:10 a.m. **Lv. Lummi Island** every hour 7 a.m.-midnight.

RESTRICTIONS: Trailers, pickup-campers, and RVs permitted. Load limit 20 tons (25 with special permission). Maximum combined vehicle length 60 ft.

FACILITIES: No

FARE: Round-trip fares. Car $3.25; driver and passengers $1.50 ea. Trailer under 10 ft. $2.25; pickup-camper under 8,000 lbs. $3.25; RV 8,000 lbs. $6.50 (higher rates according to size and weight)

RESERVATIONS: No; if there are too many vehicles for the ferry, the vessel will double back immediately.

DIRECTIONS: Ferry leaves from Gooseberry Point, Bellingham.

MAP LOCATION: P. 465, WA, 5

CONTACT: Chief Engineer, Lummi Island Ferry, Whatcom County Engineering Dept., c/o Whatcom County Courthouse, Bellingham, Washington 98225, (206)676-6730

STATE:	Washington
PLACES SERVED:	Chelan—Lucerne—Stehekin
BODY OF WATER:	Lake Chelan

FERRY SERVICE HISTORY: Passenger boats have operated on Lake Chelan since the end of the nineteenth century. The *Belle* was the first; she was owned and operated by the Lake Chelan Railroad and Navigation Company and began service in 1891. The *Stehekin*, a paddlewheel boat, began service in 1892 and was the freight and mail boat in 1901. Several other steamers, including the *Dexter*, the *Flyer*, the *Chechacko*, the *Tourist*, and the original *Lady of the Lake*, also operated at the turn of the century. The first *Lady* was built in 1900, measured 115 feet in length and was in service on the lake until 1915. She stopped at farmhouses to deliver groceries, mail, and supplies, as no road had been built at that time. The *Comanche* was in service from 1915-1943, and the *Speedway* began operation in 1926; she is still occasionally used. The all-steel *Lady of the Lake II* was put in service in June 1976. She is one hundred feet long, weights one hundred tons, is twenty-four feet wide at the beam, yet has only a six-foot draft. She was built on Lake Chelan by the Lake Chelan Boat Company.

LOCAL POINTS OF INTEREST: Lake Chelan is the deepest and longest lake (fifty-five miles) in the state, at the south end of a scenic recreation area with waterfalls, mountains extending to the shoreline, and a picturesque lakefront; the area is known for its rugged beauty. Surrounding the northern end is the North Cascades National Park. Here, the terrain, with its canyons, jagged peaks, and many rivers, is the result of glaciation. A nine-mile drive from Chelan affords a view of the Lake Chelan Valley and the Inland Empire wheat country. In Chelan, the Log Church, designed by Stanford White in 1898, the restored Whaley Mansion, and the Chelan Museum (1902) are all of interest. At Stehekin, a four-mile bus trip may be taken to the 320-foot drop of Rainbow Falls.

CROSSING TIME:	4 hrs.
FERRY TYPE:	Pedestrian
VESSEL CAPACITY:	350 passengers
OPERATING SEASON:	All year

SCHEDULE: **Apr. 15-Oct. 15:** One round trip daily. **Lv. Chelan** 8:30 a.m., **lv. Stehekin** 2 p.m. **Oct. 16-Apr. 14; *Sun., Mon., Wed., Fri. Lv. Chelan** 8:30 a.m.; **lv. Stehekin** 12:30 p.m. **(Flag stops at Manson, Field's Point, Prince Creek, & Moore; stops at Lucerne & Port of Holden.)** *No Sun. boat Jan. 1-Feb. 15. Freight barge operates April-Nov. every week, carrying cars, horses, canoes, etc. (all types of freight), but no passengers.

RESTRICTIONS: Pets permitted winter schedule only (Oct. 16-Apr. 14); must provide cage.

FACILITIES: Restrooms; snack bar (summer only).

FARE: Chelan/Field's Point-Stehekin $12 ($18 round-trip); to Lucerne $11.00 ($15 round-trip); children (6-11) half-fare.

RESERVATIONS: Not necessary except for groups of over 15.

DIRECTIONS: The landing is 1 mile south of Chelan on SR 97.

MAP LOCATION: P. 465, WA, 6

CONTACT: Lake Chelan Boat Co., 1418 W. Woodin Ave., Box 186, Chelan, WA 98816, (509)682-2224

STATE: Washington

PLACES SERVED: Edmonds-Kingston

BODY OF WATER: Puget Sound

FERRY SERVICE HISTORY: The ships on this service are the *Yakima* (meaning "to become peopled"), a super-class ferry built in San Diego in 1967, and the *Chelan* (derived from "Tsill-ane," or "deep water"). The *Chelan* is of the Issaquah class and was built in Seattle in 1981. This route carries heavy tourist traffic from the mainland to the Kitsap Peninsula and to the Olymic Peninsula via the Hood Canal Bridge.

**LOCAL POINTS
OF INTEREST:** Kingston is a small community on the North Kitsap Peninsula. Visitors here can enjoy views of Mt. Rainier and the Olympic Mountains. There is a 270-slip marina, a historic schoolhouse in Kola Kole Park, and a July 4 celebration which dates from 1889. Another town of interest on the Kitsap Peninsula is Port Gamble, which has unusual New England-style architecture; replicas of gas lamps have replaced street lighting and the entire town is a historic district. Poulsbo, called "Little Norway," is a unique town rich with Nordic traditions; it has buildings decorated with Norwegian rosemaling (painted peasant designs) and a noted Scandinavian bakery.

Edmonds is a quiet town about fifteen miles north of Seattle. It was founded by Pleasant H. Elwell, who built the first cabin here in 1868; George Brackett then purchased the Elwell Claim and the settlement became a logging and sawmill center. When it was incorporated in 1890, the town fell short by two names of enough residents, and the names of two oxen, Bill and Bolivar, were added. There are beautiful views of Puget Sound from Edmonds.

CROSSING TIME: 30 mins.

FERRY TYPE: Vehicle

VESSEL CAPACITY: *Yakima* 160 cars; *Chelan* 100 cars

OPERATING SEASON: All year

SCHEDULE: Daily. Lv. Edmonds *5:50 a.m., 7:10, **8, 8:40, 9:25, 10:10, 10:50, 11:30, 12:10 p.m., 12:55, 1:40, 2:30, 3:10, 3:50, 4:30, 5:10, 5:50, 6:30, 7:20, 7:55, ˜8:40, 9:15, ˜10, 10:35, ˜˜11:20, 11:45. **Lv. Kingston** *5:10 a.m., 6:30, **7:10, 7:50, 8:40, 9:25, 10:10, 10:50, 11:30, 12:10 p.m., 12:55, 1:40, 2:25, 3:10, 3:50, 4:30, 5:10, 5:50, 6:30, 7:15, ˜8, 8:35, ˜9:20, 9:55, ˜˜10:40, 11:10, (12:20 a.m. also, all Mondays & mornings of July 5 & Labor Day Monday.) *Not Sundays. **Saturdays only. ˜Fri., Sat., Sun., holidays only. ˜˜Fri., Sun., holidays only

RESTRICTIONS: Trailers, pickup-campers, and RVs permitted. Auto deck clearance 16 ft.

FACILITIES: Coffee shop, restrooms

FARE: Car and driver $5.40 (**$6.50), adult passenger or walk-on pedestrian *$3.20, over-
sized vehicle (to 28 ft.) $8.10 (**$9.70;
higher rates for larger vehicles), bicycle and rider $2.25, children (5-11),
senior citizens (65 +), and handicapped half-fare; children under 5 free.
*Includes return fare. **Summer surcharge.

RESERVATIONS: No

DIRECTIONS: Edmonds: From I-5 take exit 177A; follow
SR 104 west to ferry terminal. Kingston:
Kingston is 9 miles east of the Hood Canal
Bridge via SR 104.

MAP LOCATION: P. 465, WA, 7

CONTACT: See CONTACT, p. 496.

STATE: Washington

PLACES SERVED: Fauntleroy (Seattle)—Vashon Island—
Southworth

BODY OF WATER: Puget Sound

FERRY SERVICE   Half the paychecks on Vashon-Maury Island
HISTORY: are brought back from Seattle and Tacoma
via Washington State Ferries, according to
Island Life — 1982: Focus on Ferries, published by the *Beachcomber*, the
island's weekly newspaper. "Anyone who commutes is nuts, but the
nuttiest commuters are found on ferryboats on Puget Sound," says the
paper's owner/editor, Jay Becker. Another commuter says it's an island of
"70-second minutes." The coin of the realm is ferry anecdotes, and an
extraordinary Muse of Maritime Legend seems to have settled here, for
islanders have a genius for rendering haunting vignettes of life aboard the
ferries. One of the earliest commuters was Ed Babcock, who has a
certificate showing he has ridden the equivalent of twice around the world
on Washington State Ferries; he was interviewed for *Focus on Ferries* by
Mary G. L. Shacklelford. Marjorie Drum talked with Ken Moore, an
immigrant to the island from Marin County in California; he commutes to
Seattle on his motorcycle and boards the ship in the evening with great
relief. "I start winding down when I get on the ferry." Eve Dumovich
marveled at the make-up artists among the women commuters who

"apply the day's paint job with contortions Houdini would envy." (The days of female cabin attendants may have vanished, but ladies' rooms on Washington State Ferries have gilt oval mirrors, blow-dryer outlets, and vanity-sized counters to rival Elizabeth Arden's. Not to be outdone, men shave and also use blow-dryers.)

Another Vashon Island resident, Joyce Delbridge, has collected many more stories in her recently published *Ferry Tales from Puget Sound*. She says the ferry is a better place than the grocery store for running into old friends and catching up on the news and worries that bridges might make the island overly inviting, destroying its rural character. Blanche Caffiere, a Vashon Island writer recalls, in *Ferry Tales*, the sale of a $250 West Highland Terrier puppy in the ladies' room (the seller had placed a classified ad, and the ferry was the most logical place for the transfer). Reva Sparkes, a calligraphy teacher, also of Vashon Island, recalls, in "The Rambling Pram," a lady who carefully parked an old-fashioned baby carriage on the car deck and repaired to the cafeteria. Curious children released the brake and it almost went overboard; rescued just in time, it was found to contain a silver coffee service taking its annual cushioned ferry ride to the owner's grandmother's birthday party. Junius Rochester, a Seattle writer and historian, in "Who Needs the Ferries," mentions some of the pastimes enjoyed by riders, ranging from sun-bathing to chamber music and business law courses. He says, "Whizzing hovercraft or the arched girders of a bridge can never replace the natural, measured rhythm of a cross-Sound ferry." It would be a rare rider who could disagree. Washington State service was inaugurated here in 1951. The vessels used on this run are the *Klahowya* ("greetings"), the *Tillicum* ("friend"), and the *Nisqually*.

LOCAL POINTS OF INTEREST: Fauntleroy is a residential section of what is commonly called West Seattle; here, there is the Fauntleroy Community Church and a YMCA operation in the church building.

Southworth is a small community with a post office, gas station, and grocery store; the ferry terminal is a dominant landmark in town.

Vashon and Maury Islands were formed by recurring glaciers and welded together by a natural sand bar and a man-made fill. Capt. George Vancouver discovered Vashon Island on his historic 1792 voyage; he named it for Capt. James Vashon of the British Navy. Maury Island was separately identified and named for a member of the Wilkes survey party in 1841. The combined shoreline of the two islands is more than sixty-five miles. Today, the area has a quiet, rural character, though businesses welcome visitors. The island has bed-and-breakfast inns, but it is best to reserve well ahead, especially if you plan to come on the busiest week-end, in late July, when the Strawberry Festival is held, with hundreds of booths, musical performances, and a parade.

CROSSING TIME:	Fauntleroy to Vashon 15 mins.; Southworth to Vashon 10 mins.; Fauntleroy to Southworth 35 mins.
FERRY TYPE:	Vehicle
VESSEL CAPACITY:	80-100 cars
OPERATING SEASON:	All year
SCHEDULE:	**Daily. Mon.-Fri., except holidays: Lv. Fauntleroy for Vashon** 5:25 a.m., 6:20, 6:50, 7:45, 8:15, 8:45, 9:40, 10:20, 11:05,

12:30 p.m., 1:15, 2:35, 3:20, 3:55, 4:30, 4:50, 5:20, 5:40, 6, 6:30, 6:35, 7:20, 7:50, 8:10, 9:30, 11, 12:30 a.m., 1:40. **Lv. Vashon for Fauntleroy** 5:05 a.m., 5:40, 6, 6:25, 6:45, 7, 7:20, 7:50, 8:15, 9:10, 9:45, *10:35, 11:20, noon, 12:50 p.m., 1:35, 2:20, 2:55, 3:40, 5:15, 5:40, 6:20, 7:05, 7:35, 8:30, 9:50, 11:20, 12:50 a.m., 2. **Lv. Southworth for Vashon** 4:50 a.m., 5:20, 6:45, 7:35, 8:55, 9:25, *10:20, 11, 11:45, 12:30 p.m., 1:15, 1:55, 2:40, 3:15, **4, 5, **5:30, 6, 6:40, 7:25, 8:50, 10:10, 11:35, 1:05 a.m. **Lv. Vashon for Southworth** 4:55 a.m., 6:25, 7:45, 8:35, 9:05, 10, 10:40, 11:25, 12:10 p.m., 12:50, 1:35, 2:20, 2:55, 3:40, 5:15, 5:40, 6:20, 7:05, 7:35, 8:30, 9:50, 11:20, 12:50 a.m., 2. **Lv. Fauntleroy for Southworth** 5:25 a.m., 5:55, 7:10, 8:15, 8:45, 9:40, 10:20, 11:05, 11:50, 12:30 p.m., 1:15, 2, 2:35, 3:20, 4:20, 4:50, 5:20, 6, 6:45, 7:20, 8:10, 9:30, 11, 12:30 a.m., 1:40. **Lv. Southworth for Fauntleroy** 4:50 a.m., ˜5:20, 6:10, ˜˜6:45, 7:35, 8, 8:55, 9:25, **10:20, 11, 11:45, 12:30 p.m., 1:15, 1:55, 2:40, 3:15, 4, 5, 5:30, 6, 6:40, 7:25, 8:50, 10:10, 11:35, 1:05 a.m. *Does not operate Tues. or Thurs. **Via Fauntleroy. ˜Limited to 30 vehicles. ˜˜Limited to 40 vehicles. **Sat., Sun., holidays: Lv. Fauntleroy for Vashon** 5:40 a.m., 7, 7:40, 8:25, 9, 9:45, 10:30, 11:15, noon, 12:45 p.m., 1:30, 2:15, 2:55, 3:45, 4:30, 5:15, 6, 6:45, 7:30, 8:15, 8:55, +10:15, 11, 12:30 a.m., 2. **Lv. Vashon for Fauntleroy:** 5:10 a.m., 6:30, 7:10, 8, 8:30, 9:20, 10, 10:45, 11:30, 12:15 p.m., 1, 1:45, 2:30, 3:15, 4, 4:50, 5:30, 6:15, 7, 7:45, 8:30, 9:05, +9:45, 10:30, 11:50, 1:30 a.m. **Lv. Southworth for Vashon** 4:50 a.m., 6:15, 7:40, 8:15, 9:05, 10:30, 11:15, noon, 12:45 p.m., 1:30, 2:15, 3, 3:40, 4:30, 5:15, 6, 6:45, 7:30, 8:15, 8:50, +9:30, 10:10, 11:35, 1:15 a.m. **Lv. Vashon for Southworth** 6 a.m., 7:20, 8, 8:50, 9:25, 10:10, 10:55, 11:40, 12:25 p.m., 1:10, 1:55, 2:40, 3:20, 4:10, 4:55, 5:40, 6:25, 7:10, 7:55, 8:35, +9:15, 9:50, 11:20, 12:50 a.m., 2:20. **Lv. Fauntleroy for Southworth** 5:40 a.m., 7, 7:40, 8:25, 9, 9:45, 10:30, 11:15, noon, 12:45 p.m., 1:30, 2:15, 2:55, 3:45, 4:30, 5:15, 6, 6:45, 7:30, 8:15, +8:55, 9:30, 11, 12:30 a.m., 2. **Lv. Southworth for Fauntleroy** 4:50 a.m., 6:15, 7:40, 8:15, 9:05, 9:45, 10:30, 11:15, noon, 12:45 p.m., 1:30, 2:15, 3, 3:40, 4:30, 5:15, 6, 6:45, 7:30, 8:15, 8:50, +9:30, 10:10, 11:35, 1:15 a.m. +Saturday only.

RESTRICTIONS: Trailers, pickup-campers, and RVs permitted. Auto deck clearance 16 ft.

FACILITIES: Restrooms, coffee shop

FARE: Fauntleroy/Southworth: Car and driver $5.40 (**$6.50), passenger or walk-on pedestrian *$3.20, oversize vehicle & driver (to 28 ft.) $8.10 (**$9.70); higher rates for larger vehicles; bicycle and rider $2.25; children (5-11), senior citizens (65 +), and handicapped half-fare; children under 5 free. *Includes return fare. **Summer surcharge. Fauntleroy/ Vashon and Southworth/Vashon: Round-trip only. Car and driver $7.25 (*$8.70); passenger in vehicle or walk-on pedestrian $2.10; bicycle & rider $3.10; oversize vehicle to 28 ft. & driver $11.10 (*$13.30); higher rates for larger vehicles; children (5-11), senior citizens (65 +) and handicapped half-fare; children under 5 free. *Summer surcharge.

RESERVATIONS: Not necessary.

DIRECTIONS: The Fauntleroy terminal is in West Seattle next to Lincoln Park.
The Vashon terminal is on the north end of Vashon Island at a location called Vashon Heights.
The Southworth terminal is in South Kitsap County at the Eastern terminus of SR 160.

MAP LOCATION: P. 465, WA, 8

CONTACT: See CONTACT, p. 496.

Columbian Princess

STATE: Washington

PLACES SERVED: Inchelium—Gifford

BODY OF WATER: Franklin Roosevelt Lake

FERRY SERVICE HISTORY: The *Columbian Princess* plies the Franklin Roosevelt Lake in western Washington (which begins in eastern Washington as the Columbia River), connecting the town of Inchelium, on the edge of the Colville Indian Reservation, with Gifford. According to R. H. Ruby and J. A. Brown, who have recounted the history of the Inchelium-Gifford ferry in *Ferryboats on the Columbia River*, the first ferry service at Inchelium-Gifford was begun by Thomas Stansgar in 1898; Stansgar, who was an employee of the Hudson Bay Company, had married into an Indian family. In 1900, a steam-powered side-wheeler guided by a cable, was put into service by Frank Rail and a Mrs. Harrison. Throughout the early 1900s ferry service was under private ownership. Among the owners were Scotty Lang, Francis Ward, Bert Jennings, Ivar Gifford, Walter McAviney, and Herbert Lang. Other ferries were at Daisy, Washington, four miles north of Gifford, and also at a site five miles downstream. In 1940, when waters began rising behind Grand Coulee Dam (said to be the largest concrete structure in the world) and the shorelines widened, the cable controls on the ferries were abandoned. More recent operators of the ferry service were James Arnold and Donald Larson; in 1974, a permit to operate a ferry was granted to the Colville Confederated Tribes. It is used by tribal members, truck drivers, softball players, resort owners, residents, commuters, tourists, campers, and business people, carrying about 105,000 cars annually.

The *Columbian Princess* was built in 1981.

LOCAL POINTS OF INTEREST: Inchelium means "between the waters" or a town surrounded by water. The old town of Inchelium was moved up to its existing site in 1939, and some of the buildings in the former town were moved also. In 1976 the Colville Indian Housing Authority had 120 HUD homes constructed reservation-wide; twenty-seven are in Inchelium. It has a population of just over 1,150 and is bounded by the Kettle River mountain range to the west and the Franklin D. Roosevelt Lake on the east and south. Gifford has a post office.

The lake itself is a rapidly developing recreational area, with fine beaches and striking lava flows and terraces, ornamented with wildflowers. The formations are the result of volcanic activity. Nearby is Twin Lakes, also a pleasant leisure area, with rental cabins and boating activities.

CROSSING TIME: 5 mins.

FERRY TYPE: Vehicle

VESSEL CAPACITY: 17 cars

OPERATING SEASON: All year

SCHEDULE: Daily, 6 a.m.-10 p.m.; on the hour and half-hour from the Inchelium side; on the quarter hour from the Gifford side.

RESTRICTIONS: Trailers, pickup-campers and RVs permitted. No drop center low boys. Load limit 30 tons. Size limit 100 ft.

FACILITIES: None

FARE: Free

RESERVATIONS: No

DIRECTIONS: Ferry access roads run from Inchelium and Gifford.

MAP LOCATION: P. 465, WA, 9

CONTACT: Colville Confederated Tribes, Box 150, Nespelem, WA 99155, (509)634-4711; Or: Mel Tonasket, Chairman, Colville Business Council, Box 150, Nespelem, WA 99155; Or: George Davis, BIA Superintendent, Box 150, Nespelem, WA 99155

STATE:	Washington
PLACES SERVED:	Keller—Republic (north of Wilbur)
BODY OF WATER:	Franklin Roosevelt Lake

FERRY SERVICE HISTORY: Ferry service here is aboard the *Martha S.*, the only free ferry operated by Washington State. In the 1890s, a cable ferry operated here; the Department of Transportation took over the previous ferry September 1, 1930. The *Martha S.* is a steel-hulled, double-ended vessel, with no passenger cabin. She usually carries local traffic, agricultural machinery, animals, and crops.

LOCAL POINTS OF INTEREST: Keller, Republic, and Wilbur are in the Coulee Dam Recreation Area. The dam was built to divert the Columbia River from its original course, down the deep water Grand Coulee ravine. It is one of the largest concrete structures in the world, 550 feet high with a 5,223-foot crest. Franklin Roosevelt Lake was formed by the dam; it is now a major recreation area with good motorboating, picnicking, and camping available. Keller is in the Colville Indian Reservation. Wilbur is west of Spokane, the nearest large city.

Old Fort Spokane is on the south shore of the lake near Miles; it is the last frontier military outpost of the 1800s, with four buildings remaining, including a museum and visitor center housed in the brick guardhouse.

CROSSING TIME:	10 mins.
FERRY TYPE:	Vehicle
VESSEL CAPACITY:	12 cars
OPERATING SEASON:	All year
SCHEDULE:	Daily, 6 a.m.-11 p.m.
RESTRICTIONS:	Trailers, pickup-campers, and RVs permitted. Load limit 40 tons. Max. combined vehicle length 75 ft. Max. vehicle width 8 ft.
FACILITIES:	None

FARE: Free

RESERVATIONS: No

DIRECTIONS: The ferry connects SR 21.

MAP LOCATION: P. 465, WA, 10

CONTACT: See CONTACT, p. 496.

STATE: Washington

PLACES SERVED: Mukilteo (Columbia Beach)—Clinton (Whidbey Island)

BODY OF WATER: Puget Sound

FERRY SERVICE HISTORY: This route is the second most popular in the Washington State system, despite the fact that people can drive around via the Deception Pass bridge. The vessels on this run are the *Cathlamet* ("stone") and the *Kitsap* (named for a war chief and medicine man under Chief Seattle). Both ships are of the Issaquah class; the *Cathlamet* was built at Seattle in 1981 and the *Kitsap* at Seattle in 1980. Washington State Ferries began this service in 1951. Many residents of Whidbey Island commute on these ferries, as do many residents with summer cabins and campers. Among the unusual things carried have been hundreds of oil-covered birds and ducks, victims of a major oil spill involving a freighter, which were transported off Whidbey Island to the cleaning station at Mukilteo.

LOCAL POINTS OF INTEREST: Mukilteo ("good camping ground," in Indian language) was where the Point Elliott Treaty was signed in 1855; the leaders of twenty-two Indian tribes relinquished land claims to white settlers. Next to the state park here is a nice lighthouse, and there is access to a beach.

[For notes on Whidbey Island, please see entry under Port Townsend-Keystone, p. 517.]

CROSSING TIME: 20 mins.

FERRY TYPE: Vehicle

VESSEL CAPACITY: 100 cars

OPERATING SEASON: All year

SCHEDULE: **Daily. Lv. Mukilteo** *5:05 a.m., 6, *6:30, 7, *7:30, then every 30 mins. until **9:30 p.m., 10, **10:30, 11, 12:10 a.m., 1, **2. **Lv. Clinton** *4:40 a.m., 5:30, *6, 6:30, *7, then every 30 mins. until **9 p.m., 9:30, **10, 10:30, 11:35, 12:30 a.m., **1:30. *Except Sat., Sun., & holidays. **Sat., Sun., & holidays only

RESTRICTIONS: Trailers, pickup-campers, and RVs permitted. Load limit 35 tons. Overhead clearance 16 ft.

FACILITIES: Restrooms, cafeteria.

FARE: Car & driver $3.65 (*$4.40); passenger in car or foot passenger **$2.10; bicycle & rider $1.55; motorcycle & driver $2; vehicle & trailer to 28 ft. $5.55; half-fare for children (5-11), senior citizens (65 +), handicapped persons; varying rates for larger vehicles. *Summer surcharge. **Includes return; fare collected westbound only.

RESERVATIONS: No

DIRECTIONS: The Mukilteo dock is 26 miles north of Seattle (take exit #189 from I-5 and follow SR 526 and signs to terminal).

MAP LOCATION: P. 465, WA, 11

CONTACT: See CONTACT, p. 496.

Coho

STATE:	Washington/British Columbia, Canada
PLACES SERVED:	Port Angeles, WA—Victoria, BC
BODY OF WATER:	Strait of Juan de Fuca

FERRY SERVICE HISTORY: This is the last regular crossing on the west coast between Canada and the United States. Service was inaugurated by Black Ball Transport, Inc., in December 1959 (previous service on this route was by the Puget Sound Navigation Company). The vessel on this run is the *Coho*, 341 feet in overall length, with a crew of from thirteen to twenty aboard at any one time. The ship handles everything from tricycles to bulldozers. She was built by Black Ball Transport at Puget Sound Bridge & Drydock Company, Seattle, in 1959. H. W. McCurdy, in his *Marine History of the Pacific Northwest*, wrote that the *Coho*, when launched, "resembled a small ocean liner more than a conventional inland ferry." The largest percentage of vehicles and passengers are handled during the summer season and are from all parts of the United States and Canada.

LOCAL POINTS OF INTEREST: Port Angeles, "Where the Olympics greet the sea," has a natural protected harbor formed by Ediz Hook, a long curved sand- USCG Base. bar; it makes Port Angeles a port of entry for ships coming from the Pacific. The name is an abbreviated form of the designation given the harbor in 1791 by a Spanish captain, "Port of Our Lady of the Angels." Tourism, fishing, and paper and lumber mills are the chief industries. Sights include the Arthur D. Feiro Marine Laboratory, with displays of flora and fauna and "touch tanks," and the Clallam County Museum, with local history displays. Port Angeles is the headquarters of the Olympic National Park. You can take a beautiful drive up to Hurricane Ridge, winding over mountain roads above deep valleys; it is worth taking, even in a foggy mist, because it may well not be foggy once you break through at the top, above the timberline. Here, there is a National Park Service visitor center; activities include nature walks, climbing, hiking, picnicking. Wildflowers are at their best in mid-July.

[For notes on Victoria, please see entry under Anacortes-Sidney (Victoria), p. 497.]

CROSSING TIME: 1 hr. 35 mins.

FERRY TYPE: Vehicle

VESSEL CAPACITY: 85-100 vehicles

OPERATING SEASON: All year

SCHEDULE: *This is the 1987 schedule; consult company for exact dates in other years.* **Jan. 1-Jan. 24: Lv. Port Angeles** 8:30 a.m.; **lv. Victoria** 3 p.m. **Jan. 25-Feb. 8:** Out of Service. **Feb. 9-Mar. 12: Lv. Port Angeles** 8:30 a.m.; **lv. Victoria** 3 p.m. **Mar. 13-May 14: Lv. Port Angeles** 7:30 a.m., 2 p.m.; **lv. Victoria** 9:30 a.m., 4 p.m. **May 15-Sept. 30. Lv. Port Angeles** 8:30 a.m., 12:45 p.m., 5:15, *9:30. **Lv. Victoria** **6:30 a.m., 10:30, 3 p.m., 7:30. *June 11-Sept. 15 only. **June 12-Sept. 16 only. **Oct. 1-Nov. 30: Lv. Port Angeles** 7:30 a.m., 2 p.m. **Lv. Victoria** 9:30 a.m., 4 p.m. **Dec. 1-Dec. 31: Lv. Port Angeles** 8:30 a.m. **Lv. Victoria** 3 p.m.

RESTRICTIONS: Trailers, pickup-campers, and RVs permitted. Load limit 40 tons. Vertical clearance 14 ft.

FACILITIES: Restrooms, snack bar.

FARE: US funds. Car & driver $22; passengers $5.50; children (5-11) $2.75 (under 5 free); bicycles $2.40; motorcycles & driver $12.25; camper, motor home & driver under 17 ft. $22 (higher rates for larger vehicles).

RESERVATIONS: Reservations not accepted. To assure space during peak travel periods, vehicles departing Port Angeles must be at the dock several hours in advance of desired sailing. Because the lead time varies, motorists are urged to call the Port Angeles office for current information.

DIRECTIONS:
The dock in Port Angeles is at the foot of Laurel St.; in Victoria the dock is at 430 Belleville St. Each is in the central part of its city (in Victoria the dock is within two or three blocks of the Capitol Building and the Empress Hotel).

MAP LOCATION:
P. 465, WA, 12

CONTACT:
Black Ball Transport, Inc., 106 Surrey Bldg., 10777 Main St., Bellevue, WA 98004, (Bellevue) (206)622-2222; (Port Angeles) (206)457-4491; (Victoria) (604)386-2202

STATE:
Washington

PLACES SERVED:
Port Orchard—Bremerton

BODY OF WATER:
Sinclair Inlet

FERRY SERVICE HISTORY:
The ferry service, known locally as the "foot ferry," was incorporated in 1924; the current owners purchased it in the late 1930s. There are five vessels: the *Retsil*, the *Thurow*, the *Carlisle II*, the *Spirit of 76*, and the *Eagle*.

LOCAL POINTS OF INTEREST:
Bremerton is best known as the site of the Puget Sound Naval Shipyard, northern headquarters of the Pacific Fleet, by whose tempo the city is measured. The shipyard is its principal industry. The Naval Shipyard Museum, in the Ferry Terminal Building, has ship models, early steam engines, carved bowsprits, paintings, and naval artifacts from the US and Japan.

Port Orchard is the county seat, across Sinclair Inlet. The Log Cabin Museum is well worth visiting, and the Sidney Art Gallery has paintings, watercolors, pottery, weaving, and jewelry of Northwest artists for sale. There are a number of other interesting shops with antiques and collectibles, as well as one specializing in miniatures.

CROSSING TIME:
10 mins.

FERRY TYPE:
Pedestrian

VESSEL CAPACITY:	*Retwil* and *Thurow*: 80 passengers; *Carlisle II* and *Eagle*: 150 passengers; *Spirit of 76*: 250 passengers
OPERATING SEASON:	All year
SCHEDULE:	**Daily. Lv. Port Orchard** on the hr. and half-hr. 6:30 a.m.-12:30 a.m. **Lv. Bremerton** on the 1/4-hr. and 3/4-hr. 6:45 a.m.-12:45 a.m.
RESTRICTIONS:	None
FACILITIES:	Restrooms on *Eagle* and *Spirit of 76*
FARE:	Adults $.60
RESERVATIONS:	No
DIRECTIONS:	The ferry terminal is at the foot of Sidney St. in the main part of Port Orchard.
MAP LOCATION:	P. 465, WA, 13
CONTACT:	Port Orchard-Bremerton Ferry, Port Orchard, WA 98366, (206)876-2300

STATE:	Washington
PLACES SERVED:	Port Townsend—Keystone (Whidbey Island)
BODY OF WATER:	Puget Sound
FERRY SERVICE HISTORY:	The vessels on this run are the *Klickitat* ("beyond"), and, in summer only, an extra seventy-five-car ferry. The *Klickitat* is a

refurbished steel electric-class ship; she was built in San Francisco in 1927 and refurbished in 1958 and 1981. This is a recreational route to and from the Olympic Peninsula. Many riders from Bellingham find this a convenient connection if they are going north to Vancouver.

LOCAL POINTS OF INTEREST:	Port Townsend was discovered by Capt. George Vancouver in 1792; he named what he called a "very safe and capacious harbor"

in honor of the English Marquis of Townshend. By 1890, the settlement was a thriving seaport; it was at this time that the imposing Victorian buildings, which have earned the waterfront and the residential area on the bluff designation as a National Historic District, were erected. It is considered the best example of a Victorian seacoast town north of San Francisco. Many dwellings, such as the Rothschild house, have been restored. The historic area contains a number of majestic mansions, some of them serving as bed-and-breakfast inns. Among them a number of ship captains' houses survive, some in ornate style. The Jefferson County Courthouse (1892) is an imposing brick structure with a clock tower that is a mariners' homing landmark. In Fort Worden State Park, Victorian officers' residences may be seen along with a handsome parade ground. In 1890, the northern terminus for the Northern Pacific Railroad was built at Seattle instead of Port Townsend, causing a decline in the city's fortunes, but you would never know it today, with the bustling shops, restaurants, and port amenities. The city also has a variety of annual events, such as the Wooden Boat Festival, the Olympic Music Festival, jazz festivals, regattas, and conferences for writers, quiltmakers, square dancers, and other groups.

Whidbey Island, also discovered by the intrepid Capt. Vancouver in 1792, is the largest in Puget Sound and is said to be the second longest in the US (forty-five miles long). Capt. Vancouver named the island for his sailing master, Joseph Whidbey. He proved the island was not a peninsula by sailing through Deception Pass; today, the view of the swirling water from the Deception Pass Bridge is a major tourist attraction.

Keystone has a protected shoreline often explored by kayakers; it is near the Ebey's Landing National Historical Reserve and just below Coupeville. Established in 1853, Coupeville is a town with many historic buildings; Madrona Drive, along Penn Cove, is a scenic drive.

CROSSING TIME: 35 mins.

FERRY TYPE: Vehicle

VESSEL CAPACITY: 75 cars

OPERATING SEASON: All year

SCHEDULE: **Daily. Lv. Port Townsend** 7 a.m., *7:45, 8:30, 9:15, 10:05, 10:55, 11:45, 12:35 p.m., 1:20, 2:15, 3:05, *3:55, 4:45, *5:30, 6:15, *7, 7:45, *8:30, 9:10, *10. **Lv. Keystone** 7:45 a.m., *8:30, 9:15, 10:05, 10:55, 11:45, 12:35 p.m., 1:25, 2:10, 3:05, 3:55, *4:45, 5:30, *6:15, 7, *7:45, 8:30, *9:10, 10, *10:40. *Fri., Sat., Sun., Mon.

RESTRICTIONS: Trailers, pickup-campers, and RVs permitted. Load limit 30 tons. Overhead clearance 13 ft. 10 in.

FACILITIES: Restrooms, cafeteria

FARE: Car and driver $5.40 (**$6.50), adult pas-
                           senger or walk-on pedestrian *$3.20, over-
                           sized vehicle (to 28 ft.) $8.10 (**$9.70;
higher rates for larger vehicles), bicycle and rider $2.25, children (5-11),
senior citizens (65 +), and handicapped half-fare; children under 5 free.
*Includes return fare. **Summer surcharge.

RESERVATIONS: No

DIRECTIONS: Ferry landing in Port Townsend is on Water
                           St. next to Rotary Park.

MAP LOCATION: P. 465, WA, 14

CONTACT: See CONTACT, p. 496.

STATE: Washington/Oregon

PLACES SERVED: Puget Island, WA—Westport, OR ("Wah-
                           kiakum Ferry")

BODY OF WATER: Columbia River

FERRY SERVICE   There has been a ferry chugging back and
HISTORY: forth between Westport and Puget Island (in
                           Wahkiakum County, Washington) since 1925
(except for four and one-half months in 1958). There were eight different
vessels before the present blue and white steel *Wahkiakum*, built in 1961
at Hood River. The first ferryman was Walter Coates; other owners
followed, until Wahkiakum County took over the service in 1960. Of
those connected with the ferry over the years, the name of the late Oscar
Bergseng is the most prominent; he, his wife, and two sons ran the ferry
for many years. Oscar used to tell of a foggy night when a freighter
passed so close he "could have reached out and touched it." Maxine
Beck, whose husband, now retired, was a skipper along with Gary
Bergseng, is still a deckhand, along with Capt. Danny Eaton; there are
three other employees. They work twelve-hour shifts, two days on and
then two off, according to Ruth Holland of the Wahkiakum County Road
Department. She says the ferry is especially needed when SR 4 on the
Washington side is closed due to mud and rock slides. Cathy Lindsley
interviewed Danny Eaton for the Longview, Washington, *Daily News*; he
told her of the time they diverted the ferry to assist a stranded pleasure

boat stuck on an island. The ferry passengers from California cheered. "You won't see anything like that in Los Angeles!" they exclaimed. The crossings are not without drama; often, the skipper must dodge ship traffic (he and the deckhand monitor the river by radio).

LOCAL POINTS OF INTEREST: Westport is a quiet little hamlet; the main commercial establishment is the King Salmon Lodge, which offers bed and breakfast. If other vehicles are not waiting, the ferry landing assumes the air of a mirage; will a vessel really appear from behind the island? In the fog? It will and it does.

Puget Island has a pleasant rural atmosphere, with a few dwellings clustered near the ferry landing. It was discovered in 1792 by Lt. W. R. Broughton and named after his friend Lt. Peter Puget. Islanders have pursued dairy farming, cattle-raising, mint crops, salmon fishing, and canning. There are several historic churches and roads good for bicycling. At Cathlamet, just over the bridge, the Wahkiakum County Historical Museum has exhibits of early life in the area. A good spot for coffee and doughnuts before or after the ferry, especially on a wet day, is the Ranch House on Route 4.

CROSSING TIME: 15 mins.

FERRY TYPE: Vehicle

VESSEL CAPACITY: 15 cars

OPERATING SEASON: All year

SCHEDULE:	**Daily: Lv. Westport** every hour on the half-hour 7:30 a.m.-5:30 p.m., 12:15 a.m. **Lv. Puget Island** every hour on the quarter-hour 7:15 a.m.-5:15 p.m., 11:15.
RESTRICTIONS:	Trailers, pickup-campers, and RVs permitted. Load limit 30 tons. Maximum width 22 ft. Maximum length 65 ft.
FACILITIES:	Restrooms
FARE:	Car and driver $2; each additional passenger $.25; trailer $1 under 10 ft.; $1 each additional 5 ft.; pickup-camper $1-$2; RVs $4 under 25 ft.; $1 each additional 5 ft.
RESERVATIONS:	No
DIRECTIONS:	Westport is just off SR 30 between Portland and Astoria. From Puget Island there is a bridge to Cathlamet, which is on SR 4 west of Longview and Kelso.
MAP LOCATION:	P. 465, WA, 15
CONTACT:	Wahkiakum County Engineer's Office, Box 97, Wahkiakum County, Cathlamet, WA 98612, (206)795-3301

STATE:	Washington
PLACES SERVED:	Seattle—Bremerton
BODY OF WATER:	Puget Sound

FERRY SERVICE HISTORY: The vessels on this run are the Issaquah Class *Issaquah*, built in Seattle in 1979, and the *Sealth*, built in Seattle in 1982. According to Issaquah historian Harriet Fish, the name came from the Indian pronunciation "Isquowh." Indians called it "sqwak" because of the squawking sounds of flying birds and animals. Indians habitually said "ish" before words, and formed "isquowh" in the back of the throat. The white man interpreted the Indian word as "Issawquah." "Sealth" is the Indian spelling of Seattle. Many oddities have been carried on this service, including an entire circus moving to a new location and a shipment of live seals (barking all the way).

LOCAL POINTS OF INTEREST: Seattle is the seat of the ferry mania which pervades the state, its very heartbeat throbbing engines and clarion whistles. From its bustling waterfront a variety of ferries, from steamers to water-jet catamarans, ply their intrepid way to Puget Sound harbors, Canada, and Alaska. A number of cruises also depart from Seattle. One wishes, at the Colman Dock, that more of the historic ferries might have been preserved (such as the streamlined *Kalakala*, now a crab-processing plant in Kodiak, Alaska). One vessel of the old Mosquito Fleet of steamboats does survive, though, the 1922 *Virginia V* (saved by the *Virginia V* Foundation); she may be seen at Pier 55, Monday through Friday, when not out on a cruise. And there is no doubt that the spirit of the grand old Colman Dock, portal to so much waterborne travel, survives in the verve and zest of the passengers thronging the present terminal.

Seattle is a lively city, its citizens rising above the often wet and misty weather with witty T-shirts and a determined air more akin to New England than to most of the West Coast. The Space Needle is a dominant landmark, a 605-foot spire, a legacy from the 1962 World's Fair (as is the Monorail). It houses a good revolving restaurant, but reserve ahead to avoid waiting. The Needle is in the Seattle Center, which also houses the Seattle Opera House and Playhouse, the Pacific Science Center, and the Fun Forest Amusement Park. Pike Place Market is the oldest continuously operating farmer's market in the country; it has as many levels (covered) as devastating temptations, from croissants to Dungenness crabs to exotic produce. The Charles and Emma Frye Art Museum has an outstanding collection of American and European paintings, as well as Alaskan art. Special tours may be made through the Boeing assembly plant and to Tillicum Village on Blake Island (birthplace of Chief Seattle), as well as to Mt. Rainier National Park.

[For notes on Bremerton, see entry under Port Orchard—Bremerton, p. 515.]

CROSSING TIME: 1 hr.

FERRY TYPE: Vehicle

VESSEL CAPACITY: 100 cars

OPERATING SEASON: All year

SCHEDULE: **Mon.-Fri. (excluding holidays): Lv. Seattle** 5:50 a.m., 6:50, 8, 9:10, 10:20, 11:30, 1:20 p.m., 2:30, 3:55, 5, 6:10, 7:15, 9:30, 11:45, *2:10 a.m. **Lv. Bremerton** 5:40 a.m., 6:55, 8, 9:10, 10:20, 11:30, 1 p.m., 2:30, 3:55, 5, 6:10, 7:15, 8:20, 10:35, 12:50 a.m. **Sat. Sun., holidays: Lv. Seattle** 6:35 a.m., 7:45, 9:15, 10:10, 11:45, 1:20 p.m., 2:30, 4:15, 5, 6:30, 7:15, 9:30, 11:45, 2:10 a.m. **Lv. Bremerton** 5:30 am., 8, 9, 10:30, 11:20, 1:20 p.m., 2:30, 3:55, 5:25, 6:10, 7:35, 8:20, 10:35, 12:50 a.m. *Via Winslow.

RESTRICTIONS: Trailers, pickup-campers, and RVs permitted. Load limit 35 tons. Overhead clearance 16 ft.

FACILITIES: Coffee shop, restrooms

FARE: See FARE, p. 516.

RESERVATIONS: No

DIRECTIONS: Ferry leaves Seattle from Pier 52 (Colman Dock); it leaves Bremerton at the foot of First St., near Pacific Ave. and Washington Ave.

MAP LOCATION: P. 465, WA, 16

CONTACT: See CONTACT, p. 496.

Princess Marguerite

STATE:	Washington/Canada
PLACES SERVED:	Seattle, WA—Victoria, BC (BC Steamship Company, Ltd.)
BODY OF WATER:	Puget Sound

FERRY SERVICE HISTORY: The vessel on this run is the *Princess Marguerite*. She is the last of the great coastal steamers that used to ply the waters of the Pacific Northwest and one of the very few steamships still in operation on the West Coast. A classic, she was built in 1948, and, except for a year-long and well-deserved sabbatical, she has been operating on the Seattle-Victoria run since 1949. She is an institution in both Seattle and Victoria and has been proclaimed an honorary citizen of Washington, of Seattle, and of Victoria. The *Princess Marguerite*, or "the Maggie," as she is affectionately called, has been commissioned a Washington General as well as an Ambassador of Goodwill for the State of Washington. With a length of 369 feet, she was built by Fairfield Shipbuilding and Engineering Company, Ltd., Gavan, Glasgow, Scotland, and launched May 26, 1948. She was christened by Mrs. R. W. McMurray, wife of the managing director of Canadian Pacific Steamships (Captain McMurray had brought the first *Princess Marguerite* to Victoria from the Clyde in 1925). Service was originally started on this route in 1904. Most riders on this ferry come from Seattle and King County, Washington, California, and Oregon.

LOCAL POINTS OF INTEREST:	[For notes on Seattle, please see entry under Seattle-Bremerton, p. 521. For notes on Victoria, please see entry under Anacortes-Victoria, p. 497.]
CROSSING TIME:	4 hrs. 15 mins.
FERRY TYPE:	Vehicle
VESSEL CAPACITY:	50-60 cars; 1800 passengers
OPERATING SEASON:	May-early Oct.
SCHEDULE:	**Lv. Seattle** 8 a.m. **Lv. Victoria** 5:30 p.m.
RESTRICTIONS:	Trailers, pickup-campers, and RVs *not* permitted. Max. vehicle height 6 ft. 8 in.
FACILITIES:	Restrooms (including one for the handicapped), cafeteria, luxury dining room, gift and duty-free shops, newsstand.
FARE:	US funds. Adults $18 (round-trip $29); automobiles $27; motorcycles $9; bicycles $2; children (5-11) $11 (round-trip $18); children

under 5 free; senior citizens $15 ($25 round-trip). ("Sale Sail" fares offered Mon.-Thurs., round-trips only, early May-mid-June and mid-Sept.-early Oct. Consult company brochure.)

RESERVATIONS:	Advisable for autos and dayrooms.
DIRECTIONS:	In Seattle, ferry leaves from Pier 69; in Victoria, from 390 Belleville St.
MAP LOCATION:	P. 465, WA, 17
CONTACT:	British Columbia Steamship Co., Ltd., Pier 69, Seattle, WA 98121, (206)441-5560; 390 Belleville St., Victoria, BC, Canada, V8V 1W9 (604)386-1124

Victoria Clipper

STATE: Washington/Canada (British Columbia)

PLACES SERVED: Seattle, WA—Victoria, BC (Clipper Navigation)

BODY OF WATER: Puget Sound

FERRY SERVICE HISTORY: The vessel on this service, the *Victoria Clipper*, was built in Norway; it cruises at more than thirty knots. It is a 127-foot jet-propelled catamaran. Service began in 1986, in time for the Expo 86 World's Fair in Vancouver. Amenities include a concierge/cruise director, two enclosed decks, surrounded by windows with comfortable seating, and outdoor deck areas also. The vessel has three crew on the bridge and six cabin attendants.

All passengers must clear Canadian immigration upon arrival in Canada and US customs and immigration on arrival back in the US.

LOCAL POINTS OF INTEREST: [For notes on Seattle, please see entry under Seattle-Bremerton, p. 521. For notes on Victoria, please see entry under Anacortes-Victoria, p. 497.]

CROSSING TIME: 2 hrs. 30 mins.

FERRY TYPE:	Pedestrian
VESSEL CAPACITY:	300 passengers
OPERATING SEASON:	All year
SCHEDULE:	**Daily. May 1-Sept. 30: Lv. Seattle** 8:30 a.m., 3 p.m. **Lv. Victoria** 11:45 a.m., 6:15 p.m. **Oct. 1-Apr. 30: Lv. Seattle** 8:30 a.m.
Lv. Victoria 5:30 p.m.	
RESTRICTIONS:	No pets except Seeing Eye dogs.
FACILITIES:	Restrooms, galley and bar service, duty-free shop, cellular telephones (used with credit cards)
FARE:	US funds. May 16-Sept. 15: Adults $35 (round-trip $59); children, senior citizens $29 (round-trip $49). Sept. 16-May 15:
Adults $29 (round-trip $49); chidren, senior citizens $25 (round-trip $39).	
RESERVATIONS:	Required.
DIRECTIONS:	In Seattle, the *Victoria Clipper* leaves from Pier 63. In Victoria, it leaves from Ogden Point.
MAP LOCATION:	P. 465, WA, 17
CONTACT:	Clipper Navigation, 2701 Alaskan Way, Pier 69, Seattle, WA 98121, (800)521-0714 or (206)447-8000

Spokane

STATE:	Washington
PLACES SERVED:	Seattle—Winslow (Bainbridge Island)
BODY OF WATER:	Puget Sound

FERRY SERVICE HISTORY: The Winslow route is the busiest of all the Washington State Ferries, carrying 4.8 million people per year. Among the ferries on this run are the *Spokane* and *Walla Walla*, jumbo ferries built in 1972. They are 440 feet long, the largest of the fleet, carrying two thousand passengers.

The most theatrical of ferries, the Winslow-Seattle ships virtually have plays within plays, with babies born on board, cyclists racing off the dock, contests, and trophies, all ferry-oriented. Schoolchildren might draw piglets, airplanes, and butterflies in some places, but in Puget Sound they draw ferry boats (in Winslow the winning entries are made into notepaper and Christmas cards). Bainbridge Island riders elect their favorite ferry employee as Grand Marshal for the Fourth of July parade in a contest sponsored by the Bainbridge Island Chamber of Commerce (Cindi Amo in 1986). Cyclists in the annual Chilly Hilly Bicycle Tour on the hills of Bainbridge Island assemble on the ferry; when it docks in Winslow, they zoom off *en masse*, fifteen hundred strong. Even the Wing Point Golf and Country Club awards a golf trophy in the form of a ferry boat model, and the Bainbridge Island Winery has a ferry as part of its logo. It is not unknown for late-night departures to be delayed so that patrons may see the end of the Mariners' games (a thank-you note is promptly published in the paper). Office express-mail schedules are geared to ferry timetables. Many of the anecdotes in Joyce Delbridge's recently published *Ferry Tales from Puget Sound* concern this route. Mae Swofford, a babysitting Seattle grandmother, desperate on a rainy Sunday, escorted her four lively grandchildren on a "mystery trip," making three Puget Sound crossings in what she calls "the world's largest floating playpen." A two hundred-foot Christmas tree was once shipped on one of the ferries on this run.

LOCAL POINTS OF INTEREST: [For notes on Seattle, please see entry under Seattle-Bremerton, p. 521.]

Winslow is the ferry port on Bainbridge Island, a seaside village which traces its history to the nineteenth century and the days of tall-masted sailing schooners and steamers. The town has interesting antique shops, art galleries, and waterside restaurants such as the Saltwater Cafe, next to the Pegasus Coffee House, which has excellent espresso. European pastries are made at the Bainbridge Bakery, and, appropriately, the Genie dress shop specializes in separates and accessories for "lady travelers." What lady, in Winslow, is not a traveler, with the jumbo green and white ships gliding in twice an hour, ready to transport her past snow-capped romantic mountains to Seattle and beyond?

Bainbridge Island itself is remarkably pastoral, considering the astonishing number of ferry riders it harbors within its sheltered byways. There are beaches and parks, and many protected harbors inviting mariners.

Poulsbo has a special Norwegian ambience, with timbered houses with fretwork balconies and Norwegian place names. Here, the Marine Science Center has educational exhibits and marine specimens. An excellent attraction enroute to Poulsbo is the Suquamish Museum, in Suquamish; this museum depicts the history of the Pacific Northwest from the perspective of Chief Seattle and his descendants, the Suquamish people. The premier exhibition, *The Eyes of Chief Seattle*, received international acclaim when it travelled to Nantes, France, as part of Seattle's Sister City exchange. Quotes from tribal elders are incorporated in the museum exhibits, giving them a powerful voice, as are artifacts made by the Suquamish people.

CROSSING TIME: 35 mins.

FERRY TYPE: Vehicle

VESSEL CAPACITY: 206 cars; 2,000 passengers

OPERATING SEASON: All year

SCHEDULE: **Daily. Lv. Seattle** 6:20 a.m., *6:55, 7:55, **8:30, 9:25, 10:10, 11:10, 12:10 p.m., 1:10, 2:10, 3, 3:50, 4:40, 5:25, 6:15, 7, ˜7:45, 8:30, ˜9:10, 9:50, 11:15, 12:30 a.m., 2:10. **Lv. Winslow** 5:40 a.m., *6:15, 7:10, **7:45, 8:40, 9:15, 10:10, 11:10, 12:10 p.m., 1:10, 2:10, 3, 3:50, 4:35, 5:25, 6:10, ˜7, 7:45, ˜8:25, 9:10, ˜˜9:55, 10:30, +11:50, 1:10 a.m. *Except Sat., Sun., holidays. **Except Sun., holidays. ˜Fri., Sat., Sun., holidays only. ˜˜Sun., holidays only. +Fri., Sat. only.

RESTRICTIONS: Trailers, pickup-campers, and RVs permitted.

FACILITIES: Restrooms, cafeteria

FARE: See FARE, p. 522.

RESERVATIONS: No

DIRECTIONS: Ferry leaves Seattle from Pier 52 (Colman Dock). In Winslow the dock is in the center of town.

MAP LOCATION: P. 465, WA, 18

CONTACT: See CONTACT, p. 496.

STATE: Washington

PLACES SERVED: Steilacoom—Ketron & Anderson Islands

BODY OF WATER: Puget Sound

FERRY SERVICE HISTORY: This line was originally served by Mitchell and Joe Skansie, brothers who owned the Washington Navigation Company. They obtained a contract from Pierce County in 1922 to operate a ferry on the run between Steilacoom-Anderson Island-McNeil Island-Long Branch. Later the ferry was run by the Olson Company; Pierce County contracted with that company to run the ferry in 1943. Service is provided by the regular vessel, the *Steilacoom*, and the backup ferry, *Islander*. The *Steilacoom* was built in Bath, Maine, in 1936; she has a steel hull and is 119 feet long, weighing 420 gross tons. The *Islander* was built in Astoria,

Oregon, in 1924; she has a wooden hull and is ninety-eight feet long with a weight of ninety-five gross tons. Most of the riders come from Anderson Island, with some from Ketron Island. McNeil Island, nearby, is not served by this ferry, but by boats and barges owned and operated by the Washington State Department of Corrections.

LOCAL POINTS OF INTEREST: Steilacoom (pron. "Stillakum") is Washington's oldest incorporated town, chartered in 1853. It was established by Lafayette Balch, a Maine sea captain. It was established as a National Historic District in 1974; it has thirty-two buildings and sites listed on the National Registry of Historic Places, including the Nathaniel Orr Residence, built in 1857. The E. R. Rogers Restaurant is in a Victorian mansion built in 1891. The museum, housed in the town hall, focuses upon the pioneer period (1860-1900). The town was the site of the state's first library. McNeil and Anderson Islands are visible from its streets.

CROSSING TIME: Steilacoom-Ketron 10 mins.; Steilacoom-Anderson 15-20 mins.

FERRY TYPE: Vehicle

VESSEL CAPACITY: *Steilacoom*: 30 cars; *Islander*: 20 cars

OPERATING SEASON: All year

SCHEDULE: **Daily. Lv. Steilacoom for Ketron** 7 a.m., 4:20 p.m. **Lv. Ketron for Steilacoom** 7:10 a.m., 4:30 p.m. **Lv. Steilacoom for Anderson** *6 a.m., 7:40, 9, 10, **noon, 2 p.m., 3:15, 5, 6. **Lv. Anderson for Steilacoom** *6:30 a.m., 8:10, 9:30, 10:30, 12:30 p.m., 2:30, 3:45, 5:30, 6:30. *Except Sat., Sun., & holidays. **Not the first Wed. of each month.

RESTRICTIONS: Trailers, pickup-campers, and RVs permitted. For *Steilacoom* all legal loads permitted; for *Islander* max. vehicle length of 60 ft.; max. gross weight 30,000 lbs.

FACILITIES: Restrooms on *Steilacoom*; no facilities on *Islander*.

FARE: Car and driver $4.30 (includes pickup trucks without extended bumpers or load); adults $1.25; children (5-11) $0.65; senior citizens

(65 +) or Medicare card-holders or handicapped persons $0.62; bicycle & rider $1.80; motorcycle & driver $2.25; trailers to 10 ft. $2.50, to 20 ft. $4.75; varying rates for larger vehicles. Checks not accepted; cash only.

RESERVATIONS: No. Cars must be in position 10 mins. before departure time.

DIRECTIONS: Ferry leaves from Steilacoom dock at the end of Union Ave.

MAP LOCATION: P. 465, WA, 19

CONTACT: General information: Pierce County Public Works Dept., 2401 South 35th St., Tacoma, WA 98409-7487, (206)591-7250; Operations information: Steilacoom Dock Launch, Steilacoom, WA 98388, (206)588-3127

STATE: Washington

PLACES SERVED: Tacoma (Point Defiance)—Tahlequah (South Vashon Island)

BODY OF WATER: Puget Sound

FERRY SERVICE HISTORY: The ferry on this run is sometimes the *Hiyu*, the smallest of the Washington State Ferry Fleet, and sometimes the *Tillikum* ("friend"), the *Klahowya* ("greetings"), and sometimes the *Evergreen State*. Service by Washington State Ferries was inaugurated in 1951.

LOCAL POINTS OF INTEREST: Tacoma (the Indian name for Mt. Rainier) is Washington's third largest city; it is a shipping and industrial center; many industries are closely related to the lumber industry for which Tacoma is known. It is the closest city to Mt. Rainier, which can be reached in one long day trip (two leisurely days would be better). Just across the Narrows Bridge is Gig Harbor, once a fishing village and, with posh nautical supply, curio, and clothing shops, a mecca for boating people. In the boutique Carousel Horse are T-shirts commenting on the wet climate: "People in Gig Harbor Don't Tan, They Rust." On good days, though, Gig Harbor has a beautiful view of Mt. Rainier. Tacoma has avenues of fine old

Victorian homes, some built by lumber tycoons, and excellent parks. Point Defiance, near the ferry landing, has nearly seven hundred acres and miles of woodland roads and trails. A portion of the first steamship on the Pacific Ocean, the *S.S. Beaver*, is displayed here; there are also a forest industries outdoor museum and an outstanding zoo and aquarium with specimens in their "natural" habitats; rare muskox roam the lush tundra environment.

[For notes on Vashon Island, see entry under Fauntleroy (Seattle)—Vashon Island—Southworth, p. 505.]

CROSSING TIME: 15 mins.

FERRY TYPE: Vehicle

VESSEL CAPACITY: *Hiyu*: 40 cars, 200 passengers; Others: 100 cars; 1000-1140 passengers

OPERATING SEASON: All year

SCHEDULE: **Daily. Lv. Pt. Defiance** *6:20 a.m., *7, 7:40, 8:30, 9:30, 10:30, 11:30, 12:30 p.m., 1:30, **2:30, 3:40, 4:25, 5:05, 5:45, 6:25, 7:05, 7:45, 8:35, 9:35, 10:35. **Lv. Tahlequah** *6 a.m., *6:40, **7, *7:20, 8, 9, 10, 11, noon, 1:10 p.m., **2:10, 3:10, 4, 4:45, 5:25, 6:05, 6:45, 7:25, 8:10, 9:05, 10:10. *Does not run Sundays and holidays. **Runs Sundays and holidays only.

RESTRICTIONS: Trailers, pickup-campers, and RVs permitted. Load limit 36 tons. Overhead clearance 16 ft.

FACILITIES: Restrooms; vending machines

FARE: Round-trip only. Car and driver $7.25 (*$8.70); passenger in vehicle or walk-on pedestrian $2.10; bicycle & rider $3.10; oversize vehicle to 28 ft. & driver $11.10 (*$13.30); higher rates for larger vehicles; children (5-11), senior citizens (65+) and handicapped half-fare; children under 5 free. *Summer surcharge.

RESERVATIONS: No

DIRECTIONS: The ferry landing in Tahlequah is at the foot of Tahlequah Road. In Tacoma take Pearl St. to Ruston.

MAP LOCATION: P. 465, WA, 20

CONTACT: See CONTACT, p. 496.

ACKNOWLEDGMENTS

In assembling material for this project, I have been aided by many generous-hearted people. Among those who have written histories of individual ferries, or recorded anecdotes about them and shared them with me, are Ken Stein and Jill Forstell, Sayville Ferry Service, Long Island; Frank Mina, Fire Island Ferries, Long Island; Johnny Brooks, Marshallville, Georgia; Mary Richter and Dick Purinton, Washington Island Ferry Line, Washington Island, Wisconsin; James R. Bullard, Larrabee's Point, Shoreham, Vermont; Carl Wittmond, Brussels, Illinois; Richard W. Klebs, St. Johns River Ferry Service, Mayport, Florida; Joyce Delbridge and Jay Becker, Vashon, Washington; Capt. William R. Shepler and Nancy Campbell, Mackinaw City, Michigan; Patricia J. Patterson, Washington State Ferries, Seattle, Washington; Joel Overholser, Fort Benton, Montana; William Market, Put-in-Bay, Ohio; Diane Campbell, Boothbay Harbor, Maine; Capt. Richard G. Spear, Maine State Ferry Service, Rockland, Maine; Agatha Cabaniss, Islesboro, Maine; Kathleen Waterman, Islesboro, Maine; Libby Lovatt, Squirrel Island, Maine; David Clough, Prince of Fundy Cruises, Maine; Luther Blount, Blount Marine, Warren, Rhode Island; Jeannette Tanner, Mobile Bay Ferry, Alabama; Sr. Ferry Captain Howard S. Lussen, Rocky Hill-Glastonbury Ferry, Connecticut; Tom Shanley, Alaska Marine Highway System, Juneau, Alaska; Diane Speers, Woods Hole Steamship Authority; Charlotte Damsten, Grand Portage Isle Royale Transportation Company, Grand Portage, Minnesota; Capt. Robert F. Ewels, Ferry Operations Manager, Galveston, Texas; Ernest Hinojosa, Jr., Ferry Operations Manager, Port Aransas, Texas; Theodore Bratz, Golden Gate Ferry System, California; David Schermerhorn, Lake Champlain Ferries, Burlington, Vermont; David Chapman of the Cape May-Lewes Ferry; Helen Dobrunick, Fredericktown, Pennsylvania; Winifred French, Eastport, Maine; and Frederick A. Hall of the Bridgeport and Port Jefferson Steamboat Company, New York.

Particular recognition is due a number of local, state, and federal tourism and transportation officials who patiently answered multiple queries: Edward L. Ellicott, Illinois; B. K. Cooper, Craig Ogilvie, Kerry Kraus, and Garland V. Land, Arkansas; Beth Cooke, R. K. Capito, and Charles E. Parrish, Kentucky; Commander C. G. Hill, US Coast Guard, Paducah, Kentucky; K. O. Morgan and Jerry M. Stargel, Georgia; Amanda Sessel Legare, Vermont; Greg Yon, William Cutts, and Ruth B. Jones, Florida; Jett Peterson, Maine; D. Douglas Brown, Connecticut; Robert L. Woodward, Missouri; Harvey G. Ramsey and W. J. Owens, North Carolina; Ardis Stevenson and Terrie Justice, Oregon; Nancy

Michel, Inchelium, Washington; Fred Sater, Don Freitas, and Dan Parker, California; Jeanne Shaw and Charles V. Anderson, Utah; Richard F. Moreno, Nevada; Ruth Holland, Washington; Michelle Merchant, New York; Don Wick, Tennessee; Nancy Buckingham, West Virginia; Donna Purcell Mayes and Martha Steger, Virginia; Suzanne Spellman and Maynard Scarborough, Massachusetts; Commander G. M. Harben, US Coast Guard, Cincinnati, Ohio; John P. MacBean of New York City; and Laddie L. Bolden of Carville, Louisiana.

I am greatly indebted to the staff members of a number of museums, libraries, and historical societies who have supplied invaluable material: Dan Owen of the Boat Photo Museum, Maryville, Illinois; Harriet Callahan, Louisiana State Library, Baton Rouge, Louisiana; the Mariners' Museum, Newport News, Virginia; the New York Public Library; the Library of Congress; Dave Snyder, Historian, and Bruce E. Weber, Park Naturalist, Isle Royale National Park; Margot McCain, Maine Historical Society; John P. Ingle, Jr., Jacksonville Historical Society; Connie Newkirk, Rose Hawley Museum, Ludington, Michigan; Rebecca Bormann, Speer Memorial Library, Mission, Texas; Nijole Etzwiler, Sauk County Historical Society, Baraboo, Wisconsin; the Rev. Dr. Robert E. H. Peoples, President, Hilton Head Historical Society, South Carolina; A. J. Goldwyn, Dukes County Historical Society, Massachusetts; Alden P. Stickney, Boothbay Region Historical Society, Maine; Lloyd F. Brimigion, Penobscot Marine Museum, Searsport, Maine; George Carpenter, Calhoun County Historical Society, Illinois; Erin Urban and Alice Ladziak, the John A. Noble Collection, Staten Island, New York; William Olesen, Los Angeles Maritime Museum; and Henry O. Pope, Earth Science Museum, Loma, Montana.

I have profound debts among friends and family. Jane and Tom Talamini introduced me, with an unflagging enthusiasm which would do credit to Baedeker himself, to the San Francisco ferries and have kept me posted on ferry service developments within the state. My cousins Rose and John Langenheim, indefatigable archivists and gallant hosts, amassed extensive information about the Puget Sound ferries, which glide almost to their door on Bainbridge Island, and escorted me on a memorable grand tour of the Seattle ferries and the Olympic Peninsula. I owe special thanks to Ruth Doumlele, Leanne Beorn, Martha Edmonds, and Janet Schwarz, all of Richmond, Cynthia Rubin of New York, and Sarah Lapinel of Charlotte, North Carolina, for the windfall of knowledge of specific ferries in various locations. I am also indebted to Jean Davis, Betty Scott, Barbara Griffin, and Welford D. Taylor of the University of Richmond for their constant interest and support. Lois Reamy, of New York, has generously shared her expert knowledge of travel writing and book publishing, made excellent suggestions, and directed ferry news my way. Pauline Guetta, of Montreal, encouraged the project from its inception and provided me with much helpful material about US-Canadian ferries. I am deeply grateful to Mary Ann Caws, who, over a lifetime, has communicated her conviction that writing is the only reasonable gloss for each day's reading and experience and who offered poetic perspectives on the Staten Island and Jamestown ferries. Warmest thanks are due my Aunt Dorothy Williams, who has loyally supported me in this enterprise and who has been my cheerful and intrepid companion on ferries large and small on the West Coast, and my Aunt Nora Weigel, who has also accompanied me in ferry searches and voyages and illuminated their role in her Virginia childhood. I owe the book's genesis in part to my brothers, Martin and Oscar Grant, who shared a boat-saturated childhood at Wrightsville Beach, North Carolina; Oscar and his wife, Jane, later travelled with me on North Carolina crossings and told me of hitherto unknown ferries they had detected along the Intracoastal Waterway.

I am indebted to Tom Roberts of Richmond for his careful work in preparing the sectional maps. I am particularly grateful also to my son, Alexander, for his editorial assistance, and to my mainstay, Estelle Crump, who has dissolved countless burdens. Finally, I must thank my husband, Lewis, for photographic odysseys on the Jamestown ferry, for imaginative research suggestions, and, above all, for exceptional domestic forbearance.

SOURCES FOR FURTHER READING

Bowen, Dana Thomas. *Memories of the Lakes Told in Story and Picture*. Cleveland, OH: Freshwater Press, 1969.

Boyer, Dwight. *Ships and Men of the Great Lakes*. New York: Dodd, Mead, 1977.

Brewington, M. V. *Chesapeake Bay: A Pictorial Maritime History*. New York: Bonanza, 1956.

Carpenter, George W. *Calhoun Is My Kingdom: The Sesquicentennial History of Calhoun County, Illinois*. Board of County Commissioners, Calhoun County, IL: Dan Merkle Printing, 1967 (first published in 1933; reissued and enlarged).

Cass, Earle M. "History of Horne's Ferry." *Bulletin of the Jefferson County* (NY) *Historical Society*, Vol. 2, No. 5, March, 1961.

Clark, Earl. "The Mosquito Fleet Chuffed You There from Here." *American West*, May/June 1986, 48-53.

Corning, Howard McKinley. *Willamette Landings: Ghost Towns of the River*. Portland: Oregon Historical Society, 1973.

Delbridge, Joyce. *Ferry Tales from Puget Sound: A Collection of Stories, Poems, and Anecdotes*. Vashon Island, WA: Vashon Point Productions, 1986.

Dickens, Charles. *American Notes and Pictures from Italy*. First published 1842; rpt. New York: Macmillan, 1903.

Directory of Toll Bridges, Ferries, Domestic Steamship Lines, and Auto/Passenger Land Carriers. Falls Church, VA: Highway Information Services; American Automobile Association; 8111 Gatehouse Road, Falls Church, VA 22047 (1985 ed.).

Frederickson, Arthur C. and Lucy F. *Pictorial History of the C & O Train and Auto Ferries and Pere Marquette Line Steamers*. Ludington, MI: 1955; revised ed. 1965.

Fuscus, David A. "A History of the Bemus Point-Stow Ferry." Unpublished; written in 1982; available from Sea Lion Project, Ltd., R.D. One, Sea Lion Drive, Mayville, NY 14757.

Gaby, Stan. *The Orient Point Passage*. Privately printed, 1984; available at Mohegan Community College Bookstore, Norwich, CT.

Harlan, George H. *San Francisco Bay Ferryboats*. Berkeley, CA: Howell-North, 1967.

Hesse, Anna Kemper. *Centenarians of Brick, Wood and Stone: Hermann, Missouri*. Privately printed, 1969; annotated 1981.

Hesse, Anna, and Marion South. *Gasconade County Tours*. Privately printed 1968; revised ed. 1975.

Hill, Ralph Nading. *Two Centuries of Ferry Boating on Lake Champlain*. Burlington, VT: Lake Champlain Transportation Co., Inc., 1972. Originally published in *Vermont Life*, Summer 1959 and Summer 1962.

Hilton, George Woodman. *The Great Lakes Car Ferries*. Berkeley, CA: Howell-North, 1962.

Houston, John M. *Early Excursion Ships to Catalina*, in *Accounts and Stories of Old San Pedro*. San Pedro, CA: San Pedro Historical Publications, printed by Advertising Ink, San Pedro, 1978. Reprinted 1980.

Ishmael, Susan. "Ferry Operations." *Arkansas Highways*, Fall 1978, 16-19.

Island Life — 1982: Focus on Ferries. Vashon, WA: Beachcomber Press, 1982. (This number, in an annual series published by the weekly *Vashon-Maury Island Beachcomber* newspaper, dealt with ferries.)

James, Henry. *The American Scene*. First published 1907. New York: Scribner's, 1946.

Kazin, Alfred. *A Walker in the City*. New York: Harcourt, Brace, 1951.

Kemble, John Haskell. *San Francisco Bay: A Pictorial Maritime History*. New York: Bonanza. Reprint of original edition published by Cornell Maritime Press, 1947.

Kline, M.S., and G.A. Bayless. *Ferryboats: A Legend on Puget Sound*. Seattle: Bayless, 1983.

Lifeline to the Islands: Sketches and Memories of Steamers Past and Present on the Woods Hole, Martha's Vineyard, Nantucket Run. Woods Hole, MA: Published by the Woods Hole, Martha's Vineyard, and Nantucket Steamship Authority, 1977.

Miller, Peter. "The Susquehanna: America's Small-Town River." *The National Geographic*, March 1985, 352-383.

Miller, William E., Jr. *A Ferry Tale: Crossing the Delaware on the Cape May-Lewes Ferry*. Wilmington, DE: Delapeake, 1984.

Peacock, Christopher M. *Rosario Yesterdays: A Pictorial History*. Eastsound, WA: Rosario Productions, 1985.

Perry, John. *American Ferryboats*. New York: Wilfred Funk, 1957.

Ranville, Judy, and Nancy Campbell. *Memories of Mackinaw* (A Bicentennial Project of Mackinaw City Public Library and Mackinaw City Woman's Club). Mackinaw, MI; Little Traverse Printing, E. Mitchell, Petoskey, MI: copyright Mackinaw City Public Library, 1976.

Ruby, R. H., and J. A. Brown. *Ferryboats on the Columbia River*. Seattle, WA: Superior Publishing, n.d.

Stevenson, Robert Louis. *From Scotland to Silverado*, ed. James D. Hart, The Belknap Press of Harvard University Press, Cambridge, MA, 1966, pp. 146-147. (According to Hart, Stevenson was misquoting Spenser's line from *The Faerie Queene*, "And the high hils Titan discoured.")

Stick, David. *Bald Head: A History of Smith Island and Cape Fear*. Wendell, NC: Broadfoot Publishing, 1985.

————. *The Cape Hatteras Seashore*. Charlotte, NC: McNally and Loftin, 1964.

————. *The Outer Banks of North Carolina*. Chapel Hill, NC: University of North Carolina Press, 1958.

Tucker, George Holbert. *Norfolk Highlights 1584-1881*. Norfolk, VA: The Norfolk Historical Society, 1972 (printed by Printcraft Press, Inc., Portsmouth, VA).

Whittlesey, Charles W. *Crossing and Re-Crossing the Connecticut River*. No place; privately printed, 1938.

PHOTO CREDITS

INDEX

Note: **Abbreviations in brackets indicate which states have ferries on that particular body of water.**

Photo by Lewis Wright

SARAH BIRD WRIGHT's travel writing
has appeared in the *Christian Science
Monitor, Woman's World,* the *New
York Times, London Free Press,*
and dozens of other publications.
She teaches at the University of
Richmond and makes her home
in Midlothian, Virginia.